IN PURSUIT OF CIVILITY

IN
PURSUIT OF
CIVILITY

MANNERS AND CIVILIZATION IN
EARLY MODERN ENGLAND

KEITH THOMAS

YALE UNIVERSITY PRESS
NEW HAVEN AND LONDON

The excerpt from Richard Wilbur's translation of Molière's *The Misanthrope* is reprinted by permission of Houghton Mifflin Harcourt Publishing. F. R. Scott's poem 'Degeneration' is reprinted by permission of William Toye, literary executor for the estate of F. R. Scott.

US edition published by Historical Society of Israel / Brandeis University Press, an imprint of the University Press of New England.

For information about this and other Yale University Press publications, please contact:
US Office: sales.press@yale.edu yalebooks.com
Europe Office: sales@yaleup.co.uk yalebooks.co.uk

Set in Adobe Caslon Pro by IDSUK (DataConnection) Ltd
Printed in Great Britain by Gomer Press Limited

Library of Congress Control Number: 2018934836

ISBN 978–0–300–23577–7 (hbk)

A catalogue record for this book is available from the British Library.

10 9 8 7 6 5 4 3 2

To John, Richard and Madeline

CONTENTS

PLATES

7 Thomas Gainsborough, portrait of Captain William Wade, 1771. Victoria Art Gallery, Bath and North East Somerset Council / Bridgeman Images.

8 Marco Ricci, 'View of the Mall in St James's Park', *c.* 1710. National Gallery of Art, Washington, Ailsa Mellon Bruce Collection.

9 Nathan Drake, 'The New Terrace Walk, York', eighteenth century. York Museums Trust (York Art Gallery), UK / Bridgeman Images.

10 'Interior of a Coffee-House', *c.* 1700. © The Trustees of the British Museum.

11 William Hogarth, 'A Midnight Modern Conversation', 1733. © The Trustees of the British Museum.

12 'Schismaticorum in Anglia crudelitas', from Richard Verstegan [Richard Rowlands], *Theatrum Crudelitatum Haereticorum Nostri Temporis*, 1592.

13 Caricature of Gustavus Adolphus's forces, *c.* 1630. Stadt Ulm, Stadtbibliothek, E 231.

14 John White, 'Warrior neighbour of the Picts', *c.* 1585–93. © The Trustees of the British Museum.

15 John White, 'Pict Warrior', *c.* 1585–93. © The Trustees of the British Museum.

16 'Triumphant Return of the English Soldiers', from John Derrricke, *The Image of Ireland*, 1581, ed. John Small, 1883.

17 'The Revenge of the "Wild Irish"', from James Cranford, *The Teares of Ireland*, 1642. British Library, London, UK / © British Library Board. All Rights Reserved / Bridgeman Images.

18 'Captain Smith taketh the King of Pamaunkey prisoner', from John Smith, *The Generall Historie of Virginia, New England, and the Summer Iles*, 1624. Science History Images / Alamy Stock Photo.

19 John White, 'The skirmish at Bloody Point, Frobisher Bay', *c.* 1588. © The Trustees of the British Museum.

20 James Barry, 'Orpheus teaching barbarous Greeks the Benefits of Civilization', mural at the Royal Society of Arts, London, *c.* 1777–83. RSA, London / Bridgeman Images.

21 William Hamilton, engraving of Julius Agricola, from Edward Barnard, *The New, Impartial and Complete History of England*, 1790. © The British Library Board (9502.i.6.).

22 Nicholas Dixon, 'A Lady, possibly Lady Ann Rich, nee Cavendish and later 5th Countess of Exeter, with a youth and a black page', 1668. The Burghley House Collection.

23 Reproduction of a handbill advertising a slave auction in Charleston, South Carolina, 1769.

24 Thomas Watling, portrait of an aboriginal boy named Nanbree, *c.* 1792–97. The Natural History Museum / Alamy Stock Photo.

25 Robert Smirke, 'The Cession of the District of Matavai in the Island of Otaheite to Captain James Wilson for the use of the Missionaries Sent Thither by that Society in the Ship Duff', 1798. Art Collection 2 / Alamy Stock Photo.

26 Thomas Rowlandson, 'Two women fighting watched by rowdy spectators', from *Miseries of London*, 1807. Guildhall Library & Art Gallery, Heritage Image Partnership Ltd / Alamy Stock Photo.

27 'Stand Coachman, or the haughty lady well fitted', 1750. © The Trustees of the British Museum.

28 John Collet, 'The Frenchman in London', 1770. Courtesy of The Lewis Walpole Library, Yale University.

PREFACE

This book is a revised and much expanded version of three Menahem Stern lectures given in Jerusalem in November 2003. I thank the Historical Society of Israel for inviting me to deliver them; and I am very grateful to my hosts, particularly the late Michael Heyd, the late Elliott Horowitz and Yosef Kaplan, for their kindness and hospitality. I also thank my alert and critical audience for listening so attentively and for offering many helpful comments in the ensuing discussions. I am particularly grateful to Maayan Avineri-Rebhun for the exceptional patience with which she has waited for the deplorably late delivery of my manuscript.

Warm thanks are also due to my two publishers, Richard Pult of the University Press of New England and Heather McCallum of Yale University Press, for their brisk efficiency and generous encouragement. I owe my introduction to Yale to the kindness of Ivon Asquith and Richard Fisher. In Rachael Lonsdale I have had an exceptionally helpful editor. She and her colleagues have saved me from many infelicities. Steve Kent has assisted me with the plates. They have made publishing with Yale an enjoyable experience.

When I was invited, it was suggested that I might speak about manners in early modern England. I was happy to do so, for this enabled me to return to themes that I had discussed in previous lectures and seminars at British, North American, Japanese and Australian universities. It is a tricky topic, however, for the word 'manners' has several different meanings. Today it is most commonly used as a term for polite social behaviour. This is what the elderly have in mind when they say of some young people that they have very good manners, of others that they have very bad manners, and of some that they have no manners at all. The history of manners in this sense of the word was once regarded as a rather trivial subject, but in recent years it has come to be recognized as one of considerable social and moral importance, fundamental, indeed, to understanding the way in which people think of themselves and their relationship to each other. The French sociologist Pierre Bourdieu even claimed that it is possible to infer 'a whole cosmology, an ethic, a metaphysic, a political philosophy, through injunctions as insignificant as "Stand up straight" or "Don't hold your knife in your left hand"'.[1]

Much of the credit for this enhanced valuation of the topic is due to the German sociologist Norbert Elias (1897–1990), whose great work, *On the Process of Civilisation*, first published in Switzerland in 1939 but largely unnoticed until its reissue in 1969, followed by translations in French (1973–75) and English (1978–82), did so much to show that the everyday conventions of bodily comportment and social behaviour are part of a larger process by which human beings adapt themselves to the demands of living peacefully with each other. Elias's interpretation of the history of manners has some well-known limitations. But it is impossible to discuss the topic without being conscious of his looming intellectual presence. I am still embarrassed to recall that, on the only occasion when I met this world authority on the history of table manners, I managed to disgrace myself by carelessly knocking a jug of water over the table we were sharing for lunch.

Since Elias's day there has been a huge amount written about the history of manners and politeness in many different parts of the world, some of it by my former undergraduate pupils and graduate students. Outstanding among recent studies of manners in early modern England is Anna Bryson's monograph *From Courtesy to Civility* (Oxford, 1998), a work so nuanced and assured as to deter anyone from attempting to follow in her footsteps. Valuable material can also be found in Fenela Childs' unpublished Oxford doctoral thesis of 1984, 'Prescriptions for Manners in English Courtesy Literature, 1690–1760'. I have learnt a great deal from the fine essays contained in *Civil Histories*, edited by Peter Burke, Brian Harrison and Paul Slack (Oxford, 2000). A list of other scholars who have fruitfully explored some aspect of the subject would run into the hundreds.

The French distinguish *manières* (social behaviour) from *moeurs* (morals and customs). But until the nineteenth century the English used the same word for both. During the sixteenth century 'manners' came to mean the conventions governing polite interaction, but long before then the term had been employed in the much wider sense of mores, a people's habits, morals, social conventions and mode of life. That was what the fourteenth-century bishop William of Wykeham meant when he prescribed for his school at Winchester the motto 'Manners makyth man'.[2] For him, 'manners' meant a boy's whole moral and educational formation, not just his behaviour in polite social intercourse. *The Book of Good Manners*, published in 1487 and often reprinted, was William Caxton's translation of a treatise by the French monk Jacques Legrand: it was a guide to virtuous living, outlining the duties appropriate to an individual's social position, warning readers against the seven deadly sins, and instructing them how to prepare for death and the Last Judgment.

It was this wider sense of the word that the eighteenth-century philosopher David Hume had in mind when he said in his essay 'Of National Characters' that each nation had its peculiar set of manners. The same was true of his younger contemporary, the historian Edward Gibbon, when he devoted part of a chapter of *The Decline and Fall of the Roman Empire* to 'The Manners of the Pastoral Nations'. Used in this all-embracing way, the term was very close to what the late-Victorian anthropologist E. B. Tylor called 'culture or civilization', which he defined as 'that complex whole which includes knowledge, belief, art, morals, laws, custom, and any other capabilities and habits acquired by man as a member of society'.

A similar ambiguity attached to the closely associated term 'civility'. This, too, could mean everyday politeness. But it was also the name for the most desirable condition of organized human society, what would come to be called 'civilization', the opposite of barbarism. Samuel Johnson's *Dictionary* (1755) gave both meanings: civility meant both 'politeness' and 'the state of being civilized'. The new term, 'civilization', was slow to enter the English language because the older word, 'civility', seemed to serve the purpose perfectly well.

In pursuing the broader meanings of 'manners' and 'civility', as well as the narrower ones, I have tried to identify just what it was that the people of early modern England regarded as distinctive and superior about their way of living, particularly in contrast to that of so-called barbarians and savages: in other words, what they thought it meant to be 'civilized'. I have also tried to show how these assumptions affected their relations with the other peoples with whom they came into contact, and how their early colonial and imperial activities were shaped by the ancient polarity between the 'civil' and the 'barbarous'.

This is a subject that has been powerfully illuminated over the last seventy years or so by an enormous volume of historical writing devoted to European encounters with other peoples in the New World, Asia, Africa and the Pacific. There has also been much distinguished work on the relations of the English with their supposedly less civilized neighbours, the Welsh, the Scots, and especially the Irish. Scholarship on these subjects has continued to pour out during the years since these lectures were delivered. My debts to previous historians are large, and I have tried to indicate them in the copious endnotes. I must particularly acknowledge the stimulus I have drawn from the published writings of, among others, David Armitage, Robert Bartlett, Nicholas Canny, Sir Rees Davies, Sir John Elliott, John Gillingham, Margaret T. Hodgen, Anthony Pagden, J. G. A. Pocock, Quentin Skinner and Richard Tuck. Their work has left me only too aware that in my concern to sketch the broad outlines of my theme and to engage the interest of the general reader I have had to pass cursorily over many complex matters which deserve a much more nuanced treatment. Throughout, my approach is illustrative rather than comprehensive.

As always, I owe a great deal to the enormously helpful and obliging staff in all of the Bodleian Libraries, but especially in the Upper Reading Room, Duke Humfrey's Library as it used to be, and now the Weston Library. I am equally indebted to Norma Aubertin-Potter and Gaye Morgan in the Codrington Library. I also thank the friends and colleagues who have helped me on particular points. They include Thomas Charles-Edwards, Jeremy Coote, Cécile Fabre, Patrick Finglass, James Hankins, Neil Kenny, Giles Mandelbrote, Jim Sharpe and Parker Shipton. At All Souls I have depended heavily on the skill and readiness of two successive Fellows' Secretaries, Humaira Erfan-Ahmed and Rachael Stephenson. I am profoundly grateful to the college for providing me with so congenial an environment in which to work. Finally, I thank my children, Emily Gowers and Edmund Thomas, for help, advice and intellectual stimulus, and above all, my wife, Valerie, for her constant encouragement, sagacious criticism and selfless support.

All Souls College, Oxford
July 2017
K. T.

INTRODUCTION

The epithets *barbarous* and *civilized* occur so frequently in conversation and in books, that whoever employs his thoughts in contemplation of the manners and history of mankind will have occasion to consider, with some attention, both what ideas these words are commonly meant to convey, and in what sense they ought to be employed by the historian and moral philosopher.

James Dunbar, *Essays on the History of Mankind in Rude and Cultivated Ages* (1780)

In later seventeenth-century England it was common for contemporaries to refer casually to what they called 'the civil world', 'the civilized part of mankind', 'the civilized nations' or 'the civilized world'.[1] They did not always identify the countries concerned. 'How many do most of the civillest nations of the world amount to?' asked the philosopher John Locke in 1690, 'And who are they?' He did not provide an answer, though he rejected the notion that the 'civillest' nations were necessarily Christian ones, and he instanced the Chinese, 'a very

1

great and civil people'. For one of Charles II's bishops, 'the civil world' included Babylon, Aleppo and Japan.[2]

By the later eighteenth century, the orientalist William Marsden was able to divide humanity into a single hierarchy of five classes of more or less 'civilized' people, with the 'refined nations of Europe' at the top, closely followed by the Chinese, and at the bottom, the Caribs, Laplanders and Hottentots, who, he said, 'exhibited a picture of mankind in its rudest and most humiliating aspect'. His contemporary Edmund Burke observed that 'there is no state or gradation of barbarism, and no mode of refinement which we have not at the same instant under view: the very different civility of Europe and of China; the barbarism of Persia and Abyssinia; the erratic manners of Tartary, and of Arabia; the savage state of North America, and of New Zealand'.[3] It was a conceptual scheme that would have a long subsequent history. As E. B. Tylor observed in 1871: 'The educated world of Europe and America practically settles a standard by simply placing its own nations at one end of the social series and savage tribes at the other, arranging the rest of mankind between these limits according as they correspond more closely to savage or to cultured life.'[4] This was a view of the world that John Locke's contemporaries would have recognized. For them, 'civilized' people were those who lived in a 'civil' or 'polished' fashion, by contrast with the 'uncivilized', who were 'wild', 'barbarous' or even 'savage'.[5]

This way of dividing up humanity had an ancient pedigree. In the Athens of the fifth century BC, all foreigners who did not speak Greek were labelled 'barbarians' (*barbaroi*), persons whose speech was incomprehensible. Neutrally descriptive at first, the word became increasingly derogatory. Barbarians were seen not just as linguistically handicapped, but also as deficient politically, morally and culturally. There was no consensus about what these defects were, though intemperance, cruelty and submission to despotic rule were frequently cited. The Hellenic sense of identity depended on this contrast between the values of the Greeks and those of the barbarians. Yet different writers stressed different attributes of the foreigner, and there was no single concept of barbarism as such.[6] Plato was one of those who thought it absurd to bracket all non-Greeks together in this way, regardless of whether they were ignorant Scythian nomads or highly cultivated Persians and Egyptians.

In the Hellenistic period (336–31 BC) the distinction between Greeks and barbarians dwindled in significance. Stoic philosophers emphasized the unity of the human race; and the scientific writer Eratosthenes (c. 285–194 BC) rejected the division of mankind into Greeks and barbarians, observing that many Greeks were worthless characters and many barbarians highly civilized.[7] In practice, the attitude of the Greeks to other peoples was often more nuanced than that implied by the simple opposition of Hellene/barbarian.[8]

For the Romans, the barbarians were the peoples outside the frontiers of the empire. They were often, though not invariably, seen as violent and lawless, notable for their brutal cruelty (*feritas*) and lack of *humanitas*, that is to say gentleness, culture, and intellectual refinement. These barbarian attributes, particularly *feritas*, were put together to constitute the notion of barbarism (*barbaria*), an amalgam of antisocial impulses to which even the civilized might succumb. In practice, the empire's boundaries were permeable, and 'barbarous' outsiders were easily absorbed within them. But the stereotype had been established. In the fourth to sixth centuries the recurring invasions of the Western Empire by Germanic peoples did nothing to dispel it, even though many of these so-called barbarians were in fact highly Romanized.[9]

With the spread of Christianity and the disintegration of the old Roman world, the concept of the barbarian became increasingly irrelevant. The threat posed from the mid-seventh century onwards by the Arab conquests in North Africa and the Iberian Peninsula made it even more so, for Islamic culture was intellectually more sophisticated than that of Western Europe and could not plausibly be regarded as 'barbarous'. This was not the case with the Vikings, whose repeated raids on the British Isles and Northern Europe between the ninth and eleventh centuries led to their sometimes being denounced as barbarians.[10] The crucial division until the seventeenth century, however, was that between Christians and non-Christians, between 'christendom and hethennesse', as the fourteenth-century poet Geoffrey Chaucer put it. The idea of Christendom as a geographical area had been in circulation since the late ninth century and was consolidated by the Crusades of 1095–1270 against Muslim control of the Holy Places in Jerusalem.[11] In Chaucer's time the conflict with Islam was intensified by the rise of the Ottoman Turks, who would go on to conquer the Balkans, capture Constantinople, destroy the Byzantine Empire, and threaten to overrun Central Europe and the Mediterranean.

Yet alongside this enduring opposition of Christian and pagan, the old polarity of 'civil' and 'barbarous' had not been totally forgotten. The two ways of dividing mankind were sometimes conflated, with Christians seen as civilizers and paganism equated with barbarism (the Latin word *paganus* meant both pagan and rustic). In the twelfth and thirteenth centuries urbanization and economic progress in Western Europe made it possible to contrast its material prosperity with that of less developed societies. The simultaneous rediscovery of classical learning, especially the works of Aristotle, which had long been studied by Arab scholars, meant the resurrection of Greek and Roman concepts of barbarism and civility. Marked out by their alien languages, barbarians were once again associated with irrationality, lawlessness, ferocity and a low level of mental and material culture. The quintessential barbarians now were the nomadic peoples of the Eurasian Steppes, but the label was also attached to some Christian peoples: in the twelfth century, the Celtic regions of the British Isles were regarded by the English as fundamentally barbarous.[12]

The military conflict between Christians and Muslims had always been regarded as a Holy War between competing religions, but in the fifteenth century Renaissance humanists drew on classical stereotypes to represent it in more secular terms, portraying it as a contest between a civilized Western Europe and a barbarous (*immanis*) Islam, despotically governed and merciless in warfare. Civility slowly began to supersede religion as the crucial index of a country's diplomatic acceptability.[13]

In the sixteenth century, most Europeans still regarded the distinction between Christian and non-Christian as crucial. Yet although the travellers and proto-ethnographers who encountered the newly discovered worlds of America and Asia were highly conscious of the paganism of their inhabitants, their accounts of them were mostly written in the secular terms of barbarism and civility.[14] Confronted by a wide diversity of Native American cultures, the Spanish writers Bartolomé de Las Casas and José de Acosta created a typology of barbarism with which to construct a hierarchical classification of non-European peoples, ranging from those at the top who, like the Chinese, possessed laws, rulers, cities and the use of letters, to nomadic 'savages' at the bottom, such as the Caribs, who, it was thought, had no form of civil organization and lacked any means of communication with other peoples.[15] The criteria by which barbarism was identified changed over the centuries, and so did the terminology employed.[16] Scholars, travellers and those with experience of other continents regarded barbarism not as an absolute condition, but as a matter of degree. They thought in terms of a graduated hierarchy of cultures rather than a single, binary distinction between the 'civil' and the 'barbarous'. But for many people, the basic polarity remained. It was applied loosely and without reference to the finer distinctions offered by ethnographers and philosophers.

In seventeenth-century England, 'civil' people were increasingly referred to as 'civilized'. This was a more complex term because it implied both a condition, that of being civil, and a process, that of having been brought to that state by casting off barbarism. To 'civilize' was to effect the transition from the one condition to the other. This could happen to a people, as with the ancient Britons, who were said to have been made civil by the Romans, or to wild plants, which, when cultivated and improved, were described by seventeenth-century gardeners as 'civilized'.[17] By the later seventeenth century the process of civilizing was beginning to be called 'civilization'. In 1698, for example, a writer remarked that 'Europe was first beholding to Graecia for their literature and civilization'; and in 1706, Andrew Snape, Fellow and later Provost of King's College, Cambridge, described the gathering of human beings into 'societies and bodies politic' as 'the civilization of mankind'.[18] The lawyers also used the term to denote the process of turning a criminal case into a civil one.[19] Initially employed to characterize the process or action of civilizing, the term 'civilization' also came to be used to mean the end product of that process, a civilized condition. It is hard to say when exactly the word acquired this new sense. The first meaning gradually slid into the other. In his sermons of the 1740s, for instance, Henry Piers, vicar of Bexley in Kent, came very close to the idea of civilization as a condition rather than a process, when he spoke of 'civilization and polite behaviour' and 'outward decorum, or decent civilization'.[20] But only from the 1760s onwards did English writers unambiguously describe the state of those who had been civilized as one of 'civilization'.[21] As late as 1772, Samuel Johnson famously refused to admit the new word into his *Dictionary*. To convey the condition of the civilized, i.e., 'freedom from barbarity', he stuck to the older term, 'civility'.[22]

Civility was (and is) a slippery and unstable word. Yet although it was employed in the early modern period in a variety of senses, they all related in one way or another to the existence of a well-ordered political community and the appropriate qualities and conduct expected of its citizens. In the early sixteenth century, civility, like its Italian and French predecessors *civiltà* and *civilité*, also took on the larger connotation of a nonbarbarous way of living, what would eventually be known as 'civilization'.[23] 'Civility' implied a static condition, however, and lacked any suggestion of civilizing as a process.

During the sixteenth century, it also came to denote the narrower concept of good manners, courtesy and polite behaviour – treating people with 'common civility', as the expression had it.[24] It was this ambiguity that led James Boswell to make his unsuccessful attempt to persuade Johnson to restrict his dictionary's definition of 'civility' to 'politeness' or 'decency', and to express the state of being civilized with the new term 'civilization'.[25]

Despite Johnson's recalcitrance, 'civility' in the later eighteenth century fell back to its more restricted meaning of good manners and good citizenship, whereas 'civilization' came into general English usage, both as the word for the civilizing process and also as a description of the cultural, moral and material condition of those who had been civilized. The word was widely employed with unembarrassed ethnocentricity to suggest that the 'civilized' nations exemplified the most perfected state of human society, in comparison with which other modes of living were more or less inferior, the products of poverty, ignorance, misgovernment or sheer incapacity. This assumption would prove to be of crucial importance in shaping relations between Western Europeans and other peoples.

When, in the nineteenth century, the European states sought to define the conditions on which they would admit other countries to membership of international society, they invoked a 'standard of civilization' to which Asian and African governments were required to conform if they wished to be recognized as sovereign bodies. This was an updated version of the *ius gentium*, or law of nations, which had been invoked by jurists in the early modern period. Naturally, it was a standard that embodied the legal and political norms of Western Europe. It made no allowance for alternative cultural traditions. If other peoples failed to meet its formal criteria, international law denied them recognition as sovereign states and permitted foreign intervention in their domestic affairs.[26]

In the eyes of the European powers this was not so much a question of asserting their superiority as of achieving a necessary degree of reciprocity between nations. A 'civilized' government was expected to be capable of making binding contracts, conducting honest administration, protecting foreign nationals and adhering to the rules of international law. The Europeans were right in thinking that these were requirements that 'uncivilized' peoples were usually unable to meet. Yet international law itself was a European creation and it reflected the interests of advanced commercial states. Countries lacking representative government, private property, free trade and formal legal rules were seen not as possessing their own distinctive form of civility, but as 'backward', waiting to be cast into a Western mould. The Eurocentric idea of a single standard of civilization reflected contempt for the norms of conduct in other cultures; and the notion of Western superiority was invoked to justify the forcible colonization or commercial exploitation of supposedly barbarous peoples in the name of a 'civilizing mission' to export European standards of legality and proper administration to benighted parts of the globe.

The League of Nations, set up after the First World War, purported to consist of only 'civilized' states and upheld the notion that it was their responsibility to spread civilization to the rest of the world.* Only with the creation in 1945 of the League's successor, the United Nations, was this formal distinction between 'civilized' and 'uncivilized' states finally abandoned. In the words of a leading jurist at the time, 'Modern international law knows of no distinction, for the purposes of recognition, between civilized and uncivilized States, or between States within and outside the international community of civilized states.'[27]

In early modern England, the ancient and long-enduring opposition between the 'civil' and the 'barbarous' was frequently invoked as a way of expressing some of the essential values of the time. Contemporary expositions of the ideal of civility were exercises in the rhetoric of self-

---

* This did not prevent the League from recognizing Soviet Russia, Nazi Germany and Fascist Italy.

description. When explorers and colonists deplored the 'savagery' and 'barbarism' they encountered in the non-European world, they were implicitly articulating what it was that they valued about their own way of life. They defined themselves by elaborating on what they were not. Like the other great bogeys of post-Reformation England, 'popery' and 'witchcraft', the idea of 'barbarism' embodied what many contemporaries found repugnant and, by implication, revealed what it was they admired. Just as theologians explored the meaning of sin in order to show what was good,[28] so 'civilized' people needed the concept, and preferably the actual existence, of 'barbarians' in order to clarify what was distinctive about themselves. The notion of civilization is essentially relative: it has to have an opposite to be intelligible. As the philosopher and historian R. G. Collingwood wrote in the 1930s, 'We create the mythical figure of the savage, no actual historical person but an allegorical symbol of everything which we fear and dislike, attributing to him all the desires in ourselves which we condemn as beastly and all the thoughts which we despise as irrational.' Or in today's academic jargon, 'Identity is constituted by the creation of alterities.'[29] To ask what early modern English people thought was civil and what was 'barbarous' is to probe their fundamental assumptions about how society should be organized and how life should be lived. It also provides a perspective from which to reconsider our own ideas on the subject.

This book seeks to demonstrate the importance of the ideals of civility and civilization in England during the years between the Reformation of the early sixteenth century and the French Revolution of the late eighteenth. It shows the extent to which they coloured the thinking of the time and describes the uses to which they were put. It also explores some of the ways in which they were challenged and even rejected. So far as possible, it takes into account the views of the population at large, but it cannot avoid being heavily dependent on the opinions expressed by the more articulate people of the time. As a result, the text is thickly studded with direct quotations. Some may find this practice ungainly. As the natural philosopher Robert Boyle remarked in 1665, 'I know it would be more acceptable to most readers, if I were less punctual and scrupulous in my quotations; it being by many accounted a more genteel and masterly way of writing, to cite others but seldom, and then to name only the authors, or mention what they say in the words of him that cites, not theirs that are cited.'[30] This warning notwithstanding, I side with Boyle in thinking it better to quote contemporaries in their own words rather than resorting to the inevitable distortions of paraphrase.

It is important, of course, to remember that all observations on civility and barbarism, as on any other topic, were made in some specific context, and usually with a particular agenda in mind. Many early modern pronouncements on the subject arose in the course of an intercultural encounter and frequently had a polemical purpose. Ever since the Roman historian Tacitus wrote his *Germania* in order to expose the vices of the civilized by describing the virtues of the barbarous, discussions of alien ways of life have usually had an ulterior motive. In early modern England, many of those who elaborated on the barbarism of the Irish or the Native Americans were seeking to profit by expropriating them from their lands, whereas those who stressed the civility of these peoples wanted to impose restraints on their conquerors. In either case, the implicit definitions of what constituted civility or barbarism, good or bad manners, were constructed so as to serve a particular interest. The meaning of these terms varied according to the context, the person employing them, and the literary form of the document in which they occurred. Allowance also has to be made for the constraints imposed by the particular 'language' or 'discourse' in which the argument was cast.[31] Puritan theologians, natural lawyers, classical republicans, conjectural historians and political economists each wrote within a particular intellectual tradition and approached their subject in a different way. Juxtaposing quotations taken from widely differing sources can mislead if insufficient attention is paid to the context and form of their source; as one academic critic puts it, it is necessary to avoid the dangers implicit in treating the propositions contained in a text as integers to be assessed in their own right and compared with similar items elsewhere.[32]

Nevertheless, I believe that in the early modern period there was a common stock of ideas and assumptions about what was civil and what was barbarous and that it can be reconstructed by attending to what people said and wrote, however varied the context. It was, of course, a period of very considerable change – economic, political, religious and cultural. But there was also a great deal of continuity so far as ideas about manners and civility were concerned. I have tried to be sensitive to chronological change, but I have not hesitated to 'bunch' evidence drawn from different centuries when that seemed justifiable.

Many of the received notions about what constituted good manners and civilized life were common to other Western European countries. English notions of civility were particularly indebted to the literature and practice of Italy and France, which became increasingly familiar, partly through translations of printed books and partly through the experience of continental travel. English attempts to 'civilize' other parts of the world were made in the wake of the Spanish experience in Central and South America; and English ideas about what we now call international law were shaped by continental thinkers such as the Spanish theologian Francisco de Vitoria (*c.* 1483–1546), the Dutch jurist Hugo Grotius (1583–1645) and the German natural lawyer Samuel, Baron Pufendorf (1632–94).

Nevertheless, my focus is on England until the union with Scotland in 1707, and thereafter on Britain. Although Wales had been united politically to England in the early sixteenth century, it long remained, like Scotland after 1707, in many ways culturally distinct, and I have largely neglected it here. I do, however, take into account the highly self-conscious reflections on civility and civilization offered by the Scottish philosophers and historians of the eighteenth century.

To concentrate on one particular country in this way is deeply unfashionable at a time when 'transnational' and 'global' history are all the rage. In the United States, early modern English history used to be widely studied because it was from Britain that the first waves of immigration came. English cultural influences, notably Protestantism, the common law and representative government, did much to shape the early development of that nation. Today's multicultural America, however, no longer has a special relationship with the United Kingdom, and at a time when Britain, like the United States, seems to be attempting to detach itself from the rest of the world, English history is understandably regarded as a narrow specialism rather than an essential part of the historical curriculum.

Yet the study of early modern England continues to be instructive because it offers an example, unique in early modern Europe, of a highly integrated society, whose people spoke a single language, were arranged in a hierarchical but relatively fluid social structure, and had long been unified by strong political and legal institutions. It was a time of economic transformation, intellectual innovation and exceptional literary accomplishment. In the eighteenth century, Britain developed the most advanced economy in the world and extended its empire into other parts of the globe.

These are all good reasons for continuing to study English history in the early modern period. But my main justification for concentrating on the centuries between 1530 and 1789 is that this enquiry into manners and civility is part of an attempt to construct an historical ethnography of early modern England which has occupied me on and off for many years. As a Welshman, and therefore something of an outsider, I have tried to study the English people in the way an anthropologist approaches the inhabitants of an unfamiliar society, seeking to establish their categories of thought and behaviour and the principles that governed their lives. My aim is to bring out the distinctive texture and complexity of past experience in one particular milieu.

My first two chapters are devoted to early modern notions of good manners: they examine their place in the self-definition of the ruling elites, their role in the lives of the rest of the population and the extent to which they reinforced the prevailing social structure. The third chapter explores the changing ideas of contemporaries on what it meant to be 'civilized'; and the fourth discusses their views on how it was that England had come to be a civilized country. The fifth examines the ways in which the belief of the English in their superior civility affected their relations with 'uncivilized' peoples, particularly by legitimizing international trade, colonial conquest and slavery. In the last two chapters, I show how early modern ideals of civility and civilization, far from being universally accepted, were subjected to a sustained barrage of contemporary criticism. Finally, I consider how far those ideals remain relevant in modern times and ask whether social cohesion and human happiness are possible without them.

〜 1 〜

Civil Behaviour

Those little civilities and ceremonious delicacies which, inconsiderable as they may appear to the man of science, and difficult as they may prove to be detailed with dignity, yet contribute to the regulation of the world by facilitating the intercourse between one man and another.

Samuel Johnson, *The Rambler*, 98 (23 February 1751)

The Chronology of Manners

From Elizabethan times onwards the word 'manners' was often used to mean polite behaviour. Edmund Spenser wrote in *The Faerie Queene* (1596) that

the rude porter, that no manners had,
Did shut the gate against him in his face.

Similarly, in the 1690s, John Locke stressed the need for children to learn 'manners, as they call it'.[1] At the same time, the term 'manners' also continued to be employed in the older and much wider sense of the customs, morals and mode of life prevailing in any particular society. In 1651, for example, the philosopher Thomas Hobbes explained that by 'manners' he did not mean 'decency of behaviour, as how a man should salute another, or how a man should wash his mouth, or pick his teeth before company'; his concern was with 'those qualities of mankind that concern their living together in peace and unity'.[2] That was what contemporary moralists meant by 'manners' when they called, as they repeatedly did, for their 'reformation'. They wanted public authorities to take action against swearing, drunkenness, prostitution, gambling and Sabbath-breaking.[3] By contrast, Joseph Addison, writing in the *Spectator* in 1711, took the restricted view, explaining that 'by manners, I do not mean morals, but behaviour and good breeding'.[4] It is manners in Addison's narrower sense of the conventions governing personal interaction, what Hobbes called 'decency of behaviour', that are the subject of this chapter.

In the later Middle Ages, the idea of good manners was conveyed by such terms as 'courtesy', 'nurture' and 'virtue'. From the mid-sixteenth century onwards, the word 'civility' began to be used in their place: Archbishop Cranmer's *Catechism* of 1548 referred to 'the nurture and civility of good manners'. Thereafter, 'civil' and 'civility' gradually came into circulation. 'If you were civil and knew courtesy, / You would not do me thus much injury', says Shakespeare's Helena in *A Midsummer Night's Dream* (*c.* 1595–96). In the seventeenth century 'civility' overtook 'courtesy' in popularity; and in the eighteenth century it remained the term most commonly employed to convey the notion of good manners, more often than the increasingly popular expression 'politeness', and much more often than 'courtesy' and 'good breeding'.[5] Until at least the 1770s, 'civility' also retained its broader meaning as a synonym for what would come to be called 'civilization'.

'Courtesy', as the word suggests, related initially to the behaviour associated with the court, whether of monarchs or of feudal lords. It

15

was the essential attribute of courtiers.[6] 'Civility', by contrast, was the virtue of citizens.[7] The term derived from the classical notion of an organized political community or *civitas*, which for Aristotle and Cicero was the only place where the good life could be lived. As an Elizabethan translator explained, the Greek word πολιτεια (polity) 'in our tongue we may term "civility"'.[8] In late medieval Italy *civiltà* (civility) expressed the values of the independent city-states, where, as has been well said, *la vita civile* (the civil life) was 'a life that was at once civilized, civilian, and civic'.[9] In his *Dictionary* (1538), the diplomat Sir Thomas Elyot equated 'civility' with 'politic governance' and explained that to be 'civil' was to be 'expert in those things that appertain to the ministration of a commonweal'.[10]

By extension, 'civility' came to epitomize the way of life of good citizens. In Tudor times this involved the dutiful acceptance of established authority. The early sixteenth-century humanist Thomas Starkey declared that 'obedience' had always been 'reputed the chief bond and knot of all virtue and good civility'.[11] Elyot also associated civility with 'courtesy' and 'gentleness in speech'.[12] It involved tactful behaviour, the repression of anger and insult, and a determined attempt to reduce the combative aspect of social interaction. In this respect, its prescriptions overlapped with those of good neighbourliness and Christian charity. The 'chief signs' of civility, thought the Elizabethan schoolmaster Richard Mulcaster, were 'quietness, concord, agreement, fellowship, and friendship'. Citizens were expected to display tolerance, mutual respect and self-control by ordering their actions in such a way as to ease the task of living harmoniously with their fellows. For the translators of the King James Bible, 'civility' distinguished humans from 'brute beasts led by sensuality'. As the Recorder of Exeter told his son in 1612, it was 'by courtesy and humanity' that 'all societies among men are maintained and preserved'. 'Society,' he explained, was 'nothing else but a mutual and reciprocal exchange of gentleness, of kindness, of affability, of familiarity, and of courtesy among men.' John Locke agreed: civility was 'that general good-will and regard for all people, which makes any one have a care not to show, in his carriage, any contempt, disrespect, or neglect of them'.[13]

In ordinary parlance, to be 'civil' was to behave in a decent, law-abiding fashion. Civility involved consideration and accommodation to the needs of others. It was closely associated with notions of kindness and amiability, and it taught the importance of hospitality and the friendly reception of strangers. 'Civility money' was what people paid to jailers and bailiffs to ensure goodwill and preferential treatment.[14] 'Common civility' involved care of the body, so as to avoid exposing fellow citizens to unpleasant sights and smells. By extension, it called for 'decency and gracefulness of looks, voice, words, motions, gestures, and of all the whole outward demeanour'; and it came to mean being easy and agreeable in company.[15] These modes of behaviour were all seen as necessary ingredients of what came to be called 'civil conversation', a concept that related as much to actions as to speech, 'conversation' being a synonym for social interaction of every kind. In 1707 a lexicographer regarded 'civility' and 'courtesy' as interchangeable terms, both meaning 'a kind and obliging behaviour and management of one's self'.[16] 'As 'civility' became increasingly the word for everyday courtesy, its political and governmental connotations gradually withered away; and in the later eighteenth century they were transferred to the new word 'civilization'.

The rules of civility were set out in a huge prescriptive literature, much of it derived from continental originals, for writing on the subject was a phenomenon of the European Renaissance and the English were intensely aware of being relative latecomers to the genre. Works on civility took many forms. There were 'books of nurture', teaching manners to children, of which far and away the most influential was the one by the great Dutch humanist Desiderius Erasmus, whose *De Civilitate Morum Puerilium* (1530) was translated into English in 1532 as *A Lytell Booke of Good Maners for Chyldren* and reissued half a dozen times in the sixteenth century. There were guides to conduct at court, of which the most famous was the Italian

Baldassare Castiglione's *Il Cortegiano* (1528; first English translation, 1561); and there were Italian works on the civil behaviour appropriate for everyday life more generally, such as Giovanni della Casa's *Galateo* (1558; first English translation, 1576) and Stefano Guazzo's *La civil conversazione* (1574; English translation, 1581–86). In the seventeenth century, French models predominated, led by Nicolas Faret's *L'Honnête homme* (1630; translated, 1631), which was about 'the art of pleasing at court', and Antoine de Courtin's *Nouveau traité de la civilité* (1671; translated in the same year and offering detailed guidance on correct behaviour in a wide range of social situations).

These books and others like them were reissued frequently, paraphrased, adapted, imitated, plagiarized and extensively read (Plate 1).[17] There were also many English treatises on the nurture of children, the education of nobles and gentlemen, and on conversation, letter writing and other social accomplishments. There were innumerable letters of parental advice on manners, both published and unpublished, the most celebrated example being the collection of letters written to his illegitimate son between 1738 and 1768 by the diplomat and politician Lord Chesterfield, which were posthumously published in 1774 and repeatedly issued or excerpted thereafter. It has been estimated that there were, at the very least, five hundred separate editions of works on good manners published in England from 1690 to 1760 alone.[18] In the eighteenth century the novel emerged as another influential guide to conduct: Samuel Richardson saved readers the trouble of ploughing through his multivolume narratives of *Pamela, Clarissa* and *Sir Charles Grandison* by issuing in 1775 a separate *Collection of the Moral and Instructive Sentiments, Maxims, Cautions and Reflexions* they contained.

This mountain of published literature of advice has received a great deal of attention from modern historians.[19] But it is important to remember that civility was a social phenomenon rather than a literary one. Civil behaviour preceded the literature of civility; and although many individuals conscientiously followed the precepts set out in the manuals, those precepts were usually codifications and rationalizations of previously existing social practices and attitudes. Huge though it was, the volume of publication gives only a faint indication of the amount of time and attention that was devoted by early modern parents, teachers and others to the training of the young in bodily comportment and civil behaviour.

Writing in the 1930s, Norbert Elias regarded this activity as part of what he called 'the civilizing process', by which he meant the increasing self-regulation of bodily drives and emotional impulses.[20] He saw the Middle Ages as a time of unchecked impulses, when people lacked self-control and were given over to childlike oscillations of mood, accompanied by carelessness about the bodily functions and a disposition to spontaneous violence.[21] It was only during the early modern period, he thought, that Western European monarchs managed to achieve something approaching a monopoly on physical violence,* by pacifying their warlike nobility and forcing them to abandon their old military values, to learn civil modes of behaviour, and to look to the court for their advancement and to the law for the resolution of their disputes. Elias suggested that in the later Middle Ages those of high social rank imposed a stricter control of emotions and bodily impulses on their social inferiors. It was regarded as offensive to belch, say, or to wipe one's nose on one's sleeve in the presence of the king or some great man. Later, with the increasing division of labour in society at large and the lengthening of chains of social and economic interdependence in the world outside the court, the pressure for self-restraint intensified, violent emotional outbursts became less frequent, inhibitions were internalized, and enhanced feelings of shame and disgust surrounded the public performance of the bodily functions, so that their concealment ultimately became second nature to most people. In this way, Elias argued, polite manners, which had originated as a form of deference to rulers and other superiors, percolated

---

* It could never be a complete monopoly, of course, for masters continued to beat their servants, husbands their wives, parents their children, and schoolteachers their pupils.

society at large and came to express an enhanced capacity to empathize with other people.[22]

Elias exaggerated and misunderstood the inclination of medieval people to violent and unrestrained behaviour. The publicly expressed anger of medieval kings and aristocrats did not necessarily indicate an inability to contain their emotions; it was a stylized form of behaviour regarded as appropriate to their status – a political convention rather than a psychological condition.[23] This suggests that what changed in the early modern period was not the degree of personal self-control, but the prevailing conventions about how and when emotions should be publicly expressed.[24]

The author of the best subsequent study of English civility has a more sophisticated view of medieval people than did Elias, but she also sees the sixteenth century as marking a new departure in the history of manners. In the Middle Ages, she suggests, most rules for polite behaviour related only to the performance of dinner rituals in royal and noble households, and to conduct in the presence of superiors. They tended to be mere injunctions and prohibitions, unsupported by much in the way of philosophical justification. In the sixteenth and seventeenth centuries, she argues, the laws of civility were put into a wider moral and intellectual context. There was a new emphasis on civility as a form of self-presentation and on the indispensability of manners for social harmony.[25]

Early modern writing about manners did indeed achieve a complexity and sophistication unequalled in the medieval past. Thanks to the invention of printing, it also gained a much wider readership than that of its predecessors. But it would be wrong to regard the preoccupation with polite behaviour as in any way a sixteenth-century invention. There never has been a society without any conventions about proper modes of bodily comportment and social interaction. All stratified societies have their rules of etiquette and self-control. Such conventions existed long before they were written down, and the early modern period was certainly not the first to codify them. Elias's viewpoint was limited in both time and space. He took no account of social behaviour in classical antiquity, and he had little to say about the practices of extra-European societies, such as the Chinese, celebrated for their 'courtesy, compliments and ceremonies', or the Ottomans, with their elaborate code for behaviour in social gatherings.[26] Rather than exemplifying a steady 'civilizing process', history can be seen as the story of how different patterns of conventional restraint have succeeded each other.[27] Elias was right to emphasize that those conventions differed in their content, with some permitting more expression of the passions than others. But no people has ever managed without any socially prescribed inhibitions or implicit code of behaviour. As one of Elias's critics has remarked, if 'control of affect' is the essence of the civilizing process, then so-called primitives would rank very high. The author of an eighteenth-century account of the Native Americans reported that 'no people have their anger, or at least the show of their anger, more under their control ... This is one of the principal objects of their education.' The Scottish philosopher and political economist Adam Smith similarly pointed out that 'the rules of decorum among civilized nations admit of a more animated behaviour than is approved of among barbarians'; the latter were 'obliged to smother and conceal the appearance of every passion', whereas 'polished' peoples were frank and open.[28]

Later in his life, Elias conceded that 'as far back as one can see, human beings have internalised some constraints'. In his opinion, however, earlier societies were often characterized by fluctuations between an extreme level of constraint and an extreme level of nonconstraint. The civilizing process, by contrast, he saw as 'the advance towards a stable, uniform and moderate level of constraint'.[29]

Throughout the European Middle Ages, elaborate codes of courtesy and behaviour had been inculcated at royal courts and in noble households, cathedral schools, monasteries and nunneries. Such institutions were recognized places for the nurture of the young and their training in urbanity and correct social demeanour.[30] There was a continuous current of didactic writing on manners, particularly table manners, directed primarily at the children of the well-to-do. The twelfth-century treatise *Urbanus Magnus* by Daniel of Beccles covers behaviour in a wide range of social situations: in its preoccupation with propriety and bodily restraint it stands comparison with the Italian archbishop Giovanni della Casa's hugely influential *Galateo*, written three hundred and fifty years later.[31] Ideals of self-control, refinement, polished speech and affability, inherited from Rome, were conspicuous in the Latin and Anglo-Norman literature of the twelfth and thirteenth centuries; and they recurred in the English prose and poetry of the fourteenth and fifteenth centuries. Medieval writers invoked not just *civilitas*, but also such associated concepts as *urbanitas* (suavity), *facetia* (witty speech), *curialitas* (courtliness), *modestia* (moderation), *mansuetudo* (mildness), *verecundia* (modesty), and *dulcedo* (agreeableness). They also had words such as *incultus* (uncouth), *sordidus* (squalid), and *incompositus* (unruly) to indicate their opposites.[32]

The precondition of this writing on manners was the existence of a public realm of sociability. A recent study concludes that face-to-face politeness 'may not have played a major role in Anglo-Saxon England'.[33] Yet the halls of the Anglo-Saxon kings had protocols that, in their way, may have been as stylized as those of the court of Charles II.[34] Medieval courtiers had to have appropriate social skills if they were to win royal favour, just as the communities of monks and nuns needed rules of considerate and decent behaviour, not least concerning their bodily emissions, if they were to live together harmoniously.[35] In the statutes for the Oxford college he founded in 1517, Bishop Richard Fox ruled that its members should avoid all forms of insulting behaviour and strive to live lovingly together, for there was nothing more necessary for his community than proper manners (*morum honestas*).[36] In later medieval England, a rich associational life, focused on crafts, guilds and religious fraternities, generated conventions of civil interaction that, in order to outlaw quarrelling and ensure social harmony, stressed the importance of courtesy, self-restraint and mutual respect.[37] In the provincial towns and cities of the early modern period, the freemen had their own codes of civility, enjoining them to perform their civic duties responsibly, to conduct their meetings in a dignified manner, to avoid 'opproprious words' and insulting speeches and to ensure decent order and public peace.[38] Whenever individuals came together in some form of public space, they required the personal skills conducive to peaceful and effective social intercourse.[39] Early modern manuals on civility were heavily indebted to classical antiquity: to the ethics of Aristotle and the teachings of Cicero and the Stoics on controlling the passions and the need for *modestia, humanitas, honestas* and *decorum*. As the Elizabethan poet George Gascoigne wrote,

> In Aristotle somewhat did I learn
> To guide my manners all by comeliness,
> And Tully taught me somewhat to discern
> Between sweet speech and barbarous rudeness.[40]

But Renaissance writings on good manners, like Erasmus's influential work on civility for children, also followed in the wake of a long medieval tradition of injunctions for polite behaviour.[41] The notion that modern manners originated with the Renaissance is an optical illusion, created by the invention of printing, the replacement of Latin by the vernacular, and the readiness of Renaissance humanists to ignore or disparage their medieval predecessors.

Of course, ideals about how to behave evolved over the centuries; and there are distinctions to be drawn between the *urbanitas* of the Romans, the 'courtesy' of medieval chivalry, the 'civility' of the Renaissance, the aristocratic and virtuous *honnêteté* of seventeenth-century France,[42] the 'politeness' of the eighteenth century, and the 'etiquette' of the nineteenth. Medieval discussions of good manners were much concerned with behaviour at the royal court and in noble households, or with life within religious communities; their primary objectives were to teach people to show respect to their lords and to avoid offending those with whom they had to live in close proximity. Although they had a wider circulation outside the court and the monasteries, particularly among schoolboys learning Latin, the ideals of refined conduct that were current in the twelfth century do not seem to have been proposed as a model for those who were not members of the upper ranks of society or involved in serving them; and concern for the feelings of those who were socially inferior did not enter into the discussion.

Early modern treatises, by contrast, tended to envisage a wider range of contexts and to take into account the totality of social relationships. They suggested that civil behaviour was incumbent on everyone, not only the social elite and their servants; and increasingly, they emphasized not just the negative prohibition on giving offence to superiors, but also a positive injunction to seek to please everybody with whom one came into contact. For the seventeenth-century theologian Henry More, 'civility' was 'a virtue that minds us of our tie to all men in the common link of humanity; and bids us with such cheerfulness of voice, countenance, and gesture to salute whom we meet; as that when we ask them how they do, they may think themselves even the better for our asking'. Civil behaviour, agreed John Locke, was a way of expressing the 'internal civility of the mind'. The 3rd Earl of Shaftesbury (1671–1713) also favoured 'that sort of civility which rises from a just sense of the common rights of mankind, and the natural equality there is among those of the same species'. The mid-seventeenth-century judge Sir Matthew Hale believed that without the rudiments of natural justice, charity and benignity, human society was impossible.[43]

Good manners thus came to be seen as a branch of morality, a religious duty to live 'honestly and civilly'.[44] Bodily comportment and emotional restraint were generally agreed to be outward signs of the inner dispositions of the soul. Injunctions to children to keep their hands clean or comb their hair were intermingled with reminders about the need to perform their religious duties.[45] One Elizabethan philosopher remarked that a man who served God devoutly and dealt uprightly with everyone was rightly called 'a civil man'. Another defined 'civility' as nothing 'but the manners of men grounded upon moral virtue and the precepts of wise men'.[46] Many of the early modern guides to manners and civility were written by deeply religious people. Castiglione's *Il Cortegiano* was translated by Sir Thomas Hoby, who went into exile during the reign of Mary I for the sake of his religion;[47] and in the eighteenth century a large chunk of an English paraphrase of Della Casa's *Galateo* was reissued by the founder of Methodism, John Wesley.[48] The Elizabethan divine Robert Shelford maintained that it was God's command that parents should teach their children 'good manners and civil behaviour'. 'Good manners are a very comely and seemly thing', agreed the Jacobean preacher William Gouge: 'The Holy Ghost himself hath prescribed many rules of good manners, and much urged and pressed the same.' This was not 'a mere complimental matter; it was a bounden duty'. Did not Christ preach the Golden Rule of 'Do as you would be done by' (Matthew 7:12)? And did not St Peter in his First Epistle (1:8) urge his readers to be 'courteous'? 'When all is done,' concluded the pious Lady Guilford (d. 1699), 'religion forms us to the best manners in the world.'[49] In this way the teachings of traditional religion were readjusted to fit the social priorities of the day.

Less overtly religious thinkers agreed that manners and morality were closely related. For Thomas Hobbes, moral philosophy was 'the science of what is good and evil in the conversation and society of mankind'. It was embodied in the laws of nature, prescribing the rules of behaviour that fitted citizens for 'civil society' and governing their 'manners and conversation one towards another'. These laws prohibited revenge, cruelty, hatred, contempt, insult and arrogance, and required citizens to behave in a 'modest and tractable' way, by maintaining 'a constant civil amity with all those with whom the business of the world constrains us to converse'.[50] Hobbes had read the Italian works on civil courtesy and was indebted to them. For him, as for Norbert Elias, self-control and forbearance were as important causes of peace as the coercive power of the sovereign.[51] Hobbes also described the conventions for good manners in company as 'the small morals'. His admirer William Petty used the same term to describe 'the arts and offices of civility'. So did the future bishop Samuel Parker when referring to 'the arts of behaviour and conversation'.[52] For the *Spectator* in 1711 the 'great foundation of civil virtue' was 'self-denial'.[53] The virtuoso Roger North regarded 'good breeding' as 'a branch of that we call morality', a sentiment that would be echoed by David Hume, who described the laws of good manners as 'a kind of lesser morality, calculated for the ease of company and conversation'. Half a century later, the Utilitarian reformer Jeremy Bentham classified manners as a 'branch of morality' relating to those trivial matters 'by which the greatest portion of that part of every man's time which is passed in the company of another or others is occupied'.[54]

In the eighteenth century 'good breeding' was held to include the duty of 'contributing, with our utmost power, to the satisfaction and happiness of all about us', 'showing men, by external signs, the internal regard we have for them'.[55] It meant, as the elder Pitt, later Earl of Chatham, explained, 'benevolence in trifles, or the preference of others to ourselves in little daily, hourly occurrences in the commerce of life': offering them a better seat, letting them go through the door or help themselves first. David Hume and Lord Chesterfield both stressed that civility involved sacrificing one's own self-love to that of others, and Chesterfield added that 'good breeding' taught men how to do so 'with ease, propriety and grace'. The emphasis was on affability, easiness and making oneself agreeable.[56] For this, tact was essential, though few can have matched that of the actor Thomas Betterton (d. 1710), who was said to have been 'so indirect in his reproofs that he had an art of showing men their foibles without their seeing that this was what he intended'.[57]

Chesterfield was more concerned with external appearances than with internal sentiment, but others held that civil behaviour should spring spontaneously from a benevolent and good-natured 'sweetness of mind', what John Locke had characterized as a 'general good will and regard for all people'.[58] An early model of this kind of civility was the learned Norwich physician Thomas Browne (1605–82), who was especially commended by the diarist John Evelyn for his 'extraordinary humanity' and 'communicable nature', and who brought up his son Thomas to be 'patient, civil, and debonair unto all'.[59]

By contrast, nineteenth-century rules of etiquette, about how to address letters or whether one should use fish knives, were purely arbitrary prescriptions, peculiar to a particular social milieu and lacking any moral or mental foundation, though of intense interest to the upwardly mobile, anxious to verse themselves in the habits of polite society.[60]

'Good breeding', like the closely associated notion of 'politeness', was often defined as 'the art of pleasing in company', but these terms alluded to something much broader than mere good manners. In the eighteenth century they implied not just courteous demeanour and considerate behaviour, but taste, sophisticated conversation and mental cultivation more generally. The word 'polite' derived from the Latin *politus*, meaning polished. Any object with a smooth or glossy surface, such as a pearl or a jewel, might be described as 'polite'. The anatomist Samuel Collins even wrote in 1685 of 'the elegant politeness and lovely colour' of the human skin.[61] By analogy, the term had been applied since the early sixteenth century to language, whether written or spoken, when it was meticulously correct, pleasingly composed, and free from any hint of 'rudeness' or linguistic 'barbarism'. The best spoken English was that which was 'clean', 'perfectly and articulately pronounced', and 'polite'; and the best writing was praised for its 'exquisite politeness'.[62]

As late as 1691, it was claimed that 'most people confine politeness to language only'.[63] But since the 1640s and 1650s, the English had, largely through translations of French works, become familiar with wider connotations of the term than those of mere linguistic virtuosity.[64] Politeness came to be associated with education, erudition and knowledge of the arts and sciences. Contemporaries spoke of 'the solid politeness of the Greek and Hebrew learning'. In 1687 a writer could congratulate his patron on the 'politeness' of his knowledge, which extended to 'the whole circle of sciences'.[65] The more usual tendency, however, was to assume that 'polite' learning and literature were different because they were designed to please, unlike less ingratiating forms of erudition that were technical in content and inelegant in expression. The Elizabethan literary historian Francis Meres remarked that admirers of 'polite literature' were offended by the 'intricate', 'crabbed' and 'obscure' sophistries of the medieval schoolmen; while his contemporary, the legal writer William Fulbecke, associated 'the more polite learning' with the 'milder sciences'. By contrast, Edward Martin, the Restoration dean of Ely, studied 'the exact sciences, logic and mathematics', 'his nature inclining to solidity rather than politeness'.[66]

Politeness was a form of social distinction and self-advertisement. As the French political philosopher Montesquieu remarked, 'It is pride that renders us polite; we are flattered with being taken notice of for a behaviour that shows we are not of a mean condition and that we have not been bred up with those who in all ages are considered as the scum of the people.'[67] Politeness involved distancing oneself from the culture of the populace and being in tune with the latest cultural fashions of the European elite. It required a refined taste and a degree of literary and artistic education. In 1656 an English visitor to Paris praised the French Queen Mother's house, then under construction in the Faubourg St Germain, for the 'elegancy and politeness of the fabric'.[68] Shaftesbury ruled that good breeding involved learning whatever was decent in company or beautiful in the arts. The painter Jonathan

Richardson thought that the progress of politeness was such that 'the time will come when it shall be as dishonourable for a gentleman not to be a connoisseur, as now 'tis not to be able to read any other than his own language, or not to see the beauties of a good author'.[69]

Although a writer referred to 'politeness of manners' as early as 1654,[70] it was not until the end of the seventeenth century that it became common to describe civil and well-mannered behaviour as 'polite'. A French/English dictionary explained that the word *politesse*, when used of conversation rather than of language, meant the opposite of 'rude', and implied 'gallantry' and a 'handsome carriage'. In 1694 another manual defined 'politeness' as 'a mixture of civility, decency, discretion and complaisance, accompanied with a gentle and pleasant air, overspread upon all our words and actions'.[71]

This ethic of urbane sociability was wholly French in inspiration. It was partly because of the influence of Charles II, who, according to John Evelyn, 'brought in a politer way of living', that 'politeness' became increasingly the vogue in later seventeenth-century England.[72] Its appeal was reinforced in the reign of Anne by the influential journalism of the *Spectator* and *Tatler*. It did not displace 'civility' as the more usual term for mannerly behaviour, but it became a central value in the upper- and aspiring middle-class culture of the eighteenth century.[73]

As the word suggested, politeness stood for what was smooth and polished, conducive to social harmony and supportive of the established order. It implied the superiority of the elegant and pleasing to the useful and economically productive,* of belles lettres ('polite literature') to learned treatises, and of decorous religious conformity to disruptive enthusiasm. It proscribed all forms of dissent and angularity. It was a way of asserting the superiority of the leisured upper ranks of society and distancing them not just from the vulgar, but also from the worlds of commerce, provincialism and nonconformity.[74] It implied a

---

* Though Jonathan Richardson claimed that if polite English gentlemen were to build up their art collections, they would benefit the country by attracting foreign tourists; *Two Discourses* (1719), vol. 2, 49.

sensibility so exquisite that the pain arising from a transgression of civility or good breeding could prove overwhelming.[75] Civility was a social duty expected of everyone, but politeness was a distinctive hallmark of the elite. It was portrayed as a state of refinement equivalent to 'civility' in its widest sense, that is to say 'civilization'.[76]

The conventions of civil behaviour were subject to incessant changes of fashion. The funeral monument for an Oxford academic who died in 1665 commended him for his 'agreeable, albeit old-fashioned courtesy'; and when Anthony Wood visited his fellow antiquary William Prynne in 1667, he was received with 'old-fashion[ed] compliments, such as were used in the reign of K[ing] James I'.[77] Yet there was much underlying continuity over the centuries. That was why versions of sixteenth-century conduct books were still being reissued and read two hundred years later.[78] In 1683 a writer noted that, although polite ceremonies changed 'almost every year', the 'true rules of civility' were constant.[79] The late-eighteenth-century art collector Richard Payne Knight agreed that the principles of good breeding or politeness were 'the same in all ages and all countries, how much soever the modes of showing them may vary'.[80] Many modern sociolinguists accept this conclusion: the concept of politeness, they say, is universal; what differs from culture to culture and from time to time are its specific manifestations.[81]

Eighteenth-century politeness served as an ideology that justified the wealth, elegant living, leisured consumption and social privileges of a rentier oligarchy in face of the challenge presented by austere, neoclassical objections to 'luxury'.[82] It also helped an increasingly wealthy class of merchants and financiers to consolidate their social pretensions. But rather than being 'an explicitly innovative concept of social refinement', as is sometimes claimed, it was essentially a developed version of medieval and Renaissance notions of courtesy and gentlemanly education.[83] As one eighteenth-century historian remarked, doubtless with Geoffrey Chaucer's paragon in mind, it was in the Middle Ages that 'politeness became a knightly virtue'.

And of his part as meeke as is a mayde.
He nevere yet no vileynye [rudeness] ne sayde
In al his lyf unto no maner wight.
He was a verray, parfit gentil knight.[84]

Manners and Gentility

Far from being an eighteenth-century novelty, the concern of the social elite to distinguish itself by its manners, deportment and cultural accomplishments had been in evidence since Anglo-Saxon times.[85] Although the original basis of aristocratic power was military prowess, those seeking royal favour or public office had long been expected to have other qualities as well. Medieval romance literature suggests that a high value was set on eloquence, personal charm, conversational skills and emotional sensitivity.[86] In the later Middle Ages, it was regarded as 'mannerly' for young gentlemen to play the harp, sing, dance, learn languages, read 'books of eloquence' and be instructed in 'the schools of urbanity and nurture of England'.[87] In the Tudor period, gentlemen aspiring to preferment at court were expected to excel not just at riding, hunting and fighting, but also in literature, music, dancing, conversation and all forms of 'courtly behaviour'.[88] The vocabulary of manners, courtesy, civility and politeness was constantly evolving, but the prescriptions offered remained in many ways the same.

What did change during the early modern period was the increasing readiness of the nobility and gentry to adopt the ethic of civility and, later, of politeness as a way of modifying the more asser-tive notions of honour, military prowess and superiority of lineage that had dominated aristocratic culture in earlier ages. The values of sociability and urbanity, articulated by the courtesy writers of Northern Italy, appealed to English gentlemen who were spending more time in London, participating in metropolitan society and meeting regularly in the county towns for the conduct of judicial business. Their enhanced social interaction made the culture of civility increasingly relevant; and so did the growing centrality of the royal court as the place where favours were granted, marriages made and careers advanced.

In the past, widely dispersed landowners, living relatively isolated lives in hierarchically organized households and exercising lordship over a chain of semifeudal dependants, had less incentive to adopt these new styles of social behaviour or to acquire the cultural baggage required by metropolitan standards of politeness. Their rules of courtesy were largely concerned with the provision of hospitality and the protocol governing dinner in their halls. But the opening up of new forms of public interaction made the need for other social skills increasingly imperative. As the courtesy writers repeatedly stressed, ancient lineage was not enough to sustain the authority of the aristocracy; gentlemen also needed to show that they were intrinsically worthy of exercising power; and for that, an impressive personal manner and a cultivated style of life became ever more desirable. The landed elite was becoming conscious of itself as a unified class rather than as an amalgam of competing alliances and affinities. Its military function was not as central as it had been. A distinctive code of manners helped the nobility and gentry to define themselves as the ruling elite, to coexist harmoniously and to be respected by their plebeian inferiors for their merit rather than just their ancestry.[89]

The early modern period was a transitional phase in this civilizing of the aristocracy. The nobility and gentry were still quick to move from words to blows, but the feuding between rival families that had been such a feature of sixteenth-century life on the Borders with Scotland gradually declined after the Union of the Crowns;[90] and although aristocratic involvement in affrays and violent assaults did not disappear in seventeenth-century England, it was less frequent than it had been.[91] This was true of the Western European upper classes more generally.[92] It was not, as Elias argued, a sign of growing self-control. Some medieval violence was, no doubt, the result of sudden impulse, but most was a matter of purposeful and deliberate action.[93] The reason that homicide rates dwindled was not that the aristocracy had become capable of greater self-mastery, but that their values were changing in response to the growing power and legitimacy of the Tudor monarchy. Increasingly exposed to humanist notions of civil virtue, they were readier to seek honour by serving the Crown than by manipulating their retinues in pursuit of private feuds and vendettas.[94]

Yet although the upper classes were less physically ferocious than they had been, the demands of personal honour remained insistent. The sixteenth century saw the appearance of the formal duel as an accepted means of avenging insult. Despite legal prohibitions, thousands of duels were fought by nobles, gentlemen and army officers in the ensuing centuries; and the practice continued until the reign of Queen Victoria. These stylized and rule-bound encounters are usually seen as marking a step forwards from the uncontrolled violence of the feud or vendetta. Their formality served as a check upon immediate impulse; and although an insult had to be requited by a challenge, it was thought essential that it be issued and received 'with perfect calm and composure', any asperity or invective being regarded as 'a sign of unmanly weakness'.[95] It has even been argued that duels were positively encouraged by the idea of civility. The duelling ethic, it is said, was part of the theory of civil behaviour imported from Italy; and since the risk of being challenged to fight was a strong incentive to treat other people with respect, the duelling code could be represented as a means of encouraging the practice of good manners. In the early eighteenth century, the physician-philosopher Bernard Mandeville claimed that, without it, thousands of 'mannerly' gentlemen in Europe would have been 'insolent and insupportable coxcombs': the nation, he argued, should not grudge losing perhaps half a dozen men a year in order to obtain so valuable a blessing as 'the politeness of manners, the pleasure of conversation, and the happiness of company in general'. David Hume thought that nothing was more 'absurd and barbarous' than the practice of duelling, but he conceded that 'those who justify it claim that it begets civility and good manners'.[96] The twentieth-century philosopher R. G. Collingwood remarked that 'the most beautiful manners I have met with are in countries where men carry knives, and, if anybody gives them a nasty word or a nasty look, stick them into him'.[97]

In 1606 the travel writer Sir Thomas Palmer lamented that the duelling ethic was one of several 'inconveniences and corruptions' brought in by 'the civility of Italy'; and in 1614 a royal proclamation declared that 'this bravery was first born and bred in foreign parts, but after conveyed over into this island'.[98] In fact, some Italian authorities on civility had, like Giovanni della Casa, author of *Galateo*, expressed hostility to the duel; and many of the English exponents of Italian-style civility refused to condone what they regarded as a 'licentious and brutish custom'.[99] The Elizabethan gentleman who wrote *The Courte of Civill Courtesie* (1577) conceded that there were circumstances in which a duel was unavoidable; but he regarded such an outcome as a 'tragedy' and gave extensive advice on how to avoid it.[100]

In his *Discourse of Civil Life* (published in 1606, but composed in the 1580s), the administrator Lodowick Bryskett denounced duelling as a barbarous legacy of the Middle Ages, unknown to the ancients, 'contrary to all equity, and all civil and honest conversation', and destructive of 'civil society'. This was a near-verbatim translation of a section in Giraldi Cinthio's dialogues on *la vita civilè* (1565), in which the Italian dramatist strongly attacked duelling in the name of civility.[101] As a means of enforcing good manners, the duelling ethic had obvious limitations. Sir Walter Ralegh protested that 'all that is rude ought not to be civilized with death', while Thomas Hobbes observed that the code of honour meant 'civility towards men that will not swallow injuries, and injury to them that will'. The philosopher George Berkeley noted in 1732 that those who would not risk offending some bullying duellist had no hesitation about insulting a clergyman.[102] Opponents of the duel made a point of explaining that the practice was incompatible with 'true civility' and repeatedly denounced it as 'wicked' and 'barbarous'. Duelling, claimed an experienced traveller in 1678, was 'now forbidden by all civilized nations'.[103] Its survival into the early nineteenth century revealed that the conversion of the British ruling class to the new ethic of civility was only partial. Honour and reputation remained attributes to be cherished and, if necessary, preserved by violence. Nevertheless, although aristocratic involvement in drunken brawls, rape and even murder was not uncommon in the later seventeenth century, quarrels over honour and precedence seem to have become less frequent thereafter. Samuel Johnson related in 1773 how, when his mother lived in London in the late seventeenth century, there were 'two sorts of people, those who gave the wall and those who took it: the peaceable and the quarrelsome'. But 'now it is fixed that every man keeps to the right; or if one is taking the wall, another yields it; and it is never a dispute'.[104]

Most courtesy writers agreed that governing elites should cultivate refined manners which would distinguish them from their social inferiors and symbolize their right to rule. Superior bodily comportment had been thought important since the fourth century BC, when the Greek upper classes adopted an upright posture and an unhurried gait, regarding the strict control of emotion as essential to their authority.[105] It was still so regarded in nineteenth-century Britain, where, as a contemporary put it, 'a gentleman [held] himself differently from a labourer, and his features express[ed] altogether a different class of emotions and recollections'.[106] In the early modern period, those who wished to rule others needed the right sort of 'carriage' or 'mien', of the kind described by contemporaries as 'noble', 'stately', 'graceful' or 'winning'. As the Eton schoolmaster William Horman told his pupils, 'Goodliness of person increaseth authority.'[107]

There was an ethical dimension to this advice, for early modern commentators shared the medieval belief that physical demeanour was a moral indicator. What Erasmus called 'the outward honesty of the body' (*externum corporis decorum*) was a guide to the inward disposition of the soul. Simon Robson thought that 'to show a certain stateliness in going' was a sure sign of pride, and the poet Richard Brathwait wrote in 1630 that he had 'seen in the gait [of some men] such arguments of a proud heart that if the body had been transparent it could not have been clearer'.[108]

The primary purpose of training in bodily deportment was social differentiation. In the words of the English translator of Guazzo's *La civil conversazione*, 'We are so much the more esteemed by how much our civility differeth from the nature and fashions of the vulgar.'[109] The aristocracy did not just dress more opulently than their social inferiors, live in grander houses and have more servants and possessions. They also moved and spoke differently. Speech, manners, posture and gesture were instant social distinguishers, an essential element in the self-definition of the ruling elite, and reliable proof of their superior breeding (Plates 5 and 7). As a writer commented in 1649, 'Persons of a truly gentle and perfect education in points of civility can easily perceive, at the first interview, by manner of salutation, of obeisance, of posture, gesture and speech, whether a youth have been well educated or not.'[110]

Just as Erasmus had repeatedly urged his schoolboy readers not to behave like *rustici* or *agricolae* ('carters' and 'ploughmen' in the translation of 1532), so his English imitators stressed the importance of being different from 'the unpolished and illiterate rout'.[111] The seventeenth-century poet Thomas Traherne thought that 'a clown and a courtier' were 'known by their postures'; and the eighteenth-century aesthete Archibald Alison explained that the expression on the face of a great merchant was as different from that of a small shopkeeper as were the features of a landlord from those of a tenant.[112] A gentleman was someone who knew how to move, how to enter a room, how to doff his hat, what to do with it when he had doffed it, and how to take his leave. To come into company 'without some civil or affable speech' savoured of 'rusticity', and to depart 'without taking of leave or salutation' suggested 'incivility and contempt'. 'How few there are,' lamented Lord Clarendon, 'who make an entry into a room where much company is with that grace and assurance that becomes them, especially if they feel the eyes of men upon them, which disorders their countenance, makes them go faster, [and] put their heads and hands and feet into twenty antic motions.'[113] 'Moving and speaking,' thought the Scottish judge Lord Monboddo, 'distinguish a gentleman and lady in company, more than any other thing I know.'[114] Even handwriting, it was claimed, should display 'what we admire in fine gentlemen: an easiness of gesture and disengaged air, which is imperceptibly caught from frequently conversing with the polite and well-bred'.[115] The ideal was of someone whose manners, facial expression and gestures had been fashioned into a work of art marked by elegance and self-control.

The ingredients of polite bodily deportment changed over time.[116] In the early eighteenth century, the fashionable way for a gentleman to stand for his portrait was with his right hand tucked into his waistcoat and the other in his pocket or resting above his sword hilt, and with his feet turned outwards. Crossed legs were an alternative (and long-established) symbol of lordly insouciance. Today the classical ballet preserves many of these now obsolete modes of deportment: standing splayfooted or leading people by the hand. By the 1760s these mannerisms had come to seem vulgar because they had been disseminated by dancing masters and adopted by the middling classes when they had themselves painted. Sir Joshua Reynolds rejected all formal postures, and crossed legs were dismissed as 'a very trivial position'.[117]

But certain features of deportment were constant. It was agreed that the well-bred man should stand upright. He should not scratch, wriggle, pick his ears, crook his back or hold his head on one side. He should not sing or whistle in public places. He should not display curiosity, for example, by reading other people's letters over their shoulders. Above all, he should always appear unhurried and relaxed. A gentleman should never be seen running in the street.[118] 'Many men seeing you pass by them,' warned a Jacobean authority, 'will conceive presently [i.e., immediately] a good or bad opinion of you. Wherefore ye must take very good heed unto your feet, and consider with what grace and countenance you walk.' 'Fast going becometh not grave men', agreed another. Any impression of haste or agitation was to be avoided. To be in a hurry, warned a nineteenth-century conduct book, 'may appear well in a mechanic or tradesman, but ill suits the character of a gentleman or man of fashion'.[119] This notion reached its apotheosis in the pronouncement by the twentieth-century writer and socialite Nancy Mitford that 'any sign of haste, in fact, is apt to be non-U, and I go so far as preferring, except for business letters, not to use air mail'.[120]

The importance attached to bodily 'carriage' helped to create a market for corsets, trusses, artificial limbs and other devices for concealing or correcting physical defects.[121] It also made dancing an essential part of polite education. Since at least Tudor times, aristocratic families had employed dancing teachers for their children.[122] They did so not just because the ability to dance was a necessary social accomplishment and an essential aid to courtship, but because they believed it would shape the way their offspring moved and held themselves. 'Young men are taught to dance,' wrote an authority in 1660, 'not so much for to tread such a measure of steps to the tune played, as to carry their bodies well at all times and places; so that you may easily see whether any one has been taught that art ... by the neat and graceful deportment of his body.' Dancing masters taught 'gesture' and how 'to walk and make a leg'; they wiped off 'all that plainness of nature, which the à-la-mode people call "clownishness"'.[123] Lord Chesterfield urged his son to attend particularly to 'the graceful motion of your arms', together 'with the manner of putting on your hat, and giving your hand ... It will give you an habitual genteel carriage and manner of presenting yourself.' Dancing, he claimed, along with riding and fencing, would 'civilize and fashion' the body.[124] In 1772 the Lancashire flax merchant Thomas Langton urged his son to learn dancing because it gave young people 'a pretty easy manner and an agreeable behaviour'.[125] It was important, however, to avoid the slickness of a professional: to dance *too* exquisitely, thought one authority, was not polite (Plate 6). The best tactic was to dance with 'a kind of artful carelessness, as if it were a natural motion, without a too curious and painful practising'.[126]

If one wished to acquire superior manners, there was no substitute for moving in the right circles. In 1596 the Earl of Pembroke, president of the Council in the Marches, held 'a good Christmas in the castle of Ludlow'. By attending so honourable a gathering, it was said, a young Welsh gentleman could expect to learn 'as much behaviour and good manners as should have stuck by him ever after whilst he lived'.[127] Until the end of the sixteenth century, training in deportment was offered in noble and gentry households, where children were regularly boarded out as servants, specifically in order to learn good manners.[128] In the 1580s, John Smyth, the future steward to the Berkeley family in Gloucestershire, was a serving boy in the household of Lady Katherine, wife of the first Lord Berkeley. On one occasion, he passed her when he was hastening to deliver breakfast to her son. He acknowledged her with only a perfunctory curtsy, whereupon she called him back and made him do it a hundred times. 'And such was her great nobleness to me therein,' he records, 'that to show me the better how, she lifted up all her garments to the calf of her leg that I might better observe the grace of drawing back the foot and bowing of the knee.'[129] Similarly, in an Elizabethan play by Thomas Heywood, Mistress Arthur instructs her servants:

There was a curtsey. Let me see't again.
Ay, that was well.[130]

In 1599, when the vicar of Amwell, Hertfordshire, was looking for a tenant to farm his house and glebe, he settled on 'an ancient and honest man, who had a good comely and cleanly woman to his wife'; they had both in their youth been brought up in a gentleman's service 'in good fashion' and 'by that means savour[ed] somewhat of civility'.[131] Courtesy and civility became necessary qualifications for those seeking employment in gentry households; and servants, by imitation and out of deference, often adopted genteel standards of appearance and behaviour, sometimes more genteel than those of their masters (as can be seen in some modern Oxford senior common rooms, where black-coated butlers wait impassively on gesticulating Fellows clad in sweaters and jeans).[132]

In genteel families, conscientious parents attached much importance to early training in deportment, putting their children under tutors and governors who, it was hoped, would 'break their natural rudeness and mould them into some form of civility'.[133] In the early 1660s, Dr Thomas Browne of Norwich, anxious that his son Thomas should acquire 'a good garb of body', repeatedly urged him to 'put on a decent boldness and avoid *pudor rusticus* [rustic bashfulness]'. Twenty years later, Sir William Petty was similarly concerned that his ten-year-old son Henry should know how to make 'a leg salute' when he came into company; he advised his other son, Charles, to 'pitch upon ten good families whereupon to practise civility and conversation'.[134] In the eighteenth century, Lord Chesterfield stressed that 'perfect good breeding' could be acquired only by 'keeping the best company'. His contemporary, the floral artist Mrs Delany, agreed: 'To acquire a gracious manner' a young girl needed to see 'a variety of good company' in Bath or London, preferably when she was between the ages of seven and fourteen.[135]

In the grammar schools, training in civility and good manners was a regular part of the syllabus, even to the extent of being regarded by many as more important than academic learning. Here too there was heavy emphasis on gesture and demeanour. One educational writer recommended that schoolteachers should give practical demonstrations of the right way of standing, walking, entering a room and delivering a message.[136] School plays and other forms of oral work were meant not just to teach elocution, but also to overcome ungainliness and inculcate a graceful posture. When the young Robert Boyle acted in a school play at Eton in 1635, he had only a nonspeaking part; but his father was reassured that, 'for the gesture of his body and the order of his pace, he did bravely'.[137] In 1693 some of the Catholic gentry who sent their sons overseas to be educated in the Jesuit College of St Omer's in Flanders wanted the school uniform to be changed because the long cassocks or gowns then in use encouraged boys to develop 'a slovenly manner of walking, much like rustics, not as is expected of them in polite society'.[138] The Quaker Benjamin Furly poured scorn on parents who sent their sons to schools 'to learn them to walk and shail [shuffle] their legs in dancing, to doff their hats, and wring their bodies in congees [ceremonious leave-taking], and how to hold their hands, heads, necks, and make fine courtesies backwards, and such like things'.[139]

By the eighteenth century, the essence of correct deportment had become a high degree of bodily control and a strict inhibition on the display of inappropriate feeling. Civility, as one authority put it, consisted in 'containing one's self'.[140] This marked a departure from the earlier assumption that there was no emotion that could not be decently displayed when circumstances demanded it. For the literary critic George Puttenham in 1589, there was 'a comeliness' to be discerned in all passions: 'To be angry, or to envy, or to hate, or to pity, or to be ashamed decently: that is none otherwise than reason requireth.'[141] For Adam Smith in 1762, by contrast, politeness consisted in 'composure, calm and unruffled behaviour'. His contemporary, the actor Thomas Sheridan, agreed: good breeding involved 'suppressing all visible emotions of nature'.[142]

Even those who, like Puttenham, allowed the 'decent' display of emotion set limits to its expression. Just as in the twelfth century the courtesy writer Daniel of Beccles had condemned noisy laughter, so in the sixteenth Erasmus taught that it was unseemly to express mirth in such a way that the body shook with passion; one should never open one's mouth when laughing. The early Tudor schoolmaster William Horman warned his pupils that 'uncleanly and lewd laughter disworshippeth thee [robs you of respect]', and that it was a 'rebuke' for an honest man at a great feast to laugh 'indiscreetly'. The author of a late-seventeenth-century book of advice agreed that 'he which tells a merry passage without laughing appears to have some politeness'. In the following century, Lord Chesterfield regarded loud laughter as 'low and unbecoming', 'not to mention the disagreeable noise that it makes and the shocking distortion of the face'. The elder Pitt similarly thought it was 'better to smile than to laugh out loud', and the journalist Richard Steele ruled that the most that 'men of wit' should allow themselves was 'but a faint, constrained kind of half-laugh'.[143] In practice, of course, even the most meticulously correct gentleman would relax and permit himself a belly laugh when among his intimates.[144]

Tears were also suspect when shed by men. In a culture that still put a high value on military prowess, it was acceptable for males to express emotions of anger or pride, but tears were usually regarded as a sign of impotent weakness. It was not decent for a man to 'weep like a woman' or 'cry like a child'.[145] This assumption was reinforced by neo-Stoic doctrines of resignation in the face of misfortune. In Ben Jonson's Roman tragedy *Sejanus* (1603) a character calls for

> honourable sorrow, soldiers' sadness,
> A kind of silent mourning, such as men
> (Who know no tears, but from their captives) use
> To show in so great losses.[146]

More bathetically, James I's eldest son, Prince Henry, was praised because as a child he wept much less than other children of his age when he fell over and hurt himself.[147] The floggings that were for centuries an integral part of upper-class schooling were intended to teach pupils to endure pain without complaint: for the English gentry, as for the North American Indians, this was one of the principal objects of their education.[148]

Tears, however, were permissible for men on solemn public occasions, such as the death or disgrace of great public figures, as when the demise of King Henry VIII was reported to Parliament in 1547; or at the fall of Cardinal Wolsey in 1530, of Sir Thomas More in 1534, of Thomas Cromwell in 1539, and of the 2nd Earl of Essex in 1601. They might also accompany moments of high political tension, as in 1628, when 'most part of the House [of Commons] fell a-weeping'; in 1629, when the Speaker collapsed into an 'extremity of weeping' with an 'abundance of tears'; in 1657, when General Charles Fleetwood passionately opposed the offer of the kingship to Oliver Cromwell; and in 1710 at the trial of the fiery High Church preacher Henry Sacheverell, whose 'elegant and pathetical' speech in his defence brought tears to the eyes of his supporters, male and female.[149] Tears were common in the theatre when tragedies were performed. They were also permitted when shed by mourners at funerals, but only in moderation, for there was a Protestant reaction against the Catholic notion that abundant weeping could help to speed the deceased's passage through purgatory.[150] In Shakespeare's *Henry VI, Part 2*, the virtuous Warwick weeps for his country's dishonour, while in *Hamlet* it is the wicked usurper Claudius who deplores his stepson's grief for his late father as 'unmanly'.[151]

Weeping by repentant sinners, whether men or women, had long been regarded as an acceptable sign of their contrition. Medieval nuns were urged to confess their sins 'with weeping tears or at the least with mourning, sobbing and sorrows for the doing of them'.[152] In the century after the Reformation, some clergy, and not just Puritans, adopted an emotional style of preaching designed to produce tears in both preacher and congregation. The Puritan minister Samuel Torshell declared that there were 'no eyes more lovely in God's sight than the eyes that are full of tears'; and the Laudian divine Thomas Lushington thought weeping was a 'kind of praying'.[153] In the eighteenth century, Methodists and evangelicals continued this tradition. The *Tatler* declared in 1709 that 'to be apt to shed tears is a sign of a great as well as a little spirit'.[154] This notion that a readiness to weep at the distress of others was an indication of a superior sensibility had seventeenth-century roots. The great Jacobean judge Sir Edward Coke, for example, never pronounced a sentence of death without weeping.[155] But the 'man of feeling', whose tears flowed freely, did not become a publicly acknowledged ideal until the mid-eighteenth century.[156] Henry Fielding was characteristic of his age when he told his fellow novelist Samuel Richardson in 1748 that he had been so moved by the plight of Clarissa that he had 'melted' with compassion and found 'what is called an effeminate relief'.[157] This literary affectation proved only a phase, for at the end of the century it was still widely believed that weeping was 'unmanly'.[158] Yet eighteenth-century hanging judges were often in floods of tears when passing death sentences.[159]

The general movement of polite masculine culture between the sixteenth and eighteenth centuries was in the direction of greater bodily reserve. As the protoanthropologist John Bulwer observed in 1645, each country had its own 'national decorum', and the English rhetorical style was more reserved than that of France or Italy.[160] Along with the inhibitions surrounding tears and laughter went the prohibition of gesticulation (which was regarded as an unpleasant foreign habit)[161] and the replacement of the kiss and other forms of close bodily contact on meeting (which seem to have gone out of fashion in the later seventeenth century) by a bow or a handshake.[162]

By the early seventeenth century, it had become a common practice for polite education to be rounded off by a period of travel in France and Italy, ideally accompanied by a tutor or 'governor' who had moved in the best circles in Europe and thereby 'polished and civilized himself'. In this way it was hoped that the sons of the nobility and gentry would learn 'sweetness of deportment' and achieve 'the glory of a perfect breeding and the perfection of that which we call civility'.[163] Italy and France, it was claimed, would 'teach us fine and fair carriage of our body, good and discreet delivery of our mind, civil and modest behaviour to others'.[164] Like many others, Sir John Digby, who set off for Flanders in 1619, was said to have 'reaped the true fruits from his travels by carefully and exactly polishing and civilizing his exterior man by the quaint gentleness of foreign nations'. In Lord Chesterfield's view, the 'true object' of foreign travel was to learn 'the best manners of every country',[165] for the essential ideals of politeness and civility were common to the social elites of Western Europe. Increasingly, it was the French who set the tone, while the English long retained a residual sense of cultural inferiority. A speaker in a mid-seventeenth-century dialogue claimed that foreign travel had 'filed off much of that roughness which used to appear in our behaviour and demeanour; we are more civil and courteous to strangers, and to one another, than the age before us was accustomed to be'. But in 1689 John Evelyn thought his fellow countrymen were still 'exceedingly defective in our civil addresses, excuses, apologies, and forms'; the Italians and Spaniards, he believed, 'exceed us infinitely in this point of good-breeding'.[166]

The growing popularity of the Grand Tour in the later seventeenth century reflected the gentry's diminishing faith in the universities as schools of politeness. During the fifteenth century, Oxford and Cambridge had laid growing emphasis on the moral and cultural formation of their students, who were trained to become cultivated clergy or silver-tongued public servants.[167] After the Reformation, the universities became an attractive destination for the sons of the landed classes. But whereas the Elizabethan and early Stuart nobility and gentry came to acquire a considerable respect for learning and often engaged in serious legal and antiquarian study, the beau monde of the later Stuart era tended to dismiss the Latinate erudition of humanist scholarship as 'pedantry', preferring belles lettres in the vernacular because they were more immediately pleasing and therefore 'polite'.

Academics were increasingly regarded as 'clownish' and lacking in 'urbanity'. It was because of their 'ill-breeding and unaccomplishments' that 'gentlemen of quality' were forced to send their sons abroad to learn how to behave. The learning of university scholars, it was said, was 'only a pedantic way of disputing and wrangling, which makes them ungrateful to all well-bred company'; and their manners were so 'rude' that when students came down from the university, 'a man would think by their behaviour that they had never been amongst gentlemen; at best, that they are so out of countenance and blush when they come into the company of ladies that they are even ridiculous'.[168]

The ladies themselves, of course, did not make the Grand Tour, any more than they went to grammar schools or universities. Instead, upper-class girls were trained in distinctly feminine modes of deportment at home, in another household or, occasionally, at a finishing school.[169] Before the Reformation, the nuns of Syon Abbey were subject to rules of deportment as elaborate as any of those later devised by Erasmus for the instruction of young men. They were told how to stand, how to sit, how to walk, how to behave at meals, how to laugh, and where to spit. In all their bodily behaviour they were never to 'exceed the bounds of honesty'.[170] As a speaker in Castiglione's *Book of the Courtier* explained, a woman 'in her fashions, manners, words, gestures and conversation' ought to be 'much unlike the man'.[171]

Prescriptions for women's behaviour reflected the contemporary belief in the inherent weakness of the female sex and their inability to control their passions. So whereas it was usually thought indecent for men to weep in public, save on special occasions, it was held that for females to 'shed tears at every little grief' was 'nothing uncomely, but rather a sign of much good nature and meekness of mind, a most decent property for that sex'. Compassion and tenderheartedness were regarded as natural to women, and they were allowed more freedom to express their emotions. There was, however, a male suspicion of the manipulative purposes to which women could put their 'gift to rain a shower of commanded tears'.[172] In the physiological theory of the period, women were thought to be colder and moister, and therefore more prone to be lachrymose anyway. As the proverb had it, as much pity was to be taken of a woman weeping as of a goose going barefoot.[173]

Gentlewomen were expected to be graceful and dignified in their persons and to develop a pleasing, pliable manner, what one conduct book called a 'charming air and winning agreeableness'. Anne Boleyn first attracted the attention of Henry VIII because of 'her excellent gesture and behaviour'. Susanna Perwich, who died in 1661 at the age of twenty-four, was praised for 'her handsome sitting at her music':

> No antic gestures, or bold face,
> No wriggling motions her disgrace,
> While she's at play, nor eye, nor head,
> Hither or thither wandered.
> Nor nods, nor heaves in any part,
> As taken with her own rare art.
> All vain conceited affectation
> Was unto her abomination.
> With body she ne'er sat askew,
> Or mouth awry, as others do.
> Careless she seem'd, as if her mind
> Were somewhere else; and yet we find
> Performances to admiration,
> And our exceeding delectation.[174]

The overwhelming concern was to safeguard female chastity, for on that depended the preservation of the bloodline and, with it, the inheritance of family property. Discretion and modesty were the qualities to be inculcated. As one influential guidebook put it, 'civility' for women was 'nothing but a certain modesty and pudor required in all your actions'. The key female attributes were 'affability and submission'.[175] Married women were expected to display the 'civility and respect that behoves a wife to her husband', and all women were urged to be bashful, 'shamefast' and unassertive in their demeanour. They were expected to eat less than men, so as to discourage any lustful impulses,* and to ride horses sidesaddle rather than with their legs apart, which would have been sexually provocative.[176] In 1585 Simon Robson thought that women should be allowed to speak at banquets, but only softly.[177] In 1664 Margaret Cavendish, Duchess of Newcastle, complained that the education of wellborn women was 'only to dance, sing and fiddle, to write complimental letters, to read romances, [and] to speak some language that is not their native: which education is an education of the body, and not of the mind'.[178] By the later seventeenth century, it had become customary at polite dinner parties for the ladies to withdraw at a certain point, leaving the men to their drink and uninhibited conversation.[179]

In return, females were permitted greater extravagance in dress and the freer use of perfumes and cosmetics. They were also to be treated with greater courtesy and deferred to in social encounters: they had 'precedency in sitting', were allowed to go first through the door and were supposed to be given priority in the street.[180] One Jacobean thought that Englishmen were alone among nations in giving 'the higher place and way to women, though of lower degree than themselves'. They did it, he thought, 'out of a noble mind to give honour and support to weakness'. The caustic lawyer John Selden was nearer the mark when he commented that if ladies were not 'used with ceremony, with compliments and addresses with legs and kissing of hands, they were the pitifullest creatures in the world'.[181]

During the later seventeenth century, women came increasingly to be regarded as exercising a softening and civilizing influence on the manners of men. The example was cited of France, whose salon

---

* In the 1760s, a widowed physician warned his daughters, in what after his death became a widely reprinted and highly influential guide to women's education, that 'the luxury of eating' was 'a despicable, selfish vice in men, but in your sex it is beyond expression indelicate and disgusting'; John Gregory, *A Father's Legacy to His Daughters* ([1774]; 1828 edn), 31–32.

culture made it axiomatic that a man could not be 'well civilized' unless he was accustomed to mixing socially with the other sex. Women, it was now claimed, were innately more refined: 'Ladies of a noble education and great quality' were 'the best schools of civility' because they were 'naturally enemies of all kind of rudeness'; they introduced men to that 'air of the world and that politeness which no counsel nor lecture' could give them.[182] In the countryside, 'great ladies' were said to be 'reverenced and loved' for their 'civility and courtesy' and their 'exercise of bounty and charity'. Young men, thought the politician and political writer the Marquess of Halifax, needed to be 'brushed and civilized in women's company'. 'What better school for manners,' asked David Hume, 'than the company of virtuous women?' By Lord Chesterfield's time it was accepted that the experience of female society was essential for men wanting to acquire polite manners.[183] Officially excluded from politics and public affairs, well-to-do women were encouraged to concentrate on the niceties of social life. In the nineteenth century, it was they who determined the etiquette of visits and dinner parties.

Of course, innumerable women ignored or defied the conventional inhibitions on their behaviour by participating vigorously in the social and economic life of the time and setting aside all notions of female meekness, diffidence and submission. A huge volume of modern historical research has shown that there was a mismatch between the prescriptions of the courtesy writers and the realities of daily living.[184] The accepted rules of polite behaviour for women were based on the unambiguous belief that gender should be a decisive principle of social differentiation. But at all social levels women found ways of evading such constraints.

Refinement

For both sexes, knowledge of the rituals of polite society was indispensable for anyone with social ambitions. This included mastery of genteel table manners (Plate 2). It was generally accepted that to cram one's mouth, to smack one's lips, to lick the dish or to eat in the street was boorish and plebeian. In the twelfth century, Daniel of Beccles ruled that it was wrong for those who dined together to spit, cough, blow their noses, lick their fingers or blow on the soup. In the late fourteenth century, Chaucer's hyper-refined Prioress was a model of delicate table manners, remarkable because she never let food fall from her fingers or dipped her hand deep into the sauce; and she wiped her lips so that no grease was left on the cup from which she drank.[185] The modern habit of providing everyone with their own knife, fork, spoon and glass did not begin to reach English polite society until the mid-seventeenth century and did not become general until at least a hundred years later. 'Strangers ... tax us for ... not using forks but fingers', lamented a writer in 1673.[186] Forks were rare before the 1730s and mostly confined to wealthy households. Well into the eighteenth century, people continued to bring their own pointed knives to the table. A popular eighteenth-century jest book told of the Leicestershire farmer at a dinner party who, never having previously seen a fork, declined the offer of one, asking whether he could please have a spoon without any slits in it.[187] In 1816 an Essex farmer, carving a piece of fowl for himself, 'unluckily helped himself to a gentleman's middle finger'. This accident, it seems, was 'occasioned by the eagerness of the company, who all had their hands in the dish at the same time'.[188]

Some social differences in comportment at the table were slow to emerge. At the end of the seventeenth century, a Huguenot refugee who had lived in the country for more than a decade noted that the English belched as readily as they coughed or sneezed; when challenged, one man demanded to know why one should abstain from belching at the dinner table any more than spitting or blowing one's nose.[189] The practice of sharing the same drinking vessel nauseated the Italian Giordano Bruno when he visited Elizabethan England, but it long survived, despite the disapproval of the courtesy manuals.[190] Nevertheless, the trend by the later seventeenth century was for the well-to-do to multiply the items of cutlery, to forbid the use of fingers and to show increasing aversion to anything that had been near anyone else's lips. In 1671 it was noted that 'some people' were now 'so delicate' that they would not eat from a dish into which other people had dipped their spoons without wiping them.[191] Yet when the antiquary William Cole, who had been educated at Eton and King's College, Cambridge, visited Paris in 1765, he thought it worth noting, 'as a thing worthy of imitation', the practice of giving everyone at the table their own tumbler or goblet, 'which cleanly method entirely avoids the disagreeable circumstance of drinking after other people'. A French visitor to England in 1784 was revolted to find twenty people at the table all drinking beer out of the same glass. This was more than two centuries after Della Casa's *Galateo* had proscribed the sharing of drinking vessels, save by unusually close friends.[192]

By the early eighteenth century, social differences in table manners were becoming more obvious. An illustrated work explained that the higher one's social position, the lower on the stem of the wine glass one placed one's fingers, and the fewer fingers one used. It also contrasted a peasant holding a spoon with his thumb and fingers with a gentlewoman holding one 'with the tips of three fingers ... in a very agreeable manner' (Plates 3 and 4).[193] The use of cutlery became a shibboleth. For Lord Chesterfield in 1741, one of the attributes of 'an awkward fellow' was that he held 'his knife, fork and spoon differently from other people'.[194] 'Nothing shews the difference between a young gentleman and a vulgar boy so much as the behaviour in eating', ruled an authority in 1778.[195]

Carving meat was an important gentlemanly accomplishment with its own particular rules. In 1661 a cookery book specified that one should not put more than two fingers and a thumb on a joint when carving; by 1670 it was said that 'the neatest carvers' never touched the meat at all, save with a knife and fork.[196] John Hough, Bishop of Lichfield, was described in 1716 as a notably 'nice carver'; renowned for his 'courteous affability and engaging condescension', he was said to have been invited to become Archbishop of Canterbury in the previous year.[197] Lord Chesterfield attached much importance to carving 'adroitly and genteelly, without hacking half an hour across a bone; [and] without bespattering the company with sauce'.[198] In 1776 Dr Samuel Johnson had to endure a particularly obsequious display of fine carving by the renegade John Wilkes: 'Pray give me leave, Sir—It is better here—A little of the brown—Some fat, Sir—A little of the stuffing—Some gravy—Let me have the pleasure of giving you some butter—Allow me to recommend a squeeze of this orange—or the lemon, perhaps, may have more zest.'[199]

The etiquette books of the early nineteenth century reveal a maze of subtle distinctions in table manners, calculated to cause maximum social embarrassment, ranging from such delicate questions as how to eat peas (use a dessert spoon), to that of the size of the bread served with soup, which, according to a work of 1836, should never be less than an inch and a half thick: 'There is nothing more plebeian than *thin* bread at dinner' (an injunction that, many years later, the historian George Macaulay Trevelyan (1876–1962) conveyed to his grandchildren).[200] The result of all these developments was to create a widening gap between the table manners of the social elite and those of provincials and the populace.

A further index of genteel status was bodily cleanliness. In principle, this was a moral virtue that everyone ought to possess because it indicated respect for the comfort of others. It was also a religious duty because the human body was God's creation and should be respected accordingly: as the pious Elizabeth Walker told her grandson in 1689, all cleanly persons were not good, but there were few good persons who were not cleanly.[201] It was also good for trade. The draper William Scott commented on how distasteful it was to come into a shop and see the proprietor 'stand as if he were drowned in phlegm and puddle'.[202]

In practice, cleanliness was regarded as a sign of social superiority. A Tudor authority ruled that gentlemen should 'pass and excel all others' in cleanliness; while, for Chesterfield, nothing looked 'more ordinary, vulgar and illiberal than dirty hands and ugly, uneven and ragged nails'. 'The ends of the nails', he ruled, should be kept 'smooth and clean, not tipped with black, as the ordinary people's always are.' Bodily cleanliness became a social marker. A statistician discovered in 1690 that the higher on the social scale people were, the more soap they used and the more often they changed their clothes. A hundred years later it was said that 'habits of cleanliness and delicacy . . . mark the gentlewoman and her family far more than all other distinctions of an exterior kind'.[203]

Social differences also extended to more intimate matters. The desire to conceal some of the body's natural functions and private parts was, up to a point, universal. Lack of modesty when urinating and defecating had long been thought offensive at every social level. In the first century BC, Cicero regretted that the Cynic philosophers mocked people for feeling shame about the natural functions; he himself took it for granted that private parts of the body should be concealed, that calls of nature should be answered in private, and that it was unfitting to speak of such matters. Norbert Elias was surely wrong to suggest that in medieval times 'these functions and the sight of them were invested only slightly with feelings of shame or repugnance' and that they 'were therefore subjected only mildly to isolation and restraint'. In fact, they were surrounded by a huge range of euphemisms and were generally expected to be performed in private, as 'privy', the accepted term for a lavatory, suggests and the rules for monastic communities make clear. Nudity was shameful and even 'vile jesters' were said to be careful to keep their private parts covered.[204]

At first, the emphasis was on the duty of inferiors to do nothing shameful when in the presence of their betters, for that would have indicated a lack of respect or an unjustified presumption of intimacy on their part. In the late twelfth century, Daniel of Beccles accordingly ruled that, although the head of a noble household was entitled to urinate in the hall, others should find relief in some secret place;

and they should be careful not to expose themselves when doing so. In the sixteenth century, Della Casa in *Galateo*, though stressing the importance in polite company of doing nothing suggestive of the needs of nature, conceded that masters need not conceal their private parts when only their servants and social inferiors were present. Antoine de Courtin said the same a century later.[205] Yet Erasmus taught that boys should avoid such exposure, even if no one else was there, for the angels were always present; and the Elizabethan military commander and aristocrat Lord Mountjoy attracted favourable comment for his unusual modesty when performing the necessities of nature: 'His most familiar friends never heard or saw him use any liberty therein, out of the privilege of his private chamber, except perhaps on Irish journeys, when he had no withdrawing room.' The pious Nicholas Ferrar believed that one should 'with great modesty go about the performance of the daily necessities which nature exacteth'; he was shocked by 'the plain impudence of our age and nation', which he thought compared unfavourably with practice in other countries.[206]

For although they became more inclined to seek privacy when they relieved themselves, the upper ranks of society were still far from fastidious about where they did it. James I stayed in the saddle all day when hunting; Samuel Pepys defecated in the chimney on one occasion; and when Parliament met at Oxford in 1665–66, Charles II's courtiers left behind 'their excrements in every corner, in chimneys, studies, coal-houses, cellars'.[207] It was related of the 'rough, unpolished divine' Josiah ('Joe') Pullen (1631–1714), vice-principal of Magdalen Hall, Oxford, that, when showing some ladies around Oxford and taking the chief one by the hand, he had a motion to make water. 'He turned his face to a wall, performed the discharge, still holding the lady fast by the hand, to her no small confusion.'[208] As late as 1751, a writer claimed that it was 'no indecency for a man in the streets, and even before women, to turn his face against the wall and do what it would be reckon'd very immodest in any lady to do, how loaded and uneasy soever she might be'.[209]

Yet in the 1590s a traveller had noted that 'our women will not be seen to do in private houses' the necessities of nature which the 'young wenches' of Leiden had no shame about performing in the open street; and by the mid-seventeenth century, medical writers were expressing concern that some people were so embarrassed at the prospect of attracting attention by leaving the company to relieve themselves that they were endangering their health. Individuals had lost their lives, it was said, and others had brought on incurable disorders through 'the decency of not going to necessary conveniences, especially among the ladies, when it is dangerous often to abstain from it'.[210] English ladies, remarked an eighteenth-century traveller, would be ashamed even to be seen going to the necessary house, 'whereas I have known an old woman in Holland set herself on the next hole to a gentleman, and civilly offer him her mussel shell by way of scraper after she had done with it herself'.[211]

Even when men urinated in the street, there were decent and indecent ways of doing so. Passers-by were supposed to pretend not to notice, and companions were expected to take off their hats and stand back in a protective manner. For some, even these precautions were not enough. As the poet John Gay urged in 1716:

Do thou some court, or secret corner seek,
Nor flush with shame the passing virgin's cheek.[212]

The eighteenth-century philosopher David Hartley thought that the shame attached to 'natural evacuations' had been 'much increased by education, custom, and the precepts and epithets of parents and governors'.[213] At the royal court, the Groom of the King's Stool (who attended the king when he relieved himself) was from 1669 onwards increasingly referred to euphemistically as the Groom of the Stole; and in the Hanoverian age, he ceased to be present at these intimate occasions.[214] A gap between aristocratic habits and those of other people is suggested by Sarah Churchill, Duchess of Marlborough's account of her visit to the spa at Scarborough in 1732. She was appalled to discover that, when the ladies who had taken the waters began to feel the effects, they were ushered into a room 'where there is above twenty holes with drawers under them to take out; and all the ladies go in together and see one another around the room, when they are in that agreeable posture, and at the door, there's a great heap of leaves which the ladies take in with them ... I came home as fast as I could, for fear of being forced into that assembly.' Eighteenth-century sideboards contained chamber pots that gentlemen would use in full sight of their dinner companions and social equals. But the genteel Norfolk parson James Woodforde was typical of his age and class when he erected a partition in his garden to prevent his kitchen servants from 'seeing those who had occasion to go to Jericho'.[215]

Norbert Elias was right to identify a steady trend in the early modern period towards 'the weeding out of natural functions from public life'.[216] In 1703 the author of a new translation of Della Casa's *Galateo* reflected with satisfaction that his contemporaries now considered certain actions to be indecent, which had been regarded as such nearly 150 years ago in what was then 'the most polite country in the world'. In 1774 another translator observed that many of the precepts in *Galateo* now seemed 'ridiculous', since they cautioned against 'indelicacies which no one of any education can, in this age, be guilty of'. Samuel Johnson remarked a few years later that, if the works of Castiglione and Della Casa were read less than they used to be, it was 'only because they had effected that reformation which their authors intended, and their precepts now are no longer wanted'.[217]

Yet some habits were slow to disappear. It was a sign of her new royal status that at Anne Boleyn's coronation banquet in 1533, two ladies-in-waiting held a cloth before the queen's face 'when she list to spit'. When Samuel Pepys went to the theatre in 1661, a lady spat backwards on him 'by a mistake' ('but after seeing her to be a very pretty lady, I was not troubled at it at all'). The Jacobean traveller Fynes Moryson thought it remarkable that in Turkish mosques it was 'no small trespass so much as to spit', while in 1678 a writer considered the Dutch practice of keeping a pot of sand in the corner of the room to serve as a spittoon to be proof of their exceptional cleanliness. 'My friend may spit upon my curious floor', sang the poet George Herbert in the early 1630s. A hundred years later, with the spread of floor carpets, such an act would have tested friendship severely.[218]

The upper classes also set themselves apart by their distinctive speech habits. 'In all ages and in all countries', thought an eighteenth-century authority on rhetoric, there were two dialects, one of the superior ranks, one of the vulgar.[219] In fact, there were many dialects, for regional and social differences generated numerous idiosyncrasies of accent, grammar and vocabulary. In the reign of Henry VIII, the head-master of Eton thought that 'the best and most pure and true English' was spoken in London. The Elizabethan expert George Puttenham contrasted the fine English spoken at the royal court or in 'the good towns and cities' with that of 'the marches or frontiers, or in port towns, where strangers haunt for traffic['s] sake'. His near-contemporary the historian William Camden remarked that 'we have Court and we have Country English, we have Northern and Southern, gross and ordi-nary'. The speech of country people was repeatedly denigrated as 'rude' and 'barbarous'. The constant factor, as Thomas Hobbes observed, was that 'the dialect of the inferior sort of people . . . [was] always different from the language of the court'.[220]

During the early modern period, there was a growing tendency to regard provincial pronunciation and regional dialect as 'uncivil'. Puttenham declared that the inhabitants of 'uplandish villages and corners of the realm, where there was no resort but of poor, rustical or uncivil people', abused the language by 'strange accents or ill-shapen sounds, and false orthography'. In his view, the standard should be set by 'men civilly and graciously behavioured and bred'. In 1597, accord-ingly, the Master of Bury St Edmunds School, Suffolk, warned his pupils against 'the barbarous speech of your country people'.[221] In the seventeenth century, the Verneys, a gentry family, did not speak in the local Buckinghamshire dialect.[222] By the later eighteenth century, the movement towards a standard pronunciation had become fiercely prescriptive. All dialects, other than that which prevailed at court, were 'sure marks of a provincial, rustic, pedantic or mechanic education', asserted a lecturer on elocution in 1762, 'and therefore have some degree of disgrace attached to them'. 'I . . . take it for granted,' declared another self-proclaimed expert in 1783, 'that the first requisite for reading or speaking agreeably is to be free from provincial pronunciation.' At a time when the upper classes were no longer so easily distinguished by dress from their social inferiors, 'purity and politeness of expression' were alleged to be the only remaining external distinction between a gentleman and his valet or a lady and her mantua maker. The persistent assumption was that differences in linguistic usage mirrored the social order and that strong self-discipline was necessary if social distance was to be maintained.[223]

The apotheosis of politeness was elegant conversation. Indeed, David Hume claimed that it was 'in order to render conversation and the intercourse of minds more easy and agreeable' that 'good manners' had been invented.[224] In his day the term 'conversation' could still refer to social intercourse of any kind, but its narrower meaning of spoken exchange between people had long been familiar. In Elizabethan times, 'discourse and conversation' were notoriously 'the principal end of a courtier's life'. In the seventeenth century, they became 'the greatest pleasure of well-bred people'.[225] It was in conversation that the participants demonstrated their 'urbanity', a word that originally meant 'pleasantness of speech', but which quickly became a synonym for civility and courteous behaviour more generally. In the eighteenth century, Daniel Defoe regarded conversation as 'the brightest and most beautiful part of life'.[226] There was a proliferation of places and practices to facilitate conversation: coffeehouses, clubs and societies, assembly rooms, social visits and dinner parties. According to a late eighteenth-century essayist, 'mixing with society on a footing of equality' was the only way that 'men can learn to rub off those rude inattentions to others which self-love so naturally produces in every individual when confined to solitude; and to acquire that suavity of manner, and attention to others which constitutes the highest pleasure of social life, that is now denominated *urbanity*'.[227]

The aim of this urbane conversation was less to transmit information than to give and derive pleasure from making oneself agreeable to others. One did this by being interesting and amusing; not interrupting; not engaging in malicious gossip; not boasting about oneself; avoiding pedantic, technical or disputatious issues; and if one had to contradict, doing so civilly, and never allowing disagreement to jeopardize personal relationships.* Although flattery was to be eschewed, every opportunity should be seized to indicate the high esteem in which one held the persons with whom one was conversing.[228] For this purpose, as a contemporary remarked in 1632, 'a new art of words called "compliments"' had been invented.[229]

A compliment had originally been any ceremonial act of courtesy and deference, but the word came particularly to mean a polite expression of praise or respect. The many 'Helps to Discourse' published in the seventeenth century gave guidance on appropriate compliments, along with suggestions for aphorisms and repartee with which to interlard one's remarks. Some study 'compliments and get 'em by heart', noted an observer, a practice that did not escape the eyes of contemporary satirists.[230] By modern standards, the compliments recommended were distinctly florid. Manuals on letter writing (which was conversation carried on by other means) similarly advised the use of extravagant subscriptions: 'your most faithful, humble servitor'; 'your most ready to be commanded'; 'yours ever to love and serve you'.[231] Yet conventions kept changing: in 1609 English readers were

---

* Boswell tells us that even Samuel Johnson, who usually talked to win, when a dinner guest of the Duke of Argyll, 'politely refrained from opposing directly an observation which the Duke himself had made'; James Boswell, *The Journal of a Tour to the Hebrides with Samuel Johnson, LL.D.* (1785), 25 October 1773.

informed by a French author that to start a letter with 'God keep you in health' was now regarded as 'clownish'.[232]

In polite society, socially demeaning topics of conversation were prohibited. One should not converse about business, for example, because talking shop was unacceptable to those who were pretending not to be tradesmen. For the same reason, one should not talk about the weather, on whose vagaries so many livelihoods depended: to do so, it was said in 1716, was 'low, mean and peasantly'.[233] 'Fine bred people' made it a rule never to talk about their wives.[234] Women were similarly discouraged from discussing their domestic affairs or their children, or their clothes. Personal issues of all kinds were to be avoided: 'when you carve out discourse for others', advised a writer in 1670, 'let your choice be rather of things than of persons'.[235] Gossip was potentially too disruptive. For the same reason 'over-great wagers' were regarded as 'against good manners'. Good breeding required that conversation should, above all, be 'agreeable and inoffensive'. In 1725, Lady Mary Wortley Montagu remarked of the Duchess of Marlborough, with whom she was not on good terms, that 'we continue to see one another, like two people that are resolved to hate with civility'.[236]

It hardly needs to be said that the prescriptions for civil conversation were seldom followed to the letter. Only too often, human vanity, egotism, aggression and impatience would have interposed themselves. So would the inability to resist a joke at someone else's expense, for 'wit' was generally admired.[237] Even so, polite conversation was something very different from that of ordinary people. It involved discarding lower-class conversational habits, in the same way that polite literature involved dissociation from the popular culture of ballad and folksong. The constant aim of the well bred was to be 'more courteous and civil upon all occasions in conversation than the rustic, untutored part of mankind can be supposed to be'.[238] Joseph Addison complained in 1711 that there were some 'men about town, especially those polished in France', who had taken to employing 'the most coarse, uncivilized words in our language'. Well-bred persons, he thought, should use 'modest' expressions, leaving 'homely' terms to the vulgar.[239]

The general tendency was for language to become more refined. 'As politeness increases,' remarked Samuel Johnson, 'some expressions will be considered as too gross and vulgar for the delicate.' In 1768 the bluestocking Elizabeth Carter was shocked to discover that in the reigns of Henry VIII and Elizabeth the letters of 'the greatest personages' contained 'expressions which would hardly be tolerated in the lowest companies at present'. The Latin textbook produced by the grammarian John Stanbridge for schoolboys at the beginning of the sixteenth century was not the kind of work that Lord Chesterfield would have pressed on his son two hundred years later, for it did not hesitate to translate Latin anatomical terms into robust English equivalents of the kind which, until quite recently, were not uttered aloud by witnesses in a magistrates' court, but passed up on little slips of paper.[240] The 'delicate sensibility' which Adam Smith regarded as the most appropriate characteristic of 'one who lives in a very civilized society' led inevitably to euphemism and hyper-refinement.[241]

In due course, the codes of civility and politeness took on a life of their own. They reinforced aristocratic rule, but they also required grandees to conform to the prevailing conventions. A Jacobean satirist claimed that a rich man, however hideous his behaviour, could be sure to have his 'reverence, courtesy, cap and knee'.[242] Riches made up for a great deal.* Yet in practice, the wealthy usually had to learn manners

* Compare the comments of a nineteenth-century poet:

There's something undoubtedly in a fine air,
To know how to smile and be able to stare.
High breeding is something, but well bred or not,
In the end the one question is, what have you got.

So needful it is to have money, heigh ho!
So needful it is to have money.

'Spectator ab extra', in *The Poems of Arthur Hugh Clough* (2nd edn, ed. F. L. Mulhauser, Oxford, 1974), 700.

like everyone else. William Cavendish, Marquess (later Duke) of Newcastle, complained that the tyranny of fashion at Charles I's court was such that the greatest nobleman in England would be ridiculed if he had not learnt 'the last month's reverence *à la mode* that came with the last dancer from Paris, packed up in his fiddle-case'.[243]

In practice, the hierarchy of manners and the social hierarchy never exactly coincided. Sometimes those in authority exemplified everything the courtesy writers hoped for, as did Walter Devereux, 1st Earl of Essex (1539–76), of whom it was recalled that 'he had a special grace to entertain all states of men, superior, equal and inferior, with such comeliness and decency that for civility, honesty, manners and honourable behaviour he was a pattern and an example for nobility'; or Thomas Howard, 2nd Earl of Arundel (1586–1646), who 'was of a stately presence and gait, so that any man that saw him, though in never so ordinary habit, could not but conclude him to be a great person'; or Sir Kenelm Digby (1603–65), who had 'a wonderful graceful behaviour, a flowing courtesy and civility, and such a volubility of language, as surprised and delighted';* or in the eighteenth century, John Churchill, Duke of Marlborough (1650–1722), of whom Lord Chesterfield wrote that 'his figure was beautiful' and his manner 'irresistible by either man or woman'; it was this 'engaging, graceful manner' that enabled him to hold together the Grand Alliance that defeated Louis XIV. A quintessential exemplar of refined politeness was the author, politician and collector Horace Walpole (1717–97), who 'always entered a room in that style of affected delicacy which fashion had then made almost natural—*chapeau bras* between his hands, as if he wished to compress it, or under his arm, knees bent, and feet on tip-toe, as if afraid of a wet floor'.[244]

---

* John Aubrey wrote of Digby that 'he was of such a goodly handsome person, gigantic and great voice, and had so graceful elocution and noble address that had he been dropped out of the clouds in any part of the world he would have made himself respected'; *Brief Lives*, ed. Kate Bennett (Oxford, 2015), vol. 1, 325–26.

Yet though the upper ranks sought to mark themselves out by their 'wonderful graceful behaviour', their 'ease of address' and their 'civil, courteous and obliging carriage',[245] there were *parvenus* who successfully acquired the social polish of their superiors; and there were high-ranking figures who were uncouth in their behaviour, sloppy in their speech, and filthy in their personal habits. Godfrey Goodman, Bishop of Gloucester before the Civil War, had a strong distaste for the animal side of man's nature, declaring on one occasion that 'of all the noisome scents, there is none so rammish [rank smelling] and so intolerable as is that which proceeds from man's body'. Yet in 1638, Sir Francis Windebanke found the bishop weeping for the death of his elderly mother, but without a handkerchief with which to wipe his eyes and nose. 'His Lordship did it with his fingers and then wiped them upon his velvet coat . . . which I confess,' recalled Windebanke, 'did take off much of my compassion.'[246] In the following century, the novelist Richard Graves claimed to have seen at one time or another: a country gentleman borrowing someone else's toothpick, using it, and returning it with thanks; the mayor of a respectable borough startling the company by his vigorous expectorations; an eminent physician spitting on the carpet; and a rich merchant helping himself to some waste paper in the sight of everyone, selecting a piece of the softest and most pliable, and putting it in his pocket for immediate use.[247]

To realize how frequently the great failed to conform to the highest standards of polite deportment one need only read Lord Chesterfield's comments on some of the leading politicians of his day: Sir Robert Walpole ('inelegant in his manners'); Lord Townshend ('his manners were coarse, rustic and seemingly brutal'); the Duke of Newcastle ('he was always in a hurry, never walked, but always run'); the Duke of Bedford ('he had neither the talent nor the desire of pleasing'); and Charles James Fox ('inelegant in his language, hesitating and ungraceful in his elocution').[248]

Periodically, moreover, there were fashions for rakish and assertively violent or indecent behaviour among upper-class youths – 'hectors', 'rodomantoes', 'blades', 'scourers', 'swaggerers', 'roaring boys', 'roisterers', 'the damned crew', 'rakehells', 'mohocks', 'sons of Belial, flown with insolence and wine' – who proclaimed their social superiority not by conforming to the established conventions of civility and polite deportment, but by deliberately flouting them. The courtiers of Charles II were particularly notorious for their drunkenness, flamboyant sexuality and hedonistic libertinism.[249] Some university students similarly had a counterculture that involved violence, heavy drinking, sexual promiscuity and nocturnal disorder.[250] The more firmly the norms of good behaviour were established, the greater was the thrill of their transgression. When in 1667, at the sumptuous supper that followed the St George's Day service for the king and the Knights of the Garter, the guests began to fling the 'banqueting stuff' about the room 'profusely', by way of 'sport', John Evelyn left hastily 'for fear of disorder'. In 1696 an English visitor to Amsterdam noted with surprise how different at night the Dutch city was from London, for there were 'no quarrels, no heads broke, no watch-men scour'd [attacked] or assailants knocked down, no swords drawn, no sending to the Counter [prison] to lodge there all night, no breaking of windows, pulling down of signs and barbers' poles'.[251]

It was not a coincidence that later seventeenth-century England saw both growing politeness and the birth of pornography, or that good breeding in the eighteenth century was accompanied by sexual libertinism, heavy drinking, brutal sports, bawdy and scatological humour and scurrilous gossip.[252] The values of civility and politeness were all-pervasive in early modern England, but their influence on the behaviour of the upper classes was never complete.

2

Manners and the Social Order

They teach us, how to each degree and kind
We should ourselves demean, to low, to high,
To friends and foes, which skill men call Civility.
Edmund Spenser, The Faerie Queene (1590–96)

The Social Hierarchy

In the early modern period, the concept of good manners was in-extricably bound up with the existence of a social hierarchy which it was the business of the codes of civility to reinforce. The essence of good behaviour was what French rhetoricians termed *bienséance* and the English called 'decorum': doing what was fitting, decent and seemly. In his Latin dictionary of 1538, Sir Thomas Elyot defined *decorum* as 'a seemliness, for that which becometh the person, having respect to his nature, degree, study, office or profession, be it in doing or speaking . . . Sometime it signifieth honesty.' Over a century later, the influential French authority Antoine de Courtin agreed that civility was 'nothing else but the modesty and decorum to be observed by everyone according to his condition'.[1]

Decorum required behaviour appropriate to the time, place and occasion. Working clothes were different from Sunday clothes; behaviour in church was unlike behaviour in an alehouse; dress and demeanour were not the same for a wedding as for a funeral.[2] A sense of decorum obliged people to conduct themselves in a way befitting their age and their sex. As David Hume remarked in his discussion of what he called 'decency', effeminate behaviour in a man or a rough manner in a woman were 'ugly, because unsuitable to each character, and different from the qualities which we expect in the sexes'.[3] Above all, decorum required people to relate to each other differently, according to their respective social positions. 'One principal point of this art,' explained Jonathan Swift, 'is to suit our behaviour to the three several degrees of men: our superiors, our equals, and those below us.'[4]

This was an abiding principle in early modern notions of good manners and it was endlessly reiterated in the books of advice. To one's superiors, one should display deference and respect; with one's equals, one should be open, generous and frank; to one's inferiors, one should be affable and condescending (a word that had not yet acquired its pejorative overtones). As the Elizabethan statesman William Cecil, Lord Burghley, advised his son: 'The first prepares thy way to advancement. The second makes thee known for a man well bred. The third gains a good respect, which, once got, is easily kept.' In the later seventeenth century, the Marquess of Halifax put it crisply: there was 'nothing more unmannerly than to be civil to everybody alike'.[5]

An elaborate repertoire of modes of address expressed the gradations of social superiority – 'your lordship', 'your honour', 'your worship', etc. – and an equally complex set of gestures displayed deference: standing up, taking off one's hat, bowing, kneeling, letting the superior speak first, not getting too close, and not looking into his eyes.[6] Breach of these conventions could cause deep offence.* Many of these reverential gestures were the same as those employed in the churches of the time, for it seemed appropriate to honour God in the way one would pay respects to a great monarch; hence, the insistence of many High Churchmen that one should take off one's hat in church and kneel when praying rather than sit. John Hacket, the Restoration Bishop of Coventry and Lichfield, could not 'endure to see, in this complimental age, men ruder with God than with men, bow lowly and often to one another, but never kneel to God'. As one Laudian cleric remarked, 'Good carriage is as well a point of religion as of civility, and must be learned no less in the temple than in the court.' When Nicholas Ferrar, head of the devout little community at Little Gidding, entered a church, he made a 'low obeisance, then took four paces and made another, and a few paces further made a third'. These he regarded as 'courtesies' to God.[7]

Similar rules governed polite behaviour between women and men, and between the old and the young. An Elizabethan cleric recommended that children should be taught 'good manners and civil behaviour: to rise up to their betters [and] uncover the head to make obeisance; to be courteous towards their equals; to be gentle and loving to their inferiors'. Schoolboys were expected to take off their caps to those they met in the street and to give way to passers-by as a 'point of civility'.[8] Many held that age should be honoured, regardless of social position, though the popular Restoration preacher and former provost of King's College, Cambridge, Benjamin Whichcote urged that, 'in converse', 'age and education' should speak first.[9] Those at the top could always break the rules and gain popularity by dispensing their inferiors from such requirements, but that was their privilege. Superiors could choose whether or not to be 'courteous' to

---

* On 10 June 1642, the House of Commons deemed a print of Charles I and Sir John Hotham, the parliamentary governor of Hull, to be scandalous because it showed Hotham on horseback on the town wall, with the king on foot and bareheaded below him; *Journals of the House of Commons* 2 (1803), 617.

their inferiors, but the inferiors had always to be 'civil' to them. An Elizabethan manual on boxing advised gentlemen to rebuke any 'saucy lout' or 'loitering lubber' in their household with three or four blows 'well set on, a span long on both cheeks'.* In 1718, Sir Edward Longueville, a Buckinghamshire gentleman, was killed when his horse stumbled as he leant over with his whip to lash a 'clown' who had given him 'some affront', and whom he was pursuing 'on purpose to teach him better manners'.[10] In well-ordered communities, however, such violence was prohibited: in All Souls College, Oxford, a Fellow was punished in 1615 for striking the underbutler.[11]

Good manners thus sustained the social order by requiring people to behave in accordance with their place in the hierarchy. Civility, as one manual, plagiarizing de Courtin, put it, was 'nothing else but the modesty and handsome decorum to be observed by everyone according to his or her condition'. In his advice to drapers, William Scott stressed that it would be 'uncomely' to kiss a ploughman's hand as one would that of a lord, or to bow low to a chambermaid as one would to her lady. Sir Robert Brooke's widow, Elizabeth, who died in 1683, was said to have had the virtue of courtesy 'in a high degree' because she entertained all persons, but 'with civilities proper to their several qualities'.[12] 'What is good breeding?' asked the eighteenth-century philosopher Thomas Reid. 'It consists of all the external signs of due respect to our superiors, condescension to our inferiors, politeness to all with whom we converse ..., joined in the fair sex with that delicacy of outward behaviour which becomes them.' King George III gave the same advice to his son, the future William IV: obey your superiors, be polite to your equals, and show good nature to your inferiors.[13]

The idea was still there in the twentieth century. In *The Longest Journey* (1907), the novelist E. M. Forster describes the estate agent Mr Wilbraham:

---

* A popular Victorian manual on etiquette, *The Habits of Good Society* (1859 edn, 9), urged gentlemen to learn to box so that they could punish a cabman or bargee who insulted a lady: 'One well-dealt blow settles the whole matter.'

He knew his place, and kept others to theirs: all society seemed spread before him like a map. The line between the county and the local, the line between the labourer and the artisan—he knew them all, and strengthened them with no uncertain touch. Everything with him was graduated—carefully graduated civility towards his superiors, towards his inferiors carefully graduated incivility. So—for he was a thoughtful person—so alone, declared he, could things be kept together.[14]

What is particularly striking about the endless repetition of this advice through the centuries is the implicit assumption that superiors, equals and inferiors could be easily identified as such. Everyone knew, or was expected to find out, just where he or she stood in the social hierarchy. People had to be certain of their 'station and rank' before it was clear how they ought to behave. It was everyone's duty, thought Whichcote, 'to consider their ages, places, relations, function, education, and to proportion themselves accordingly'.[15]

This assumption that people should be treated differently according to their social position was an enduring strand in the concept of civility. But it had to be reconciled with the almost equally tenacious, and potentially egalitarian, notion that the well-mannered person should extend to everyone the polite deference which had originally been reserved for superiors. As the writer Robert Ashley put it in 1596, 'It is the part of civil courtesy and modest humanity to speak gently to all, to salute, embrace and entertain them without difference.'[16]

A mid-eighteenth-century essayist even recommended being *more* civil to social inferiors than to equals or superiors, 'because there is always a sort of jealousy amongst our inferiors; and if they are not taken particular notice of, they think themselves despised'. It was important to humour them, he explained, because 'we cannot subsist without these poor people. Our tenants cannot use our farms, or pay us any rent, without their assistance to cultivate the earth. Trades and manufactures could never be carried on without them.'[17] Whichcote had made the same point in the previous century: 'If it were not for the poor, for aught I know, the higher must do the lowest drudgeries themselves, and none are to despise a necessary instrument.'[18]

These unusually realistic admissions are a reminder that the practice of civility was as likely to be prudential as altruistic. At the Tudor court, where men's fortunes depended on the caprice of royal favour, polite dissimulation was essential for survival.[19] In the world at large, good manners helped ambitious individuals to make their way. 'Civil courtesy,' claimed a writer in 1577, would enable men 'to purchase worthy praise of their inferiors, and estimation and credit among their betters.' Robert Ashley agreed that 'nothing doth more easily draw the good wills of men than this gracious and courteous kind of behaviour', while an early-eighteenth-century writer defined politeness as 'a dextrous management of our words and actions, whereby we make other people have better opinion of us and themselves'.[20]

Just as Castiglione had taught that the courtier needed polite accomplishments if he was to gain the prince's ear, so Lord Chesterfield believed that one object of politeness was to secure the individual's social advancement: 'It is by manners only that you can please and consequently rise.' He claimed to know of a hundred instances of 'a very shining fortune and figure, raised upon no other foundation than that of address, manners and graces'. James Boswell concurred: 'The talent of making people with whom we converse each pleased with himself is possessed by few, but ... [it] ought to be cultivated as much as possible, because it leaves an agreeable reflection, and gains for the person who practises it an advantageous situation in the minds of those upon whom it is practised.' He could have cited the example of Sir Joshua Reynolds, the great painter of Hanoverian society, whose ability to attract a large and illustrious clientele owed almost as much to his unruffled affability and complaisance as to his artistic skill.[21]

The upper ranks of society had long been aware that dignity needed to be accompanied by more amiable qualities (*affabilitas*) if their rule was to be palatable to those below them. In his *Boke Named the Gouernour* (1531) Sir Thomas Elyot included a chapter on 'affability and the utility thereof'. In it, he argued that magnates with 'a proud and haughty countenance' were 'vehemently' hated, 'be they never so high in estate or degree', whereas 'a gentle and familiar visage' worked wonders for a nobleman: 'All do grant that he is worthy all honour that may be given or wished him.' His contemporary Sir Thomas More said the same: 'a little courtesy' could often do more to win the support of the common people than 'a great benefit'.[22] In the reign of James I, the lawyer William Martyn observed that the most successful rulers were those who were affable, courteous and pleasant; and the Lord Keeper, Francis Bacon, reminded the judges that 'power is ever of greater strength when it is civilly carried'.[23] The gentry were repeatedly urged to be 'affable and courteous in speech and behaviour'. The didactic writer Richard Brathwait declared in 1630 that 'mildness' was 'a quality so inherent … to a gentleman, as his affability will express him, were there no other means to know him'. 'Cherish affability', the Yorkshire gentleman Sir Henry Slingsby advised his sons in 1651. 'There is nothing that purchaseth more love with less cost.' In the same year Thomas Hobbes informed his readers that 'affability of men already in power is increase of power, because it gaineth love'.[24]

The future regicide John Cook declared that courtesy was 'the most precious pearl that any man in authority can wear, for it buyeth men's hearts'. The 2nd Earl of Carbery (*c.* 1600–86) told his son that 'the civility of a hat, a kind look or word from a person of honour, has brought that service which money could not'. Similarly, in the early 1650s the Marquess of Newcastle advised the future Charles II to be 'courteous and civil to everybody … and, believe it, the putting off your hat and making a leg pleases more than reward or preservation, so much doth it take all kind of people'. A decade earlier, a translator had dedicated a version of Della Casa's *Galateo* to the young Prince Charles, promising that if he observed its rules of civility he would secure the love of all men and command their obedience.[25] This was advice that Charles would be careful to follow, mindful perhaps of the tradition that every time William of Orange, the leader of the sixteenth-century Dutch revolt, raised his hat, he won a subject from the king of Spain.[26] Charles may also have been aware that his father, Charles I, had helped to bring about the Civil War by alienating the Scots, a people notoriously lacking in 'complimental courtesy', with his imperious manner and rigidly formal 'keeping of state'.[27]

Courtesy towards subordinates was advisable for all those in authority at whatever level. Soldiers, for example, were much more likely to venture their lives if they had a friendly officer. The failure of most of Charles I's commanders to be acquainted with their troops was said to have been 'an extraordinary prejudice to the King's cause'. An exception was Colonel Charles Cavendish, who, though of noble birth, 'used the same familiarity and frankness amongst the meanest of his soldiers, the poorest miner, and amongst his equals; and by stooping so low he rose the higher in the common account, and was valued accordingly as a prince and a great one'.[28] Gentleman farmers were advised to be affable when calling their hired labourers to work in the morning and 'kindly to incite them to their business'. The agricultural writer Gervase Markham believed that a successful husbandman needed 'an affable and courteous nature' to rule his household and get the best from his employees, 'since out of harshness proceeds more rebellion than good obedience'.[29] Some employers seem to have taken this advice so seriously that one Jacobean clergyman felt it necessary to warn them of the danger of taking pride in their lack of pride, for example, by ostentatiously declining to be 'lofty in carriage, apparel, or contempt of inferiors' and by choosing to be called 'goodman' rather than 'master' or 'master' rather than 'Sir Knight'.[30]

More commonly, anxiety lest familiarity should breed contempt led many magnates to affect a 'proud and haughty countenance'. The Jacobean nobility and gentry, thought the antiquarian John Aubrey, were 'damnable proud and insolent'.[31] Modesty could sometimes be necessary, conceded one aristocratic author, but it was also important to 'know when to be high'. As Sir William Wentworth advised his son in 1604, a gentleman who wished to be honoured and feared in his locality had to 'bear countenance and authority'.[32] The 2nd Earl of Arundel was 'a person of great and universal civility, but yet with that restraint as that it forbade any to be bold and saucy with him'. He did not court popularity, but sought to 'let the common people know their distance and due observance'. An eighteenth-century writer remarked that titles were 'apt to turn men's brains and make them imagine that the inferior people are not of the same species with themselves, and that none but the rich or great are entitled to the return of any civilities or good manners from them'.[33]

Despite warnings against undue familiarity with inferiors, the style of aristocratic rule normally recommended in the early modern literature of advice was ostentatiously unassertive. The author of *The Compleat Gentleman* (1678) repeatedly stressed that mildness, courtesy and affability were far and away the most effective means of winning hearts and thereby consolidating obedience. 'What is true breeding among the civilized,' asked Bishop Gilbert Burnet in a sermon before the queen in 1694, 'but the putting on the appearances of modesty and humility?'[34]

In the seventeenth century it became increasingly common, in memoirs and on funeral monuments, to praise the gentry for their *'suavitas morum'* (smooth manners), 'courtesy', 'civility', 'winning address', 'affability' and 'condescension'.[35] Lucy Hutchinson, widow of the regicide Colonel John Hutchinson, wrote proudly of her husband's 'general affability, courtesy, and civility . . . to all persons'; while it was said of the Earl of Huntingdon's daughter Lady Mary Jolife, who died in 1678, that 'she was pleased to converse with infinite benignity and condescension, even to the meanest people'.[36]

By the eighteenth century, these qualities had become de rigueur. 'Speaking low' was a distinctively English form of good breeding;

and good manners required understatement.[37] Moreover, a man of 'real politeness' was expected to be more attentive to his inferiors than to his equals. 'In good company,' wrote David Hume, 'you need not ask who is the master of the feast. The man who sits in the lowest place, and who is always industrious in helping everyone, is certainly the person.' This had not been the case a century earlier: a French visitor to England noticed in 1678 that the mistress of the house always sat at the upper end of the table, a place which in France was customarily given to guests.[38]

Of course, social differences were too great for civility to be extended to everyone equally. A polite gentleman could not treat his servant in the same way that he treated his equals. When John Locke recommended 'general goodwill and regard for all people', he added that this meant expressing 'respect and value for them, *according to their rank and condition*'.[39] For all his belief in the little courtesies of daily life, the Earl of Chatham would not have opened the door for his footman. The Catholic writer Timothy Nourse claimed in a work posthumously published in 1700 that it was a mistake for a gentleman to try to win the common people 'by civilities': too many of the lower orders, he warned, were 'very rough and savage in their dispositions, being of levelling principles, and refractory to government, insolent and tumultuous'. The best way was 'to bridle them and to make them feel the spur'.[40] In 1779 an essayist complained that politeness was not expected to enter into the treatment of those in a lower station of life: 'He may be esteemed the best-bred man in the world who is a very brute to his servants and dependants.'[41] Yet though it was severely qualified by the imperatives of social hierarchy, the idea of good manners as universal benevolence was undoubtedly there.

The German philosopher Friedrich Nietzsche once remarked that the masses would submit to slavery of any kind so long as those in charge 'constantly legitimize themselves as higher, as *born* to command – by having noble manners'. By contrast, he thought, industrialists with vulgar personal habits encouraged the worker to think that it was only luck or accident which elevated one person above another, 'and thus is socialism born'.[42] In early modern England, the social authority of the upper classes was reinforced by superior manners and bodily appearance. They gave them poise and self-assurance and made others feel inferior in their presence. As Adam Smith wrote of the young nobleman: 'His air, his manner, his deportment: all mark that elegant and graceful sense of his own superiority, which those who are born to inferior stations can hardly ever arrive at. These are the arts by which he purposes to make mankind more easily submit to his authority and to govern their inclinations according to his own pleasure; and in this he is seldom disappointed. These arts, supported by rank and pre-eminence, are, upon ordinary occasions, sufficient to govern the world.' Smith cited the example of the French king Louis XIV, whose talents and virtues were 'not much above mediocrity', but who was regarded as the model of a perfect prince because of his graceful shape, the majestic beauty of his features, his 'noble and affecting' voice, and a 'step and deportment' that suited his rank, but 'would have been ridiculous in any other person'.[43]

Many contemporaries believed that, without 'ceremonious fashions of manners', 'all civil order' would collapse. 'Take away good nurture and civility,' wrote an Elizabethan clergyman, 'and there will be no quiet and orderly living, either in the Church of God or [the] commonwealth.' Good manners, it was said, helped to keep the peace in families, among neighbours and throughout the nation.[44] In the later seventeenth century, after the social upheavals of the Civil War and Interregnum, civility seemed even more essential as a prop to the existing hierarchy. The rules of classical decorum were a barrier against the excesses of sectarian enthusiasm. By treating the expression of a contentious opinion in politics or religion as a social faux pas, an error of taste, the norms of politeness had a powerfully conservative effect. They made political and religious unorthodoxy appear as unacceptable instances of bad manners. The guiding principle of civility was that people should behave in such a way as to make human relations as smooth and trouble free as possible. They should be considerate and complaisant so as to avoid causing unnecessary pain. In early modern England, this meant accepting the social differences of rank and class and not attempting to challenge the established order.

The Topography of Manners

Where, then, did this leave those at the bottom of the pile? What impact did these genteel doctrines of courtesy, decorum and politeness have on the culture of the populace: the artisans, small farmers, servants and labourers?

It goes without saying that many modes of polite behaviour were wholly beyond their reach. In the eighteenth century 'politeness' involved the display of refined taste in everything from houses and gardens to literature, music and art. It required education, travel and wealth. Readiness to acquire an ever-expanding range of goods had long been seen as an essential attribute of a 'civil' existence. One could live without wine, spices, linen and silks, thought a Tudor writer, 'yet very far from civility should it be'.[45] In 1602 the antiquary Richard Carew recalled how Cornish farmers used to live very simply: their houses had earthen walls, low thatched roofs, few partitions, no glass windows and, instead of chimneys, a hole in the roof to let out smoke; they slept on straw with a blanket but no sheets; and their domestic equipment amounted to a wooden drinking bowl and a few pans. But now things had changed, 'and the Cornish husbandman conformeth himself with a better-supplied civility to the Eastern pattern'.[46] A royal proclamation of 1615 lamented that the manufacture of glass windows and glass drinking vessels involved chopping down precious woods to provide fuel for the glassworks. But it stressed that there could be no going back to stone vessels and latticed windows (proverbial for keeping out the light and letting in the wind) if 'the civility of the times' was to be maintained.[47] The usages of polite society presupposed suitable dress, houses and furniture, along with servants to clean rooms, carry hot water, wash clothes and prepare food. 'Needless curiosity about rooms, and furniture, and accommodations', lamented the Presbyterian divine Richard Baxter, was defended 'under the honest name of decency', and 'a world of need-nots' excused because they were 'civilities'.[48] In 1723 a visiting preacher to a village near Kibworth, Leicestershire, encountered what he thought 'one of the most unpolite congregations I ever knew', because there was 'not so much as a tea-table' for miles around and 'but one hoop-petticoat'.[49]

Politeness required early immersion in the habits of the fashionable world. It called for the leisure in which to pay social visits, attend dinners, stand around chatting in aristocratic salons, and acquire the cultural baggage that gave one topics to chat about.[50] No one who had not been educated in 'a free behaviour in company' could attain the correct demeanour by 'mere aping'.[51] To be truly polite it was essential to have regular experience of polite society, especially the society of women. Those who usually moved in exclusively male company, such as naval officers, who spent long periods at sea, were notoriously lacking in politesse.[52] As an eighteenth-century clergyman reflected after entertaining to dinner a Suffolk farmer who was wealthy but 'of uncultivated manners', 'How discernible is the want of polish! It is only company that can give that facility and smoothness of manner.'[53]

In all these obvious ways, politeness was wholly inaccessible to the great majority of the population. An agricultural labourer might learn to be civil to his betters, but he could never hope to be 'polite'. Indeed, it would only evoke derision if he made the attempt.[54] To the poor, struggling to find the means of subsistence, the refinements of politeness were utterly irrelevant.

Degrees of civility thus mirrored the inequalities of the social order. A sixteenth-century Dutch traveller observed that, in all countries, the 'common sort and multitude' were 'in behaviour and manners gross and unnurtured'; whereas, thanks to their education and upbringing, the nobility and gentry displayed a 'very commendable order and civil behaviour'. A later writer praised the gentry's kindly attitude to strangers, whom they would invite to their houses and feast them 'merrily, heartily, and bountifully', out of what they termed 'courtesy' or 'neighbourhood'.[55] In Jacobean Cornwall, the topographer John Norden discovered that the gentry 'and such as have tasted of civil education' were 'very kind, affable, full of humanity and courteous entertainment', but many of 'the baser sort' of people were 'harsh, hard, and of no such civil disposition'.[56] 'By reason of poverty,' noted a writer in 1641, 'many men, as also their children, become ill-tutor'd, rude, uncivil.'[57] In Edward Chamberlayne's annual reference book *Angliae Notitia*, the nobility, gentry, scholars, merchants and chief tradesmen were flatteringly described as 'extremely well-polished in their behaviour', but 'the common sort' were labelled 'rude and even barbarous', especially in their attitude towards strangers.[58] Polite writers assumed that country folk who didn't read, didn't travel, and were unacquainted with fashionable society lived in a state of semi-barbarism little different from that of the inhabitants of Africa or the New World. Some even referred to them as 'Indians' or 'savages'.[59] Indeed, the Native Americans were sometimes said to be less 'rude' than English rustics.[60]

Since classical times, 'rusticity' (*rusticitas*) and good manners had always been polar opposites, for civility was essentially urban, the ethic of civic communities. For the ancient Greek character writer Theophrastus, the 'rustic' was notorious for his lack of any sense of decorum; his body smelled and his posture was indecent.[61] In the early modern period, it was generally assumed that 'the civiller sort' lived in cities and towns. The Elizabethan town clerk of Tewkesbury believed that the 'special kind of society and fellowship of one people, gathered together in one town' was 'the beginning of all civility' and 'the lively precedent of behaviour to the rustic and ruder sort'.[62] Civility could not be learnt by those who were 'mere hedge-hogs of the fields, and never saw other behaviour but what is in use at a country church door'. The diplomat Sir William Temple believed that those who lived among woods, fields and herds of cattle and had little converse with human beings were bound to remain ignorant and more reliant on their senses than their reason.[63] It was notorious that a person who came into the company of two gentlemen, one brought up in the country and one in the court or city, could immediately tell which was which 'by their speech, gesture and behaviour'. Elizabethan sophisticates despised rural gentry for the 'rusticity of their houses and garments', their 'ungentle gestures' and their 'clownish speech': 'as, for example, someone will laugh when he speaketh; another will cough before he tells his tale; and some will gape or yawn'.[64] Town dwellers regarded farm labourers as 'barn-door savages', 'country hawbucks', mannerless 'gubbins', bumpkins born and bred in Hogs Norton.[65] When young George Dobson was sent to the choir school in Elizabethan Durham, he was cruelly persecuted by his school-fellows, who knew him to have been bred in the country and 'so rustic-like that he could not cover his clownish and wayward manners'.[66]

The seventeenth-century herald Randle Holme carefully distin-guished the various types of 'country clown': the 'churl', who rever-enced no one; the 'boor' or 'swain', who knew nothing of civil behaviour; the 'rustic fellow', who had 'neither been civilized or brought into good manners'; and the 'plebeian', 'of vulgar speech or language'. Other contemporary terms associating the country dweller, especially the peasant farmer or labourer, with a total lack of refinement or good manners included 'churl', 'clodhopper' and 'clunch'.[67]

Just as the social structure was envisaged as a descending hierarchy of civility, so it was common for travellers to divide England into zones of politeness. The further from the city and the court, the greater the rudeness. 'Urbanity', as an Elizabethan explained, was derived from the Latin *urbanus*, 'which is civil, courteous, gentle, modest or well-ruled, as men commonly are in cities and places of good government'. London, which in Tudor times already exceeded all other cities and towns 'in manners and good fashions, and courtesy', was proverbially more civil than Lincolnshire.[68] In 1577 the Bishop of London wanted to get troublesome Puritan preachers out of London by sending them off to combat popular ignorance in Lancashire, Staffordshire, Shropshire 'and such other barbarous countries'.[69] Riding on circuit in the late 1670s, Roger North remarked that the counties near London had 'little singular to be noted', but that when he got to Dorset, 'what we call gentility of everything began to wear off'.[70]

Some manufacturing towns were also regarded as lacking in 'urbanity of manners'. The streets of Birmingham were described in 1690 as 'dirty, dangerous and full of ill examples'; though when the historian William Hutton visited the town in 1741, the inhabitants appeared 'strongly marked with the modes of civil life': 'I had been among dreamers, but now I saw men awake.'[71] In the eyes of those used to London society, even a large provincial city could seem lacking in urbanity: Alexander Pope found Bristol in 1739 'very unpleasant', 'with no civilized company in it'.[72]

Yet since the later seventeenth century, most county towns had come to be recognized as centres of politeness and public sociability, particularly those on main roads and with nobility and gentry resident in the vicinity, such as Norwich, which the literary clergyman Thomas Fuller praised for its 'urbanity and civility'. Richard Baxter thought that 'their constant converse and traffic with London' did 'much promote civility and piety' among the tradesmen of Kidderminster.[73] As MP for King's Lynn, Horace Walpole was bored by the provincialism of the inhabitants, but he conceded that 'to do the folks justice, they are sensible, and reasonable, and civilized . . . I attribute this to their more frequent intercourse with the world and the capital, by the help of good roads and post-chaises, which, if they have abridged the King's dominions, have at least tamed his subjects.' Many of Walpole's contemporaries commented on the way in which improved roads were opening up the remoter parts of the country to trade and the influence of metropolitan manners.[74]

The result was that in the eighteenth century numerous provincial towns had a cultivated middle class who lived in some style, with a well-developed sense of what was 'civil' behaviour and what was 'vulgar'. Though claiming to be uncorrupted by metropolitan fashions, they led a rich associational life, with assembly rooms, race meetings, lectures, walks and theatres (Plate 9).[75] These public spaces were deliberately created as arenas where the social order could be made visible and rituals of polite sociability conducted. With the proliferation of clubs, coffeehouses and societies, habits of civil behaviour developed as a matter of course. 'I lately took my friend Boswell and showed him genuine civilized life in an English provincial town', said Samuel Johnson in 1776. 'I turned him loose at Lichfield, my native city, that he might see for once real civility.'[76]

Maritime districts were also thought to be more refined because they were more accessible to strangers; the Romans had regarded Kent as the most civil part of England. But the so-called uplandish or rural areas remote from London* and lacking an educated bourgeoisie were seen as benighted.[77] Dwellers in nucleated villages were acknowledged as more affable and sociable than those who lived solitary lives on lonely farms.[78] The nobility and gentry engaged in much coming and going, exchanging compliments and visiting each other's houses.[79] But most ordinary country folk seemed to lack the social virtues, because they were 'surrounded with impassable roads, having no intercourse with man to humanise the mind, no commerce to smooth their rugged nature'.[80]

Most barbarous of all were those who lived in the countryside but were not part of the normal rural hierarchy: the squatters and cottagers in the fens, forests and wastes, who were largely exempt from the social discipline provided by squire and parson;[81] the unsettled

---

* Correspondingly, 'inland', the term for districts nearer the capital and centres of population, came to mean 'refined' or 'civilized'. In Shakespeare's *As You Like It*, Orlando, charged with being 'a rude despiser of good manners', explains that although 'the thorny point / Of bare distress hath ta'en from me the show / Of smooth civility, yet I am inland bred / And know some nurture' (act 2, scene 7). Similarly, Rosalind, pretending to be Ganymede, explains that she learnt her fine accent from an uncle who 'was in his youth an inland man' (act 3, scene 2).

working poor with no fixed abode, whom the government dismissed as 'rogues' and 'wandering persons', living 'like savages';[82] the bargees on the rivers and canals, who were proverbially coarse and disorderly;[83] the 'robustick wild people' of the Forest of Dean;[84] 'the rude and ill-nurtured people' of Romney Marsh; and the inhabitants of the Cambridgeshire Fens, who were 'rude, uncivil, and envious to all others', whom they derided as 'upland men'. The geographer Nathanael Carpenter thought that the thick vapours rising from the marshes produced 'men of blockish and hoggish dispositions and natures, unapt for learning and unfit for civil conversation'.[85] Miners were seen as especially uncouth. In Somerset they were described as 'wild brutish people', 'savage and depraved, . . . brutal in their natures, and ferocious in their manners';[86] in Derbyshire they were, allegedly, 'of a brutish nature and behaviour', notorious for their 'rudeness, incivility and disobedience';[87] in Northumberland they were 'little better than savages';[88] and in Cornwall, they were 'the roughest and most mutinous men in England'.[89] Some mining communities were indeed havens for criminals, but these stereotyped descriptions did not always rest upon close acquaintance.[90]

As great as the contrast between country and city was that between North and South. The Highland zone of England was seen by Southerners as backward and uncivil; the 'uplandish' people who lived there were notorious for their rudeness.[91] In 1537 Archbishop Cranmer described the inhabitants of the Scottish border as barbarous and savage brigands, ignorant of agriculture, and living on pillage, just as his successor Matthew Parker feared in 1560 lest the 'rude' Northerners should become 'too much Irish and savage'. The values of the Tudor state were those of peaceful and agricultural lowland England, not the pastoral and turbulent North.[92] As an Elizabethan writer complained, 'We boast much of civility and nurture in the South parts of this land, namely in London, and dispraise and despise the North as rude and uncivil.' His own experience convinced him that this was an error of judgement.[93] Yet Viscount

Wentworth, the Lord President of the North, and himself a Yorkshireman, could refer in 1629 to 'the barbarous Northern folk'. Bishop Hacket, on his travels in the Midland counties of Staffordshire and Shropshire, 'discovered in places remote a Northern rigour and churlishness among our villagers, wanting that southern sleekness that is usually found in cities and great towns, the metropolis especially'.[94] The Northerners of Yorkshire, Lancashire and Cumbria were notorious for their dour plain speaking and blunt, uncourtly manner. On Tyneside, the keelmen, who loaded the coal onto the big ships, were equally notorious for their cursing, swearing, drunkenness and violence: the 'can houses' supplying them with beer kept an inferior brew for them, which they called 'savage beer' or 'beer for savages'.[95] The rudeness of the miners who lived in the Peak district of Derbyshire contrasted with the superior manners of the dwellers in the agricultural and manufacturing southern half of the county. An eighteenth-century writer thought that this was because 'civilization does not take place so early in a mountainous as in a champaign [flat, open] country'. But he also attributed it to the miners' lack of intercourse with the rest of the world and their resulting lack of that 'polish, which a free and extensive commerce with neighbouring countries [districts] frequently gives'.[96]

The Civility of the Middling Sort

Whether they lived in London or the provinces, the professional and commercial middle classes of early modern England had codes of refinement and polite behaviour that were often independent of those of the court and the gentry, and in some ways exceeded them.[97] Urban traders had always set a high value on courteous, honest and sober dealing, and shopkeepers were noted for their 'extreme civility', bordering on obsequiousness.[98] This was not invariably the case, for in 1552 the Privy Council found it necessary to warn the butchers of London that their wives and servants should use gentle and honest language with their customers.[99] Normally, however, 'obliging behaviour' and 'genteel deportment' were accepted as important qualifications for anyone engaged in commerce. 'They who would enfavour themselves for the advantage of any business,' noted a contemporary in 1638, 'must show themselves affable, smooth and courteous.' The man who stood behind the counter had to be 'all courtesy, civility, and good manners'. No discourteous trader, it was claimed, had ever risen to a great fortune; and the economic expansion of eighteenth-century England would have been impossible without a widespread ethic of honesty, courtesy and trustworthiness.[100] When the traveller Richard Pococke visited the pottery towns in 1750, he encountered 'much civility and obliging behaviour, as they look on all that come among them as customers'.[101] Similarly, a Swiss visitor warned against what he called 'the dangerous civility' of the people of Paris, with which they encouraged people to buy more than they had intended.[102]

Bernard Mandeville has left us a fine description of the ingratiating and gentlemanlike manner of a mercer as he sets out to entrap a fine young lady into buying his expensive silks. Anyone who wanted grand ladies as his customers had to be 'a very polite man, and skilled in all the punctilios of City good-breeding ... He must dress neatly and affect a court air.'[103] In 1774 the great hosiery manufacturer Jedediah Strutt gave a copy of Lord Chesterfield's *Letters* to his son, urging him to acquire 'the manners, the air, the genteel address, and polite behaviour of a gentleman' as they would prove essential when he came to do business in the world.[104]

Eighteenth-century defenders of the commercial interest would argue that trade refined and polished manners, because it encouraged more extensive contact with the rest of the world. Their claim was fully borne out by the behaviour of contemporary merchants, salesmen and innkeepers. To sell goods it was important to have an empathetic feeling for the needs and desires of others. An essential precondition of this polite style, however, was commercial competition. When, as in the case of the ferrymen on the River Severn, the seller had a monopoly, there was no 'stimulus to ensure civility'; and the ferrymen could be as rude and offensive as they wished.[105] The same was true of porters, wagoners and carriers, who were 'the rudest and most uncivilized part of the nation', and of seamen, who were 'as rough, surly, and ill-natured as the element they live upon'. Customs officers were another occupational group who had nothing to gain by being civil.[106] For rather different reasons, surgeons were noted for 'a strange kind of rusticity of manners and ill-nature, which they contract by their continued austerity and necessary cruelty to their patients in performing their operations'.[107]

An important civilizing role was played by the thousands of voluntary clubs and societies that sprang up all over the country in the seventeenth and eighteenth centuries.[108] They included associations of like-minded friends who met in taverns and eating places to drink, dine and converse. Some of these became aggressively masculine gatherings, bawdy and drunken. Others, such as the Jacobean meetings of poets, lawyers and politicians associated with Ben Jonson and his friends, were self-conscious agents of cultivated sociability. The rules for Jonson's Apollo Club in the early 1620s pointedly dissociated its members from the aristocratic rowdies of the day:

And let our only emulation be
Not drinking much but talking wittily.
. . .
To fight and brawl (like Hectors) let none dare,
Glasses or windows break, or hangings tear.[109]

Peaceful conviviality could also be achieved in a domestic context. In the reign of Henry VIII, the historian Polydore Vergil noted that the 'common sort' of London citizens were in the habit of inviting their friends to dine or sup in their houses, 'accounting it a great part of gentleness (*humanitas*)'. During the ensuing two centuries, the middle-class home became better equipped for entertaining visitors. As houses were enlarged, room spaces were differentiated and expenditure increased on tables, linen, cutlery and tableware, domestic eating and drinking became an important aspect of what contemporaries regarded as 'civility'.[110] The authors of the cookery books of the period took it for granted that their readers would want to entertain at meals 'their kindred, friends, allies and acquaintances'; and the frequency of such domestic entertaining is confirmed by the diaries of the time.[111] Mild intoxication was accepted as a helpful aid to convivial conversation, though in the eighteenth century the new nonalcoholic drinks of coffee, tea and chocolate also played a central role in public sociability. The tea party became a ubiquitous social ritual, while it was claimed that the coffeehouses attracted such 'civil' and 'intelligent' company that they could not fail to 'civilize our manners, enlarge our understandings, refine our language, [and] teach us a generous confidence and handsome mode of address' (Plate 10).[112]

Urban sociability of all kinds was much recommended by the courtesy writers. It was a recognized code of civility among 'the ordinary civil sort of people', as one contemporary called them,[113] though not everyone adhered to it. An observant writer explained in 1585 that there were three sorts of men whose manners were to be reprehended: those who neither invited neighbours to dinner nor accepted invitations from them; those who invited them, but declined return invitations; and those who accepted invitations, but never issued any themselves.[114]

It was with good reason that Richard Baxter regarded 'freeholders and tradesmen' as 'the strength of religion and civility in the land'.[115] For they were certainly more civil in their behaviour than many aristocrats, whose conduct in public places was often noisy, boorish and inconsiderate.[116] Most of the middling classes were hostile to aristocratic values; they rejected duelling and the gentleman's code of honour that went with it; and they preferred diligence and thrift to conspicuous leisure and profligate expenditure.[117] They also exceeded their superiors in personal cleanliness and linguistic propriety. Indeed, their characteristic error was that of excessive refinement. Shakespeare's Hotspur, son of the Earl of Northumberland, rebukes his wife for saying 'in good sooth': 'You swear like a comfit-maker's wife . . . Swear me, Kate, like a lady as thou art, / A good mouth-filling oath, and leave "in sooth" / And such protest of pepper-gingerbread / To velvet-guards and Sunday-citizens.'[118] When the politician George Canning, who had been a brilliant scholar at Eton and Christ Church, composed the inscription for the younger Pitt's monument in the Guildhall, he wrote: 'He died poor.' It was an alderman who wanted to substitute: 'He expired in indigent circumstances.'[119]

For the eighteenth-century middle class, the crucial distinction was between the 'genteel' and the 'vulgar'. This was partly a matter of money: in 1753 a contemporary defined the 'genteel trades' as those that, unlike the 'common trades', required 'large capitals'.[120] But differences of manners and taste were also involved. The inevitable outcome was that 'in dress, furniture, deportment, &c, so also in language, the dread of vulgarity, constantly besetting those who are half conscious that they are in danger of it, drives them into extremes of affected finery'.[121] As a result, the word 'genteel', which had long been used to denote the style of life appropriate to gentlefolk, came to acquire its modern connotations of false pretension.

The Manners of the People

What about those below this social level, the small farmers, journeymen and labourers? Did they subscribe to upper-class standards of civil behaviour? Or were they indifferent to the prevailing notions of civility and politeness? These are not easy questions to answer, but there are some pointers.

It might be thought, for example, that the lack of privacy in public lavatories like the common house of easement at Queenhithe in the Port of London, with its long rows of forty unpartitioned seats for men and forty for women, and the survival into the twentieth century of two- and three-seater privies, suggest that lower down the social scale attitudes to defecation and urination were more relaxed.[122] The saltpetre hunters of the early modern period assumed that the floors of houses would be saturated with urine and excrement. In 1628 they wanted to dig under the churches because 'the women piss in their seats, which causes excellent saltpetre'. (Some allowance should perhaps be made for the length of seventeenth-century sermons.)[123] When the sexual adventurer Giacomo Casanova visited England in 1763, he was startled to see people defecating in the street and doing so with their backs to the passers-by rather than facing them (which, as his companion explained, would have robbed them of their anonymity).[124] Yet although ordinary people relieved themselves against church walls, on the stairs of public buildings and in the corners of rooms, the evidence of the church courts suggests that the populace at large had definite standards of physical propriety. The exposure of the private parts of the human body was universally regarded as 'uncivil' and 'beastly'.[125] The eighteenth-century antiquarian Francis Grose even claimed that a person who defecated near a highway or a public footpath could, by an ancient custom, be required by passers-by to take off his hat with his teeth, 'and without moving from his station to throw it over his head, by which it frequently fell into the excrement'. A man refusing to obey this rule might be pushed backwards into his own deposit.[126]

The general assumption among the upper classes was that in all parts of the country the lower ranks of the population were 'clownish', coarse in behaviour and lacking in self-control. They did not set out to please in the way recommended by the manuals of civility, but were surly and uningratiating. They were unused to any 'ceremonies of courtesy', and their gestures were graceless, 'hoggish' and 'unrestrained'.[127] Ignorant and inarticulate, they were incapable of polite discourse. If they met people of quality, they could be overcome by 'rustic bashfulness' and run away, 'ashamed or afraid'. Clumsy in body, they stood cap in hand, with rough arms hanging loose and toes turned in.[128] The gentry were advised to keep their children away from 'barbarous nurses, clownish playing-mates, and all rustical persons' lest they be contaminated by their bad manners.[129] 'Peasantry,' warned a courtesy writer, was 'a disease like the plague, easily caught by conversation [i.e., company].'[130] Elizabethan entrepreneurs envisaged exporting to America the 'poorer sort of people', who troubled 'the better sort' with 'their sundry disorders'; and the royal palaces employed porters to keep out those who were 'uncivil, uncleanly and rude'. As the twentieth-century Italian communist intellectual Antonio Gramsci would remark, subordinate groups have, in the eyes of the social elite, always appeared barbarous and pathological.[131]

Whether artisans and labourers were quite as lumpish, awkward and heavy-handed as the commentators maintained we may reasonably doubt. But account has to be taken of the distinctive posture and bearing that their superiors achieved by education and from the physical advantages arising from differences in diet, clothing, furniture and occupation. Undernourished persons, engaged in manual labour, could hardly be expected to conform to aristocratic standards of physical elegance. In Elizabethan times, it was acknowledged that 'the bodies of the gentlemen of England and [of] poor labouring men [were] of divers dispositions'. The experience of campaigning in Ireland convinced the writer Gervase Markham that a gentleman could endure extremes of hunger and cold that would kill off 'a hundred clowns'.[132] In the later eighteenth century, the lower classes were, on average, shorter and thinner than their social superiors; and army officers were both stronger and more handsome than the men.[133] As David Hume observed in 1739, 'The skin, pores, muscles and nerves of a day-labourer are different from those of a man of quality . . . The different stations of life influence the whole fabric.'[134] Miners, blacksmiths and other industrial workers were often warped physically by their occupations; and their hands were rough and calloused. In Elizabethan Pembrokeshire, it was said that 'hard labour, parching of the sun, and starving with cold' were 'a chief cause

89

of the unseemliness of the common people'.[135] John Locke thought that 'a middle-aged plough-man' could 'scarce ever be brought to the carriage . . . of a gentleman, though his body be as well proportioned, and his joints as supple'.[136]

Despite these physical differences, the concepts of civility and incivility seem to have been familiar at even the humblest social levels. The lower classes had for centuries been expected to practise self-control in the presence of their superiors: deference and obedience were integral to their lives.[137] Copyhold tenants might be explicitly required to be 'of honest conversation'. Seventeenth-century overseers of the poor frequently made the distribution of relief conditional on the recipients behaving themselves 'civilly', not using 'uncivil language', and not comporting themselves in an 'unruly or uncivil' way.[138] In the 1660s, the vicar of Bruton, Somerset, wrote testimonials certifying that applicants for poor relief had 'always lived civilly' or were 'of civil life and conversation'. In Lancashire twenty years later, one applicant claimed that he had been 'a very civil, painful, and laborious workman', while another said that he had 'civilly demeaned himself against his neighbours'. Others chose to represent themselves as 'decent', 'painful' or 'honest'. Whether or not they used the word 'civil', the qualities of honesty, industry and sobriety to which they laid claim closely resembled what contemporaries understood by the term.[139]

'Honesty' was the virtue of those who supported themselves by their own labour and lived in a peaceable, orderly and inoffensive way.[140] It also meant sexual propriety. This was a fundamental requirement, and not just for women: it was almost as insulting to call a man a 'whoremaster' as to label a woman a 'whore', and both parents of a bastard were liable to censure.[141] Fornication, adultery and sexual harassment were all regarded as 'incivilities': a Devonshire woman complained in 1655 that a would-be rapist 'took up her clothes in a very uncivil way'.[142]

The idea of civility thus had plenty of popular resonance. It implied deference to superiors, respect for the elderly, and orderly, law-abiding behaviour towards friends, relations and neighbours. In the towns, it encouraged polite sociability and involved a code of street etiquette that prescribed rules of precedence and outlawed pushing, shoving and jostling.[143] In church, worshippers were expected to wear their best clothes and behave in a 'decent', 'comely' and 'orderly' fashion. The 'unmannerly' behaviour and 'rude and immodest' acts of those who 'uncivilly' disturbed services were said to cause offence to 'all honest and civil people', and the culprits were often prosecuted in the church courts, along with talebearers, troublemakers and sexual offenders.[144] Secular courts similarly indicted individuals for 'opprobrious' or 'uncivil' speeches to JPs and others in authority, 'in breach of good manners'. Scolding women were charged with reviling their neighbours 'in most barbarous and uncivil manner', while slanderers were described as 'undecent' and 'unmannerly'.[145]

The language of vulgar abuse reveals that it was generally thought shameful for anyone, however poor, to be 'drunken', and 'barbarous' for them to be 'turbulent' or 'disordered.[146] Householders might require their lodgers to be 'civil, and not drunkards, who do nothing but pot it and quarrel'.[147] Printing houses had customs designed to ensure 'civil and orderly deportment'; they punished swearing, fighting, drunkenness and abusive language among the workforce, along with 'affronts or indignities' offered by visitors. Like many other trade associations, the Stationers' Company insisted on the 'good behaviour and civil conversation' of its members. When the East India Company was in search of young English women who would agree to be shipped to India to become wives of the company's employees, it insisted that they should be 'of honest and civil behaviour'.[148]

Civility also included the courteous reception of strangers. The Elizabethan writer Thomas Churchyard boasted of the 'kindness', 'courtesy', 'fair words' and 'reverence' of the 'plain people' of Shrewsbury and North Wales, who saluted visitors in 'civil manner', yielded cap and knee to their betters, and held it 'a duty to follow a stranger's stirrup (being out of the way) to bring him where he wisheth'. He had similarly kind things to say about the 'manifest courtesies' and 'reverent manners' with which the ordinary people of Suffolk and Norfolk received a visit in 1578 by Elizabeth I. The mid-Tudor agricultural writer Thomas Tusser similarly thought it important that country folk should answer strangers 'civilly' and show 'no discourtesy' to their neighbours.[149]

In practice, however, foreign visitors seem to have encountered an unfriendly reception throughout the early modern period, whether at ports like Dover and Gravesend, where they were rudely received and extortionately charged, or in the streets of London, where they were regularly subjected to jeers and insults from 'the baser sort of prentices, serving men, draymen and like people'. 'None is so derided, mocked, and laughed at, as strangers, now in England', lamented an Elizabethan, who saw it as 'an occasion of slander to this our native soil'.[150] In the 1620s James I issued two proclamations condemning the 'many insolencies of rude and savage barbarism' directed by 'the inferior and baser sort of people' against visitors from abroad. But they seem to have had little effect.[151] Only in the later eighteenth century did the demeanour of the capital's populace towards foreigners become more civil.[152] Before then, even English travellers might be subjected to the same treatment. When in 1754 the novelist Henry Fielding, bloated, disfigured and dying of cirrhosis, was carried on board a ship to Portugal at Rotherhithe, he was subjected to a torrent of insulting mockery by the sailors and watermen.[153]

Writing in 1700 about the Shropshire village of Myddle, Richard Gough commended some of the inhabitants for being 'courteous' and 'peaceable', and condemned others as 'rude', 'quarrelsome' and 'untowardly'.[154] Conversely, many humble persons were praised for being 'of civil behaviour and carriage' or 'of an honest and civil life'.[155] As a modern historian sagely remarks of the language employed by ordinary people in their depositions before the church courts, 'The particular face of civility that is exposed here is less to do with the niceties of polite behaviour than with conduct and qualities that a later age would term respectability, propriety, and decency.'[156]

The poorer members of society were not a homogeneous class. There had long been a tendency to distinguish the 'honest poor' from their more disreputable counterparts. In eighteenth-century London, the poor who were working and of fixed abode were differently regarded from those who were unemployed and unsettled.[157] In the industrial age, the distinction between 'respectable' and 'rough' became fundamental to working-class culture. Robert Roberts, in his classic account of life in a Lancashire slum at the beginning of the twentieth century, emphasized that the poorest classes were sharply stratified by different levels of respectability. Many working-class women struggled to keep their doorsteps and windows clean and imitated what they thought to be middle-class refinement in dress and language. Even in prison, there were men who took their food alone because they were afraid they lacked the 'proper manners' for eating with the others.[158]

Long before then, it had been customary to distinguish those members of the lower orders who comported themselves in what was regarded as a 'decent' fashion from those who were unruly and unrestrained, such as the 'idle and disorderly' beggars, whom seventeenth-century commentators condemned for their 'most beastly manners', or the apprentices and young artisans of late eighteenth-century London, many of them notorious for their brawling, pilfering and sexual promiscuity.[159] The concern of many artisan communities to demonstrate their civility can be seen in the eighteenth-century friendly societies that aimed to promote 'good manners and conversation'. The drunken woman, who in 1801 pissed into a man's hat and put it on his head, was not untypical of the more demoralized members of the Nottinghamshire working class; but in the eyes of her respectable neighbours, her behaviour was reprehensible.[160]

Civilizing Agents

People in authority had long been concerned to regulate the personal behaviour and 'civilize' the manners of those sections of the population whom they regarded as 'rude', 'barbarous' and a threat to public order. They did so in response to the pressure of the respectable, as in Norwich in 1604, where 'the better sort of people' were said to be 'much grieved and offended' that 'the ruder sort' were not 'restrained'.[161] Of course, by 'civilizing' the populace, the authorities did not mean that they wanted them to master the arts of fashionable self-presentation and to engage in polite conversation. Rather, the aim was to ensure that 'the common sort' would be deferential, law abiding, obedient to the commands of their political and social superiors and, above all, industrious. As Bernard Mandeville remarked, 'It is not compliments we want of them, but their work and assiduity.'[162]

Work itself was thought to have a therapeutic effect on popular behaviour, for hard-working men were 'civil' men. In Jacobean times the enclosure of the royal forests was urged in order to 'bring the former unprofitable inhabitants to a civil and religious course of life': 'civilizing these unhappy persons' was a 'strong argument in favour of enclosing the wastes and commons'.[163] Parliamentary enclosure of open fields in the later eighteenth century was also regarded as, in part, a civilizing project, designed to root out the indolence, immorality and pauperization associated with common land.[164] The republican pamphleteer John Streater urged in 1653 that care should be taken 'to increase manufacture, for that enricheth and civilizeth the people'. With similar objectives in mind, the mid-seventeenth-century activist Samuel Hartlib wanted reformed workhouses to become schools for 'civilizing' the children who 'lie all day in the streets in playing, cursing, and swearing'. Child labour was believed to have an intrinsically 'civilizing' effect. Daniel Defoe recommended that vagrant street urchins be gathered up from the streets and placed in hospitals, where they would be fed, clothed, governed and taught 'good letters and good manners', until they were aged fourteen, when they would be ready for service as seamen in the King's Navy or on merchant ships.[165]

Grammar schools were regarded as 'a principal means to reduce a barbarous people to civility', by softening manners, accustoming children to a disciplined routine and teaching them to obey authority. In the belief that a lack of education led to 'rustic impudence and clownish untractableness', much effort went into inculcating 'decent and proper behaviour', both in and outside school.[166] When Archbishop Harsnet founded two schools at Chigwell, Essex, in 1629, he declared that he was more concerned that his scholars should be 'nurtured and disciplined in good manners than instructed in good arts'. John Locke agreed that priority should be given to teaching manners and good habits: that was indeed 'the main point' of education.[167] This conviction lay behind the founding of many new grammar schools in the supposedly backward north of England. But no one envisaged that the poor should receive a 'polite' education. Although they were ready to make exceptions for bright boys who could be trained for the ministry, most well-to-do contemporaries were opposed to educating the common people beyond a minimal level lest they develop ambitions above their station.

In the civilizing of the population, the upper ranks were expected to play a crucial role. The royal court had traditionally been the place 'where true manners grow', especially from the sixteenth century, when under the Tudors it was thought to have become 'much greater and more gallant than in former times'.[168] The 7th Earl of Derby justified his disastrous appointment of a rude sea captain as governor of the Isle of Man in the 1630s on the grounds that he was 'excellent company' and had 'civilized himself [by spending] half a year at court, where he served the Duke of Buckingham'. When the future James II held court in Edinburgh from 1679 to 1682, it was claimed that the citizens 'laid down the greatest part of their former roughness ... by his daily example'.[169] Queen Caroline, wife of George II, cultivated the fine arts in a self-conscious belief that the royal court should be a civilizing influence on the nation; and in the mid-eighteenth century, Lord Chesterfield still believed that courts were 'unquestionably the seats of good-breeding'. But the truth was that, after the Revolution of 1688, the English court lost its centrality to polite society and ceased to set the fashions of the day.[170] Long before then, royalty had often failed to set an example. The court of Henry VIII was chaotic and informal, while that of James I was, in John Aubrey's opinion, 'unpolished and ill-mannered'. Under Charles I, the Stuart court became more refined, but Puritans were reluctant to accept it as the arbiter of good manners; and after 1660, the louche example of Charles II robbed it of any moral authority it had once possessed. Looking back at the previous century, Jonathan Swift concluded that royal courts were 'the worst of all schools to teach good manners'.[171] Politeness was not the same as courtliness; and under the Hanoverians, it was largely unaffected by that concern to please the ruler which was so overriding in the absolute monarchies of the continent.

The aristocracy, however, continued to exert an influence on the manners of the populace. The heralds even claimed that one of the main purposes of having a nobility was 'to draw the rude people unto a more civil kind of life and courtesy of behaviour'.[172] The future Leveller Richard Overton was less enamoured of the aristocracy, but he too believed that it was the task of magistrates to 'preserve public modesty, comeliness and civility, that there may be a general comely demeanour as rational creatures'. The exiled royalist Margaret Cavendish noted on her continental travels that towns where the prince did not reside or which the nobility and gentry did not frequent were 'most commonly . . . but little civilized'.[173] Hence the government's constant pressure on English gentlemen to reside in their own localities rather than spending all their time in London. The theory was that in the metropolis they would pick up appropriate forms of polite behaviour, dress and speech, and then return to the shires to instruct their inferiors. From the example of the gentry, yeomen farmers would learn to 'savour of some good fashion', and the great aristocratic country houses would bring urban civilization to rural areas.[174]

In 1617 Sir Henry Widdrington hoped that the example of resident justices of the peace would reform the 'uncivil and rude manners' of the Northumberland dalesmen, while a Lincolnshire gentleman was praised in 1634 because he 'doth daily civilize the rudeness of the people'.[175] Artificers and labourers had been 'much improved and bettered by conversing with gentlemen', thought a Jacobean commentator; he urged sceptics to witness for themselves 'the civility now generally practised amongst us'.[176] Similarly, in 1780 it was claimed that one of the beneficial effects of the Vauxhall Gardens in London was that 'the manners of the lower orders have, by almost imperceptible degrees been humanized by often mixing with their betters'.[177]

Norbert Elias denied the civilizing effect of organized religion on the grounds that religion is never more or less 'civilized' than the society or class that practises it.[178] This ignores the possibility that, at any one time, the values of the clergy may be more 'civilized' than those of the lay population. Certainly, in England the established Church was an active agent of civility. In the later Middle Ages, the clergy did much to check violence and keep the peace in the parishes.[179] The Tudor preacher Bernard Gilpin was famous for having helped to pacify the northern people of Redesdale and Tynedale, calming their 'savage demeanour' and reducing them to 'civility and better order of behaviour'.[180] The clergy regarded good manners as important and incivility as a breach of Christian charity. They urged their flocks to defer to superiors, check the expression of anger and contempt, and practise the golden rule of doing as you would be done by.[181] The civilizing implications of the Christian message were stressed by a London preacher in 1641 when he described the peaceable kingdom foretold in Isaiah 11:6–8 as 'the turning of fierce and brutal men, and people who, in regard of their savage and cruel nature, differ nothing from beasts, unto sweet and calm and sociable manners and conversation'.[182] When Thomas Hall arrived at his parish of King's Norton, Worcestershire, in 1640, he found an ignorant flock of disorderly drunkards; but he set to work and, we are told, 'in a short time they were civilized'.[183] During the Commonwealth and Protectorate, the concerted drive by Puritan clergy, in alliance with godly magistrates, to reform the people's manners, from their drinking habits to their sexual behaviour, was as much concerned with inculcating civility as with encouraging godliness. The same was true of the continuing attempts of lay and ecclesiastical authorities since medieval times to regulate personal behaviour and of the Societies for the Reformation of Manners of the 1690s and thereafter.[184]

Before the Civil War, a bishop had defended church ales (alcoholic fund-raising parties) 'for the civilizing of the people, ... for the composing of differences by occasion of the making of friends, [and] for the increase of love and unity'. The ales were seen by many as a means of 'conforming of men's behaviour to a civil conversation, composing of controversies, [and] appeasing of quarrels'. The Puritans, however, disliked these occasions because they were held on Sundays and tended to be boisterous and drunken. After the Restoration, Charles II's master of the revels thought that a licensing system could reduce the disorders at church ales and thereby 'much civilize the people'.[185] A hundred years later, Archbishop Secker claimed that Sunday worship greatly helped to 'civilise' the populace 'by uniting neighbourhoods in formed assemblies ... with hearts disengaged from selfish attentions, and open to friendly regards'. Joseph Addison observed in the *Spectator* that country people would 'soon degenerate into a kind of savages and barbarians, were there not such frequent returns of a stated time, in which the whole village meet together with their best faces, and in their cleanliest habits, to converse with one another upon indifferent subjects, hear their duties explained to them, and join together in adoration of the Supreme Being'. The Scottish divine Hugh Blair claimed in 1750 that religion 'civilizes mankind. It tames the fierceness of their passions, and wears off the barbarity of their manners'; and the dean of Carlisle remarked to Samuel Johnson that 'it might be discerned whether or no there was a clergyman resident in a parish by the civil or savage manner of the people'.[186]

The Sunday school movement, which grew up in the last two decades of the eighteenth century, embodied the ethics of the 'respectable' working class. Its intention was that the children of the poor should be 'humanized and civilized' by absorbing the values of honesty, punctuality, cleanliness, 'decorum' and 'civility'. In 1789 it was claimed that the introduction of Sunday schools was improving the inhabitants of South Derbyshire in 'kindness to each other, in civility to strangers, and in the practice of modesty and decency'; and when in 1797 the religious writer Hannah More visited a Sunday school in a Mendips mining village, she was greatly impressed by the 'civilised manners' and 'handsome Sunday clothes' of two young colliers who were teaching scripture to the children.[187]

The Methodist revival had a similar influence. At the end of the eighteenth century, it was reported that, thanks to the efforts of the Wesleyan preachers, the miners of the Forest of Kingswood, Gloucestershire, who forty or fifty years earlier had been 'so barbarous and savage, that they were a terror to the city of Bristol', were now 'much civilized and improved in principles, morals, and pronunciation'.[188] In Tyneside the Methodists were said to have 'greatly civilized' the 'semi-barbarians' of the coalpits, who had, in Thomas Bewick's opinion, been 'like Cherokees or Mohawks'. In Wales, the propagation of this same gospel of hard work, temperance, thrift, self-education and religious knowledge has been aptly dubbed 'chapel civility'.[189]

Partly because of the efforts of these various 'civilizing' agencies, and even more because of the growth of towns, trade, industry and the improvement of communications, the manners of the common people were generally agreed to have softened between the early sixteenth and late eighteenth centuries. Higher wages, more regular working habits and the spread of consumer goods were all helping to 'civilize' the lower classes. Looking back over the previous sixty years, the radical tailor Francis Place concluded in 1823 that 'the progress made in refinement of manners and morals' had 'gone on simultaneously with the improvements in Arts, Manufactures, and Commerce'.[190]

Plebeian Civility

Their subjection to the authority of others meant that the common people had always been aware of the survival value of self-discipline. This did not, however, necessarily involve emulating the manners of their betters. On the contrary, their codes of bodily comportment and social interaction were radically different. Of course, habits, values and customs varied greatly according to region, locality and occupation. Nevertheless, it is possible to offer some tentative generalizations about the distinctive civility of the populace.

For example, labouring people tended to have a different attitude to the body. Typically, they prized not elegance, but strength and endurance. Their standards of physical beauty were not the same as those of their superiors: gentlemen disliked sunburn and preferred their women to be pale and interesting, whereas 'the honest rustic' liked a woman 'of a good strong make' and 'sun-burnt, frowsy complexion'.[191] The lower orders were dirtier than their masters, and they were alleged to be habitually flatulent. Notoriously, they stank. William Bullein, a mid-Tudor medical writer, noted that 'plain people in the country, as carters, threshers, ditchers, colliers and ploughmen, use seldom times to wash their hands, as appeareth by their filthiness, and as very few times comb their heads, as it is seen by flocks, nits, grease, feathers, straw and such like, which hangeth in their hairs'.[192] The Elizabethan topographer John Norden warned his readers against letting 'drudges, as housekeepers or labourers, or suchlike, come near thy person, or thy table, for either their rude behaviour or ill smell will be offensive'.[193]

Yet even at the humblest level, it was an insult to call anyone 'filthy' or 'lousy'. Dirty or ragged clothes brought disgrace to their wearers, and it has been calculated that there were over a thousand different terms in the various English dialects for a slattern.[194] Clean linen was a crucial source of self-respect. Ordinary people had a strong sense of decorum, of what was neat and decent, and appropriate to their station. Even the very poor could go to great lengths on special occasions to avoid appearing disreputably dressed.[195] The most macabre example is that of the criminal in 1721 who deliberately chose to be pressed to death rather than plead at his trial: 'No one shall say that I was hanged in a dirty shirt and ragged coat.'[196] Plebeian dirt was less a matter of choice than a consequence of poverty, lack of spare time and the scarcity of hot water.[197] Making a virtue of necessity, however, manual workers tended defensively to treat cleanliness as an effeminate affectation, hailing the dirt of the miner or farm labourer as a mark of virility. In the Elizabethan countryside, where women did agricultural work, it was said that if a gentlewoman 'be more fine or delicate', 'she is misliked . . . and called a clean-fingered girl, as though that were a great ignominy'.[198]

Dirt could even be seen as protective. An Elizabethan writer recorded the opinion, held 'by many nowadays, and especially among the common sort', that it was 'not good for the head to be washed'; he cited an old saying that, he claimed, was 'common in almost every man's mouth': 'Wash thy hands often, thy feet seldom, but thy head never.' In one seventeenth-century Surrey village, the 'poorest sort' were said to keep their children 'very nasty and unclean, scabbed or lousy or both, or else without change of apparel'. Eighteenth-century doctors discovered there was a 'vulgar notion, familiar only to common people', that a frequent change of linen would weaken newborn children by robbing them of 'nourishing juices' and that it was dangerous to wash a child's hair. As William Buchan, author of the enormously influential *Domestic Medicine* (1769 and frequently reissued), declared, 'Peasants in most countries seem to hold cleanliness in a sort of contempt.'[199]

There was also a greater readiness among the populace to resort to physical violence. Like Tudor aristocrats, working men regarded fighting as a source of status and masculine identity. When Captain Robert Dover founded the annual 'Cotswold games' in the reign of James I, he provided fencing and horse racing for the gentry, but wrestling, single-stick fighting and shin kicking for the common people. The cleric Thomas Fuller believed that 'the ruder sort of people scarce count anything a sport which is not loud and violent ...It is no pastime with country clowns that cracks not pates, breaks not shins, bruises not limbs, tumbles and tosses not all the body.' Even in their dancing, the lower orders were thought to be more boisterous, with much flailing of limbs and whooping with joy.[200]

By the late eighteenth century, the gentry and middling sort had largely abandoned the extreme interpersonal violence that had been common among their sixteenth-century predecessors. Henceforth, those accused of homicide were most likely to be working-class labourers. Their murderous attacks were usually spontaneous and uncontrolled, the fatal outcome of a sudden quarrel.[201] But much popular violence was carefully regulated and as subject to laws of etiquette as the gentleman's duel. In late medieval England, there had been informal conventions governing fights between individuals: provided the rules were observed, a degree of violence had been regarded as entirely acceptable.[202] In early modern times, impromptu boxing and wrestling were recognized methods of resolving differences. 'A ring! A ring!' was the cry. Strict rules governed the conflict, and heavy emphasis was laid on the importance of fair play and 'standing up and fighting like a man'. In 1659 the soldiers of the rival armies commanded by Generals Monck and Lambert said that they would not fight each other, but would 'make a ring for the officers to fight in'.[203] In the later seventeenth century, it was not unusual for a coachman who had a dispute about the fare with the gentleman who had hired him to agree to a fight to resolve the issue (the gentleman almost always won). A man who was willing to fight was never short of admirers. This was a lower-class code of honour, which in the opinion of Voltaire had no counterpart in other countries.[204]

Respectable women had always regarded female violence as improper and uncivil, though in the seventeenth century even they were capable of it under certain circumstances.[205] Their social inferiors were less inhibited. At the Westminster quarter sessions between 1680 and 1720, thousands of men and women were charged with assault.[206] Yet plebeian violence seems to have declined during the eighteenth century, particularly after the introduction of street lighting made London and other cities safer at night. Popular sports grew less dangerous and fistfighting was increasingly regarded as 'savage' and 'barbarous'.[207] But even in the nineteenth century, physical violence, particularly in 'fair fight' and by women as well as men (Plate 26), continued to be seen by the less 'respectable' poor as an acceptable form of retaliation for offensive words. Working-class men could not afford to resolve their disputes by litigation and, like the members of today's gangs of delinquent youth, were usually egged on to fight by their peers. Drink and sexual jealousy were the most common causes of these affrays.[208]

Verbal violence by husbands towards wives occurred at all social levels, but physical violence was a different matter. William Blackstone remarked in his *Commentaries* (1765–69) that wife-beating began to be challenged legally 'in the politer reign of Charles II', but that in his day it was still to be found among 'the lower rank of people'. Mandeville thought that lasting harmony between husband and wife was very uncommon among 'the lowest vulgar and those of meanest education', because the passions of the 'uncivilized' were fleeting and inconstant; whereas well-educated people had learnt that life was easier when they tied themselves up to 'rules and decorums'. In the nineteenth century, wife-beating was (wrongly) associated exclusively with the rougher part of the working class and much disapproved of by the respectable. The judge Sir John Nicholl declared in 1827 that 'even among the very lowest classes, there is generally a feeling of something unmanly in striking a woman'.[209]

For the middling classes, fornication, adultery and illegitimacy had long been seen as incompatible with social respectability. Their notions of sexual morality coincided with those of the church courts, which until the Civil War were vigorous in their prosecution of sexual delinquency. The subsequent decline of the courts and a less vigorous prosecution of bastard bearers by the lay magistrates enabled something like an alternative morality to come into the open. Its key feature was the long-held and widely accepted notion that fornication, and sometimes even cohabitation, were permissible if the couple involved were planning to marry.[210] This sentiment was reflected in a huge increase during the eighteenth century in bridal pregnancy and illegitimacy. By the end of the century, it is probable that a quarter of all first births were illegitimate and a further quarter conceived before marriage.[211] It is also likely, though more evidence on this point is needed, that the rise in illegitimacy was particularly evident among the lower ranks of the population.[212] It was ironic if so, for it brought the poor closer to the sexual ethics of the aristocracy than to those of the middling classes, for whom marital fidelity and domesticity had become crucial ingredients of a civil life.[213]

In their daily behaviour, the common people tended to be more spontaneous than their superiors. Their sociability was more relaxed and less constrained by formalities than the carefully orchestrated interaction of the well-to-do. They did not make genteel 'visits', but went to see each other unannounced, as the mood took them; and their behaviour in company was less subject to polite inhibition. Margaret Cavendish, Duchess of Newcastle, noted that although the nobility and gentry got drunk more frequently than the peasantry, because they could afford to, they were careful to stay sober on important occasions; whereas peasants were 'for the most part, drunk at their departing'.[214] There was more singing at work among the lower orders, more whistling, more horseplay, more personal remarks, more gossip about other people, more tears, more obscene language and bawdy jokes, more 'smutty phrases' and 'excessive laughter'. Only beggars, it was said, were, 'by a kind of toleration', permitted to sing in the street.[215] Among 'the meaner sort of husbandmen and country inhabitants', lamented one Elizabethan, 'he is thought to be the merriest that talketh . . . most ribaldry',[216] an observation fully borne out by reported speech in the defamation suits in the church courts. In 1649 John Bulwer thought that those 'most apt to laughter' were 'children, women, and the common people'; and a later Stuart divine lamented that 'foolish jesting' was most common 'when the youth of both sexes' met together, 'especially among such of lower rank … who have not been blest with the best education and breeding'. Obscenity made a gentleman contemptible, thought the Oxford cleric Obadiah Walker in 1673, 'but amongst clowns he is most accepted … that useth it most'.[217] A linguistic expert explained in 1702 that there were 'base, low words, such as are never met with but in the mouth of the vulgar, and never used, either in conversation or writing, by the better and more polite sort of people. The French call them *des mots bas*.'[218]

The rural population did not aspire to the niceties of polite conversation. The 'character' writer John Earle observed in 1628 that 'a plain country fellow' did not affect elegant gestures or pretty speeches: 'His compliment with his neighbours is a good thump on the back; and his salutation commonly some blunt curse.' When a countryman came out of church, said a Stuart preacher, he fell 'immediately into a discourse about his cattle, or his ground, or the price of corn, or anything of that nature'. 'His ordinary discourse,' agreed the Jacobean writer Henry Peacham, 'is of last year's hay, which he hopes will give six pounds the load in Smithfield, and of the rate of swine in Romford market.'[219] Another contemporary reported that when 'the ruder sort of people' were gathered in an alehouse, they could be heard 'speaking altogether, and with such a confusion that you shall hear none of them distinctly. They call aloud one another by their names or nick-names, in a rustic and homely manner, and make commonly such a noise that those who pass by stand to listen if they quarrel not.'[220]

In the following century, Adam Smith contrasted 'the most polite persons', who 'preserve the same composure' throughout a public entertainment, with 'the rabble about them', who 'express all the various passions by their gesture and behaviour'. Immune from the pressure of good breeding to suppress all visible emotion, the populace allowed themselves the hearty laughter that the gentlemen were supposed to shun. In the nineteenth century, the novelist George Eliot would remark that 'the last thing in which the cultivated man can have community with the vulgar is their jocularity'.[221]

Yet Bernard Mandeville thought that 'plain, untaught people, the lowest vulgar and those of the meanest education' were more honest and less deceitful than their social superiors; and the Romantic writers of the later eighteenth century felt that there was an authenticity about popular discourse which the 'polite' part of the nation had lost. As the Scottish poet James Beattie wrote in 1776, 'The conversation of the common people, though not so smooth, nor so pleasing as that of the better sort, has more of the wildness and strong expression of nature. The common people speak and look what they think, bluster and threaten when they are angry, affect no sympathies which they do not feel, and when offended are at no pains to conceal their dissatisfaction. They laugh when they perceive anything ludicrous, without much deference to the sentiments of their company; and, having little relish for delicate humour, because they have been but little used to it, they amuse themselves with such pleasantry as in the higher ranks of life would offend by its homeliness ... These passions in a clown or savage may be natural, which in the polite world men are very careful to suppress.'[222]

The language of the populace was different from that of the polite world. They spoke in their local dialect rather than 'talking fine'; and they had their own demotic vocabulary. By the later seventeenth century, for example, Westmorland speech had come to be regarded by outsiders as 'uncouth', but the locals regarded it as 'the true English'.[223] The language of lower-class quarrels was usually colourful, and sometimes witty enough to become a popular form of street theatre.[224] Scolding and scurrilous name calling were what Bernard Mandeville called a 'half-civilized' alternative to physical violence.[225]

So too was that rich repertoire of expressive gestures which conventional good manners prohibited. Winking, pointing, yawning, nudging, mimicking, spitting, sniggering, 'mooning' and farting were recognized weapons of plebeian defence and subversion. The fingers of the hand alone offered a lively vocabulary of derision and insult, whether by extending the middle finger and drawing back the others into a fist, or by putting the thumb to the nose and wagging the outstretched fingers.[226] When one turbulent Jacobean villager was urged by his neighbours to keep the peace, he retorted by 'casting up his leg and laying his hand on his tail, making a mouth in a very contemptuous manner'. The patience of the godliest man, thought an observer, would be sorely tried by these 'dumb shows, winking eyes, wry mouths, bended brows, pointed fingers, touch of feet and other apish tricks'.[227]

In the *Spectator*, Richard Steele noted how the different social groups expressed contempt in different ways: 'The proud and prosperous ... by the scornful look, the elevated eye-brow, and the swelling nostrils...The prentice speaks his disrespect by an extended finger, and the porter by stealing out his tongue.'[228] Even the conventional gestures of deference to superiors could be ironically converted into forms of insult. In 1594 Thomas Clement of Englishcombe, Somerset, was charged with 'mockingly' saying to the local clergyman, 'If it like your worship, or your lordship if you will.' In 1620, Anne Lea, walking through Nantwich churchyard, passed Anne Lewis, a former servant whom she had dismissed; Anne acknowledged her by making 'a curtsy in a scornful and deriding manner'.[229]

The poorer people also had their own distinctive rules of hospitality. They were thought to attach more importance to food and drink than to conversation, preferring 'the fire of a good kitchen' and a 'spread table' to 'cringes', 'congees' and 'such discourses as only fill the ear'.[230] They were highly conscious of the obligations of 'neighbourhood'. Even the humblest parents were expected to invite 'gossips' and neighbours to the lying-in at childbirth and to the celebrations accompanying churchings, weddings, funerals and housewarmings. Such events were usually accompanied by the reciprocal exchange of gifts. Yet although it was often the guests who provided the refreshments, the financial burden could be considerable.[231] 'The churching dinners pinch the poor sort', remarks a character in a Jacobean dialogue. 'Their husbands labour some three weeks or a month to get some noble [a coin worth a third of a pound], and that must be spent upon one dinner, to keep custom and because they will do as others do; and so, after they have done groaning, their husbands must groan too.'[232] Just as tippling at higher social levels had its 'common rules of civility', so in the common alehouses, there were conventions about whose turn it was to buy a round or pay their 'shot'. 'Let them meet in an inn or tavern, upon business, or in a way of kindness,' said a preacher, 'then what striving is there who shall pay, and who shall pay most! What throwing down their money on the table!'[233]

Everywhere great importance was attached to conviviality. This was true at all social levels: the Gloucestershire gentleman Christopher Guise confessed that, when still a young man, he learnt to drink more than was good for him, 'believing it a point of civility'.[234] Puritan ministers who wanted to curb popular drunkenness had to contend with the 'common opinion' that 'drinking and bezzling [tippling] in the ale-house or tavern is good fellowship and shows a good kind nature, and maintains neighbourhood'. In the eyes of their social superiors, the poor might seem to be recklessly extravagant, wasting money on drink rather than trying to save it. But it was this very conviviality that strengthened the bonds of kinship and neighbourhood and thus provided some protection against possible misfortune.[235] In eighteenth-century London, it was the custom for most working men who could afford it to spend their evenings in a public house or tavern. Drink was a powerful catalyst of masculine solidarity.[236]

In small communities there were strong codes of neighbourly behaviour that involved keeping livestock out of other people's corn, lending goods and services, respecting the elderly and rallying round at times of need in a network of mutual support.[237] As a preacher remarked in 1687, 'They which have the least of that we call breeding' were 'prone to pity and commiseration': 'Men of a simple and rustic education, and of mean professions, easily fall into compassion, and seldom fail of relieving one another, if the consideration of their own interest does not prevail against it.'[238] Unlike town dwellers, country folk customarily greeted people when they passed them on the road. A Jacobean clergyman in Cornwall reproached those 'malcontents' who could not 'afford a cheerful look unto their brother or neighbour, nor spare him a merry thought or friendly word'.[239]

Too little is known about the eating arrangements of ordinary people. The sixteenth-century commentator William Harrison said of 'the poorest sort' that they had no regular mealtimes, but 'generally sup and dine when they may'.[240] Yet two hundred years later, when the housing and furnishings of the labouring classes were still rudimentary, and when meals for many of them were inadequate and irregular, it is revealing that the social investigator Sir Frederic Morton Eden should have asserted that not only could 'the lowest peasant' eat his meal at a table, but also that his table was 'covered with a table-cloth'. 'The sitting together at a table,' he remarked, 'is, perhaps, one of the strongest characteristics of civilization and refinement.'[241] On small farms, however, it is likely that the mistress of the house did not join the menfolk at the table, but hovered behind them to ensure that they were properly fed.*

Some of the lower orders were still eating with their fingers when their superiors had gone over to forks, and many of them were resistant to the assumption of the fashionable world that one should converse all the time while eating. But even in the later Middle Ages their meals were not necessarily without ceremony. There might be a

---

* A practice common in the Vale of Glamorgan farmhouses of my youth, and among the Breton peasants of a century ago; Pierre-Jakez Hélias, *Les Autres et les miens* (Paris, 1977), 69.

chair at the table for the head of the house; and one late fourteenth-century peasant is even known to have possessed a basin, ewer and towel, so that his meal could be preceded by a handwashing ceremony.[242] In the later eighteenth century, tea drinking, with its overtones of moderation, sobriety and polite civility, became universal among the working classes. The labouring poor also acquired a greater variety of household goods.[243] 'Much true politeness may often be found in a cottage', thought the radical philosopher William Godwin.[244] In the nineteenth century, a working-class home would symbolize its respectability by an accumulation of decorative knick-knacks and, eventually, a carefully furnished but uninhabited front room in which to receive company.[245]

So, though the lower orders often failed to meet genteel standards of civility, they were not without their own codes of proper behaviour. An observer accurately summarized the position in 1655: 'Amongst the rich and nobles of the earth, it is called "court-like breeding", but of those of the lower degree it is called "country-breeding", and amongst the lower sort of the world it is called "neighbourhood" and "civil respect" to one another.'[246] There were obvious differences between these various modes of civility. Courtliness was not the same as gentility, and middle-class manners differed from those of the poor. As a writer remarked in 1658, 'That urbanity which becomes a citizen would relish of too much curiosity [excessive care] in a country-man; and that compliment which gives proper grace to a courtier would cause derision if presented by a merchant or factor.' Lord Chesterfield said the same a century later: 'What is good breeding at St James's would pass for foppery or banter in a remote village; and the homespun civility of that village would be considered as brutality at court.'[247] He also drew a distinction between 'bare common civility' ('everyone must have that who would not be kicked out of company') and '*manières*', by which he meant 'engaging, insinuating, shining manners; distinguished politeness, an almost irresistible address; a superior gracefulness in all you do'.[248]

For Chesterfield, of course, the primary value of politeness was that it was a form of social distinction, accessible only to gentlemen and designed to reinforce their authority. It could be intimidating rather than conciliatory; for as the philosopher Abraham Tucker observed, many people behaved politely so as to show their own breeding rather than to please the company. Common civility, by contrast, was more egalitarian, designed to achieve social harmony by enjoining the courteous treatment of everyone, regardless of rank. This tension between manners as an agent of social differentiation and manners as a source of peaceable living runs through the early modern period. The difference was well expressed in 1838 by the American novelist James Fenimore Cooper when he divided 'deportment' into 'that which, by marking refinement and polish, is termed "breeding"; and that, which, though less distinguished for finesse and finish, denoting a sense of civility and respect, is usually termed "manners"'.[249]

In early modern England, every social group needed its own form of manners and civility if it was to avoid dissolving into anarchy. Much of the necessary restraint on human impulse was imposed from above. The laws of the state punished crimes against property and the person, and provided remedies for civil damage, while the church courts prosecuted offenders against social harmony. But even before the Church began to withdraw from this role in the later seventeenth century, it had never been possible for public authorities to regulate all aspects of personal behaviour. Much depended, therefore, upon the voluntary adherence of individuals to prevailing codes of civility.

To live together peaceably, individuals had of their own accord to make a whole range of personal concessions and adjustments. That was why Thomas Hobbes declared in 1651 that one of the laws of nature conducive to human preservation was 'compleasance: that is to say, that every man strive to accommodate himself to the rest'.[250] For Joseph Addison in 1713 this 'complaisance' was an essential social virtue: 'It produces good nature and mutual benevolence, encourages the timorous, soothes the turbulent, humanises the fierce, and distinguishes a society of civilized persons from a confusion of savages.'[251] For David Fordyce, professor of moral philosophy at Aberdeen in the 1740s, it was courtesy, neighbourhood, affability and the associated virtues that supplied the defects of the law and maintained 'the harmony and decorum of social intercourse'.[252] For Chesterfield in 1749, 'mutual complaisances, attentions, and sacrifices of little conveniences' were 'as natural an implied compact between civilised people, as protection and obedience are between kings and subjects'.[253]

Of course, the forms of accommodation, and the degree of pressure to accept them, differed according to the context. In late medieval England, the codes that imposed the greatest inhibition on personal impulse were associated with the royal court, noble households and religious communities. Later, they were matched or exceeded in the worlds of commerce, retailing and the learned professions. London and the provincial towns generated their distinctive forms of urban sociability and middle-class politeness. Lower down the scale, individuals dependent on others for employment or poor relief also had to practise self-control and accommodation, though their manners did not have to be flowery. The spread of genteel codes of behaviour owed something to social emulation, for the middling and lower-middling orders were notoriously imitative of their superiors in dress and behaviour. But the incentive to that emulation came from their social circumstances.

To find a theory that explains the spread of civility, we need look no further than the French political philosopher Montesquieu, who wrote in 1748 that 'the more people there are in a nation who need to deal with each other and not cause displeasure, the more politeness there is'.[254] Or, following Norbert Elias, whose work is essentially a brilliant elaboration of that insight, we could say that what led people to restrain their impulses was not the spread of courtesy literature or the desire to imitate the habits of the great, but the growth of human interdependence.[255] The more indispensable the goodwill of landlords, employers, patrons, neighbours and business associates, the greater was the need for accommodating behaviour. The more extensive the market, the more developed the division of labour; and the more elaborate the network of communications, the more widely dispersed was the practice of civility. As people moved out of their local milieus, where their relationships were known and prescribed by tradition, into the open, unstructured social space of towns and cities, where they had to make their way as undifferentiated individuals, the more crucial for their welfare did civil behaviour become. Works of advice, such as Erasmus Jones's *The Man of Manners, or Plebeian Polish'd* (1735), were explicitly intended for the upwardly mobile: 'persons of mean births and education, who have unaccountably plunged themselves in wealth and power'.[256]

It was among the middling classes that the pressure was most intense, whether on professionals who had to please their clients or traders who sought to ingratiate themselves with their customers. In the 1790s, accordingly, the theologian and natural philosopher Joseph Priestley thought that there was 'most true politeness in the middle classes of life'. Because they spent more of their time in the society of their equals, they were more used to governing their tempers; they attended more to the feelings of others and were more disposed to accommodate themselves to them. By contrast, 'The passions of persons in higher life, having been less controlled, are more apt to be inflamed; the idea of their rank and superiority to others seldom quits them; and though they are in a habit of concealing their feelings, and disguising their passions, it is not always so well done.'[257]

The common people were usually regarded as living closer to nature and less in control of their animal passions; and it is true that the pressure to inhibit the expression of antisocial emotion was least intense on those whose main obligation was to engage in manual labour. Yet just as Western travellers discovered on closer acquaintance that the Native Americans were not savages but had 'their own sort of civility',[258] so historians are coming to appreciate that the English lower orders had their own codes of manners and civil behaviour. Some were derived from the teaching and example of their superiors. Some were a prudential response on the part of those dependent on the goodwill of others for their subsistence. Others stemmed from the demands imposed by life in small groups and communities. Many were simply what a modern historian has called 'broadly non-divisive standards of common decency', that minimum of self-control which is a feature of any human society: what Richard Overton in 1645 termed 'the laws of common modesty and civility which nature hath written in the hearts of all men'.[259] As yet, we can recover these forgotten codes of civility in only the most rudimentary outline, but closer interrogation of the surviving evidence may allow future historians to say more.

ᘉᕤᐃ 3 ᘉᕤᐃ

The Civilized Condition

The term *polished*, if we may judge from its etymology, originally referred to the state of nations in respect to their laws and government. In its later applications, it refers no less to their proficiency in the liberal and mechanical arts, in literature, and in commerce.

Adam Ferguson, *An Essay on the History of Civil Society* (Edinburgh, 1767)

Civil Society

The idea of civility did not just imply polite behaviour and tactful accommodation to the feelings of others. When Elizabethan and Jacobean commentators said of the native Irish or the North American Indians that they wanted to reduce them to 'civility', they did not mean that they wished to improve their table manners (though some certainly hoped to do that). They had in mind a much larger process: emancipation from a state of barbarism and a transition to a 'civilized' way of life. Only then, they thought, would the

Irish become more obedient subjects and the Native Americans more accommodating neighbours.

This polarity between the civil and the barbarous was deeply embedded in the language of the time. In his *Briefe Description of the Whole Worlde* (1599, and frequently reprinted), the future archbishop George Abbot offered assessments as to how 'civil' or 'rude' were each of the peoples he described. The geographer Richard Hakluyt divided nations into the 'civil' and the 'less civil'; and when Sir Thomas Palmer published a guide for English travellers in 1606, he recommended that the first question they should ask about any country they visited was 'whether the people be civil or barbarous'.[1] In New England, Roger Williams, the founder of Providence, Rhode Island, maintained that mankind was divided 'into two sorts': 'first, the wild and pagan, whom God hath permitted to run about the world as wild beasts'; and, second, 'the civil', who were 'brought to clothes, to laws, &c, from barbarism'.[2]

But what did these terms mean? What was 'barbarism'? And how did one recognize a state of 'civility' when one saw it? Early modern discussions of the subject drew heavily on stereotypes inherited from Greek and Roman writers. They were also influenced by increasing acquaintance with the peoples of other parts of the world, whose modes of life were described, with varying degrees of accuracy, in a huge contemporary literature of travel and exploration. It was from such literature that readers like the republican Algernon Sidney (d. 1683) gained an impression of 'the bestial barbarity in which many nations, especially of Africa, America, and Asia, do now live'.[3]

The Greek conception of barbarism as a state of linguistic inadequacy still survived, and the term was regularly employed by Renaissance humanists to signify ignorance of classical Greek and Ciceronian Latin. When Richard Fox founded Corpus Christi College, Oxford, in 1517, he provided for a Reader in Latin (*humanitas*), whose task it was to root out and expel any 'barbarity' (*barbaries*) from his college. In Scotland, the humanist scholar George Buchanan

(1506–82) claimed that the substitution of Latin for the ancient Scottish tongue would enable his fellow countrymen to pass from rusticity and barbarism to culture and civilization (*ad cultum et humanitatem*).[4] The term could also denote an uncertain grasp of the vernacular: a word 'faultily or spokenly written' was a 'barbarism'.[5] It was by the standard of rhetorical excellence that the early sixteenth-century antiquary John Leland judged the age of the religious writer Richard Rolle (early fourteenth century) to be 'barbarous', that of the poet John Gower (late fourteenth century) to be 'semi-barbarous', and his own age as 'flourishing' and 'cultivated'.[6] But a broader connotation of barbarism was becoming familiar. In his dictionary of 1538, Sir Thomas Elyot explained that the epithet *barbari* (barbarians) had originally referred to those 'which do speak grossly, without observing of congruity, or pronounce not perfectly, especially Greek or Latin'. But he went on to say that the term could also signify those 'that abhor all elegancy' or 'be without letters, fierce or cruel of manners or countenance'.[7]

The use in England of the adjective 'barbarous' in this wider, nonlinguistic sense grew more frequent in the later sixteenth century and became standard in the seventeenth. The parallel employment of the noun 'barbarism' as a term for the uncivilized condition was current from the 1570s.[8] The narrower linguistic concept of 'barbarian' did not disappear altogether: in the later eighteenth century, the historian William Robertson dismissed all the vernacular languages of medieval Europe as 'barbarous' on the grounds that they were 'destitute of eloquence, of force, and even of perspicacity'.[9] But early modern dictionaries increasingly associated 'barbarous' people with 'rudeness', not just of speech but also of behaviour, defining them as 'churlish', 'uncivil', 'without letters', 'enemies of learning' and, above all, 'fierce' and 'cruel'.[10] Barbarism was 'a wilderness of life and manners'.[11]

An alternative word for 'barbarian' was 'savage' (from the Latin *silvaticus*, 'of the woods'). In the eighteenth century, 'savages' came to be regarded as more backward and lower on the scale of humanity than 'barbarians'. They were thought to be hunter-gatherers, lacking private property and any political organization, by contrast with 'barbarians', who typically were nomadic shepherds and herdsmen led by a chief. The former were remote from civilization, the latter a potential threat to it. Savagery was commonly associated with the indigenous peoples of Africa and America, whereas supposedly uncivilized peoples nearer home, such as the Russians, were seen not as savages but as barbarians.[12] But throughout the early modern period, the terms were often used interchangeably: contemporaries spoke of 'savage barbarians' and 'barbarous savages'.[13] Moreover, there was seldom a simple polarity between the barbarous and the civil: there were degrees of barbarism, and some barbarians were seen as less uncivil than others.

Although non-Christians were often regarded as barbarians, the criterion was not necessarily a religious one. In the early Middle Ages, 'barbarous' was usually synonymous with 'pagan'. But the patristic writers had accepted that non-Christians could be culti-vated and humane; and in twelfth-century England, the historian William of Malmesbury took the religious component out of the notion of barbarism and redefined it as consisting in a lack of learning and a poverty of material culture.[14] Not everyone was converted to this view that civility was a matter of culture rather than religion. In the early sixteenth century, the historian Polydore Vergil spoke for many when he equated civilization or, as he put it, the perfect way of life, with Christianity.[15] But the enhanced awareness of Greek and Roman civility that came with the Renaissance made it impossible to dismiss the world of classical antiquity as barbarous merely because of its paganism. There was also increasing respect for the ancient, but non-Christian, civilizations of India and China. From the fifteenth century onwards, the idea of 'Christendom' began to be challenged, though faintly at first, by that of 'Europe';[16] and in the following century, the Protestant Reformation dealt a mortal blow to the medi-eval concept of a united Christian world. It even became possible for

118

some Western European powers to open diplomatic and commercial relations with the Ottomans, rather than regarding them as infidels against whom to launch yet another crusade.

In practice, the two criteria, religion and civility, frequently overlapped, as when the Turks were described as both 'barbarous' and 'sworn enemies of the Christian faith'.[17] But the secular terms 'civil' and 'barbarous' increasingly came to be seen by many as a more instructive way of categorizing other peoples than that of dividing them into Christians and non-Christians. In the eyes of many seventeenth-century commentators, there were Christians who were 'barbarians', such as the Irish, and heathens who were 'civilized', such as the Chinese. In 1661 a writer could refer to 'all civilized nations, whether heathens, Turks, Jews or Christians'.[18] John Locke drew a firm distinction between a 'civil society' and a 'religious society'; and his contemporary the Quaker William Penn urged the total separation of church and state. This had long been the goal of Protestant sectaries, who wanted religion to be a matter of voluntary association, while rulers concerned themselves exclusively with civil and secular matters.[19] Roger Williams, whose religion led him to emigrate to New England, maintained that 'Christianity adds not to the nature of a civil commonweal; nor doth want of Christianity diminish it'.[20]

Yet many contemporaries felt uneasy when confronted by non-Christian peoples and had difficulty in regarding a pagan society as fully civilized. Islam, in particular, continued to be associated with 'barbarous' cruelty and despotic rule. In 1615 the poet and traveller George Sandys described Mahomet as 'wicked, worldly, treacherous and cruel' and his religion as the enemy of 'all civility and liberty'.[21] The continuing military threat presented by the Ottoman Turks meant that the old ideal of a united Christendom was slow to die, and indeed retained much resonance well into the eighteenth century.[22] Yet whereas in 1674 the instructions to the English ambassador to Constantinople still referred to 'Christians' and 'Christendom', those given to his successor in 1710 concerned 'the Affairs of Europe'. The

Treaty of Utrecht was the last European peacemaking document to refer to the *respublica Christiana* (the Christian commonwealth).[23] It continued to matter whether other nations were Christian or not,* but it was becoming more important to know whether they adhered to the principles of 'the common law of humanity'.[24]

Strictly speaking, the discourse of 'humanity' was distinct from that of 'civility', but in practice the two were closely related and their injunctions overlapped. For Cicero and Seneca, *humanitas* was the cultural refinement that came from a broad education in the liberal arts; it could also imply kindness, benevolence and human feeling. For them, these were qualities that distinguished the civilized Roman from the *feritas* (ferocity) and *immanitas* (savagery) of the barbarian.[25] In early modern England *humanitas* was associated with love for one's fellow men and was closely related to the idea of Christian charity. Sir Thomas Elyot defined the principal qualities of humanity in 1531 as benevolence, beneficence and liberality.[26] It became usual to bracket together 'the rules of civility and humanity' on the assumption that they pointed in the same direction.[27] The oriental scholar Thomas Smith held that the Turks were justly seen as barbarous, not because of their cruel punishments, which he thought necessary because of their 'natural fierceness', or for want of 'civil behaviour among themselves', for they were respectful and submissive to superiors, but because of their lack of 'common humanity', evident in the 'intolerable pride and scorn' with which they viewed the rest of the world.[28]

At the heart of the idea of 'civility' was the idea of an orderly and peaceful political community. For a Tudor humanist such as Thomas

---

* In his essay 'Of the Standard of Taste' (1757), David Hume declared that in the Koran the Prophet 'bestows praise on such instances of treachery, inhumanity, cruelty, revenge, [and] bigotry as are utterly incompatible with civilized society'. The Whig bishop Gilbert Burnet, however, believed that 'the Mahometans' had greatly softened since the days of the Prophet and become so gentle that they allowed even those who believed their religion to be an imposture to live safely among them; 'Preface' to his translation of Lactantius, *A Relation of the Death of the Primitive Persecutors* (Amsterdam, 1687), 24.

Starkey, 'civility' meant 'living together in good and politic order', unlike wild beasts 'without laws and rules of honesty'. It involved being ruled by 'marvellous good laws, statutes and ordinances, devised by man by high policy, for the maintaining of civil life', and 'to keep the citizens in unity and peace'.[29] This was what Starkey's contemporary the diplomat Richard Morison thought of as a 'commonwealth' and what the Elizabethan theologian Richard Hooker, echoing Cicero, called 'civil society'.[30] It was a condition, he thought, that did 'more content the nature of man than any private kind of solitary living'; and it brought 'most happy days' by comparison with 'those times wherein there were no civil societies'.[31]

This, of course, was quite different from the late twentieth-century concept of 'civil society' as comprising the forms of voluntary associational life that are distinct from the state, such as churches, trade unions, charitable organizations, pressure groups and, according to some definitions, the capitalist market. This meaning of the term did not emerge before the early nineteenth century, when the German philosopher G. W. F. Hegel in his *Philosophy of Right* (1821) redefined civil society (*bürgerliche Gesellschaft*) to include all social life between the family and the state. It is true that both Hobbes and Locke believed that human society antedated the state, and the idea of social life as something distinct from public affairs on the one hand and the private sphere of family and friends on the other was implicit in much early modern writing about manners and sociability. Contemporaries sometimes spoke of 'civil society' as a synonym for the sociability of the well-to-do ('keeping civil society') or for polite company (not 'fit for any civil society').[32] But the term 'civil society' normally meant an organized political community, usually a state, but sometimes a smaller unit, such as a town or, occasionally, even a family.[33]

Civil society, it was claimed, was founded on 'good and wholesome laws, made for the preservation of the public peace and tranquillity'.[34] It gave its members security for their lives and possessions, and provided formal procedures for punishing crime and resolving disputes. A firm legal and political framework, backed up by powers of enforcement and effective means of defence against outside attack, was the essential basis for any civil society. Law was what George Sandys called 'the ordination of civility', and a 'civil life' was one lived in accordance with the law. As the Marquess of Halifax remarked in the late seventeenth century, 'The civilized world hath ever paid a willing subjection to laws.'[35] In John Locke's classic definition, 'Those who are united into one body, and have a common established law and judicature to appeal to, with authority to decide controversies between them, and punish offenders, are in civil society, one with another.'[36]

The formation of civil society was thus seen as the founding condition of civilized life. As Bernard Mandeville put it, 'When once men come to be governed by written laws, all the rest comes on apace.'[37] In Sir Walter Scott's tale of 'The Two Drovers' (1827), the judge explains that 'the first object of civilization is to place the general protection of the law, equally administered, in the room of that wild justice which every man cut and carved out for himself, according to the length of his sword and the strength of his arm'. It was also crucial that the criminal law should be administered equitably, rather than following the practice of the Ottoman Turks, who, according to Sir William Temple in 1690, believed that it was better that two innocent men should die than that one guilty one should live.[38]

If the government was unable or unwilling to punish 'scandalous offenders', then, in Roger Williams's view, the civil state would 'dissolve by little and little from civility to barbarism'.[39] This was the situation in Gaelic Ireland where there was no criminal law as such and victims or their families were left to seek some form of compensation.[40] This was also said to be the condition of the Native Americans, who had no system of criminal jurisdiction, but left crimes against the injured person to be avenged by that person's family and friends. In 1748 Governor James Glen of South Carolina proclaimed it 'a great step towards civilizing savage and barbarous nations when they can be brought to do public acts of justice upon their criminals'.[41] Matters were even worse in many parts of the world where there seemed to be no recognizable government, and the people lived, like the Numidians, with 'no civility at all, nor any laws prescribed unto them'. Without justice, thought Adam Smith, 'the immense fabric of human society ... must in a moment crumble into atoms'.[42]

Judged by these criteria, early modern England was indubitably a civil society. Not only was it a much governed country, it was also one in which the access of ordinary people to justice was often easier than it is today.[43] It had long been unified by strong political and legal institutions. Rather than leaving homicides to be revenged by the kin of the deceased or treating them as a matter for financial compensation, the Angevin kings, building on the work of their late Anglo-Saxon predecessors, had classified them as felonies to be punished by the Crown.[44] Theft and robbery were likewise deemed to be public crimes rather than private wrongs.* The impulse to take private revenge was not easily extinguished, for feudal lords had waged war against their enemies throughout the Middle Ages; but by the mid-sixteenth century, the blood feud, still practised in parts of Wales and Scotland, was in England largely confined to the counties on the Northern Marches. In what has been called a transition from 'lineage society' to civil society, fidelity to the local magnate was being succeeded by loyalty to the monarchical state.[45] The medieval office of coroner was developed as an effective means of investigating violent deaths and prosecuting those responsible.[46] Offences against life, property and public order were dealt with by an elaborate system

---

* The French jurist and political philosopher Jean Bodin (1530–96) thought that the treatment of theft as a capital crime rather than a civil damage was proof of the refinement of the customs (*morum humanitas*) of the modern age, by contrast with the savagery (*feritas*) and barbarism (*barbaries*) of the past; Jean Bodin, *Methodus ad Facilem Historiarum Cognitionem* (Amsterdam, 1650), 319.

of royal justice, stretching up from the village constables by way of manorial courts, borough courts, JPs, quarter sessions and assize courts to the Court of King's Bench at Westminster. An equally complex hierarchy of courts handled civil disputes. A close alliance between the Crown and most of the nobility and gentry enabled the early modern English state to provide increasingly effective legal means of checking disorder. There was more use of recognizances to keep the peace, extensive recourse to arbitration and quasi-formal methods of settling quarrels, and a huge increase in civil litigation.[47]

It was, however, only from the 1770s that the courts began to take a serious view of common assault. Previously, acts of moderate violence had been widely tolerated on the grounds that they could be a justifiable response to undue provocation. Alternatively, they were treated as a civil offence, for which the plaintiff could seek damages, preferably by a settlement out of court.[48] The criminalization of assault in the late eighteenth century and its punishment by fines or imprisonment reflected a new intolerance of interpersonal violence (though not of the beating of wives, apprentices, servants and schoolchildren). It took two statutes, in 1803 and 1828, to ensure summary punishment for minor assaults and heavy penalties for more serious cases.[49]

The foundation of the whole system was the state's claim to a monopoly on physical force. In the sixteenth century, uprisings against the government, such as the Pilgrimage of Grace in 1536, Kett's Rebellion and the Prayer Book Revolt in 1549, and the rising of the Northern Earls in 1569, were all brutally suppressed with extreme violence and scant concern for legal process. The same was true of the Monmouth Rebellion in 1685 and the Jacobite Risings of 1715 and 1745.[50] The Crown's dependence upon the troops raised by the great magnates from their tenants, friends and relations was crucial until the later sixteenth century, but diminished thereafter with the development of a trained militia and the fading away of the nobles' military power.[51] After 1689 the state had a permanent standing army, legalized annually by parliamentary statute. In Adam

Smith's opinion, it was only by means of such a force that the civilization of a country could be preserved for any length of time.[52] Smith was also said to have asserted that little else was needed to 'carry a state to the highest degree of opulence from the lowest barbarism, but peace, easy taxes, and a tolerable administration of justice; all the rest being brought about by the natural course of things'.[53]

Good laws, and the means of enforcing them, however, were not sufficient on their own to ensure civil behaviour. The inhabitants of civil society were also expected to tame their aggressive impulses and to exercise self-restraint in their daily lives. As a dictionary of 1707 explained, to 'civilize' was to 'make courteous and tractable'.[54] For Latin authors, civilized people were those who were milder or gentler (*lenior, mitior, moratior*) and more humane (*humanior*). They were encouraged to emulate the Athenians, who, according to Thucydides (in Thomas Hobbes's translation, published in 1629), were the first among the nations of Greece that 'laid by their armour, and, growing civil, passed into a more tender kind of life'.[55] Benjamin Whichcote urged that citizens should be 'of a pacifying, peace-making and reconciling spirit'. Meekness, agreed a New England pastor, was 'a virtue most necessary to fit for society, making us gentle, tractable, persuadable, willing to bear the yoke': the 'meek spirits' were 'the glue and solder that unites societies'.[56] The author of the standard seventeenth-century manual for JPs wanted the justices not merely to punish disorder, but to eliminate its causes by intervening in advance to prevent the kind of behaviour that might threaten 'amity, quiet and good government'. He instanced 'scoffs, jests, taunts', offensive songs, and the practice of hanging outside a neighbour's door 'tokens of shames and disgrace', such as drawings of gallows or cuckold's horns. Church, borough and manorial courts regularly prosecuted scolds, malicious gossips, talebearers, railers, cursers and 'sowers of discord'.[57]

Violent behaviour, other than that authorized by the state (of which there was a great deal), was seen as intrinsically uncivilized.

Those engaged in the popular uprisings of 1549 were accused of dealing 'uncivilly' with their neighbours; and the men and women who participated in the numerous riots against the enclosure of the commons or the high price of corn were regularly accused of behaving in an 'uncivil', 'rude', 'barbarous' and 'savage' manner.[58] James VI and I was determined to suppress the private feuds of Scottish nobles because he regarded them as smelling of 'barbarity and savageness' and as incompatible with the 'comeliness and decency that is required in a civil and well-governed people'.[59] Similarly, the Jacobean Earl of Northampton proposed that anyone who offered to fight a duel should be ostracized as 'a barbarous, rude and uncivil person, unmeet and unfit for civil company'.[60] Distaste for interpersonal violence was the official ethic of a country that had been internally pacified, with an effective judicial system and an increasingly unmilitary aristocracy. It was also the ethic of urban living, for commerce depended on a peaceful relationship between buyer and seller. Since at least the sixteenth century, the founders and governors of grammar schools had forbidden pupils to bring swords, daggers or other weapons to school.[61] In the later seventeenth century, travellers in England were ceasing to carry weapons, and the high walls that had protected medieval towns were beginning to be pulled down.[62]

The decline of violence as a means of settling disputes between ordinary people is reflected in the steady fall from around 1630 in the number of homicide accusations heard by the courts. There was also a marked drop in the number of cases of unpremeditated murder, a suggestive indication of a trend towards greater individual self-control.[63] It is likely that nonlethal violence declined at the same time, but since most cases were unreported, it is impossible to measure.[64] What can be said is that the decline of weapon carrying made assaults less deadly and that everyday violence was increasingly seen by the respectable classes as disreputable. Women were far ahead of men in this respect: they were much less likely to be charged with crimes of violence, and their involvement in criminal charges of any

kind dropped sharply during the eighteenth century.[65] The one exception to this rule was infanticide, a crime to which unmarried mothers
were uniquely tempted and which achieved high rates throughout
the period.[66]

Barbarians, however, being supposedly uninhibited by legal or
moral restraints, were alleged to be given over to more or less continuous violence and warfare, external and internal, waged for plunder
or for sheer delight in bloodshed, and conducted with the utmost
ferocity (Plate 13). Early modern writers drew heavily on Greek and
Roman representations of barbarian life as characterized by uncontrolled passion and violent disorder.[67] They observed that shepherds
and pastoralists took naturally to fighting because their nomadic life
was well adapted to the rhythms of warfare. This was the case with
the ancient Germanic war bands, which had such a 'conceit of
manhood [martial courage]' that they created 'barbarism at home
and desolation abroad'. Barbarians could not be trusted to keep their
word; they settled disputes by force, not law, and they lacked what
the Jacobean administrator Sir Clement Edmondes regarded as 'the
sovereign happiness' – peace and tranquillity.[68] A central feature of
'all uncivilized nations', agreed the Scottish historian John Dalrymple
in 1757, was that their government was 'exceeding lax'.[69]

Civil society was generally agreed to be the essential precondition
of human fulfilment. Economic and cultural life could not hope to
flourish without internal peace and the rule of law. As the future
bishop William Warburton wrote in 1736, 'The arts of life owe their
original to civil society; and the more perfect the policy [i.e., the
system of government] is, the higher do those improvements rise.'[70]
David Hume believed that 'from law arises security; from security
curiosity; and from curiosity knowledge'. For him, law and government were fundamental to the civilizing process.[71] William Robertson
agreed that without regular government and personal security there
could be no progress in science or refinement in taste and manners.
Edmund Burke similarly believed that it was only civil society that

127

made it possible for man to 'arrive at the perfection of which his nature is capable'.[72] In Britain, as in so many other parts of the world, to be 'civilized' one had to be incorporated within a state.[73]

In the early modern period, some commentators regarded any autonomous political unit as a civil society, including even the 'barbarous' kingdoms of Asia and Africa.[74] But most claimed that a civilized form of government had to meet certain specifications. The nature of those specifications differed according to the political views of those prescribing them. Thomas Starkey's reflections on 'perfect civility' were conditioned by his dislike of arbitrary rule and his belief that power should be exercised for the common good and shared among king, nobility and an active citizenry.[75] Appalled by the tsar's despotic regime, Elizabeth I's envoy to Russia reported that if only the people were 'civilled', they would bear it no longer.[76] By contrast, a Royalist preacher during the Civil War maintained that 'by moral civility we are bound to be subject to him who protects us'.[77] It was in reaction to such assertions that John Locke in 1690 ruled flatly that absolute monarchy was 'inconsistent with civil society'.[78] After the Revolution of 1688, parliamentary government became the norm. Yet David Hume defied his Whig contemporaries in 1742 when he held that the absolute government of France should be regarded as 'a civilized European monarchy' because it guaranteed the security of its subjects and encouraged the arts and sciences. The more conventional view was expressed later in the same decade by King George II's chief minister Henry Pelham when he remarked of the Highland Scots that 'till they are governed in the same manner as in England, it is not to be presumed that they will entirely become civilized'.[79]

These disagreements about the forms of government consistent with civil society reveal that 'civil' and 'barbarous' were rhetorical terms, carrying a high emotional charge, but distinctly protean and often lacking any universally agreed content. They were used polemically to justify or to oppose some particular attitude or course of action, and their meaning shifted over time and varied according to the context. The ancient polarity was constantly invoked, but the meaning given to it depended on the speaker's interests and pre-occupations. Competing groups and interests appropriated these emotive and highly malleable terms to serve their particular agenda, regularly redefining them to incorporate new values and meet changing circumstances.

Almost anything of which one strongly disapproved might be called 'barbarous'. King James I regarded tobacco smoking as a 'barbarous' custom because it had been learnt from 'the wild, godless and slavish Indians'. The traveller Thomas Coryat described excessive health drinking by Jacobean gallants as 'a custom ... most barbarous, and fitter to be used among the rude Scythians and Goths than civil Christians'. Sir John Vanbrugh thought that the medieval practice of burying the dead in churches was 'a custom in which there is something so very barbarous ... that one cannot enough wonder how it has ever prevailed amongst the civiliz'd part of mankind'. When his fellow architect Nicholas Hawksmoor opposed a plan for 'barbarously' altering the old quadrangle at All Souls College, Oxford, he would have had in mind the needless destruction of old buildings by Goths and Vandals.[80] In all cases the practice denounced was vaguely associated with 'barbarian' peoples, but the association was a loose one. The real force of the word 'barbarous' was that it expressed animosity, indignation or disgust. In the same way, a practice of which the speaker approved might be termed 'civil' or 'civilized'. Samuel Johnson, for example, declared that 'the true test of civilization' was 'a decent provision for the poor'.[81] It is common for people today to declare portentously that 'the hallmark of a civilized society' is the way it treats animals, say, or children, or the universities, or refugees, or whatever cause they happen to be championing. Sometimes such assertions reflect a considered view as to what an ideal form of society should look like. More often, they are just bids for sympathy.

Although the terminology of 'civil' and 'barbarous' was extensively invoked for its polemical effect, there was a good deal of agreement in the early modern period about what the essential ingredients of 'civilized' existence might be. In a country where the notion of a 'freeborn Englishman' had by the mid-seventeenth century come to be seen as a unique feature of its constitution, it was widely asserted that a civil society should never permit slavery or serfdom, because, as Sir Clement Edmondes put it, its 'chiefest end' was the 'free disposition of ourselves and our possessions'.[82] In the twelfth century, William of Malmesbury had cited the continuance of slavery in Ireland as proof that the Celts were barbarians.[83] In the sixteenth century it was a matter of national prestige to assert that, unlike the Turks, the English had no slaves.[84] Subsequently, it was claimed that slavery had been abolished 'throughout the world amongst civilized people'. As Fynes Moryson put it, slavery dated from the time 'when might was right, and the weaker and poorer were made subject to the stronger and richer'; it was 'more cruelly or more gently exercised as the nations were or became more barbarous or civil'.[85] In the eighteenth century, it was common to urge that a country could not be civilized if it had domestic slavery.[86] Slavery in the colonies was, of course, another matter.

There was never a consensus about what was the most civilized form of government. But there was general agreement that civil society was incompatible with the violently despotic rule thought to be typical of many barbarian regimes (though others were associated with an anarchic degree of personal liberty, 'without king, governor, [or] commonwealth').[87] Since classical times it had been assumed that all the great Asian powers were despotically governed.[88] William Thomas, clerk of the council to Edward VI, lamented the plight of the 'barbarous people' of Persia and Tartary: 'What miserable lives they lead, what servitude and subjection they endure.'[89] A visitor to Russia in the 1660s compared the tsar's tyrannical rule to that of the ancient barbarians or the Ottoman Turks of his own day.[90]

Sir Thomas Roe reported in 1616 from the court of the Great Mogul in India that his government was 'uncertain, without written law, without policy, the customs mingled with barbarism'. The republican Algernon Sidney inveighed against the 'monstrous tyranny of Ceylon, an island in the East-Indies, where the King knows no other laws than his own will'. As for the much-praised government of China, it was, thought Daniel Defoe, an 'absolute tyranny'.[91] The Earl of Clarendon believed that the 'savage people' of America lived 'under a most entire subjection and slavery to their several princes'.[92] Only those countries with a temperate climate, thought Sir William Temple, could expect to have a moderate government ruling by law. Extremes of temperature, whether the freezing cold of Tartary and Muscovy or the unbearable heat of India and Africa, were believed to lead inexorably to despotism.[93]

For classical republicans such as Algernon Sidney, no 'civilized nation' could ever bind itself to obey a tyrant. Writing in the same tradition, the Scottish philosopher Adam Ferguson regarded active civic participation in government as a crucial index of a civil society, much more so than material progress: Sparta and republican Rome, he thought, had lacked trade and industry, but had undoubtedly been civil societies; whereas China and India, though commercially advanced, were despotically governed and therefore were not. His criterion of a civil society was strictly political, and it excluded rule by a single person.[94]

Everyone agreed that civil society had to secure the private property of its members, a central preoccupation in early modern England, but one to which barbarians were supposedly indifferent. Hunter-gatherers had no property, and nomadic herdsmen were unconcerned to accumulate material possessions. The 'wild Irish', for example, were said to have no care for riches, not even for 'pot, pan, kettle, nor for mattress, feather bed, nor such implements of household'; and their system of landholding vested ownership in the clan rather than in the individual.[95] Clarendon excluded the Turks from the civilized world, not because of their religion, for he thought that a non-Christian society could still be a civil one, but because of the sultan's absolute power over his subjects' property. Paul Rycaut, who had spent time in Constantinople and Smyrna in the 1660s, urged his English readers to thank God that they lived in a free country, where their wives, their children and the fruits of their labour could be called their own.[96] The Elizabethan Jesuit Robert Persons thought that it was security of tenure in their tiny landholdings that enabled most of the common people to 'maintain themselves decently and bring up their children in civility'.[97]

For Clarendon, property rights were the foundation of civilized society: 'Whatsoever is of civility and good manners, all that is of art and beauty, or of real and solid wealth in this world, is the product of this passion ... Nothing but the joy in propriety [property] reduced us from ... barbarity; and nothing but security in the same can preserve us from returning into it again.'[98] Hence John Locke's celebrated dictum that 'government has no other end than the preservation of property'. For him, 'the civilized part of mankind' were those who had made positive laws to protect it.[99] The concept of property as something distinct from mere possession, however, was a sophisticated one, beyond the comprehension of savages, and also, it was alleged, of the 'vulgar' in eighteenth-century Britain. As for testamentary succession, the right of men to dispose of their goods after their death, that, thought Adam Smith, was a 'refinement ... which we are not to expect from a people who have not made considerable advances in civilized manners'.[100] Notoriously, barbarians had no respect for the property of others; and the prohibition of theft and rapine formed no part of their moral code. For David Hume, this meant that the enjoyment of possessions, which he ranked as one of the three human goods along with the pleasures of the mind and the body, was wholly insecure among 'rude and savage' peoples.[101]

A key attraction of civil society, therefore, was, as Adam Ferguson observed, that it brought about a 'certain security of person and property', to which 'we give the name of civilization'. The political economist Robert Malthus agreed: it was 'to the established administration of property, and to the apparently narrow principle of self-love that we are indebted for . . . every thing indeed that distinguishes the civilized from the savage state'. The historian Thomas Babington Macaulay echoed these sentiments in a parliamentary speech of 1832. 'The great institution of property,' he claimed, was the source of 'all civilization, all that makes us differ from the tattooed savages of the Pacific Ocean.'[102]

In the credit-based economy of early modern England, trustworthiness, reliability and a readiness to keep contracts were seen as essential aspects of civility. Barbarians, by contrast, were said to be perfidious and unreliable, particularly if they lacked a settled and continuous political authority capable of honouring agreements entered into by its predecessors.[103] In the later seventeenth century, the Royal African Company defended its slave-trading monopoly by explaining that commerce with Africa had to be backed up by expenditure on forts and warships because of 'the natural perfidiousness of the natives, who, being a barbarous and heathen people, cannot be obliged by treaties without being awed by a continuous and permanent force'. George III's advocate general declared in 1764 that a ruler who held that his people were not bound by a treaty made by a predecessor would be returning them to 'original barbarism'.[104] In the nineteenth century, accordingly, a crucial test of whether or not a state should be recognized internationally as 'civilized' was the ability of its government to make and keep binding contracts.[105]

The ideal of civilized behaviour also came, though slowly and by degrees, to encompass the notion of polite interaction between citizens of rival faiths and toleration for religious minorities, so long as they behaved 'civilly'. Elizabethan Catholics were advised by their casuists that, when dining in a Protestant household, they should bow their heads at grace 'out of civility and politeness' to their hosts: not to do so was a sign of 'incivility' and 'rusticity'.[106] In the following century, the author of one antipapist polemic conceded that, although the Catholics mistakenly adhered to a false Church, many of them were 'civil in their dealings about common affairs, courteous, loving, kind-natured, free-hearted, true and trusting in matters of account betwixt man and man'. While maintaining their religious separateness, Catholics often socialized with their neighbours and took their share of local responsibilities.[107] Similarly, many Puritan clergy, while urging their flock to avoid as far as possible the company of the profane and the unregenerate, stressed that they should be courteous to all people they met: however much one disapproved of their sins, the obligations of 'humanity and intercourse of civil society' had still to be honoured.[108]

The Cambridge preacher Richard Sibbes held that 'a kind of complacency, a sweet familiarity, and amity' should be reserved for the few in whom could be seen 'the evidences and signs of grace', and thought it wrong to consort with sinners out of mere politeness. But he accepted that 'a benevolence and a beneficence' were due to everyone, however unregenerate.[109] Roger Williams similarly believed that strong disapproval of the views of others and a determination to convert them to the truth could nevertheless be combined with treating them with a decent minimum of respect; he regarded religious persecution as an evil, 'opposite to the very tender bowels of humanity' and 'stabbing ... at the heart of all civil peace and civil magistracy, and civility itself'. Commonwealths, he thought, could flourish despite religious differences, if men would 'walk but by the rules of humanity and civility'. Moreover, peaceful coexistence with the ungodly was a necessary precondition for the frank conversation in which their attention could be drawn to the error of their ways.[110]

Many leading churchmen also thought that civil obligations took priority over religious differences. Urging Catholics not to separate themselves from their Protestant neighbours, the future Irish bishop William Bedell flatly rejected the view that it was unlawful to have social relations with those of a contrary religion; indeed, it was a sin to break off 'civil society with men of a false religion or wicked life to whom we are necessarily bound by the law of God or man'.[111] The Restoration Bishop of Lincoln, Robert Sanderson, advised against undue familiarity with schismatics, but he too conceded that 'the rules of neighbourhood and common civility' had to be observed. Thomas Browne, author of *Religio Medici*, was not a Catholic, but he conceded that everyone owed 'the duty of good language' to the pope. In the later seventeenth century, some Protestant visitors to Rome even reconciled themselves to kissing the pontiff's toe because it was 'a civil and usual compliment'.[112]

One of Sanderson's successors at Lincoln, Thomas Barlow, welcomed the readmission of the Jews in 1655 because they had been 'not only unchristianly, but inhumanely and barbarously used'; in his view, England was bound by 'kindness and civility' to make amends for the injuries done to the Jews in the past. After the 1688 Revolution, he noted with pleasure that Protestant Dissenters had been given 'the civility and courtesy of a moderate toleration'.[113] The motives for the limited Toleration Act of 1689 were essentially political, but some supported it on principle. John Locke, who set high store by civility, believed that 'courtesy, friendship and soft usage' could influence men's opinions in a way that force could not.[114] For him, civility was not just a matter of outward behaviour: 'inward civility' involved sincere 'respect and goodwill to all people' and 'a care not to show any contempt, disrespect, or neglect of them'. Only the establishment of equal religious liberty for all those who shared this attitude could provide 'a bond of mutual charity' by which everyone might be 'brought together into one body'.[115] Those whose principles were believed to threaten the civil order, however, such as Roman Catholics and atheists, continued to be excluded.

The *Spectator*, that great organ of civility, pronounced firmly against 'intemperate zeal, bigotry and persecution'.[116] Yet few thought that religious pluralism was desirable in itself and the civil disabilities of non-Anglicans would last into the nineteenth century. In practice, however, Dissenters and Catholic recusants were frequently well-integrated members of their local communities. When Daniel Defoe visited Dorchester, the county town of Dorset, in the early eighteenth century, he found Anglican and Dissenting clergy 'drinking tea together, and conversing with civility and good neighbourhood'.[117] The sixteenth and seventeenth centuries had witnessed much bitter religious hatred, but by Defoe's time de facto religious toleration, at least of Christian denominations, had come to seem expedient on pragmatic, prudential grounds. As a necessary precondition of social harmony, it was celebrated in genteel society as indispensable for a trading country, an essential part of civility and politeness, and a hallmark of civilized behaviour.[118]

A closely associated attribute of civility was the peaceful conduct of theological and scientific debate, free from ill temper and personal abuse and marked by readiness to acknowledge error. A French visitor to England in the 1660s was much impressed by the proceedings of the early Royal Society: speakers were never interrupted 'and differences of opinion cause[d] no manner of resentment, nor as much as a disobliging way of speech . . . Nothing seemed to me to be more civil, respectful and better managed.'[119] In the later seventeenth century, the civil exchange of information and the courteous discussion of conflicting views became the accepted norm within the wider scientific community and the international republic of letters. As the authors of *The Independent Whig* remarked in 1721, gentlemen had learnt to conduct their controversial writing 'for the most part with humanity, and always with good manners'. The correspondence of men of letters was expected to be 'civil and polite'.[120] In aspiration, at least, this made a marked contrast to the virulent personal abuse that had been such a feature of post-Reformation theological controversy and had characterized the heated exchanges in the 1650s between John Milton and his fellow scholars Claude Saumaise and Peter du Moulin over the legitimacy of the English republic.[121]

Crucial for the peaceful resolution of disagreements was the existence of formal or informal conventions for the conduct of meetings and political debates. In England, national and local assemblies had established such conventions by late Anglo-Saxon times.[122] The sixteenth- and seventeenth-century House of Commons had long-standing rules of debate: prohibiting violence; banning 'offensive' or 'irreverent' speeches; forbidding whispering, interrupting or hissing; and requiring members when leaving the chamber to turn and make a low curtsy, as they did on entering it. Similar procedural conventions governed the conduct of business by trading companies and other local bodies. Even a village meeting might have its by-laws setting out the procedure for decorous discussion.[123]

In the eighteenth century, civility came to require that political disputes should be peacefully resolved and that unsuccessful politicians could be dismissed from office without having to face subsequent exile or execution. Even parliamentary opposition to the king's ministers gradually came to be accepted as legitimate and respectable rather than factious, though the prejudice against it lingered on.* Every 'polished and commercial nation', thought Adam Ferguson, had to learn how 'to decide every contest without tumult'.[124]

Civility also had an international dimension. As one Elizabethan put it, 'the society of nations' was part of civil society and was 'maintained by ambassadors, intercourse of traffic, justice ministered [to] strangers, open denouncing of war, and mercy to the vanquished'. In this spirit Sir Philip Sidney invoked what he called 'the universal civility, the law of nations (all mankind being as it were co-inhabiters or world citizens together)'. All peoples, agreed Sir Clement Edmondes, were 'linked together in the strict alliance of human society'. These were echoes of Cicero's Stoical concept of a single human society (*hominum societas*) transcending state boundaries.[125]

---

* As late as June 2017, UK Prime Minister Theresa May and one of her ministers suggested that opposition to her government's policy for Brexit was 'unpatriotic'; *Daily Mail Online*, 1 June 2017; *Guardian*, 24 June 2017.

Early modern jurists believed that humankind was bound by a universal law of nature, accessible to human reason without the aid of divine revelation. It was accepted by all the more civilized nations (*moratiores*), though some other peoples were too savage or ignorant to recognize it: the exiled French jurist Jean Barbeyrac (1674–1744) remarked that he knew from experience that the term 'law of nature' was as much unknown to the common people as the *Terra Australia incognita*.[126] From this law of nature the jurists deduced a wide range of human rights and obligations. They also revived and developed the Roman concept of a *ius gentium*, a law of nations. According to many authorities, this overlapped with the law of nature and was common to all peoples, though in the opinion of others it was a set of conventions observed by only the 'more civilized' nations and ignored by or even inapplicable to others.[127] In what he claimed was the first book on the subject, William Fulbecke based his *Pandectes of the Law of Nations* (1602) on the practice of only the 'most civil' nations. The Royalist bishop Jeremy Taylor agreed that this law was observed especially by 'all wise and civil nations that communicate with each other'.[128]

Founded on what were taken to be the principles of natural justice, but increasingly on the treaties made between individual countries, the law of nations was meant to govern military, diplomatic and commercial relations between the European states. In the eighteenth century, some German natural lawyers dismissed the *ius gentium* as neither law nor morality, but merely rules of diplomatic courtesy.[129] But the great British authority Sir William Blackstone declared the law of nations to be 'a system of rules, deducible by natural reason, and established by universal consent among the civilized inhabitants of the world'.[130] The barbarians were those who deliberately broke these rules or were wholly ignorant of them. The Ottoman Turks, for example, were said to honour in peacetime the conventions for the 'civil' and 'courteous' treatment of ambassadors; but if war broke out, they ignored the law of nations, imprisoning ambassadors and treating them violently, 'contrary to the custom of the ancient Romans, and other gallant and civilized people'.[131]

Civil society could thus be envisaged as what one writer called 'the uniting cement of the world'.[132] For Richard Hooker, the laws of nature involved 'the courteous entertainment of foreigners and strangers' and 'a kind of society and fellowship even with all mankind'.[133] The friendly reception of foreign visitors had been an essential test of civility since classical times.[134] In the early modern period, it became increasingly important, with the growth of travel, the migration of religious refugees and the vast expansion of international trade. 'If a man be gracious and courteous to strangers,' thought Francis Bacon, 'it shows that he is a citizen of the world.' The exiled Catholic priest Thomas Wright observed in 1604 that 'it is held for great civility, and as a sign of a noble nature, to entertain strangers kindly, and, contrariwise, for extreme barbarousness to abuse or use them currishly'. Similarly, one of Locke's correspondents declared that inhospitality to foreigners was 'a barbarous sort of inhumanity', worthier of the Scythians than of 'civilized men'.[135]

The Spanish theologian Francisco de Vitoria was the first to turn the ancient custom of hospitality into a law of nature. He was followed by Richard Hooker, who believed that the nations of the world should practise hospitality 'for common humanity's sake'. The great Dutch jurist Hugo Grotius ruled that the common duties of humanity prescribed by natural law included permitting strangers' ships to anchor on a foreign shore for reasons of health or provisioning and allowing foreign immigrants to settle if they had been expelled from their own country.[136] In practice, such hospitality conflicted with the interests of the host countries and was increasingly denied. When in 1677 William Penn was refused entrance to a German city and forced to sleep in the fields, he wrote an explosive letter of protest to the local ruler: 'Is this the law of nations, or nature, or Germany, or of Christianity? Oh! Where is nature? Where is civility?'[137]

Civilized Warfare

Nowadays, the word 'civil' is the opposite of 'military': we contrast soldiers with 'civilians' and the armed services with the 'civil service'. In the early modern period, 'civil' and 'martial' were similarly regarded as opposites.[138] Although there were few decades between 1500 and 1800 when their country was not at war, many contemporaries regarded armed conflict, other than of a strictly defensive kind, as intrinsically uncivil. For Erasmus and the early Tudor humanists John Colet, Richard Pace and Thomas More, warfare was irrational, 'beastly' and 'depraved'. William Cecil, Elizabeth I's chief minister, warned his son Robert that war was 'of itself unjust, unless the good cause make it just'. Sir Clement Edmondes, in his *Observations upon Caesar's Commentaries*, one of the seventeenth century's most frequently reissued books, remarked that civility involved an 'indisposition to warlike practices': civil people had no taste for fighting. The Puritan casuist William Ames ruled in 1639 that desiring and delighting in war was 'a sign of a barbarous and cruel man'. In 1653 Margaret Cavendish, the future Duchess of Newcastle, regarded war as the enemy of 'civil society'.[139] In 1680 the Earl of Mulgrave, an experienced campaigner, described war as 'the common nurse of barbarism', while his contemporary the physician Humphrey Brooke considered that no people were 'more barbarously savage and relentless' than soldiers.[140]

In the age of the Enlightenment, war was said to appeal only to 'unpolished minds'.[141] Adam Smith contrasted barbarian societies, where everyone was a warrior, with civilized ones, in which fighting was left to paid professionals.[142] The essayist Vicesimus Knox, writing in 1782 on 'the folly and wickedness of war', declared that 'while we are warriors, with all our pretensions to civilization, we are savages'.[143]

In the later seventeenth century, the Marquess of Halifax held it to be 'no small mark of this latter age being more civilized, that the brutal animosities between several nations are very much lessened, even with the vulgar; with the better sort, quite extinguisht'.[144] This was unduly optimistic. But when war did break out, the law of nations demanded that it be conducted, so far as possible, with humanity and civility. This meant, among other things, allowing safe conduct to heralds and ambassadors, being merciful to the defeated and respecting the immunity of non-combatants. The wars of antiquity, by contrast, had been total: despite the existence of theoretical constraints on what might decently be done,[145] defeated leaders were usually executed and their followers and families enslaved. With the decline of domestic slavery after the Norman Conquest, enslavement ceased to be practised by English armies. The growth of towns, trade and a monetized economy encouraged a shift to ransoming the wealthier prisoners. It also stimulated a concern to limit the destruction accompanying military victory lest it be reciprocated by the enemy. As Edward Gibbon would point out, such considerations were unknown to nomadic barbarian pastoralists because their property travelled with them.[146]

Restraints on the conduct of late medieval warfare derived from a mixture of Roman law and the customary rules observed by professional soldiers. The most effective sanction was the chivalric code of the knightly classes, which, though glorifying military prowess and thereby helping to make warfare endemic, was moved by a combination of honour and reciprocal self-interest to set limits on what was acceptable behaviour during and after battle. Later, this code was supplemented by royal ordinances and formal articles of war issued on particular occasions.[147]

To flout the rules of war was, in the words of Sir Clement Edmondes, to 'break the bonds of civil conversation'. Yet only too often the rules were ignored: as Richard Hooker remarked, the laws of arms were 'much better known than kept'.[148] Late medieval ordinances prohibiting attacks on non-combatants did not prevent Henry VIII from pursuing a scorched-earth policy in northern France in 1544, killing civilians and creating starvation for all.[149]

Such ordinances gave little protection to the local populations, who were frequently ravaged, and none at all to rank-and-file soldiers, who, being unable to offer a ransom when captured, were routinely slaughtered.

During the Hundred Years War with France, however, it had become increasingly common to extend the practice of ransoming to prisoners lower down the military hierarchy.[150] As the early modern state assumed greater control over armies that had previously been raised by private contractors so the restraints on the conduct of war multiplied, and rank-and-file prisoners were more frequently ransomed or exchanged. These conventions were embodied in Dutch and, later, Swedish military codes, both published in England in the 1630s. Exceptions were made for members of garrisons who had caused needless loss of life by prolonging a siege after being called on to surrender, and it was not deemed an atrocity to pursue and kill enemy soldiers flying from the battle. Mercenaries acting without the authority of a legitimate ruler were also denied quarter; this was how Lord Grey of Wilton, Elizabeth I's Lord Deputy of Ireland, justified his cold-blooded slaughter in 1580 of six hundred Spaniards and Italians at Smerwick, County Kerry.[151]

In 1593, in a treatise based on 'ancient and later precedents of most expert warriors', the theologian Matthew Sutcliffe ruled that it was 'savage cruelty' and 'contrary to the nature of fair wars' to 'massacre' those who threw down their weapons and confessed themselves vanquished. In 1598 the Italian exile and legal philosopher Alberico Gentili asserted in his treatise *De Iure Belli*, dedicated to the Earl of Essex, that the rights of humanity and the laws of war required that the lives of prisoners taken in war should be spared. As a herald explained in 1602, 'It is unlawful to kill a man having yielded himself, because that act is inhumane, and all great captains have forbidden it.' In the same year William Fulbecke agreed that it was 'beastly' and a 'part of immanity [savagery] and cruelty' to murder prisoners just because they had fought in defence of their country. In 1629 the preacher Richard Bernard declared that 'to slay poor prisoners in cold blood' was a sign of 'a savage and implacable nature'.[152] It was in order to rebut the charge that the Scots were less civilized (*minus culti*) than their English neighbours that in 1605 a Scottish writer pointed to their moderation in victory, exemplified by the merciful treatment of prisoners after their success at Otterburn in 1388.[153] The exchange of prisoners became increasingly common in the later seventeenth century when manpower was economically more precious. The German jurist Samuel von Pufendorf regarded this as in accordance with 'the law of humanity' and observed by 'most people pretending to civility'.[154]

These rules contrasted with the practice of supposed barbarians, such as the Ottoman Turks, who allegedly killed every prisoner who was unfit to be sold as a slave,[155] or the Native Americans, who enslaved captured women and children. Even in England, the notion lingered that captives taken in a just war might rightfully be made slaves by their conquerors because they were indebted to them for their lives. The Elizabethan merchant adventurer Sir George Peckham believed that the law of nations allowed prisoners of war to be condemned to servitude. So did the leading Puritan theologian William Perkins. In the early seventeenth century, Grotius asserted that, by the law of nations, the victors were perfectly entitled to kill their prisoners unless the laws of their own state forbade it.[156]

At the end of the seventeenth century, the enslavement of prisoners of war was still seen as acceptable by such champions of liberty as Algernon Sidney and John Locke. It was left to William Blackstone in the eighteenth century to point out that once the right to kill captives was withdrawn, the associated right to enslave them lost its moral justification.[157]

English military ordinances of the sixteenth and early seventeenth centuries were more concerned with the distribution of ransoms than with the welfare of the captives. With the notable exception of Henry VIII's ordinances for the expedition to France in 1513,[158] they did not explicitly ban the killing of prisoners, though they ordered that it should not happen without the commander's authority. At Coruña in 1589 English troops cut the throats of some five hundred unransomable Spanish captives.[159] In 1639 the author of a handbook on military practice advised that if one side had taken many prisoners only for the vanquished side to launch a new attack, then the prisoners should be killed to prevent them from joining the attackers.[160] In the English Civil Wars, however, the articles governing the conduct of both Parliamentary and Royalist armies were notable for their explicit requirement, on pain of death, that, under normal circumstances, quarter was to be given to defeated enemies. This injunction seems to have been first issued by the Earl of Northumberland for the army sent north in 1640 to fight against the Scots.[161] It was regularly reiterated thereafter.

The contending parties in the English Civil Wars shared a common culture and were often linked by ties of kinship and friendship. Their leaders combined a strong commitment to honourable conduct with a keen awareness of the likelihood of retaliation. Both sides agreed accordingly that it was important to show 'good nature and civility' to the defeated. John Milton praised the New Model Army as 'the civillest and best ordered in the world', while the Parliamentary preacher Hugh Peter claimed that, at the sack of Basing House in October 1645, the Royalist gentlewomen were treated 'somewhat coarsely, but not uncivilly'. When negotiating the Royalist surrender of Worcester in 1646, the Parliamentary commander Thomas Rainsborough was careful lest he be 'found wanting in anything which is civility'; and the Parliamentary general Sir William Waller claimed that during his service, 'I constantly endeavoured to express all the civilities I could to those of the adverse party.' In 1649, when a shortage of money meant that one of the new Commonwealth's regiments was still demanding free quarter from reluctant householders, their colonel did what he could 'to see that civil demeanour by the soldiers be used'.[162] Even the Royalist Sir John

Oglander admitted that Parliament 'took all course possible to civilize their soldiers'. The contemporary historian of the New Model Army, Joshua Sprigg, praised it for its orderly behaviour, arrears of pay notwithstanding, adding that 'had they not had more civility than money, things had not been so fairly managed'.[163] Similarly, Charles I's preachers urged the Royalist troops to do nothing 'that savour[ed] of immodesty, barbarousness or inhumanity'. The Parliamentarian officer Edmund Ludlow confessed that when taken prisoner during the war, he had been treated 'very civilly'.[164] During the Anglo-Dutch War of 1652–54, the same rules applied: in 1653 it was ordered that captured Dutch naval officers be carefully guarded, but treated 'with civil respect'.[165]

Of course, the Civil Wars involved very heavy slaughter on both sides, with the number of deaths proportionately comparable to that in the First World War.[166] Prisoners were often handled roughly and sometimes real atrocities occurred, though in England (as opposed to Ireland) much less frequently than in the contemporaneous Thirty Years War, and, by contrast with that conflict, seldom involving civilians.[167] In his history of the Rebellion, the Earl of Clarendon stressed the horrors of the wars and listed many instances of 'rudeness', 'barbarity' and 'inhumanity.[168] The accepted convention that a defeated garrison which had refused to surrender was not entitled to quarter sometimes led to mass killings, particularly if the defenders were Catholics, as at Basing House in 1645.[169] When atrocities did happen, the injured side would invariably accuse the other of 'barbarously' breaching the accepted code of civil behaviour.[170] The numerous protestations of their 'civility' by both sides are not in themselves reliable guides to what took place, but they do show how seriously the ideal of civilized conduct in wartime was taken, even in what contemporaries sardonically regarded as 'our uncivil, civil wars'.[171]

When dealing with pirates, rebels, deserters and traitors, however, 'courteous dealing', as one Elizabethan called it, had always been regarded as inappropriate. By opting out of the political community such people were deemed to have lost their right to consideration. They were therefore denied the privileges that the law of nations gave to combatants who had the formal status of enemies. The laws of war did not protect those who violated them.[172] In 1642 the initial inclination of the Royalists was to treat their opponents as rebels who deserved no quarter, though it was quickly curbed when Parliament threatened to hang Royalist prisoners by way of reprisal. In the Second Civil War, it was the turn of the Royalists to be cast in the role of rebels or traitors, and some of them were treated accordingly.[173] A brutal application of this doctrine came a hundred years later, when the defeated Jacobites were mercilessly hunted down after the Battle of Culloden.[174] Yet the British Isles never saw anything comparable to the horrors of the War of the Holy League (1683–99), when a European coalition drove the Ottoman Turks back into the Balkans after their unsuccessful siege of Vienna. In this conflict between Christians and Muslims, the laws of war were totally suspended, with both sides enslaving or massacring their prisoners and committing innumerable atrocities against the local population.[175]

Most eighteenth-century commentators congratulated themselves on the civilized manner in which the European wars of their day were conducted. In the 1760s, Adam Ferguson remarked that, whereas the maxims of war in the time of Homer had resembled those which prevailed 'in the woods of America', modern European nations sought 'to carry the civilities of peace into the practice of war'; they 'mingled politeness with the use of the sword'. Like David Hume, Ferguson regarded humanity in warfare as the chief characteristic that distinguished a 'civilized age from times of brutality and ignorance'.[176] Modern wars were 'waged without hatred', thought the philosopher Abraham Tucker in 1777: 'Battles [are] fought without rancour and barbarity, laws of war established by general agreement, and measures kept between the greatest enemies: the estates of the conquered are not taken from them, nor their persons made slaves, nor slaughter and extirpation practised in cold blood.'[177] Gibbon complacently observed that 'the laws and manners of modern nations' protected 'the safety and freedom of the vanquished soldier' and ensured that 'the peaceful citizen' was seldom 'exposed to the rage of war'. Adam Smith similarly believed that modern laws of war were 'superior in moderation and humanity' to those of ancient times.[178] 'In our age of humanity,' declared George III's advocate general in 1764, 'war itself is civilized.' Among 'civilized nations', agreed the historian William Robertson, war was 'disarmed of half its terrors'.[179]

This was to ignore the unprecedented volume of slaughter that occurred from time to time, as during the battles of the Seven Years War (1756–63), when massed infantry were confronted by murderous firepower.[180] Yet a comparison of the laws of war as expounded by Hugo Grotius in 1625 with those set out by the Swiss-born jurist Emmerich de Vattel in 1758 suggests that the rules of European warfare had indeed become more humane during the intervening years. So, in some ways, had actual practice. There was greater respect for civilians, more concern for prisoners and the wounded, and a new acceptance of the right of besieged garrisons to quarter, despite their having put up a determined resistance.[181]

The officers of most European armies shared a similar aristocratic background and subscribed to a common military etiquette.[182] By comparison with the total war waged by the French revolutionary armies in the 1790s, much eighteenth-century warfare was in spirit more like medieval trial by combat. It tended to be strictly contained; its sieges and pitched battles took on a formal quality and their outcome was usually accepted by both sides.[183] Protests were quick to follow when the rules were broken and warfare conducted in what was regarded as a 'barbarous' manner. Ambushes, for example, were outlawed as the way in which 'the uncivilized part of mankind' made war against each other. The American Indians were notorious for putting self-preservation first and avoiding any conflict that carried with it an element of risk. Their object was to weaken and destroy their enemies with the least possible loss to themselves. The Indian warrior's ideal was to 'lie in wait day after day, till he can rush upon his prey when . . . least able to resist him; to steal in the dead of night upon his enemies, set fire to their huts, and massacre the inhabitants, as they fly naked and defenceless from the flames'.[184]

Hence the indignation aroused when the British recruited the natives to assist them when the American colonists revolted in 1775. The American Declaration of Independence of the following year accused George III of enlisting 'merciless Indian savages, whose known rule of warfare is an undistinguished destruction of all ages, sexes and conditions', and of sending armies of foreign mercenaries to America in 'circumstances of cruelty and perfidy scarcely paralleled in the most barbarous ages, and totally unworthy [of] the head of a civilized nation'. British critics of George's government echoed this complaint.[185] The colonists gained further legitimacy for their cause by denouncing the atrocities committed on the battlefield by British troops, who sometimes killed prisoners, bayoneting them in cold blood and mangling their bodies.[186]

A Civilized Compassion

Whether in war or peace, civility involved abstaining from any conduct that could be labelled 'cruel', that is to say, which was callously indifferent to the pain of others or took pleasure in its infliction. Such abstention was not required when the pain was considered to be necessary, as in the practice of surgery or the waging of just war or the punishment of criminals or the correction of delinquent schoolchildren. But unnecessary cruelty had been regarded as a defining attribute of barbarism since classical times. What was barbarity, asked a Jacobean writer, if 'cruelty and inhumanity be not special points of it?'[187] The medieval Church, however, did not list cruelty as one of the Seven Deadly (or Cardinal) Sins, though Thomas Aquinas regarded those who took pleasure in inflicting pain as brutish and inhuman.[188] In early modern England, cruelty was regularly denounced as 'inhuman', because incompatible with humanity; 'unnatural' because against natural law; 'effeminate' because indicative of a weak surrender to passion;[189] 'unchristian' because against the teachings of the Gospel; and 'savage', 'barbarous' or 'uncivil' because incompatible with the norms of civil society. These intellectual traditions were distinct, but they reinforced each other in their practical implications; and they all contributed to buttressing the notion that cruelty was unacceptable in a 'civilized' society. Michel de Montaigne regarded it as 'the extremest of all vices'.[190] Thomas Hobbes, who believed that cruelty was a breach of the law of nature, defined it as the infliction of pain without regard to 'future good' or 'without reason'.[191] This made 'cruelty' an intrinsically unstable concept because there was obvious room for disagreement as to what was or was not reasonable.

The archetypal barbarians were the 'Scythians', originally inhabitants of territory to the northeast of the Black Sea, but in practice a generic term for Eurasian nomads of any kind. Herodotus told how they blinded and enslaved their prisoners of war, cut off their enemies' heads and drank out of their skulls.[192] Other barbarians were equally notorious for their supposed cruelty. The Picts were remembered as 'a cruel nation and marvellous prone to fight' (Plate 15); the Irish were said to be 'very cruel' and 'bloody-minded'; the Turks (who were supposedly Scythian in origin) were notorious for their 'beastly cruelty', as were the Aztecs for their 'cruel' and 'horrible' sacrifices; the cruelties of the Russians 'would scarcely be believed'.[193] English historians recounted the horrid cruelties committed in the wars of the past by the Scots and the Welsh; and David Hume regarded cruelty as a vice 'peculiar to uncivilized ages'. It was thought to be an inevitable feature of societies that lived by hunting wild animals.[194] 'All barbarous nations have been observed to be revengeful and cruel', thought the American botanist Cadwallader Colden. 'The curbing of these passions is the happy effect of being civilized.' Dr Johnson agreed: 'Savages are always cruel.' Captain Cook, when voyaging in the Pacific, was said to have assumed that 'almost every tribe of uncivilized men' would treat their enemies with 'brutal cruelty'.[195]

To some extent these perceptions reflected cultural differences in the accepted conventions governing the conduct of warfare. Many Native Americans, for example, thought revenge killing important and declined to return their prisoners, whom they tortured in their rage and grief for the losses they had sustained during the fighting. They were also notorious for scalping their enemies.[196] Adam Smith suggested that their harsh living conditions diminished the humanity of savages, by contrast with civilized people, who enjoyed 'security and happiness' and therefore had more developed sensibilities.[197] There was possibly some justification for this view. A distinguished anthropologist has written that 'In some primitive societies there is often no category of behaviour expressly recognized as cruel. It is violence rather than the infliction of pain that is stigmatized ... Pain in human beings outside the social circle or in animals tends to be a matter of minimal interest.' There is no reason to think that human beings were less sensitive to pain in the past than they are today, but their readiness to accept it was infinitely greater.[198]

When supposedly civil people committed acts of cruelty, they were accused of emulating these barbarians. During the Wars of the Roses the Lancastrian army was alleged to have acted with such 'detestable ... cruelness as hath not been heard done amongst the Saracens or Turks'.[199] In Elizabethan times, Catholic writers denounced the hanging, drawing and quartering of Jesuit missionaries as 'barbarous, worthy of Turks or Scythians' (Plate 12): 'There was never Scythian, nor savage Tartar, that could use more inhumane cruelty than to rip up the bodies of innocent men, being perfectly alive, to tear out their entrails to be consumed with fire.' They also complained bitterly of the 'rude', 'uncourteous', 'clownish' and 'uncivil' manners of the investigating magistrates.[200] In 1645, when three hundred Irish female camp followers, infants and children were butchered by the Scottish Covenanters at Philiphaugh, it was said that they had been 'cut in pieces with such savage and inhuman cruelty, as neither Turk nor Scythian was ever heard to have done the like'.[201]

For the Protestants, however, the Marian burnings memorialized by John Foxe, the St Bartholomew's Day massacre in France and the activities of the Inquisition were all proof of the 'savage cruelty and brutish barbarism' of the Catholics. 'The badge of the gospel', said an Elizabethan MP, 'is clemency and gentleness', and 'the fruits of the contrary religion . . . is sourness and cruelty'.[202] It was widely believed that if the Spanish Armada of 1588 had been successful, English civilians would have been tortured and killed.[203] Preaching on the first anniversary of the Gunpowder Plot of 1605, Lancelot Andrewes, Bishop of Chichester, declared that the conspirators were 'not men, no, not savage wild men: the Huns, the Heruli, the Turcilingi [barbarian invaders of fifth-century Italy], noted for inhumanity. Even among those barbarous people, this fact would be acounted barbarous.'[204] In 1646 a Weymouth mariner declared that 'he fought not against the Papists for their religion, for 'twas lawful for every man to use his conscience, but he fought against them as bloody men'.[205] A Restoration preacher thought that the tortures of the Inquisition were 'an instance of barbarity beyond the practice of any uncivilized nation'.[206]

Particularly notorious was the 'savage cruelty' of the Spaniards in America, whose treatment of the Native Americans was given wide publicity from 1583 onwards by English versions of the account given by the Dominican missionary Bartolomé de Las Casas, and retailed in such later works as Sir William D'Avenant's opera of 1658 entitled *The Cruelty of the Spaniards in Peru*.[207] Although most Indian deaths in Spanish America were attributable to disease rather than Spanish violence, the 'Black Legend' was widely disseminated. 'Within forty years,' a Reading preacher told his audience in 1596, 'they [the Spaniards] butchered about twelve millions of men, women, and infants.' For Algernon Sidney writing in 1680, the total had become forty million.[208] In the early eighteenth century, Daniel

Defoe described Spanish 'barbarities' as 'a bloody and unnatural piece of cruelty, and such as for which the very name of Spaniard is reckon'd to be frightful and terrible to all people of humanity'. He conceded, however, that just as the cruelties of the Israelites committed against the peoples of Canaan were carried out in response to commands from heaven, so the cruelty of the Spaniards towards pagan practitioners of human sacrifices, 'however abhorred by us, was doubtless an appointment of God, for the destruction of the wickedest and most abominable people upon earth'.[209]

The depiction of other sects or nations as 'cruel' could be a way of legitimizing violent action against them. Much of the literature on the supposed cruelty of the Turks was produced in connection with attempts to launch a new crusade in the fifteenth century.[210] In justifying the mid-seventeenth-century wars against the Dutch, a great deal was made of their torture and execution of ten English employees of the East India Company in 1623 (the 'Amboyna massacre').[211] Aggression against those who were barbarously cruel to others could be plausibly represented as humanitarian intervention. In an early and largely unnoticed instance, Oliver Cromwell, having in 1655 launched an unprovoked attack on Spanish possessions in the West Indies, cited as part of his justification the 'utmost barbarity' with which the Spaniards had treated the Native Americans. He claimed that, since all men were brothers, 'All great and extraordinary wrongs done to particular persons ought to be considered as in a manner done to all the rest of the human race.'[212] This was a doctrine that went back to the Roman Stoics, had been held by Thomas More's Utopians, was endorsed in Elizabethan times by Alberico Gentili, and would reverberate down to the twenty-first century.[213]

In Ireland, the atrocities accompanying the rebellion of the Ulster Catholics in 1641 were retailed in exaggerated form by Sir John Temple in his *History of the Irish Rebellion* (1646). The civil war that followed the revolt was said to have involved both sides in 'cruelties such as are not usual even among the Moors and Arabs' and 'unheard of among pagans, Turks or barbarians'.[214] In England, at the battle of Nantwich in 1644, Irish Catholic women were accused of carrying 'such horrid, bloody instruments that the eye of man never held before, being long knives, above half a yard in length, with a hook and a point at the end of them, made not only to stab, but to tear the flesh from the very bones'. They had 'deadly weapons, newly made, which were to be struck into the body, and could not be pulled out again', noted a London tradesman in his diary.[215]

This fear of an enemy armed with ingeniously sadistic equipment was a recurring fantasy. It featured prominently in the numerous reports of Catholic plots that coursed through Restoration England. In the months leading up the 1688 Revolution, there were repeated rumours of an approaching Irish-Catholic army, equipped with hideous instruments of torture.[216] Bishop Gilbert Burnet wrote of the Roman Catholic Church that, 'notwithstanding all the polishings of learning and civility that are in it, it is now the cruellest and the most implacable society that has ever yet appeared in the world'.[217] In the Palatinate and elsewhere, Louis XIV's armies were said to have committed 'cruelties unheard of among civilized nations'. As for his persecution of the Huguenots, it was astonishing that 'in an age so clear-sighted and so civilized as ours, a nation which passes for polite could ever come to such cruel extremities'.[218] In the mid-eighteenth century, a philosopher thought it worth asking why Roman Catholics were 'more cruel and guilty of more horrid barbarities than other persons of a civilized and learned education'.[219] Yet in Scotland in 1650 it was the invading English Protestant army of whom it was rumoured that they would amputate the right hands of all youths between six and sixteen, burn women's breasts with hot irons, and cut the throats of everyone between sixteen and sixty.[220]

In the eyes of many observers, the incessant corporal punishment practised in the grammar schools was another instance of unnecessary cruelty. Some contemporaries wanted legislation to bring it to an end because it was 'barbarous'.[221] Others used the word to describe the

153

ill-treatment of animals. Warning against 'our natural propensity to cruelty', the Puritan preacher Robert Bolton condemned the 'barbarous inhumanity' of blood sports. The London Bear Garden was denounced by its enemies in the 1640s as a 'nurse of barbarism and beastliness', while the 'inhuman practice' of Spanish bullfighting was notorious for its 'rudeness and barbarity'.[222] In the following century, Gibbon noted that the cruelties of animal slaughter for food were 'disguised by the arts of European refinement', whereas 'in the tent of a Tartarian shepherd' they were 'exhibited, in their naked and most disgusting simplicity'.[223]

Theology was also affected by these sentiments. The early seventeenth-century reaction against Calvinist doctrines of reprobation was stimulated by the conviction that God could never have been capable of such 'extreme cruelty' as to predestine human beings to eternal torment in hell for no fault of their own. The increasing disbelief of theologians in the reality of everlasting punishment reflected a new disinclination to accept so 'cruel', 'barbarous and savage' a notion. The unorthodox mathematician and divine William Whiston (1667–1752) was not alone in rejecting a conception of God that 'supposed him to delight in cruelty and barbarity, the most savage cruelty and barbarity possible'.[224]

The same belief that cruelty was intrinsically 'barbarous' lay behind the repeated, but highly debatable boast that English judicial punishments were less ferocious than elsewhere. The fifteenth-century chief justice Sir John Fortescue was one of many who criticized the inhumanity of the investigative torture that was routinely practised across the Channel; while the Tudor statesman Sir Thomas Smith claimed that 'tormenting, demembering either arm or leg, breaking upon the wheel, impaling, and such cruel torments as be used in other nations by the order of their law, we have not'.[225] He was drawing an implicit contrast with the Ottoman Turks, who were notorious for their hideous punishments, particularly 'staking' (impaling) and 'gaunching' (dropping from a height on to sharp hooks).[226] He could also have cited the ferocious penalties meted out by the Russian tsar Ivan IV ('the Terrible'): an English traveller witnessed a man who had been impaled, languishing in 'horrible pain'.[227]

Torture was more regularly employed on the continent because the civil law required a confession as proof of guilt if two witnesses were not forthcoming, whereas in England the common law relied on the jury system. In practice, however, torture was used in only a minority of cases in France; and its employment declined further during the seventeenth century.[228] In England, despite its illegality in common law, torture was repeatedly authorized under royal prerogative by the Elizabethan and Jacobean privy councils when investigating particularly serious crimes, especially plots against the monarch. Its purpose was usually to extract information rather than to establish guilt, and its defenders were sensitive to the charge of 'unnecessary' cruelty. They claimed, somewhat disingenuously, that what was done was 'but gentle and merciful', and that those who administered the rack were required 'to use it in as charitable a manner as such a thing might be'.[229] In 1648 the laws of Massachusetts permitted those convicted of capital crimes to be tortured to make them reveal their confederates, 'but not with such tortures as be barbarous or inhumane'.[230] After the reign of Charles I, torture under the royal prerogative disappeared altogether, though harsh imprisonment, involving manacling, starvation and sleep deprivation, was sometimes used to force accused persons to plead: in 1681 it was said that there was 'a hole in Newgate which never any man could endure two days without confessing any thing laid to his charge'.[231]

The English penal system remained a great deal more ferocious in its assaults upon the body of the criminal than Fortescue and Smith had claimed. Standard punishments in the early modern period included hanging (i.e., slow strangulation),* branding, pillorying, flogging, amputation of hands and ears, and slitting of noses – not to mention the *peine*

---

* For the macabre suggestion that many of those executed did not die on the gallows, but were only half-hanged and killed subsequently by anatomists on the dissecting table, see Elizabeth T. Hurren, *Dissecting the Civil Corpse* (Basingstoke, 2016).

forte et dure, i.e., the pressing to death of those who refused to plead. Traitors, including those who murdered their employers, were drawn by horses along the ground or on a litter to the gallows, hanged, taken down when still alive, castrated, disembowelled and quartered. Females convicted for killing their husbands or employers were deemed guilty of petty treason, for which the penalty was to be burned alive. In the eighteenth century, there were suggestions that the introduction of perpetual slavery, castration, vivisection, whipping to death, and breaking on the wheel should also be considered.[232]

In the fifteenth century, Sir John Fortescue had boasted that more men were hanged in England in a year for robbery and manslaughter than were hanged in France for those crimes in seven years. A French visitor in the reign of Mary I was predictably appalled by the English practice of indiscriminately killing criminals for offences that in France would have merited no more than a whipping.[233] It has been estimated that in the hundred years before 1630 some 75,000 felons were executed, and that more people were hanged in England between 1580 and 1630 than between 1630 and 1967.[234] 'Strangers judge us a wicked or cruel nation, in regard we hang more in a year than others do in seven', thought one Jacobean.[235] In 1767 the English translator of the Italian penal reformer Cesare Beccaria declared that the number of criminals put to death in England was 'much greater than in any other part of Europe'.[236]

This regime seemed as 'cruel' and 'uncivilized' to many contemporaries as it does to us. In the 1530s Thomas Starkey believed that many 'barbarous and tyrannical' laws would have to be rescinded before England could attain 'true civility'. After Henry VIII's demise, the 'cruel and bloody' statutes (which included a provision for boiling convicted poisoners to death) were repealed as 'very strait, sore, extreme and terrible'.[237] In 1535 a London correspondent of Lady Lisle, wife of the governor of Calais, knew her to be so 'pitiful' that he forbore to give her details of the latest executions; and when a woman was burned at Smithfield in 1632 for poisoning her husband, Lady

(Judith) Barrington, an Essex gentlewoman, commented that 'the cruelty' was 'wondered at'.[238] In the reign of Elizabeth I, a government agent warned that Catholic accounts of the execution of missionary priests were giving 'a barbarous opinion of our cruelty: I could wish that in these cases it might please Her Majesty to pardon the drawing and quartering'.[239] In 1585 the House of Commons wanted a 'more severe punishment' for the failed assassin William Parry than mere hanging, drawing and quartering, but the queen rejected their request. On learning in the following year that the first batch of conspirators in the Babington Plot had been castrated and disembowelled when still alive, she ordered that the second lot should be allowed to hang until they were dead.[240] At the execution of the Jesuit poet Robert Southwell in 1595, the executioner made three attempts to cut him down in time to be disembowelled when still alive, but on each occasion the crowd cried, 'Stay! Stay!' After witnessing the hanging, drawing and quartering of Father Hugh Green at Dorchester in 1642, Mrs Elizabeth Willoughby recorded that 'Methought my heart was lifted out of my body to see him in such cruel pains.'[241]

Lord Chief Justice Coke confessed that, if a man could see all those hanged in one year gathered together, 'it would make his heart to bleed for pity and compassion'.[242] The Oxford antiquary Anthony Wood recalled his horror when in 1654 at the age of twenty-one he witnessed the public execution of two highwaymen: 'This was the first or second execution that A. W. ever saw, and therefore it struck a great terror into him to the disturbance of his studies and thoughts.'[243] During a stay in France, the diarist John Evelyn witnessed the torture of a suspected robber, but he found the spectacle so 'uncomfortable' that he was 'not able to stay the sight of another'.[244]

In 1584 the Kentish gentleman Reginald Scot denounced the 'outrageous and barbarous cruelty' of 'witch-mongers and inquisitors', whose 'unnatural and uncivil discourtesy' led them to persecute harmless old women for an impossible crime.[245] The hanging of convicted witches became an increasingly controversial matter during the ensuing century. There was also a long-running, though ineffective, opposition to executing thieves for stealing goods worth more than a shilling, a practice which Thomas Starkey in the 1530s regarded as 'against nature and humanity' and incompatible with 'good civility'. The banking projector William Paterson denounced it in 1701 as 'a destructive and unsuccessful piece of cruelty'.[246] Judges allowed many convicted criminals to escape the death penalty by pleading benefit of clergy and successfully passing a reading test, and juries frequently undervalued stolen goods in order to save the accused from conviction as a felon. Their motive, however, may sometimes have been to ensure that the offender was publicly whipped for his misdemeanour instead of being allowed to plead clergy and escape with a token branding on the thumb. Some of those in authority thought there was 'too much lenity' and lamented such 'foolish and fond pity'.[247] But the standard punishments for treason were criticized by many as 'inhumane', 'cruel' and 'barbarous'. During the Commonwealth and Protectorate, any death sentences imposed by the High Courts of Justice had to be for beheading or hanging only. 'I take all executions of justice further than simple death to be purely cruelties', was one seventeenth-century reader's translation of a passage in Montaigne's *Essays*.[248]

The practice of burning religious heretics had long evoked horror. Several early Protestant writers thought it wrong, whatever the victim's religious persuasion.[249] In the seventeenth century, this 'pious cruelty' (as a later reformer called it) was increasingly attacked as 'barbarous'. Temporarily abolished by the Long Parliament in 1648 and the Rump in 1650, it was finally brought to an end in an act of 1677 by which heresy ceased to be a capital offence.[250] As for pressing to death, a contemporary denounced it in 1651 for its 'barbarity and inhumanity'; he would not 'for all the world' be a witness of 'any man's suffering in such kind'.[251]

In 1689 the authors of the Bill of Rights outlawed all 'cruel and unusual punishments'. They had in mind the treatment of the Popish

Plot informer and perjurer Titus Oates, who had been sentenced to be fined, imprisoned, pilloried and whipped four times a year for the rest of his life. But they were also following the precedent set by the colony of Massachusetts, which, as early as 1641, had prohibited all bodily punishments that were 'inhumane, barbarous or cruel'.[252] From the 1690s it became customary to mitigate the penalty for treason by strangling the women before lighting the fire and letting the men hang until they were dead before they were cut down and disembowelled. This was proof, thought the great lawyer William Blackstone, of the English nation's humanity.[253]

The annual number of executions in England declined dramatically after the 1630s. Capital convictions increased and, in the eighteenth century, so did the creation of new capital offences; but though subject to occasional fluctuations, the proportion of the convicted who were put to death diminished steadily between 1630 and 1740.[254] In the northern and western parts of the country, there was a marked reluctance to hang those convicted of offences against property.[255] A growing number of convicts were reprieved and transported to the American colonies to work on the plantations. By 1700 this was the most common fate of those convicted of a serious felony. In two acts, of 1718 and 1720, transportation became the standard penalty for some noncapital crimes as well.[256] Despite the numerous calls for the introduction of more ferocious punishments, the eighteenth century saw the end of judicial branding and mutilation, the abolition of the burning of women for treason,[257] the decline of public whipping and, save for a sharp rise in London executions in the 1780s, an increasing recourse to imprisonment as an alternative to capital and corporal punishment. It was not until the 1820s and 1830s, however, that the old bloody code was formally dismantled.[258]

Although the execution rate in late eighteenth-century England was still far higher than that in most continental countries, and remained so until well into the nineteenth century,[259] this shift from bodily punishment, first to transportation and then to an emphasis on incarceration and reform, was hailed by many contemporaries as evidence of a new and 'civilized' compassion. The 3rd Earl of Shaftesbury remarked on 'the genius of our nation against keeping anything in pain or putting out of pain: above all, praise our laws for rack abolished, no wheel'; and the moralist John Brown reflected complacently on 'the lenity of our laws in capital cases; our compassion for convicted criminals; even the general humanity of our highwaymen and robbers, compared with those of other countries'. Adam Smith saluted 'the humanity of a civilized people', which, he thought, led them to mitigate punishments. Blackstone applauded the abolition in 1772 of the *peine forte et dure*, that 'cruel process', so repugnant to 'the humanity of the laws of England'.[260]

The growing aversion to punishments involving the infliction of physical pain may have reflected a new preoccupation with felicity in this world rather than the next. When in 1677 a writer proposed the total abolition of the death penalty, his argument was that capital punishment was unacceptable because it put 'an end to all earthly happiness'; and in the eighteenth century there are signs of mounting unease about punishments involving the taking of human life.[261] The medieval assumption that pain had a positive spiritual value because it enabled human beings to experience the sufferings of Christ was rejected by most Protestants.* Much more common was the notion that pain was a divine chastisement, a means of expiating sin and a way of bringing people nearer to God. To that extent, afflictions of any kind were a blessing and, in the eyes of some, even a sign of divine approval. But by the later seventeenth century, the appeal of this idea was also diminishing.[262] Instead, pain was coming to be seen as something intrinsically undesirable. In the past, contemporary accounts of executions and other forms of bodily punishment only occasionally mentioned the pain they inflicted, preferring instead to stress the shame they

---

* Though not by the Quakers, who defined themselves as a persecuted people and attached much importance to recording their 'Sufferings' because of their spiritual value; Robert Barclay, *An Apology for the True Christian Divinity* (5th edn, 1703), 254.

involved. 'Our forefathers,' thought the Scottish judge Lord Kames in 1778, 'could bear without much pain what would totally overwhelm us.'[263] But the same changes that made people more protective of their bodily inviolability, more concerned with concealing their bodily odours and emissions, and more sensitive to those of others, made them readier to identify with the agonies of the sufferer and more reluctant to inflict or witness them. As the French traveller and *philosophe* Baron Lahontan wrote of the Canadian Iroquois practice of burning their prisoners to death in a slow fire, nothing was more painfully affecting to 'a civil man' than to be obliged to witness such torments.[264] By 1836 John Stuart Mill could note that 'the spectacle, and even the very idea, of pain, is kept more and more out of the sight of those classes who enjoy in their fulness the benefits of civilization'.[265]

The overall shift to imprisonment instead of execution and other bodily punishments was as much the product of a new penal strategy as of a new sensibility. Intended to be a more effective method of controlling and reforming criminals, it has been dismissed in recent times as merely a substitution of one method of exercising state power for another, in which 'humanity' played little part.[266] It is undeniable that penal reform was in part driven by circumstances unconnected with humanitarian sentiment.[267] The expanding demand for labour, both at home and in the colonies from the later seventeenth century on, made it appear increasingly wasteful to execute healthy young criminals for trivial offences: the Quaker John Bellers calculated in 1699 that every time an able-bodied man was cut off by an untimely death it cost the country £200.[268] An ever more powerful state no longer needed to demonstrate its strength by exposing its penal repertoire to the public gaze. Greater certainty of punishment was a more effective deterrent than its severity. The concern that public floggings and executions attracted disreputable and disorderly spectators, combined with evidence that sanguinary punishments were ineffective, helped to propel the shift to transportation and imprisonment. Long sentences, solitary confinement and hard labour inflicted pain, but they did not do so in the public view. Prisons, like abattoirs, became invisible. So, in the mid-nineteenth century, did executions. It is hard not to conclude that the objection was less to the fact of judicially inflicted pain than to the sight of it.

Yet even if practical considerations were decisive in bringing about changes in the penal system, it is striking to see how frequently the arguments for reform were couched in the language of 'barbarism' and 'civilization'. Sanguinary punishments were still thought necessary for 'barbarous' peoples (because, it was assumed, only their bodies and not their minds were sensible to pain), but they were increasingly held to be inappropriate for the civilized. 'The severity of our criminal law might perhaps be very proper in the days of Gothic tyranny and ferocity of manners,' wrote Dr William Smith in 1777, 'but at this period of civilization and refinement, a milder mode of punishment would be more adequate.'[269] Another reformer declared that the treatment of traitors involved 'such savage butchery as might even stain a Hottentot'; it was intolerable, he thought, that such penalties, devised in an age of ignorance and barbarity, should be allowed to continue in 'the present civilized and enlightened period'. In the nineteenth century, it was standard for abolitionists to describe the death penalty as 'a barbarous relic'.[270]

In Hanoverian England it became axiomatic that the most 'polite' nations were the most 'humane'.[271] The ancient Athenians had art and philosophy, noted the bluestocking Elizabeth Carter, but their 'brutal cruelty' in warfare showed that 'their hearts were the hearts of barbarians'.[272] Admiration for the Romans was severely qualified by the memory of their 'savage and barbarous inhumanity': their conquest of England had been 'very violent and horrible'.[273] As for the more immediate past, it was notorious that medieval people were cruel and unfeeling.[274] For Adam Smith, sympathy for others was a quality unique to 'a humane and polished people'; 'the delicate sensibility required in civilized nations' was not to be found among savages. The animal lover John Lawrence commented on 'the superior humanity of the present over any former period', and the Birmingham historian William Hutton rejoiced that 'the whole generations of faggots and torture are extinct in this age of light'.[275]

Whether eighteenth-century reformers were right to believe themselves more compassionate than their ancestors is debatable.[276] What is certain is that they wanted to think that they were. Pity, sympathy, benevolence and compassion were seen as distinctively modern emotions, unknown either to the people of the past or to the 'barbarians' of foreign climes. They had the power to 'refine' and 'civilize' human nature. A greater sensitivity to physical pain, whether one's own or that of others, and a distaste for causing or witnessing its infliction had come to be seen as essential attributes of civility. Humanity was the virtue of a man 'civiliz'd', who was 'gentle, benevolent, purged of all rage and every unsociable passion'. Cruelty, by contrast, was associated with a specific type of depraved human being, one who lacked all feelings of humanity and was wholly insensitive to the sufferings of others.[277] The contemporary taste for cruel jokes directed against dwarfs, the deaf, the blind and other disabled persons suggests that there were many inhabitants of eighteenth-century England whose civility still had some way to go.[278]

Civilized Manners

Dislike of cruelty was potentially of universal applicability. So were the rule of law, the safeguarding of life and private property, and the orderly conduct of war and international relations. But many of the other criteria advanced as tests of a people's civility reflected narrower English or, at most, Western European preconceptions. In 1606 Sir Thomas Palmer advised travellers that the best way of discovering whether nations were civil or barbarous was to study their 'gesture, apparel, decency, conversation, diet, feeding, giving of honour, and all other actions of the people of a country, one to another'.[279] Unfamiliar forms of dress, hairstyles and bodily ornament or, worse still, no dress at all, were readily perceived as proof of a barbarous condition. 'The custom of wearing clothes,' reflected an early eighteenth-century antiquary, 'grew as people grew more polite and civil.' He thought it probable that 'the ruder nations' went half-naked until they came to be 'more civilized'. The fact that Patagonians now wore drawers, agreed the traveller Thomas Pennant in 1767, was a sign that they had taken 'a few steps farther towards civilization'.[280]

Sir Philip Sidney criticized the Indians for wearing jewels in their noses and lips rather than in what he called 'the fit and natural place of the ears'.[281] Roger Williams noted that it was 'the foolish custom of all barbarous nations to paint and figure their face and bodies'. The poet Edmund Spenser regretted that Irish women rode sidesaddle on 'the wrong side of the horse', facing right rather than left. Fynes Moryson noted 'twenty absurd things' practised by the Irish, 'only because they would be contrary to us'. Their matted hairstyles ('glibs') aroused disgust and, by covering their faces, enabled malefactors to escape unrecognized. Their voluminous 'mantles' served as a garment by day and a mattress by night, making it possible for a nomadic people to live out 'in bogs and woods' and giving their wearers a hint of menace similar to that aroused by the 'hoodies' of modern times.[282]

The standard of personal cleanliness, already an accepted criterion of civility at home, also became a way of distinguishing between peoples abroad. 'The more any country is civilized,' ruled the *Spectator*, 'the more they consult this point of politeness.' There was said to be more disease in barbarous countries because impolite people had inferior hygiene. The eighteenth-century medical writer William Buchan declared that 'what[ever] pretensions people may make to learning, politeness or civilization, we would venture to affirm that so long as they neglect cleanliness, they are in a state of barbarity'. The demographer Robert Malthus similarly associated 'savages' with dirt and stench.[283] Arriving in Riga after a diplomatic visit to Muscovy in the 1660s, the English ambassador's secretary commented on what a joy it was for him and his colleagues, 'after a tedious association with a people barbarous and rude', to find themselves once more among those who were 'civil and urbane', notable for 'exquisite neatness and cleanliness in all things'.* When Lord Macartney led an embassy to China in 1792, he was disgusted to find that there were no proper 'places of retirement': the 'necessaries' were quite open and public; ordure was constantly being removed, and the stench was everywhere.[284] In Islamic countries, by contrast, English visitors were constantly astonished by the frequency and thoroughness with which the people washed themselves. Even so, Lord Kames thought that the English were 'remarkable for cleanness the world over'.[285]

Urbanity, courtesy and politeness were, of course, an integral part of being civilized. As one conduct theorist remarked, children were taught manners in order to make them fit members of civil society: by inculcating mutual respect and affection, good manners helped to keep the peace in families, among neighbours and between nations.[286] In the New World, European travellers were shocked to find that some Native Americans appeared unaware of the first principles of polite decorum: although they obeyed their chiefs and respected their elders and parents, they used the same mode of address for everyone, regardless of their social position.[287] Only after she had learnt English and been converted to Christianity did the Indian princess Pocahontas become 'very formal and civil, after our English manner'.[288] Disgusted by the apparent incivility of the Quakers he encountered in America, Roger Williams reminded them 'that in our native country, and in all civilized countries, . . . civility, courteous speech, courteous salutation, and respective behaviour, was generally practised, opposite to the carriage of barbarous and uncivilized people'.[289]

Unfamiliar foodstuffs and methods of food preparation were also taken to be proof of incivility. The Spaniards were disgusted to find Native Americans eating insects and reptiles. An early settler in New

---

* Travelling in Russia in 1805, the future Bishop of Calcutta Reginald Heber reported that 'to pass leeward of a Russian peasant is really so terrible an event that I always avoid it if possible'; *The Life of Reginald Heber by His Widow* (1830), vol. 1, 107.

England thought that if anything could bring the natives to civility it would be the use of salt to preserve fish and corn for the winter, 'which is a chief benefit in a civilized commonwealth'.[290] Eating uncooked meat was a sure sign of barbarism.[291] So were unfamiliar table manners. As Robert Boyle remarked, 'The circumstances of eating and drinking are those which make men with the greatest confidence term other nations brutish and barbarous.'[292] The Elizabethan explorer Martin Frobisher lamented that the Indians of northeast America did not use either 'table, stool, or table-cloth for comeliness', while an early emigrant to Massachusetts observed that those of New England ate 'in a rude manner . . . without either trenchers, napkins or knives'.[293] Sir Thomas Sherley, who had been their prisoner in Constantinople, reported that the Turks ('the most inhumane of all other barbarians') tore their meat and bread with their hands, 'neither using knife nor trencher'.* The Jacobean merchant William Finch thought the inhabitants of Socotra (in the Arabian Sea) 'unmannerly' because they ate their meat on the ground with no knives or spoons but only their fingers, and the trav- eller Thomas Herbert found the eating habits of Persian women 'strange and offensive': when overcome by sudden laughter, they would eject the meat from their mouths back into the dish from which they had taken it. Edward Long similarly reported that black slaves in Jamaica, 'at their politest entertainments', would 'thrust their hands all together into the dish, sometimes returning into it what they had been chewing'.[294] Charles II's ambassador to Muscovy was shocked not to be provided with a napkin at dinner; while during his embassy to Peking, Lord Macartney discovered that the Chinese were all 'foul feeders', drinking out of the same cup, spitting about the room, blowing their noses in their fingers and wiping them on their sleeves.[295]

Throughout the early modern period, indissoluble monogamous marriage was widely regarded as an essential feature of a civilized

---

* One of the reasons why the Victorian politician Richard Cobden maintained that the Turks could not be regarded as Europeans was that 'they use their fingers still, in place of those civilized substitutes, knives and forks'; *Political Writings* (1867), vol. 1, 270–71.

society, for by it 'wild and unbridled affections' were 'reduced to humanity and civility'.[296] Hence the battle fought, until the later seventeenth century, by the church courts against all forms of sexual irregularity. Savages, by contrast, were alleged to gratify their appetites without 'those artificial rules of decency and decorum which might lay a restraint upon their conduct'. An Elizabethan sailor reported that the natives of Florida were 'so brutal and base' that they did not 'forbear the use of their wives in open presence'.[297] In 1774 Lord Kames reflected with satisfaction that women, formerly regarded as mere 'objects of animal love', were now valued 'as faithful friends and agreeable companions', or as a later versifier put it:

Each sensual joy with social bliss combined,
And appetite with intellect refined.[298]

Physical violence between the spouses was a violation of civilized standards. Although the right of husbands to subject their wives to 'moderate' chastisement was upheld by the courts until 1828, it had long been regarded by many as wholly unacceptable. A Jacobean pamphleteer associated wife-beating with 'some ancient ages of barbarism before civility was fully embraced'; and at the end of the seventeenth century, a feminist writer denounced the 'barbarous' tyranny of men over women, not just in 'all the Eastern parts of the world, where the women, like our negroes in our Western plantations, are born slaves, and live prisoners all their lives', but also in 'some parts of Europe, which pretend to be most refin'd and civiliz'd'.[299] In the *Spectator*, Richard Steele urged that husbands should treat wives with 'civility', not 'barbarous disrespect'. For the eighteenth-century middle classes, marital violence was shameful, an unspeakable 'barbarity'.[300]

As early as 1670, a writer declared that 'by how much each nation is more civilized and refined from barbarism, so much greater liberty and honour do women there enjoy'.[301] English travellers disapproved of the Turkish practice of segregating women and letting them emerge only when heavily veiled. Fynes Moryson thought that the Turks valued women only for their sexual allure and had no regard for 'learning or qualities of mind'. Turks were barbarians, agreed an eighteenth-century traveller: their love was 'sensuality, without friendship or esteem'.[302] Deploring Islamic polygamy, Richard Baxter remarked in 1673 on 'the great slavery that the women are kept in, making them like slaves that they may keep them quiet'. He added that since women played a large part in the education of children, by which 'all virtue and civility' were maintained, their enslavement could lead only to 'the debasing and brutifying of mankind'.[303]

In the following century, it became common to lament the adverse effect of polygamy on the position of women. 'Barbarism', thought David Hume, was its 'inseparable concomitant'.[304] Adam Smith linked polygamy to despotism because it prevented the emergence of a hereditary nobility, a class which he saw as an essential bulwark against monarchical despotism. He also commented on the miserable plight of the polygamist's wives.[305] Lord Kames claimed that it was only in temperate climes that women were treated as rational beings; and the dramatist Richard Sheridan told Queen Charlotte that in Java and Japan the women were 'absolute slaves': 'The East, which has always been the seat of tyranny to women, has always been the seat of barbarism and ignorance.'[306] China was not a seat of ignorance, but there too women occupied a totally subordinate position.[307]

The immolation of Indian widows on their husbands' funeral pyres had at first evoked a mixture of revulsion and admiration: in 1618 William Methwold, an agent of the East India Company, noted that the practice was intended to deter wives from poisoning their spouses, but he regarded it as a 'cruel and heathenish custom'.[308] Yet for all its horror, it seemed touching evidence of conjugal fidelity and noble heroism. So long as the Company was only a trading corporation, it was reluctant to interfere with local customs. But by the early nineteenth century, when it had acquired a territorial empire and become the dominant political authority in the subcontinent, it was ready to take action against *sati*, which was now regarded as an indisputably 'barbarous' practice. Its abolition in 1829 was seen as giving some legitimacy to the British presence in India.[309]

In 1673 Bathsua Makin, regarded by some as the greatest female scholar in England, denounced the practice of denying young women a proper education as a 'barbarous custom' appropriate only for countries where women were oppressed, such as 'Russia, Ethiopia, and all the barbarous nations of the world'. Her sentiment was echoed in 1697 by Daniel Defoe, who regarded it as 'one of the most barbarous customs in the world, considering us as a civilized and a Christian country, that we deny the advantages of learning to women'.[310] In the eighteenth century, these sentiments became commonplace. With only a few exceptions, most contemporaries believed that the history of women was the story of their gradual emancipation as society became economically and socially more complex: Lord Kames called it 'the gradual progress of women from their low state in savage tribes to their elevated state in civilized nations'.[311] 'Savages', thought Malthus, degraded the female sex: in North America, the native men were idle, save when they were hunting or fighting, while the women led lives of incessant toil. This, as others pointed out, was the case in most barbarian societies. 'Barbarous nations', according to David Hume, reduced their females to 'the most abject slavery, by confining them, by beating them, by selling them, by killing them'. This was a great contrast with the polite society of his day, where the sexes met sociably and where male authority was exercised 'in a more generous, though not a less evident manner', namely, by condescending gallantry.[312]

John Dalrymple explained in 1757 that 'in all barbarous ages, where courage and strength of body are more necessary than the virtues of the mind, the rights of women must be but little regarded'; only with the 'softening of manners' did they come to be respected.[313] The Scottish jurist John Millar attributed this softening of manners and the resulting freedom of women to the introduction of regular government and the subsequent rise of manufacturing and commerce.[314] In 1771 Edmund Burke felt able to tell the House of Commons that 'the civilization that is amongst us turns upon two things: the indissolubility of marriage and the freedom of the female sex. To these we owe every advantage that Europe has over every state in the world.'[315]

Of course, these new 'rights of women' were not usually envisaged as extending much further than freedom of movement, succession to property, some limited educational opportunity and an entitlement to be treated with polite deference. By the standards of aristocratic French ladies, ruling their salons and acting as 'the umpires of polite letters', their English counterparts were relatively subordinate.[316] By modern standards, their emancipation had barely begun. Despite these limits, English commentators aligned themselves with the philosophers of the European Enlightenment in regarding the condition of women as a reliable index of the progress from barbarism to civility. Each stage of social development was seen as bringing new benefits to females.[317] James King, the astronomer on Captain Cook's third voyage, and William Anderson, the ship's surgeon, were both certain that the treatment of women was the best criterion by which to assess the degree of civilization to be found among the different peoples of the South Seas.[318] In the words of William Alexander:

> The rank ... and condition in which we find women in any country mark out to us with the greatest precision the exact point in the scale of civil society to which the people of such country have arrived; and were their history entirely silent on every other subject, and only mentioned the manner in which they treated their women, we would, from thence, be enabled to form a tolerable judgment of the barbarity or culture of their manners.[319]

Hence Lord Macartney's conclusion that 'the genuine politeness which distinguishes our manners ... cannot be expected in Orientals, considering the light in which they regard the female world'.[320]

The Fruits of Civility

By the eighteenth century, what above all made 'civilized' peoples conscious of their difference from 'barbarians' was their material superiority, signalled by the possession of a whole range of skills that brought visible benefits, economic, technological, artistic and intellectual: all the goods that were absent in Thomas Hobbes's famous description of the state of nature, where there was 'no place for industry ...; no culture of the earth; no navigation, nor use of the commodities that may be imported by sea; no commodious building; no instruments of moving, and removing, such things as require much force; no knowledge of the face of the earth; no account of time; no arts; no letters; no society'.[321] Hobbes did not mention money, which John Locke would later regard as an indispensable spur to productivity, particularly silver money, which he saw to be 'the instrument and measure of commerce in all the civilized and trading parts of the world'. Bernard Mandeville similarly thought money 'absolutely necessary to the order, the economy, and the very existence of civil society', while Montesquieu declared that its presence was a sure sign of a civilized country.[322] Nevertheless, in agriculture, navigation, industry, technology, trade, architecture, literature and learning, Hobbes enumerated virtually all the accepted activities that, as he put it, distinguished 'the civility of Europe from the barbarity of the American savages'.[323] By implication, he defined barbarism in wholly negative terms, not as an alternative way of life, but as the simple absence of civil society and its accompanying benefits. This was a widespread attitude, reflected later in Samuel Johnson's *Dictionary*, where definitions of the word 'civil' were largely couched in negatives. Adam Ferguson justifiably accused his contemporaries of imagining 'that a mere negation of all our virtues is a sufficient description of man in his original state'.[324]

Like other proponents of civility, Hobbes stressed the priority of state formation, of 'laws and common-wealth, from whence proceedeth science and civility'.[325] Once a political society had been created, he thought, as did his French contemporary René Descartes, that almost all the subsequent advantages of civilized life were the product of 'true philosophy', particularly mathematics, without which the English would not have differed 'from the wildest of the Indians'. From that philosophy came all that was 'beautiful or defensible in building, or marvellous in engines and instruments of motion', along with 'whatsoever commodity men receive from the observation of the heavens, from the description of the earth, from the account of time, from walking on the seas'. It was only 'want of leisure from procuring the necessities of life and defending themselves against their neighbours' that prevented the Native Americans and other 'savage' people from developing these sciences. Here Hobbes was echoing the French historian and geographer Pierre d'Avity, who had previously observed that 'human sciences flourish in peaceable towns and among men which live at their ease'.[326]

Many of Hobbes's contemporaries shared his belief in the fundamental importance of calculation and measurement, skill in the arts and sciences, and technological knowledge. Without the arts and sciences, thought the Elizabethan translator Thomas Hacket, mankind had been 'but naked, barbarous, and brutish'. Francis Bacon regarded their presence as the crucial difference between the most civilized (*excultissima*) province of Europe and the most savage and barbarous (*fera et barbara*) region of the New World. Samuel Purchas, who edited the narratives of contemporary travellers, believed that the great empires of Persia, India and China had failed to expand because they lacked the crucial art of navigation.* It was their seafaring skills, their shipbuilding and their cartography that had given Europeans their advantage.[327] The philosopher Richard Cumberland considered that 'civil society, mutual commerce and aid' had been

---

* This was hard on China, which in the early fifteenth century had sent ships through the Indian Ocean to the very tip of South Africa, but then deliberately gave up such expeditions.

made possible by knowledge of numbers, weights, measures and coins.[328] Adam Smith would add that the invention of firearms had ensured civilization's continuance: in ancient times the opulent and civilized found it difficult to defend themselves against the poor and barbarous nations, whereas in modern times the poor and barbarous were defenceless against the opulent and civilized. The Scottish philosopher Dugald Stewart agreed: firearms and the science of fortification had given civilized nations a security against the eruptions of barbarians which they had never previously possessed.[329]

Metalworking was particularly important. John Locke attributed the poverty of the Native Americans to 'their ignorance of what was to be found in a very despicable stone, I mean the mineral of iron'; and the great naturalist John Ray thought that metals and minerals were 'necessary instruments' of 'culture' and 'civility': without their exploitation, life would be 'barbarous and sordid'.[330] In the later eighteenth century, iron was described as 'the mainspring perhaps of civilized society'. Gibbon regarded it, along with money, as essential if a people were to emerge from 'the grossest barbarism'. Jean-Jacques Rousseau thought that Europe was more civilized than the rest of the world because it had both iron and corn. The historian William Robertson remarked that neither the Aztecs of Mexico nor the Inca of Peru could be regarded as civilized: not only did they make little progress in domesticating animals, but they were totally unacquainted with the useful metals.[331]

A written language was, of course, seen as crucial to civility. Without it, there could be no laws as opposed to customs, no impersonal administration, no record keeping, and no sophisticated commerce. England had had all these things since late Anglo-Saxon times, but it was not until the later Middle Ages that greater lay literacy had made possible the accumulation and transmission of knowledge far beyond the confines of a specialized clerical class. Functional literacy was essential not just for members of the learned professions of medicine, law and theology, but for an increasing number of other occupations. Contemporaries saw this as a key distinction between them and the barbarians. 'Amongst men,' wrote Samuel Purchas, 'some are accounted civil . . . by the use of letters and writing, which others wanting are esteemed brutish, savage, barbarous.' The judge Sir Matthew Hale noted that those peoples who were 'better instructed in letters and writing' were more 'civilized' than the others. Bernard Mandeville believed that civil society was impossible without written laws; William Robertson observed that 'in civilized states' all transactions of any importance were conducted in writing; and Gibbon agreed that 'the use of letters' was 'the principal circumstance that distinguishes a civilized people from a herd of savages, incapable of knowledge or reflection'.[332] By these standards, early modern England was only half-civilized, since it is generally agreed that, at the beginning of the eighteenth century, barely half the men and only a quarter of the women could sign their names, though a distinctly larger proportion would have been able to read.[333]

With literacy went printing, for, as Samuel Johnson remarked, without it, knowledge could not be diffused and 'the mass of every people must be barbarous'. In 1792 Dugald Stewart concluded that the growth and spread of learning, made possible by the invention of printing, had been 'by far the most important' of all the circumstances which distinguished 'the present state of mankind from that of ancient nations'. His contemporary Sir James Mackintosh agreed: it meant that knowledge could never again be lost in the way it had been after the fall of Rome.[334]

It was a commonplace that, before mankind had learnt to form civil societies, human beings had lived in a state of barbarous ignorance.[335] In the century after the Reformation, defenders of the universities and the well-endowed bishoprics and cathedral chapters fended off their critics by claiming that robbing the Church would lead to 'the decay of learning' and a return to ancient barbarism.[336] People were 'civilized' by literature, declared the future Restoration bishop John Gauden in 1653; and without education they would degenerate to 'brutish barbarity'. The civility Gauden had in mind was of a distinctly Anglican and Royalist flavour, for he cited the sectaries and lay preachers of the Interregnum as a disastrous instance of what could happen if power fell into the hands of 'the unlearned sort'. So, later, did the poet John Dryden.[337] But the belief in the civilizing value of learning was shared by those whose case for supporting intellectual inquiry was less self-interested. As Roger North, lawyer and historian, would point out, it was from their superior knowledge that 'the civilized parts of the world' derived all their advantages; he divided mankind into three classes: '1. Learned. 2. Unlearned. 3. Barbarous.'[338] Thomas Sprat in his history of the Royal Society similarly appears to have equated 'the civil world' with 'the learned world'. Skill in numeration, a capacity for generalization, an understanding of causal regularity and a language abounding in abstract terms were becoming widely accepted indicators of a people's civility.[339]

The *philosophes* of the eighteenth-century Enlightenment followed Bacon, Hobbes and Descartes in regarding the sciences as the primary motors of human progress. For Montesquieu, the key difference between a barbarous people (*un peuple barbare*) and a civilized one (*un peuple policé*) was that civilized societies seethed with new ideas, whereas the only ideas in barbarous ones were about how to survive.[340] Savages were notoriously lacking in curiosity, and a sure sign of barbarism was an indifference to intellectual inquiry, as manifested in England by some Protestant sectaries, in Russia by general ignorance of natural philosophy and 'all good learning', and in Africa by a collective failure to improve knowledge.[341] The Scythians, according to Benjamin Whichcote, 'were called barbarians because they had no culture [i.e., education] amongst them'.[342] Nothing did more to consolidate the notion of Ottoman barbarity than the destruction of books and dispersion of Greek scholars that accompanied their conquest of Constantinople in 1453. Thereafter, it became a fixed conviction that the 'unlettered Turk' was an enemy of all learning and hostile to the acquisition of new knowledge.[343] George

Sandys, who had spent a year in Turkey, reported that the Ottomans rejected printing, perhaps because they thought that to make learning universal would be to subvert their religion and system of government, which were best preserved by universal ignorance.[344]

The flourishing of the fine arts of painting, sculpture and architecture was a further index of civilization. When in 1719 the portraitist Jonathan Richardson proposed the foundation of an academy to educate gentlemen in the art of painting, he claimed that it would 'complete the civilizing and polishing of our people'.[345] For David Hume, there was scarcely 'any other ground of distinction between one age and another, between one nation and another, than their different progress in learning and the arts'. This was not just because of their practical utility. More fundamentally, he believed that 'a serious attention to the sciences and liberal arts soften[ed] and humanize[d] the temper, and cherishe[d] those fine emotions, in which true virtue and honour consists'. The more the refined arts advanced, he wrote, the more sociable men became. 'Enriched with science, and possessed of a fund of conversation', they were no longer content to live 'in that distant manner which is peculiar to ignorant and barbarous nations'. They flocked into cities and loved to receive and communicate knowledge, to show their wit, their breeding and their taste in conversation, clothes or furniture (Plate 8). 'Clubs and societies are everywhere formed. Both sexes meet in an easy and sociable manner; and the tempers of men, as well as their behaviour, refine apace. So that, beside the improvement which they receive from knowledge and the liberal arts, it is impossible but they must feel an increase of humanity from the very habit of conversing together ... Thus industry, knowledge, and humanity are linked together by an indissoluble chain.' This humanity was for Hume 'the chief characteristic' that distinguished a civilized age from times of barbarity and ignorance.[346] It arose from the social intercourse of equals that distinguished most Western European cities, by contrast with the more hierarchical conventions of their Asian counterparts.[347]

The sophisticated social life of eighteenth-century England would have been impossible without steady advances in the knowledge and exploitation of the natural world. This was the period when Western Europe was about to overtake Asia in science and technology. Paper, printing, gunpowder and the mariner's compass had all been invented in China, and its people were admired for their skill in ceramics and the manufacture of silks. India was equally famous for its textile industries. But by the later eighteenth century, it was becoming obvious that European achievements in industrial technology were surpassing those of the Asian countries and that it was on these achievements that the culture and civilized life of the period increasingly depended.[348] If as the anthropologist Claude Lévi-Strauss once claimed, a society's level of development is best measured by the quantity of energy available to each member of the population, then the agrarian and fossil-fuelled revolutions of the eighteenth century constituted a huge step forwards for Great Britain, with its rise in agricultural productivity and its rich coal deposits, its new technology for deep mining and its improved roads, navigable rivers and canals for the transport of goods.[349]

Contemporaries did not articulate the concept of energy capture, but they were well aware of the changes that were taking place. 'Consider the gradual steps of civilization from barbarism to refinement,' urged a pamphleteer in 1780, 'and you will not fail to discover that the progress of society from its lowest and worst to its highest and most perfect state has been uniformly accompanied and chiefly promoted by the happy exertions of man in the character of a mechanic or engineer. Let all machines be destroyed, and we are reduced in a moment to the condition of savages.'[350] The social theorist Charles Hall defined 'civilization' in 1805 as 'the improvement of the sciences, and . . . the refinements of manufactures, by which the conveniences, elegancies, and luxuries of life are furnished'.[351]

Consciousness of this advantage in wealth and living conditions underpinned most contemporary reflections on the differences between civilization and barbarism. As early as the reign of Edward VI, the clerk to the royal council, William Thomas, rejoiced in his country because it compared so favourably with the rest of the world, not only in 'justice' and 'civility', but also in 'wealth and commodity'.[352] For Malthus, two hundred and fifty years later, the defining features of 'savage' life were, above all, poverty, famine and disease; whereas in Adam Smith's 'well-governed society', the division of labour brought about 'that universal opulence, which extends itself to the lowest ranks of the people'. In drawing a contrast between that 'opulence' and 'the lowest barbarism', Smith revealed his essentially economic criterion of civilization.[353] In the nineteenth century, the physical mastery of nature was widely regarded as the essential precondition of civilized life, even by those whose who, like John Stuart Mill, believed that true civilization required not just the improvement of material conditions, but also the enlargement of mankind's mental and moral faculties.[354]

In all these different ways, educated contemporaries defined and refined what they regarded as the essential ingredients of civility and the civilized condition. They did so in the course of their growing interaction with people on other continents and in their relations with the lower classes at home. By invoking the concept of 'civilization' they were, of course, celebrating their own way of life and what it was about it that made them feel it was superior to that of others. At every stage civilization was defined as much by what it was not as by what it was. In the process, the original, political notion of civility broadened out to embrace many other aspects of human culture on which value was set. Civilization continued to mean the possession of the laws and political arrangements that enabled people to live peacefully together. But it also involved the life of the mind and the intelligent exploitation of the resources of the natural world.[355]

For civilizing was not a single process but a combination of several different processes. As the late nineteenth-century Cambridge historian J. R. Seeley would point out, the word 'civilization' was regularly invoked as the explanation of a large number of phenomena that, despite being contemporaneous, were not necessarily connected with each other: 'sometimes the softening of manners, sometimes mechanical inventions, sometimes religious toleration, sometimes the appearance of great poets and artists, sometimes scientific discoveries, sometimes constitutional liberty'. There was, he suggested, no reason to believe that all these things had one single cause.[356] This was to ignore the diagnosis by Marx and Engels, for whom 'civilization' covered all these things and was just another name for the bourgeois method of production.[357]

According to the context and their own ideological preferences, therefore, commentators continued to stress the constitutional, or the economic, or the intellectual, or the moral dimensions of the civilized condition. It is not surprising that the Scottish philosopher James Dunbar concluded in 1780 that, since there was no simple, agreed criterion distinguishing civilization from barbarity, it might be better to dispense altogether with the terms 'barbarous' and 'civilized' as being much too general to be informative. Instead, he proposed that they should be replaced with 'expressions of more definite censure and approbation'.[358] Unfortunately, Dunbar overlooked the emotional appeal of this ancient terminology and the innate human disposition to see the world in terms of binary opposites. The notion of what it meant to be 'civilized' went on expanding, but the polarity of 'barbarism' and 'civilization' would retain its rhetorical utility.

∂ 4 ∂

The Progress of Civilization

We look back on the savage condition of our ancestors with the triumph of superiority; we are pleased to mark the steps by which we have been raised from rudeness to elegance.

Thomas Warton, *The History of English Poetry* (1774–81)

The Ascent to Civility

Implicit in the notion of civility was a model of social development, the process of becoming civil, of being 'civilized'. Barbarians were seen as still living in something approaching the original state of mankind, whereas civilized peoples were assumed to have a history in a way that barbarians did not.

Many Tudor humanists embraced a classical notion that went back to Aeschylus, Protagoras, Moschion and other Greeks, but in early modern times was known chiefly through its elaboration by the Roman writers Cicero, Vitruvius and, especially,

Lucretius. This was the belief that mankind had originally lived like wild beasts in caves and forests and only later discovered fire, invented language, created civil societies and developed the arts and sciences.[1] It taught, as Thomas Starkey understood it, that early men, 'without city or town, law or religion', had 'wandered abroad in the wild fields and woods' before forsaking that 'rudeness and uncomely life' for 'this civility which you now see established'.[2]

Opinions differed as to the nature of the initial stimulus that had impelled human beings to come together to form political societies. Some suggested that it was the need to safeguard themselves against wild animals or, as Thomas Hobbes maintained, to secure protection against each other. Others postulated some natural cataclysm that had forced mankind into new modes of living, such as a great flood or a devastating forest fire. Some, following Cicero, attributed the change to the eloquence of heroic leaders such as Hercules, whose rhetorical power supposedly persuaded men to abandon their savage mode of life, or Orpheus, who employed his music to tame wild beasts and bring people 'from the violent current of natural cruelty to affability and courtesy': 'binding savage lives in civil chains', as the poet George Chapman put it in 1605 (Plate 20).[3] It was thanks to these founders of civil government, thought Sir William Temple in 1692, that the native inhabitants were brought from savage and brutish lives 'to the safety and convenience of societies, the enjoyment of property, the observance of orders, and the obedience of laws', which were followed by security, plenty, civility, riches, industry and all kinds of arts.[4]

Regardless of its particular variations, the theory that mankind had originally lived in a brutish condition was highly contentious. It clashed with the respected teaching of Aristotle, who held that human beings had always been naturally sociable. It also offended the Church because it conflicted with the biblical narrative in

Genesis, according to which the first men led a settled life, Adam as a gardener, Abel as a shepherd, and Cain as a tiller of the soil;* though some commentators attempted to reconcile the two narratives by arguing that it was only after the Flood that mankind had degenerated into becoming 'untame and uncivil'.[5] At first, people lived on the tops of mountains, thought the Jacobean poet George Sandys; then, little by little, they descended, 'changing their conditions with their places, and by how much nearer the sea, so much the more civil'.[6] This idea that civil society was a relatively late and entirely human construction was a secular one. It had appealed to a number of late medieval radical thinkers who were concerned with subjecting papal or monarchical power to constitutional control;[7] and for the same reason, it was vigorously condemned by seventeenth-century High Churchmen, anxious to preserve a sacred aura around royal authority.

In a canon of 1606, Convocation, the Church's legislative body, declared the idea of an original state of anarchy to be a serious error, on the grounds that Adam and the patriarchs who followed him had exercised a God-given political authority. That canon was republished in 1690 by Archbishop Sancroft on behalf of his fellow Nonjurors, the clergy who had refused to take the oath of allegiance to William III because he had ousted the lawful king, James II.[8] Earlier, in 1681, when Charles II was embarking on his period of absolute rule, a Wiltshire clergyman, preaching a sermon on 'The Necessity of Subjection', felt it necessary to deny the existence of an original state of nature: even the cruellest barbarians, he held, were sociable among themselves and had 'some kind of government'.[9]

---

* In his *Introductory Lectures on Political Economy* (1831), Richard Whately, Oxford's second professor of the subject, cited Genesis as proof that the first men did not live in a savage condition. He added that, since there was no record of a savage people rising to a civilized condition without the assistance of others who were already civilized, it followed that the first human beings must have owed their civility to divine agency. A similar argument had been made earlier by the Scottish schoolmaster Daniel Doig in his *Two Letters on a Savage State* (1792).

Bishop John Bramhall similarly sought to refute Thomas Hobbes's conception of the natural condition of mankind by maintaining that there never was 'such degenerate rabble of men without all religion, all government, all laws, natural and civil', not even 'amongst the most barbarous Americans'.[10] These defenders of divine hereditary right were very uncomfortable with the notion that there had ever been a time when people had roamed free from any form of government or subjection. They also maintained that, even if there had been such a time, human beings would still have shown kindness and compassion to each other.[11] But they failed to dislodge the widely held belief that the growth of civility had been a long, drawn-out process. As one of them admitted in 1670, Hobbes's picture of the original state of nature had been 'swallowed down . . . as an article of faith' and become 'the standard of our modern politics'.[12]

The suggestions made by classical thinkers about the nature of the civilizing process were resurrected in early modern times in the context of English relations with the Scots, the Irish and the Native Americans. A self-interested concern to find out how these supposedly barbarous or semibarbarous peoples could best be 'reduced to civility' (to 'reduce to' was to bring to) generated a keen interest in what Dugald Stewart would call a 'conjectural history' of the human ascent to a civilized condition.[13]

Civility, it was said, began when humans ceased to live by hunting wild creatures and started to domesticate them. 'Keeping some kind of cattle', thought Roger Williams, was 'some degree' of 'civility'; in 1656 the government of Virginia gave cows to the Native Americans in return for wolves' heads as 'a step to civilizing them'.[14] But pastoralists, always on the move with their herds and flocks, were perpetually involved in plunder and warfare. That had been the condition of the Scythians described by Herodotus and the northern barbarians in the writings of Caesar and Tacitus. According to one Elizabethan geographer, it was still that of the Tartars of central Asia, who lived 'after the manner of the old Scythians', sleeping under their carts, never staying long enough in any one place to justify sowing corn, but following their droves of cattle, drinking their milk and eating horseflesh.[15] This also had some resemblance to the Welsh and Irish ways of life as perceived by the twelfth-century author Gerald of Wales. Apparently echoing Varro, Lucretius and other classical sources, yet with only the faintest demonstrable debt to them,[16] Gerald asserted that mankind had progressed from the woods to the fields, and from the fields to settlements and towns. Portraying the Irish as the classical barbarians reborn, he identified pastoralism as 'the first mode of living' and, it has been claimed, identified its structural links with warfare in a manner that anticipated Edward Gibbon's celebrated analysis of the 'manners of pastoral nations' nearly five hundred years later. As Gibbon ironically remarked, 'The pastoral manners which have been adorned with the fairest attributes of peace and innocence are much better adapted to the fierce and cruel habits of a military life.'[17] Another twelfth-century work, the *Gesta Stephani*, similarly associated the warlike habits of the Welsh and the Scots with their pastoral mode of subsistence.[18]

In the sixteenth century, this interpretation was revived. 'Look into all countries that live in some sort by keeping of cattle,' urged Edmund Spenser, 'and you shall find that they are both very barbarous and uncivil, and also greatly given to war.'[19] The Bedouins of Arabia, who lived by grazing their cattle, were described in one of the accounts published by Samuel Purchas as 'wild men, amongst whom is no civil society, no truth nor civility': vagabonds, who had no towns or certain habitation, ate raw flesh and were constantly at war with everyone.[20] The traveller Fynes Moryson, who had served with English troops in Ireland, recalled that keeping cattle had been popular with 'the most strong and able bodies, and men given to spoils and robberies'; it suited their slothful dispositions, he thought, and made it easy for them to elude justice by taking their cattle to graze in the woods.[21]

There was, of course, a great deal more order to these apparently nomadic lives than hostile observers appreciated. The Irish were transhumant, moving their livestock seasonally, but they were not nomadic; and the notion that they had no agriculture was erroneous: in 1600 the English forces in Ireland deliberately cut down their corn so as to starve them into submission.[22] But like Gerald of Wales before them, English commentators approached the Irish with classically derived preconceptions about the nature of barbarism.[23] They recalled the Roman myth of the goddess Ceres, who, it was said, had invented the plough, tamed oxen to draw it and taught men to sow and grind wheat, thereby bringing 'those that lived afore after the manner of wild beasts into honest civility'.[24] Dislike of what appeared to be Irish nomadism was intensified by the suspicion among the English governing classes of 'masterless men' and vagrant poor. At home and abroad, their firm preference was for a population of fixed abode, firmly locked into a disciplined and hierarchical social structure.

The vital step towards civility, therefore, was the transition to settled agriculture and the cultivation of the soil, for it was notoriously the inhabitants of the forests and uncultivated wastes who were the most disorderly. Elizabethan propagandists for colonization in Ireland urged that the spread of arable farming would emancipate the natives from the endemic violence to which they were accustomed. Elizabeth I's secretary of state Sir Thomas Smith thought that civility would increase 'more by keeping men occupied in tillage than by idle following of herds, as the Tartarians, Arabians and Irishmen do'. Tillage, he argued, required the cultivators to be settled in one place and thus easier to control, by contrast with nomads, who were constantly on the move and intrinsically anarchic: it 'settleth the occupier, and what with tending his fallow, reap-tide, seed-time and threshing, it bindeth always the occupier to the land, and is a continual occupation of a great number of persons [and] a maintainer of civility'. It was also a great 'enemy to war'. There were accordingly a number of proposals that the Irish should be made to reduce their herds of cattle and prohibited from converting arable land into pasture.[25]

Tillage accustomed people to work all the year round, a way of life to which the 'uncivilized' were notoriously indisposed. The Welsh were said to dislike digging or indeed any form of physical labour; the 'wild Irish' were supposedly 'slothful, not regarding to sow and till their lands, nor caring for riches'; the Hebrideans were described as 'enemies of tillage', who 'wear out their days in hunting and idleness after the manner of beasts'; and in North America the Indian males, who similarly devoted their time to hunting and fighting, were said to be ready to 'fly into the woods' at any suggestion that they should engage in hard work.[26] Laziness bred poverty, and poverty was the source from which all other miseries proceeded: it enervated the spirits and made men dull, ignorant, brutish and dirty.[27] By contrast, regular employment, as the physician Peter Chamberlen explained in 1649, 'civilized' men and made them 'tractable and obedient to superiors' commands'. That was why Spenser wanted to have the Irish people 'tithed* and ordered, and every one bound to some honest trade of life'.[28] It was also why English colonists were shocked to discover that Native American men appeared to prefer starvation to work: 'We labour and work in building, planting, clothing ourselves, &c, and they do not.'[29] The Restoration divine Isaac Barrow believed that intensive labour raised people 'above rude and sordid barbarism' and generated 'all those arts whereby human life is civilized, and the world cultivated'. Productive industry was described by one commentator as 'the first step to civility'.[30]

A further step along the road from barbarism was the establishment of towns. For Thomas Starkey, civility was possible only in cities or castles.[31] The Elizabethan Lord Deputy of Ireland, Sir Henry Sidney, regarded towns as 'nurseries of civility'. Sir Thomas Smith thought that the more men resorted together, the more civil and obedient they became; and Edmund Spenser agreed: 'Nothing doth sooner cause civility in any country than many market towns.'[32]

---

* I.e., organized in 'tithings' (groups of householders answerable for each other's conduct).

The lawyer Richard Hakluyt stressed the need to gather raw materials: stone, slate and timber were 'things without which no city may be made nor people in civil sort be kept together'. To be 'scattered in small companies' was a 'hindrance to civility'.[33]

This was not a new idea. Aristotle had ruled that it was only in the city-state that the highest form of life could be lived. When the ancient Gauls began to encircle their towns with walls, the Romans took it as a sign that that they were moving towards a more civilized way of life (*ad usum vitae cultioris*).[34] In England from at least the twelfth century the association between market towns and cultivated living was generally recognized.[35] This was partly because their defensive structure provided their inhabitants with the security necessary for a collective life, what one seventeenth-century writer called 'the urbanity of walled towns'; partly 'by reason that people repairing often thither for their needs' would 'daily see and learn civil manners of the better sort'; and partly because they provided a market for agricultural produce, thus stimulating tillage and husbandry in the countryside.[36] An Elizabethan scholar explained that in the reign of Mary Tudor good behaviour was called *urbanitas* (urbanity) because it was 'rather found in cities than elsewhere': town life reduced barbarous ferocity and generated 'a certain mildness of manners'; trade and handicrafts were invented in towns; and only there did learning and the liberal arts flourish.[37] A sixteenth-century traveller in Africa assumed that those people who lived in towns and cities were 'likely to be somewhat more addicted to civility'.[38] In the eighteenth century, it was a commonplace that 'polished manners' arose in cities and spread outwards to the rest of society.[39]

True civility thus came to be seen as impossible without an adequate degree of economic development. Civil society needed husbandmen to till the soil and merchants to exchange necessary goods.[40] In Elizabethan times the accepted model was that of lowland England, a countryside of neatly cultivated fields, enclosed gardens and verdant pastures, dotted with fine manor houses for the gentry and punctuated by walled towns, where commerce could flourish.[41]

Propagandists for English colonization in Ireland were convinced that with orderly cultivation, the introduction of heritable private property in place of clan ownership and the growth of a market-oriented economy, the turbulent tribal society, dominated by a warrior aristocracy, would inexorably give way to a new, peaceful regime, with people locked into a disciplined and hierarchical social structure and animated by the profit motive.[42]

Most commentators, accordingly, agreed with James I's Lord Deputy of Ireland, who held that the love of money and goods would 'sooner effect civility than any other persuasion whatsoever'.[43] That was why the crew on one of Martin Frobisher's voyages in search of the Northwest Passage left behind for the 'brutish' Inuit a collection of 'bells, glasses, and other toys'. These objects, they thought, would 'embolden the barbarous people to use some courtesy'.[44] Samuel Purchas noted that people 'in the more southerly parts of Arabia' were 'better civilized' than the Bedouins in the north, because they had cities and trade, whereas the Bedouins continued to reckon their wealth in camels and flocks of sheep. The former English chaplain in Tangier observed in 1671 that the reason for the apparent 'stupidity and barbarism' of the Barbary Moors was that their whole time was 'spent gaining whereon to live, through a deficiency whereof the politest nations will soon degenerate into ignorance and rusticity'. It was, he thought, because of their poverty that the Moors had no equivalent of Europe's colleges and universities.[45]

Seventeenth-century England, by contrast, was seen as abounding not only in such necessities as meat, drink, clothes, houses and coaches, but also in 'wines, spices, drugs, fruits, silks, pictures, music, silver, gold, precious stones and all the other supports of grandeur and delight'. This abundance, claimed Sir Dalby Thomas in 1690, showed her to be 'a truly civilized and glorious nation indeed'.[46]

The conviction that commerce was a civilizing force is sometimes regarded as a late seventeenth- and early eighteenth-century phenomenon, a response by defenders of the merchant interest to the charge, levelled by devotees of the classical republican tradition, that the vast expansion of English foreign trade in the later seventeenth century had corrupted manners, weakened 'ancient virtue' and sapped the martial spirit by encouraging 'luxury' and, with it, a readiness to rely on a professional (and expensive) standing army to defend the country, rather than a national militia. It has also been linked to the need to defend paper credit and state borrowing against the allegations of corruption launched by country squires and political pamphleteers in an attempt to discredit the so-called moneyed interest – the stock-jobbers and investors in the public debt, whose numbers had multi-plied in response to the financial demands on governments made by the wars against France between 1689 and 1714. This 'ideological need' to defend commerce, it has been suggested, was responsible for launching the notion that it was trade that led to the refinement of manners,[47] a doctrine that was subsequently given wider circulation by Montesquieu in his *L'Esprit des lois* (1748).[48]

It is not surprising that some of the pamphleteering about trade and traders during these years should have provoked a response from the champions of Britain's role as a trading nation. The political econ-omist Charles Davenant defended the East India Company's export of bullion to pay for imports of Indian silks and calicoes, and he believed that it was in the country's interest to expand its foreign commerce as much as possible. Yet even Davenant was capable in 1699 of describing trade as 'a necessary evil'. 'In its nature a pernicious thing, it brings in that wealth which introduces luxury; it gives a rise to fraud and avarice, and extinguishes virtue and simplicity of manners; it depraves a people and makes way for that corruption which never fails to end in slavery, foreign or domestic.'[49] This indictment had a long tradition behind it. As a legal writer pointed out in 1602, both Plato and Aristotle had regarded 'merchandizing' as 'an enemy to virtue'.[50]

The defence against such charges drew on similarly ancient argu-ments, for the association of commerce with civility was very much older than the party politics of the reigns of William III and Anne.

Since at least the fourth century AD, it had been a Christian common-place that God had deliberately refrained from making any country self-sufficient in its natural resources so as to ensure that international trade would have to take place, thus encouraging 'love and society' and 'sociable conversation' between the peoples of the world.[51] In 1547 the future clerk of Edward VI's council boasted that 'our merchants do now traffic abroad', and had thereby 'obtained such knowledge of civility' that foreign visitors to England were as courteously received as in any other European kingdom. 'Traffic of one country with another,' agreed a sixteenth-century French historian and experienced traveller, was 'marvellous profitable and necessary, for by it civil society is kept.'[52] As Samuel Purchas explained in 1625, 'mutual commerce' was the mechanism by which the superfluity of one country supplied the necessities of another so that 'the whole world might be as one body of mankind'. Trade, it was urged, broadened people's horizons, softened their manners, made them more respectful towards foreigners, and bound the human race together in 'communion and fellowship'. It acquainted each nation with the language, manners, behaviour and customs of others; and it turned merchants into 'citizens of the world'. This, urged a writer in 1654, was 'a kind of community . . . which ought to be countenanced and encouraged'.[53] For the Jacobean chronicler Sir James Perrott, commerce with foreign nations was 'the chiefest means to beget civility'.[54]

In a world where Christians traded freely with Jews and Turks, and where seafaring nations observed a shared code of maritime etiquette, these were plausible claims.[55] Defenders of the merchant interest could reasonably argue that commerce fostered friendship, encouraged sociability and disseminated learning and the arts, even if their further claim that trade was also the greatest enemy of war was less convincing in an age of belligerent commercial competition between the Western European powers.[56] They could also point out that a civilized readiness to keep promises and to adapt tactfully to local customs was an essential ingredient of commercial success.

'Wherever commerce is introduced,' Adam Smith would write, 'probity and punctuality always accompany it. These virtues in a rude and barbarous country are almost unknown.'[57]

Stress on the civilizing power of trade became more insistent during the course of the seventeenth century. Bishop Sprat believed that 'traffic and commerce' had brought to mankind 'civility and humanity itself'. The antiquary Aylett Sammes declared that 'learning and science' were 'especially got by commerce'. John Evelyn agreed that it was trade that 'cultivated our manners' and civilized barbarous nations.[58] 'The great design of God Almighty,' thought the press licenser Edmund Bohun in 1696, was 'to civilise the whole race of mankind, to spread trade, commerce, arts, manufactures, and by them Christianity, from pole to pole round the whole globe of the earth.'[59] 'The more trade', said the ex-buccaneer William Dampier, 'the more civility', and 'the less trade, the more barbarity and inhumanity'.[60]

These sentiments became commonplace in the following century. Bernard Mandeville thought that 'the whole superstructure' of civil society was 'made up of the reciprocal services which men do to each other'. The economic writer Malachy Postlethwayt declared in 1751 that, in every country, the progress of trade advanced the arts and sciences, civility and urbanity. The historian William Robertson regarded merchants as 'the guardians of public tranquillity'.[61] Contemporaries spoke in the same breath of 'civil society and commerce', or 'the civilized and trading parts of the world'. The two practices – trade and civility – naturally went together, and the accumulation of individual wealth by commerce was persuasively justified.[62]

In the mid-eighteenth century, a number of writers, led by Adam Smith in Scotland and Anne-Robert-Jacques Turgot in France, formulated the 'stadial' theory: that mankind achieved civility by progressing through successive stages of development, each characterized by a distinctive mode of subsistence that shaped the nature of a society's government, laws, 'manners' and cultural life, and each carrying with it the seeds of further development into the next phase.

First came the Age of the Hunters, 'a way of life highly inimical to thought and reflection',[63] and one requiring few laws or regulations because there was no conception of property; then the Age of the Shepherds, which brought with it property in livestock and therefore the introduction of laws against theft; then the Age of Agriculture, with which came fixed settlement, property in land, and therefore more laws and regulations; and finally, as the most advanced stage, the Age of Commerce, and, with it, even more laws, together with the 'softening' of manners and the flourishing of literature, science and the arts.[64] Parallel to these phases of economic development went a corresponding enlargement in the intellectual powers of the human mind.[65]

This theory was based not on historical evidence, but on intelligent guesswork as to what was most likely to have happened in the past. Its ingredients had a long prehistory, going back to classical antiquity, with its many competing accounts of the social and economic evolution of mankind.[66] The theory also drew upon more recent essays in conjectural history. In 1520, for example, the German humanist Johannes Böhm (Boemus) (c. 1485–1535) offered a remarkable description of human progress from an original beastlike existence to a world of productive agriculture and handicraft, international trade, great cities, magnificent buildings, books, learning and refined behaviour. His work was translated into English in 1555 and again in 1611.[67]

The stadial theory was also influenced by the attempts of sixteenth- and early seventeenth-century Spanish thinkers to develop a taxonomy of barbarism in response to their encounter with the native peoples of Central and South America. It owed something to the speculations about the ascent from barbarism to civility offered at the same time by such French thinkers as Louis Le Roy and Pierre d'Avity, and it may have been influenced by the impressively coherent theory of social evolution put forward in the late sixteenth century by the Italian Giovanni Botero.[68] Implicit in Elizabethan proposals to make Ireland 'civil' by stimulating agriculture and trade, it was further developed in the writings of seventeenth-century natural lawyers, especially the German Samuel von Pufendorf, on the origins of property rights and their social and economic consequences,[69] and in Sir Isaac Newton's posthumously published *Chronology of Ancient Kingdoms Amended* (1728), which portrayed human evolution after the Flood as the story of successive phases of development based on changing modes of subsistence.[70] The decisive intervention was Montesquieu's crisp summary in 1748 of the four modes of subsistence and their different implications for law making.[71]

The mid-eighteenth-century version of the stadial theory was partly animated by a reforming desire to show that the entails which prevented the estates of the Scottish aristocracy from entering the land market were absurdly out of date in a commercial world and a hindrance to economic progress.[72] It drew its greatest strength from the long-standing readiness of the champions of the merchant community to represent trade as the culmination of the civilizing process.

An alternative version of the theory postulated only three stages: savagery, barbarism (or 'half-savagery'), and civility, based respectively on hunter-gathering, pastoralism and agriculture, with commerce as a necessary part of the age of agriculture rather than a separate stage.[73] This was Turgot's view. Lord Kames related the three stages to the evolution of property: hunter-gathering permitted only temporary possession; barbarism involved property in animals; and agriculture created property in land. Only the third stage brought with it a regular system of government and connected individuals in 'an intimate society of mutual support'.[74] Adam Ferguson distinguished between savages with no property, barbarians with property but no laws, and those in civil society with property and laws.[75]

The concept of civility thus offered a historical perspective as well as a geographical one. Most proponents of the stadial theory presupposed the original uniformity of mankind and the subsequent development of all peoples in the same direction, though at differing speeds. Cultural differences were the result of some societies being further ahead than others: their styles of music, dance and poetry, for example, reflected the stage they had reached in the ascent from savagery to civilization.[76] The aboriginal inhabitants of North America were thus said to present 'a very striking picture of the most distant antiquity'.[77] Some commentators discerned a cycle in which civility periodically fell back into barbarism, just as human beings rose to maturity only to dwindle away in old age. Greece, for instance, 'of old, the seat of civility, mother of sciences and humanity', was 'now forlorn, the nurse of barbarism, a den of thieves'. Imperial Rome had also reverted in later centuries to weakness and obscurity: 'the brand which had filled the world with its flames sunk like a taper in the socket'.[78] Nearer home, there was the example of the Anglo-Norman settlers of Ireland (the 'Old English'), who had degenerated under the bad influence of the Gaelic Irish.[79] As the learned clergyman George Hakewill remarked in 1635, 'the most civil nations' of his day might in the future become barbarous again, and 'the most barbarous be civilized'.[80]

Nevertheless, a Jacobean Oxford tutor could assure his pupils that 'in these late ages nations generally throughout the world have been more civilized than heretofore, commonwealths and learning more flourished, and mutual commerce more used'.[81] Francis Bacon thought that the improvement of navigation and trade meant that intellectual horizons had vastly widened since the days of classical antiquity; superior work in natural philosophy could be expected as a result. In 1667 the historian of the Royal Society was equally certain that the 'arts and civility' of his age far exceeded those of the Greeks and Romans. It was true, he admitted, that many peoples in northern Europe and Asia, and almost all the population of sub-Saharan Africa, were still in the state of nature; but there was no reason to think that in the course of time they would not lay aside 'the untamed wildness of their present manners'. Ten years later, Sir William Petty reflected, 'If man hath improved so much in the several past centuries and ages of the world, how far he might proceed in six thousand years more.' By this time an optimistic belief in the possibility of unceasing social, economic and intellectual progress was widespread.[82] This conviction would become a crucial feature of Western civilization.[83] Moreover, there was no telling what improvements had already been effected in faraway countries. The future bishop Joseph Hall thought in 1609 that there might be people 'still more civil than we are' in 'Terra Australis'.[84]

The social philosophers of the eighteenth century discerned what they called 'a natural progress from ignorance to knowledge, and from rude to civilized manners'; and they saw it as a potentially endless process. 'What we now admire as the height of improvement,' wrote the Scottish preacher Hugh Blair, 'may in a few ages hence be considered as altogether rude and imperfect.'[85] It was also coming to be accepted that a nation which did not advance was doomed to fall backwards. In the seventeenth century, it was recognized that China and India had manufacturing techniques in, respectively, porcelain and textiles from which the West had much to learn. Sir William Temple noted in 1690 that 'the greatest, richest, and most populous kingdom now known in the world' was China. He described it as 'framed and policed with the utmost force and reach of human wisdom, reason, and contrivance', exceeding 'all those imaginary schemes of European wits', such as Plato's *Republic*, More's *Utopia* or Harrington's *Oceana*.[86] Yet in the eighteenth century, most Enlightenment philosophers regarded India, China and Japan as commercial societies that had atrophied. The British ambassador to Peking in 1792 reported that the Chinese, once 'a very civilized people' by comparison with their European contemporaries, had failed to sustain their progress: 'Whilst we have been every day rising in arts and sciences, they are actually become a semi-barbarous people in comparison with the present nations of Europe.'[87]

Despite this discouraging example, the advance from rudeness to refinement, from barbarism to civility, was the guiding preoccupation of eighteenth-century Scottish social philosophers.* From David Hume onwards, historians similarly came to see their central task as charting the history of 'manners' in order to explain what T. B. Macaulay in 1848 would call 'the long progress from poverty and barbarism to the highest degrees of opulence and civilization'.[88] Lord Kames, for example, sought to trace the history of law 'from its rudiments among savages, through successive changes, to its highest improvements in a civilized society'.[89] This progress was also a popular theme for poets.[90] Cultural and material differences between peoples were perceived as varying points on one single scale, with Western Europe, and Britain in particular, at the very peak. 'I may say without any vainglorious boast, or without great offence to anyone,' declared the mid-Victorian prime minister Lord Palmerston, 'that we stand at the head of moral, social and political civilization.'[91]

In the early modern period, it was believed that civility had moved over the centuries from East to West. The architect John Webb noted that Sir Walter Ralegh, in his *History of the World* (1614), had related that 'from the East came the first knowledge of all things, and that the East parts of the world were the first civilized, having Noah himself as an instructor, whereby the farther East to this day, the more civil, the farther West, the more savage'.[92] Samuel Purchas thought that the long train of cultural transmission had originated in Armenia (where Noah's Ark had settled) and eventually reached England via Assyria, Egypt ('as it were an university to all the world'), Greece, Rome, the Saracens (Muslims), Italy and France.[93] Civility, it was generally agreed, had begun in Asia and North Africa, but when those areas succumbed to barbarism, it had found a new home in

---

* When the young James Boswell went to dinner in 1762 with George Home, son of Lord Kames, he was disconcerted to find that the conversation was about the differences between a 'rude' and a 'polished' state of society: 'I kept up a *retenue* [i.e., restrained myself] and spoke only when I was sure that I was right'; *Boswell's London Journal 1762–1763*, ed. Frederick A. Pottle (1950), 48.

Europe, 'in civility . . . the youngest' of the three continents.[94] Europe, noted a Gloucestershire gentleman in the 1660s, 'hath in civility and knowledge, at least in our opinions who are inhabitants thereof, outstripped her sister Asia, where we are taught that man was first planted'. Though vaguely conscious of their debt to the Islamic learning of the early Middle Ages, his contemporaries celebrated Europe's superior forms of government, her productive industry, her extensive trade, and the unmatched politeness of her inhabitants, which made other continents seem rude and barbarous in comparison.[95] Western Europe, in particular, stood out, for the Eastern part of the continent was regarded as distinctly lower in the scale of civilization.[96] A Scottish writer declared in 1700 that England, France and Italy far excelled other countries 'for politeness and civility, for grandeur and magnificence, and for arts and inventions, and the public encouragement of them'. His compatriot David Hume took it for granted that French and English gentlemen were the most civilized rank of men in the world's two most civilized nations.[97]

It seems clear that during the seventeenth century Western Europeans forged ahead in navigation, military capacity, property rights, commercial organization and financial institutions. They took the lead in literature, natural science and technological inventiveness; they had unique access to the resources of the New World; and their women enjoyed more personal freedom than elsewhere. It is, however, far from certain that calorific consumption, life expectancy and overall productivity were higher in Europe than everywhere else until, at the earliest, the middle of the eighteenth century.[98] Yet from the late sixteenth century onwards, the visual representation of Europe by Europeans, whether in maps or ceramics or pictorial imagery, was unashamedly triumphalist.[99] Two hundred years later, as the writings of Edmund Burke reveal, the notion of a distinctively European civilization was common currency.[100]

For a reminder of what life had been like without civility one had only to look back to the ancient Britons. No people had been more barbarous than they: naked, filthy, ignorant and 'almost as savage', thought John Aubrey, 'as the beasts whose skins were their only raiment'. For the future bishop John Bridges, preaching in 1571, they were 'naked like Irishmen, painted like devils, fierce like Scythians'. The Elizabethan historian William Camden described them as 'altogether uncivilized, perfectly rude and wholly taken up in wars', while the Jacobean geographer Nathanael Carpenter asserted that they lived 'almost in the condition of wild beasts in woods and deserts, feeding like swine on herbs and roots, without law or discipline'.[101] There was disagreement as to whether 'our uncivilized predecessors' (as Sir Thomas Browne called them) had been quite as uncivil as the Native Americans or whether they were perhaps 'two or three degrees less savage'. But 'uncivilized' they undoubtedly were (Plate 14).[102] In the later eighteenth century, Edmund Burke believed that, 'like all barbarians', the Britons had been 'fierce, treacherous and cruel'.[103]

Although there was a legend that civility had been brought to Albion by the Trojan Brutus, most educated persons believed, after reading Caesar, Tacitus and other classical sources, that it was the Roman Conquest which had civilized the Britons by subjecting them to law and introducing them to the liberal arts. 'The Romans with their victories,' wrote the Elizabethan mathematician Thomas Digges, 'drove barbarism out of our countries by leaving us a pattern of more civil life.' A Jacobean author put it more strongly, declaring that, but for the Romans, his fellow countrymen would have remained 'overgrown satyrs, rude and untutored in the woods, dwelling in caves, and hunting for our dinners (as the wild beasts in the forests for their prey), prostituting our daughters to strangers, sacrificing our children to idols, nay eating our own children'.[104] Echoing Tacitus, the architect Inigo Jones asserted that the Romans had taught the Britons 'the knowledge of the arts, to build stately temples, palaces, public buildings, to be elegant in foreign languages, and by their habits and attire attain the qualities of a civil and well-ordered people' (Plate 21).[105] The Romans 'beat us into some civility', agreed John

Milton, 'likely else to have continued longer in a barbarous and savage manner of life, if God had not sent the Romans to civilize us'. But for them, thought Edmund Bohun, the English might still be going naked and painted with woad.[106]

When the Romans left Britain, it was said, the country had reverted to barbarism. The Anglo-Saxons were notoriously ignorant, uncultivated, feud-ridden and violent. Edmund Spenser thought that, in the first centuries after their arrival, England was infested by robbers and outlaws, 'very like to Ireland as it now stands'. Milton regarded the Anglo-Saxons as a barbarous and heathen nation, famous for nothing else but robberies and cruelties, while David Hume described them as 'in general a rude, uncultivated people, ignorant of letters, unskilled in the mechanical arts, untamed to submission under law and government, addicted to intemperance, riot and disorder'.[107]

The twelfth-century historian William of Malmesbury had traced the emergence of a gentler mode of life, beginning in the sixth century with the introduction of Christianity to the court of King Ethelbert of Kent, and advancing further in the ninth century with King Egbert of Wessex, who had been to France, a country whose polished manners were unrivalled, and his grandson King Alfred, who established internal peace and fostered learning. After them, things went into reverse and, in William's opinion, it was only with the arrival of the Norman conquerors that the civilizing process was renewed.[108] His views were frequently echoed in the early modern period. The Earl of Clarendon believed that, in Anglo-Saxon times, 'civility was hardly admitted into the nation', whereas Norman manners 'did very much polish the roughness of our native temper ... We grew possessed of that civility and discretion that made us fit for commerce and conversation with the other parts of the world.' Sir William Temple similarly declared that, as result of the Norman Conquest, 'we gained more learning, more civility, more refinement of language, customs and manners, from the great resort of other strangers, as well as [the] mixture of French and Normans'.[109] Looking back on England's history, Edmund Burke in 1775 attributed the country's 'progressive increase of improvement' to 'a succession of civilizing conquests and civilizing settlements'.[110]

This view of the Romans and Normans as civilizing agents was highly contested. Conventional assumptions about civility and barbarism had been much influenced by the Roman model. But they were challenged by a strongly anticlassical current of thought, driven partly by the belief that the Romans' values were intrinsically pagan and partly by the feeling that their civilization had been marked by 'excessive cruelty'. The connoisseur Roger North confessed that he preferred the morality of the Goths to that of the Greeks and Romans. Daniel Defoe thought that their taste for gladiatorial sports and throwing criminals to wild animals showed that the Romans were 'very far from a people civilized'; their invasion of Britain was 'an unjust, bloody, tyrannical assault upon the poor Britons, against all right and property, against justice and neighbourhood, and merely carried on for conquest and dominion'.[111] The seventeenth-century physician and writer Philip Kinder dismissed the Romans as 'uncivilized' on the bizarre grounds that they did not know what gloves were until they learnt about them from the Greeks and that their surnames were 'beggarly, rude, [and] barbarous'.[112] At the end of the eighteenth century, Joseph Priestley agreed that the Romans 'long remained strangers to true politeness': they 'had no visiting days, no balls, no assemblies of noblemen and persons of distinction at ladies' houses'. Mary Wollstonecraft regarded them as 'half civilized' because of their cruelties and their 'unnatural vices'.[113]

Welsh historians claimed that the Britons were civilized before the Romans ever arrived. Writing in the mid-sixteenth century, Sir John Price declared that there had never been a time when ancient Britain lacked learned men skilled in the liberal arts: the Britons had become literate as early as the Romans, and possibly earlier. His compatriot Humphrey Llwyd asserted in 1573 that 'philosophy and the liberal sciences were known to the Celtae and Britons before they were to the Greeks and Latins'.[114] The Britons, agreed the common lawyer George Saltern in 1605, had not been 'barbarous', but were a 'civil' people living under 'good laws', with 'many good cities, kings, nobles, governors, discipline of war and peace, commerce, and traffic with foreign nations, and all other parts of civility'. The poet Michael Drayton concurred:

So barbarous nor were we, as many have us made,
And Caesar's envious pen would all the world persuade.[115]

In 1695 Edward Lhwyd's contributions to the 1695 edition of Camden's *Britannia*, based on his researches into Celtic archaeology, revealed the existence before the Romans arrived of silver and gold coins, elaborate metalwork and huge stone monuments whose erection must have required considerable political organization and technical skill. Lhwyd admitted that these structures were 'rude' and 'barbarous', but claimed that they were no more so than 'those of our neighbour nations before they were conquered by the Romans'; and he confessed that he had originally assumed that some of the metal artefacts were Roman, 'supposing them too artificial to have been made by the Britons before the Romans civilized them'.[116]

The notion of Anglo-Saxon barbarism was rejected by apologists for the Church of England, notably the Elizabethan archbishop Matthew Parker, who saw in the Anglo-Saxon Church a proto-Protestant institution largely independent of the papacy. William Camden noted the Anglo-Saxons' receptivity to Christianity and their contribution to the English language; he praised their 'valour and prowess' and regarded them as a 'warlike, victorious, stiff, stout and vigorous nation'.[117] Similarly, many English common lawyers maintained that it was the Anglo-Saxons who had founded Parliament, the jury system and other bulwarks of English freedom. The Normans, by contrast, were, like the Romans, widely disparaged as people of 'a certain martial barbarousness', cruel tyrants who had conquered

England by violence, introduced barbarous land laws, and abridged the nation's liberties.[118]

Nationalist sentiment of a vaguely racial kind led many eighteenth-century English antiquarians to take an intense interest in the ancient Britons, Goths and Anglo-Saxons, all of whom could be seen as embodying satisfactory alternatives to the ideals of classical civilization. Henry St John, Lord Bolingbroke, thought that their laws and system of government revealed that the Goths and Lombards, whom the Romans had represented as barbarous, were not barbarians at all. The poet William Blake believed that the ancient Britons had been 'naked, civilized men, plain in their acts and manners, wiser than after-ages', but 'overwhelmed by brutal arms'.[119]

The progress of civility in the centuries following the Norman Conquest was widely asserted to have been very slow. In the sixteenth century, classically minded humanists, zealous Protestants and apologists for the Tudor dynasty united in portraying the Middle Ages as a barbarous era of Gothic ignorance, popish darkness, feudal oppression and political disorder.[120] Early Italian humanists had maintained that it was not until the fourteenth century that art and literature began to recover from the darkness into which Europe had been plunged after the barbarian invasions of the Roman Empire. In their eyes, whatever was not classical, whether language or architecture or philosophy, was to be regarded as 'barbarous'.[121] Their influence can be seen on the many Tudor scholars who saw themselves as living in a more cultivated age, one fully at home in Greek and Latin literature. Edmund Spenser claimed that the English had been 'brought unto that civility that no nation in the world excelleth them in all goodly conversation and all the studies of knowledge and humanity'. Francis Bacon asserted that in 'manners, civility, learning and liberal sciences', as well as in other respects, 'the state of this nation was never more flourishing'. The Elizabethan town clerk of Tewkesbury, John Barston, thought that no country in the world enjoyed so much internal peace and quietness, the people displaying 'more humanity and civil behaviour' than in the 'unhappy times past'.[122]

Nevertheless, Tudor humanists continued to express concern about the lingering 'barbarity' of the English language, English poetry and English law. They were very conscious of being relatively late converts to Renaissance learning and to the Italian code of civil behaviour. In the preface to his translation of Castiglione's *Il Cortegiano* (1560), Sir Thomas Hoby lamented that England had been regarded as barbarous 'time out of mind'. In the 1590s Edmund Spenser remarked that it was 'but even the other day since England grew civil', and the poet Gabriel Harvey observed that it was 'not long since' that 'eloquence in speech and civility in manners arrived in these parts of the world'. Francis Osborne, author of the popular *Advice to a Son* (1655–58), agreed: the English were 'the last arrival within the pale of civility'. 'To whatever politeness we may suppose ourselves already arrived,' wrote the 3rd Earl of Shaftesbury fifty years later, 'we must confess that we are the latest barbarous, the last civilized or polished people of Europe.' England's 'arts and civil accomplishments', he thought, had come at second or third hand 'from other states, courts, academies, and foreign nurseries of wit and manners'. In 1758 David Hume put it more strongly: every improvement in agriculture and manufactures over the previous two centuries had arisen from imitation of foreigners: 'Had they not first instructed us we should have been at present barbarians.'[123]

In the century after the Reformation, therefore, it was usual to claim that it was only recently that the country had emerged from a time of mental, religious and political darkness. Catholics might look back wistfully to the medieval centuries as an age of faith and charity, lawyers respect them as a crucial period of judicial innovation, scholars admire their philosophers, and the common people cherish the myth of a bygone Merry England. The exiled Jesuit Robert Persons even claimed in 1582 that no Christian people had been 'better framed to courtesy and humanity' or 'more disposed to beneficence and friendly behaviour' than the English, until the Protestant heresy 'dissolved the bonds of love and amity'.[124] But the official view of the Protestant establishment was expressed by Sir Henry Wotton, who believed that 'the combustions and tumult of the Middle Age' had 'uncivilized' English literature, and by the Restoration bishop Simon Patrick, who rejoiced that in his day 'monastic barbarism' had been superseded by 'politeness and elegancy'.[125]

In the late seventeenth and eighteenth centuries, many features of medieval life were denounced as 'barbarous', from chivalric jousting to trial by ordeal or combat.[126] Sir Christopher Wren's son agreed with John Evelyn that Gothic architecture had been introduced by 'those truculent people from the North ... overrunning the civilized world'; the preacher Hugh Blair thought that the duelling code of honour derived from 'the ferocious barbarity of Gothic manners'; and the agriculturalist Arthur Young regarded open-field farmers as 'Goths and Vandals'.[127] The poet William Julius Mickle elaborated on the 'mental darkness' of the 'monkish ages', the medieval 'ferocity of manners' and the 'most absolute tyranny' of 'the feudal system'.[128] The historian William Robertson offered a more balanced view of the medieval period, stressing its contribution to the regular administration of justice, the establishment of representative government and the end of domestic slavery. Yet he also thought of it as the time when people had not yet attained 'that degree of refinement which introduces a sense of decorum and propriety in conduct, as a restraint on those passions which lead to heinous crimes'. The most common view was that the nation did not begin to be 're-civilized' until the sixteenth century: only then did England shake off its 'Gothic rust' and begin 'to imitate its neighbours in politeness'.[129]

Contemporaries were very conscious that the supply of goods and amenities had hugely increased since the medieval period. In 1702 a writer remarked that no people had ever advanced so many arts, sciences and trades to such a high point and so rapidly as the English of his day: he pointed to the progress made over the last half-century in weaving, glassmaking, building, japanning, sugar making, distilling and navigation.[130] By contrast, the English at the beginning of the sixteenth century were, in David Hume's opinion, still 'an uncultivated nation'; he cited the 5th Earl of Northumberland (d. 1527), whose castle had few fires, no chimneys, no glass windows but only glimmering candles, 'ragamuffins of servants and retainers', no vegetables, and salt beef and mutton for nine months of the year. Just as John Locke (and after him Adam Smith) said that an English day labourer was better fed, lodged and clad than an American Indian king, so Hume declared that a footman in the current Duke of Northumberland's household was better off than the head of the family had been two hundred and fifty years previously. In his influential *History of England* (1754–61), he dated 'the dawn of science and civility' to the reign of Henry VII: thereafter, 'men gradually attained that situation with regard to commerce, arts, science, government, police, and cultivation in which they have ever since persevered'.[131]

Even so, the country's progress towards civility was far from straightforward. Hume thought that the absolute government of Elizabeth I was as authoritarian as that of eighteenth-century Turkey: if the royal power to grant monopolies had not been subsequently abridged, 'England, the seat of riches, and arts, and commerce, would have contained at present as little industry as Morocco or the coast of Barbary'. By contrast, the Revolution of 1688, establishing limited monarchy, was accomplished by what had become 'a great and civilised nation'; its makers compared very favourably with the 'turbulent and barbarous aristocracy' who had dethroned Richard II in 1399.[132] Most of Hume's contemporaries agreed that their era was indeed more 'civilized' and 'polished' than any of its predecessors, and they felt the better for it. As Bernard Mandeville put it, the more that men were civilized, the happier they became. 'Elegant living may hurry mankind into luxury and licentiousness,' reflected a Westmorland clergyman in 1770, 'but God be praised that I was not born in the days of ignorance, cruelty and barbarism.'[133]

Barbarous Neighbours

It was in this conviction that their own refined civility had been achieved only by a long process of historical evolution that the English contemplated the other peoples of the world. Most of them would have agreed with the geologist John Woodward, who in 1695 regarded 'the far greater part of the world' as 'still barbarous and savage'.[134] Those with some academic education thought this retarded condition was caused by the physical environment: climate, soil and altitude supposedly shaped the temperature of people's bodies and 'natural dispositions'. A cosmology inherited from Aristotle and Hippocrates taught that those who lived either too near the sun or too far away from it were cruel and barbarous by nature, lacking laws, sciences and civility, and unable to govern themselves in an orderly and rational fashion.[135] It was because he subscribed to this notion that those who inhabited the intemperate zones, whether hot or cold, were 'more brutish, simple and savage' that Sir Thomas Palmer concluded in 1606 that the people of Africa, America, Magellanica (the Southern Pacific), northeast Europe and Asia were 'by nature barbarists'. Similarly, John Ogilby in 1671 thought that the natives of the Andes came much nearer to 'the civility and ... subtlety of the Europeans' than did other Americans because their climate resembled that of Europe.[136] Diet was also important, for it was believed that the humoral balance of the body was affected by the foodstuffs it ingested. 'One of the chiefest causes of the savages' inhuman cruelty', wrote the colonial promoter Sir William Vaughan in 1630, was their habit of eating the flesh of wolves and bears. In Sir Matthew Hale's opinion, it was the abundance of easily accessible wild fruit in hot and fertile countries that robbed the inhabitants of any incentive to engage in cultivation.[137]

'Less civilized' people were increasingly seen as stuck at an earlier stage of development. The 'new found lands', it was said, contained many peoples resembling 'the first men, without letters, without laws, without kings, without commonwealths, without arts'. The Tartars still lived by hunting, just as the ancient Germans had done; and the Inuit women painted their faces blue like the ancient Britons. Thomas Hobbes was typical in regarding the Native Americans as an example of what other nations had been 'in former ages' before they became 'civil and flourishing'.[138]

Some examples of this retarded development were nearer home. In the Middle Ages, the Welsh appeared barbarous to their English neighbours because of their pastoral economy, their kin-based social structure and the way in which they made warfare a way of life: all very different from the English ideal of arable cultivation, towns, markets and a monetized economy, governed by local gentry and overseen by a powerful monarch. Moreover, Welshmen ignored the laws of war, killing male captives and enslaving women and children.[139] Edward I's defeat of the Welsh princes in 1282–83 was followed by the English Crown's annexation of their principality, which covered half of Wales, the rest remaining split between the various marcher lordships. At the same time, Welsh law and administration were partly converted to the English model. In the fourteenth century, a chronicler reported that the Welsh had begun to cultivate fields and gardens, live in towns, wear shoes and sleep in beds in the English manner.[140] Yet in the early sixteenth century, the historian Polydore Vergil could still report that, because Welsh land was mostly barren or uncultivated, the people lived on oaten bread and watered milk and supplemented their income with theft and robbery. Wales contained 'many rude and beastly people', agreed Vergil's contemporary, the physician Andrew Boorde.[141]

The change came with the Tudor statutes of 1536 and 1543, which extended the principality and the common law to the whole of the country, thereby making the monarch the largest landowner, bringing the marcher lordships into the shire system created for the principality in 1284, and consolidating Wales into a single political, judicial and administrative unit overseen by the Council in the

Marches and the Court of Great Sessions.[142] 'By the union of these shires in traffic [commerce], alliances, and common justice', wrote Francis Bacon, Wales was 'reduced' to 'civility and peace'. Bishop Rowland Lee found Wales 'very wild' when he became president of the Council in the Marches in 1534, but his draconian law enforcement was said to have brought the country to 'good civility' before he died in 1543.[143] His colleague, the Bishop of St David's, urged the founding of grammar schools and the moving of his remote see to Carmarthen with the aim of eliminating the people's 'barbarous ignorance' and replacing their 'Welsh rudeness' by 'English civility'.[144] According to one of Elizabeth I's administrators, however, it was Henry VIII's introduction of itinerant justices that proved crucial in bringing Wales 'to know civility'. Between 1550 and 1600, the Court of Great Sessions hanged some four thousand Welsh thieves. In 1576 the vice president of the Council in the Marches rejected complaints about continuing disorder, declaring that 'in Wales universally' there were 'as civil people and [as] obedient to law as are in England'. Indeed, the Welsh took to litigation so enthusiastically that they clogged up the courts with petty suits.[145] When in 1640 the Long Parliament proposed to abolish the criminal jurisdiction of the Council in the Marches, its defenders claimed that it had played a key role in 'reducing and civilizing' the king's subjects in Wales.[146]

Common to contemporary discussions of Welsh society was the assumption that 'civility' meant being law abiding and obedient to the regime. But the term also had wider implications. In the late 1560s it was said that the Welsh had begun 'to inhabit towns, to learn occupations, to exercise merchandise, to till the ground well, and to do all other kinds of public and necessary functions as well as Englishmen'. Upwardly mobile Welshmen got on well in English society because they were supposedly 'more given to the culture and trimming of their bodies (like Spaniards) . . . and . . . very apt to learn court-like behaviour'.[147] In 1612 Sir John Davies (English-born, but

THE COVRT
of ciuill Courtesie.

Fitlie furnished vvith

a pleasant port of stately phrases and pithy
precepts: assembled in the behalfe of all
young Gentlemen, and others, that are
desirous to frame their behauiour
according to their estates, at
all times, and in all
companies.

Therby to purchase worthy praise
of their inferiours: and estimation and credite among
their betters.

Out of the Italian, by
S. R. Gent.

Imprinted at London
by Richard Ihones.
1 5 9 1.

1 The publisher of this Elizabethan guide to courteous behaviour enhances its appeal by claiming
that it is a translation of a treatise by an Italian nobleman. The author urges young men to cultivate 'a
comely audacity without a saucy presumption'.

2 Medieval table manners: a fifteenth-century Flemish artist contrasts the sedate comportment of temperate diners with the unrestrained greed of their social inferiors.

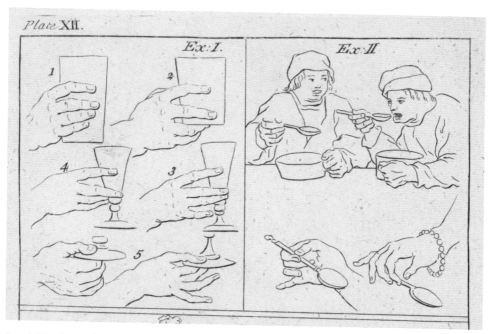

Plate XII.

Ex: I.

Ex: II

3 and 4 In this guide for early-eighteenth-century artists, a 'clownish peasant' is seen putting his elbows on the table, grasping his porringer, and eating in a greedy and disorderly way, whereas a 'better bred' person sits upright and holds the porringer by one ear and the spoon by three fingers.

Social differences are similarly reflected in the different ways of holding a wine glass. Note how the Earl of Godolphin, formerly Queen Anne's first minister (third from the right), holds his in the approved, though distinctly precarious, manner.

5 Elizabethan aristocratic swagger: the queen's favourite, Robert Dudley, Earl of Leicester, portrayed by an unknown Anglo-Netherlandish artist around 1575.

6 The mannered posture of a fashionable French dancing master, depicted by William Hogarth in 1735.

7 The epitome of politeness: Captain William Wade, master of ceremonies at the Bath assembly rooms, and much admired for the elegance of his dress and manners, painted by Thomas Gainsborough in 1771.

8 Designed in the reign of Charles II as a grand processional route, the Mall in St James's Park soon became a place of fashionable resort.

9 Provincial cities and towns also had their promenades for polite society, as here in York, with its New Terrace Walk, constructed in the 1730s on the banks of the River Ouse.

10 This London coffeehouse of *c.* 1700 is shown as a place where men read the newspapers and discuss politics.

11 In Hogarth's 'A Midnight Modern Conversation' (1733), the polite sociability of the St John's Coffee House, Temple Bar, has degenerated into a drunken orgy.

12 Protestant cruelty: the fate awaiting Catholic missionary priests in Elizabethan England, as depicted by an exiled sympathizer.

13 Barbarous Northerners: a hostile view of the Laplanders, Livonians and Scotsmen whom Catholics believed to be part of the army assembled by the Swedish king Gustavus Adolphus for his invasion of Germany in 1630.

14 and 15 The ancient inhabitants of Britain as imagined by the Elizabethan artist John White. 'Warrior neighbour of the Picts' (left) carries a sixteenth-century sword, but has no shoes. The bodily decoration of the ancient 'Pict Warrior' from northern Scotland (below) echoes that of the Native Americans whom White had encountered in the Roanoke Colony.

16 Elizabethan troops return with their trophy heads after wiping out a band of kerns ('wild Irish' foot soldiers).

English Protestantes stroped naked & turned
into the mountaines, in the frost, & snowe, whereof many hundreds are perished to death,
& many liynge dead in diches & Sauages
upbraided them saynge now are ye wilde
Irisch as well as wee.

17 In the rebellion of 1641 the 'wild Irish' had their revenge.

C. Smith taketh the King of Pamavukee prisoner 1608

18 One of the daring encounters with Native Americans of which John Smith, leader of the Virginia colonists between 1607 and 1609, subsequently boasted.

19 This copy of a lost drawing by John White shows the attempt of the Eskimos (Inuit) in 1577 to repel Martin Frobisher's men in their quest for gold on Baffin Island. It accurately depicts the Eskimos' dress, weapons, tents and kayak.

20 Orpheus charms savage people into accepting civilized life: the first scene in James Barry's decorative scheme, *The Progress of Human Knowledge and Culture*, painted for the Royal Society of Arts in 1777–83.

21 William Hamilton's late-eighteenth-century representation of Julius Agricola, the first-century AD governor of Britain, introducing Roman arts and sciences to the British. The caption observes that the 'astonished' inhabitants 'soon became fond of the arts and manners of their cruel invaders'.

Julius Agricola a Roman Governor in Britain under the Emperor Domitian, introducing the Roman Arts & Sciences into ENGLAND, the Inhabitants of which are astonished & soon become fond of the Arts & manners of their cruel Invaders.

22 Many high-born ladies in the seventeenth and eighteenth centuries kept a black child as an exotic toy. This unidentified woman is possibly the young widow, Lady Anne Rich, future wife of the 5th Earl of Exeter.

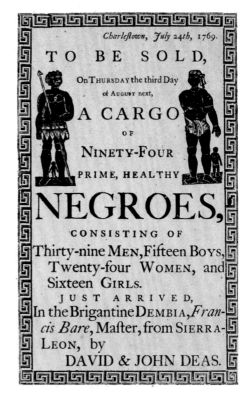

23 A handbill advertising a South Carolina slave auction in 1769.

24 The parents of this nine-year-old Australian aboriginal boy died of smallpox in 1789, and he was adopted by an English surgeon. Thomas Watling's poignant drawing is remarkable for its human sympathy.

25 Robert Smirke's painting of the cession of Matavai to Captain Wilson shows the local chief and his docile people in 1797 granting a shipload of Christian missionaries access to a district of Tahiti.

26 Fights between women were not uncommon in Hanoverian London. This is Thomas Rowlandson's depiction of a 'brawling and scratching' match between two 'drunken drabs'.

27 Plebeian lack of deference: when the driver refuses to move the haughty lady's coach from blocking the road, a bespattered London mob ignores her protests and tramples its way through the carriage itself.

28 Xenophobic masculinity: in this engraving of 1770, a pugnacious butcher, purveyor of the national dish, roast beef, offers to fight a richly dressed but cowardly and effeminate Frenchman, while a prostitute pulls his pigtail.

of Welsh ancestry) could claim that Wales 'hath attained to that civility of manners, and plenty of all things, as now we find it not inferior to the best parts of England'. Yet his contemporary Sir Clement Edmondes thought that the Welsh custom of 'Hooboub' (*hwbwb*, i.e., hue and cry) savoured of 'barbarism rather than of any civil government'; and in 1611 it was said of the Welsh that 'though they be much improved, yet do they not equal the English in civility'.[148] Hostile English writers and travellers continued to regard the inhabitants of Wales as rude, boorish and dirty.[149] A visitor to the 'wild mountainous country' of Radnorshire in 1756 reported that his trip had given him 'an idea of our nation before it became better cultivated and more civilised'. Twenty years later, an American traveller to Wales encountered 'remains of barbarism and uncivilization'. The Hon. John Byng, touring Wales in the 1780s and 1790s, found the inhabitants still 'inferior to the common English in civility' and was greatly repelled by the 'filth and nastiness' of Welsh bodies.[150]

When discussing the Scots, informed contemporaries drew a sharp distinction between Highlanders and Lowlanders. The latter, explained William Camden, were 'more civilized' and used 'the language and habit of the English; the other more rude and barbarous, and use[d] that of the Irish'. As a clan-ridden and warlike society, the Highlanders possessed all the standard barbarian attributes, for their primary loyalty was to their kindred rather than to the state. Although they engaged in cultivation when the terrain permitted it, they relied principally on hunting, fishing and keeping cattle and sheep.[151] King James VI and I thought that, within the Highlands, the mainlanders were 'barbarous for the most part, and yet mixed with some show of civility', whereas the islanders were 'all utterly barbarous, without any sort or show of civility'. The first sort would come to heel if the laws were strictly enforced, but the others needed to have colonies planted among them 'that within short time may reform and civilize the best inclined', while 'rooting out or transporting the barbarous sort'.[152] The union of crowns in 1603 was followed by the eventual pacification of the Borders, the colonization of Orkney and Shetland, and an assault on Gaelic cultural distinctiveness.[153] In 1616 the chiefs were made to promise to obey the law, reduce their retinues, adopt Lowland farming methods, and abandon the Gaelic language, which was regarded as one of the chief causes of 'the continuance of barbarity and incivility in the Highlands'.[154]

The Highland chiefs thus gradually came to accept the government's authority, but their clansmen retained their military ethic and remained violent and lawless.[155] At the end of the seventeenth century, the Lowlanders were said to have 'civilized' themselves 'by their travels and by their commerce with France and England', whereas the mountain dwellers were still reputed to be barbarians, 'cruel, revengeful, living by fishing, hunting, and plunder'. Much contemporary reflection on the nature of civility and barbarism took its origin from this contrast between the two Scotlands.[156]

Despite the Act of Union in 1707, clanship and lawlessness continued in the Highlands until the Jacobite rebellions of 1715 and 1745, which, in the novelist Henry Fielding's opinion, drew their support from 'the savage inhabitants of wilds and mountains, ... outlaws, robbers, and cut-throats, who live in a constant state of war, or rather robbery, with the civilized part of Scotland'.[157] In the aftermath of the Forty-Five Rebellion, there was a concerted attempt to pacify and 'civilize' the region in order to safeguard the Hanoverian dynasty. The confiscation of the rebels' estates was accompanied by legislation encouraging linen manufacture, banning Highland dress, and forbidding the carrying or possession of 'broad sword or target, poignard, whinger, or durk, side pistol, gun, or other warlike weapons'.[158] The effect of these acts 'for the further civilizing of the inhabitants of the Highlands of Scotland' is debatable; but when Samuel Johnson visited the Western Isles in 1773, he reported that the ferocity of the clans was softened, their military ardour diminished, and their contempt for government subdued.[159]

South of the border, there was a tendency to ignore these distinctions and to regard all Scots as 'rude and barbarous'. Scottish soldiers were reputed to be particularly savage in warfare; Scottish houses were said to be 'dirty and unswept, like stables or hogs-sties'; and the Scots themselves boorish at the table, lousy, smelly and lacking what the wit Sydney Smith would call 'all faecal propriety and excremental delicacy'. Samuel Pepys asserted in 1682 that 'so universal a rooted nastiness hangs about the person of every Scot (man and woman), that renders the finest show they can make nauseous, even among those of the first quality'.[160] A traveller to Edinburgh in 1705 found the city almost totally without any houses of office and excrement lying in heaps in every street: 'The scent was so offensive that we were forced to hold our noses as we passed the streets and take care where we trod, for fear of disobliging our shoes.'[161] 'It is the ostentation of a Scotsman,' sneered the politician John Wilkes, 'to let the world know he has a handkerchief.'[162] With such witticisms did the English reassure themselves of their superior civility in an age when Scottish universities and philosophers were the ornament of the European Enlightenment.

Lower in the scale of civility came the Irish. It was said that, until the English conquest in the twelfth century, the Irish had no stone houses, no money, no foreign trade, no learning other than saints' legends, no science, no mathematics, no manufacture, and no navigation.[163] The classic account of Irish incivility was composed by Gerald of Wales in the late 1180s in the wake of Henry II's conquest of 1171–72, itself an event that bore witness to English military superiority and had been legitimized by Pope Alexander III as a rightful attempt to evangelize a 'rude and unlettered people' and reform their manners. Gerald's description of the Irish as idle pastoralists who lived like beasts was deeply influential in the early modern period.[164] At the beginning of the sixteenth century, the English monarch was nominally lord of all Ireland. In practice, he controlled no more than a third of the country and governed through the Anglo-Irish lords (the 'Old English'), who, despite fourteenth-century attempts to stop them from going native, were increasingly Gaelicized in language, dress and manners. The rest of the island was ruled by native Irish chiefs, hostile to English ways. Ignoring the social and cultural differences among the members of what was in fact a complex society, Henry VIII's lord chancellor dismissed the native Irish as 'a people barbarous and savage'. So did Elizabeth I.[165] Sir Thomas Elyot recommended reading Caesar's *Commentaries*, 'that thereof may be taken necessary instructions concerning the wars against Irish men or Scots, who be of the same rudeness and wild disposition that . . . the Britons were in the time of Caesar'. Edmund Spenser, who served as the Lord Deputy's secretary from 1580 to 1589, believed that the Irish were lineally descended from the Scythians and were 'the most barbarous nation in Christendom'.[166] An entertainment performed before the queen in 1588 portrayed a wild Irishman, 'bareheaded, with black, long-shagged hair down to his shoulders', and 'a threatening countenance'. 'All the world knows their barbarism', said Oliver Cromwell.[167]

Much of this animosity towards the Irish stemmed from Protestant distaste for their tenacious adherence to the Catholic Church. In practice, however, attitudes varied according to the circumstances. When the Irish made rebellious war, they were depicted as barbarians; when there was a prospect of peaceful reconciliation, they were portrayed more favourably: hence Henry VIII's willingness in the 1540s to contemplate making Gaelic chiefs peers of the realm. Ever since Gerald of Wales had depicted Irish barbarism by way of justifying Henry II's conquest, the most extreme denunciations of the Irish as savages were almost always proffered as legitimations, retrospective or prospective, of violent action against them.[168] From time to time there were sympathetic attempts to understand the peculiarities of this pastoral society with its nomadic transhumance, its weak central authority, its powerful lordships, its kin-based social structure and its constant feuding.[169] In 1676 Sir William Petty rebutted the notion that the Irish were descended from the Scythians,* while Irish antiquarians of the seventeenth and eighteenth centuries vigorously refuted Gerald's hostile description of their medieval ancestors. Instead, they celebrated the piety and learning of ancient Gaelic culture, portraying Ireland as a land of saints, scholars and musicians long before the Normans arrived.[170] In the eighteenth century, the recovery and vindication of Gaelic culture would become an important part of the campaign by Catholics for the relaxation of the penal laws against them.[171]

But most English visitors to Ireland recoiled in face of the violence and disorder, and what they saw as the idleness of the people and the filthiness of their dress, food and personal habits.[172] The Irish, claimed Barnabe Rich in 1609, were 'more uncivil, more uncleanly, more barbarous, and more brutish in their customs and demeanours than in any other part of the world that is known'. Fynes Moryson recorded that it was 'no rare thing to see the wives of great men to make water as they stood talking with men, and some in the rushes of the Presence Chamber in Dublin, and to do openly the most secret necessities of the body'. A writer in the 1640s concluded that the natives of Ireland were called 'the Wild Irish' because 'in all manner of wildness they may be compared with the most barbarous nations of the earth'.[173]

---

*This did not prevent Edmund Burke from asserting that it was the legacy of Scythian manners, as much as the nature of the soil, that made the Irish addicted to pasturage rather than agriculture; *Writings and Speeches*, ed. Paul Langford et al. (Oxford, 1981–2015), vol. 1, 512.

༺ 5 ༻

Exporting Civility

Among all nations of the world, they that be politic and civil do master the rest.

> Sir Thomas Smith (attrib.), *A Discourse of the*
> *Commonweal of This Realm of England* (1581), ed.
> Mary Dewar (Charlottesville, VA, 1969)

Confronting the Barbarians

In the early modern period, the relations between the 'civilized' powers of Western Europe and the 'barbarian' or 'savage' peoples whose lands they sought to penetrate provoked a great deal of learned and philosophical argument. Some maintained that those who were so barbarous as to refuse to trade with outsiders should be punished for violating 'the mutual society and fellowship between man and man prescribed by the law of nations'. Since God had intended the peoples of the world to trade with each other, it was claimed that foreigners were entitled to travel, trade and even reside in other countries; and they could use force if they were denied access.

214

This right to make a violent entry into countries that, despite attempts at peaceful persuasion, persisted in refusing to allow foreigners to trade with them was originally expounded in the 1530s by the Spanish theologian Francisco de Vitoria. He saw it as part of the laws of nature and nations commanding communication, sociability and hospitality. The right was invoked by the Spaniards in their dealings with the Amerindians.[1] It was also invoked in 1583 by the English adventurer Sir George Peckham, who claimed that it was permissible to use force against the 'savages' of Newfoundland if they 'barbarously' resisted those who merely sought 'just and lawful traffic'; this action, he maintained, would 'no whit transgress the bonds of equity or civility'.[2] Others who endorsed this opinion included two Regius Professors of civil law at Oxford, Alberico Gentili and Richard Zouche; the common lawyer Richard Hakluyt; the colonist William Strachey; the Jacobean travel writer Samuel Purchas; the Caroline Bishop of Exeter Joseph Hall; and, though only in the first version of his political philosophy, Thomas Hobbes.[3] As a recent commentator has remarked, these writers were prepared to authorize what seems to modern eyes a 'quite astonishing degree of permeability of one state by the inhabitants of others'. It was a crude rationale for forcing non-European peoples into commercial relations against their will; and it drew strength from the conviction that those who resisted these incursions were, in Purchas's words, 'barbarians, borderers, and outlaws of humanity'.[4]

In the eighteenth century, Daniel Defoe saw the world as divided between civilized nations, who traded, and barbarous ones, who did not. North Africa, for example, had in ancient times been the centre of a flourishing commerce, but it had subsequently been overrun by 'barbarous nations'. The followers of Mahomet in the kingdoms of Fez and Morocco were 'the destroyers both of commerce and cultivation'. Having 'very little inclination to trade' and 'being a rapacious, cruel, violent and tyrannical people, void of all industry and application, and neglecting all culture and improvement', they had become thieves, robbers, pirates and slave traders. Defoe urged that the seafaring powers of Western Europe should join together to expel the Moors ('the most barbarous people in the world') from the coastal areas and drive them up-country, where they would be unable to continue their depredations on other nations and be obliged to seek subsistence by honest labour.[5]

The law of nature was also invoked in support of the claims of Western invaders to take possession of land that their 'uncivilized' native owners did not cultivate. This was an argument used by English adventurers in Elizabethan Ireland. Sir Thomas Smith explained in 1572 that his proposed colony in County Down would not be 'a conquest', but an 'inhabiting of waste and desolate grounds'.[6] Farmers, it was claimed, had rights in land, but hunter-gatherers did not. Uncultivated land was what would later come to be called *res nullius*, the property of no one.[7] As Sir Thomas More's Utopians had believed, it was perfectly justifiable to take land by force from people who left it waste yet denied others their right by natural law to take it over and cultivate it.[8] In 1629 John Winthrop, the first governor of the Massachusetts Bay colony, asserted that land which had never been 'replenished or subdued' was free 'to any that possess and improve it'; the colonists could, therefore, go and dwell among the Indians 'in their waste lands and woods, leaving them such places as they have manured for their corn'. The influential New England divine John Cotton similarly claimed that, by the law of nature, 'the void places of the country' became the property of those who chose to occupy them.[9]

More aggressively, John Rolfe, the author of a prospectus for the colonization of Virginia, informed his readers that they were 'a peculiar people marked and chosen of the finger of God to possess it. For undoubtedly he is with us.' In practice, however, Rolfe, like most North American colonists, accepted that the Indians had property rights in land merely by occupying it, regardless of whether or not it was under cultivation. As a result, purchase became a normal method of acquiring territory. Whether the Indians fully understood the nature of these transactions and were free agents in making them is another matter.[10]

Back at home, the preachers and lawyers took a harder line. If the English evicted the Indians and introduced their own superior agricultural methods, claimed Samuel Purchas, they could make American land a hundred, 'perhaps a thousand', times more productive. They had a right 'by the law of nature and humanity' to replenish the unoccupied parts of another country, especially when the inhabitants were 'wild' and had no fixed abode. It was surely wrong to leave 'so good a country' in the hands of 'so bad [a] people, having little of humanity but shape, ignorant of civility, of arts, of religion, more brutish than the beasts they hunt, more wild and unmanly than that unmanned wild country which they range rather than inhabit'.* The poet and preacher John Donne assured the Virginia Company in 1622 that 'many cases may be put when not only commerce and trade, but plantation in lands not formerly our own, may be lawful'.[11] Thomas Hobbes modified this position, but only to a small extent. He was in favour of the transplantation of the English poor to 'countries not sufficiently inhabited'; but he ruled that these immigrants were not entitled to 'exterminate' those they found there, although they were allowed to 'constrain them to inhabit closer together', that is, to move up and make room for the newcomers. He may have been influenced by the views of his onetime employer Francis Bacon, whose preference was for 'a plantation in a pure soil, that is where people are not displanted … For else it is rather an extirpation than a plantation.'[12]

---

* The mid-nineteenth-century Archbishop of Dublin Richard Whately described 'the lowest and rudest races that inhabit the earth' as 'sunk to the level of the brute creation, and in some points, below the brutes': 'Ignorant and thoughtless, gross in their tastes, filthy in their habits, with the passions of men, but with the intellect of little children, they roam, half-naked and half-starved, over districts which might be made to support, in plenty and in comfort, as many thousands of Europeans as there are individuals in the savage tribes'; *Miscellaneous Lectures and Reviews* (1861), 26–27.

Others, however, were prepared to contemplate extirpation. When one people deemed another to be uncivilized, the consequences could be devastating. The Romans had believed that their cultural superiority entitled them to engage in the wholesale slaughter of barbarians, men, women and children.[13] King James VI and I, in his campaign to rid the Scottish state of 'thieves', 'murderers' and 'oppressors', ordered the 'full extermination' of such 'vermin'; he also commanded a Scottish nobleman to 'extirpate and root out' three whole clans from the Isles of Skye and Lewis and replace them with a plantation of 'civil' people.[14] In the mid-eighteenth century, the leading European authority on the law of nations, the Swiss lawyer Emmerich de Vattel, did not merely maintain the right of the civilized to appropriate uncultivated land belonging to others, while permitting them to leave land waste for defensive or other purposes. He also advocated the genocide of peoples without agriculture: in his opinion, those (such as the ancient Germans and 'some modern Tartars') who lived in fertile countries yet failed to cultivate the soil and lived by plundering others deserved 'to be extirpated as savage and pernicious beasts'.[15]

Vattel was echoing sentiments that had long been expressed. From the mid-seventeenth century onwards, there were repeated proposals by English settlers in the West Indies that the native people, the Caribs (Karifuna), should be utterly destroyed because these 'barbarous savages' were an obstacle to the spread of more sugar plantations. Successive attempts at their 'extirpation' were authorized by the home government, but they were only partly successful; and a much reduced community of Caribs survived.[16] In 1763 the commander-in-chief of the British army in America sanctioned a plan to eliminate hostile Indian tribes on the Pennsylvania frontier by distributing blankets infected with smallpox, along with any other available method that might serve to 'extirpate this execrable race'.[17] In the nineteenth century, the assumption that 'savage' peoples were doomed to extinction became widespread; and

218

the process was sometimes deliberately accelerated, as in the case of the indigenous Australians.[18]

Violent intrusion on the uncivilized was also justified by the assumption, articulated by both Hobbes and Locke, that most barbarians were still living in the state of nature and their forms of government were too rudimentary to be recognized as constituting independent states. As a speaker in a dialogue by Francis Bacon put it, there were 'nations in name' that were 'no nations in right, but multitudes only, and swarms of people': when these 'heap[s] of people' were unable to govern themselves, another nation that was 'civil or policed' could justly invade and subdue them.[19] In New England, accordingly, it was confidently asserted that the natives had no government or law among them, save 'club law'.[20] When James I granted a portion of southeast Newfoundland to Sir George Calvert in 1623, his charter recognized that the land was 'in some parts thereof inhabited by certain barbarous people', but ruled that they were to be regarded as piratical invaders; the laws of war entitled the settlers to kill those responsible for these 'incursions'. Other royal grants dismissed the indigenous inhabitants as 'not worthy of the name of a nation, being wild and savage'.[21]

The Native Americans did indeed lack civil societies possessing sovereignty in the Hobbesian sense of the word, but they were held together by complex alliances and political structures. Whether those observers who described them as living in a state of anarchy failed to understand these arrangements, dismissed them as inadequate or were simply disingenuous, it is hard to say.[22] Certainly, it was difficult to reconcile the assertion that the natives had no corporate identity with the common practice of making treaties and buying land from them.

Civilizing by Force

Some scholastic theologians and natural lawyers maintained that civilized people were not justified in using force against barbarians unless they had been injured by them in some way or because intervention was necessary to protect the innocent.[23] But an alternative view, proclaimed by the late medieval papacy, was that it was sufficient to show that the barbarians' way of life blatantly flouted the law of nature and nations (defined, of course, in Eurocentric terms). In the early modern period, Gentili, Grotius and other authorities modified this view, but did not reject it altogether. Just as they authorized war against pirates and brigands, so they supported action against those who committed especially atrocious breaches of natural law such as cannibalism or bestiality.* They were careful to emphasize that the motive for intervention in another people's affairs should be high-minded and not a mere cover for plunder. But if the crimes of the barbarians really were major ones, then by 'the common law of mankind' it was acceptable to use violence in order to correct them.[24]

In the early modern period, therefore, differences in levels of civility were regularly invoked to justify the invasion, conquest and colonization of 'uncivilized' countries. It was usually claimed that in this way the inhabitants would be introduced to a higher form of existence. Aristotle had maintained that Greeks were entitled to make war against barbarians in order to rule them; and the Romans had shown that violent conquest, followed by authoritarian rule, could be a necessary preliminary to the growth of civility (*cultus* and *humanitas*). The Romans had brought nomadic peoples to a settled existence and suppressed barbarous practices such as human sacrifice. Sir Matthew Hale regarded them as a 'civilized' people 'with great knowledge in arts and sciences, and in civil and military government', which they transmitted to the barbarous people they conquered.[25] Gerald of Wales had expressed the same idea in the twelfth century, when he claimed that the Irish, by being forced to

---

* In a dialogue by Francis Bacon, one speaker, a 'Roman Catholic zealant [zealot]', argues that if an Amazon state were to be discovered, it would be right to attack it because government by women was a perversion of the law of nature; *The Works of Francis Bacon*, ed. James Spedding et al. (new edn, 1879), vol. 7, pt 1, 33.

submit to the kings of England, were being introduced to 'a better form of life' (*meliorem formam vivendi*).[26] Sir William Temple envisaged the early history of mankind as the story of how successive conquests succeeded in 'reducing barbarous nations unto civil and well-regulated constitutions' and 'subduing those by force … who refused to accept willingly the advantages of life or condition that were offered them'.[27] In 1713 Joseph Addison's tragedy *Cato*, with its stirring evocation of the civilizing mission, played to packed houses:

A Roman soul is bent on higher views:
To civilize the rude unpolished world,
And lay it under the restraint of laws;
To make Man mild, and sociable to Man;
To cultivate the wild licentious Savage
With wisdom, discipline, and liberal arts;
Th'embellishments of life: virtues like these
Make human nature shine, reform the soul,
And break our fierce barbarians into men.[28]

Although some early American colonists hoped to convert the natives by 'piety, clemency, courtesy, and civil demeanour',[29] the notion that it was permissible to impose civilization by force quickly became a commonplace. Francis Bacon assured the Earl of Essex, on the eve of the latter's departure in 1599 to be Lord-Lieutenant of Ireland, that the Romans had held that the most honourable form of military victory was the conquest of people who, like the Irish, were 'barbarous and not reduced to civility'.[30] The Elizabethan captain Haly Heron noted that, 'by the painful travails of worthy conquerors', 'barbarous people' had been 'brought to a most civil government'; and a Jacobean preacher claimed that it was lawful for a Christian king to fight and conquer 'barbarous and savage people, and such as live under no lawful or warrantable government', provided that his object was 'to reclaim and reduce those savages from their barbarous kinds of life'.[31] The historian Edmund Bolton declared that it was 'no infelicity to the barbarous' to be 'subdued by the more polite and noble: however precious 'wild freedom' might be, it was 'merely brute and savage' without 'liberal arts and honourable manners'. James I's attorney general for Ireland, Sir John Davies, held that 'a barbarous country must be first broken by war before it will be capable of good government'. The prominent Interregnum lawyer Bulstrode Whitelocke noted that, although Nimrod was 'a cruel and wicked man', God had used him as an instrument 'to force the barbarous people to obedience and civility'.[32]

The Roman achievement was an inspiration to some of those who wished to subjugate the native Irish and destroy their unruly way of life; and, though they must have passed over the heads of many of those involved, classical precedents were frequently cited during the 'plantation' of Munster under Elizabeth I and of Ulster under James I.[33] These colonial settlements, involving the expropriation of the native possessors, were modelled on the English shires and intended to be exemplary units of civility, which would encourage the local population to adopt a better way of life.[34] In practice, however, the colonizers were primarily concerned with their own enrichment. Their conception of 'civility', unlike that of the Romans, who had admitted conquered peoples to citizenship, was strictly limited.

The aims of successive English governments were also restricted. In the sixteenth century, their essential objective was to secure the collaboration of the Irish living outside the Pale (the Anglicized area surrounding Dublin). Henry VIII abandoned the practice of appointing Irish-born deputies, took on the title of King of Ireland in 1541, and set about persuading the Gaelic and Old English lords to renounce the papacy and accept his authority in return for confirmation of their titles and estates.[35] In the reign of Elizabeth I, however, a sequence of rebellions by Irish chiefs, and the accompanying risk that Catholic Ireland might become a Spanish satellite and a base for invading England, forced the Elizabethan government into asserting its direct authority over the whole of the island. Opinions differed as to whether this would be best achieved by a policy of peaceful assimilation, or by expropriating the Irish by military conquest and establishing plantations of English and Scottish settlers throughout the country, or by reforming the Gaelic Irish through the introduction of the English language, English laws, new walled towns, arable farming, grammar schools and Protestant clergy. Different policies were followed at different times, and there were long periods of sanguinary warfare involving brutal executions of Irish rebels, real or supposed, and the confiscation of their lands (Plate 16).[36] Some of the officials who favoured conciliation protested against the extortionate behaviour of the English troops, who 'with their harlots, their boys, their horses and dogs' billeted themselves on the local population, causing 'great outrage among the common people'.[37] But for others, the ultimate goal was the reshaping of Irish society to fit an English model, to keep the Irish 'in order, in virtuous labour, and in justice, and to teach them our English laws and civilities and leave robbing and stealing and killing of one another', as Sir Thomas Smith put it in 1572.[38]

This commitment to what was seen as a civilizing mission arose out of the need for security, since in practice 'civility' was equated with acceptance of English rule, what Shakespeare called 'civil discipline'.[39] Henry VIII had sought to reduce Ireland to 'a due civility and obedience'; and it was with the aim of ensuring national security that Elizabeth I had encouraged her representatives to 'allure and bring in that rude and barbarous nation to civility'.[40] In his *Description of Ireland*, written for Holinshed's *Chronicles* (1577), the Latin scholar and future Catholic exile Richard Stanihurst urged that the Irish should be brought 'from savageness to civility' so that they could 'frame themselves pliable to the laws and ordinances of Her Majesty'. 'Where the country is subdued,' he argued, 'there the inhabitants ought to be ruled by the same law that the conqueror is governed, to wear the same fashion of attire wherewith the victor is vested, and speak the same language that the vanquisher parleth.'[41] When in 1592 Henry Bagenal proposed to found a school at Newry to educate the youth of Ulster in 'civility and learning', his object was less to give the children an academic training than to ensure that 'they may be taught their duty to their prince and country'. Similarly, James I's worries about Irish 'barbarity and want of civility' reflected his fear that they were 'so easily stirred ... to break forth in rebellions'.[42] Time and again in discussions of policy towards Ireland, the words 'civility' and 'obedience' were bracketed together. The guiding assumption was that if only the Irish could be converted to civility, they would then become 'faithful, obedient and true subjects'.[43]

In North America it was sometimes claimed that the English mission was to bring the Indians 'from their wild manner of life to the civil and polite customs of Europe'. Sir George Peckham hoped that they would make the transition 'from brutish ignorance to civility and knowledge, from unseemly customs to honest manners, from disordered routs and companies to a well-governed common-wealth, and withal should be taught mechanical occupations, arts and liberal sciences'.[44] The Virginia Charter of 1606 expressed the wish that, 'in time', the colonists would 'bring the infidels and savages living in those parts to human civility and to settled and quiet govern-ment'.[45] Samuel Purchas echoed the hope that the English in Virginia would 'play the good Samaritan' and convert the natives 'by humanity and civility from barbarism and savageness to good manners and human polity'. So did Thomas Hariot.[46] But always the main concern was to make the 'savages' 'tractable' and 'subject to civil authority', so that the invaders could trade and colonize, safe from attack. As John Eliot, the 'Apostle to the Indians', claimed, by 'civi-lizing' as well as converting his Native American pupils he secured their 'submission to the King's government'.[47]

There was also a keen awareness that by 'civilizing' people it was possible to create a new source of importable commodities and a new market for English goods. Elizabethan projectors envisaged that, once they forsook their 'barbarous and savage living', the Native Americans would want to buy English cloths and 'desire to live in the abundance of all things, as Europe doth'. It was well known, thought Sir George Peckham, that all savages, 'so soon as they shall begin but a little to taste of civility will take marvellous delight in any garment, be it never so simple, as a shirt, a blue, yellow, red or green cotton cassock, a cap or such-like, and will take incredible pains for such a trifle'.[48] In 1728 Daniel Defoe argued that the best way of increasing commerce was to instruct barbarous nations in the arts of living: 'clothing with decency, not shameless and naked; feeding with humanity, and not in a manner brutal; dwelling in towns and cities, with economy and government, and not like savages'. He pointed out that the result of this policy was that the Native Americans now bought 'an infinite number of things for the abundant accommodation of life; and those that are more civilized do it more'.* In the eighteenth century, it became axiomatic that an increase of 'civilized' people meant an increase in commerce.[49]

Defoe believed that it was a duty 'to subdue the barbarous and idolatrous nations of the world'. He thought that the Roman conquest, though 'unjust, bloody [and] tyrannical', was 'the kindest thing that could have befallen the British nation'; and he was not against the use of (preferably moderate) violence to inculcate civility and spread Christianity throughout the world. Proposing a 'universal war against paganism and devil-worship', he claimed that if the Christian powers could only unite, they could 'beat the very name of Mahomet out of the world'. He even contemplated a 'crusade' against the Japanese: they were, he admitted, 'a most sensible, sagacious people under excellent forms of government'; but their Buddhist priests, temples and idolatrous images cried out for destruction.[50]

---

* In the *Communist Manifesto*, Marx and Engels would write that 'the cheap prices of its commodities are the heavy artillery with which it [the bourgeoisie] batters down all Chinese walls, with which it forces the barbarians' intensely obstinate hatred of foreigners to capitulate'; Karl Marx and Frederick Engels, *Selected Works* (1969), vol. 1, 36–37.

There was nothing new about Defoe's assumption that violence was a legitimate accompaniment of the civilizing mission. The Elizabethan philosopher John Case accepted that tough military action was necessary if barbarians were to be made orderly and civil, though he repudiated excessive cruelty of the kind used by the Spaniards and Portuguese in the New World.[51] By contrast, the colonial promoter Richard Eden in 1555 had applauded the 'manhood' of the Spaniards, as displayed in their 'slaughter of such as could by no means be brought to civility'. Eden was probably seeking to ingratiate himself with the Spanish nobles at Mary Tudor's court, to whom he owed his preferment. His attitude lends strength to the suggestion that differences over policy, whether in America or Ireland, owed as much to circumstances and the patronage connections of individuals as to conflicting ideological preferences.[52]

In the 1590s, after the failure of alternative policies, many of those involved in the English government of Ireland came to agree with Edmund Spenser that the 'savage brutishness and loathsome filthiness' of the native Irish justified a policy of wholesale dispossession and killing, though not until they had first been given a final opportunity to submit voluntarily.[53] Only when nine years of fighting between 1594 and 1603 were brought to a successful conclusion did the English return to the brutal, but relatively more peaceful 'plantation' policy of selective eviction of Irish peasants to make way for English and Scottish settlers; and for this a more favourable image of the Irish had to be painted in order to attract immigrants. At the same time, a determined effort was made to introduce the English common law in place of Irish customary law. The latter had been held responsible for the country's disorder because it punished murder, rape and robbery with no more than a fine. It had also been blamed for Ireland's poverty because its kin-based rules of inheritance denied sons the right to succeed, thus depriving occupants of an effective incentive to improve their estates; hence, the government's attempt to introduce primogeniture.[54] By 1633 the Anglo-Irish antiquary James Ware could claim that, during the previous thirty years, the Irish had become law-abiding; and trade, agriculture, civility and learning had flourished. Clarendon similarly believed that in the 1630s Ireland was on the way to being so 'civilized' as to constitute a jewel in the English crown. On the eve of the Ulster Rebellion of 1641, the so-called New English settlers owned at least 40 per cent of Irish land and had developed a market economy with a huge increase in exports of wool and live cattle.[55]

Just as Spenser's support for an aggressive policy had been provoked by what he saw as Irish recalcitrance, so in North America the secretary of the Virginia Company came to an equally draconian view after a violent Indian insurrection in 1622: the attempt to civilize the natives, he declared, was too laborious and time consuming, and should be replaced by a policy of simple conquest. In his opinion, the 'treacherous violence' of the Indians entitled the English, 'by the right of war and the law of nations', to invade and destroy those who had sought to destroy them. Samuel Purchas agreed that 'future dangers' should be prevented by 'the extirpation of the more dangerous of the savages'; and the Virginia Company duly ordered that, as 'a sharp revenge upon the bloody miscreants', they should be rooted out 'from being longer a people upon the face of the earth'.[56] The attempt to bring civility to the native peoples was abandoned: 'Show [me] one man that was converted or civilized', demanded a pamphleteer in 1644.[57] The 'inhuman barbarities' of the armed Indian rising of 1675–78 ('King Philip's War') further confirmed the settlers in their view that the natives were 'barbarous men of blood'. By 1721 a writer could boast that seven or eight 'fierce and populous tribes' had been 'subdued and utterly extirpated'.[58] The English did not need the labour of the Indians in the way they did that of the Irish and therefore made very little effort to assimilate them into their colonial settlements. Whereas the Spaniards incorporated the indigenous people into their American empire, the English banished them to the margins.[59] They also persuaded themselves that they had done the

Indians no wrong. In 1776 a poet predicted a glorious future for British America, 'the greatest glory of the British crown', and one, he claimed, that had been acquired 'without guilt or bloodshed'.[60] Since these words were published in what would prove to be the year of the American Declaration of Independence, this was a double irony.

In Ireland, the plantation policy and the uncompromising Protestantism of the Dublin government provoked Gaelic lords and Catholic peasants into the Ulster rising of 1641. It spread to the other provinces, leading to brutal sectarian violence, and was followed by a prolonged civil war. In 1649 Oliver Cromwell reverted to the aggressive policy proposed by Spenser fifty years earlier. 'Ireland looks like a fallow ground', wrote the radical Welsh preacher Morgan Llwyd: 'thou must be ploughed again.' John Milton defended Cromwell's military subjugation of the country as 'a civilizing conquest' that would teach the natives to abandon their 'absurd and savage customs' and 'wax more civil'.[61] One estimate puts the number of Irish deaths between October 1641 and October 1652 as a result of war, famine or plague at 618,000, as against a total prewar population of 1.5 million.[62] In the ensuing scramble for Irish land by Cromwell's soldiers and financial backers (the 'Adventurers'), the civilizing mission, never supported by everyone, was only intermittently pursued.

After Charles II's restoration, a new policy was followed with its emphasis on developing the Irish economy, encouraging commercial links between the two countries, and securing them by protectionist legislation. In the later seventeenth century, Sir William Petty could claim that the English had brought 'arts, civility and freedom' to Ireland: even the poorest Irishman, he declared, now rode on horseback. Yet in the 1690s a French observer reported that, although some of the native Irish were civilized enough, others continued to live in a 'wild' and 'brutish' manner. In the 1720s and 1730s, the dean of St Patrick's Cathedral, Dublin, complained that whereas the colonists in Ireland were 'more civilized' and 'much better bred' than their counterparts in many English counties, the Irish people lived in 'filthy cabins' and were 'miserable, tattered, half-starved creatures, scarce in human shape': politeness was 'as much a stranger as cleanliness'. These evils, he added, were 'the effect of English tyranny'.[63]

Oddly enough, religion was regarded as less central to the civilizing process than one might have supposed. Of course, many contemporaries were as anxious to convert the heathen to what they regarded as the true religion as they were to civilize them. They wanted to give them 'civility for their bodies' and 'Christianity for their souls'. The 'inhumanity' of barbarous peoples was said to result from their ignorance of the true God: the moral rules to be found in the Bible were seen as 'well adapted to civilize the world'.[64] In the seventeenth century, a synthesis of piety and civility was implicit in the proposals of Thomas Hobbes, James Harrington and other political thinkers for a 'civil religion' that would not come under the jurisdiction of the clergy, but would be an organ of the state.[65] A hundred years later, Edmund Burke still believed that 'the first openings of civility' had everywhere been made by religion: it was 'the basis of civil society' and 'one great source of civilization amongst us'.[66]

Though Christianity and civility were often seen as interlinked, the two conditions were distinct; and it was usually recognized that 'to civilize' was not the same as 'to gospellize'.[67] A London preacher claimed in 1641 that 'the doctrine of the Gospel, sincerely obeyed, first Christianizeth men and then civilizeth them'.[68] But most churchmen thought that this was putting the two processes in the wrong order: there was no point in trying to bring Christianity to a barbarous people until they had been tamed by laws and refined by education. Their 'brutishness' and 'stupidity' made barbarians 'incapable of understanding' celestial things. So the inculcation of civility took priority. 'The way to make them Christian men', as Samuel Purchas put it, was 'first to make them civil men'.[69]

In 1695 the Archbishop of Canterbury was urged to send missionaries to India, where there were said to be 'civilized, polite and ingenious people' who were 'very capable of all manner of instruction' and 'very docile to receive it'. By contrast, one could not expect to convert the 'savage and wild nations' of the Western Plantations until they were 'better civilized'.[70] In North America, the secretary of the Society for the Propagation of the Gospel in Foreign Parts (SPG) reported in 1730 that it was impossible to teach Christianity to the Mohawks until they were 'in some degree civilized'; and that soon became the general view. As Bishop Warburton explained, Christianity required 'an intellect above that of a savage to comprehend. Something then must be previous to it. And what is that but civil society?'[71] Religion for him was not a cause of civilization; it was an effect.

Meanwhile there was an enduring tendency to assume that non-Christians were not full members of international society and had no legal status until they had been converted, not even a right to the territory they occupied. Pope Innocent IV (1243–54) had ruled that infidels could legitimately hold territory and govern themselves, but this doctrine was challenged by the Italian canon lawyer Hostiensis (Henry of Segusio, d. 1271), who came to the view that they could do so only if they recognized the pope's supremacy.[72] Such doubts about the legitimacy of infidel states were alive and well in the sixteenth century. In 1578 Elizabeth I felt able to authorize the adventurer Sir Humphrey Gilbert to search out 'remote heathen and barbarous lands' not already in the possession of 'any Christian prince or people', which he and his heirs could occupy and enjoy in perpetuity. Gilbert's half-brother, Sir Walter Ralegh, received a similar commission in 1584, as did other colonial projectors in the reigns of James I and Charles I. Lands inhabited only by 'savages having no knowledge of the divine being' were seen as fair game for Christian expropriators.[73]

In the same spirit, a late Elizabethan proclamation cited the paganism of the blacks in England as one of the reasons for ordering their expulsion from the country; and in the case of *Butts* v. *Penny*

(1677), the King's Bench accepted it as a justification for enslaving them, a view that was reaffirmed in 1694.[74] Gentili had been in favour of making war against atheists, but not against infidels. He agreed that the English were right to regard the Turks as their enemies, but explained that the reason was not the Turks' religion: it was their threatening behaviour and their seizure of English merchants' goods. If the Ottomans kept the peace, there would be no justification for seeing these infidels as enemies. As it was, however, he held that a Turk who was captured or took refuge in England should automatically become a slave.[75]

The idea of Christendom as a society whose members were entitled to preferential treatment retained its resonance well into the eighteenth century. Protestant clergy maintained, as had the medieval Church before them, that they had a right to preach the Gospel to the heathen and to use force if their missionaries were denied access. Gentili had rejected this claim, but Richard Baxter had a long tradition behind him when he maintained that 'if a poor barbarous Indian nation, like the cannibals, would not consent to hear the gospel, or suffer preachers to come among them', then the evangelizers had the right to 'force them to admit the preachers'.[76] Serious missionary work in North America and the West Indies had got under way in 1701 with the foundation by High Anglicans of the Society for the Propagation of the Gospel in Foreign Parts. But the SPG, like subsequent Dissenting missions, concentrated on the white population, and its achievements before 1790 were modest.[77]

It was, of course, an issue as to whether all barbarians were capable of being civilized, or whether some, like Prospero's Caliban, were not. The climatic theory of human difference implied that true civility was possible only in the temperate zone. But many contemporaries rejected this notion as contrary to common sense and daily experience. Human nature, they believed, was everywhere the same. For Francis Bacon, the differences between civilized Europe and the barbarous regions of the New World arose not from soils, climate or bodily constitutions, but from European superiority in the arts and sciences. Fynes Moryson agreed that geographical circumstances were irrelevant to cultural differences: all virtues sprang from knowledge and religion, and all vices from ignorance, atheism and superstition.[78]

In 1703 the medical writer Peter Paxton pointed out that the children of 'the most brutal savages' were indistinguishable in infancy from those of 'the more polite Europeans'. Where, therefore, he asked, did the subsequent diversity of manners and ways of living come from? His answer involved a firm rejection of all natural and environmental hypotheses; the differences, he maintained, were not 'to be derived from our natures, nor from any physical causes': they were 'the blessed effects of society'.[79] Bernard Mandeville believed that the influence of climate was 'soon overbalanced by skilful government': with the establishment of internal peace, wealth would increase and, with it, the arts and sciences. In that way, a band of savages could in time turn into 'a well-civilized nation'. James Adair, a trader who had spent over thirty years living with the Native Americans of the Southeast, urged that, with 'a proper cultivation', they were 'capable of attaining all the liberal arts and sciences' and of shining 'in higher spheres of life'.[80] The notion that degrees of civility had physical causes was dealt the coup de grâce by David Hume in his essay 'Of National Characters': 'No one attributes the difference of manners in Wapping and St James's to a difference of air or climate.'* Yet Edward Gibbon continued to believe that 'the influence of food or climate, which, in a more improved state of society, is suspended or subdued, most powerfully contributes to form, and to maintain, the national character of barbarians'.[81]

---

* In his essay 'Of Commerce' (1752), however, Hume conceded that a likely reason why people living in the tropics had never 'attained to any art or civility' was that they had less need for clothes and housing and therefore lacked a 'spur to industry and invention'. Having fewer goods, they also had less incentive to establish 'a settled police or regular authority', whether to protect them from foreign enemies or from each other.

It did not follow, however, that uncivilized peoples were incapable of 'improvement'. The Aristotelian notion that some people, especially barbarians, were natural slaves was popular with Renaissance humanists and influential in the early years of Spanish America. It was, however, firmly rejected by Alberico Gentili and seems to have had comparatively little resonance in England.[82] The sternly republican John Milton scorned the many English citizens who chose to submit to a king rather than be members of a free commonwealth. But when he described them as 'by nature slaves, not fit for liberty', he was not suggesting that nature had originally intended them to be enslaved.[83] Similarly, the guiding assumption of the early colonial promoters was that, however rude and uncultivated the native peoples were, they could eventually be civilized in the way the English had been. In Sir Thomas Palmer's words, there was 'no nation in the world but may be reduced to civility, and forced in time to put off barbarousness'.[84]

The preacher Robert Gray expressed a contemporary commonplace when he remarked in 1609 that it was not the nature of men, but their education, which made them 'barbarous and uncivil'. 'Change the education of men,' he claimed, 'and you shall see that their nature will be greatly rectified and corrected.'[85] Morgan Godwyn, author of *The Negro's and Indian's Advocate* (1680), who had lived in Barbados, rejected the idea that black slaves were stupid, 'divers of them being known and confessed by their authors to be extraordinarily ingenious and even to exceed many of the English; and for the rest, they are much the same with other people, destitute of the means of knowledge and wanting education'. In his *Essay Concerning Human Understanding* (1690), Locke provided the epistemological underpinnings for this view, remarking that had the Virginian king Apochancana been educated in England, he would perhaps have been 'as knowing a divine and as good a mathematician as any in it'. In 1728 Bernard Mandeville stated flatly that there was 'no difference between the original nature of a savage and that of a civilized man'.[86]

Inventing Race

In this view of mankind there was no room for any presumption of immutable racial difference, let alone a hierarchy of races. The official religious orthodoxy was that humanity was a single species, with a common ancestor, and only superficially differentiated by environmental influences and cultural traditions. As Roger Williams reminded his fellow colonists in 1643:

> Boast not proud English, of thy birth and blood.
>   Thy brother Indian is by birth as good.
> Of one blood God made him, and thee, and all,
>   As wise, as fair, as strong, as personal.[87]

In practice, however, differences in bodily appearance frequently aroused suspicion. Blackness, in particular, was regarded unfavourably: this was the period when Europeans increasingly came to think of themselves as 'white', and to regard that as the natural condition from which other peoples had degenerated. For the Elizabethan navigator George Best, the blackness of the Ethiopians was a pollution, an 'infection of blood', stemming from Noah's curse on the sons of Ham.[88] The best-known account of Africa, composed by the Moorish traveller Al Hassan Ibn-Mohammed Al-Wezaz Al-Fasi, better known as John Leo Africanus, declared that 'negroes ... lead a beastly kind of life, being utterly destitute of the use of reason, of dexterity of wit, and of all the arts'.[89] In the 1590s, the members of a Japanese embassy to Rome were assured by their hosts that black Africans were ignorant and stupid: they lived like cattle and were by nature cruel, barbarous, unable to control their desires, and devoid of all refinement; as Aristotle had said, they were born only to serve.[90]

In late medieval Europe, it had been common for political and religious conflicts to be thought of as conflicts between different peoples, Germans and non-Germans, Spaniards and Muslims,

English and Welsh. But if there was a biological dimension to this kind of thinking, it was overshadowed by an emphasis on cultural and religious differences. The Aristotelian thought of the day had no coherent theory of heredity.[91] When, in the seventeenth century, Thomas Browne described the Jews as a distinct 'race and nation', he had religion and culture in mind as much as biological ancestry.[92] Medieval and early modern thinking, however, was also shot through with assumptions about the importance of 'birth', 'blood' and 'lineage'. The standard explanations of human differences, whether climatic, humoral, physiognomical or astrological, had protoracialist implications; and so had the habit of referring to nations as peoples who shared a common descent.[93] The Elizabethan Jesuit Robert Persons, for example, could attribute quarrels between Welshmen and 'true Englishmen' to their 'being of the stock of different peoples'.[94]

In the seventeenth century, Irish barbarism was often regarded as an innate characteristic. The Jacobean traveller Fynes Moryson deplored intermarriage between the English settlers and the native Irish on the grounds that the children 'of mingled race' were bound to degenerate from their English parents. In 1646 Sir John Temple referred in his history of the Ulster rising of 1641 to the 'perverse dispositions' of the Irish, 'transmitted down, whether by infusion from their ancestors or natural generation'.[95] Similar assertions were sometimes made about the Native Americans. When news of the Indian massacre in Virginia reached England in 1622, a lawyer associated with the Virginia Company composed a poetic denunciation of the Indians as 'men monsters', 'no better than a herd of beasts', not descendants of Adam, but 'errors of nature, of inhuman birth, the very dregs, garbage and spawn of earth', who had sprung up after the Flood 'like vermin of an earthly slime'.[96]

In the West Indies, the English planters appear from the start to have regarded their black slaves as intrinsically brutish, inferior and, above all, different. Likewise, in Virginia, an act of 1691 condemned the 'abominable mixture and spurious issue . . . by negroes, mulattoes or Indians marrying with English or other white women'. Slavery in the Anglo-American world came to be inextricably linked to the blackness of the slaves.[97] Racist practice long preceded racial theory, and theoretical monogenism proved to be entirely compatible with notions of racial inferiority.

In due course, theoretical backing for racial discrimination began to emerge. Sir William Petty opined in 1677 that there seemed to be 'several species' of men: the Negroes of Guinea and the Cape, he held, differed from Europeans not just in their manners, but also 'in the internal qualities of their minds'. Like many of his contemporaries, however, Petty was probably using the word 'species' in a loose sense, to indicate the varieties within a single human race. He recognized the influence of climate on cultural differences and never doubted the humanity of black Africans, though he clearly regarded them as a lower form of it.[98] Samuel Pepys took a keen interest in Petty's inquiries and the question of 'where the brute ends and man begins'. Sir William Temple also thought that Africa produced 'a race of men that seem hardly of the same species with the rest of mankind'. Their contemporary, the language reformer Francis Lodwick, was another who believed that blacks and whites had different ancestors. His reflections, like those of Petty, remained unpublished until modern times; but in 1684 the French doctor François Bernier published an article dividing humankind into four or five different species.[99]

It was only in the mid-eighteenth century that it became at all common for European intellectuals to uphold publicly the notion of intrinsic racial difference, independent of social and environmental circumstances; and it was only then that 'scientific' racial explanations began to be offered for cultural peculiarities.[100] Enlightenment critics of Christianity began to challenge the notion that all mankind had a single ancestor. In 1753 David Hume publicly declared that there were four or five different species of men and that the nonwhites were 'naturally inferior'. 'There never was,' he added, 'a civilized nation of any other complexion than white.' In the last edition of the essay in which this statement occurred, Hume altered 'never' to 'scarcely ever'.

He also retracted his assertion about there being several species of men. But he reaffirmed his negative view of blacks.[101]

This became a widespread prejudice. There were no white savages, thought the traveller John Ledyard, and few uncivilized people who were not brown or black.[102] In the late eighteenth century, it became more common (though very far from universal) to suggest that there were several different branches of mankind and that some were intrinsically incapable of rising to the cultural level of the Europeans.[103] In 1773 the absentee Jamaican planter Edward Long asserted that African Negroes were a different and more bestial species of the human race: 'I do not think that an orang-outang husband would be any dishonour to an Hottentot female.'* A year later, Lord Kames agreed that there were indeed different races of men, fitted by nature for different climates. He confessed that he used to think that blacks were inferior in understanding, but he now recognized that in Africa they had no incentive to improve their powers and that abroad they were slaves: 'Who can say how far they might improve in a state of freedom?' Such optimism was far from universal. In the late eighteenth century, the old opposition between the barbarous and the civil was beginning to be superseded by that between the black and the white.[104]

Fighting and Enslaving

Whatever their colour, when war was waged against the 'uncivilized', it usually assumed a particularly brutal character. The medieval law of arms had applied only to peoples who had been part of the old

---

* After a visit to Tunis in 1718, Lady Wortley Montagu wrote of the women living in tents around the ruins of Carthage that 'their posture in sitting, the colour of their skin, their lank black hair falling each side of their faces, their features, shape and limbs differ so little from their own country people the baboons, 'tis hard to fancy them a distinct race, and I could not help thinking there had been some ancient alliances between them.' Yet in 1752 she concluded that 'mankind is everywhere the same: like cherries or apples, they may differ in size, shape, or colour, from different soils, climates or culture, but are still essentially the same species'; *Letters of Lady Mary Wortley Montagu*, ed. Robert Halsband (Oxford, 1965–67), vol. 1, 427; vol. 3, 15.

Roman Empire; and in the early modern period, the laws of war were frequently suspended in extra-European clashes between rival imperial powers, as in the Caribbean or the East Indies.[105] They were discarded altogether in conflicts with those deemed to be barbarians, since it was assumed (often correctly) that they would not be reciprocated. As David Hume explained, 'Were a civilized nation engaged with barbarians who observed no rules, even of war, the former must also suspend their observance of them, where they no longer serve to any purpose, and must render every action or rencounter [skirmish] as bloody and pernicious as possible to the first aggressors.'[106] Restraint in warfare was possible when the contending parties shared a common culture, but it was quickly abandoned when one side regarded the other as 'enemies to human society', which was how Oliver Cromwell described the rebellious Irish in 1650.[107]

By invoking this Roman concept of the *hostis humani generis* (enemy of the human race), it was possible to set limits to the notion that all peoples were to be regarded as members of one single human society. Along with pirates, brigands and professional murderers, it excluded barbarians, who did not recognize the law of nations.* An enemy had to be acknowledged as a lawful opponent before he could be entitled to fair treatment in accordance with the laws of war.[108] In the Middle Ages, English wars against the Welsh and the Scots were not subject to the restraints that were meant to operate in the conflicts with the French.[109] In the seventeenth and eighteenth centuries, fighting against the Native Americans followed a pattern that would have been unacceptable in Europe. As the Council of Virginia resolved in 1623, 'neither fair war nor good quarter' should be offered to 'these barbarous and perfidious enemies'.[110] Similarly, the treatment of seafaring privateers until the mid-eighteenth century depended on

---

* Henry VIII's brutal devastation of the civilian population of the Boulonnais in northern France stands comparison with anything the English ever did in Ireland. It was justified by labelling the victims 'robbers' and 'brigands', and denouncing the peasants who fled to the woods as 'wild'; Neil Murphy, 'Violence, Colonization and Henry VIII's Conquest of France, 1544–1546', *P&P* 233 (2016).

whether or not the state that backed them was deemed to be 'civilized' or 'barbarous'.[111]

In Ireland warfare had always been exceptionally brutal. The Irish in the sixteenth century were seen as rebels, to be punished by the same instruments of martial law and mass executions as Tudor governments employed to suppress rebellions at home. Such measures, it was claimed, were necessary 'until such time as the people shall become civil or embrace the laws and peaceable living'.[112] The Elizabethan Lord Deputy, Lord Grey of Wilton, boasted that he had hanged almost 1,500 people 'of note' during his three years in Ireland, 'not accounting those of the meaner sort, nor yet executions by law, and killing of churls, which were innumerable'.[113] The palisades of dead men's skulls, which had shocked the Spaniards who encountered the Aztecs of Mexico and horrified eighteenth-century English visitors to the rulers of Dahomey, had their counterpart in the row of rebel heads with which Sir Humphrey Gilbert lined the path to his tent when engaged in subduing Elizabethan Ireland.[114]

After the atrocities committed by the Ulster rebels of 1641, which, though exaggerated by propagandists (Plate 17), were real enough, the attitude to the Irish became one of undisguised hatred. In October 1644 Parliament ordered that every Irishman or Irish-born Catholic captured fighting against the Parliamentary forces on land or sea should be immediately put to death. This spectacular departure from the accepted laws of war occasioned a good deal of unease among Parliamentarians and evoked justified protests by the Royalists. It was not always observed, partly because of fear of retaliation.[115] But it was defended on the grounds that the rules of civility did not apply to dealings with the uncivilized: in the wars in Ireland quarter had never been given or received, and in wars against the Irish it was regarded as 'a dishonour to use those civilities practised by soldiers in foreign parts'.[116] Clarendon was appalled by the 'barbarous manner' in which the Earl of Warwick had ordered that all captured Irish seamen should be bound back-to-back and thrown into the sea.[117] The Welsh and the Cornish were sometimes subject to similar ill-treatment during the Civil War on account of their supposed barbarism.[118]

In the late sixteenth century, Alberico Gentili had explained that international conventions about the rights of ambassadors and the fair treatment of prisoners did not apply to rebels because they were trying to drag the world back to the savagery of former times.[119] The Irish in the 1640s were seen as both rebels and barbarians. A government-sponsored pamphlet of 1650 described them as 'a people so exquisitely savage, so barbarously loathsome, so monstrously inclined' that 'we may therefore warrantably and righteously endeavour the extirpation of them'.[120] A century later, the Duke of Cumberland's slaughter of the Scottish Jacobites after their defeat at Culloden in 1746 was defended on similar grounds.[121] Well into the twentieth century, it continued to be asserted that wars against 'peoples possessing a low civilization' could be conducted more brutally than would normally have been acceptable. The standards obtaining in the 'civilized' wars between European powers were disregarded in the 'savage' wars against native peoples. As John Stuart Mill explained in 1859, it was 'a grave error' to suppose that the same rules of international morality could obtain between civilized nations and barbarians as between one civilized nation and another.[122]

Civility thus stopped short when it reached the frontiers of the civilized community. The England that devoured guides to civil behaviour and polite social intercourse was also the England that was involved in the forcible transportation of black Africans to slavery in North America and the West Indies. By 1700 British ships had carried over 350,000 of them. In 1807, when the trade was abolished, the total had reached 3.4 million (Plate 23). Perhaps a fifth of them died en route.[123]

In principle, the institution of slavery had been unknown in England since the twelfth century. In *Cartwright's Case* (1569), it was resolved that England boasted 'too pure an air for slaves to dwell in'.[124] The medieval system of villeinage, which made landholding conditional on the payment of feudal dues and the performance of labour services, also withered away in the Tudor period. As late as 1698, Chief Justice Holt ruled that villeinage was still technically legal, but the general view was that free socage (i.e., paying rent) was, in the words of an eighteenth-century lawyer, 'a tenure better accommodated to the more civilized dispositions of mankind'.[125] In 1769 the leading abolitionist Granville Sharp described medieval villeinage as a 'disgraceful and uncivilized' practice, brought in by 'uncivilized barons in an age of darkness'.[126]

In practice, Tudor governments were reluctant to abandon slavery altogether. In the early sixteenth century, there were royal proclamations ordering that vagabonds and spreaders of seditious rumours should be enslaved in the galleys, and a short-lived act of 1547 made slavery a punishment for those who refused to work.[127] The Elizabethan Privy Council occasionally sent felons to serve in chains in the galleys; in 1602 it ordered that this should be the fate of all condemned criminals who were not 'notorious or dangerous offenders'. In the same year the Star Chamber sentenced the libellers of Lord Buckhurst to lifetime servitude in the galleys.[128] Until the mid-eighteenth century, there were intermittent proposals that enslavement should become a recognized part of the penal code and the poor law.[129] From the early seventeenth century, vagrants, military prisoners and criminals were regularly deported to North America and the West Indies, where as indentured labourers (i.e., temporary slaves) they were often cruelly treated. In the 1650s they were joined by Scottish and Irish prisoners of war and in the 1680s by the Duke of Monmouth's defeated rebels. A majority of the voluntary migrants to North America in the seventeenth century went as indentured servants.[130]

Enslavement as an exceptional punishment for grave forms of delinquency could be reconciled with prevailing notions of civil society. Quite different was the slavery on a huge scale of Africans whose only crime was to have been born in the wrong place. Unlike indentured servants, slaves were slaves for life; they had no access to legal protection, and their children became slaves too. When Richard Jobson, who had been sent from England in 1620 to explore trading possibilities in Gambia, was offered some female slaves, he replied that 'we were a people who did not deal in any such commodities; neither did we buy or sell one another, or any that had our own shapes'. Similarly, Robert Sanderson, the future Restoration bishop, preached in 1638 that trading in human beings was a sin; he thanked God that 'in these times we scarce know what it meaneth', though he was aware that it had been practised the world over 'in some former times' and still was among Turks and pagans.[131]

Yet in a very short time slavery and the slave trade came to be widely regarded as acceptable, and not only by the planters of Barbados and Virginia, who depended on African slave labour and enacted legislation in the 1660s to make it legal.[132] Nearer home, Charles II's government ran a concentration camp for enslaved Moorish captives at Tangier.[133] John Locke, who, like many legal philosophers of the day, allowed the enslavement of prisoners taken in a just war, seems to have assumed that slave-raiding expeditions fell into that category; he helped to include slavery in the draft laws for the colony of Carolina.[134] The African Company, which supplied slaves to the West Indies, was given a royal charter in 1672, thereby implicating the English state in the trade, an involvement that was extended in 1713 when the Treaty of Utrecht gave Britain the right to provide black slaves to the Spanish empire.[135] In 1703 an ingenious projector proposed that blacks and mulattoes from America, and Tartar slaves from Russia, should be imported to England as an agricultural workforce and the medieval laws of villeinage revived to control them.[136]

Paradoxically, the English were deeply involved in the slave trade at a time when their enthusiasm for personal liberty had never been greater. 'How is it,' asked Samuel Johnson, 'that we hear the loudest yelps for liberty among the drivers of negroes?'[137] In the 1760s

William Beckford, the radical Lord Mayor of London, was attacked as a hypocrite for campaigning in the name of liberty when he was also a wealthy West Indian slave owner. His brother Richard, a fellow slave owner, could even exclaim, 'Thank God that we have no slaves in this kingdom!' Civility at home, it seemed, was wholly compatible with barbarism abroad.[138] The irony, as Adam Smith explained, was that the more cultivated the society, and the greater the freedom and opulence of the inhabitants, the worse was the treatment of their slaves. In a barbarous country, by contrast, slaves were more on a level with their masters; and because individual masters had fewer of them than did owners of large sugar plantations, less discipline was needed to keep them in order.[139]

Black slavery was often justified on the grounds that its victims were not Christian and that their enslavement was necessary if they were to be converted.[140] But their conversion to Christianity did not lead to the slaves' emancipation. What above all made slavery tolerable to those who might otherwise have been opposed to it was the belief that its victims were barbarians, for whom liberty was inappropriate.[141] This argument had been a crucial consideration for the ancient Greeks,[142] and it retained its persuasiveness in the early modern period. Most of those shipped in the 1650s from England to the New World as indentured labourers were Irish and Scots prisoners, whose homelands were notoriously uncivilized. The Africans transported to West Indian slavery were, as the Barbados Assembly explained in an act of 1688, 'of such barbarous, wild and savage nature and such as renders them wholly unqualified to be governed by the laws, customs and practices of our nation'.[143] They were, thought Bernard Mandeville, 'people that have not yet made a great hand of their sociableness'.[144] Drawing on the long geographical tradition that the people of sub-Saharan Africa were 'most barbarous, without laws, sciences or civility', eighteenth-century defenders of West Indian slavery dwelt on the depravity of African manners and the despotism of their native rulers: the people, they claimed, had 'no rules of civil polity', 'no knowledge of civility, arts, or science',* and were 'utterly unacquainted' with 'everything which constitutes civilized life'.[145]

In the later seventeenth century, Sir Thomas Browne predicted that when African countries were 'well civilized', they would cease to sell their people to labour in the American plantations. A later writer defended the enslavement of Africans by saying that they lived in a state of 'brutish barbarism'; but he added that 'when they become civilized, it must cease, of course'.[146] Meanwhile, it was claimed that the slave trade took Africans away from a continent given over to murderous warfare into 'lands where no such barbarities were known' and introduced them to 'a much happier state of life', 'as comfortable a state' indeed as that enjoyed by 'the lower orders in any country in Europe'.[147] Slavery was even regarded by some as a necessary civilizing stage through which barbarians had to pass. 'Through slavery and bondage,' thought the waterman poet John Taylor in 1638, 'many people and nations that were heathens and barbarous have been happily brought to civility and Christian liberty.'[148] The West Indian planters, however, were predictably hostile to any attempts at 'civilizing' their slaves. By the end of the eighteenth century, it was they who had increasingly come to be seen as the barbarians.[149]

*　*　*

Nowadays it is usual to regard the claim of English colonists and missionaries that they were bringing 'civility' to barbarous peoples as a self-serving pretext for physical violence and cultural aggression against those they regarded as lower in the scale of civilization. By portraying their own social norms as 'civilized', and those of others as backward, cruel and ignorant, the travel writers and propagandists

---

* The irrelevance of this argument was exposed by the American Founding Father Benjamin Rush, who asked whether it would 'avail a man to plead in a court of justice that he defrauded his neighbour because he was inferior to him in genius or knowledge'; Benjamin Rush, *A Vindication of the Address to the Inhabitants of the British Settlements on the Slavery of the Negroes in America* (Philadelphia, PA, 1773), 32–33.

created an implicit justification for unsolicited intervention in the lives and livelihoods of other peoples. Conscientiously worked out as an application of the 'law of nature', the embryonic international law that developed between the sixteenth and eighteenth centuries helped to legitimize the commercial and colonizing interests of those Western European powers who had defined themselves as 'the civilized world'. Unsurprisingly, some modern critics see the rhetoric of 'civility' and the whole notion of 'Western civilization' as an ideological invention designed to destroy aboriginal cultures and thereby facilitate the worldwide expansion of capitalist relations.[150] They follow in the wake of Karl Marx, who described what he called 'the great civilizing influence of capital' and, with Friedrich Engels, evoked the process by which capitalism forced 'all nations, on pain of extinction, to adopt the bourgeois mode of production', thus compelling them 'to introduce what it calls civilization into their midst, i.e., to become bourgeois themselves. In one word, it creates a world after its own image.'[151]

Yet many people in early modern England sincerely believed that the civilizing mission was a moral obligation, 'a godly and commendable deed'.[152] Sixteenth-century humanists thought it was good to bring people from 'barbarism' to a 'civilized' way of living, for that would enable them to fulfil their nature. Thomas More related how the founder of his Utopia had introduced a rude and wild population to *cultus* and *humanitas* (freely rendered by Ralph Robinson in 1551 as 'all good fashions, humanity, and civil gentleness', and by a later translator in 1684 as 'politeness'). Edmund Spenser believed that the introduction of agriculture would bring the Irish 'sweetness and happy contentment'.[153] Richard Hakluyt thought that there was 'no greater glory' than 'to conquer the barbarian, to recall the savage and the pagan to civility.' 'What hath ever been the work of the greatest princes of the earth,' asked the Jacobean governor of Virginia, Captain John Smith (Plate 18), 'but planting of countries, and civilizing barbarous and inhuman nations to civility and humanity?'[154] The Commonwealth government claimed in 1649 that by 'reducing

Ireland to civility' they would bring its people 'things tending to their good and happiness'. A few years later James Harrington portrayed the aspiration to empire as a 'duty ... to put the world into a better condition than it was before'.[155] In 1738 Bishop William Warburton declared that 'civilizing a barbarous people' was 'a work of exalted charity'; and in 1773 the Scottish historian Robert Henry opined that no one could be better employed than 'in civilizing the barbarous', taking them out of 'a sordid and miserable' existence and putting them into 'a decent and comfortable way of living'.[156] Even the great abolitionist William Wilberforce believed that 'the arts and sciences, knowledge and civilization' were never the native growth of any country: 'They have ever been communicated from one nation to another, from the more to the less civilized.'[157] The same could be said of modern attempts by Western powers to export democracy and human rights to the rest of the world.

Yet in the early modern period not everyone subscribed to the implicit assumption of the civilizers that there was only one acceptable form of civility and that their own legal, political and cultural standards were uniquely appropriate for all other human beings. It is time to consider those who took a different view.

Civilization Reconsidered

When Indians hear the horrid filths
    Of Irish, English men,
The horrid oaths and murders late,
    Thus say these Indians then:
We wear no clothes, have many Gods,
    And yet our sins are less.
You are barbarians, pagans wild,
    Your land's the wilderness.
        Roger Williams, *A Key into the Language of America* (1643)

Cultural Relativism

During the past hundred and fifty years or so, many features of what was once regarded as the distinctive civilization of Western Europe and North America have been adopted in most parts of the world. Whether it be medicine and public health, science and technology, democracy and human rights, or jeans, pop music, mobile phones and football, the culture of the West has permeated countries that were once dismissed as 'barbarous' and 'uncivilized'. In the name of 'modernization' and 'development', the richer countries pour 'aid' into poorer ones in order to accelerate this process of reducing the world to one single 'civilization'.

Nowadays, however, it is by no means unusual to be sceptical, not to say cynical, about attempts, however well intentioned, to export Western modes of life to other peoples. As globalization reduces the nations of the world to cultural homogeneity, we increasingly prize the values of difference and diversity.[1] We accept, at least in theory, that there may be many valid ways of living, even if most of us remain firmly committed to the one to which we are accustomed. The very concept of 'civilization' has come to be offensive to many because of its legitimizing role in the history of colonialism. It is seen as a camouflage for capitalist ambition, political aggrandizement and the contentious assumption that Western ways of life are intrinsically superior to all others. That was why the old division between 'civilized' countries and 'barbarous' ones was officially discarded in the late 1940s, when the United Nations declared that the world was composed of a plurality of civilizations.[2] As for the supposed superiority of the civilized present to the barbarism of the remote past, archaeologists have taught us to recognize that the inventions of the Neolithic era – agriculture, stock rearing, pottery and weaving – were at least as momentous as those of the Industrial Revolution.[3] Similarly, anthropologists remind us that Eskimos and Australian Aborigines survived and flourished without the aid of modern technology in a physical environment that would have defeated their 'civilized' contemporaries. If we still speak of barbarism, it is no longer as a way of describing the condition of some 'undeveloped' society. Rather, we regard it as a morally reprehensible state of mind into which, as in the case of Nazi Germany, even the most civilized people may sometimes fall.

The notion that every culture is worthy of respect is often assumed to have been an invention of the Romantic era, given classic formulation by the German thinker Johann Gottfried von Herder (1744–1803). It was he, it is claimed, who best articulated the view that cultures were incommensurable. Instead of representing 'savage' or 'barbarian' societies as situated at the bottom of a ladder leading step by step to higher and more 'civilized' modes of existence, Herder rejected the whole attempt to construct such a hierarchy. Each culture, whether in the present or the past, was unique: it had its own validity and was not to be judged by the standards of another or measured against a single universal scale.[4] Herder was not consistent in this view, for he also believed in the universal values of cultural progress and human fulfilment (*Humanität*).[5] A Christian, whose later work abounds in value judgements about the superior bodily appearance of Europeans and their unprecedented achievements in the arts and sciences, he had a clear notion about what was 'civilized' (*gesittet*) and what was 'barbarous' (*barbarisch*). He condemned the Hindu practice of widow burning as 'barbarous' and 'inhuman', and he welcomed the progress (*Fortgang*) of civilization.[6] In short, he was a pluralist but not a relativist. He thought it important to recognize that there were many different cultures, each of which deserved to be understood on its own terms. But although one should try to comprehend their values, one did not have to share them.

Despite this ambivalence, Herder's writings constitute a profound critique of traditional ethnocentrism, a belief in the singularity of each people, and a vigorous defence of cultural diversity. Denouncing the slave trade and all forms of colonial conquest, he issued a vigorous challenge to European complacency. As he explained, he had no wish to disparage the quality of life in the civil society of his day; but he wanted justice to be done to different ways of living, which were appropriate for people living in other times or in other places. This required empathy (*Einfühlung*) and an ability to understand other cultures and their values in their own terms.[7]

Like so much else, the germ of Herder's attitude can be traced back to classical antiquity. The observation that each social group thinks its own customs are the best and despises those of others is as old as Herodotus. The legendary Scythian prince Anacharsis was alleged to have said in the sixth century BC that the Scythians laughed just as much at the Athenian way of speaking as the Athenians did at his. Exiled to the shores of the Black Sea at the beginning of the first century AD, the Roman poet Ovid complained that he was regarded as a barbarian there because the locals could not understand him. Later in the century, St Paul wrote, 'If I know not the meaning of the voice, I shall be unto him that speaketh a barbarian, and he that speaketh shall be a barbarian unto me.'[8] In the early modern period, this became a common rhetorical trope. 'The Scythians were barbarians among the Greeks,' wrote the French poet Joachim du Bellay in 1549, 'but the Athenians were also barbarians among the Scythians.' Similarly, the Spanish Dominican missionary Bartolomé de Las Casas, writing in the 1550s, observed that 'just as we regard the people of the Indies as barbarians, they also judge us to be barbarians because they do not understand us'.[9]

At the same time, many European intellectuals were led by their training in classical rhetoric and their rediscovery of the philosophical scepticism of Sextus Empiricus (*c.* AD 100–200) into a half-playful, half-serious questioning of the conventional values of the time, which they suggested were the peculiarities of their particular society rather than universal truths.[10] Such an attitude was powerfully reinforced by the travellers, explorers and ethnographic writers of the sixteenth and seventeenth centuries. As new knowledge about other peoples of the world poured into Europe, it was impossible for well-informed contemporaries not to become increasingly self-conscious about the peculiarities of their own brand of civility. It is well known how descriptions of the natives of Central and South America who had been subjugated by the *conquistadores* helped to foster a nascent sense of cultural relativism among sixteenth-century Spanish moralists and philosophers. The lawyer Alonso de Zorita (1512–85), for example, observed that all peoples tended to describe as 'barbarian' whatever it was they found different.[11]

The most influential expression of this relativist way of thinking was to be found in the *Essais* (1580–88) of Michel de Montaigne, which became well known in England through John Florio's translation of 1603. Drawing on the legacy of the classical sceptics, and demonstrating a remarkable freedom from ethnocentricity, the French author concluded that there were no universal standards of beauty or religion or morality which were accepted by all peoples, not even a rule for the division of labour between the sexes. There were just many different customs; and as Herder would later say, each custom had its own reason. It followed that 'barbarism' was merely a pejorative name for what any particular people found unfamiliar in the habits of others.[12] Montaigne's disciple Pierre Charron, in his book *Of Wisdome* (translated into English five years after Florio's *Montaigne*), poured scorn on those who condemned as 'barbarous and beastly' anything that did not accord with 'the common use and custom of their country'.[13]

Of course, Montaigne was not really an ethical relativist. He was a devout Catholic, who had his own set of values by which he judged the behaviour of others. These enabled him to suggest in his essay 'On the Cannibals' that his contemporaries were the true barbarians, for it was greater barbarism to burn people alive for heresy, as was their practice, than to eat them when they were dead, as the 'savages' supposedly did. Similarly, Charron was applying his own assumptions about rationality when he argued that many exotic practices that at first sight appeared savage and inhumane could be seen to be perfectly reasonable when examined more closely.[14] Nevertheless, he and Montaigne were influential propagators of the notion that the Western European way of looking at the world was not a uniquely valid one.

This assumption was more common in early modern Britain than is sometimes appreciated. In 1550, several decades before Montaigne, an anonymous Scottish writer, probably the Dundee clergyman Robert Wedderburn, repudiated English slurs on his fellow countrymen by remarking that every nation regarded others as barbarous if their 'natures and complexions' were 'contrary' to theirs.[15] The

English author George Puttenham suggested in 1589 that the word 'barbarous' was a relative term, stemming from the 'great pride' of the Greeks and Romans, which had led them to regard 'all nations beside themselves' as 'rude and uncivil'.[16] In 1603 the poet Samuel Daniel, brother-in-law of Montaigne's translator John Florio, called it 'a touch of arrogant ignorance to hold this or that nation barbarous, these or those times gross'; in his view, even the Goths and Vandals had great achievements to their credit, since their laws and customs were 'the originals of most of the provincial constitutions of Christendom'. Daniel also offered a notable defence of the learning of the Middle Ages, so despised by many of his contemporaries.[17]

Travellers had long noticed that even in Western Europe peoples differed from each other in their characteristic ways of walking, speaking and gesturing, and that they had conflicting notions of what constituted civil behaviour. The merchant-economist Gerard de Malynes observed in 1601 that men's idea of what was 'civil' reflected the practice of their particular country. 'That which is civility in one nation,' agreed Sir Thomas Palmer in 1606, 'is unaccustomed and rejected in other states.' 'Our deformity is others' beauty,' noted John Locke, 'our rudeness, others' civility.'[18] With the increasing awareness of other cultures, thanks to the travellers, and of other ages, thanks to the growth of antiquarian studies, it was a sentiment frequently repeated.[19] As Adam Smith would remark, 'A degree of politeness which in Russia would be highly esteemed, even regarded as positively effeminate, would be seen as rudeness and barbarism at the court of France.'[20]

It followed that it was wrong to call other nations 'barbarous' simply because their standards were different.* Robert Boyle thought

---

* When two Japanese boys were sent to Europe by the Jesuits in the 1580s, they returned to report that in Portugal it was thought polite to sit on chairs and boorish to sit on the ground, whereas the Japanese thought the opposite. They concluded that each country had customs appropriate to its circumstances: the Japanese way of sitting suited their modest financial resources, whereas the furniture of the Europeans reflected their greater spending power; *Japanese Travellers in Sixteenth-Century Europe*, trans. J. F. Moran, ed. Derek Massarella (Hakluyt Soc., 2012), 137–38.

it absurd that the Greeks and the Romans had given the name of 'barbarian' to each other, as well as to the rest of the world, when both peoples were 'highly civilized'.[21] The traveller Paul Rycaut thought that readiness to dismiss the manners and habits of other nations as 'barbarous' stemmed from ignorance and unfamiliarity; the historian John Oldmixon put it down to 'vanity'; and the Cambridge orientalist Simon Ockley thought it was 'childish'.[22] In John Dryden's play *The Indian Emperour* (first performed in 1665), one of the Spanish commanders involved in the conquest of Mexico remarks that

No useful arts have yet found footing here,
But all untaught and savage does appear.

To which his leader, Hernán Cortez, retorts that

Wild and untaught are terms which we alone
Invent, for fashions differing from our own.[23]

As a pamphleteer concluded in 1695, 'One nation calls another barbarous, because different in habit [i.e., dress], manners, diet and ceremonies.'[24]

It was also widely recognized that, even within the same nation, ideals of civil behaviour did not stay constant, but changed over time. When, at the beginning of the eighteenth century, Roger North sat down to consider what was meant by 'good breeding', he rapidly concluded that no part of it was founded in nature, but that 'all of it' was 'relative': there was 'no universal character of good breeding: the currency whereof is purely from the stamp of custom and opinion'. His contemporary the Welsh antiquarian Henry Rowlands agreed: what was thought barbarism in one age was deemed civility in another. The author of an English dictionary of 1749 pointed out that the same was true of linguistic propriety: one era regarded as 'polite and elegant' what another accounted 'uncouth and barbarous'.[25]

Another Kind of Civility

The sense of relativism that came from a sharpened historical consciousness was reinforced by face-to-face encounters with other societies. In 1634 the traveller Henry Blount set out on a tour of the Levant to determine 'whether, to an unpartial conceit, the Turkish way appears absolutely barbarous, as we are given to understand, or rather another kind of civility, different from ours, but no less pretending'. As a stranger in the Bulgarian city of Sofia, he found that he was less troubled by 'affronts or gaping' than in any other town he had ever visited; and he was overwhelmed by the 'incredible civility' of the Turkish sailors. He returned to report that it was the vanity of all nations to esteem themselves civil and others barbarous.[26]

In 1644 the protoanthropologist John Bulwer observed that each nation had its own standards of bodily decorum; he tentatively suggested a climatic explanation: for example, the inhabitants of northern countries such as England and Germany did not gesticulate in the way that the Italians did because the colder weather forced them to keep their hands in their pockets.[27] In 1671, Lancelot Addison, who during his seven years as a chaplain in Tangier had closely observed the Moors and the Jews, echoed Henry Blount's opinion that what was commonly called 'barbarous' was 'only another kind of civility'. He knew of no nation 'so rude and barbarous, as to be utterly devoid of all rites of civility and respect'; and he found that the allegedly barbarous people of West Barbary were remarkable for their order, civility and religion. At the time of childbirth, for example, they observed a 'decency conformable to the best civilized people' (by which he meant that they avoided sexual relations during pregnancy and for forty days after the birth).[28]

Other travellers discovered that supposedly barbarian societies had their distinctive rules for polite eating, drinking and conversing. Those who ate with their fingers, for example, counted it 'the greatest incivility in the world' to let any food fall or to spit or cough while eating.[29] Sir Thomas Palmer reported that, although 'the Turks and Indians and other barbarians of Africa' ate their meat on the ground, they were neater and cleaner than the 'Dutchmen' [i.e., the Germans], who were 'slovenly and sluttish in their apparel and feeding'. He also thought that the Islamic inhabitants of subequatorial Africa who practised daily bathing could instruct the 'Dutchmen' in bodily cleanliness. Although firmly of the view that 'of all civil nations' the English were preeminent, he believed that there was 'no nation in the world, how court-like soever, but hath the dregs and lees of barbarous incivility'.[30] Conversely, there was no nation so barbarous that it had nothing to offer which was worthy of imitation: the English, Scots, French, Italians and Spanish, despite being 'the most reformed and court-like people', were all 'tainted with some blemish of barbarousness' which the heathen nations could teach them how to reform. In their notorious incivility to foreign visitors, the common people of England compared very unfavourably with the 'African heathen negroes', who were 'so charitable to strangers that nothing shall be denied them, if it rest in their powers to relieve their distress and wants'. The people of 'East India' were said to be equally hospitable and considerate; and there were similar lessons to be learnt from the Turks, Tartars, Persians, Parthians and Egyptians. Even the Scythians were more restrained in their drinking than the Germans, whose drunkenness made them 'more uncivil than beasts'.[31]

A probably fictitious account in 1670 of a merchant who had supposedly been captured and forced to serve in the Algerian army represented him as confessing that he had seen nothing of 'that rudeness which our people imagine to be in all the parts of Africa': on the contrary, he had found the people to be 'very polite and well bred; ... They are affable, hospitable, courteous, kind and very liberal.' The surveyor William Smith was sent out by the Royal Africa Company in 1726. As he moved through the West African kingdoms, he described the various peoples he met as, respectively, 'civil' and 'good-natured', 'very civilized', 'most courteous and civil to strangers', 'gentleman-like', 'abounding with good manners and ceremony to each other', and 'exceedingly civil and courteous'. Later English visitors to West Africa found the natives of Cape Verde 'civilized and hospitable to strangers'.[32] Initially repelled by African polygamy, some came to see it as reminiscent of the Biblical patriarchs, and far preferable to the European practice of permitting married men to keep mistresses.[33]

Travel dispelled many of the prejudices disseminated by armchair geographers. Sailors, merchants and diplomats who had practical experience of dealing with alien peoples tended to be much more pragmatic and tolerant when confronted by unfamiliar manners and customs. This was particularly true of those who lived and traded in the Ottoman Empire, the traditional enemy of Christian Europe, notorious for its alleged cruelty and despotic rule. Many English merchants and travellers interacted closely with Ottoman subjects and often formed a sympathetic view of what appeared to be a well-ordered, efficiently administered and militarily formidable society, as well as a remarkably tolerant and pluralist one.[34] As consul to the Levant Company in Smyrna, Paul Rycaut reported in 1668 that the Turks were not 'so savage and rude as they are generally described'. Travellers commented favourably on their neatness, cleanliness and sobriety; their respectful submissiveness to their superiors; and their civility to foreign visitors.[35] In the reign of James II, would-be repealers of the Test Acts against Catholics and Dissenters held up the Turks, Persians and Mughals as setting an example of religious toleration that the English would be well advised to follow.[36]

As the Turkish threat to Europe receded at the end of the seventeenth century, denunciations of Ottoman barbarism became less common, and a vogue arose for Turkish fashions in dress, decoration and coffee drinking.[37] The Cambridge University professor of Arabic commented in 1717 on the 'folly of the Westerlings in despising the wisdom of Eastern nations, and looking upon them as brutes and barbarians, whilst we arrogate to ourselves everything that is wise and polite'. He conceded that the West had recently seen greater advances in the sciences, but there had not been the least improvement in areas where the Easterners excelled, namely, 'things of universal necessity', such as 'the fear of God, the regulation of our appetites, prudent economy, decency and sobriety of behaviour in all conditions and emergencies of life'.[38] His contemporary Lady Mary Wortley Montagu, wife of the English ambassador to Constantinople, remarked on the 'obliging civility' of the Turkish women, declaring that, contrary to what was usually thought, they were freer than their English counterparts because they were concealed by their dress and therefore able to go anywhere. Later in the century, the diplomat Sir James Porter reported that the Turkish government, although not ideal, was 'much more perfect and regular, as well as less despotic' than most writers had represented it.[39]

The Native Americans similarly impressed many early colonists with their courtesy, 'civility' and physical modesty. They were 'in their behaviour as mannerly and civil as any of Europe', claimed the first travellers to Virginia. Roger Williams, reflecting on his years 'among the barbarians', concluded that the natives were 'of two sorts (as the English are)': some were 'rude and clownish', but most had 'a savour of civility and courtesy ... both amongst themselves and towards strangers'; and he praised them for their warm hospitality.[40] The Quakers were alone among the early colonists in ignoring the traditional civil/savage dichotomy and treating the natives simply as the children of God.[41] But many other English settlers admired the gravity, dignity and hospitality of the Indian chiefs. Some compared their dwellings, with the fire in the middle of the floor, to the old baronial halls of England, and their wigwams to the English gentry's 'summer-houses'. They also noted that they did not spend all the year in the same place, but 'after the manner of the gentry of the civilized nations, remove[d] for their pleasures, sometimes to their hunting places, where they remain, keeping good hospitality'.[42] Others, like the Quaker William Penn, found the appearance and ritual practices of the Indians more reminiscent of the London Jews: 'A man would think himself in Duke's Place or Berry Street in London when he seeeth them.'[43] (Since Oliver Cromwell's day, large numbers of Jews had lived at these addresses in Aldgate.)

In 1605 Sir Ferdinando Gorges was presented with three captured Native Americans. He found that they had 'an inclination to follow the example of the better sort and in all their carriages manifest shows of great civility, far from the rudeness of our common people'. Gorges was not the only colonist to regard the natives as in many ways 'less rude' than English rustics or to believe that some of the customs of this 'uncivilized' people, such as their respect for the elderly, were 'fit to serve for models to the most civilized Europeans'.[44] Early descriptions of the good-humoured way in which the Native Americans played football would have pleased the headmaster of a nineteenth-century public school: 'They never strike up another's heels, as we do, not accounting that praiseworthy to get a goal by such advantage … If any man … be thrown, he laughs … There is no seeking of revenge, no quarrelling, no bloody noses, scratched faces, black eyes, broken shins, no bruised members or crushed ribs. But the goal being won, … friends they were at the football, and friends they must meet at the kettle.'[45]

Allowance has to be made for the contexts in which such assessments were offered. In their eagerness to attract emigrants, traders and investors, the authors of the early colonizing literature went out of their way to represent the Native Americans as friendly, courteous and welcoming. Later, when disillusion had set in after some violent encounters, accounts of the habits and dispositions of the natives were usually less favourable.[46] One of the most sympathetic portrayals of their way of life, *New English Canaan* (1637), was by Thomas Morton, whose anti-Puritan sentiments and rival involvement in the beaver trade had brought him into conflict with the colonists of Plymouth and Massachusetts Bay. His praise of the Indians was a way of hitting back at his enemies, who, he claimed, had failed to emulate the natives' skills. Roger Williams, who warmly commended the natives for their humanity and civility in his *Key into the Language of America* (1643), had been banished from the colony of Massachusetts in the midwinter of 1635–36 and given shelter by a tribe of Native Americans. He noted that they had no beggars and no fatherless children unprovided for; robberies, murders and adulteries were also much less frequent than among the English.[47]

Even those with no previous axe to grind came to accept that there was much to admire about these so-called barbarians. Some respected their practical abilities. Arguing that there was 'no nation so barbarous, no people so brutish, but there is something among them worthy of imitation', one Restoration writer urged the English to follow the example of the American Indians by growing potatoes to feed the poor. Similarly, Sir Thomas Browne noted that some of 'the most barbarous nations' were addicted to fishing and very knowledgeable about it.[48] Others admired their morality. The political writer James Tyrrell remarked that the Native Americans did not steal from each other, and the physician Humphrey Brooke observed that 'the Turks, Indians, and many other people we are pleased to account barbarous' were much kinder to animals than his fellow countrymen.[49] John Locke drew upon his extensive reading in travel literature when he reported that 'the [American] Indians, whom we call barbarous, observe much more decency and civility in their discourses and conversation, giving one another a fair silent hearing, till they have quite done; and then answering them calmly, and without noise or passion'.[50]

Numerous observations of this kind preceded the protoanthropological work of Joseph-François Lafitau, French Jesuit missionary to Canada, who, in his desire to confute the atheists at home by showing that the principles of religion were universal, demonstrated in 1724 to a European public that the Native Americans had their own forms of civility ('*une espèce de civilité à leur mode*'), distinguished by respect for the aged, deference to equals, affability and hospitality.[51]

Later in the century, the fashionable London obstetrician William Smellie gave it as his opinion that 'savages and the ruder nations' often displayed more discernment in the upbringing of infants than was to be found 'in the most polished stages of society'. Captain James Cook frequently recorded during his voyages in the South Seas that he was received 'with great civility'. He found the Maoris 'as modest and reserved in their behaviour and conversation as the most polite nations of Europe'; while the Tongans, although lacking metals and having no communication with other nations, proved in the opinion of Cook's surgeon William Anderson to be 'in every respect almost as perfectly civilized as it is possible for mankind to be'. Later in Alaska, Cook encountered 'the most peaceable, inoffensive people I ever met with, and, as to honesty, they might serve as a pattern to the most civilized nation upon earth'.[52]

Adam Smith took a less rosy view of the life led by savages and barbarians, but he noted that no people showed more respect for women as rational beings than did the North American Indians. He also firmly refuted the notion that the natives were the creatures of uncontrollable passion. On the contrary, he believed that the very harshness of the conditions in which they lived led them to excel in the virtue of self-control. In their patient enduring of labour, hunger and pain; their contempt for torture and death; and their absolute command of their passions, the Native Americans set an example of 'heroic and unconquerable firmness'. In 'civilized societies', by contrast, people were readily forgiven if they complained when in pain, grieved when in distress, were overcome by love or were discomposed by anger.[53]

Of course, what most of such comments reveal is the readiness of British visitors to spot similarities between the practices of other peoples and their own ideas of civility. As the influential cleric Jeremy Taylor remarked in 1660, it was the observer's own assumptions that determined which nations were to be regarded as *moratiores* (better mannered). 'If they be like our customs, our laws, and manners of living, then we approve them, else we condemn them.'[54] This was not the same as accepting that when 'barbarian' notions of civil behaviour were radically different from familiar ones they might nevertheless be equally valid. That remained a minority view confined to the intellectually sophisticated. Most of the English were as slow to recognize that supposedly barbarous people might have their own forms of civility as were the upper ranks of society to accept that their social inferiors at home had their own kinds of politeness.

Nevertheless, the reports of seventeenth-century travellers to the Levant reveal that, long before Herder or even Lafitau, the subversive opinion was already circulating that the standards of civility which the Europeans upheld as universal were merely their own cultural peculiarities; they were not intrinsically superior to those of other countries, and they were subject to constant change over time. As the politician and writer Sir Thomas Pope Blount put it in 1692, a wise man should suspend his judgement and not be overforward in censuring and condemning the laws and customs of other nations: many practices that, on first acquaintance, seemed savage and inhumane would, when examined more closely, prove to be perfectly rational. In the *Spectator*, Joseph Addison (son of the Lancelot Addison who had found in Tangier not barbarism, but a different mode of civility) censured the 'narrow way of thinking' that led his fellow countrymen to regard the customs, dress and manners of other countries as ridiculous if they did not resemble their own.[55]

In the eighteenth century, it became a central tenet of Montesquieu, Diderot and other *philosophes* of the French Enlightenment that it was wrong to judge other societies by the standards of one's own. While simultaneously proclaiming universal principles of politics and morality, these thinkers somehow managed also to suggest the relativity of cultural values and the incommensurability of different ways of life.[56] Similarly, in Britain, the philosopher David Hartley lamented 'the opinions of savageness, barbarity, and cruelty, which ignorant and unexperienced persons are apt to entertain concerning

261

some distant nations'; and Adam Ferguson dismissed the term 'barbarian', 'in use with one arrogant people, and that of "gentile" with another', because they served to distinguish only the stranger whose language and pedigree differed from theirs. 'Savages we call them,' said Benjamin Franklin of the Native Americans, 'because their manners differ from ours, which we think the perfection of civility; they think the same of theirs.' Lord Macartney, George III's ambassador to China, agreed: 'How little right we have to despise and ridicule other nations on the mere account of their differing from us in little points of manners and dress, as we can very nearly match them with similar follies and absurdities of our own.'[57]

Neither Macartney nor Franklin would for a moment have thought of ranking these other ways of life as on a par with their own.[58] Even so, the radical notion that the civilization of Western Europe was only one among many was beginning to take shape. Asia, in particular, had been known since Elizabethan times to be 'full of civil people'.[59] China, despite its failure to make further intellectual or technological progress, was particularly celebrated for its effective government and obsequiously elaborate code of behaviour.[60] Persia was known and admired thanks to the very full account of its manners and customs published in 1686 by the Huguenot Sir John Chardin, who reported that 'the polite men amongst them are upon a level with the politest men of Europe'. Even earlier, the Jacobean traveller Sir Anthony Sherley had claimed that Shah Abbas's government differed 'so much from that which we call barbarousness' that it was as good a model for a monarchy as was Plato's for a republic.[61] As for the Arabs, the great oriental scholar Sir William Jones observed in 1787 that 'men will always differ in their ideas of civilization, each measuring it by the habits and prejudices of his own country', but 'if courtesy and urbanity, a love of poetry and eloquence, and the practice of exalted virtues be a juster measure of perfect society, we have certain proof that the people of Arabia, both in the plains and in cities, in republican and monarchical states, were eminently civilized for many ages before their conquest of Persia' (in the mid-seventh century).[62]

India was also regarded with some respect, particularly in the later eighteenth century, when Sir William Jones considered its ancient literature to be only slightly inferior to that of Greece and Rome and described the Sanskrit language as 'more perfect than Greek, more copious than Hebrew, and more exquisitely refined than either'. He also thought that Hindu teachings on the afterlife were superior to those of Christianity. As Edmund Burke remarked in 1783, the Indians were a civilized and cultivated people when the British were still in the woods.[63] The East India Company prided itself on not interfering with the country's civil and religious institutions. It preferred to propagate Christianity by example rather than overt evangelization. It did not necessarily object to missionaries, provided they were firmly under the Company's control, but it was not until 1813 that Christian missionaries were given free access to the country, and then only in response to Evangelical pressure from home. By that time, new ideas of European moral and racial superiority were in the ascendant.[64]

The early modern period was marked by an increasing awareness that Western Europeans could appear as barbarous to other peoples as other peoples did to them. In the eyes of the Islamic world, the pork-eating and wine-drinking West appeared filthy and sexually profligate. The Ottomans were sometimes praised for making no distinctions of status in their empire between those they regarded as civilized and those they regarded as barbarians.[65] This did not stop the Turks from regarding Western Europeans as 'unwashed dogs' who did not bathe.* A Moor who had been to England told Lancelot Addison that he was scandalized to see women, dogs and dirty shoes brought into places

---

* George Sandys commented, with evident surprise, that the Turks never urinated without washing their hands and privities, 'at which business they sequester themselves, and crouch to the earth, reviling the Christian, whom they see pissing against a wall'; George Sandys, *A Relation of a Journey Begun An. Dom. 1610* (1615), 64.

where God was worshipped. True civility for him required conversion to Islam.[66] 'We are apt to call "barbarous" whatever departs widely from our own taste and apprehension,' wrote David Hume, 'but [we] soon find the epithet of reproach retorted on us.'[67]

In India, Europeans wearing hats were seen as ridiculous; and their taking them off as a mark of respect was positively offensive, since for Indians the action was the conventional prelude to a challenge.[68] The Japanese regarded the Portuguese traders as barbarians because they entered temples without removing their shoes and defiled their straw mats by spitting and blowing their noses on them.[69] The Chinese had a repertoire of ceremonious bodily gestures that far exceeded anything to be found in Europe.[70] They believed themselves to be 'the only reasonable and civilized people' and were notoriously contemptuous of Westerners, whom they classified, along with the rest of the non-Chinese world, as barbarians and required to pay tribute money if they wanted access to their country.[71] Hence Adam Ferguson's sagacious comment on 'that mutual contempt and aversion' with which nations at different stages of economic development regarded each other, and the complacency with which all of them believed their own condition to be the epitome of human felicity: 'We are ourselves the supposed standard of politeness and civilization; and where our own features do not appear, we apprehend that there is nothing which deserves to be known.'[72]

An important feature of the new disposition to take other cultures more seriously was the willingness of some observers to accept that many so-called savages and barbarians did not exist in a condition of anarchy, as Thomas Hobbes and others had maintained, but had their own forms of government and regulation. This was a critical concession, since the level of a people's political organization was an accepted index of their civility. The French philosopher Pierre de La Primaudaye, in a work available in English translation from 1586 and often reprinted, observed that although there were people in some parts of the world who lived like beasts, lacking houses or money and eating raw flesh, there were none with 'no kind of policy established amongst them, or that use[d] no laws or customs, where-unto they willingly submit themselves'.[73] The Jacobean leader of the English colonists in Virginia, Captain John Smith, explained that although the native people were 'very barbarous', yet they had 'such government as that their magistrates, for good commanding, and their people, for due subjection and obeying, excel[led] many places that would be counted very civil'. Only a minority of the colonists shared this belief that the North American Indians lived in some form of civil society. Yet without it, the practice of buying land from Indian tribes, which presupposed their ability to make binding contracts, would have made no sense.[74]

In the same way, John Ogilby's *Atlas* (1670) showed Africa as made up of distinct kingdoms; even the inhabitants of Madagascar, though much addicted to theft and robbery, were said to have 'some kind of government or law among them'.[75] In his treatise of 1703 on govern-ment, Peter Paxton noted that modern explorers had never found even 'the most rude and barbarous savages' living alone in woods or deserts: when their numbers were 'not sufficient to raise larger and more powerful governments', they belonged to 'small septs or hordes, with some marks of order or economy amongst them'.[76] David Hume believed that the Native Americans lived in amity without an established government, but submitted in time of war to the leadership of one of their number, who relinquished his authority when the war was over.[77]

Inevitably, this increasing understanding of the extra-European world had the effect of casting doubt on the age-old, binary distinc-tion between the 'civil' and the 'barbarous'. One of the reasons leading the philosopher James Dunbar to reject it was his conviction that it rested on an unjustified belief in European superiority. Anticipating the great anthropologist Claude Lévi-Strauss, he argued that the very survival for so long, without any threat of extinction, of 'even the simplest and rudest race of men inhabiting the frozen shores of Greenland, or placed between the fervour of a vertical sun along the

Guinea coast, or on the banks of the Orinoco', was proof that they had attained 'a measure of worth and of felicity' not much inferior to that of 'the most admired nations'.[78]

Despite this growing sense among educated contemporaries of the relativity of custom and the variety of cultural practices to be found in the world, the 'conjectural' historians of the eighteenth century never spoke of 'civilizations' in the plural. 'Civilization' for them was still an ideal, not a neutral term of analysis. They tended to think of all peoples as going through the different stages of development on the same, single evolutionary scale. Only the final stage, their own 'commercial society', was regarded as fully mature. In their eyes, all other modes of subsistence underpinned lower forms of life that could never claim to be more than partially 'civilized'. It is true that in the later eighteenth century it was not uncommon for contemporaries to use the word 'civilization' as a neutral, value-free concept by referring to such entities as 'Gothick civilization' or 'modern European civilization'. But not until the early nineteenth century did the word 'civilization' come to be employed in the plural, first in France and only later in Britain.[79]

In practice, this new sense of the simultaneous existence of numerous distinct 'civilizations' was quickly overshadowed by a new and accelerated phase of Western imperialism, which represented itself as advancing 'Civilization' in the singular.[80] In the nineteenth century, the idea of a plurality of civilizations was very much a minority view. Yet in that belief we can see the origins of what would become the orthodoxy of early twentieth-century social anthropologists, namely, that differing customs, manners and ways of living were to be regarded not as stages in an upward progression, but as independent and coexisting 'cultures'. As John Stuart Mill wrote in 1840, 'great thinkers from Herder to Michelet' had shown that 'even barbarians, as the [ancient] Germans, or still more unmitigated savages, the wild Indians, and again the Chinese, the Egyptians, the Arabs, all had their own education, their own culture; a culture which, whatever might be its tendency upon the whole, had been successful in some respect or other'.[81] Herder had said that there was no people on earth without a culture; and as the French anthropologist Marcel Mauss (1872–1950) would explain, societies with certain attributes in common with each other could be usefully identified as forming a single and distinct 'civilization'.[82] In his preface of 1929 to a study of Maori economics, the historian R. H. Tawney cautiously observed that the anthropologists had proved that 'what are called primitive peoples are not necessarily, it appears, uncivilized. Some of them . . . are merely peoples with a different kind of civilization.'[83] For Claude Lévi-Strauss, the real barbarians were now those who believed in the existence of barbarism.[84] The irony of this celebrated aperçu is that, by making this unprecedented willingness to regard other cultures as of equal value into an essential attribute of modern civility, it implicitly proclaims the superiority of our own broad-minded outlook to the narrowly parochial prejudices of less-enlightened peoples.*

The Civilizing Mission Disputed

In the early modern period, the recognition that most American, African and Asian peoples, whether 'barbarian' or not, had their own forms of political organization generated a sustained debate about the limits on the incursions into their territory that European powers could legitimately make. Many authorities followed the Spanish theologian Francisco de Vitoria in maintaining that strangers had a presumptive right to enter other countries, trade with them and dwell there. Alberico Gentili had agreed, though he conceded that a ruler was entitled to forbid trade in certain commodities and could prohibit access to the interior. The Spanish Jesuit Luis de Molina (d. 1600) went further by

---

* Contrast the robust view of the American philosopher Richard Rorty (1931–2007), who declared that 'some cultures, like some people, are no damn good: they cause too much pain and so have to be resisted (and perhaps eradicated) rather than respected'; 'In a Flattened World', *London Review of Books* 15, no. 7 (8 April 1993), 3.

maintaining that rulers had the right to prohibit access altogether, save in cases of extreme necessity.[85] His views were cited in England by the learned lawyer John Selden, who similarly held that a people could exclude foreign traders if they so wished.[86] That principle was, after all, implicit in the mid-seventeenth-century Navigation Acts confining English goods to English ships. Accordingly, both civil and common lawyers upheld the Crown's right to restrain trade with certain countries or in particular commodities.[87] In his *Elements of Law* (completed in 1640), Thomas Hobbes declared it to be a law of nature 'that men allow commerce and traffic indifferently to one another'. But in *Leviathan* (1651), he ruled that it was for the sovereign to determine where, and in what commodities, foreign trade should be conducted. He would, no doubt, have denied the existence of any legitimate Amerindian or African sovereign capable of exercising similar powers.[88] His argument was continued by Samuel von Pufendorf, whose work was well known in England. Pufendorf affirmed that the ruler of a country that had no relations with other countries was entitled either to deny entry altogether or to charge foreigners for access; he accepted that hospitality to strangers was a charitable act, but he maintained that the strangers could not claim it as a right.[89]

In the eighteenth century, Enlightenment thinkers such as Diderot and Kant further modified the ancient ethic of 'hospitality'. They continued to allow the right of voyagers to visit, to seek sanctuary from persecution and, in cases of extreme necessity, to take on basic provisions; but despite their own cosmopolitan dislike of isolationism, they maintained that countries were fully entitled to repel those with whom they did not wish to have commercial relations. They therefore endorsed the right of China and Japan to keep out Western traders. Similarly, Captain Cook, in accordance with instructions issued by the president of the Royal Society, accepted that the New Hebrideans were justified in trying to protect the islanders from foreign ships; though in practice, his need for water and fresh food forced him to land and kill the natives who tried to stop him.[90]

There was also mounting opposition to the doctrine that those who did not cultivate their land were obliged to let it be taken over by an invader who wished to do so. Drawing a pointed analogy with aristocratic game reserves in England, Roger Williams argued in the 1630s that even if the American Indians did not farm the territory they occupied, it was still theirs because they hunted over it: the English nobility reserved some of their estates for hunting and no one denied their ownership.[91] In the later seventeenth and early eighteenth centuries, many natural lawyers, including Pufendorf and his fellow German Christian Wolff, the Huguenot Jean Barbeyrac and the Cambridge professor of divinity Thomas Rutherforth, firmly repudiated the idea that hunters and nomadic shepherds could not collectively own land unless they cultivated it.[92] When, between 1769 and 1772, the new British owners of the West Indian island of St Vincent set about clearing away the native Caribs on the grounds that these 'uncivilized' and 'lawless' people had failed to cultivate the land they occupied, there was a howl of parliamentary protest at such 'cruelty'.[93]

The assumption of English monarchs that they were entitled to license their subjects to appropriate lands occupied by non-Christian peoples had been bolstered in the reign of James I by Sir Edward Coke's assertion that infidels were natural enemies, who could be legitimately attacked and with whom it was forbidden to trade, unless the monarch specifically permitted it.[94] His opinion, though disseminated in some legal textbooks, was dismissed as irrelevant by Lord Chief Justice Jeffreys in the court of King's Bench in 1685,[95] rejected in 1698, and definitively repudiated in the same court in 1774 by Lord Mansfield, who described it as an 'absurd' notion that 'in all probability arose from the mad enthusiasm of the Crusades'.[96]

Coke's dictum would, of course, have made it impossible to preach Christianity to the heathen. Worse still, it was wholly incompatible with the expansion of English commerce. In 1745 a leading chancery judge dismissed Coke's further assertion that the testimony of an infidel was unacceptable in the courts as 'a most impolite notion', which 'would at once destroy all that trade and commerce from which this nation reaps such great benefits'. The doctrine had originated, he said, 'in very bigoted Popish times, when we carried on very little trade, except the trade of religion, and consequently our notions were very narrow, and such as I hope will never prevail again in this country'.[97]

Natural lawyers had long held that paganism did not in itself diminish a ruler's authority. They rejected the view that Christians were entitled to make unprovoked war on infidels or to impose their religion by the sword.[98] Of course, the exposition of natural law was an academic and theoretical pursuit that had relatively little influence on the actual practice of traders and colonizers. Even so, Sir George Peckham felt it necessary in 1583 to offer a lengthy refutation of the objection made by some 'as do take upon them to be more than meanly learned' that it was 'scarce lawful' for Europeans to plant colonies by violence.[99] He would have had in mind the Spanish Dominican theologians of the early sixteenth century, who maintained that pagans could be legitimate rulers and denied the right of the Spaniards to make war on those they believed to be natural slaves. Bartolomé de Las Casas held that all peoples, however barbarous, were entitled to defend themselves against those who sought to attack them and take away their freedom.[100] The Jesuit Francisco Suárez (1548–1617) ruled that war against those of inferior talents was unlawful, unless they lived like wild beasts, naked, cannibalistic and without any form of government. If there really were such people, war could be waged against them, but its aim should be to organize them in a more human fashion, not to destroy them.[101]

In the seventeenth century, there were some vocal opponents of colonization by force. Roger Williams inveighed in 1652 against the 'sin' of the royal patents whereby kings were 'invested with right by virtue of their Christianity to take and give away the lands and countries of other men'.[102] Bishop Joseph Hall expressed the same viewpoint: 'The barbarous people', he said, were 'lords of their own' and were entitled to live peaceably, 'without the intermeddling [of] other nations'.[103] The Royalist clergyman Jeremy Taylor noted disapprovingly in 1660 that many nations had believed, and some still believed, that they were fully entitled to attack 'barbarous and savage people', particularly if they were rich and 'the possessors of far distant countries': 'The Romans, who were the wisest of all nations, did so ... All people whom they called barbarous, or whom they found rich, were their enemies.'[104]

Although classically educated authors such as Sir Thomas More drew on Roman precedents to justify European expansion, there was always an anti-imperialist strain in humanist thought, exemplified by Montaigne's blistering attack on the horrific slaughter that had accompanied the Spanish conquest of Mexico and Peru.[105] In England in 1649 it was a hatred of 'inhuman cruelties', augmented by a belief in the right of all peoples to govern themselves, that led some of the Levellers and their associates to condemn the 'robbing of the poor Indians' and the hunting of 'the poor Irish'. They wanted peace to be restored to Ireland by negotiation, not by 'murdering poor people'. For one of their leaders, William Walwyn, the Cromwellian conquest of Ireland was 'an unlawful war, a cruel and bloody work'. Another pamphleteer denied the right of the English to encroach upon the freedoms of the Irish or to deprive them of the land that God and nature had given them.[106] Later in the century, the republican Algernon Sidney denounced the Spanish conquest of Native Americans as a 'most unjust and detestable tyranny'. Even John Locke, who upheld the right of victors in a just war to enslave the defeated, did not extend the right of conquest to include the appropriation of their land.[107]

The ruthless exploitation of defenceless populations was strongly attacked by some religious leaders. In 1678 the dean of St Paul's preached to the House of Commons against the 'fraud and violence', 'injustice and cruelty' and 'rapine and oppression' by which the 'mighty empires of the world' had been raised and maintained. Eleven years later, the sailor Edward Barlow, son of a small farmer, wrote in his journal on a voyage to the East Indies that 'for foreign nations to come and plant themselves in islands and countries by force, and build forts and raise laws, and force the people to customs against the true natives and people of the said places without their consent, how this will stand with the law of God and the religion we possess, let the world judge'.[108]

The European Enlightenment's lack of sympathy for imperialism was famously expressed by Diderot in his *Supplément au voyage de Bougainville* (1772) and his contributions to the Abbé Raynal's *Histoire philosophique et politique des Deux Indes* (1770–81), which were promptly translated into English and widely read.[109] Diderot had a tradition of writing on natural law behind him when he claimed that the only country which could be lawfully appropriated by an outside power was an uninhabited one.[110] In stressing the cruelties and injustices of European colonialism, he was articulating opinions that had long had their British supporters. In 1709 John Lawson, the surveyor general of North Carolina, denounced the unjust treatment of the Native Americans by the English settlers, who had 'abandoned their own country in order to drive them out and possess theirs'. Samuel Johnson repeatedly expressed his uneasiness about the oppression of other peoples involved in overseas conquest and colonization, denouncing 'the enormous wickedness of making war upon barbarous nations because they cannot resist, and of invading countries because they are fruitful'. In 1738 he informed readers of the *Gentleman's Magazine* that Europeans, because of their superiority in 'arts, arms and navigation', 'have made conquests and settled colonies in very distant regions, the inhabitants of which they look upon as barbarous, though in simplicity of manners, probity and temperance, superior to themselves'. '[They] seem to think that they have a right to treat them as passion, interest, or caprice shall direct, without much regard to the rules of justice or humanity. They have carried this imagined sovereignty so far that they have sometimes proceeded to rapine, bloodshed and desolation.'[111]

Like Johnson, David Hume lamented that 'the great superiority of civilized Europeans above barbarous Indians' had 'tempted us ... to throw off all restraints of justice, and even of humanity, in our treatment of them'.[112] Similar concern was shown by the president of the Royal Society in 1768 when, in his 'Hints' to Captain Cook on the eve of his voyage to Tahiti, he stressed that 'the utmost patience and forbearance' should be shown towards the natives of the South Pacific: they were 'the legal possessors' of the regions they inhabited and to shed their blood would be 'a crime of the highest nature'.[113]

In the later eighteenth century, Robert Clive's conquest of Bengal, Bihar and Orissa in 1757 on behalf of the East India Company, and the company's authoritarian rule of its new territories thereafter, provoked a mounting stream of protest at home. A parliamentary inquiry set up in 1772 received evidence of the company's 'unheard-of cruelties' and 'open violations of every rule of morality'.[114] The traveller William MacIntosh urged in 1782 that Britain should treat the Hindus 'not as slaves or inferior animals, but as fellow-men, entitled to protection, liberty and justice'. In the same year Thomas Parker, a Lincoln's Inn lawyer, published a devastating account of the cruelties involved in Clive's conquests and the human misery caused by the East India Company's 'mercantile avarice'. These and similar protests led to the India Act of 1784, which placed the company under government control and culminated in the protracted trial (1786–95), though eventual acquittal, of the former governor general of India, Warren Hastings, for corruption and oppression.[115]

This was the context for Edmund Burke's impassioned attack on the implicit assumption that the norms of civilized society did not apply to relations with peoples outside Europe.[116] In 1791, when the Hastings trial was still running, William Robertson concluded what would prove to be his last work of historical scholarship with the hope that his account of 'the early and high civilization of India and of the wonderful progress of its inhabitants in elegant arts and useful science, may have some influence on the behaviour of Europeans towards that people'.

Like Burke before him, he reminded his readers that the Indians had 'attained a very high degree of improvement many ages before the least step towards civilization had been taken in any part of Europe'.[117]

The campaign against the trade in African slaves from the 1760s onwards ran parallel with the agitation about India. Just as the critics of the East India Company regarded its brutality and oppression as fundamentally uncivilized, so the abolitionists denounced slavery as incompatible with the norms of civil society. How, asked the economic writer Malachy Postlethwayt, could 'civilized and polite Europeans' think that the Africans were intended to be slaves? It was surely much better to have a 'friendly, humane and civilized commerce' with them. The abolitionist Granville Sharp pointed out that, if slavery had been allowed within England, 'we should no longer deserve to be esteemed a civilized people'; the same in his view was true when the English tolerated 'the uncivilized customs which disgrace our colonies'.[118]

Sharp was right to invoke the long-standing English hostility to domestic slavery. Strong objections to the selling of men had been expressed in March 1659, when Parliament debated the legitimacy of sending captured Royalists as indentured labourers to Barbados.[119] Sectarian radicals objected to the enslavement of 'freeborn' Englishmen, and their influence lay behind a remarkable Rhode Island ordinance of 1652 declaring that 'no black mankind or white' should be bound to serve for more than ten years and that the conditions of their service should be 'as the manner is with English servants'.[120] Richard Baxter accepted the legitimacy of slavery as a punishment for criminals, but he thought that 'to go as pirates and catch up poor negroes or people of another land that never forfeited life or liberty, and to make them slaves and sell them, is one of the worst kinds of thievery in the world, and such persons are to be taken as the common enemies of mankind'.[121] In the later seventeenth century, there were other notable published protests against the 'cruelty', 'inhumanity' and 'barbarousness' of Negro slavery in the plantations, and not only by those who had witnessed it.[122]

When the abolitionist campaign got under way in the later eighteenth century, it had several distinct arguments. Slavery was attacked on economic grounds as an inherently inefficient method of production made obsolete by the advance of civilization, which depended on free labour and was motivated by self-interest.[123] It was regarded as 'absolutely inconsistent with Christianity': in its cruelty and inhumanity, it violated the rule that we should love our fellow human beings.[124] It was also seen as incompatible with the principles of justice because it denied its victims their natural right to personal freedom: 'A stronger and more wanton violation of man's right', thought one radical in 1776, could not possibly be conceived.[125] Lord Mansfield's judgment in *Somersett's Case* (1772) had made it clear that chattel slavery had no legal basis in England. Why then should British ships be allowed to carry slaves from Africa to British plantations in the West Indies?

The conventional answer was that Africans were barbarians and were therefore not entitled to the liberties enjoyed by Britons. If emancipated, they would fall into a life of idleness and crime.[126] Some abolitionists denied this, arguing that the Africans were not 'wild and unsettled' like the Native Americans, but were civil and affable people who engaged in agriculture and commerce. It was the degrading condition of slavery itself that turned them into barbarians. Hence William Cowper's description of the slave's plight:

> to deep sadness sullenly resign'd,
> He feels his body's bondage in his mind,
> Puts off his gen'rous nature, and to suit
> His manners with his fate, puts on the brute.[127]

But the more radical answer was that, even if they were barbarous, they were also human beings and entitled to be treated as such. Hence Tom Paine's denunciation of British incursions on 'the hapless shores of Africa, robbing it of its unoffending inhabitants, to cultivate her stolen dominions in the West'.[128] What the abolitionists were urging was a fundamental reconsideration of the traditional relationship between 'civilized' peoples and those at a lower stage of social development.[129] The long delay of the abolition of the slave trade (1807) and of slavery itself (1833) showed how difficult it was for those with a vested interest in the trade to accept this argument. When slavery was eventually abolished, the Slave Compensation Commission distributed £20 million (£2 billion in modern money) to British slave owners.[130]

One of the influential objections to the African slave trade had been, as Malachy Postlethwayt put it, that it 'obstructed the civilizing of these people'.[131] The Quakers and Evangelicals, who spearheaded the campaign, were passionately concerned to save souls. In accordance with Christ's command to teach all nations (Matthew 28:19 and Mark 16:15), they envisaged abolition as a necessary prelude to intense missionary activity to convert the Africans to Christianity and 'civilize' them in the process.[132]

The concept of a civilizing mission, however, had never commanded unanimity. Spanish Dominican thinkers of the sixteenth century denied that the *conquistadores* were entitled to force the Native Americans to change their way of life. They maintained that every people, however barbarous, had the right to defend itself against such attempts, for only God had the right to punish sin. In the ensuing centuries, the much-repeated claim by the natural lawyers that 'civilized' people were entitled to punish nations for breaking what they regarded as the laws of nature was strongly contested.[133] Besides, as John Donne observed, it was far from clear just what the law of nature was: 'This term, the Law of Nature, is so variously and unconstantly delivered, as I confess I read it abundant times before I understand it once or can conclude it to signify that which the author should at that time mean.'[134]

The view of most natural lawyers was that foreign powers could intervene in another country's affairs only if it was in order to suppress major crimes, such as piracy or cannibalism. Even then, they needed to proceed very cautiously, as any military action that was not provoked by a prior injury to the invading power was prima facie suspect. Gentili had firmly rejected Aristotle's notion that barbarians were natural slaves against whom war could justly be waged. Grotius several times cited Plutarch's warning that the claim to be 'civilizing' barbarians could be a mere cover for greedy acquisition.[135] From the later seventeenth century on, a series of European thinkers reiterated their challenge to the notion that one nation had the right to invade another in order to 'civilize' it.[136]

A particularly notable statement was contained in Pufendorf's *De Jure Naturae et Gentium (Law of Nature and Nations)* (1672), of which the English translation of 1703, supervised by Basil Kennett, subsequently president of Corpus Christi College, Oxford, went into four further editions by 1749. Based first in Heidelberg and then at Lund, Pufendorf could afford to view the activities of the colonial powers with some detachment. Acknowledging his debt to Montaigne and Charron, he rejected the assumption of Grotius and others that the law of nature could be derived solely from the practices of 'the most civilized nations'. For no people regarded themselves as 'uncivilized' or 'barbarous', and some non-European powers, such as the Chinese, assumed that they were infinitely more civilized than any other nation. It was, Pufendorf argued, only vanity that led some European nations to regard their own manners as the standard by which others should be judged and to denounce any people who did not exactly conform to their model as 'barbarous and savage'. 'For, according to this doctrine, if we had a mind to destroy any nation differing from us in customs and manners, it were only [necessary] to brand them with the reproachful name of "Barbarians", and then to invade them without further colour or excuse.' In Pufendorf's opinion, not even cannibalism justified foreign intervention unless it involved killing innocent strangers.[137]

A similar view was expressed in 1705 by the Halle professor Christian Thomasius, who declared that all nations had equal standing and that the term 'barbarian' originated in the 'stupid contempt' of the Greeks and Romans for other peoples.[138] Awareness that they themselves were the descendants of people whom the Romans had regarded as barbarians may well have coloured the views of these two German philosophers. The Swiss lawyer Emmerich de Vattel followed in their footsteps when in the 1750s he explicitly rejected the claim that one people had the right to invade another in order to 'civilize' them. Criticism of this kind would culminate in Raynal's *Histoire des Deux Indes*. This comprehensive indictment of colonialism showed that civilization was not something that could be exported by 'civilized' Europeans, since they invariably turned into barbarians when they invaded other continents.[139]

The views of these continental intellectuals were shared by many English writers. Few went as far as the barrister Robert Ward, who in the late eighteenth century proposed that there should be different laws of nations in other parts of the globe so as to fit the varying requirements of societies at differing stages of development.[140] But Sir William Temple followed Pufendorf in arguing that Europeans had arrogated to themselves the task of defining the laws of nature and nations and had treated those peoples they regarded as barbarous as if they did not belong to the human race. In his opinion, these supposed barbarians had a right to have their views taken into account.[141] The theologian Thomas Burnet observed in 1690 that it was 'commonly the vanity of great empires to uncivilize, in a manner, all the rest of the world; and to account all those people barbarous that are not subject to their dominion'.[142] In his *Civil Polity*, Peter Paxton condemned the error of supposing that 'all the rest of mankind, whose conditions or circumstances are in most respects extremely unlike ours, should notwithstanding stand in need of what we do'.[143] The poet Ambrose Philips, in his play *The Briton* (1722), depicted a British prince indignantly rejecting the claim that the Romans had civilized his people:

The Civilizers!—the Disturbers, say;
The Robbers, the Corrupters of Mankind!
Proud Vagabonds! who make the world your home
And lord it when you have no right.[144]

Jonathan Swift in *Gulliver's Travels* (1726) explained sardonically that 'if a prince sends forces into a nation where the people are poor and ignorant, he may lawfully put half of them to death, and make slaves of the rest, in order to civilize and reduce them from their barbarous way of living'.[145] Denouncing the African slave trade, the poet Richard Savage issued a stern warning in 1736:

Let by my specious name no tyrant rise,
And cry, while they enslave, they civilize![146]

The Defects of Civilization

The failure of supposedly civilized people to live up to the standards they claimed to exemplify did not go unnoticed. In 1653 John Bulwer pointed to the irony that civilized ladies called other peoples 'barbarous' for mutilating their bodies, when they themselves pierced their ears and hung jewels from them. A century later, Adam Smith commented that the women of 'some of the most civilized nations which, perhaps the world ever beheld' had for nearly a century been struggling to 'squeeze the beautiful roundness of their natural shape into a square form of the same kind'.[147] More seriously, it was evident that the progress of civility in Europe had not brought an end to the cruelty and inhumanity that had been thought of as distinctively 'barbarian' characteristics. Thomas Bastard, the Elizabethan satirist, believed that the conquest of the New World had made its native inhabitants loving, meek and virtuous, but that in the process the conquerors had become 'savage, fierce and barbarous'. The Quaker George Bishop contrasted the 'most courteous entertainment' that was extended to the Friends by the supposedly 'savage' Susquehanna Indians with the 'barbarous inhumanity' shown them by the New Englanders.[148] Colonists repeatedly showed themselves to be capable of ferocious brutality. When they burned the Pequot village in 1636, their Narragansett Indian allies, whom they regarded as 'savages', were horrified, crying that 'it is too furious and slays too many men'.[149]

The contrast between the nobility of the 'barbarians' and the barbarity of their 'civilized' conquerors would become a regular theme in critical histories of European imperialism.[150] The royalist clergyman Thomas Fuller deplored the practice of filling the colonies with criminals, 'dissolute people' and other 'scum'.[151] Bernard Mandeville thought that 'the most civiliz'd people' had often been guilty of 'studied cruelties' that savages would never have thought of; and the sceptical politician and philosopher Henry St John, Lord Bolingbroke, agreed: 'In our civilized and enlightened age . . . there are some that exceed in injustice and inhumanity all that we are told of Iroquois, Brasilians, or the wildest inhabitants of African deserts.'[152]

Roger Williams correctly pointed out that the Native American way of making war was 'far less bloody and devouring than the cruel wars of Europe'.[153] In Africa also, as one experienced trader reported, warfare was 'infinitely less bloody than ours'.[154] For though the wars of eighteenth-century Europe were often conducted with a great show of civility, they involved huge slaughter all the same.[155] Defoe's Robinson Crusoe was appalled to encounter evidence of cannibalism by naked savages. But on mature reflection, and no doubt under the influence of Montaigne, he concluded that the custom was no worse than the common Christian practice of refusing quarter to defeated enemies in battle.[156]

At the end of the eighteenth century, the vast death toll resulting from European warfare provided the theme for a lacerating poem by the Presbyterian minister Joseph Fawcett, sardonically entitled 'Civilized War': 'refined barbarism', he thought it. In 1805 the scholarly Liverpool banker William Roscoe declared that the treachery, cruelty and ferocity of the war against Napoleon would 'disgrace an age of barbarians'.[157] All this suggested that 'barbarism' and 'civility' might be less the distinctive attributes of particular societies than a way of characterizing actions or modes of behaviour that could at one time or another be found anywhere.

The progress of commerce, so frequently lauded for its civilizing effects, was also viewed with marked ambivalence. Few went as far as Gerrard Winstanley, the mid-seventeenth-century Digger, who described trade as 'the thieving art of buying and selling'.[158] But generations of critics, influenced by classical notions of republican virtue, alleged that the multiplication of consumer goods brought in by international trade had a corrupting effect, sapping the people's civic commitment, lessening their military spirit and leading to what the mid-eighteenth-century writer John Brown called 'gross luxury' and 'effeminate refinement'.[159] Adam Smith was hardly an enemy of trade, but he too noted the unfortunate effects of commerce on a people's mental and moral character. It was because of their involvement in trade, he thought, that the minds of men were 'contracted and rendered incapable of elevation'; education was 'despised or at least neglected'; and the heroic spirit was 'almost utterly extinguished', for commerce sacrificed the courage of mankind. He reminded his audience at Glasgow University that in 1745 'four or five thousand naked, unarmed Highlanders took possession of the improved parts of this country without any opposition from the unwarlike inhabitants'.[160]

Many eighteenth-century *philosophes* expressed a similar suspicion of trade and traders. Commerce might foster agreeable manners, but it also elevated self-interest into a guiding principle and encouraged people to do nothing, save for money.[161] The claim that it brought humanity together into one great society was falsified by the succession of trade wars which had convulsed Europe since the later seventeenth century. As the great merchant and economic writer Josiah Child told a House of Lords committee in 1669, all trade was 'a kind of warfare'. The American statesman Alexander Hamilton argued in

The Federalist (1787–89) that commerce, far from extinguishing the flames of conflict, merely substituted one object of warfare for another.[162] Edmund Burke even maintained that good manners were not the result of trade, as was usually claimed, but the cause of it.[163]

Others observed that the traffic in drink and firearms had a positively malign influence on Africans, whose condition had deteriorated as a result of European contact. In 1807 William Roscoe told Parliament that the British traders who purchased slaves in return for guns and alcohol had prevented 'that civilization and improvement in Africa which might otherwise have taken place'. Over thirty years earlier, Captain Cook, after a second visit to a community in South Island, New Zealand, reflected on the damage that commerce with Europeans and 'civilized' Christians had done to the Maoris:

> We debauch their morals ... and we introduce among them wants, and perhaps diseases, which they never before knew, and which serves only to disturb the happy tranquillity they and their forefathers had enjoyed. If any denies the truth of this assertion, let him tell me what the natives of the whole extent of America have gained by the commerce they have had with Europeans.[164]

It would be left to later generations to discover that international trade, aggravated by urbanization, was a major cause of the spread of infectious diseases throughout the globe.[165]

By the later eighteenth century, several key aspects of civilized existence had come to appear seriously retrogressive. Adam Smith pointed out that it involved the subordination of the lower classes, who were required to labour in order to keep the rich in comfort. 'In a civilized society,' he wrote, 'the poor provide both for themselves and for the enormous luxury of their superiors.' The division of labour benefited the economy and made even the poor better off than they would have been elsewhere, but in his view it severely cramped the mental lives of those condemned to spend their existence in the performance of mechanically repetitive tasks. As even the act of thinking threatened to become a specialized occupation,[166] Smith lamented 'that drowsy stupidity, which, in a civilized country seems to benumb the understanding of almost all the inferior ranks of people', 'whereas in the barbarous societies, as they are commonly called', 'every man has a considerable degree of knowledge, ingenuity, and invention'. Smith's hope was that schools provided by the state and affordable to the common people would remedy the situation.[167] His younger contemporary Dugald Stewart, who similarly regretted the way in which the division of labour turned men into 'living automatons', looked forward to the invention of machines that would take over their repetitive tasks.[168] Yet another Scottish philosopher James Dunbar thought that the lower classes in most of the 'civilized' countries of Europe were 'in a state of intellectual debasement' to which there was 'scarce any parallel in the history of rude barbarians'. He concluded that when it came to comparing their respective levels of virtue and happiness, Europeans were little better off than 'the simplest and rudest race in Greenland or Guinea'. Their contempt for such peoples resembled the readiness of the ancient Greeks to disparage all other nations. In both cases, prejudice was founded on ignorance.[169]

Analyses of this kind were paralleled by radical criticism of the sort levelled by Diderot and Rousseau in their passionate exposure of what they saw as the injustices, endless toil, sexual frustrations and artificial desires of civilized society. For Jean-Jacques Rousseau, it was above all the institution of private property and its subsequent inequalities that had corrupted mankind.[170] For whereas barbarism was a great equalizer, the effect of civilization was, as the Scottish conjectural historians had shown, 'to introduce a distinction of ranks, and to sink the lower orders of men far beneath that station to which by nature they are entitled'.[171] George Forster, who served as a naturalist on James Cook's second voyage, contrasted the 'happy equality' of the people of Tahiti with the miseries of the lower classes in some

civilized states and the 'unbounded voluptuousness' of their superiors. But he noted that, even in Tahiti, social distinctions were
growing: he prophesied that the common people there would eventually perceive what was happening and, 'a proper sense of the general
rights of man awakening in them', would 'bring on a revolution'.[172]

In the 1790s Mary Wollstonecraft declared that civilization could
be 'the first of blessings, the true perfection of man', but only if it was
enjoyed by everyone; as it was, 'the preposterous distinctions of rank'
rendered civilization 'a curse'. Tom Paine similarly lamented that
so-called civilization had the effect of making one part of society
more affluent and the other more wretched than either would have
been in a natural state. The result was that a large proportion of those
who lived in supposedly 'civilized' countries were 'in a state of poverty
and wretchedness far below the condition of an Indian': their plight
was 'far worse than if they had been born before civilization began'.[173]
The demographer Robert Malthus was clear that 'in every civilized
state' there had to be 'a class of proprietors and a class of labourers';
and in 1805 the doctor Charles Hall agreed that without the existence of a poor class, civilization would have been impossible.[174]
When Alexis de Tocqueville visited industrial Manchester in 1835,
he found low-paid workers living in filthy squalor; it was a place, he
wrote, where civilized man was turned back almost into a savage.[175]

Civilization Rejected

It was only too obvious that few of the natives of the New World or
the inhabitants of the Celtic fringe had any desire to be 'civilized' by
their invaders. When the navigator Martin Frobisher encountered
the Inuit of Baffin Island in 1577, he discovered that they preferred
to hurl themselves into the sea rather than submit to a conqueror
(Plate 19). He could not but admire the commitment of this 'brutish
nation' to their liberties and their 'miraculous manliness' in defending
them.[176] In Ireland, as Edmund Spenser lamented, the people hated

the English and saw no reason to copy their manners: having been brought up 'licentiously and to live as each one listeth', they regarded English laws as 'most repugnant to their liberty and natural freedom, which in their madness they affect'. In his play *The Queen's Arcadia* (performed in 1605), Samuel Daniel represented the inhabitants of an idyllic, pastoral country resisting the attempts of sophisticated outsiders to corrupt it:

> How they implanted have their battery here,
> Against all the main pillars of our state,
> Our rites, our customs, nature, honesty,
> T'imbroil, and to confound us utterly,
> Reckoning us barbarous, but if thus their skill
> Doth civilize, let us be barbarous still.[177]

In the same vein, the Catholic Bishop of Ossory David Rothe claimed that the Irish were already 'sufficiently civilized': they were not barbarians, but men with reason and language. He appealed to King James I to govern them in accordance with their own 'manners, customs and habit of their inclinations'. Other Irish apologists declared that it was not they, but the English, who were the barbarians.[178] Hostile accounts of the Irish Rebellion of 1641 related that 'those barbarians, the natural inhabitants of Ireland' wanted to 'extinguish the memory' of the English newcomers, 'and of all the civility and good things by them introduced amongst that wild nation'. They demolished the houses built by the English; the gardens, orchards and enclosures they had planted; and the ironworks they had constructed. In their determination to 'deliver themselves from their long-continued subjection to the English nation', they even destroyed whole herds of English cows and flocks of English sheep.[179]

In North America, according to George Savile, Marquess of Halifax, the Indians preferred their 'slovenly liberty' to 'that which we call a civilized way of living'. As Benjamin Franklin observed, their wants were supplied by bounteous Nature, so they had no incentive to learn the arts that would enable them to change their way of life.[180] Several observers noted that their social and political arrangements were marked by relative egalitarianism and a communal ethic of sharing, which resulted in the absence of beggars. Their reports were confirmed by the colourful account of the Huron and Iroquois Indians offered to English readers in 1703 by the Baron Lahontan, who had fought and travelled extensively in French Canada. Projecting early Enlightenment values on Native Americans, he suggested that they were far too rational to accept the tenets of Christianity and portrayed them as 'strangers to *meum* and *tuum*, to superiority and subordination': they lived, he said, 'in a state of equality, pursuant to the principles of nature'.[181] The ex-slave Ottobah Cugoano claimed that in West Africa also the poor were never allowed to fall into destitution.[182]

A mid-seventeenth-century observer remarked that 'the wild people count[ed] none free but such as graze cattle and follow their wars; [they held] that ploughing, sowing, reaping, and the trades of artificers were but inventions to reduce a people to servitude by labour and call it "civilizing" them'.[183] The 'wild people' were quite right, for in such contexts the object of introducing 'civility' was to establish political subservience and a regime of continuous labour.* Instead of the arduous work of ploughing with oxen, the Native Americans preferred the less intensive regime of slash and burn, planting their crops in the rich, weed-free ashes and moving on after a year or two. Like the Irish, they sometimes expressed their hatred of the English way of life by attacking the colonists' livestock.[184] In his *History of America* (1777), William Robertson explained that the Native Americans regarded their own customs as the standard of

---

* In the eyes of James Macpherson, admirer of the Scottish Highland past and publisher of poems he attributed to the legendary Gaelic bard Ossian, the agricultural labourers buried in the poet Thomas Gray's country churchyard were 'damned rascals that did nothing but plough the land and sow corn'; *Boswell's London Journal, 1762–1763*, ed. Frederick A. Pottle (New York, 1950), 110.

excellence and preferred their freedom, independence and egalitarianism to the cares, constraints and inequalities of civilized society. A British soldier who had been an envoy to the Cherokee Indians in 1761 confirmed that their older people still looked back nostalgically to the days before the white settlers had arrived.[185]

Particularly embarrassing was the case of those English colonists, men and women, who either ran away to the American Indians or, having been captured by them, elected to stay, even though they had the chance of returning home. Some, no doubt, were victims of what would today be called Stockholm syndrome, the process by which hostages develop sympathetic feelings towards their captors, to whom they feel irrationally grateful for not treating them as badly as they had feared. Others, who had been captured as young children, were absorbed into Indian culture and reluctant to re-join their families. Similarly, captive women who had married into the Indian community refused to leave their husbands.[186]

These desertions occurred from the very start of the English settlements and remained a persistent problem despite the severe punishments for 'runagates' devised by the governor of Virginia in 1611. As a modern historian has remarked, their flight raises the possibility that significant numbers of the early settlers were 'so indifferent to the extension of English civility that they happily integrated themselves into the indigenous society'.[187] In 1642 the Connecticut General Court complained that 'divers persons depart from amongst us and take up their abode with the Indians, in a profane course of life'. During the Seven Years' War, British soldiers who had been captured by the Indians and forcibly inducted into their culture often found it difficult to return to English ways: some even fought alongside their captors against their former comrades. By 1782 it was said, though with some exaggeration, that 'thousands' of Europeans had become Indians, 'and we have no examples of even one of those aborigines having from choice become Europeans'.[188] Benjamin Franklin thought that when an Indian child was brought up among the colonists, he would, given the chance, return to his people; whereas a young white person who had been rescued from captivity by the Indians would flee back to the woods at the first opportunity. He attributed this to the preference of all concerned for a life of ease, free from care and labour.[189]

A similar problem was presented by the so-called renegadoes, the English seamen, captured by the Moors, who converted to Islam and settled in Turkey or North Africa, like the pirate Sir Francis Verney, who based himself in Algiers and carried out raids on his native country's shipping.[190] Many were frightened into conversion by the hardships of their captivity and the prospect of better treatment. Others were said to have converted 'out of choice, without any terror or severity shown them' and to have become more inveterate enemies of Christianity than the Turks themselves.[191] A Jacobean traveller who had himself been captured and imprisoned in Turkey thought that the renegadoes were 'for the most part rogues, and the scum of people, which being villains and atheists, unable to live in Christendom, are fled to the Turk for succour and relief'.[192] Such conversions were doubtless made easier by the misleading report that the Muslims did not require their converts to be circumcised. (In fact, only the elderly, for whom the operation might have proved fatal, were excused from this ordeal.)[193] Conversion was essential for those hoping to join the Barbary pirates or seeking admission to the Ottoman military elite. Others changed their allegiance to fit their location: 'Many hundreds are Musselmans in Turkey and Christians at home', noted a preacher in 1628.[194]

Without going so far as to opt out of civilized society, many contemporaries felt that, with the growth of civility and the enhanced availability of 'luxury' goods, something had been lost. Already present in sixteenth-century Scotland,[195] an affected nostalgia for the simple life became increasingly common. An English translation of the account by the French explorer Marc Lescarbot of the Iroquois of Acadia was published in 1609. It portrayed the Indians as an ingenious people who, in the author's opinion, could achieve a great deal if only they could be converted to Christianity and persuaded to take up new handicrafts. But he conceded that they enjoyed a more contented life than that of his fellow Frenchmen: they lived in common, without money, and shared their food; they lacked ambition, had no lawsuits and seldom quarrelled; and they were a happy people, always singing and dancing.[196] Similarly, after extensive travels in Europe and the Near East, Fynes Moryson concluded in 1617 that the happiest people on earth were the nomads, who lived in tents and by being constantly on the move escaped 'the heat of summer, the cold of winter, the want of pastures, all diseases, and all unpleasing things, but at their pleasure enjoy[ed] all commodities of all places'.[197] Thomas Morton claimed that the Native Americans, though an 'uncivil' people, led a happier and freer existence 'void of care' because they were indifferent to 'baubles' and 'superfluous commodities'. William Walwyn, an admirer of Montaigne, regretted that people no longer lived 'according to nature', but chased after 'superfluous subtleties and artificial things' (later, however, he changed his mind and came to believe that it was only 'plenty of trade and commerce' that could produce 'happiness and prosperity').[198]

The Catholic priest John Lynch defended the innocent pastoral life led by the native Irish before the English arrived: they were uncorrupted by such ostentatious luxuries as mock-marble palaces, tessellated floors and carved chimney pieces; and though their manners were rustic and unpolished, they were free from the crouchingly obsequious displays of servility so fashionable in his own day. The poet Thomas Traherne claimed in his *Centuries of Meditations* that the real barbarians were the modern Christians, whereas the savages who went naked and subsisted on water and roots were living as Adam and Eve had done. He admitted that some barbarians shared a taste for material goods and coveted beads, glass buttons and feathers; but, he added, 'We [sur]pass them in barbarous opinions and monstrous apprehensions, which we nickname "civility" and "the mode".' The antiquarian John Aubrey similarly looked back to 'older times before wealth and arts had introduced luxury and vanity'; he admired 'this primitive simplicity, which civilized nations call barbarity'.[199]

In *Winter* (1726), the first part of his hugely popular *The Seasons*, the poet James Thomson celebrated the innocence of the Laplanders:

> They
> Despise th'insensate barbarous trade of war;
> They ask no more than simple nature gives.
>
> . . .
>
> No false desires, no pride-created wants,
> Disturb the peaceful current of their time.
>
> . . .
>
> Their reindeer form their riches. These their tents,
> Their robes, their beds, and all their homely wealth
> Supply.

His source was a German account that described Lapland as an 'unpolished' and somewhat 'barbarous' place, but one where theft, murder and adultery were virtually unknown.[200] Similarly, Captain Cook believed that the natives of 'New Holland' (Australia) were much happier than his fellow Europeans because they were unacquainted with 'the inequality of condition' and indifferent to such superfluities as 'magnificent houses' and 'household stuff'. In Tonga, he reported, 'Joy and contentment is painted in every face.'[201] When the American John Ledyard visited Siberia in 1787–88, he found a people with few wants who were undistracted by the difficulties that 'the luxury of civilization' had created for 'even its ordinary members'. Instead, he encountered 'one continued flow of good nature and cheerfulness'.[202]

In a society like eighteenth-century Britain, whose more dynamic members were committed to the idea of material and intellectual progress, this idealization of a simpler way of life could never be more than a minority opinion. Yet many early modern intellectuals flirted with a primitivist tradition according to which all forms of civilization were a regrettable departure from mankind's original simplicity; and barbarians were to be admired for their courage, robustness, freedom and happiness. The Christian doctrine of the Fall preserved the notion of an original age of innocence from which sinful man had degenerated. The classical myth of the Golden Age of primeval innocence had been described by Hesiod, Lucretius and Virgil, but was best known from the many translations of Ovid's *Metamorphoses*. It took several forms, some suggesting that the first men had crops and herds, others that they subsisted on the spontaneous bounty of nature. In either case the myth perpetuated the notion that people had once lived peacefully, uncorrupted by avarice and ambition, and without the need for laws and government.[203] William Watreman wrote in 1555 that, 'in the rude simplicity of the first world', they 'gaped not for honour nor hunted after riches, but each man was contented with little'. The Elizabethan poet Michael Drayton recalled how an innocent age, unacquainted with gluttony, drunkenness, luxurious fashions or 'slaughtering broils and bloody horror', had been ended by the discovery of gold and silver, the invention of coinage, the manufacture of weapons and the building of ships capable of exploring unknown lands. Benjamin Whichcote, a former vice-chancellor of Cambridge University, remarked that although 'culture and education' led to 'the civilizing of men's manners', they often rendered them 'more villainous than by the uncultivated principles of nature they would ever have proved'. Even John Locke wrote of 'the innocence and sincerity' of 'the Golden Age', before men had been corrupted by 'vain ambition' and 'evil concupiscence'.[204]

The moral superiority of the simple life long remained a popular theme. Edward Gibbon conceded that although the progress of civilization had helped to assuage the fiercer passions of human nature, it had been much less conducive to the practice of chastity. His fellow historian William Robertson noted that 'some philosophers' (he instanced Rousseau) had supposed 'that man arrives at his highest dignity and excellence long before he reaches a state of refinement; and in the rude simplicity of savage life displays an elevation of sentiment, an independence of mind, and a warmth of attachment for which it is vain to search among the members of polished society'. Mary Wollstonecraft regarded 'a barbarian, considered as a moral being', as 'an angel, compared with the refined villain of artificial life'.[205]

Many of the accounts of human evolution inherited from classical antiquity contained the radical message that theft, murder, warfare and social oppression were the inexorable consequences of the transition to civilized life. The multiplication of desires and the craving for distinction led only to unhappiness. This was the belief of Lucretius, whose view of civilization has been fairly described as 'deeply ambiguous'. In the fourth century BC, it had also been the doctrine of the Cynics, who chose to live in a state of primitive simplicity and adhere to a philosophical programme that articulated a revolt against most of the attributes of what their contemporaries would have regarded as civilized life.[206]

In the early modern period, the notion that social and economic progress could bring misery in its wake was frequently reiterated. Particular stress was laid on the damaging effects of private property, an institution that, it was said, had not existed in Eden, but had come into being as a remedy for man's wickedness. The first Christians were believed to have practised the community of goods; and the legitimacy of private property was frequently questioned during the subsequent history of the medieval Church, most notably by St Francis, who claimed to renounce all property, whether privately or communally owned.[207] These religious inhibitions were paralleled by the doubts about property transmitted by classical mythology. In 1543, for example, Henry Parker, later Lord Morley, presented Henry VIII with his translation of a work by Boccaccio. It included the myth of how the Roman goddess Ceres converted mankind from wild vagabonds into settled farmers and town dwellers, thus bringing them to 'honest civility'. With agriculture, however, came the enclosure of fields and the beginnings of private property, expressed in 'these two bitter words *meum* and *tuum*, that is to mean *mine* and *thine*, the names enemies as well to the private wealth as to the common wealth'. After that, there 'arose poverty, bondage, strife, hate and cruel battle, and burning envy'. 'The life of man [was] shortened thereby by famine, hunger, and battle, which afore that time was unknown to them that lived in the woods.'[208] A few years later, the same idea was expressed by the leading French poet Pierre de Ronsard. His compatriot Marc Lescarbot also declared that 'of possessing of land cometh warfare'.[209]

Many subsequent commentators endorsed this alleged association between the rise of private property and the growth of human conflict. It became proverbial that *meum* and *tuum* were the cause of all the wars and quarrels in the world. Pufendorf vainly tried to refute the notion by pointing out that private property had been introduced to prevent contention rather than encourage it.[210] Yet in a work dedicated in 1703 to the spectacularly wealthy Duke of Devonshire, the French military adventurer Baron Lahontan declared that 'a man must be quite blind who does not see that the property of goods . . . is the only source of all the disorders that perplex the European societies'.[211] Bernard Mandeville similarly asserted that 'almost all the wars and private quarrels that have at any time disturbed mankind' had arisen from 'differences about superiority, and the *meum* and *tuum*'. The notion was implicit in the scheme of human development outlined by the Scottish conjectural historians. It appeared in the poetry of William Cowper; and it was, of course, fundamental to Rousseau's critique of civilized society.[212]

It also underlay one of early modern England's most radical assaults on the whole notion of 'civilization'. This is to be found in a short but remarkable essay appended in 1659 to an English translation of Aristophanes's play *Plutus*. In it, the author, identified only by the initials 'H. H. B.', attacked the whole notion of the progress of civility. Since the Fall of Man, he maintained, it had been downhill all the way. First came 'tyranny and blood-shedding over other creatures' and, after that, the persecution and enslavement of one another; then agriculture, which led to forced labour and slavery, and, with it, private property, 'that unhappy thing', which provoked competition and brought war into the world; and finally, new arts and inventions, which encouraged some nations to 'account themselves more civilized than others', to despise 'innocent life with the title of barbarism' and to conquer those who lived 'happy without such inventions'. If people who thought like that could have seen Adam in the Garden of Eden, he remarked sardonically, they would have wanted 'for the poor wretch's good . . . to teach him some of our good manners and good husbandry'. He added that no one had the right to spread Christianity to other peoples unless they had specific divine authority for doing so.[213]

Coming as it did a hundred years before the writings of Rousseau, this was a total rejection of the whole idea of civilized living and an absolute denial of the right of the civilized to impose their values on those they regarded as barbarous. Buried at the back of an obscure Greek play, it seems to have gone wholly unnoticed at the time.[214] It is tempting to dismiss it as merely a *jeu d'esprit*, a rhetorical exercise in paradox of a kind popular among Renaissance humanists, and comparable to the literary subversions of the accepted concept of *humanitas* by the rhetoricians of imperial Rome.[215] But the author's tone is grimly serious. His essay is a powerful reminder that in early modern England there never was unanimity about either the meaning of civility or its desirability.

It has been well remarked that this, most arrogant of civilizations, was also the one most given to radical self-criticism.[216] For it was a distinctive feature of eighteenth-century Europe, and of British society in particular, that it did not rest on a single set of principles, but was the outcome of a maelstrom of conflicting interests, traditions and values.

In this diversity lay its strength.[217] The early modern period was an age of dramatic British expansion, much of it involving the expropriation, enslavement or murder of other, supposedly 'barbarous' peoples. But it also generated a sense of cultural pluralism, a degree of respect for the cultures of the 'uncivilized', and a nascent hostility to colonialism and imperial conquest.

These were never more than the views of a minority. In the nineteenth century, the increasing dominance of Britain's economic and military power generated huge self-confidence in the superiority of Western civilization. It confirmed the widespread disdain for the 'backward' peoples of Asia and Africa and strengthened the assumption that it was entirely acceptable to suspend conventional standards of civil conduct when dealing with them.[218] Optimists believed in the benevolent, civilizing character of the British administration of the colonial territories. Turning their back on earlier notions of cultural relativism, missionaries sought to convert 'savages' to Christianity (Plate 25).[219] Even liberals tended to agree with John Stuart Mill that 'despotism' was a legitimate way of governing barbarians, 'provided the end be their improvement, and the means justified by actually effecting that end'.[220] As the British Empire rose to its zenith, more critical views had relatively little effect on government policy; and in public opinion they were largely submerged by a torrent of racially based imperialist sentiment. In the Britain of 1900, the notion that the world was divided between civilized people and those who were more or less barbarous was almost as widely held as it had been in 1500.

༺ 7 ༻

Changing Modes of Civility

What are these wond'rous civilizing arts,
This Roman polish, and this smooth behaviour,
That render man thus tractable and tame?
Are they not only to disguise our passions,
To set our looks at variance with our thoughts?

Joseph Addison, Cato (1713)

Xenophobic Masculinity

In the absence of agreement about the merits of civilization and the desirability of trying to impose it on other peoples, it is hardly surprising that the codes of manners and behaviour propounded in the name of civility should have proved equally divisive. They often appeared to conflict with deeply held beliefs about religion and morality. They were seen by radicals as politically contentious, and they were resisted by those who were attached to older assumptions about what was or was not proper behaviour.

There seemed, for example, something foppish and effeminate about politeness, repressing as it did all the traditional male qualities of aggression and self-assertiveness. A 'composed carriage' and a 'complimental tongue' were seen by some as 'the bare outsides of manhood' rather than the real thing.[1] It was said of the Puritan soldier Colonel John Hutchinson that 'there was nothing he hated more than an insignificant gallant that could only make his legs and preen himself, and court a lady, but had not bravery to employ himself in things more suitable to man's nobler sex'.[2] The growth of commerce and cultivated pursuits notoriously sapped the will to fight; and the status of military prowess, once regarded as the highest form of masculine achievement, seemed to be diminished by the value set by the teachers of civility on pacification and accommodation.[3] Instead of being the duty of all adult males, the defence of the realm had by the eighteenth century been handed over to the professionals.

It was in less polite societies that the traditional masculine values survived. The sixteenth-century inhabitants of the Western Isles of Scotland, when travelling to other parts, chose to sleep in their clothes on the ground, rejecting their hosts' offers of beds and blankets, 'lest such barbarous effeminateness (for so they call it) should taint and corrupt their native and inbred hardiness'.[4] Sir Clement Edmondes recalled that Cato, 'the Censor', warned the Romans that they would lose their empire if they allowed Greek to be taught, 'for by that means they would easily be drawn from the study and practice of war to the bewitching delight of speculative thoughts'.[5] Similarly, Sir Thomas Roe reported from Constantinople in 1621 that the Turks deliberately neglected 'the gentlest arts and sciences', lest they should 'soften and civilize' a people whose purpose was 'war, blood and conquest'. He believed that the reason they permitted English collectors to carry away their ancient sculpture was that they hoped that this taste for antiquities would 'corrupt' and 'divert' them 'from the thought and use of arms'.[6] He was quite right, for polite gentlemen recoiled from some traditional forms of quasi-military recreation, which were coming to appear coarse and boorish. The tilts and tourneys, so popular at the court of Elizabeth I, were discontinued by Charles I, whose tastes were more refined. The geographer Nathanael Carpenter noted that Alexander the Great had been able to conquer the Persians because they had been 'reduced to civility and lost their hardness'. The 'ancient courage' of the modern Turks was also said to have been much diminished through their growing 'more civil'. By contrast, no men were more 'desperate and adventurous' than those who were 'rude and barbarous, wanting all good manners and education'.[7]

The prominent role of women in polite society enhanced this belief that civility was effeminizing. Men were emasculated, it was said, by spending too much time dancing or conversing with women. The entertainment of ladies, thought a writer in 1673, should be regarded as merely 'a pleasing amusement or a school of politeness': a man who made it his whole business rendered himself contemptible. There were many warnings against over-refinement, and there was a widespread awareness that polite manners could easily turn into 'niceness' and 'delicacy'.[8] The former soldier Thomas Gainsford mocked the effeminacy of the typical Jacobean courtier, who 'as a young man, wears furred boots, dares scarce tread on the ground, smelleth of perfumes, hath a fan in his hand to keep the wind from his face, rideth too softly in the streets, and must always tread on a matted floor'. As Adam Smith drily remarked, 'The delicate sensibility required in civilized nations sometimes destroys the masculine firmness of the character.'[9]

It was in response to such sentiments that King James I advised his son to avoid undue delicacy at the table, by eating 'in a manly, round and honest fashion'.[10] At a lower social level, it was said to be common for 'clowns' to repudiate all polite behaviour, preferring to take refuge in an 'awkward bluntness' and to be 'very frequent in the repetition of the words "rough" and "manly".'[11] Defenders of good manners attempted to offer reassurance, claiming that civility did not really effeminize or threaten martial virtue.[12] David Hume pointed out that the armies of modern civilized states far surpassed those of barbarians in their discipline and military efficiency.[13] He could also have reminded critics that the chivalric tradition had valued courtesy as well as courage. Chaucer's Knight had fought with distinction all over Europe, Asia Minor and North Africa, but in bearing he was 'as meeke as is a mayde'. Yet the new emphasis on peaceful and emollient behaviour in daily life did indeed involve a redefinition of what the ideal qualities of upper-class masculinity might be. The army continued to offer an acceptable career for gentlemen until modern times, but military skill was no longer expected of everyone. In social intercourse, more value was placed upon temperance, restraint and understatement than boastful self-assertion.* One modern historian even characterizes the civilizing process in modern times as the 'feminization of the male'.[14]

Throughout the early modern period, there was a current of xenophobic hostility to the import of foreign mannerisms and modes of greeting. Some of this reflected Protestant suspicion of anything that came from a popish country. 'New-fashioned salutations below the knee' had been brought back from Italy, thought a Jacobean writer; they should be despised by 'any good, plain, honest man'.[15] Archbishop Laud disliked such 'Spanish tricks' as 'making of legs to fine ladies'.[16] Others attacked 'filthy Italianate compliment-mongers' on the grounds that a few 'words of real English truth from the heart' were better received than 'ten thousand compliments and grimaces'.[17] The character writer John Earle portrayed 'A Blunt Man' as 'a great enemy to the fine gentleman' and 'things of compliment'. 'The rare and plain speech of England' was widely regarded as preferable to 'Spanish

* It seems that some may still regard civility as a threat to their masculinity. In an article in the *London Review of Books* for 22 September 1994, I commented on the desirability of 'good manners in scholarly controversy'. The next issue (6 October) contained a letter from an indignant reader, asking, 'Who wants those? They would *emasculate* [my italics] more than the *LRB*'s letters page.'

compliments', and 'English honesty' deemed superior to the 'apish gestures' and 'false delicacy of French affected politeness' (Plate 28).[18] 'Our ancestors', wrote Barnabe Rich in 1604, 'were but plain-dealing men': 'They had not the mincing compliments now in use.'[19]

Italian manuals of courtesy were also distrusted because some of them condoned the practice of duelling. Sir Thomas Palmer remarked in 1606 that those who observed 'the civility of Italy' 'would have the world know that the civility that is in them, cannot brook uncivility proffered, without resentment in the highest nature'.[20] Part of the inscription on the marble gravestone of Henry Dunch, an Oxfordshire gentleman who died in 1686, read:

> His curious youth would men and manners know
> Which made him to the southern nations go.
> Nearer the sun though they more civil seem
> Revenge and luxury has their esteem,
> Which well observing he return'd with more
> Value for England than he had before.[21]

It was because the moral integrity of the English seemed threatened by these continental tastes and affectations that there was so much criticism of the practice of sending young gentlemen abroad to learn how 'to exchange goodness and harmless simplicity for a compliment'.[22] In 1617 Fynes Moryson, a particularly experienced traveller, advised those who visited foreign countries to adopt the manners of the people among whom they found themselves when they were there, but to shed them when they returned home; they should lay aside 'the spoon and fork of Italy, the affected gestures of France, and all strange apparel, yea, even those manners which with good judgment he allows, if they be disagreeable to his countrymen'.[23] Many travellers seem to have ignored these warnings, for there were numerous complaints about the foreign mannerisms they brought back with them. As a Nottinghamshire gentleman lamented in 1614,

'It becometh some . . . ill to personate the Pantaloon, when shrugging up the shoulders he signifieth "beware" or "patience", or by lifting up the brows, admiration, or by . . . nodding up and down the head, approbation.' Most English people disliked such gesticulation.[24] They also preferred to think of themselves as blunt, plainspoken and devoid of foreign 'craft and subtlety'; and they talked a great deal about their 'frankness' and 'sincerity'. Shakespeare's Henry V represented himself as a 'plain soldier' and a 'plain king', who could not 'mince it in love' or dance or rhyme himself into a lady's favour, but was 'a fellow of plain and uncoined constancy'. 'True English gentry' might lack 'that flattering and complimental gaiety' so natural to their neighbours the French; but theirs was the 'true English genius', which was 'plain, hospitable and debonair, without much ceremony and dissimulation', yet vastly preferable to 'modish hypocrisy accompanied with cringes and grimaces'. Even some of those at the highest social level were ready to claim that a rough, uningratiating style was an essential ingredient of national identity.[25] The Jacobite Duke of Wharton (1698–1731), founder of the Hell-Fire Club and a notorious rake and profligate, lamented that, 'by an inundation of foreigners', British honesty had been 'lost in dissimulation and politeness'.[26] In the eighteenth century, many country gentry rejected any aspirations to cultural refinement, avoided the polite world and stuck to their traditionally boisterous life of hunting, drinking and everyday brutality. Similarly, eighteenth-century London abounded in male clubs given over to drunkenness, gambling and ribaldry (Plate 11).[27]

Come, Sirrah, ne'er tell me of your ways à la mode,
How your fops treat in France, and pay visits abroad.
How formal the fools are when ever they meet,
With what nice punctilios each brings in his treat.
I hate your withdrawing rooms for choc'late and tea,
Your kickshaws and sweetmeats are lost upon me.

Give me your plain claret, and honest old soaker,
That ne'er baulks [declines] his glass, nor foh's at the smoker
[exclaims in disgust at the smoky chimney],
I shan't need you with plate then, and napkin in hand,
Whilst the dessert is eating, near the cistern to stand.
Nor blush to be seen in a dirty close room
That smells of mundungus [malodorous tobacco], and wants
the kind broom.[28]

Manners and Morality

Closely linked to the quasi-nationalistic fear of cultural domination by foreign influences was a strong current of provincial resistance to the affectations of metropolitan society. For it was from London and the court that new forms of civility were disseminated. Here too, the provincial reaction took the form of an appeal to 'plain English' and 'downright dealing', 'without compliment'. Country people, it was said, had 'more friendship than compliments, and more truth than eloquence'.[29] In Yorkshire a gruff and abrasive distaste for unnecessary civilities, bordering on downright rudeness, had been a symbol of regional identity since at least the time of the truculent hero George, the Pinner* of Wakefield, who, in the Elizabethan play of that name, tells King Edward that 'we Yorkshire men be blunt of speech, and little skill'd in court or such quaint fashions'.[30] In the name of frankness and candour, 'good, plain, honest men' repudiated the artificiality and hypocrisy of London society.

Away from the metropolis, the nineteenth-century glossaries of regional dialects suggest that a mincing walk, 'talking fine' and other 'airs and graces' indicative of affected delicacy could evoke ridicule; people who tried to shed their local accent in an attempt to pass as gentlefolk or who introduced pretentious table manners from

---

* A pinner was a local officer whose duty it was to impound stray beasts.

302

London encountered local scorn and hostility. Since the seventeenth century, such affectations had been rebuked with, 'Marry, come up, my dirty cousin!'There was no room for what later generations would call 'la-di-da'.[31] When the young John Locke paid a return visit from Oxford to his paternal home in rural Somerset, he was charmed by 'two or three bonny country girls that have not one jot of dissimulation in them'.[32] The common people seldom used the term 'politeness', which they took to mean an undesirable affectation of 'fine' behaviour. Although many tried to emulate their social superiors by dressing ostentatiously, others were suspicious of socially inappropriate finery and preferred a plain homespun style.[33]

Throughout the early modern period, a strong feeling existed in favour of language that was unvarnished and direct, and hostile to 'anticks and apish gestures', the 'art of adulation, and the skill of ceremonious speech'.[34] Its defenders claimed that theirs was a purer form of politeness, uncorrupted by metropolitan or courtly fashion.[35] Inevitably, however, what some regarded as 'honest sincerity' and 'plain dealing' was seen by others as vulgarity, coarseness and incivility. 'Thou mayest sometimes be too plain', warned a courtesy writer in 1640, rejecting the 'country objection that downright dealing is best'. As David Hume remarked, 'The ancient simplicity, which is naturally so amiable and affecting, often degenerates into rusticity and abuse, scurrility and obscenity.'[36]

Yet Hume also noted that 'modern politeness' could involve affectation, foppery, disguise and insincerity. For though good manners might indicate genuine benevolence towards others, they were usually a diplomatic way of concealing one's true feelings. Such concealment was the very essence of civility, which taught that one should always try, if possible, to please those with whom one came into contact. Inevitably, it called for simulation and dissimulation. Moreover, the emphasis on making oneself agreeable to others often stemmed from a frank, not to say cynical, recognition that this could help one to get on in life. As a writer observed in 1638, 'They that would enfavour themselves for the advantage of any business must show themselves affable, smooth and courteous.'[37] Compliments and courtesies easily degenerated into mendacious flattery. Joseph Addison imagined the ambassador of Bantam, in Java, who visited England in 1682, reporting back that the English regarded the Bantamese as barbarians because they said what they meant, but accounted themselves a civilized people because they spoke one thing and meant another.[38]

The medieval image of the courtier as an aping, fawning, sycophantic hypocrite took on new life in the early modern period;[39] and with some justification, for whereas Erasmus had regarded good manners as a sign of inner virtue, most subsequent conduct books laid all their emphasis on externals: for them, appearances were everything. Sir Walter Ralegh defined compliments as 'a courteous and court-like kind of lying'; Sir Henry Wotton regarded courtly ceremony and compliment as 'the gesture and phrase of dissemblers'; and another Jacobean writer called flattery 'dishonest civility'.[40] At James I's court, a Dutch visitor noticed that a man, 'in an outward show of reverence with cap and knee', would 'bare his head to him whose head, in his heart, he desires were smitten off'.[41] 'We love to have ... our flatteries called "civility"', observed the author of *The Gentlemans Monitor* (1665). The Marquess of Halifax duly defined civility as 'well-bred hypocrisy'. For Bernard Mandeville, the art of good manners had 'nothing to do with virtue or religion'. It consisted in flattering the pride and selfishness of others and concealing one's own.[42] Numerous eighteenth-century writers denounced

> that noble Art
> That makes the tongue to contradict the heart.
> One tells me he's my servant to command,
> Who the same moment wishes I were hang'd.
> Another hopes to see me in my grave,
> Yet swears he is my most obedient slave.[43]

For moralists, it was a commonplace that the ordinary courtesies of daily life involved innumerable petty falsehoods. William Perkins thought that 'those that live by bargaining commonly lie and dissemble. They that deal with chapmen shall hardly know what is truth, they have so many words, and so many shifts. In this respect Christians come short of Turks, who are said to be equal, open, and plain-dealing men, without fraud or deceit.' Daniel Defoe complained that 'all the ordinary communication of life is now full of lying; and what with table-lies, salutation lies, and trading-lies, there is no such thing as every man speaking truth with his neighbour'. David Hume agreed: 'Without an innocent dissimulation or rather simulation', it was 'impossible to pass through the world'.[44]

The transparent insincerities of civil behaviour led to much heart-searching by conscientious persons. In 1659 the radical polemicist Henry Stubbe attacked the notion that 'a civil man' should be expected to sign his letters to equals or inferiors as 'your servant'.[45] Over a century later, the Evangelical Hannah More elaborated on the dangers of ordering servants to tell callers that their master was not at home. This 'daily and hourly lie', she thought, corrupted young servants up from the country and unaccustomed to telling blatant falsehoods. It could not be defended by pleading that it was 'one of those lies of convention, no more intended to deceive than the "Dear Sir" at the beginning, or "Your humble servant" at the close of a letter to a person who is not dear to you, and to whom you owe no subjection'. Instead of falling back on this feeble pretence, 'some scrupulous persons' were so repelled by the practice of making servants tell lies that they made it a point of conscience to 'lay themselves open to the irruption of every idle invader who sallies out on morning visits, bent on the destruction of business and the annihilation of study'.[46]

The conflict between politeness and honesty was reflected in the classic texts on good manners themselves, which urged complaisance and accommodation on the one hand, while warning against flattery and hypocrisy on the other.[47] It was abundantly revealed to the world in 1774, with the posthumous publication of Lord Chesterfield's *Letters* to his son, in which polite behaviour was presented as cynical camouflage for self-advancement. Few were able to emulate the 4th Lord Digby of Geashill (d. 1686), who allegedly managed to get through life without ever saying more than he meant or telling a lie 'even in compliment'.[48]

Prominent among the critics of polite dissimulation were the godly. English Protestantism owed nothing to Renaissance ideas about civility and in some ways was strongly antagonistic to them. Those who attacked genuflections in church as 'cringing' or 'ducking' and derided Catholic ceremonials as 'stage plays' were, unsurprisingly, equally hostile to ritual and 'formality' in daily life.[49] If elaborate gestures of deference were unacceptable in the worship of God, they were all the more inappropriate in relations between mere humans. Hence the assertion by a hostile pamphleteer in 1641 that some held all good manners to be popery.[50] William Perkins believed that 'the courtesy of the world', with its removal of the cap, bending of the knee and paying of compliments, seldom indicated genuine affection and often concealed real enmity.[51] The Essex minister Jeremiah Dyke thought 'neater and civilified compliments of faith and troth' were as objectionable as the 'prodigious oaths of wounds and blood' and 'damned language' of ruffians.[52] The preacher Thomas Brooks declared flatly that 'civility' was 'very often the nurse of impiety, the mother of flattery and an enemy to real sanctity'. John Bunyan deplored 'the poor and beggarly art of complimenting, for the more compliment, the less sincerity'. His Pilgrim was told by Evangelist that Civility, 'notwithstanding his simpering looks', was 'but a hypocrite'.[53] He could have pointed to the playwright William Wycherley's character Lord Plausible, who protests that if he were ever to say anything unpleasant about anybody it would always be behind their back, 'out of pure good manners'.[54]

Civility thus seemed to be increasingly detached from religion. As many godly Puritans noticed, persons without 'a spark of God in their hearts' were 'able to carry themselves in their outward behaviour very orderly and mannerly'. Good manners were perfectly compatible with personal wickedness. One could be a stickler for social decorum and yet despise religion.[55] Indeed, civility was not just irrelevant to the quest for eternal life; it could positively obstruct it, for the norms of polite behaviour seemed to imply that it was more important to avoid offending others than to please God. 'Good manners' were 'an hindrance to grace': 'They who are most diligent in teaching or practising the one are commonly most negligent in the other.'[56] It was 'not sufficient for a man to live in outward civility': what mattered was the spiritual struggle with sin. 'Mere civility' was regularly denounced by Puritan preachers as 'nothing else but a fair demeanour in the world', which usually went with ignorance of Christ.[57]

To worldly people, serious religious commitment appeared impolite: 'If any man cleave a little more than ordinary to religion,' lamented John White in 1615, 'that scarce suits with the civility of our time.' To engage in religious conversation at a feast, for example, was regarded by many as 'uncivil and unmannerly'. So were attempts to evangelize neighbours or strangers.[58] To reprove sin was 'uncivil', and to wake up one's betters when they fell asleep in church was 'unmannerliness'. The same was true of a refusal to drink excessively when pressed to do so by a friend. Lucy Hutchinson praised her husband, the Puritan colonel, for his ability to criticize pride and vanity 'without any taint of incivility'; but, as the Marquess of Halifax remarked, 'a great part of the manners of the modern age' consisted in *not* speaking out against fashionable vices.[59] No wonder that conscientious ministers, in their zeal to save souls, felt it necessary to omit 'all ceremonial compliments' or that 'men of the world' were said to believe that religion made men 'rude and rustical'.[60]

The godly justified their apparent incivility with the obvious retort: 'Would you have us let them go quietly to hell for fear of displeasing them or seeming to be unmannerly or uncivil?'[61] But they sometimes went to extremes in their belief that it was better to be rude to men than discourteous to God. One zealous iconoclast was said, with some understatement, to have overrun 'even good manners in some houses that entertained him' by his disconcerting habit of immediately tearing and defacing any devotional picture he happened to notice on his host's wall.* He 'would scarce endure a cross in a gentleman's coat of arms'.[62] One godly lady rejected the polite education normally thought appropriate for well-born girls, piously announcing that she was 'willing to be despised for [her] homely and mean walking, endeavouring to cast off those high looks and mincing gait, which is gotten by dancing; both which are condemned by the prophet Esay [Isaiah] expressly'. Robert Boyle lamented that there were many such young women who were ignorant of the rules of polite behaviour and unsociably gauche in company because their parents, 'out of a mistaken zeal', regarded good breeding as 'below a Christian' and insufficient to bring them to heaven.[63]

Polite emphasis on bodily restraint and self-control also conflicted with the emotionalism of some kinds of evangelical religion. Puritans and sectaries were repeatedly mocked for their whining and weeping, their nasal twang, their uncourtly mannerisms, their lifting up the whites of their eyes, their strange gestures and their distorted facial expressions.[64] When John Rogers, vicar of Dedham, wished to represent the torments of the damned, he took hold of the canopy over the pulpit with both hands and roared hideously.[65] Such behaviour was in flagrant defiance of conventional notions of proper bodily

---

* This may have been the Parliamentarian soldier Sir William Springett (1620/22–44), who, on one occasion when he came to visit a colleague, was shocked as he passed through the hall to spy 'several large, fine, superstitious pictures, as of the crucifixion of Christ, of his Resurrection, &c. They were thought very ornamental to the hall.' He drew his sword, cut them out of their frames, and spitting them on his sword's point, carried them into the parlour to greet his host's astonished wife; Mary Penington [sic], *Some Account of Circumstances in the Life of Mary Pennington* (1821), 93–95.

deportment, as those who engaged in it were well aware. 'Till a man seems odd to the world,' boasted a preacher in 1641, 'he is never right in religion and righteousness.'[66] In 1670 Samuel Parker, who had renounced his Presbyterian upbringing and embraced the Church of England, displayed the fanaticism of the convert in an intemperate attack on the Dissenters, whom he described as 'the rudest and most barbarous people in the world', likening them to 'the savage Americans'. Sixty years later, the godly vocabulary of 'believers', 'converted persons' and 'regenerate ones' was still greatly disliked by 'the polite part of the town'.[67] It is impossible to understand the hostile feelings aroused towards the sectaries and Dissenters in the seventeenth century, or the Methodists in the eighteenth (notorious for their 'screaming with hideous noises and unbecoming gestures'),[68] unless we take account of the way in which their whole style of bodily comportment seemed to flout the accepted rules of civility. One friend of the nonconformists even suggested that the Dissenting academies should remedy the situation by employing dancing masters to teach future ministers 'gracefulness and gentility of address, and prune off all clumsiness and awkwardness that is disagreeable to people of fashion'.[69]

The godly were severe on the waste of time and money involved in observing the fashionable conventions of polite sociability. Richard Baxter despised 'that vanity which they call breeding' and deplored the resources expended on grand houses, lavish entertaining and endless courtesy visits to friends, relations and neighbours, all in the name of 'civility'.[70] The Anglican George Herbert thought it unlawful to spend the day 'in dressing, complimenting [and] visiting'. The Baptist Henry Jessey disliked this practice of what he called 'idle women wandering about', and the pious Mary Bewley (d. 1659) was praised because 'her delight was to abide at home, not spending time on needless and complimental visits, or in going about from house to house'.[71] It was an old problem: the Jesuit Richard Strange wrote in his life of the thirteenth-century bishop St Thomas

Cantilupe that the saint regarded the 'ceremonious visits of courts' as a waste of time, 'yet to avoid them would have been deemed a solecism against civility'.[72]

Other requirements of civility were equally irksome. Hospitality was an accepted social convention, but many regarded it as a cover for gluttony and intemperance. Health drinking was conventionally defended as a form of courtesy, but it was an obvious excuse for drunkenness.[73] The conventions of polite conversation were also frowned upon. The godly disapproved of small talk and deplored the practice of treating religious topics with levity or excluding them altogether lest they should cause dissension. 'In the practice of civility', it was only too easy to find oneself speaking of God 'slightly, inconsiderately or merrily'.[74] William Perkins was prepared to allocate time for 'urbanity', that is, recreational conversation, but he regarded 'a dexterity in mocking and descanting upon men's persons and names' as a sin; and he expected people at the dinner table to talk seriously about religious matters.[75]

Throughout the early modern period, therefore, there were serious tensions between the accepted code of civil behaviour and the claims of godliness and personal integrity.[76] Yet there was no suggestion in mainline Puritanism that the basic standards of civility should not be observed. Although the godly were expected to keep their distance from their unregenerate contemporaries, they played their part in the local communities and believed that it was important 'to be courteous to all men, both good and bad'.[77] Many were celebrated for their excellent manners, such as the Dissenting minister Joseph Alleine, who was as courteous, affable and civil in conversation 'as a man (subject to the common frailties of human nature) could be'. In his collected lives of Puritan ministers and godly women, the nonconformist biographer Samuel Clarke made a point of stressing their 'obliging conversation' and 'affable deportment'. The godly Elizabeth Walker even hired a French dancing master to teach her daughters.[78]

The Quaker Challenge

It was left to the Quakers to make a direct onslaught on the laws of civility in the name of religious principle.[79] This sect appeared in the late 1640s, and by 1660 had some forty thousand adherents, primarily from the middling sort. They were not the first religious group to question titles of honour or to refuse to doff their hats to their social superiors: earlier heretics and sectarians had also rejected these conventional forms of social deference.[80] But in their thoroughgoing repudiation of all the polite courtesies of social intercourse, the Quakers had no predecessors, unless one counts the Cynics of ancient Greece, who went much further by abandoning even the conventions of bodily decency.[81] Following the biblical reminder that God was no respecter of persons (Acts 10:34), and claiming that it was ungrammatical as well as obsequious to call an individual by the plural form 'you', the Quakers addressed everyone in the second person singular, 'thou' or 'thee', a salutation normally reserved for intimates or inferiors or those one intended to insult. This practice caused enormous offence, as their leader George Fox recalled: 'Thou'st "thou" me, thou ill-bred clown', some 'proud men' would say, 'as though their breeding lay in saying "You" to a singular ... This "Thou" and "Thee" was a fearful cut to proud flesh and self-honour.'[82] The Quakers refused to call anybody 'Sir' or 'My Lord', or to kneel, curtsey or perform other 'crouchings and cringings with their bodies' and 'exterior parts of politeness'. Since Christ had said that one should salute no man on the highway (Luke 10:4), they declined to say 'good evening' or 'good morrow'.[83] They would not even bid farewell when leaving someone's house, 'so that their departures and [their] going aside to ease themselves [were] almost undistinguishable'.[84]

In conversation the Quakers declined to use 'those flattering words, commonly called compliments', such as 'your servant, sir', on the grounds that they were 'frivolous, feigned and hypocritical' and indistinguishable from lies.[85] Instead, their speech was simple, unadorned, undiplomatic and outspoken; in style not unlike that 'direct, frank, no-holds barred Sabra way of talking', known in modern Israel as *dugri* and practised for much the same reasons. Like *dugri*, Quaker speech went with simplicity of dress and lifestyle and was meant to demonstrate the speaker's honesty, candour and self-confident irreverence.[86] The Friends criticized parents for training their children in 'evil manners (deceitfully called good manners nowadays)' and sending them to schools 'to learn them to walk, and shail [shuffle] their legs in dancing, to doff their hats and wring their bodies in congees and how to hold their heads, necks, and make fine curtseys backwards, with such like things as young women learn at such places, that so they may not lose one grain, hair, nor jot of that honour, renown, fame, respect, and worship among men, which their parents can purchase them by money'. They scorned polite deport-ment, refusing to employ dancing masters for their children, and developing a peculiarly awkward gait.[87] Their essential objection was to actions that did not correspond to the feelings of the heart. Like John Bunyan, they believed that 'the more compliment, the less sincerity'.[88]

Behind this attitude lay the old suspicion of metropolitan smooth-ness and preference for blunt speaking. The Friends expressed what a writer in 1653 called the 'peevishness, envy and antipathy' of 'country people' to 'men of better breeding and manners'.[89] But they went further in their rejection of all forms of verbal deference. John Whitehead remarked that the only Lord was God and the only person a man should address as 'My lady' was his wife. Edward Billing boasted that one of his coreligionists had addressed Philip, 4th Earl of Pembroke, as 'Phil'.[90]

By omitting all gestures of respect and using the same language to high and low, the Quakers flouted the whole principle of deference to superiors, which was one of the foundations upon which the laws of civility were built. As one of their critics remarked, they held that to be religious, one was obliged to be *un*civil.[91] The Friends were accused of regarding 'common civility' as 'the mark of the beast'. Their 'brutish irreverence to superiors' and their rejection of all courteous salutations were seen as threatening to 'reduce persons from civility to barbarism'.[92] Unsurprisingly, they were relentlessly persecuted as 'enemies to civility and good manners'.[93] In face of their heterodoxy, the Royalist divine Thomas Fuller thought it necessary to reaffirm the correct use of the second person singular: '*Thou* from superiors to inferiors,' he ruled, 'is proper, as a sign of command; from equals to equals, [it] is passable, as a note of familiarity; but from inferiors to superiors, if proceeding from ignorance, [it] hath a smack of clownishness; if from affectation, a tang of contempt.'[94]

Yet when their critics accused them of lack of 'courtesy' and 'civility', the Quakers retorted that such terms were merely euphemisms for an unchristian failure to treat men as equal in the sight of God. Their objection was to the social distinctions implicit in the accepted code of civil behaviour. As one early convert, James Parnel, wrote in 1655: 'If a poor man come before a rich man, it may be the rich man will move his hat; that is called courtesy and humility. But the poor man must stand with his hat off before him, and that is called honour and manners, and due respect unto him. But if the rich man do bid him put it on, it is counted a great courtesy and he gets honour to himself to be counted a courteous man. But this difference or respect of persons was never ordained by God but by the Devil.'[95]

More emolliently, another Quaker, Benjamin Furly, explained that the Friends did indeed reject 'those dirty customs of bowing the body, bidding "Good morrow" and "Good night", wagging the hat', and similar 'self-set-up customary ceremonial gestures'. Instead they expressed that 'true honour' which came from the heart by such 'true and infallible' actions as shaking hands, falling on the other person's neck, embracing and kissing.[96] In 1707 George Keith, who had been a prominent Friend before he returned to the Anglican Church, described how the Quakers greeted their familiar acquaintances by taking them by the hand, gripping it and pressing hard on the wrist as well as the hand in order 'to feel the life in the person whom they so grip'.[97] Defending the Quaker practice of addressing magistrates as 'thee' and 'thou', Henry Stubbe said that it was merely a rejection of 'a French fashion in speech' and no more implied disobedience than did wearing plain clothes rather than the 'gaudy apparel of rulers'.[98] In defence of his fellow religionists, John Whitehead vigorously rejected the charge that Quakers were uncivil and discourteous. 'For courteousness to all, both to superiors and to equals,' he asked, 'where is the man or woman among all our neighbours that hath been conversant with us, that can justly accuse us and show wherein we have not been courteous and amenable to them? Unless they count it discourtesy to reprove for evil, or not to have their persons worshipped and adored as God, with uncovering the head, and bowing the knee?'[99] For the Friends, 'true' courtesy was expressed by the golden rule.* 'Learn to do as you would have all to do unto you,' said James Parnel, 'and here is good manners and breeding, courtesy and civility.'[100]

In response to this sectarian challenge during the Interregnum, the Anglican Church made a conscious effort after 1660 to emphasize that religion taught amiability, not rudeness, and was wholly compatible with all the little courtesies of social life. John Sharp, Archbishop of York, deplored the incivilities of the Quakers and stressed the desirability of 'an easy, inoffensive, obliging way of address and behaviour'. Christ himself, he declared, had been 'the most free, obliging, and civil, and, if I durst use the word, I would say the most complaisant person that ever perhaps appeared in the world'.[101] His colleague Edward Fowler, Bishop of Gloucester, had made the same point: Christ, he said, was 'a person of the greatest freedom, affability and courtesy'. There was nothing crabbed or

---

* In the same way, *dugri* speakers in Israel are said to show true respect to those with whom they converse by tacitly implying that their interlocutors have the strength and moral integrity to be able to take the speaker's direct talk for what it is: '*Dugri* speech in the sabra culture does not violate but rather realizes a culture-specific idea of politeness'; Tamar Katriel, *Straight Talk* (Cambridge, 1986), 117.

morose about him: he was 'marvellously conversable, sociable and benign'. These assurances that Jesus would have been entirely at home in an Augustan drawing room set the tone for several decades of Anglican writing about the compatibility of polite sociability with religious principle.[102] As a writer put it in 1720, 'The world seems generally of [the] opinion now that sound sense, polite learning, good breeding, and an easy and affable conversation are not only consistent with true religion, but are most productive of it.' Virtue itself could be defined as the practice and refinement of manners.[103]

But the moral conflict to which the Quakers had so dramatically drawn attention could not be so easily evaded. Although protesting that they were not against true courtesy, the Friends themselves continued to preserve their distinguishing 'plainness of speech' and to reject all the 'exterior parts of politeness'. In practice, they were noted for their exceptional personal cleanliness and for their business honesty. Their speech and bodily deportment were, in their way, just as controlled and disciplined as those of the most sophisticated courtier.[104] Yet others found them awkward because of their insistence on elevating their religious principles above the requirements of ordinary civility. In Thomas Hobbes's view, people who obstinately refused to accommodate themselves to others were like stones collected for use in building, which had to be cast away because of their 'asperity' and 'irregularity'.[105]

The Quakers were not the only English Protestants to regard the hypocritical obsequiousness of polite speech as an enemy to 'the truth, simplicity and honesty of the heart'.[106] At the end of the seventeenth century, even the Archbishop of Canterbury deplored the vogue of 'compliment and dissimulation' and called for a return to 'the old English plainness and sincerity', which, he believed, were threatened by the taste for 'foreign manners and fashions'.[107] In the eighteenth century, sincerity was widely extolled as a distinctive national characteristic.[108] Unfortunately, sincerity and civility did not go easily together. Guides to politeness put all their emphasis on external appearance, marked by social ease and the ostentatious cultivation of good taste, rather than on inner sentiment.[109]

In France, the Jansenist Pierre Nicole (1625–95) and the educational philanthropist Jean-Baptist de La Salle (1651–1719) confronted this problem by developing different brands of what they called 'Christian civility' (*civilité chrétienne*). Nicole envisaged a civility that was 'perfectly true, perfectly sincere' and 'different from that of men of the world'. This meant, among other things, being uncivil to those who robbed others of their time by overwhelming them with unwanted letters and visits. La Salle, by contrast, sought to combine moral teaching with respect for social proprieties (*bienséance*).[110]

In Britain the issue was ultimately resolved by accepting that civilized life could not exist without a certain amount of dissimulation and that polite courtesies were not meant to be taken literally. As Bernard Mandeville remarked, in all civil societies people were taught from the cradle to be hypocrites; they could not be sociable creatures unless they had learnt to stifle their innermost thoughts.[111] All compliments were lies, but as a contemporary remarked in the 1690s, since everybody knew that they were lies, they did no harm: 'You return 'em in the same manner you receive 'em.' 'Am I a liar,' asked David Hume, 'because I order my servant to say I am not at home?'[112] By regarding complimentary forms as mere conventions, empty of any real meaning, it became possible for people to use them without undue heart searching. 'How are you?' we ask today, but we do not always stay for an answer.

Only the most scrupulous moralists, such as Immanuel Kant in the 1790s, continued to wrestle with such dilemmas as whether the phrase 'Your most obedient servant' at the end of a letter was a lie, or what one should say when a mediocre writer asked you whether you liked his book. Kant's view was that insincere compliments did not deceive the recipient; they were, however, a sign of goodwill and helped to develop genuine benevolence in those who regularly paid them. This conclusion would subsequently receive qualified endorsement from the French sociologist Émile Durkheim and the British philosopher Bertrand Russell, both of whom thought it wrong to be truthful when being so would cause unnecessary pain.[113]

Most people in early modern England, like most of us today, allowed the demands of social life to take precedence over strict adherence to truth; to be 'civilly false' rather than 'rudely honest' was not hypocrisy but necessary tact.[114] In Richard Wilbur's witty rendering of the words of Molière's Philinte:

In certain cases it would be uncouth
And most absurd to speak the naked truth;
With all respect for your exalted notions,
It's often best to veil one's true emotions.
Wouldn't the social fabric come undone
If we were wholly frank with everyone?[115]

When, in the 1790s, the radical William Godwin came to consider the laws of politeness, he took the same view. It was true, he conceded, that politeness was sometimes incompatible with sincerity. But important though it was, sincerity should be regarded as an inferior obligation to that of general benevolence. It was not necessarily wrong to criticize people to their face, provided one did so in a courteous manner, but consideration for the feelings of others came first; and no one need worry that he was jeopardizing his moral integrity by being polite.[116]

Yet by preferring to give priority to 'sincerity' and truthfulness to one's own feelings, the religious radicals of seventeenth-century England had anticipated one of the essential principles of late eighteenth-century Romanticism. Like Jean-Jacques Rousseau, they rejected artificial social forms in the name of personal integrity and the teachings of the heart. For Rousseau, heir to the ancient Cynics, the only moral failure was the betrayal of one's own inner self.[117]

317

Many later Romantics discarded polite ceremony in the name of natural feeling, individuality and authenticity. Just as Captain Cook had admired the Indians of Nootka Sound for being 'unacquainted with the various artifices by which civilized nations learn to hide their real dispositions', so the Romantics regarded the common people as more authentic in their manners than their oversophisticated superiors. For the lower classes appeared to speak from the heart, and their frank simplicity contrasted favourably with the affectations of those above them.[118]

By the end of the eighteenth century, the link between manners and morality had been decisively broken. Early nineteenth-century Evangelicals continued to regard good manners as an outward sign of an inner religious life, and Victorian educators cherished the notion of the Christian gentleman, chivalrous and decent. But it had become generally accepted that social cohesion required a degree of hypocrisy and that the normal courtesies of daily life involved innumerable petty falsehoods. Manners were important, but they were not to be confused with ethics.

Democratic Civility

Along with the moral objections to civility went a political one. In his life of his father-in-law, the Roman governor of Britain, the historian Tacitus had suggested that the civilizing culture that the Romans brought to the Britons was intended to enslave them. By encouraging the conquered people to adopt their language, tastes and manners, they consolidated the incorporation of Britain into the Roman Empire.[119] John Milton repeated Tacitus's words when he wrote in his *History of Britain* that the Romans introduced 'proud buildings, baths and the elegance of banqueting; which the foolisher sort called civility, but was indeed a secret art to prepare them for bondage'.[120] Sir Henry Wotton said the same about William the Conqueror: the 'new behaviours and habits' brought in by the

Normans 'under show of civility' were 'in effect but rudiments of subjection'.[121]

With its common law, its jury system, its civil liberties and its high level of popular participation in local government, early modern England was an unpropitious environment for hierarchical ritual. There were no longer any serfs or villeins; an Englishman's home was his castle; and the common people were relatively self-confident – notorious in eighteenth-century Europe for their lack of deference in daily life.[122] When absolutism was the rule in other European countries, Britons retained their political freedom, it was said, because of 'that natural churlishness and roughness of temper which is inherent in a true right English man'. Their rudeness to strangers, regardless of rank, symbolized their consciousness of living in a free country.[123]

Even so, the poor were well advised to display deference and respect if they wanted to secure employment or receive parish relief. One mid-seventeenth-century writer described 'labouring poor men, which in time of scarcity pine and murmur for want of bread, cursing the rich behind his back; and, before his face, cap and knee, and a whining countenance'. Another depicted a poor tenant paying rent to his landlord 'in as slavish a posture as may be, namely, with cap in hand, and bended knee, crouching and creeping from corner to corner, while his lord (rather tyrant) walks up and down the room, with his proud looks, and with great swelling words questions him about his holding'.[124]

Yet there are some signs that outward deference to superiors was on the decline well before the appearance of self-conscious popular radicalism in the 1640s and 1650s. An Elizabethan lamented that, in places where the royal court spent most time, the people used to pass the nobility in the streets 'without moving either cap or knee'; this 'stubborn stoutness' and 'unmannerly, disordered boldness' arose, he thought, from their long familiarity with the noblemen's servants and their daily view of their masters.[125] In the Shropshire town of

Ludlow, seat of the king's Council in the Marches, the common council noted in 1611 'the little respect and sometimes the contumely of lewd and presumptuous persons towards our said governors'. Sir Henry Spelman observed in the 1630s that even 'inferior gentlemen' were coming to accost the nobility with 'familiarity' rather than with the 'great respect, observance and distance' they had shown fifty years earlier.[126] In London in the century before the Civil Wars, there were many instances of plebeian insult and vandalism directed against aristocrats, mayors and aldermen. In the country at large there was a continuous undercurrent of subversive talk, especially in alehouses, about unpopular monarchs, gentlemen and clergy, and widespread hostility towards rich traders who exploited food shortages.[127] Riotous protests were common throughout the early modern period.[128] High food prices, low wages, the enclosure of common lands and the erection of tollgates could all provoke violent demonstrations. In the eighteenth century, miners and industrial workers were capable of striking in protest against low wages or unsatisfactory working conditions. But typically, the protesters were concerned to attack abuses of authority and to defend what they saw as legitimate rights. They aimed to force their social superiors and employers to perform the duties expected of them, and they seldom challenged the existence of a hierarchical social order as such. Protests rarely involved face-to-face abuse or violence against the person, though they sometimes were enlivened by insulting scatological gestures, a particularly effective way of infuriating those who had been brought up to regard the control of the body as an essential part of their civility.[129]

With the heightening of political and religious tensions in the years 1640–42, there was much local disorder and a near breakdown of the normal courtesies as affronts to the gentry and abuse of magistrates, constables and clergy reached a crescendo.[130] The historian Clarendon recalled 'the fury and licence of the common people, who were in all places grown to that barbarity and rage against the nobility and gentry (under the style of "cavaliers"), that it was not safe for any to live at their houses who were taken notice of as no votaries to the Parliament'.[131] A contemporary ballad expressed the mood of the time:

Good manners have an evil report,
  And turns to pride we see.
We'll therefore cry good manners down,
  And hey! Then up go we.[132]

The Civil Wars and their aftermath witnessed a thoroughgoing challenge to the old hierarchical conception of civil courtesy. From the boys in the Ipswich streets in the 1630s, who stared in Bishop Wren's face 'very uncivilly ... in an insolent manner', to the Fifth Monarchist plotters in 1657, described as 'very obstinate and resolute fellows', who refused to take off their hats to Protector Cromwell and addressed him as 'thou', the period was one continual assault on traditional forms of deference.[133] Lucy Hutchinson tells how her husband, the Parliamentary officer, found that his allies in Nottinghamshire distrusted civility, thinking it 'scarce possible' for anyone to continue to be both a gentleman and a supporter of the godly interest, and forcing him to behave uncivilly towards his Royalist cousin in a way that went against his natural instincts.[134] In 1646 the Presbyterian Thomas Edwards declared that in the previous two years, and especially since Parliament's victory at Naseby, the sectaries had in the most insolent and unheard-of manner abused 'all sorts and ranks of men, even to the highest'.[135]

Polite deference to superiors declined further with Charles I's defeat. In 1648 a Parliamentary MP reported to a Royalist exile in Paris that 'civility begins to be looked upon as a monster now'.[136] The subsequent abolition of the monarchy, episcopacy and the House of Lords consolidated the revolution. The Commonwealth established in 1649 shunned ostentatious display and was hostile to the obsequious rituals that had propped up kingship and aristocracy: what Milton called 'the base necessity of court flatteries and prostrations' and 'the perpetual bowings and cringings of an abject people'.[137] In 1653 a petitioner urged the Barebones Parliament to abolish 'the titles of Duke, Marquess, Earl, Lord, Knight, Esquire and suchlike ... as a vainglorious thing'; and in 1654 a carter was committed at Middlesex Sessions to the house of correction for saying in open court and 'in an uncivil manner' that he was 'as good a man as his landlord Barnes, meaning John Barnes, Esq.', a JP then sitting in the court.[138] Anthony Wood observed in 1659 that the 'upstarts' who ruled the country during the Interregnum did not give 'the common civility of a hat' to the old Royalist gentry; and in the same year John Evelyn reported that the nobility were cursed and reviled by the London carters.[139]

Writing in the year of Charles II's restoration, the future bishop John Parry observed that, in recent years, 'respectful civility' had been esteemed 'a piece of idolatry', 'common civility' looked on as the mark of the beast, and 'a seemly reverence to superiors' regarded as equivalent to worshipping the Antichrist.[140] His disgust was shared by Clarendon, who complained that the sects had 'discountenanced all forms of reverence and respect, as relics and marks of superstition'.[141] In 1663 the Lord Mayor of London issued an order forbidding any repetition of the 'rudeness, affronts, and insolent behaviour' displayed by 'the unruly and meaner sort of people' during the Interregnum towards 'noblemen, ladies, gentlemen and persons of quality passing in their coaches or walking through the streets of the City'; this 'undutifulness and contempt of their superiors', he claimed, had been encouraged by 'the late usurped powers'.[142] In fact, similar orders had been issued in 1621, for hostility to strangers and jeering at the coaches of the aristocracy were endemic in pre-Civil War London.[143] Nevertheless, it became part of post-Restoration mythology that the quarrel of the Parliamentarians, 'those barbarous rebels', had been as much with 'politeness and the liberal arts' as with monarchy and episcopacy. The Nonconformists were accused of shaking 'the very foundations of religion and good manners', while atheism and profaneness had led 'plebeians and mechanics' to abandon civility along with their religion.[144]

The return of Charles II meant the restoration of the aristocracy to their old position and the reinstatement of the conventional rituals of deference, though punctuated by periodic episodes of popular protest. There was, however, a continuing trend towards greater informality in manners and behaviour. In the first part of his reign, Charles II was a much less formal monarch than his father had been, making himself accessible to 'all sorts of people' and standing bareheaded to greet them affably.[145] Polite society had always had an ambivalent attitude towards its own rituals; it was not only Puritans or Quakers who felt unease about the theatricality implicit in the practice of politeness. In the early seventeenth century, many contemporaries deplored 'apish formality', 'cringes and compliments' and the affected manners of 'quaint crane-paced courtiers'.[146] The manuals of civility themselves warned against affectation, artificiality and what Sir Henry Wotton in 1633 called 'frothy formalities'. True politeness, they stressed, lay in 'real benevolence', not ceremonious forms; and any opening for relaxed informality should be gratefully seized.[147] Genuine respect for others was infinitely more important than outward ceremony. Colonel Hutchinson 'hated ceremonious compliment, but yet had such a natural civility and complaisance to all people as made his converse very delightful'. Jonathan Swift was in favour of good manners, which he defined as not making other people feel uneasy. But he was hostile to the cultivated mannerisms of good breeding, which he dismissed as 'pedantry': 'a courtly bow, or gait, or dress are no part of good manners'. Even Lord Chesterfield recommended an 'easiness of carriage', holding that only 'country bumpkins' and those who had never been in 'good company' were stiff and formal.[148]

The stilted postures and movements inculcated by the dancing masters were increasingly disdained by those who favoured a more 'natural' style of bodily comportment. The 3rd Earl of Shaftesbury thought that dancing masters, 'if strictly followed', taught 'a fictitious, false and affected gesture and mien'. Others, while admiring the easy and graceful movements that 'the true gentleman' had acquired by having learnt to dance, were offended by 'the coxcomb who is always exhibiting his formal dancing-bow and minuet-step'. The 'fop' was the same 'formal, stiff creature' wherever he went, whereas the 'person of breeding' knew how to leave off formality when a freer manner was appropriate.[149]

Between intimate acquaintances, polite ceremonies had always been not just superfluous, but positively inappropriate. Sir Thomas Browne dedicated *Urne-Buriall* (1658) to his friend Thomas Le Gros, 'having long experience of your friendly conversation, void of empty formality'. John Locke, writing to his friend Anthony Collins in 1704, declared that they were 'past ceremony' and 'beyond civility'; the 'sincerity' of 'true friendship' set them free 'from a scrupulous observance of all those little circumstances' of what he called 'outside civility'. He contrasted his relations with his friends, which were marked by 'sincerity', with those with other people, to whom he extended only the external civility of 'making legs' and kissing hands.[150]

The movement towards greater informality was noticed by contemporary observers, who contrasted the grave, reserved and highly formal style of the Elizabethan gentry with the more relaxed and socially accessible demeanour of their counterparts in the late seventeenth century. Bishop Sprat thought in 1667 that the 'vast distance between them and other orders of men' was 'no longer observed'.[151] Roger North noticed that, whereas 'ceremony and stiff formality' still survived in France and Italy, the English were more casual. When coaches passed each other in Hyde Park, it was sufficient for acquaintances to bow once to each other; whereas in Rome they did it every time they passed, and 'with such overstrained reverence, as if nothing less than precipitation out of the coach were sufficient'.[152]

Within the household, relations between parents and children were also becoming less formal. Clarendon's nostalgia for the vanished world of pre-Civil War England lay behind his lament that, after the Restoration, 'children asked not blessing of their parents ... The young women conversed without any circumspection or modesty ... Parents had no manner of authority over their children, nor children any obedience or submission to their parents.'[153] Perhaps every generation feels, as it grows older, that manners have become sloppier and that age is less respected than when they were young. Sir Walter Ralegh quoted the Roman moralist Seneca: 'Our ancestors have complained, we do complain, our children will complain, that good manners are gone, and that all things grow worse.'[154] In Jacobean times moralists grumbled about 'the customable rudeness of our young persons, that show no token of reverence to their elders in rising or being uncovered before them, but use such behaviour towards them as if they were their companions or play-fellows'.[155] But in the later seventeenth century, children were indeed ceasing to stand bare-headed in the presence of their parents. The distinctively English custom of their kneeling daily to receive their parents' blessing was also on the decline.[156] It had always caused some unease among the stricter Protestants, who saw it as a popish ceremony. Most of them had managed to reassure themselves that it was acceptable because it was a purely civil ritual, not a religious one, but others had their scruples.[157] In New England, where the Puritan clergy preached against it, some parents made it a matter of conscience *not* to allow their children to express reverence in word or gesture.[158] In old England it became increasingly common to regard rituals of filial respect as either superstitious or superfluous. Yet Roger North, writing in the mid-1690s, assumed that the parental blessing was still a 'universal custom'; and it was still alive in the early eighteenth century.[159] The 1703 edition of a popular conduct manual continued to advise children that they should bow whenever they approached their parents.[160] It is not clear when these conventions eventually died away.

In society at large, issues of precedence were coming to matter less; extravagant displays of deference and subordination were less common and greetings and partings less elaborate. Prescriptions for domestic entertaining reflected a parallel tendency to become less hierarchical and more convivial. Guests were often encouraged to help themselves rather than waiting to be served; and formal health drinking declined.[161] To Samuel Johnson's disgust, in the mid-eighteenth century it became a fashion (with Quaker origins) that guests should quit the company without first taking leave of the lady of the house.[162]

Writing in the *Spectator* in 1711, Joseph Addison declared that there had been 'a very great revolution' in behaviour: originally, 'the politer part of mankind' had distinguished themselves from 'the rustic part of the species' by elaborate forms and ceremonies; but as they came to find those ceremonies burdensome, they threw them off, so that 'at present ... an unconstrained carriage, and a certain openness of behaviour are the height of good breeding. The fashionable world is grown free and easy; our manners sit more loose upon us; nothing is so modish as an agreeable negligence.'[163] It was now 'the best breeding', agreed the nonagenarian Bishop Hough in 1742, to lay aside the 'ceremonious behaviour' that people had been taught as children.[164] The word 'formal' was coming to mean behaviour that was not so much socially decorous as stiff and unnatural. There was a general dislike of deep bows and bended knees. A French traveller reported in 1698 that ordinary Englishmen did not (God forbid!) raise their hats when they met each other, but at most would drop their chin a little and make a very small inclination of the head. By the end of the eighteenth century, even the most polite gentlemen were ceasing to pull their hats off when addressing someone, as would have been normal in Paris.[165]

During the eighteenth century, the gentry began to dress down. They adopted plebeian fashions, such as the frock coat, the great coat and, ultimately, trousers. Peers appeared in the House of Lords dressed like farmers. Official occupational costumes, decorations, heraldic devices, retinues and other public advertisements of status were less regularly employed; and the social order ceased to be as immediately visible as it once had been.[166]

The term 'condescension' had long been used approvingly to describe the gracious willingness of the upper ranks of society to converse amiably with their social inferiors. But by the mid-eighteenth century, the word had begun to acquire the pejorative meaning of treating others with an unconcealed sense of superiority. People were becoming more sensitive to what Samuel Johnson called 'the insolence of condescension'.[167] In the later eighteenth century, the manners of the English aristocracy were generally believed to be distinguished by their exceptional ease, informality and avoidance of ceremonial niceties. The *New Bath Directory* for 1792 declared that 'ceremony, beyond the rules of politeness, is totally exploded; everyone mixes in the rooms upon an equality'.[168] Even today the British are perplexed by the common French habit of shaking hands each morning, and their practice with moderately close acquaintants is never to shake hands at all.

Only in the last decades of the eighteenth century do the informality and accessibility of the English upper classes appear to have weakened. The economic growth of those years generated an expanding class of socially ambitious nouveaux riches. In reaction, many of those who had been born into high society fended off the new arrivals by developing an increasingly stiff, reserved, and exclusive manner. By 1835 Alexis de Tocqueville could shrewdly observe that 'Everybody [in England] lives in constant dread lest advantage should be taken of his familiarity. Unable to judge at once of the social position of those he meets, an Englishman prudently avoids all contact with them.' Foreign visitors increasingly found the English, as opposed to the Scots, Welsh and Irish, reserved, unsociable, jealous of their privacy and unresponsive to strangers.[169] That was why in Jane Austen's *Pride and Prejudice* (1813) Mr Bingley liked the Bennet girls: with them there was 'no formality, no stiffness'.[170]

It may be a general rule that any unduly formal code of speaking or moving will generate a reaction towards more relaxed behaviour, justified in terms of frankness, honesty and authenticity as against what seem the artificialities of the prevailing system. But the essential reason for growing informality in late seventeenth- and early eighteenth-century Britain was that the old status hierarchy of aristocracy and gentry was giving way to a more complex social and political structure. In the countryside, the ability of great landowners to determine the fortunes of their inferiors remained overwhelming. Their landed estates gave them immense social and political influence, and they continued to expect and receive the deference appropriate to their rank. In the nation at large, however, the growth of the professions and the expansion of commerce, industry and the financial sector so complicated the social scene that the simple hierarchy of superiors, equals and inferiors, postulated by all the textbooks on civility, ceased to be recognizable.

One notable consequence of these changes was the gradual disappearance during the seventeenth century of the use of the second-person singular ('thou') when addressing social inferiors, and its replacement by the plural form ('you'), hitherto employed for addressing only equals or superiors. In 1646 a conduct book advised young readers that 'To persons of lesser rank, one saith *You* without *thou*-ing anybody.'[171] From the later seventeenth century, the titles of 'Mr' (short for 'Master') and 'Mrs' ('Mistress') began to move down the social scale to replace more condescending terms such as 'Father', 'Widow' and 'Goodwife', or occupational names ('Ostler'). During the nineteenth century, they came to be indiscriminately applied to everyone who had no other title. The anonymity of the metropolis assisted in this process by making it uncertain just what a stranger's social status was and therefore more politic to err on the safe side.[172]

Meanwhile, the steady growth of the economy was creating a freer labour market and greater occupational mobility. As the demand for labour increased, social deference became less necessary for individual survival. Edward Chamberlayne, a careful observer of the contemporary scene, noted in 1669 that the common people had become too prosperous and self-confident to give the 'humble respect and awful reverence' to the nobility, gentry and clergy that was customary in other European kingdoms. Fifty years later, a Swiss visitor commented on their 'little regard for the grandees' and 'their unwillingness to yield them any superiority, as is usual in other countries'.[173] Commerce required courtesy in the dealings between buyers and sellers, but, as Sir Peter Pett remarked in 1661, 'the greater part of persons engaged in trade and traffic' hated 'ceremonies' because they took up too much time. Shopkeepers were polite to their customers, but they could not afford to get involved in the time-wasting rituals of polite sociability. The world had become 'more active and industrious', thought Bishop Sprat; and more of the nobility and gentry were applying themselves to trade and business than ever before.[174] As the early twentieth-century American sociologist Thorstein Veblen would explain, manners and ceremonial observances were most esteemed in an age when conspicuous leisure was highly valued. Decorum was a product of leisure-class life: the busier people were, the less room they had for social courtesies.[175] The decline in deferential rituals reflected long-term changes in the tempo of economic life.

A further solvent of traditional civilities was the growth of large cities, above all London. The mingling of ranks in the streets and at public entertainments led to greater informality. The impersonality of city life, the busyness of people hurrying through the streets, and the absence of the forms of community control that still operated in the countryside licensed brusqueness and incivility. The magistrate and novelist Henry Fielding wrote in 1753 that the London mob claimed an exclusive right to the parts of the streets set aside for pedestrians and that other people could not walk there by day without being insulted or by night without being knocked down (Plate 27). In the relatively anonymous crowds of eighteenth-century London, it was unnecessary, and indeed impossible, for the civilly inclined to give every passer-by an appropriately graduated greeting in the way that would have been usual in a rural village.[176] Even in the country-side, manners were changing. Elizabeth Ham, the daughter of a Dorset yeoman, recalled growing up in the 1780s, 'a little rustic uncouth child': 'I well remember that I used to curtsey to all the fine-dressed ladies that I met, till told not to do by the nurse-maid.' In 1790 the Hon. John Byng, travelling in the Midlands, regretted the old days, when every gentleman 'was bow'd to with reverence, and "A good morning to you, master", "Good evening, good journey to you, Sir", were always presented, with every old-fashion'd wish, and compliment of the season'. But now, alas, better roads had spread less deferential metropolitan manners.[177]

The decline of the old courtesies was also related to changes in the distribution of political power. After 1688 the role of the monarch was strictly limited and the influence of the royal court on the manners of the upper classes became correspondingly less. Government was conducted by the king's ministers working through Parliament, the departments of state, the law courts and local corpo-rations. Administration was increasingly bureaucratic and rulebound, institutional rather than personal. Authority depended less on cere-mony and public display. Rituals of precedence and respect were dwindling into empty symbols rather than living demonstrations of power and subordination.

Eighteenth-century Britain was essentially an aristocratic republic which governed within the carapace of a ceremonial monarchy and was subject to periodic pressure from the population at large. Thanks to a free press and an abundance of satirical talent, political life was robust, irreverent and undeferential. Britain's constitutional kingship differed greatly from the absolute monarchy in France; and so did its manners, for as the radical Dissenting minister Richard Price pointed out, the manners of a people were profoundly affected by the nature of the government to which they were subject.[178] In the reign of

Charles II, the Marchioness of Newcastle observed that kingship was the form of government under which people became most civil, whereas democracy was 'more wild and barbarous'. David Hume, in an essay published in 1742, explained that 'politeness of manners' arose most naturally in monarchies and courts, but 'where power rises upwards from the people to the great, as in all republics, such refinements of civility are apt to be little practised'. 'The republics of Europe,' he remarked, 'are at present noted for want of politeness.'[179]

Montesquieu made the same point a few years later: politeness originated in political regimes where it was vital not to offend one's superiors; elaborate courtliness was the product of monarchical autocracy. Republics, however, tended to be associated with 'a manner frank, abrupt and austere', as William Godwin remarked.[180] For Lord Kames, language in a democracy was generally 'rough and coarse'; in an aristocracy, 'manly and plain'; in a monarchy, 'courteous and insinuating'; and in a despotism, 'imperious with regard to inferiors, and humble with respect to superiors'.[181] The 'equality of popular states' was 'very unfavourable to politeness', agreed Joseph Priestley: monarchies generated the habit of pleasing, whereas 'the haughty republican is not likely to acquire a habit of condescension to others'.[182] When James Boswell visited Geneva in 1764, he found that when his host wanted to put him into a good seat in church, a 'fat old woman' refused to give him her place, and at supper in the town hall guests pelted each other with bread balls. He saw this behaviour as a 'nauseous example of the manners of republicans'.[183]

Appalled by their lack of deference to Louis XVI and his queen, Edmund Burke remarked sardonically of the French revolutionaries that there had been 'a considerable revolution in their ideas of politeness'. He would have been even more shocked when the *sansculottes*, following in the wake of the English Quakers, proposed a law banning the use of the second person plural, *vous*, and making it compulsory to address everyone as *tu*.[184] The *sansculottes* had their admirers nearer home, for in the later eighteenth century many

English radicals associated civility with the servile observances of absolute monarchy. Refusing to recognize the conventions of polite behaviour or to participate in subservient rituals that, in their view, helped to maintain an unacceptable social order, they despised what Tom Paine called 'the puppet-show of state and aristocracy'.[185] As William Godwin put it, they regarded politeness as 'a set of rules, founded in no just reason, and ostentatiously practised by those who are familiar with them, for no purpose more expressly than to confound and keep at a distance those who, by the accident of their birth or fortune, are ignorant of them'. Godwin's wife, Mary Wollstonecraft, similarly rejected 'politeness' and 'meretricious compliments' in the name of sincerity and 'cleanliness of mind'.[186] Some English supporters of the French Revolution deliberately cultivated an aggressive, unobsequious manner to indicate their dislike of polite formalities. By their slouching posture, they signified their social insubordination. A contemporary recalled that Samuel Taylor Coleridge's friend Tom Poole was 'rather rustic in his appearance, perhaps ostentatiously so, and provincial in his dialect ... No one would have thought that he was on the same social level as my father and uncle. I suppose, in his republican days, he cultivated clownishness, just as he left off powder.'[187] In the same period, William George Spencer, father of the sociologist Herbert Spencer, so disliked titles and formalities that he never took his hat off to anyone, declined to put 'Esquire' or 'Reverend' on an envelope, and refused to call even his acquaintances 'Mr'.[188]

It is unsurprising that radicals despised prevailing codes of courtesy. For anyone who wishes to alter the status quo will quickly discover that scrupulous civility can be a block to innovation. People would never change anything if they were worried about offending others or making them feel uncomfortable. Those who seek to alter accepted notions about how society should work will inevitably incur the charge of rudeness and discourtesy. Not just riots, but the protests, strikes and demonstrations that became an increasingly common feature of eighteenth-century industrial relations were long regarded as 'uncivil' or 'disrespectful'. So were political acts that challenged the accepted distribution of power. In the eyes of Thomas Hobbes, the Long Parliament's vote that Queen Henrietta Maria was a traitor for providing the king with military assistance from Holland was 'a bestial incivility'.[189]

Radicals and revolutionaries have always tended to despise 'respectability' because observing the proprieties reinforces the standards of what they regard as an unjust social order; they reject civility, which they see as a means of keeping dissent at bay.[190] Informal manners and contempt for polite rituals therefore become part of their equipment. 'What I like about you, Webb,' said the political psychologist Graham Wallas to his fellow Fabian socialist Sidney Webb after watching him running for a train, 'is that there is no damned nonsense about style.'[191] 'That man's a Socialist', said his grandfather to the future playwright John Osborne, explaining, 'That's a man who doesn't believe in raising his hat.'[192] A similar rejection of social hierarchy may account for the notoriously uningratiating manner adopted by many citizens of Israel in its early days.[193] The biographer of the eminent legal philosopher H. L. A Hart tells us that, after his visit to that country in 1964, he never quite got over what he saw as the rudeness of its inhabitants, which he put down to a 'misidentification of politeness with servility'.[194]

Early feminists similarly found it necessary to flout the accepted rules of polite behaviour by women because they (correctly) saw them as deriving from, and helping to sustain, an unequal distribution of power between the sexes. In the 1660s, the protofeminist Margaret Cavendish, Duchess of Newcastle, excited titters when, instead of curtseying, she made legs and bowed to the ground like a man.[195] A late eighteenth-century writer commented on 'the painful sentiments we feel when female features assume the expression of man'.[196] Quaker women were frowned upon because it was not their practice to retire at the end of dinner and leave the men drinking, a custom that other champions of female equality attacked as 'barbarous and odious'.[197] Mary Wollstonecraft believed that civilized women were ruined by 'false refinement'; her call for 'a revolution in female manners', to restore to women their lost dignity, was itself a breach of decorum.[198] In this, as in other cases, the vigorous expression of dissent was seen as incompatible with the ideal of civility.*

In the early modern period, those who wished to see the effect of democracy on manners had only to look across the Atlantic. Ever since their Puritan beginnings, the inhabitants of colonial America, living in frontier conditions, with no royal court, no nobility, no acknowledged social elite and an underrepresentation of women, had been hostile to many of the hierarchical rituals they had left behind. In the South, the values of landed gentility long survived; but in New England, there was greater emphasis on community and equality. Liberty was more important than politeness.[199] The creation of the American republic enhanced this tendency. In the early nineteenth century, the United States was notorious as a place where youth paid no respect to age and little if any deference was shown to social superiors. Plain speaking and 'a new kind of civility' replaced distance and reserve with what an earlier generation would have regarded as excessive familiarity.[200] Genteel English travellers complained of the levelling effect of the American 'want of refinement', exemplified by gross table manners and the ubiquitous spittoon; while the novelist James Fenimore Cooper, returning to his home country in 1833 after a long stay in Europe, had no doubt that Americans had 'retrograded in manners' during the previous thirty years.[201] In fact, American manners in the post-Revolutionary era were very far from those of an equal society. They rested on a firm distinction between the middle classes and their inferiors, the

* In her contempt for politeness and punctuality, the American writer and activist Susan Sontag (1933–2004) was in this tradition: 'You don't have to be there in time!' she would say. 'Don't be so servile'; Sigrid Nunez, *Sempre Susan* (New York, 2011), 8.

servants and labourers; and of course, they tacitly assumed the existence of a huge black slave population. Yet their most acute observer,
Alexis de Tocqueville, praised them for their frankness, openness,
tolerance and sincerity; and even Cooper conceded that their lack of
polish by European standards was more than made up for by their
greater kindness and sociability.[202]

In Britain the growth of democracy was a slower process, but its
contribution to the disappearance of many traditional courtesies
would be similar. Increasing social and political equality led inexorably to greater informality of language, fewer external symbols of
power, and a decline in the observance of rituals of respect.[203] In the
words of the Victorian poet A. H. Clough:

'Tis sad to see to what democracy is leading—
Give me your Eighteenth Century for high breeding.[204]

The Future of Manners

In the early twenty-first century, British society is less visibly hierarchical than it was. External symbols of deference are much less
evident, and accepted styles of speech and bodily comportment are
infinitely more relaxed. Following the lead set by the United States,
a more informal style of behaviour is favoured, justified in terms of
frankness, friendliness and truthfulness. Psychotherapists disparage
self-control and restraint as unhealthy inhibitions ('hang-ups').
Books on etiquette give way to manuals on liberation and self-
realization. Deference of any kind is increasingly repudiated, whether
of poor to rich, young to old, women to men, or men to women.
Formal titles are treated with indifference, and people tend to feel
uncomfortable unless they are immediately on first-name terms with
each other. Dress is more casual; fewer family meals are consumed
sitting round a table; and with the disappearance of domestic service,
the formal dining room ceases to be an essential feature of the

middle-class home. Every Oxford college advertises itself as 'friendly and informal'.

As the location of political and economic power shifts to global corporations and the mass media, the old established institutions, such as the monarchy, the cabinet, the House of Lords, the Church of England, political parties, the professions and the ancient universities, cease to receive the deference they once enjoyed. BBC announcers no longer find it necessary to employ received pronunciation, and privately educated politicians affect glottal stops and 'Estuary English'. Changes in the distribution of power between men and women, adults and children, employers and employees lead inexorably to new modes of behaviour. The newly rich do not need to acquire good manners in order to gain social or political acceptance. Small children push past grown-ups on the pavement; the elderly are more likely to be ignored than respected; and gallantry to women can seem positively offensive. This is the triumph of what in the eighteenth century would have been seen as republican equality; it marks the disappearance of the politeness that rested on a desire to please superiors. Old-style courtesy is distrusted as the snobbish and hypocritical legacy of a hierarchical and patriarchal age. Good manners are believed to prevent the individual from being true to his or her authentic self.

In their daily behaviour, the British middle classes are less formal, less inhibited and less phlegmatic than they were seventy years ago.[205] They freely engage in social kissing; they eat in the street; they shout and gesticulate; they use obscene language with greater freedom; they talk openly about sex and the body's natural functions; they play ear-splitting music in public places; they conduct loud conversations on their mobile phones in crowded railway carriages; and when engaged in organized sport, they show no gentlemanly restraint, but exult in victory, punching the air and hugging their teammates.

These are not symptoms of a 'decivilizing process', such as that manifested in the horrors of the two World Wars and the Holocaust. Rather, they are the signs of what Norbert Elias calls 'informalization', a change in the relations between the sexes, the generations and the social classes. The new modes of behaviour do not threaten internal law and order, and there is no reason to think that they lead to higher rates of interpersonal violence. They involve more-demanding standards of bodily cleanliness: we no longer need notices telling us that spitting is prohibited. They set a higher premium on personal amiability; and in the case of such phenomena as nudity on the beach or social kissing, they presuppose a very high level of self-control.[206] These changes reflect the weakening of social hierarchies based on tradition, inheritance, the subordination of the lower classes, the control of young people and the subjection of women. They are also accompanied by a belief in self-expression, a much greater acceptance of human diversity and an unprecedented tolerance of religious, sexual and ethnic differences. What we have now is a new and more equal form of civility.

Of course, its precepts are not always observed. The emphasis by psychologists and educators on the importance of self-esteem and personal fulfilment can encourage an atomistic form of individual selfishness that is potentially destructive of collective life. The relaxation of the social controls exerted by family and community is sometimes blamed for bad manners in the street, litter, late-night noise, graffiti, cycling on the pavement, juvenile delinquency, football hooliganism and similar forms of antisocial behaviour. It is very doubtful, though, whether these and similar incivilities are any more of a problem than were their equivalents in the past. More serious is the persistence of interpersonal violence, albeit far less than in previous centuries.[207] But that too is dwarfed by the huge achievements of a modern civility that makes it possible for pedestrians to negotiate crowded pavements without bumping into each other; for commuters in an underground train to travel uncomplainingly and without jostling when packed together with total strangers in the closest possible proximity; and for drivers to hurtle at great speed along crowded motorways without colliding with other vehicles.

The rules of the road are prescribed and enforced by the state, but there are no laws enforcing good manners on the pavement or on public transport. Manners, wrote Montesquieu, are those habits that are not established by legislators because they are unable or unwilling to do so: they appreciate that not everything needs to be corrected and that it is bad policy to try to change by law what ought to be changed by custom.[208] Despite periodic attempts by governments, especially during the Interregnum, to reform manners and personal behaviour, early modern England witnessed a steady withdrawal by church and state from the oversight of individual conduct. One legal remedy for bad manners had been the action for *scandalum magnatum*, which was meant to protect peers from verbal abuse. In the early seventeenth century, the courts awarded heavy damages for this offence; but after 1689 they ceased to do so, and recourse to the action dwindled away.[209] Many contemporaries wanted to ban uncivil speech more generally and to enforce 'signs of respect'.[210] Although the young John Locke was one of those who favoured the legal regulation of 'a courteous saluting' and 'a decency of habit [i.e., dress] according to the fashion of the place', he changed his mind in later life on the grounds that such legislation would lead to 'perpetual prosecution and animosity'.[211] The abandonment in 1604 of the sumptuary legislation regulating dress and consumption, the reduction in 1695 of press censorship, and the increasing disinclination of the church courts in the later seventeenth century to prosecute sexual offenders, scolds and troublemakers resulted in a vast enlargement of those areas in which personal behaviour was, for the first time, left to individual choice. This new domain of personal freedom included bodily appearance, dress and demeanour, sexual relationships, behaviour towards neighbours and strangers, intellectual and political debate, and social intercourse of every kind.

There were recurring attempts by private societies to achieve 'the reformation of manners', by which they meant the enforcement of statutes against such offences as swearing, sabbath breaking, gambling and prostitution. In addition, the common people continued to express their disapproval of marital irregularities by censorious gossip, written libels and shaming rituals of 'skimmington' and 'rough music'.[212] In the eighteenth century, the justices of the peace made some attempts to fill the gap left by the church courts.[213] William Blackstone, in the fourth book of his *Commentaries on the Laws of England* (1769), ruled that individual members of the state were still legally 'bound to conform their general behaviour to the rules of propriety, good neighbourhood, and good manners, and to be decent, industrious, and inoffensive in their respective stations'. But many of the statutes he cited as enforcing these duties had fallen into desuetude; those still in force were concerned with such matters as bigamy, common nuisance, vagabondage and gambling, but said nothing about the courtesies of everyday life.[214] This left informal communal pressure as the only external constraint on the individual's behaviour in social interaction with other people. Yet in London there was, from the later seventeenth century onwards, a steady decline in the monitoring, denouncing and public shaming of delinquent neighbours that had been such a feature of earlier communities.[215] In the metropolis, at least, the individual's right to personal privacy was coming to be tacitly respected, and the same process was probably occurring in other urban communities.

It is unsurprising, therefore, that it was in the mid-eighteenth century, when supervision by church and state had diminished and the area of personal space been substantially enlarged, that David Hume remarked that it was only good manners which saved old men from contempt and strangers from neglect. Similarly, Edmund Burke asserted that manners (in the wider sense of habits and customs) were more important than laws, on the grounds that 'the law touches us but here and there, and now and then', whereas manners 'barbarize or refine us by a constant, steady, uniform, sensible operation, like that of the air we breathe in'.[216] This was an old notion: in 1582 the Kentish justice of the peace William Lambarde, in his charge to a local jury, quoted the poet Horace: 'What shall we do with laws without manners?'[217] It became a central doctrine of the Scottish Enlightenment. The learned judge Lord Kames reminded the young George III in 1762 that 'depravity of manners will render ineffectual the most salutary laws'. Adam Ferguson thought that manners were as important for a nation's strength as its numbers or wealth, while for Adam Smith, 'the very existence of human society' depended on observance of the duties of justice, truthfulness, chastity and fidelity. Although Smith admitted that a commercial society would be 'less happy and agreeable' than one where beneficence was practised, he later maintained that society was kept going by self-interest and could subsist without kindness or 'any mutual love or affection'.[218]

When in the late twentieth century the constraints of civility proved inadequate to enforce new ideals of equality and diversity, it became necessary once again to turn to legislation. Today many countries have laws about human rights, race relations, equal opportunities, sexual harassment, hate speech, smoking in public places, the treatment of children, and the welfare of the disabled. Some even try through legislation to discourage lack of respect for others.[219] Recent decades have also seen a great increase in formal procedures of accountability and audit. If people cannot be trusted to behave in the desired fashion of their own accord, and if the inhibitions imposed by professional etiquette and personal honour prove unreliable, there have to be written rules and procedures together with statutory authorities to ensure that the rules are obeyed. As a result, a huge range of new torts and criminal offences has been created.[220] The guiding assumption is that if social relationships are to be regulated, then it has to be by the law, because informal codes of courtesy can no longer be relied on. If pushing past people on the pavement, or using obscene language, or queue jumping, or not replying to invitations, or not saying 'please' and 'thank you' were seen as real threats to social cohesion, there would be a law against them, in the same way there are acts of Parliament against fomenting racial hatred and local by-laws against allowing dogs to foul the pavement.* Not that those aspects of personal behaviour that are unregulated by the state are entirely left to the market. In practice, every community has its own 'micro law' involving conventions for civil behaviour in a variety of situations, whether in the street, or as passengers on a bus, or at the theatre, or at business meetings and academic seminars. In small communities, loss of respect, which is the punishment for breach of these conventions, remains a far from trivial sanction.[221]

In the early modern period, 'politeness', the sophisticated virtue of the social elite, was widely regarded as superior to the more basic 'civility', which could be displayed by anyone. In modern times this assessment has been reversed. In 1838 the American author James Fenimore Cooper dismissed good breeding, in the sense of polish and refinement, as pleasant but not essential. Basic civility and respect for others, however, he regarded as indispensable to human civilization.[222] The twentieth-century Oxford philosopher R. G. Collingwood strongly endorsed this verdict: the first constituent of civilization, he held, was the process of bringing members of the community to behave 'civilly' to each other, by which he meant respecting other persons' feelings: abstaining from shocking them, annoying them, frightening them, or arousing in them any passion or desire that might diminish their self-respect.[223] Good manners, in the sense of considerate behaviour and tactful accommodation to the feelings of others, continue to be widely regarded as serving an essential purpose. They facilitate communication between human beings.[224] A modern historian puts it well when he says that the function of civility is to act as social glue in communities when other forms of solidarity have been cast aside.[225] In order to cohere, every social group needs its own form of civility, even frontier societies such as the American Wild

* In 1997 a draft law was introduced, but not enacted, by the Israeli Knesset to prevent queue jumping. It would have made 'failing to stand in line' a criminal offence; W. Michael Reisman, *Law in Brief Encounters* (New Haven, CT, 1999), 70–71.

West or Israel in its early days. Self-restraint and the peaceful settlement of differences are a biological necessity if human beings are to survive in close proximity to each other.

Modern political philosophers, therefore, take a keen interest in civility. Like their Renaissance predecessors, they define it as the virtue of good citizenship.* But the aspect of that virtue which they emphasize has shifted. Law-abidingness, which was the central requirement of sixteenth-century civility, remains crucial: for the American philosopher John Rawls, writing in 1971, civility involved obedience to laws that have the support of a democratic majority, even if one personally regards them as unjust.[226] But the right of the state to levy taxes and enforce law and order is no longer disputed in the way it was in Tudor times.[227] Instead, much more attention is given nowadays to the role of civility in a culturally diverse society and its potential contribution to enabling citizens with very different beliefs, values and attitudes to live peacefully together. Commentators spend much time agonizing about whether the expression of critical views on serious political and religious issues is 'uncivil' because it upsets other citizens. Hence the controversy surrounding present-day attempts to ban 'hate speech' or to exclude contentious speakers from university campuses because the 'incivility' of expressing unpopular opinions makes some students feel uncomfortable.[228]

In these circumstances civility is seen as providing a 'standard of conversational decorum', of how to disagree without being disagreeable, as President Barack Obama put it.[229] Some philosophers argue that candid discussion of potentially inflammatory issues should be inhibited by the civil duty to respect the feelings of those with whom we disagree, and that this duty should, if necessary, be enforced by legislation.[230] Others maintain that this would be a dangerous inflation of the notion of respect: the open expression of opinions that

* A meaning of the term that more than half a century ago was deemed by a learned editor to be 'now obsolete': John Milton, *Complete Prose Works of John Milton*, ed. Don M Wolfe et al. (New Haven, CT, 1953–82), vol. 2, 381.

some find unacceptable, they say, is essential to the working of democracy; a 'civilized acceptance of difference' need not inhibit the frank expression of an alternative point of view, for civility requires only a minimum degree of politeness.[231] Yet most participants in the debate prize fair-mindedness, readiness to listen, respect for the dignity of others,* and that indefinable quality called 'decency', though these are seen as moral duties, not legal ones.[232] The difficulty underlying the whole discussion is that civility cannot resolve the problems facing societies riven by radically different values because it is itself a concept whose meaning and value are fiercely contested.[233]

In such a context, amiable and trivial conversation of the kind that the seventeenth-century Quakers so despised can be important as a means of establishing human solidarity, even if it is only about the weather, what Robert Boyle called 'almanac discourse'. That is why Roger Williams was appalled by the Quakers; he thought that in 'a wild and savage country' such as America, 'without manners, without courtesy', friendly greetings were particularly necessary, for 'except you begin with a "What cheer?" or some other salutation, you had as good meet an horse or a cow'.[234]

Civility in the past has tended to be a conservative force, respecting social hierarchy and outlawing the expression of radical sentiments because they endanger social harmony. But courtesy and consideration need not imply abject deference. Civility is as important in an egalitarian society as in a hierarchical one. As William Godwin observed in 1797, the abolition of servility need not imply a diminution in kindness and respect for other people.[235]

In the eighteenth century, Lord Chesterfield thought that, without good breeding, royal courts would become 'the seats of violence and desolation'.[236] In the mid-twentieth century, the military thinker B. H. Liddell Hart maintained that 'only manners in the deeper

---

* Though Ronald Dworkin famously maintained that no one in a democracy has a right not to be offended; Ronald Dworkin, 'The Right to Ridicule', *New York Review of Books*, 23 March 2006.

sense – of mutual restraint for mutual security – can control the risk that outbursts of temper over political and social issues may lead to mutual destruction in the atomic age'.* Others have suggested that everyday civility protects us from a descent into barbarous atrocity. This was the view of the Canadian poet F. R. Scott:

The first to go are the niceties,
The little minor conformities
That suddenly seem absurdities.

Soon kindling animosities
Surmount the old civilities
And start the first brutalities.

Then come the bold extremities,
The justified enormities,
The unrestrained ferocities.[237]

It is undoubtedly true that the twentieth century's collapse into total war and genocide would have astonished and appalled many of the early modern exponents of civility. Some of them would have seen the mass murder of people simply because of their ethnicity as a crime against the essential unity of the human race. They would also have regarded the abolition of any effective distinction between combatants and non-combatants, or even between war and peace, as the epitome of what they thought of as 'barbarism'. Modern technology makes total war wholly incompatible with any previous ideas of 'civilization'.[238] In such catastrophic happenings, not yet concluded, they would have seen

---

* Regrettably, Liddell Hart went on to explain that civilized societies were based on the differentiation of the sexes and that good manners, which depended on the influence of 'women as women', were threatened by the short hair, short skirts and mannish dress of 'progressive' women. He regarded the female corset as a vital agent of civilization; B. H. Liddell Hart, 'Manners Mould Mankind', *World Review*, Jan.–Feb. 1946.

the collapse of that restraint, self-control, desire for accommodation and respect for others which was central to their philosophy.

The irony, alas, is that the Holocaust would have been impossible without the technological and bureaucratic expertise to be found only in a highly civilized society. Many of those who devised and executed it were perfectly capable of courtesy and civility in their ordinary lives. There was no necessary link between genocide and bad manners. What made it possible was not an inclination to incivility as such, but a redrawing of the boundaries of the human community within which civility was required. In the same way, the German Democratic Republic (1949–90) laid great stress on the importance of everyday politeness, while ordering the relentless persecution of those they believed to be hostile to the regime.[239] In these distinctions, we see a repetition of the early modern notion that the laws of war could be suspended in conflicts with 'barbarians'. They also resemble the nineteenth-century doctrine that only 'civilized' countries were entitled to be regarded as full members of the international community. Not until it is accepted that civility means tolerance of difference, whether ethnic, religious or sexual, can it be expected to protect humanity from further disasters. Yet when some cultural differences appear incompatible with what are widely deemed to be human rights, such tolerance seems impossible to achieve. The only way forward appears to be a renewal of the civilizing mission, though this time one conducted in a peaceful and more sympathetic fashion.

In early modern England, the use of the terms 'civility' and 'barbarism' was, as we have seen, essentially rhetorical. It justified whatever course of action or mode of life the speaker happened to favour. Contemporaries upheld the political and cultural arrangements to which they were accustomed, or to which they aspired, by describing them as 'civilized', just as they rejected others by labelling them 'barbarous'.

Yet there was more to their implicit definition of a civilized society than the unthinking assumption that their own way of doing things was the right one. By stressing the importance of internal peace, legal rules, personal liberty, international trade, humanity in warfare, science, learning and the arts, the thinkers of the early modern period were outlining what would become an ever more widely accepted view of human possibilities. They were, of course, also the necessary preconditions for the spread of global capitalism. But the core idea was that civility comprised the body of beliefs, practices and institutions which made it possible for people to live together and flourish. It called for restraint, tolerance and mutual understanding. Barbarism was the opposite: it meant disorder, cruelty and ignorance. The contrast between the two conditions has not lost its meaning.

NOTE ON REFERENCES

In order to save space, I have given only the main title of books and articles, omitting their subtitles, and only the primary place of publication. Details of each source are given on its first citation in the notes to each chapter; thereafter, a shortened title has been employed. Unless otherwise stated, the place of publication is London. In quotations from contemporary sources, the spelling, punctuation and capitalization have been modernized.

By way of apology for the copiousness of the endnotes, I invoke the justification offered by the great Scottish historian William Robertson in the preface to his *History of the Reign of the Emperor Charles V* (1769):

> I have carefully pointed out the sources from which I have derived information, and have cited the writers on whose authority I rely with a minute exactness, which may appear to border upon ostentation, if it were possible to be vain of having read books, many of which nothing but the duty of examining with accuracy whatever I laid before the public would have induced me to open. As my inquiries conducted me often into paths which were obscure or little frequented, such constant references to the authors who have been my guides were not only necessary for authenticating the facts which are the foundations of my reasonings, but may be useful in pointing out the way to such as shall hereafter hold the same course, and in enabling them to carry on their researches with greater facility and success.

I have, however, tried to modify this policy in the way recommended by Anthony Ashley Cooper, 3rd Earl of Shaftesbury (1671–1713), namely, 'to place in the pages of the text no other notes beside what will be agreeable and pleasant to the reader, what will not have the air of pedantry, and what will pass with the polite people, entertain them, and adorn the text. The rest . . . by themselves at the end, in a small print.'*

---

* Cited in Lawrence E. Klein, *Shaftesbury and the Culture of Politeness* (Cambridge, 1994), 109.

ABBREVIATIONS

AHR	*American Historical Review*
Amer.	*American*
BL	British Library
Bodl.	Bodleian Library
Bull.	*Bulletin*
Cal.	*Calendar*
CSSH	*Comparative Studies in Society and History*
CultSocHist	*Cultural and Social History*
ECCO	Eighteenth Century Collections Online
EcHR	*Economic History Review*
EEBO	Early English Books Online
EETS	Early English Text Society
EHR	*English Historical Review*
Hist.	*Historical*
HistRes	*Historical Research*
HJ	*Historical Journal*
HMC	*Historical Manuscripts Commission Reports*
HWJ	*History Workshop Journal*
JBS	*Journal of British Studies*
JHI	*Journal of the History of Ideas*
JMH	*Journal of Modern History*
Journ.	*Journal*
JSocHist	*Journal of Social History*
ODNB	*Oxford Dictionary of National Biography*
OED	*Oxford English Dictionary* (online version)
P&P	*Past & Present*
Rev.	*Review*
ser.	series
Soc.	Society

ABBREVIATIONS

SocHist	*Social History*
SP	*State Papers*
TNA	The National Archives
TRHS	*Transactions of the Royal Historical Society*
WMQ	*William and Mary Quarterly*

NOTES

Preface

1. Pierre Bourdieu, *Outline of a Theory of Practice*, trans. Richard Nice (Cambridge, 1977), 94.
2. See Mark Griffith, 'The Language and Meaning of the College Motto', available on the New College, Oxford, website.

Introduction

1. The earliest reference to 'the civil world' yielded by the Early English Books Online (hereafter, EEBO) search facility (as of 29 Sep. 2016) is in 1607 and to 'the civilized world' in 1658.
2. John Locke, *Two Treatises of Government*, ed. Peter Laslett (Cambridge, 1960), 261 (bk 1, para. 141); Griffith Williams, *The Great Antichrist Revealed* (1660), 3rd pagination, 48.
3. William Marsden, *The History of Sumatra* (2nd edn, 1784), 167–68; *The Correspondence of Edmund Burke*, ed. T. W. Copeland et al. (Cambridge, 1968–78), vol. 3, 350–51. For a well-grounded survey of eighteenth-century British perceptions of the world, see P. J. Marshall and Glyndwr Williams, *The Great Map of Mankind* (1982).
4. E. B. Tylor, *Primitive Culture*, vol. 1 (1871; 5th edn, 1913), 26.
5. An EEBO search reveals that the term 'uncivilized' was in use from 1607 onwards.
6. Timothy Long, *Barbarians in Greek Comedy* (Carbondale, IL, 1986), chap. 6; Edith Hall, *Inventing the Barbarian* (Oxford, 1989); Jacqueline de Romilly, 'Les barbares dans la pensée de la Grèce classique', *Phoenix* 47 (1993); *Greeks and Barbarians*, ed. Thomas Harrison (Edinburgh, 2002); J. G. A. Pocock, *Barbarism and Religion* (Cambridge, 1999–2015), vol. 4, 11–14; Roger-Pol Droit, *Généalogie des barbares* (Paris, 2007), 31–141; *Oxford Classical Dictionary*, ed. Simon Hornblower et al., 4th edn (Oxford, 2012), s.v. 'Barbarian', by Thomas E. J. Wiedmann.
7. Plato, *Politicus*, 262 d-e; Strabo, *Geography*, bk 1, chap. 4, sect. 9 (on Eratosthenes).

NOTES to pp. 3–6

8. As argued by Erich S. Gruen, *Rethinking the Other in Antiquity* (Princeton, NJ, 2011), chaps. 1 and 2.

9. G. Freyburger, 'Sens et évolution du mot "barbarus" dans l'oeuvre de Cicéron', in *Mélanges offerts à Léopold Sédar Senghor*, ed. Association des Professeurs de Langues Classiques au Sénégal (Dakar, 1977); Yves Albert Dauge, *Le Barbare* (Brussels, 1981); Peter Heather, 'The Barbarian in Late Antiquity', in *Constructing Identities in Late Antiquity*, ed. Richard Miles (1999); Ralph W. Mathisen, 'Violent Behaviour and the Construction of Barbarian Identity in Late Antiquity', in *Violence in Late Antiquity*, ed. H. A. Drake (Aldershot, 2006); Lynette Mitchell, *Panhellenism and the Barbarian in Archaic and Classical Greece* (Swansea, 2007); Guy Halsall, *Barbarian Migrations and the Roman West, 376–568* (Cambridge, 2007), 45–57; Droit, *Généalogie des barbares*, 145–205.

10. Karl Leyser, 'Concepts of Europe in the Early and High Middle Ages', *P&P* 137 (1992), 41n.

11. Geoffrey Chaucer, 'General Prologue', *The Canterbury Tales*, line 49; Denys Hay, 'The Concept of Christendom', in *The Dawn of Civilization*, ed. David Talbot Rice (1965); Judith Herrin, *The Formation of Christendom* (1987), 8.

12. W. R. Jones, 'The Image of the Barbarian in Medieval Europe', *CSSH* 13 (1971), is a pioneering piece of synthesis. See also Rodolfo di Mattei, 'Sul concetto di barbaro e barbarie nel Medioevo', *Studi in onore di Enrico Besta* (Milan, 1937–39), vol. 4; Robert Bartlett, *Gerald of Wales 1146–1223* (Oxford, 1982), chap. 6; Anthony Pagden, *The Fall of Natural Man* (Cambridge, 1982), chap. 2; Arno Borst, *Medieval Worlds*, trans. Eric Hansen (Cambridge, 1991), chap. 1; Seymour Phillips, 'The Outer World of the European Middle Ages', in *Implicit Understandings*, ed. Stuart B. Schwartz (Cambridge, 1994); John Gillingham, *The English in the Twelfth Century* (Woodbridge, 2000), chap. 1, and 'Civilizing the English?', *HistRes* 74 (2001); Michael Staunton, *The Historians of Angevin England* (Oxford, 2017), 351–58.

13. James Hankins, 'Renaissance Crusaders', *Dumbarton Oaks Papers* 49 (1995); Nancy Bisaha, *Creating East and West* (Philadelphia, PA, 2004); Michael Wintle, 'Islam as Europe's "Other" in the Long Term', *History* 101 (2016), 45, 48.

14. On early modern ethnographic writing as a dialogue between the 'languages' of Christianity and civilization, see Joan-Pau Rubiés, 'New Worlds and Renaissance Ethnography', *History and Anthropology* 6 (1993).

15. Pagden, *Fall of Natural Man*, chaps. 6 and 7.

16. In medieval and Renaissance Latin, the contrast between the civil and the barbarous was expressed in such twin terms as *urbanus* (refined) and *agrestis* (rustic), *excultus* (cultivated) and *incultus* (uncultivated), *humanus* (humane) and *barbarus* (barbarian), *compositus* (well-ordered) and *incompositus* (disordered), *civilis* (courteous) and *incivilis* (unmannerly, though it later came to mean unjust or tyrannical). Civility was *civilitas* or *humanitas* (humanity) or *cultior genus vitae* (a more cultivated form of life); it was associated with *leniores mores* (gentler manners) and its opposite was *barbaria* or *barbaries* (barbarism) or *feritas* (savagery). For Hugo Grotius in the early seventeenth century, civilized peoples were *moratiores* (better mannered), *humaniores* (more humane) or just *meliores* (better). For Samuel von Pufendorf, there were *gentes cultae* and *gentes barbarae*.

17. John Evelyn, *Elysium Britannicum, or the Royal Gardens*, ed. John E. Ingram (Philadelphia PA, 2001), 161, 403; Frances Harris, *Transformations of Love* (Oxford, 2002), 29. *OED* records the verb to 'civilize' from 1595 and the adjective 'civilized' from 1611 (EEBO records instances of the latter from 1600). 'Cultivated', meaning refined by education, was a mid-seventeenth-century neologism.

18. *OED*, s.v. 'civilization, 1' (instances from 1656 onwards), and EEBO, s.v. 'civilization', eighty-six hits in forty-six records before 1700; J(odocus) Crull, *The Antient and Present State of Muscovy* (1698), 140; Andrew Snape, *A Sermon Preach'd before Princess Sophia at*

Hannover, the 13th/24th of May 1706 (Cambridge, 1706), 18. Apparently unaware of these numerous earlier instances, and noting that the French term *civilisation* was first used in a non-legal sense by Victor Riqueti, Marquis de Mirabeau, in the 1750s, continental scholars have disseminated the notion that the term did not appear in English until a few years later; Lucien Febvre, 'Civilisation: Evolution of a Word and a Group of Ideas', in *A New Kind of History and Other Essays*, trans. K. Folca, ed. Peter Burke (1973); Émile Benveniste, 'Civilisation: Contribution à l'histoire du mot', in *Problèmes de linguistique générale* (Paris, 1966–74), chap. 28; Jean Starobinski, 'The Word *Civilization*', in *Blessings in Disguise*, trans. Arthur Goldhammer (Cambridge, 1993) (like Benveniste, drawing on Joachim Moras, *Ursprung und Entwicklung des Begriffs der Zivilization in Frankreich* ([1756–1830]; Hamburg, 1930); Catherine Larrère, 'Mirabeau et les physiocrates', in *Les Équivoques de la civilisation*, ed. Bertrand Binoche (Seyssel, 2003), 83.

19. *OED*, s.v. 'Civilization, 2'.
20. Henry Piers, *Gospel-Repentance* (1744), 39; *Atheism, (or the Living without GOD in the World) a 'Commoner' Sin than Thought of* (1748), 83n.
21. For examples of the new usage, see ECCO and *17th–18th Century Burney Collection Newspapers* (Gale Cengage, online).
22. *Boswell's Life of Johnson*, ed. George Birkbeck Hill, rev. L. F. Powell (Oxford, 1934–50), vol. 2, 155; *Boswell for the Defence*, ed. William K. Wimsatt Jr and Frederick A. Pottle (1960), 57.
23. *OED*, s.v. 'civility, 10', gives 1531 as the first use in this sense and 1549 as the next; other early sixteenth-century examples can be found via the EEBO search facility. For the Italian and French terminology, see Rosario Romeo, *Le Scoperte americane nella coscienza italiana del Cinquecento* (Milan, 1954), 106–8, n2; George Huppert, 'The Idea of Civilization in the Sixteenth Century', in *Renaissance*, ed. Anthony Molho and John A. Tedeschi (Florence, 1971); Alain Pons, 'Civilité-Urbanité', in *Dictionnaire raisonné de la politesse et du savoir-vivre du Moyen Âge à nos jours*, ed. Alain Montandon (Paris, 1995).
24. The *OED* gives no instances of this usage before 1561, but they can be found in *The Dictionary of Syr Thomas Elyot* (1538) and other works of the 1540s and 1550s.
25. 'Civilisation', in its two meanings of a process and the end product of that process, was included in John Ash, *The New and Complete Dictionary of the English Language* (1775).
26. Gerrit W. Gong, *The Standard of 'Civilization' in International Society* (Oxford, 1984); Hedley Bull, 'The Emergence of a Universal International Society', in *The Expansion of International Society*, ed. Bull and Adam Watson (Oxford, 1984); James Tully, 'Lineages of Contemporary Imperialism', in *Lineages of Empire*, ed. Duncan Kelly (Procs. of the British Academy, 155; Oxford, 2009); Liliana Obregón, 'The Civilized and the Uncivilized', in *The Oxford Handbook of International Law*, ed. Bardo Fassbender and Anne Peters (Oxford, 2012).
27. Edward Keene, *Beyond the Anarchical Society* (Cambridge, 2002), 136–47; id., *International Political Thought* (Cambridge, 2005), chap. 6; H. Lauterpacht, *Recognition in International Law* (Cambridge, 1947), 31n1.

28.   Thus though sin itself be ill, 'tis good
        That sin should be, for thereby rectitude
        Through opposed iniquity, as light
        By shades, is more conspicuous and more bright.
                            Lucy Hutchinson, *Order and Disorder* [1679], ed.
                                    David Norbrook (Oxford, 2001), 57.

29. R. G. Collingwood, *The Philosophy of Enchantment*, ed. David Boucher (Oxford, 2005), 183; Ernst van Alphen, 'The Other Within', in *Alterity, Identity, Image*, ed. Raymond Corbey and Joep Leerssen (Amsterdam, 1991), 15.
30. 'New Experiments and Observations Touching Cold', in *The Works of the Honourable Robert Boyle*, ed. Thomas Birch (2nd edn, 1772), vol. 2, 476.

31. On the idea of political thought as a contest between competing languages, see, e.g., Anthony Pagden, 'Introduction', in *The Languages of Political Theory in Early-Modern Europe*, ed. Pagden (Cambridge, 1987); J. G. A. Pocock, *Political Thought and History* (Cambridge, 2009), chap. 6.
32. Ciaran Brady, 'New English Identity in Ireland and the Two Sir William Herberts', in *Sixteenth-Century Identities*, ed. A. J. Piesse (Manchester, 2000), 82.

1 Civil Behaviour

1. Spenser, *The Faerie Queene* (1596), bk 6, canto 3, st. 38; John Locke, *Some Thoughts concerning Education*, ed. John W. and Jean S. Yolton (Oxford, 1989), 124.
2. Thomas Hobbes, *Leviathan* (1651), ed. Noel Malcolm (Oxford, 2012), vol. 2, 150 (chap. 11).
3. Martin Ingram, 'Reformation of Manners in Early Modern England', in *The Experience of Authority*, ed. Paul Griffiths et al. (Basingstoke, 1996), and id., *Carnal Knowledge* (Cambridge, 2017), index, 'reformation of manners'; M. K. McIntosh, *Controlling Misbehaviour in England, 1370–1600* (Cambridge, 1998); Bob Harris, *Politics and the Nation* (Oxford, 2002), chap. 7; Joanna Innes, 'Politics and Morals', in *The Transformation of Political Culture*, ed. Eckhard Hellmuth (Oxford, 1990).
4. *Spectator* 119 (17 July 1711), ed. Donald F. Bond (Oxford, 1965), vol. 1, 486. Similarly, *Caxton's Book of Curtesye*, ed. Frederick J. Furnivall (EETS, 1868), 25 ('Handle your food cleanly because manners make man').
5. Thomas Cranmer, *Catechismus* (1548), fol. xlv^v; *A Midsummer Night's Dream*, act 3, scene 2, lines 147–48. EEBO records for 1500–1600 (accessed on 23 Apr. 2016), 6,818 hits (in 1,307 records) for 'courtesy' and only 959 hits (in 388 records) for 'civility', most of them in the last quarter of the century. Between 1601 and 1700, however, there were 15,506 hits (in 5,718 records) for 'civility', 12,278 of them after 1650, and 10,771 hits (in 3,079 records) for 'courtesy.' There were also 702 hits (in 514 records) for 'good breeding'; and 644 (in 328 records) for 'politeness', though only 14 of them before 1650 and only 81 before 1660. As a guide to usage, these figures have obvious limitations, not least those stemming from the shortcomings of EEBO's and ECCO's search facilities, but they suggest some modifications to the otherwise helpful discussions of changing terminology in Anna Bryson, *From Courtesy to Civility* (Oxford, 1998), 46–49, and Phil Withington, *Society in Early Modern England* (Cambridge, 2010), 186–89, 194–95.
6. Cf. Spenser, *Faerie Queene*, bk 5, canto 1, st. 1 ('Of court it seems, men courtesy do call').
7. Cf. Thomas Gainsford, *The Rich Cabinet* (1616), fol. 27 ('A citizen is a professor of civility'). For a fuller discussion of 'civility', see Bryson, *Courtesy to Civility*, chap. 2.
8. [Guillaume de La Perrière], *The Mirrour of Policie* (Eng. trans., 1598), fol. 1.
9. Peter Burke, 'A civil tongue', in *Civil Histories*, ed. Burke et al. (Oxford, 2000), 36; John Hale, *The Civilization of Europe in the Renaissance* (1993), chap. 7.
10. Sir Thomas Elyot, *The Dictionary of Syr Thomas Eliot Knyght* (1538), s.vv. '*politia*', '*civilis homo*'.
11. Thomas Starkey, *An Exhortation to the People, Instructing Them to Unitie and Obedience* [1536], fol. 5.
12. Elyot, *Dictionary*, s.v. '*urbanitas*'.
13. Richard Mulcaster, *Positions* (1581), ed. Robert Henry Quick (1887), 137; *The Bible*, ed. Robert Carroll and Stephen Prickett (Oxford, 1997), liii; William Martyn, *Youths Instruction* (1612), 80; Locke, *Some Thoughts concerning Education*, 200 (para. 143).
14. Linda A. Pollock, 'The Practice of Kindness in Early Modern Elite Society', *P&P* 211 (2011); *OED*, s.v. 'civility money'.
15. Locke, *Some Thoughts concerning Education*, 200 (para. 143); Antoine de Courtin, *The Rules of Civility; or the Maxims of Genteel Behaviour* (English trans., from 12th French

edn, 1703). The EEBO search facility suggests that the term 'common civility' came into general use from the 1580s onward.

16. *Glossographia Anglicana Nova* (1707), s.v. 'courtesie'.
17. For the use made of Castiglione's *Il Cortegiano*, see Peter Burke, *The Fortunes of the Courtier* (Oxford, 1995).
18. Fenela Ann Childs, 'Prescriptions for Manners in English Courtesy Literature, 1690–1760, and their Social Implications' (D.Phil. thesis, Univ. of Oxford, 1984), 32–33. For works published before 1690, see John E. Mason, *Gentlefolk in the Making* (Philadelphia, PA, 1935), Virgil B. Heltzel, *A Check List of Courtesy Books in the Newberry Library* (Chicago, IL, 1942); and Bryson, *Courtesy to Civility*.
19. Outstanding examples are Bryson, *Courtesy to Civility; Civil Histories*, ed. Burke et al.; and Markku Peltonen, *The Duel in Early Modern England* (Cambridge, 2003). Teresa M. Bejan, *Mere Civility* (Cambridge, MA, 2017) is an excellent study of civility as 'a conversational virtue particularly pertinent in the practice of disagreement' (209n9). There are two instructive essays by French historians: Jacques Revel, 'The Uses of Civility', in *Passions of the Renaissance*, ed. Roger Chartier (*A History of Private Life*, ed. Philippe Ariès and Georges Duby (1987–91), vol. 3); and Roger Chartier, *The Cultural Uses of Print*, trans. Lydia G. Cochrane (Princeton, NJ, 1987), chap. 3. Many useful articles are contained in *Dictionnaire raisonné de la politesse et du savoir-vivre du Moyen Âge à nos jours*, ed. Alain Montandon (Paris, 1995). Camille Pernot, *La Politesse et sa philosophie* (Paris, 1996) is a well-informed and penetrating analysis.
20. Norbert Elias, *Über den Prozess der Zivilisation* (Basel, 1939), trans. Edmund Jephcott as *On the Process of Civilisation*, ed. Stephen Mennell et al. (*The Collected Works of Norbert Elias* (Dublin (2006–14), vol. 3); *Die höfische Gesellschaft* (Darmstadt, 1969), trans. Edmund Jephcott as *The Court Society* (rev. edn) (*Collected Works*, vol. 2); *Essays II*, ed. Richard Kilminster and Stephen Mennell (*Collected Works*, vol. 15), 3. The term 'civilizing process' had been used a few years earlier by A. O. Lovejoy and George Boas in their *Primitivism and Related Ideas in Antiquity* (Baltimore, MD, 1935), 7.
21. Elias, *On the Process of Civilisation*, 13, 71, 136, 207, 274, 412, 522. He derived this view from the Dutch historian Johann Huizinga, whose *The Waning of the Middle Ages* (*Herfsttij der Middeleeuwen* (2nd edn, 1921)) he greatly admired. Marc Bloch similarly suggested that medieval men were less able to control their immediate impulses ('médiocrement capable de réprimer leur premier mouvement'); *La Société féodale* (Paris, 1939; 1968), 567–68.
22. Elias, *On the Process of Civilisation*, 105, 137–38, 149–50, 237–38; Elias, *Essays II*, 7.
23. See J. E. A. Jolliffe, *Angevin Kingship* (2nd edn, 1963), chap. 4; Stephen D. White, 'The Politics of Anger', and Barbara H. Rosenwein, 'Controlling Paradigms', in *Anger's Past*, ed. Rosenwein (Ithaca, NY, 1998); Levi Roach, *Kingship and Consent in Anglo-Saxon England, 871–978* (Cambridge, 2013), 174–76; Stephen J. Spencer, '"Like a Raging Lion"', *EHR* 132 (2017).
24. A point well made in Linda Pollock, 'Anger and the Negotiation of Relationships in Early Modern England', *HJ* 47 (2004).
25. Bryson, *Courtesy to Civility*, 26–29, 70–71, 107–8.
26. Gabriel de Magalhães, *A New History of China* (Eng. trans., 1688), 101; *The Ottoman Gentleman of the Sixteenth Century*, trans. Douglas S. Brooks (Cambridge, MA, 2003). Another instructive example is provided by Daud Ali, *Courtly Culture and Political Life in Early Medieval India* (Cambridge, 2004).
27. Jack Goody, *The Theft of History* (Cambridge, 2006), chap. 6; Rosenwein, 'Controlling Paradigms', 241.
28. Jeroen Duindam, *Myths of Power* (Amsterdam, 1994), 173; [William and Edmund Burke], *An Account of the European Settlements in America* (3rd edn, 1760), vol. 1, 172; Adam Smith, *The Theory of Moral Sentiments*, ed. D. D. Raphael and A.L. Macfie (Oxford, 1976), 207–8 (V. 2. 10–11).

29. Norbert Elias, *Interviews and Autobiographical Reflections*, trans. and ed. Edmund Jephcott et al. (*Collected Works*, vol. 17), 195–96.
30. C. Stephen Jaeger, *The Origins of Courtliness* (Philadelphia, PA, 1985); id., *The Envy of Angels* (Philadelphia, PA, 1994); Thomas Zotz, 'Urbanitas', in *Curialitas*, ed. Josef Fleckenstein (Göttingen, 1990); Aldo Scaglione, *Knights at Court* (Berkeley, CA, 1991).
31. *Urbanus Magnus Danielis Becclesiensis*, ed. J. Gilbart Smyly (Dublin, 1939). On this see Robert Bartlett, *England under the Norman and Angevin Kings* (Oxford, 2000), 582–88; Frédérique Lachaud, 'L'Enseignement des bonnes manières en milieu de cour en Angleterre d'après *l'Urbanus Magnus* attribué à Daniel de Beccles', in *Erziehung und Bildung bei Hofe*, ed. Werner Paravicini and Jörg Wettlaufer (Stuttgart, 2002); Danny Danziger and John Gillingham, *1215* (2003), 10, 30, 91–92; and Fiona E. Whelan, 'Urbanus Magnus', *Bodl. Lib. Record* 27 (2014).
32. See H. Rosamond Parsons, 'Anglo-Norman Books of Courtesy and Nurture', *Procs. of the Modern Languages Assoc.* 44 (1929); Servus Gieben, 'Robert Grosseteste and Medieval Courtesy Books', *Vivarium* 5 (1967); Diane Bornstein, *Mirrors of Courtesy* (Hamden, CT, 1975); Nicholas Orme, *From Childhood to Chivalry* (1984); Jonathan Nicholls, *The Matter of Courtesy* (Woodbridge, 1985); Claude Roussel, 'Le Legs de la Rose', in *Pour une histoire des traités de savoir-faire en Europe*, ed. A. Montandon (Clermont-Ferrand, 1994); Daniela Romagnoli, 'La Courtoisie dans la ville', in *La Ville et la cour*, ed. Romagnoli (Paris, 1995); J. A. Burrow, *Gesture and Looks in Medieval Narrative* (Cambridge, 2002), 84–91, 116, 128, 135; Frédérique Lachaud, 'Littérature de civilité et "processus de civilisation" à la fin du XIIe siècle', in *Les Échanges culturels au Moyen Âge*, ed. Danielle Courtemanche and Anne-Marie Helvétius (Paris, 2002); Michael Staunton, *The Historians of Angevin England* (Oxford, 2017), 160–63; and especially, John Gillingham, 'From *Civilitas* to Civility', *TRHS*, 6th ser., 12 (2002). For terminology, see *Dictionary of Medieval Latin from British Sources*, ed. R. E. Latham et al. (1975–2013), and for an anthology of English medieval treatises and didactic poems, *Manners and Meals in Olden Time*, ed. Frederick J. Furnivall (EETS, 1868).
33. Thomas Kohnen, 'Linguistic Politeness in Anglo-Saxon England', *Journ. Hist. Pragmatics* 9 (2008), 155.
34. David Burnley, *Courtliness and Literature in Medieval England* (Harlow, 1998), chap. 1; James Campbell, 'Anglo-Saxon Courts', in *Court Culture in the Early Middle Ages*, ed. Catherine Cubitt (Turnhout, 2003), 165–66; Stephen Pollington, *The Mead Hall* (Hockwold-cum-Wilton, 2003), 42–47.
35. See Dilwyn Knox, '*Disciplina*: The Monastic and Clerical Origins of European Civility', in *Renaissance Society and Culture*, ed. John Monfasani and Ronald G. Martin (New York, 1991).
36. 'Statutes of Corpus Christi College', 63–64, in *Statutes of the Colleges of Oxford* (Oxford, 1853), vol. 2.
37. Gervase Rosser, *The Art of Solidarity in the Middle Ages* (Oxford, 2015), 34, 143–44; Ben R. McRee, 'Religious Gilds and the Regulation of Behaviour in Late Medieval Towns', in *People, Politics and Community in the Later Middle Ages*, ed. Joel Thomas Rosenthal and Colin Richmond (Gloucester, 1987).
38. Christian D. Liddy, *Contesting the City* (Oxford, 2017), index, s.v. 'civic values'; Barbara A. Hanawalt, *Ceremony and Civility* (New York, 2017), introduction; Jonathan Barry, 'Civility and Civic Virtue', in *Civil Histories*, ed. Burke et al.; Phil Withington, 'Public Discourse, Corporate Citizenship, and State Formation in Early Modern England', *AHR* 112 (2007); id., *The Politics of Commonwealth* (Cambridge, 2005), 11–12; Cathy Shrank, 'Civility and the City in *Coriolanus*', *Shakespeare Qtly* 54 (2003).
39. Felicity Heal, *Hospitality in Early Modern England* (Oxford, 1990), 102–4.
40. George Gascoigne, *A Hundreth Sundrie Flowres*, ed. G. W. Pigman III (Oxford, 2000), 315; Aristotle, *Nichomachean Ethics*, bk 7; Cicero, *De Officiis*, bk 1, chaps. 46, 93, 96, 126; Edwin S. Ramage, *Urbanitas* (Norman, OK, 1973). On *modestia*, see Dilwyn Knox,

'Gesture and Deportment', in *Cultural Exchange in Early Modern Europe*, vol. 4, ed. Herman Roodenburg (Cambridge, 2007); on the influence of Plutarch, Richard Brathwait, *The English Gentleman* (1630), 86–89, and Helen Moore, 'Of Marriage, Morals and Civility', in *Early Modern Civil Discourses*, ed. Jennifer Richards (Basingstoke, 2003); and on classical influences more generally, Alain Pons, 'Civilité-urbanité', in *Dictionnaire raisonné de la politesse*.

41. Mary Theresa Brentano, 'Relationships of the Latin Facetus Literature to the Medieval English Courtesy Poems', *Bulletin of the Univ. of Kansas* 36 (1935), 64–65; Knox, 'Disciplina'; Gillingham, 'From Civilitas to Civility', 278.

42. On which see M. Magendie, *La Politesse mondaine et les théories de l'honnêteté, en France, au XVIIe siècle, de 1600 à 1660* (Paris, [1925]); Jean-Pierre Dens, *L'Honnête Homme et la critique du goût* (Lexington, KY, 1981); Peter France, *Politeness and Its Discontents* (Cambridge, 1992).

43. Henry More, *An Account of Virtue* (1690), 139; Locke, *Some Thoughts concerning Education*, 200 (para. 143); Anthony Ashley Cooper, 3rd Earl of Shaftesbury, *Characteristicks of Men, Manners, Opinions, Times*, ed. Philip Ayres (Oxford, 1999), vol. 1, 59; Sir Matthew Hale, *The Primitive Origination of Mankind* (1677), 368.

44. *A Golden Chaine*, in *The Workes of . . . M(aster) W(illiam) Perkins* (Cambridge, 1608–1631), vol. 1, sig. B2ᵛ.

45. A good example is *Caxton's Booke of Curtesye*. See, more generally, Scaglione, *Knights at Court*, chap. 5; Jean-Claude Schmitt, *La Raison des gestes dans l'occident médiévale* (Paris, 1990), 224–25; Nicholls, *Matter of Courtesy*, 1–2, 32, 199; Dilwyn Knox, 'Erasmus' *De Civilitate* and the Religious Origins of Civility in Protestant Europe', *Archiv für Reformationsgeschichte* 86 (1995).

46. T[homas] R[ogers], *A Philosophicall Discourse* (1576), fol. 87; Sir Richard Barckley, *A Discourse of the Felicitie of Man* (1598), 326.

47. On the likely motives for his translation, see Mary Partridge, 'Thomas Hoby's English Translation of Castiglione's *Book of the Courtier*', *HJ* 50 (2007).

48. *Arminian Magazine* 11 (1788).

49. William Gouge, *Of Domesticall Duties, Eight Treatises* (3rd edn, 1634), 538–39; Robert Shelford, *Lectures or Readings upon the 6. Verse of the 22. Chapter of the Proverbs Concerning the Vertuous Education of Youth* (1602), 14; J. C. Davis, 'A Standard Which Can Never Fail Us', in *Popular Culture and Political Agency in Early Modern England*, ed. Michael J. Braddick and Phil Withington (Woodbridge, 2017); John Knight, *A Sermon Preach'd at the Funeral of the Right Honourable the Lady Guilford* (1700), 35.

50. Hobbes, *Leviathan*, ed. Malcolm, vol. 2, 220–43 (chap. 15); vol. 3, 1132 ('Review and Conclusion'); *The Elements of Law*, ed. Ferdinand Tönnies (2nd edn, 1969), 95 (I.18.1); *De Cive, The Latin Version*, ed. Howard Warrender (Oxford, 1983), 113 (III.xii).

51. Quentin Skinner, 'Hobbes and the Social Control of Unsociability', in *The Oxford Handbook of Hobbes*, ed. A. P. Martinich and Kinch Hoekstra (Oxford, 2016); Bejan, *Mere Civility*, 98–101.

52. *Leviathan*, ed. Malcolm, vol. 2, 150 (chap. 11); *The Petty Papers*, ed. Marquess of Lansdowne (1927), vol. 2, 188–89; Samuel Parker, *A Free and Impartial Censure of the Platonick Philosophie* (Oxford, 1666), 27.

53. *Spectator* 248 (14 Dec. 1711), ed. Bond, vol. 2, 462.

54. F. J. M. Korsten, *Roger North (1651–1734)* (Amsterdam, 1981), 117; David Hume, *Essays Moral, Political, and Literary*, ed. T. H. Green and T. H. Grose (1875), vol. 2, 200; Jeremy Bentham, *Deontology*, ed. Amnon Goldworth (Oxford, 1983), 276–77.

55. Henry Fielding, *Miscellanies*, ed. Henry Knight Miller (Oxford, 1972), vol. 1, 3–4.

56. *Correspondence of William Pitt, Earl of Chatham*, ed. William Stanhope Taylor and John Henry Pringle (1838–40), vol. 1, 79; Hume, *Essays*, vol. 1, 187; Chesterfield, in *The World* 148 (30 Oct. 1755), in *British Essayists*, ed. Robert Lynam et al. (1827), vol. 17, 181; Tobias Smollett, *Travels through France and Italy*, ed. Frank Felsenstein (Oxford, 1979), 57.

57. *Biographica Britannica* (1747–66), vol. 2, 780. For earlier advice on how to reprove faults in others without causing offence, see *Youth's Behaviour*, trans. Francis Hawkins (7th imprn, 1661), 15.

58. For an acute analysis of these conflicting approaches to civility, see C. J. Rawson, 'Gentlemen and Dancing-Masters', *Eighteenth-Century Studies* 1 (1967); see also Markku Peltonen, 'Politeness and Whiggism, 1688–1732', *HJ* 48 (2005), 405–6.

59. *The Letters of Sir Thomas Browne*, ed. Geoffrey Keynes (new edn, 1946), 10. On civility and 'learned sociability' as guiding principles of Browne's life, see Claire Preston, *Thomas Browne and the Writing of Early Modern Science* (Cambridge, 2005).

60. On the etiquette books, see Michael Curtin, *Propriety and Position* (New York, 1987); Marjorie Morgan, *Manners, Morals and Class in England, 1774–1858* (Basingstoke, 1994), 19–31.

61. Samuel Collins, *A Systeme of Anatomy* (1685), 61.

62. Sir Thomas Elyot, *The Boke Named the Gouernour*, ed. Henry Herbert Stephen Croft (1883), vol. 1, 35 (I. v); Virgilio Malvezzi, *The Pourtrait of the Politicke Christian-Favourite* (Eng. trans., 1647), 38; Guy Miège, *A New Dictionary French and English* (1677), sig.*Ppp2.

63. [Jacques] L'Esprit, *The Falshood of Human Virtue* (Eng. trans., 1691), 187.

64. Its growing use before the Restoration can be traced through the search facility of EEBO.

65. David Lloyd, *The States-men and Favourites of England since the Reformation* (1665), 16; Richard Gibbs, *The New Disorders of Love* (1687), sig. A2ᵛ.

66. Francis Meres, *Palladis Tamia* (1598), fol. 246; William Fulbecke, *An Historical Collection of the Continuall Factions, Tumults, and Massacres of the Romans and Italians* (1601), sig.*3; Lloyd, *States-men and Favourites*, 461.

67. 'The Spirit of Laws', bk 4, chap. 2, in *The Complete Works of M. de Montesquieu* (1777), vol. 1, 39.

68. Peter Heylyn, *A Survey of the State of France* (1656), 75.

69. Shaftesbury, *Characteristicks*, vol. 2, 206 (VI. iii. 1); Jonathan Richardson, *Two Discourses* (1719), vol. 2, 221.

70. Richard Flecknoe, *Love's Dominion* (1654), sig. A5.

71. Miège, *New Dictionary*, sig. *Ppp 2; Abel Boyer, 'Twelve Dialogues', in *The Compleat French-Master for Ladies and Gentlemen* (1694), 2nd pagination, 32.

72. *The Diary of John Evelyn*, ed. E. S. de Beer (Oxford, 1955), vol. 4, 409–10.

73. Between 1701 and 1800, 'civility' has 28,738 hits in ECCO (accessed on 24 Apr. 2016), 'politeness' 20,435, 'courtesy' 11,434, and 'good breeding' 9,517. The failure of 'politeness' to overtake 'civility' in the eighteenth century is confirmed by the evidence of the Old Bailey Proceedings, cited in Robert B. Shoemaker, *The London Mob* (2004), 294–95, and by the Corpus of Early Correspondence (CEEC), drawn upon by Terttu Nevalainen and Heli Tissari, 'Contextualizing Eighteenth-Century Politeness', in *Eighteenth-Century English*, ed. Raymond Hickey (Cambridge, 2010).

74. Although they appear to have missed the original, linguistic use of the term, there are indispensable discussions of 'politeness' in J. G. A. Pocock, 'Clergy and Commerce', in *L'Età dei Lumi*, ed. Raffaele Ajello et al. (Naples, 1985), vol. 1, 1n72; id., *Virtue, Commerce, and History* (Cambridge, 1985), 236–37; France, *Politeness and Its Discontents*, esp. chap. 4; John Brewer, *The Pleasures of the Imagination* (1997), 99–113; Paul Langford, 'The Uses of Eighteenth-Century Politeness', *TRHS*, 6th ser., 12 (2002); and numerous studies by Lawrence E. Klein, including 'The Political Significance of "Politeness" in Early Eighteenth-Century Britain', in *Politics, Politeness, and Patriotism*, ed. Gordon J. Schochet (Washington, DC, 1993); *Shaftesbury and the Culture of Politeness* (Cambridge, 1994); 'Politeness for Plebes', in *The Consumption of Culture, 1600–1800*, ed. Ann Bermingham and John Brewer (1995); 'Coffeehouse Civility, 1660–1714', *Huntington Lib. Qtly* 59 (1997–98), and 'Politeness and the Interpretation of the Eighteenth Century', *HJ* 45 (2002). Two helpful surveys of recent writing on the topic

are Philip Carter, *Men and the Emergence of Polite Society, Britain, 1660–1800* (Harlow, 2001), chaps. 1 and 2, and Stephen Conway, *Britain, Ireland, and Continental Europe in the Eighteenth Century* (Oxford, 2011), chap. 4.

75. Henry Home, Lord Kames, *Sketches of the History of Man* (Edinburgh, 1774), vol. 2, 169.
76. Lawrence Klein, 'The Third Earl of Shaftesbury and the Progress of Politeness', *Eighteenth-Century Studies* 18 (1984–85), 213. For some early instances, see M. Le Roy, Sieur de Gomberville, *The History of Polexander*, trans. William Browne (1647), 224; [François, Duc de La Rochefoucauld], *Epictetus Junior, or, Maximes of Modern Morality*, ed. J[ohn] D[avies] of Kidwelly (1670), 128–29; Thomas More, *Utopia*, Eng. trans. [by Gilbert Burnet] (1684), 66.
77. Monument to John Meredith in the chapel of All Souls College, Oxford; *The Life and Times of Anthony Wood*, ed. Andrew Clark (Oxford Hist. Soc., 1891–1900), vol. 2, 110.
78. *Arminian Magazine* 11 (1788), 27–28; *George Washington's Rules of Civility and Decent Behaviour*, ed. Charles Moore (Boston, MA, 1926).
79. D. A., *The Whole Art of Converse* (1683), 5.
80. Richard Payne Knight, *An Analytical Inquiry into the Principles of Taste* (4th edn, 1808), 291–92.
81. Maria Sifianou, *Politeness Phenomena in England and Greece* (Oxford, 1992), 49.
82. J. G. A. Pocock, 'Gibbon and the Shepherds', *History of European Ideas* 2 (1981), 195, and 'Cambridge Paradigms and Scottish Philosophers', in *Wealth and Virtue*, ed. Istvan Hont and Michael Ignatieff (Cambridge, 1983), 243.
83. For the much reiterated view that politeness was a new phenomenon of the later seventeenth and eighteenth centuries, see Carter, *Men and the Emergence of Polite Society*, 1, 23–26.
84. Gilbert Stuart, *A View of Society in Europe* ([1778]; Edinburgh, 1813), 64. Geoffrey Chaucer, 'General Prologue', *The Canterbury Tales*, lines 69–72.
85. Julia M. H. Smith, *Europe after Rome* (Oxford, 2005), 174–75; David Crouch, *The English Aristocracy 1070–1272* (New Haven, CT, 2011).
86. Burnley, *Courtliness and Literature*.
87. Gillingham, 'From *Civilitas* to Civility', 270; *Caxton's Booke of Curtesye*, 31, 34–35; *The Household of Edward IV*, ed. A. R. Myers (Manchester, 1959), 126–27; Nigel Saul, *For Honour and Fame* (2011), 169–71.
88. *The Institucion of a Gentleman* (1555), sig. Bvij; Ruth Kelso, *The Doctrine of the English Gentleman in the Sixteenth Century* (Urbana, IL, 1929), 48, 160–62.
89. Elyot, *Boke Named the Gouernour*, vol. 2, 447; J. Gailhard, *The Compleat Gentleman* (1678), vol. 1, sig. A8ʳ⁻ᵛ. On this theme, see Heal, *Hospitality in Early Modern England*, 102–7, 151–52, 301; ead. and Clive Holmes, *The Gentry in England and Wales, 1500–1700* (Basingstoke, 1994), esp. chaps. 7 and 8; and Bryson, *Courtesy to Civility*, esp. chap. 5.
90. Michael J. Braddick, *State Formation in Early Modern England*, ca. *1550–1700* (Cambridge, 2000), 373–78.
91. Lawrence Stone, *The Crisis of the Aristocracy 1558–1641* (Oxford, 1965), chap. 5; *Glamorgan County History*, vol. 4, ed. Glanmor Williams (Cardiff, 1974), 104–5, 190, 200; Penry Williams, *The Tudor Regime* (Oxford, 1979), 235–43, 251–52, 460–61; J. A. Sharpe, *Crime in Early Modern England 1550–1750* (Harlow, 1984), 95–99; id., 'Revisiting the "Violence We Have Lost"', *EHR* 131 (2016), 305–7; Keith Brown, 'Gentlemen and Thugs in 17th-Century Britain', *History Today* 40 (2000); Gregory Durston, *Crime and Justice in Early Modern England* (Chichester, 2004), 49–54, 68–69.
92. Gregory Hanlon, 'The Decline of Violence in the West', *EHR* 128 (2013), 368–70, 382.
93. Stuart Carroll, *Blood and Violence in Early Modern France* (Oxford, 2006), 309; Michel Nassiet, 'Vengeance in Sixteenth- and Seventeenth-Century France', in *Cultures of Violence*, ed. Stuart Carroll (Basingstoke, 2007), 125–26; and see note 23 (this chapter).
94. M. E. James, *English Politics and the Concept of Honour 1485–1642* (*P&P*, supp. 8, 1978), esp. 32–45.

95. Richard Payne Knight, *The Progress of Civility* (1796), 42n.
96. Bernard Mandeville, *The Fable of the Bees*, ed. F. B. Kaye (Oxford, 1924), vol. 1, 220; David Hume, *An Enquiry concerning the Principles of Morals*, ed. Tom L. Beauchamp (Oxford, 1998), 118.
97. R. G. Collingwood, *The New Leviathan* (Oxford, 1942), 339.
98. Sir Thomas Palmer, *An Essay of the Meanes how to make our Travailes into Forraine Countries the more Profitable and Honourable* (1606), 42, 64–65; *Stuart Royal Proclamations*, ed. James F. Larkin and Paul L. Hughes (Oxford, 1973–83), vol. 1, 307.
99. Antonio Santuosso, 'Giovanni Della Casa on the *Galateo*', *Renaissance and Reformation* 11 (1975), 8; Sir Clement Edmondes, *Observations upon the Five First Bookes of Caesar's Commentaries* (1600), 198. In *The Duel in Early Modern England*, Markku Peltonen argues that 'duelling had a vital role in civility' and 'had always been taken as a chief promoter of civil courtesy' (147). He cites several English proponents of civility who held this view (17–18, 46–48, 55–57, 171, 175–76, 192–93, 247), including Bernard Mandeville, who argued in many writings from 1709 onwards that the idea of honour was crucial to the 'civilizing of mankind' (e.g., *Fable of the Bees*, chap. 5). Most of these individuals were less wholehearted supporters of the duel than Professor Peltonen suggests; they justified it in terms of honour rather than civility; and they pointed out that there were other ways in which honour could be defended, for example, by creating a special court to settle disputes. Peltonen quotes Lord Chesterfield as saying that, in a case of serious insult, there were only two alternatives for a gentleman: 'extreme politeness or a duel' (307). This comes from a distorted version of Chesterfield's advice to his son, published in Philadelphia in 1781. What Chesterfield actually wrote was 'extreme politeness or knocking down' (*The Letters of the Earl of Chesterfield to His Son*, ed. Charles Strachey (1901), vol. 2, 272). Of the two, he favoured extreme politeness.
100. S. R., *The Courte of Civill Courtesie* (1577), 17–27.
101. Lod[owick] Br[yskett], *A Discourse of Civill Life* (1606, but written in the 1580s), 64–85, a rendering of Giovanni Battista Giraldi Cinthio, *De Gli Hecatommithi* (2nd edn, Venice, 1566), pt 2, dial. 1, 23–32. Markku Peltonen acknowledges that Bryskett's book was an adaptation of Cinthio, but does not note that Cinthio, although an exponent of Italian civility, was very hostile to duelling.
102. *The Works of Sir Walter Ralegh* (Oxford, 1829), vol. 6, 460 (*History of the World*, bk 5, chap. 3); Thomas Hobbes, *Behemoth or the Long Parliament*, ed. Paul Seaward (Oxford, 2010), 157; George Berkeley, *Alciphron*, ed. Laurent Jaffro et al. (Hildesheim, 2009), 153.
103. Peltonen, *Duel in Early Modern England*, 245–62; William Ames, *Conscience with the Power and Cases thereof* (Eng. trans., n. pl., 1639), vol. 4, 183; Berkeley, *Alciphron*, 186, 187; Nicholas Rogers, *Mayhem* (New Haven, CT, 2012), 32.
104. Brown, 'Gentlemen and Thugs'; *Boswell's Life of Johnson*, ed. George Birkbeck Hill, rev. L. F. Powell (Oxford, 1934–50), vol. 1, 102. On the rules of the road for vehicles, see Hume, *Enquiry concerning the Principles of Morals*, 31n16.
105. Jan Bremmer, 'Walking, Standing and Sitting in Ancient Greek Culture', in *A Cultural History of Gesture*, ed. Bremmer and Herman Roodenburg (Oxford, 1991), 7. On the importance of bodily deportment for the upper classes of imperial Rome, see Peter Brown, 'Late Antiquity', in *A History of Private Life*, ed. Paul Veyne, trans. Arthur Goldhammer (Cambridge, MA, 1987), vol. 1, 240–86.
106. 'Gentlemen', *Cornhill Magazine* 5 (1862), 336.
107. William Horman, *Vulgaria* (1519), ed. Montague Rhodes James (Roxburghe Club, 1926), 59; *OED* and EEBO, s.v. 'carriage'.
108. Des[iderius] Erasmus, *De Civilitate Morun [sic] Puerilium*, trans. Robert Whitington (1532), sig. A2ᵛ; George James Aungier, *The History and Antiquities of Syon Monastery* (1840), 298; S[imon] R[obson], *The Choise of Change* (1585), sig. F1ᵛ; Brathwait, *English Gentleman*, 5.

109. *The Civil Conversation of M. Steeven Guazzo*, trans. George Pettie and Barth(olomew) Young (1581–86; 1925), vol. 1, 123.
110. George Snell, *The Right Teaching of Useful Knowledg* (1649; 2nd edn, 1651), 60–61. Herman Roodenburg, *The Eloquence of the Body* (Zwollen, 2004), gives an illuminating account of similar assumptions about bodily deportment among the elite of the seventeenth-century Dutch republic.
111. Erasmus, *De Civilitate Morun [sic] Puerilium*, sigs. A7ᵛ, C2ᵛ, C7ᵛ, C8; *School of Manners or Rules for Childrens Behaviour* (4th edn, 1701; Victoria and Albert Museum, 1983), 13.
112. Thomas Traherne, *Christian Ethicks* (1675), 327; Archibald Alison, *Essays on the Nature and Principles of Taste* (4th edn, Edinburgh, 1815), vol. 2, 292.
113. Thomas Wright, *The Passions of the Minde in Generall* (1601), 210; Edward Hyde, Earl of Clarendon, *Miscellaneous Works* (2nd edn, 1751), 317. Precise instructions on such matters, illustrated by drawings, were provided by F[rançois] Nivelon, *The Rudiments of Genteel Behaviour* (1737).
114. James Burnet, Lord Monboddo, *Of the Origin and Progress of Language* (Edinburgh, 1773–92), vol. 4, 295.
115. George Bickham, *The Universal Penman* (1733–41), introduction, 2.
116. A pioneering guide to these changes, designed primarily for actors and theatrical directors, is Joan Wildeblood, *The Polite World* (rev. edn, 1973).
117. Nivelon, *Rudiments of Genteel Behaviour*, plate 1; Ellen G. D'Oench, *The Conversation Piece* (New Haven, CT, 1980), 30. For crossed legs as a thirteenth-century symbol of superior status, see Lachaud, 'Littérature de civilité', 49.
118. Erasmus, *De Civilitate Morum Puerilium*; Giovanni della Casa, *Galateo of Maister John Della Casa*, trans. Robert Peterson (1576), 111; T[homas] P[ritchard], *The Schoole of Honest and Vertuous Lyfe* (1579), 44; George Puttenham, *The Arte of English Poesie*, ed. Gladys Doidge Willcock and Alice Walker (Cambridge, 1936), 296–97. Cf. Aristotle, *Nicomachean Ethics*, 1125a; Cicero, *De Officiis*, bk 1, chap. 131.
119. James Cleland, *Hero-Paideia: or the Institution of a Young Noble Man* (Oxford, 1607), 170; Wright, *Passions of the Minde*, 215; Thomas Tegg, *A Present for an Apprentice* (2nd edn, 1848), 266–67.
120. Nancy Mitford, 'The English Aristocracy', in Alan S. C. Ross et al., *Noblesse Oblige* (1956), 42.
121. Lynn Sorge-English, *Stays and Body Image in London* (2011); David M. Turner and Alun Withey, 'Technologies of the Body', *History* 99 (2014).
122. *The Lisle Letters*, ed. Muriel St. Clare Byrne (Chicago, IL, 1981), vol. 4, 488, 517; *HMC, Rutland*, vol. 4, 382; Barbara Ravelhofer, *The Early Stuart Masque* (Oxford, 2006), 18–19, 21.
123. H[enry] T[hurman], *A Defence of Humane Learning in the Ministry* (Oxford, 1660), 31–32; *Correspondence of the Family of Hatton*, ed. Edward Maunde Thompson (Camden Soc., 1878), vol. 2, 214; Locke, *Some Thoughts concerning Education*, 124 (para. 67); *Spectator* 334 (24 Mar. 1712), ed. Bond, vol. 3, 235.
124. *Letters of Chesterfield*, vol. 1, 140, 269, 239.
125. *The Letters of Thomas Langton, Flax Merchant of Kirkham, 1771–1788*, ed. Joan Wilkinson (Chetham Soc., 1994), 133–34.
126. [John Weaver], *An Essay towards an History of Dancing* (1712), 178.
127. *Glamorgan County History*, vol. 4, 100.
128. *A Relation, or Rather a True Account of the Island of England*, trans. Charlotte Augusta Sneyd (Camden Soc., 1847), 25; *The Vulgaria of John Stanbridge and the Vulgaria of Robert Whittinton*, ed. Beatrice White (EETS, 1932), 117–18; Ben Jonson, *The New Inn* (1629), vol. 1, 3; *The Memoirs of Sir Hugh Cholmley* (1787), 85–86; K. B. McFarlane, *The Nobility of Later Medieval England* (Oxford, 1973), 105; Grant McCracken, 'The Exchange of Children', *Journ. of Family History* 8 (1983), 310–11.

129. John Smyth, *The Berkeley Manuscripts: The Lives of the Berkeleys*, ed. Sir John Maclean (Gloucester, 1883–85), vol. 2, 386.

130. [Thomas Heywood], *A Pleasant Conceited Comedie, wherein is Shewed, How a Man may Chuse a Good Wife* (1602), sig. F4.

131. *The Parish Register and Tithing Book of Thomas Hassall of Amwell*, ed. Stephen G. Doree (Herts. Rec. Soc., 1989), 180.

132. Tim Meldrum, *Domestic Service and Gender, 1660–1750* (Harlow, 2000), 59; J. Jean Hecht, *The Domestic Servant Class in Eighteenth-Century England* (1956), 46, 47, 49, 54–55, 61, and chap. 8; Lawrence Stone, *Broken Lives* (Oxford, 1993), 179; Langford, 'Uses of Eighteenth-Century Politeness', 324.

133. Sir Samuel Morland, *The Urim of Conscience* (1695), 155; Gailhard, *Compleat Gentleman*, 88–90.

134. *Letters of Sir Thomas Browne*, 4, 5, 7, 15; Lord Edmond Fitzmaurice, *The Life of Sir William Petty 1623–1687* (1895), 303.

135. Chesterfield, in *The World* 148 (30 Oct. 1755), in *British Essayists*, vol. 17, 182; *The Autobiography and Correspondence of Mary Granville, Mrs Delany*, ed. Lady Llanover (1st ser., 1861), vol. 3, 219.

136. Snell, *Right Teaching of Useful Knowledg*, 55–58.

137. *The Lismore Papers*, ed. Alexander B. Grosart (2nd ser., 1887–88), vol. 3, 224. For the teaching of manners in grammar schools, see Carlisle, *Concise Description*, vol. 1, 224, 277, 408, 604, 617, 809; vol. 2, 10, 49; Foster Watson, *The English Grammar Schools to 1660* (1908), chap. 6; and of rhetorical delivery, B. L. Joseph, *Elizabethan Acting* (1951), 8–14.

138. Hubert Chadwick, *From St Omers to Stonyhurst* (1962), 235.

139. Benjamin Furly, *The Worlds Honour Detected* (1663), 8.

140. De Courtin, *Rules of Civility*, 203.

141. Puttenham, *Arte of English Poesie*, 289.

142. Adam Smith, *Lectures on Rhetoric and Belles Lettres*, ed. J. C. Bryce (Oxford, 1983), 198; Thomas Sheridan, *British Education* (1756), 437–38.

143. Bartlett, *England under the Norman and Angevin Kings*, 585; Erasmus, *De Civilitate*, sig. A6^{r–v}; Horman, *Vulgaria*, 82, 115, (and 113); [Paul Pellisson-Fontanier], *A Miscellany of Divers Problems*, trans. H[enry] S[ome] (1680), 30; *Letters of Chesterfield*, vol. 1, 213 (and 285); *Correspondence of Chatham*, vol. 1, 79; *The Guardian*, no. 29 (14 Apr. 1713). See also Keith Thomas, 'The Place of Laughter in Tudor and Stuart England', *TLS* (21 Jan. 1977); Quentin Skinner, 'Why Laughing Mattered in the Renaissance', *History of Political Thought* 22 (2001); Kate Davison, 'Occasional Politeness and Gentlemen's Laughter in 18th-Century England', *HJ* 57 (2014), 931–36.

144. Davison, 'Occasional Politeness.'

145. Puttenham, *Arte of English Poesie*, 290; Thomas Hobbes, *De Homine* (1658), vol. 9, 7; Childs, 'Prescriptions for Manners', 180. See, more generally, Bernard Capp, '"Jesus Wept" but Did the Englishman?', *P&P* 224 (2014).

146. *Sejanus*, act 1, lines 133–36.

147. Thomas Birch, *The Life of Henry Prince of Wales* (1760), 384.

148. Walter J. Ong, 'Latin Language Study as a Renaissance Puberty Rite', *Studies in Philology* 56 (1959); [William and Edmund Burke], *An Account of the European Settlements in America* (3rd edn, 1760), vol. 1, 172.

149. Stanford E. Lehmberg, *The Later Parliaments of Henry VIII, 1536–1547* (Cambridge, 1977), 237 (and cf. 230); George Cavendish, *The Life and Death of Cardinal Wolsey*, ed. Richard S. Sylvester (EETS, 1959), 160; William Roper and Nicholas Harpsfield, *Lives of Saint Thomas More*, ed. E. E. Reynolds (Everyman's Lib., 1963), 47, 49; Susan Brigden, *Thomas Wyatt* (2012), 525; Lisa Jardine and Alan Stewart, *Hostage to Fortune* (1998), 230; *Cal. SP, Domestic, 1628–9*, 153; *Commons Debates for 1629*, ed. Wallace

Notestein and Frances Helen Relf (Minneapolis, MN, 1921), 105; C. H. Firth, *The Last Years of the Protectorate* (1909), vol. 1, 148; *Remarks and Collections of Thomas Hearne*, ed. C. E. Doble et al. (Oxford Hist. Soc., 1885–1921), vol. 2, 357, 459.

150. Matthew Steggle, *Laughing and Weeping at Early Modern Theatres* (Aldershot, 2007), chap. 5; Marjory E. Lange, *Telling Tears in the English Renaissance* (Leiden, 1996), chap. 4; Ralph Houlbrooke, *Death, Religion, and the Family in England 1580–1750* (Oxford, 1998), 224–25; David Cressy, *Birth, Marriage, and Death* (Oxford, 1997), 395; Thomas Dixon, *Weeping Britannia* (Oxford, 2015), chap. 2.

151. William Shakespeare, *Henry VI, Part II* (1594), act 1, scene 1, lines 112–22; *Hamlet* (ca. 1600), act 1, scene 2, line 94; and see Martha A. Kurtz, 'Tears and Masculinity in the History Play', in *Grief and Gender, 700–1700*, ed. Jennifer C. Vaught (Basingstoke, 2003).

152. *Female Monastic Life in Early Tudor England*, ed. Barry Collett (Aldershot, 2002), 100.

153. Samuel Torshell, *The Hypocrite Discovered* (1644), 71; Bodl., MS Rawlinson E95, fol. 4ᵛ (Lushington); Raymond A. Anselment, 'Mary Rich, Countess of Warwick and the Gift of Tears', *Seventeenth Century*, vol. 22 (2007); Arnold Hunt, *The Art of Hearing* (Cambridge, 2010), 86–88, 91–93, 160; Alec Ryrie, *Being Protestant in Reformation Britain* (Oxford, 2013), 187–95, and index, s.v. 'tears'.

154. *Tatler* 28 (15 Sept. 1709), ed. Donald F. Bond (Oxford, 1987), vol. 1, 474.

155. Andrew Moore with Charlotte Crawley, *Family and Friends* (1992), 16.

156. R. S. Crane, 'Suggestions toward a Genealogy of the "Man of Feeling"', *Eng. Literary History* 1 (1934); Carter, *Men and the Emergence of Polite Society*, 94–96, 106–7, 128, 190–91; id., 'Tears and the Man', in *Women, Gender and Enlightenment*, ed. Sarah Knott and Barbara Taylor (Basingstoke, 2005); Jennifer C. Vaught, *Masculinity and Emotion in Early Modern English Literature* (Aldershot, 2008), 23; Dixon, *Weeping Britannia*, chap. 7.

157. *Correspondence of Henry and Sarah Fielding*, ed. Martin C. Battestin and Clive T. Probyn (Oxford, 1993), 70.

158. E.g., Vicesimus Knox, 'On the unmanliness of shedding tears', *Lucubrations, or Winter Evenings* 90 (1795), in *The British Essayists*, ed. Robert Lynam et al. (1827), vol. 30, 31; William M. Reddy, 'Sentimentalism and Its Erasure', *JMH* 72 (2000).

159. Douglas Hay et al., *Albion's Fatal Tree* (1975), 29; *The Journal of the Rev. William Bagshaw Stevens*, ed. Georgina Galbraith (Oxford, 1965), 140; V. A. C. Gatrell, *The Hanging Tree* (Oxford, 1994), 508.

160. J[ohn] B[ulwer], *Chirologia* (1644), vol. 2, 145.

161. Keith Thomas, 'Introduction', in *A Cultural History of Gesture*, 8–9; *A Treatise of Daunces* (1581), sig. B8ʳ⁻ᵛ; R[obert] C[awdrey], *A Table Alphabeticall* (3rd edn, 1613), s.v. 'gesticulate'; Bulwer, *Chirologia*, vol. 2, 118; D. A., *Whole Art of Converse*, 119; Mandeville, *Fable of the Bees*, vol. 2, 290–91; Joyce Ransome, '"Courtesy" at Little Gidding', *Seventeenth Century* 30 (2015), 427–29.

162. Keith Thomas, 'Afterword', in *The Kiss in History*, ed. Karen Harvey (Manchester, 2005), 192–93.

163. Gailhard, *Compleat Gentleman*, vol. 2, 10; Joseph Hall, *Quo Vadis?* (1617), sig. A5; 'Katherine Austen's Journal 1664–1666', ed. Barbara J. Todd, in *Women and History*, ed. Valerie Frith (Concord, Ontario, 1997), 221; *HMC, Salisbury*, vol. 12, ix; Stone, *Crisis of the Aristocracy*, 694–98; George C. Brauer, *The Education of a Gentleman* (New York, 1959), 157–59; Conway, *Britain, Ireland, and Continental Europe*, chap. 7; Henry French and Mark Rothery, *Man's Estate* (Oxford, 2012), 144–48.

164. [Sir John Stradling], *A Direction for Travailes* (1592), sig. C1ᵛ.

165. 'Life of Sir John Digby', ed. Georges Bernard, in *Camden Miscellany*, vol. 12 (Camden Soc., 1910), 115; *Letters of Chesterfield*, vol. 2, 262–63.

166. Clarendon, *Miscellanous Works*, 340; *The Letters and the Second Diary of Samuel Pepys*, ed. R. G. Howarth (1933), 206, 209.

167. J. I. Catto, 'Conclusion', in *The History of the University of Oxford*, ed. T. H. Aston et al. (Oxford, 1984–2000), vol. 2, 770.
168. 'Katherine Austen's Journal', 220–21; Clarendon, *Miscellaneous Works*, 322; [S. C.], *The Art of Complaisance* (1673), 119–20.
169. On finishing schools, Dorothy Gardiner, *English Girlhood at School* (1929), 209–14, 224; *The Journal of William Schellinks' Travels in England*, trans. and ed. Maurice Exwood and H. L. Lehmann (Camden, 5th ser., 1993), 59.
170. George James Aungier, *The History and Antiquities of Syon Monastery* (1840), 291, 299, 377–80, 385.
171. Baldassare Castiglione, *The Book of the Courtier*, trans. Thomas Hoby (1588 edn, Everyman's Lib., 1928), 189.
172. William Shakespeare, *The Taming of the Shrew* (ca. 1592), Induction, scene 1, lines 121–22; R[obson], *The Choise of Change*, sigs. Kiiiᵛ–ivᵛ; Samuel Purchas, *Hakluytus Posthumus* (Glasgow, 1905–7), vol. 19, 92–93.
173. Puttenham, *Arte of English Poesie*, 290–91; Timothy Bright, *Treatise of Melancholie* (1586), 143–44; Robert Burton, *The Anatomy of Melancholy*, ed. Thomas C. Faulkner et al. (Oxford, 1989–2000), vol. 3, 130–32 (3. 2. 2. 4); Ian Maclean, *The Renaissance Notion of Woman* (Cambridge, 1980), 33–35, 41–42, 46; Morris Palmer Tilley, *A Dictionary of the Proverbs in England in the Sixteenth and Seventeenth Centuries* (Ann Arbor, MI, 1950), 542.
174. Hannah Woolley, *The Gentlewomans Companion* (1673), 44; Cavendish, *Life and Death of Cardinal Wolsey*, 29; John Batchiler, *The Virgins Pattern* (1661), 53.
175. Woolley, *Gentlewomans Companion*, 45, 47; Robert Codrington, *The Second Part of Youths Behaviour, or Decency of Conversation amongst Women* (1664), 31. On didactic literature addressed to females, see Ruth Kelso, *Doctrine for the Lady of the Renaissance* (Urbana, IL, 1956), esp. chaps. 3 and 7; Childs, 'Prescriptions for Manners', chap. 5; Dilwyn Knox, 'Civility, Courtesy and Women in the Italian Renaissance', in *Women in Italian Renaissance Culture and Society*, ed. Letizia Panizza (Oxford, 2000); Laura Gowing, '"The Manner of Submission"', *CultSocHist* 10 (2013); Soile Ylivuori, 'Women's Bodies and the Culture of Politeness', *Lectio Praecursoria* (12 Dec. 2015), www.ennenjanyt.net/. . ./soile-ylivuori.
176. Withington, *Politics of Commonwealth*, 221; Bartholomew Batty, *The Christian Mans Closet*, trans. William Lowth (1581), fol. 75ᵛ; Bridget Hill, *Eighteenth-Century Women* (1984), 23–24; [John Trusler], *The Honours of the Table* (1788), 7, 119; Peter Edwards, *Horse and Man in Early Modern England* (2007), 76–77.
177. R[obson], *The Choise of Change*, sig. Liv.
178. Margaret Cavendish, Duchess of Newcastle, *CCXI Sociable Letters* (1664), 50.
179. The practice was established by 1659, when John Evelyn criticized it in his *Character of England; The Writings of John Evelyn*, ed. Guy de la Bedoyère (Woodbridge, 1995), 84–85.
180. Daniel Rogers, *Matrimonial Honour* (1642), 251; [Charles Cotton], *Scarronides: or, Le Virgile Travesty* (1664), 90–91; John Gay, 'Trivia', in *Poetry and Prose*, ed. Vinton A. Dearing (Oxford, 1974), vol. 1, 144.
181. Fynes Moryson, *Shakespeare's Europe*, ed. Charles Hughes (2nd edn, New York, 1967), 474–75; *Table Talk of John Selden*, ed. Sir Frederick Pollock (1927), 25; Hume, *Essays*, vol. 1, 193.
182. Gailhard, *Compleat Gentleman*, vol. 2, 75–77; D. A., *Whole Art of Converse*, 16; S. C., *Art of Complaisance*, 118, 120; and see [Judith Drake?], 'A Lady', *An Essay in Defence of the Female Sex* (3rd edn, 1697), 136–47.
183. *Miscellaneous Works of Clarendon*, 295; *The Works of George Savile, Marquis of Halifax*, ed. Mark N. Brown (Oxford, 1989), vol. 3, 361; Hume, *Essays*, vol. 1, 194; *Letters of Chesterfield*, vol. 1, 195, 197, 238, 385; vol. 2, 24, 34–35; Karen O'Brien, *Women and Enlightenment in Eighteenth-Century Britain* (Cambridge, 2009), 74–75.

184. See, e.g., Amy Louise Erickson, *Women and Property in Early Modern England* (1993), 235–36; Alison Wall, 'Elizabethan Precept and Feminine Practice', *History* 75 (1990); Sara Mendelson and Patricia Crawford, *Women in Early Modern England* (Oxford, 2003); Amanda Vickery, *The Gentleman's Daughter* (New Haven, CT, 1998); Bernard Capp, *When Gossips Meet* (Oxford, 2003); Ingrid H. Tague, *Women of Quality* (Woodbridge, 2002), chap. 7; Elaine Chalus, *Elite Women in English Political Life* (Oxford, 2005); Gowing, '"The Manner of Submission"'; Alexandra Shepard, *Accounting for Oneself* (Oxford, 2015).

185. *Urbanus Magnus Danielis Becclesiensis*, 37; Chaucer, 'General Prologue', *Canterbury Tales*, lines 127–36.

186. Obadiah Walker, *Of Education* (1673), 218–19.

187. *The Diary of Samuel Pepys*, ed. Robert Latham and William Matthews (1970–83), vol. 10, 144; Smollett, *Travels through France and Italy*, 34; Lorna Weatherill, *Consumer Behaviour and Material Culture in Britain 1660–1760* (1988), 152–53; David Hey, *The Fiery Blades of Hallamshire* (Leicester, 1991), 131–34; *Joe Miller in Motley*, ed. W. Carew Hazlitt (1892), 123.

188. A. J. Peacock, *Bread or Blood* (1965), 14.

189. *M. Misson's Memoirs and Observations in his Travels over England*, trans. [John] Ozell (1719), 316–17.

190. John Bossy, *Giordano Bruno and the Embassy Affair* (New Haven, CT, 1991), 224–25.

191. De Courtin, *Rules of Civility*, vol. 1, 100–101. For growing squeamishness in this area, see Bryson, *Courtesy to Civility*, 98–100.

192. William Cole, *A Journal of my Journey to Paris in the Year 1765*, ed. Francis Griffin Stokes (1931), 270; Arthur Young, *Travels during the Years 1787, 1788 and 1789* (Dublin, 1793), vol. 1, 582; *A Frenchman in England 1784*, ed. Jean Marchand, trans. S. C. Roberts (Cambridge, 1933), 44; Della Casa, *Galateo*, 9.

193. Gérard de Lairesse, *The Art of Painting* (1707), trans. John Frederick Fritsch (1738), 39.

194. *Letters of Chesterfield*, vol. 1, 93–94. Similarly, Gailhard, *Compleat Gentleman*, vol. 2, 67.

195. Charles Vyse, *The New London Spelling-Book* (1778), 174.

196. Will[iam] Rabisha, *The Whole Body of Cookery Dissected* (1661), 245; Hannah Woolley, *The Queen-Like Closet* (1670), 375.

197. *Remarks and Collections of Thomas Hearne*, vol. 5, 169; David Bindman and Malcolm Baker, *Roubiliac and the Eighteenth-Century Monument* (New Haven, CT, 1995), 283; *ODNB*, s.v. 'Hough, John'.

198. *Letters of Chesterfield*, vol. 1, 269.

199. *Boswell's Life of Johnson*, vol. 3, 69.

200. Agogos [Charles William Day], *Hints on Etiquette and the Usages of Society* (2nd edn, 1836), 28, 27; Laura Trevelyan, *A Very British Family* (2006), 186.

201. David Hume, *A Treatise of Human Nature* (1739–40), ed. David Fate Norton and Mary J. Norton (Oxford, 2000), 390 (3. 3. 4); *Letters of Chesterfield*, vol. 1, 343; [Anthony Walker], *The Holy Life of Mrs Elizabeth Walker* (1690), 291. This and the following paragraph draw on my chapter 'Cleanliness and Godliness in Early Modern England', in *Religion, Culture and Society in Early Modern Britain*, ed. Anthony Fletcher and Peter Roberts (Cambridge, 1994).

202. William Scott, *An Essay of Drapery* (1635), 95.

203. Thomas, 'Cleanliness and Godliness', 70, 77; *The Memoirs of James Stephen*, ed. Merle M. Bevington (1954), 138.

204. Cicero, *De Officiis*, bk 1, chaps. 126–28; Elias, *On the Process of Civilisation*, 134–36; J[ohn] D[avies] of Kidwelly, *The Ancient Rites, and Monuments of the Monastical and Cathedral Church of Durham* (1672), 134; Dominike Mancini, *The Mirrour of Good Maners*, trans. Alexander Barclay (1570; Spenser Soc., 1885), 70; Della Casa, *Galateo*, 5–6; Bryson, *Courtesy to Civility*, 101.

205. *Urbanus Magnus Danielis Becclesiensis*, 38–39, 44; Della Casa, *Galateo* (1576), 17; Bryson, *Courtesy to Civility*, 86–87; and see the comments of Charles Taylor, *A Secular Age* (Cambridge, MA, 2007), 139–42.

206. Erasmus, *De Civilitate Puerilium*, trans Robert Whittington (1540), sig. B1; Fynes Moryson, *An Itinerary* (Glasgow, 1907–8), vol. 2, 263; Ransome, '"Courtesy" at Little Gidding', 428.

207. J. P. Kenyon, *The Stuarts* (rev. edn, 1977), 41; *Diary of Samuel Pepys*, vol. 4, 244; *Life and Times of Anthony Wood*, vol. 2, 68.

208. *Biographia Britannica* (1747–66), vol. 6, pt. 2, 4379n.

209. [Benjamin Buckler], *A Philosophical Dialogue concerning Decency* (1751), 10. For the authorship of this curious work, see the letter of 28 Oct. 1930, from Bodley's Librarian, attached to the copy (GZ. 5. 7) in the Codrington Library, All Souls College, Oxford, and the note by Francis Douce in the Bodleian copy (Douce RR 162(1)).

210. John Cramsie, *British Travellers and the Encounter with Britain 1450–1700* (Woodbridge, 2015), 221; Humphrey Brooke, *A Conservatory of Health* (1650), 194; Sir John Floyer, *Psychrolousia: Or the History of Cold Bathing* (3rd edn, 1709), 348–50; Cole, *Journal of My Journey to Paris*, 272; William Buchan, *Domestic Medicine* (8th edn, 1784), 139.

211. Buckler, *Philosophical Dialogue*, 10.

212. *Dobsons Drie Bobbes*, 8–9; Adam Petrie, *Rules of Good Deportment, or of Good Breeding* (Edinburgh, 1720), 9; John Gay, 'Trivia', bk 2, lines 299–300, in *Poetry and Prose*, vol. 1, 152.

213. David Hartley, *Observations on Man* (1749), vol. 1, 448–49.

214. David Starkey, 'Representation through Intimacy', in *Symbols and Sentiments*, ed. Ioan Lewis (1977), 215–18.

215. *Letters of a Grandmother, 1732–1735*, ed. Gladys Scott Thomson (1943), 46; *A Frenchman in England 1784*, 31–32; *The Diary of a Country Parson*, ed. John Beresford (1924; Oxford, 1968), vol. 1, 280.

216. Elias, *On the Process of Civilisation*, 136–39; Sarah Toulalan, *Imagining Sex* (Oxford, 2007), 228–30.

217. [Giovanni della Casa], *Galateo of Manners* (Eng. trans from the Latin, 1703), sigs. A1ᵛ–2; *Galateo: Or a Treatise on Politeness and Delicacy of Manners*, [trans. Richard Graves] (1774), ix; Samuel Johnson, *The Lives of the Most Eminent English Poets*, ed. Roger Lonsdale (Oxford, 2006), vol. 3, 7.

218. *Lisle Letters*, vol. 3, 382; *Diary of Samuel Pepys*, vol. 2, 34–35; Moryson, *Itinerary*, vol. 3, 441; Gailhard, *Compleat Gentleman*, vol. 2, 167; 'Unkindnesse', in *The Works of George Herbert*, ed. F. E. Hutchinson (Oxford, 1941), 93. For 'spitting-sheets', '-cups', '-boxes', and '-pots', see *OED*.

219. Robert Eden Scott, *Elements of Rhetoric* (Aberdeen, 1802), 13.

220. *Floures for Latin Spekynge Selected and Gathered Oute of Terence*, compiled and trans. by Nicolas Udall ('1533' [1534]), fol. 112ᵛ; Puttenham, *Arte of English Poesie*, 144; William Camden, *Remains Concerning Britain*, ed. R. D. Dunn (Toronto, 1984), 42; Joseph M. Williams, '"O! When degree is shak'd"', in *English in Its Social Contexts*, ed. Tim William Machan and Charles T. Scott (New York, 1992); 'Answer to Sir William Davenant's Preface before *Gondibert*', in *The English Works of Thomas Hobbes*, ed. Sir William Molesworth (1839–45), vol. 4, 455.

221. Puttenham, *Arte of English Poesie*, 144–45; Edmund Coote, *The English Schoole-Maister* (1596), 30.

222. Henry Cecil Wyld, *A History of Modern Colloquial English* (3rd imprn, 1925), 162–64.

223. Thomas Sheridan, *A Course of Lectures on Elocution* (1762), 30; J[ohn] Walker, *Hints for Improvement in the Art of Reading* (1783), 11; [Philip Withers], *Aristarchus, or the Principles of Composition* (2nd edn, [1789?]), 160–61. See, more generally, Olivia Smith, *The Politics of Language 1791–1819* (Oxford, 1984), chap. 1; Lawrence Klein, '"Politeness"

as Linguistic Ideology in Late Seventeenth- and Early Eighteenth-Century England', in *Towards a Standard English 1600–1800*, ed. Dieter Stein and Ingrid Tieken-Boon van Ostade (Berlin, 1994); Lynda Mugglestone, '*Talking Proper*' (Oxford, 1995), chap. 1; *The Development of Standard English 1300–1800*, ed. Laura Wright (Cambridge, 2000); Katie Wales, *Northern English* (Cambridge, 2006), 75–78, 93–94.

224. Hume, *Essays*, vol. 1, 192.

225. Gainsford, *Rich Cabinet*, fol. 20ᵛ; [Madeleine de Scudéry], *Conversations upon Several Subjects*, trans. Ferrand Spence (1683), vol. 1, 1; Marc Fumaroli, *Le Genre des genres littéraires français* (Oxford, 1992); Alain Montandon, 'Conversation', in *Dictionnaire raisonnée de la politesse*, 125–51; Bryson, *Courtesy to Civility*, 153–71.

226. Thomas Cooper, *Thesaurus Linguae Romanae & Britannicae* (1573), sig. S6; EEBO, s.v. 'urbanity'; Daniel Defoe, *Serious Reflections during the Life and Surprising Adventures of Robinson Crusoe* (1721), 91; Steven Shapin, *A Social History of Truth* (Chicago, IL, 1994), 114–19; Withington, *Society in Early Modern England*, 189–96, 219.

227. James Anderson, *The Bee, or Literary Weekly Intelligencer* (1791–93), vol. 1, 170; and Jon Mee, *Conversable Worlds* (Oxford, 2011), 71.

228. D. A., *Whole Art of Converse*; Nicolas Faret, *The Honest Man*, trans. E[dward] G[rimestone] (1632), 251–89; *The Works of the Learned Benjamin Whichcote* (Aberdeen, 1751), vol. 2, 405–8; Locke, *Some Thoughts concerning Education*, 200–203 (paras. 143–44); Peter Burke, *The Art of Conversation* (Cambridge, 1993), chap. 4.

229. [W. S.], *Cupids Schoole* (1632), sig. A2.

230. BL, Sloane MS 881 (Richard Baker, 'Honor discours'd of'), fol. 5; Adam Smyth, '*Profit and Delight*' (Detroit, MI, 2004), 25–26, 29–31; James Shirley, *The School of Complement* (1631).

231. Philomusus [John Gough?], *The Marrow of Complements* (1654), 106–7, 113–14; Bryson, *Courtesy to Civility*, 169–71. On written forms of conversing, see Katherine R. Larson, *Early Modern Women in Conversation* (Basingstoke, 2011), chap. 1.

232. [Marc Lescarbot], *Nova Francia*, trans. P. E[rondelle] (1609), 242.

233. John Laurence, *The Gentleman's Recreation* (1716), sig. A5ᵛ.

234. Hume, *Essays*, vol. 1, 236n.

235. De Scudéry, *Conversations upon Several Subjects*, 1–3; R[obert] L[ingard], *A Letter of Advice to a Young Gentleman leaving the University* (Dublin, 1670), 17.

236. Gerard Malynes, *Consuetudo, vel Lex Mercatoria* (1636), 141; Hume, *Treatise of Human Nature*, 381 (3. 3. 2); *The Complete Letters of Lady Mary Wortley Montagu*, ed. Robert Halsband (Oxford, 1966), vol. 2, 512.

237. Phil Withington, '"Tumbled into the Dirt"', *Journ. of Hist. Pragmatics* 12 (2011), and id., *Society in Early Modern England*, 189–95; Hume, *Enquiry concerning the Principles of Morals*, 67.

238. *The Theological Works of the Most Reverend John Sharp* (Oxford, 1829), vol. 3, 310.

239. *Spectator* 119 (17 July 1711), ed. Bond, vol. 1, 488.

240. Samuel Johnson, *A Dictionary of the English Language* (10th edn, 1810), sig. b2; *Letters from Mrs. Elizabeth Carter to Mrs. Montagu*, ed. Montagu Pennington (1817), vol. 1, 393; *Vulgaria of John Stanbridge*, 6, 7, 17.

241. Smith, *Theory of Moral Sentiments*, 209 (V. 2. 13); G. J. Barker-Benfield, *The Culture of Sensibility* (Chicago, IL, 1992), 290–92. Yet in private correspondence with his friend Earl Waldegrave, Lord Chesterfield could display a phallic bawdiness that would have been more appropriate for a member of the Hellfire Club than the author of the *Letters to his Son*; see Davison, 'Occasional Politeness and Gentlemen's Laughter', 936–38.

242. [Nicholas Breton], *Pasquils Mad-Cap and His Message* (1600), 2.

243. S. Arthur Strong, *A Catalogue of Letters and Other Historical Documents Exhibited in the Library at Welbeck* (1903), 213.

244. Richard Davies, *A Funerall Sermon preached . . . at the Buriall of Walter, Earl of Essex* (1577), sig. Eii; Sir Edward Walker, *Historical Discourses, upon Several Occasions* (1705),

221; *The Life of Edward, Earl of Clarendon . . . by Himself* (Oxford, 1857), vol. 1, 31; *Letters of Chesterfield*, vol. 1, 293–94; Letitia-Matilda Hawkins, *Anecdotes, Biographical Sketches and Memoirs* (1822), vol. 1, 106.

245. *Life of Edward, Earl of Clarendon*, vol. 1, 31; John Prince, *Danmonii Orientales Illustres* (Exeter, 1701), 505.

246. Godfrey Goodman, *The Fall of Man* (1616), 77; Geoffrey Ingle Soden, *Godfrey Goodman, Bishop of Gloucester* (1953), 282.

247. Della Casa, *Galateo* (1774), xiii–xvi.

248. Philip Dormer Stanhope, Fourth Earl of Chesterfield, *Characters (1778, 1845)* (Augustan Reprint Soc., Los Angeles, 1990), 12, 31, 49, 51, 54.

249. Bryson, *Courtesy to Civility*, chap. 7. See also *The Institucion of a Gentleman*, sig. Biiiiᵛ; Daniel Statt, 'The Case of the Mohocks', *SocHist* 20 (1995); Jason M. Kelly, 'Riots, Revelries, and Rumor', *JBS* 45 (2000); Helen Berry, 'Rethinking Politeness in Eighteenth-Century England', *TRHS*, 6th ser., 11 (2001); Carter, *Men and the Emergence of Polite Society*, 135–37; Tim Raylor, *Cavaliers, Clubs, and Literary Culture* (Newark, DE, 1994), 75–83; Margaret J. M. Ezell, *The Later Seventeenth Century* (*Oxford English Literary History*, vol. 5, Oxford, 2017), 159–68.

250. Alex Shepard, *The Meanings of Manhood in Early Modern England* (Oxford, 2003), chap. 4; ead., 'Student Violence in Early Modern Cambridge', in *Childhood and Violence in the Western Tradition*, ed. Laurence Brockliss and Heather Montgomery (Oxford, 2010).

251. *Diary of John Evelyn*, vol. 3, 480; William Mountague, *The Delights of Holland* (1696), 138–39.

252. For pornography, see James Grantham Turner, *Schooling Sex* (Oxford, 2003), Sarah Toulalan, *Imagining Sex* (Oxford, 2007), and Julie Peakman, *Mighty Lewd Books* (Basingstoke, 2003); for libertinism, see Faramerz Dabhoiwala, *The Origins of Sex* (Oxford, 2012); and for other forms of impoliteness, see Vic Gatrell, *City of Laughter* (2006), and Simon Dickie, *Cruelty and Laughter* (Chicago, IL, 2011).

2 Manners and the Social Order

1. *The Dictionary of Syr Thomas Eliot Knyght* (1538), fol. xxxᵛ; [Antoine de Courtin], *The Rules of Civility* (Eng. trans., 1671), 2–3 (plagiarized by Hannah Woolley, *The Gentlewomans Companion* (1675), 44).

2. On the decorum of funerals, see Ralph Houlbrooke, 'Civility and Civil Observances in the Early Modern English Funeral', in *Civil Histories*, ed. Peter Burke et al. (Oxford, 2000).

3. David Hume, *An Essay concerning the Principles of Morals*, ed. Tom L. Beauchamp (Oxford, 1998), 70 (section 8).

4. Jonathan Swift, *A Proposal for Correcting the English Tongue, Polite Conversation, Etc*, ed. Herbert Davis and Louis Landa (Oxford, 1937), 213.

5. *Desiderata Curiosa*, ed. Francis Peck (new edn, 1779), vol. 1, 49; *The Works of George Savile, Marquis of Halifax*, ed. Mark N. Brown (Oxford, 1989), vol. 3, 71. For similar injunctions, see, e.g., S[imon] R[obson], *The Choise of Change* (1585), sig. Iii; Thomas Gainsford, *The Rich Cabinet Furnished* (1616), fols. 99ᵛ–100; William Scott, *An Essay of Drapery* (1635), 94; *The Works of the Learned Benjamin Whichcote* (Aberdeen, 1751), vol. 2, 229.

6. J. A. Burrow, *Gesture and Looks in Medieval Narrative* (Cambridge, 2002), 17–38; Anna Bryson, *From Courtesy to Civility* (Oxford, 1998), 88–96; Keith Thomas, *The Ends of Life* (Oxford, 2009), 149–50.

7. Alec Ryrie, *Being Protestant in Reformation Britain* (Oxford, 2013), 205–8; [Thomas Plume], 'An Account of the Life and Death of the Author', in John Hacket, *A Century of Sermons* (1675), x; *Three Sermons preached by . . . Dr Richard Stuart, Dean of St Pauls* (2nd edn, 1658), 1; *Materials for the Life of Nicholas Ferrar*, ed. Lynette R. Muir and John A. White (Leeds, 1996), 131–32.

8. R[obert] C[leaver], *A Godlie Forme of Householde Gouernement* (1598), 278 (repeated verbatim in Robert Shelford, *Lectures or Readings upon the 6. Verse of the 22. Chapter of the Proverbs* (1602), 14); F[rancis] S[eager], *The Schoole of Vertue* (1557), sig. A1ᵛ.

9. Joyce Ransome, ' "Courtesy" at Little Gidding', *Seventeenth Century* 30 (2015), 43; William Ames, *Conscience with the Power and Cases thereof* (Eng. trans., n. pl., 1639), bk 2, 154; *Works of Whichcote*, vol. 3, 417.

10. *Manners and Meals in Olden Time*, ed. Frederick J. Furnivall (EETS, 1868), 240; *Remarks and Collections of Thomas Hearne*, ed. C. E. Doble et al. (Oxford Hist. Soc., 1885–1921), vol. 6, 215.

11. *The Warden's Punishment Book of All Souls College, Oxford, 1601–1850*, ed. Scott Mandelbrote and John H. R. Davis (Oxford Hist. Soc., 2013), 39.

12. Woolley, *Gentlewomans Companion*, 44; Scott, *Essay of Drapery*, 87; Nathaniel Parkhurst, *The Faithful and Diligent Christian Described and Exemplified* (1684), 64.

13. Thomas Reid, *Essays on the Intellectual Powers of the Human Mind* (1827), 385; *The Later Correspondence of George III*, ed. A. Aspinall (Cambridge, 1962–70), vol. 5, 657.

14. E. M. Forster, *The Longest Journey* (1907; 1947), 113–14.

15. *Works of Whichcote*, vol. 3, 413. The point was emphasized in Charles Vyse, *The New London Spelling-Book* (1778), 167.

16. Robert Ashley, *Of Honour*, ed. Virgil B. Heltzel (San Marino, CA, 1947), 69. Similarly, David Hume, *Essays, Moral, Political and Literary*, ed. T. H. Green and T. H. Grose (1898), vol. 1, 187.

17. Stephen Philpot, *An Essay on the Advantage of a Polite Education joined with a Learned One* (1747), 33.

18. *Works of Whichcote*, vol. 2, 229.

19. Susan Brigden, *Thomas Wyatt* (2012), 35.

20. S. R., *The Courte of Civill Courtesie* (1577), title page; Ashley, *Of Honour*, 69; *The English Theophrastus* (1702), 108.

21. *The Letters of the Earl of Chesterfield to His Son*, ed. Charles Strachey (1901), vol. 2, 235 (also vol. 1, 93, 196); James Boswell, *The Applause of the Jury*, ed. Irma S. Lustig and Frederick A. Pottle (1982), 14; Richard Wendorf, *Sir Joshua Reynolds* (Cambridge, MA, 1996).

22. *The Boke Named the Gouernour*, ed. Henry Herbert Stephen Croft (1880), vol. 2, 39–55; 'The History of King Richard the Thirde', in *The Complete Works of St Thomas More* (New Haven, CT, 1963–97), vol. 2, 5.

23. William Martyn, *Youth's Instruction* (1612), 79–81; James Spedding, *The Letters and the Life of Francis Bacon* (1861–1874), vol. 6, 211.

24. William Vaughan, *The Golden-Grove* (2nd edn, 1608), pt 3, chap. 16; Richard Brathwait, *The English Gentleman* (1630), 61; *The Diary of Sir Henry Slingsby, of Scriven*, ed. Daniel Parsons (1836), 226 (following William Cecil's much copied advice to his son, in *Desiderata Curiosa*, vol. 1, 49); Thomas Hobbes, *Leviathan*, ed. Noel Malcolm (Oxford, 2012), vol. 2, 134 (chap. 10).

25. John Cook, *The Vindication of the Professors & Profession of the Law* (1646), 6; Virgil B. Heltzel, 'Richard Earl of Carbery's Advice to His Son', *Huntington Lib. Bull.* 2 (1937), 79; *Original Letters Illustrative of English History*, ed. Henry Ellis (1st ser., 1825), vol. 3, 289; Lucas Gracian de Antisco, *Galateo Espagnol, or the Spanish Gallant*, trans. William Styles (1640), sig. A3ʳ⁻ᵛ.

26. Ronald Hutton, *Charles the Second* (Oxford, 1989), 447–48; [N(athaniel) W(aker)], *The Refin'd Courtier* (1663), sigs. A5ᵛ–6.

27. David Stevenson, 'The English Devil of Keeping State', in *People and Power in Scotland*, ed. Roger Mason and Norman Macdougall (Edinburgh, 1992).

28. John Aubrey, *Brief Lives*, ed. Kate Bennett (Oxford, 2015), vol. 1, 95.

29. John Norden, *The Surveyors Dialogue* (1607), 231; G[ervase] M[arkham], *The English Husbandman* (1635), vol. 1, 6.

30. John Robinson, *Essayes; or Observations* (2nd edn, 1638), 506.
31. Barnabe Rich, *Allarme to England* (1578), sig. Hi^v; John Aubrey, *'Brief Lives', Chiefly of Contemporaries*, ed. Andrew Clark (Oxford, 1898), vol. 2, 317.
32. 'Advice to his sons' (attributed to William, 5th Earl of Bedford and later 1st Duke, 1613–1700), in [E. Strutt], *Practical Wisdom* (1824), 244; *Wentworth Papers 1597–1628*, ed. J. P. Cooper (Camden, ser. 4, 12 (1973)), 12.
33. Sir Edward Walker, *Historical Discourses, upon Several Occasions* (1705), 223; Philpot, *Essay on the Advantage of a Polite Education*, 244.
34. Thomas Wright, *The Passions of the Minde in Generall* (1601), 210–11; Simon Daines, *Orthoepia Anglicana* (1640), 85; J. Gailhard, *The Compleat Gentleman* (1678), vol. 2, 20, 27, 112–13, 124; Gilbert Burnet, *A Sermon Preach'd before the Queen* (1694), 17.
35. E.g., John Le Neve, *Monumenta Anglicana, 1600–1649* (1719), 108; id., *Monumenta Anglicana, 1650–1679* (1718), 41, 153, 156; id., *Monumenta Anglicana, 1650–1718* (1719), 56, 58, 227, 259; id., *Monumenta Anglicana, 1700–1715* (1719), 27, 63, 149, 173, 195, 246; John Wilford, *Memorials and Characters* (1741), 22, 296, 312, 494, 514; F. E. Hutchinson and Sir Edmund Craster, *Monumental Inscriptions in All Souls College Oxford* (2nd edn, by M. A. Screech, Oxford, 1997), 13, 16, 33, 35, 40, 43–44, 45, 48; Sir Thomas Phillipps, *Monumental Inscriptions of Wiltshire*, ed. Peter Sherlock (Wilts. Rec. Soc., 2000), 18, 120, 184, 194, 230, 252, 266, 351.
36. Lucy Hutchinson, *Memoirs of the Life of Colonel Hutchinson*, ed. James Sutherland (1973), 12; Samuel Willes, *A Sermon Preach'd at the Funeral of the Right Honble the Lady Mary . . . Jolife* (1679), 32.
37. Bernard Mandeville, *The Fable of the Bees*, ed. F. B. Kaye (Oxford, 1924), vol. 2, 291–92; William Craig, in *The Mirror* 26 (24 Apr. 1779), in *The British Essayists*, ed. Robert Lynam et al. (1827), vol. 24, 102.
38. Hume, *Essays*, vol. 1, 193; Gailhard, *Compleat Gentleman*, vol. 2, 66.
39. John Locke, *Some Thoughts concerning Education*, ed. John W. and Jean S. Yolton (Oxford, 1989), 200 (para. 143) (my italics).
40. Timothy Nourse, *Campania Foelix* (1700), 15.
41. Craig, in *The Mirror* 26, in *British Essayists*, vol. 24, 102.
42. Friedrich Nietzsche, *The Gay Science*, trans. Walter Kaufmann (New York, 1974), 107–8 (bk 1, sect. 40).
43. Adam Smith, *The Theory of Moral Sentiments*, ed. D. D. Raphael and A. L. Macfie (Oxford, 1976), 54.
44. Thomas Churchyard, *A Sparke of Frendship and Warme Goodwill* (1588), sig. Ci^v; Shelford, *Lectures or Readings upon Proverbs*, 17; S. Arthur Strong, *A Catalogue of Letters and Other Historical Documents Exhibited in the Library at Welbeck* (1903), 210–13; *Letters of Chesterfield*, vol. 2, 218; Gailhard, *Compleat Gentleman*, vol. 1, 87.
45. Sir Thomas Smith, *A Discourse of the Commonweal of the Realm of England*, ed. Mary Dewar (Charlottesville, VA, 1969), 62.
46. Richard Carew, *The Survey of Cornwall*, ed. John Chynoweth et al. (Devon and Cornwall Rec. Soc., 2004), fol. 66^v.
47. *Stuart Royal Proclamations*, ed. James F. Larkin and Paul L. Hughes (Oxford, 1973–83), vol. 1, 342.
48. *The Practical Works of . . . Richard Baxter* (1707), vol. 1, 231, 825.
49. Geoffrey F. Nuttall, *Calendar of the Correspondence of Philip Doddridge DD (1702–51)* (Northants. Rec. Soc., 1979), 12.
50. On the importance of education and reading as sources of conversational topics, see Robert Codrington, *The Second Part of Youths Behaviour* (1664), 2–3, and Woolley, *Gentlewoman's Companion*, 7.
51. F. J. M. Korsten, *Roger North (1651–1734)* (Amsterdam, 1981), 112.
52. Bernard Capp, *Cromwell's Navy* (Oxford, 1989), 219; N. A. M. Rodger, 'Honour and Duty at Sea, 1660–1815', *HistRes* 75 (2002), 433–35; William Mountague, *The Delights*

of Holland (1696), 8; William Dampier, *A New Voyage round the World* (1697), sig. A3ᵛ; [George Colman and Bonnel Thornton], *The Connoisseur* 84 (4 Sept. 1755), in *British Essayists*, vol. 19, 52–55.

53. *Diaries of William Johnston Temple 1780–1796*, ed. Lewis Bettany (Oxford, 1929), 134.
54. Peter France, *Politeness and Its Discontents* (Cambridge, 1992), 64; Chesterfield, in *The World* 148 (30 Oct. 1755), in *British Essayists*, vol. 17, 182.
55. Levine Lemnie, *The Touchstone of Complexions*, trans. T[homas] N[ewton] (1576), fol. 16ᵛ (probably echoing the report in Ioannes Boemus, *Omnium Gentium Mores* (1521); see Ed. Aston's translation, *The Manners, Lawes, and Customes of All Nations* (1611), 385); Giovanni Botero, *Relations of the Most Famous Kingdomes and Common-Wealths Throughout the World*, ed. R[obert] J[ohnson] (1630), 79 (an interpolation by Johnson).
56. John Norden, *Speculi Britanniae Pars: a Topographical and Historical Description of Cornwall* (1728), 27. His contemporary Richard Carew gave a more favourable account in his *Survey of Cornwall*, fols. 58ᵛ–62ᵛ.
57. R[obert] C[rofts], *The Way to Happinesse on Earth* (1641), 5.
58. Edward Chamberlayne, *Angliae Notitia* (20th edn, 1702), 318–19.
59. *The Works of Michael Drayton*, ed. J. William Hebel (Oxford, 1961), vol. 3, 208; *Memoirs of Sir Benjamin Rudyerd*, ed. James Alexander Manning (1841), 135–36; [Henry Whitfield], *Strength out of Weaknesse* (1652), 19.
60. John Josselyn, *An Account of Two Voyages to New-England* (1674), 124–25.
61. 'Of rusticitie or clownishnesse', in *Theophrastus Characters*, in J[ohn] Healey, *Epictetus Manuall* (1616), 15–18 (the first English translation); E. de Saint Denis, 'Evolution sémantique de "urbanus-urbanitas"', *Latomus* 3 (1939); Michael Richter, '*Urbanitas-rusticitas*', in *The Church in Town and Countryside*, ed. Derek Baker (Ecclesiastical Hist. Soc., Oxford, 1979).
62. Richard Rogers, *A Commentary upon the Whole Booke of Judges* (1615), 445; John Barston, *The Safegarde of Societie* (1576), sig. B1; James Turner, *The Politics of Landscape* (Oxford, 1979), 173–77.
63. George Snell, *The Right Teaching of Useful Knowledg* (2nd edn, 1651), 61; Sir William Temple, *Miscellanea* (1680), 52.
64. *Cyuile and Uncyuile Life* (1579), sigs. Miiiᵛ, Kiiᵛ, Niᵛ.
65. *A Glossary of Words Used in Holderness*, ed. Frederick Ross et al. (Eng. Dialect Soc., 1887), 25, 48. 'Gubbins' was the contemptuous name given to the members of a lawless and mannerless community living near Brent Tor, on the edge of Dartmoor. First mentioned in a poem by William Browne of Tavistock (see Thomas Westcote, *Devon in MDCXXX*, ed. George Oliver and Pitman Jones (Exeter, 1845), 360), they were described by Thomas Fuller, *The History of the Worthies of England*, ed. P. Austin Nuttall (1840), vol. 1, 398–99. 'Gubbins' were worthless fish parings, but the use of the word in this context may have been derived from Friedrich Dedekind's *Grobianus* (Frankfurt, 1549), an influential caricature of rudeness and incivility, of which an English translation by R. F. was published in 1605 as *The Schoole of Slovenrie* and edited by Ernst Rühl in his *Grobianus in England* (*Palaestra* 38) (Berlin, 1908); see Bryson, *Courtesy to Civility*, 40–41, 102, 196. The children's books by the American author Frank Gelett Burgess (1866–1951) on bad manners to be avoided, e.g., *Goops and How to Be Them* (1900), seem a likely echo of Grobianus. For Hogs Norton (from Hook Norton, Oxon), see Fuller, *Worthies*, vol. 3, 5, and Morris Palmer Tilley, *A Dictionary of the Proverbs in England in the Sixteenth and Seventeenth Centuries* (Ann Arbor, MI, 1950), 313.
66. *Dobsons Drie Bobbes*, ed. E. A. Horsman (1955), 13–14.
67. Randle Holme, *The Academy of Armory* (Chester, 1688), vol. 3, 72. For examples of the use of such terms, see *OED* and EEBO.
68. Angel Day, *The English Secretorie* (1586), 39; Andrew Boorde, *The Fyrst Boke of the Introduction of Knowledge*, ed. F. J. Furnivall (EETS, 1870), 119; *Wilson's Arte of Rhetorique 1560*, ed. G. H. Mair (Oxford, 1909), 13; Bodl., MS Selden supra 108,

fol. 54 (Thomas Greaves, exiled from his Cambridge college in 1648 to a Lincolnshire rectory, complaining that there was no place there for literature or the arts, unless of a rustic or very sordid kind: '*nec literis, nec artibus quisquam hic locus nisi rusticanis, atque sordidissimis*').

69. BL, Lansdowne MS 25, fol. 63ᵛ (John Aylmer to Lord Burghley).
70. *The Lives of the Rt. Hon. Francis North, Baron Guilford, the Hon. Sir Dudley North, and the Hon. and Rev. Dr John North*, ed. Augustus Jessopp (1890), vol. 3, 130.
71. Kenneth Woodbridge, *Landscape and Antiquity* (Oxford, 1970), 166; *The Records of King Edward's School, Birmingham*, ed. William Fowler Carter et al. (Dugdale Soc., 1924–74), vol. 6, 57; William Hutton, *An History of Birmingham* (3rd edn, Birmingham, 1795), 90–91.
72. *Letters of Alexander Pope*, ed. John Butt (World's Classics, 1960), 329.
73. Fuller, *Worthies*, vol. 2, 487; *Reliquiae Baxterianae*, ed. Matthew Sylvester (1696), vol. 1, 89.
74. *The Letters of Horace Walpole*, ed. Mrs Paget Toynbee (Oxford, 1903–18), vol. 5, 43–44 (31 Mar. 1761); John Spranger, *A Proposal or Plan for an Act of Parliament for the Better Paving, Lighting and Cleansing the Streets* (1754), sig. a4ᵛ; Henry Home, Lord Kames, *Elements of Criticism* (6th edn, 1785), vol. 2, 485; Hutton, *History of Birmingham*, 296.
75. R. H. Sweet, 'Topographies of Politeness', *TRHS*, 6th ser., 12 (2002); Peter Borsay, *The English Urban Renaissance* (Oxford, 1989), chap. 10; id., 'Politeness and Elegance', in *Eighteenth-Century York*, ed. Mark Hallett and Jane Rendall (York, 2003); Amanda Vickery, *The Gentleman's Daughter* (New Haven, CT, 1998), esp. chaps. 5–7; Shani d'Cruze, *A Pleasing Prospect* (Hatfield, 2008), chap. 5.
76. *Boswell's Life of Johnson*, ed. G. Birkbeck Hill, rev. L. F. Powell (Oxford, 1934–50), vol. 3, 77; Peter Clark, *British Clubs and Societies 1580–1800* (Oxford, 2000).
77. George Puttenham, *The Arte of English Poesie*, ed. Gladys Doidge Willcock and Alice Walker (Cambridge, 1936), 144; Sir John Cullum, *The History and Antiquities of Hawsted* (1784), 220. Robert Whittington translated Erasmus's *rurestris* (rustic) as 'uplandish'; *De Civilitate Morum Puerilium* (1532), sig. D3.
78. G. J. Williams, *Iolo Morgannwg* (Cardiff, 1926), 25.
79. See, e.g., Vickery, *Gentleman's Daughter*, chap. 6.
80. Hutton, *History of Birmingham*, 91; Cullum, *History and Antiquities of Hawsted*, 220n.
81. *The Agrarian History of England and Wales*, vol. 4, ed. Joan Thirsk (Cambridge, 1967), 111, 411–12; Keith Thomas, *Man and the Natural World* (1983), 194–95.
82. (Privy Council) *Orders and Directions* (1630), sig. G4ᵛ; and see Patricia Fumerton, *Unsettled* (Chicago, IL, 2006).
83. T. S. Willan, *River Navigation in England 1600–1750* (1936), 106–7.
84. Bodl., MS Rawlinson B.323, fol. 99ᵛ (Gloucestershire collections of Richard Parsons (d. 1711)).
85. *Proceedings Principally in the County of Kent*, ed. Lambert B. Larking (Camden Soc., 1862), 154; William Camden, *Britain, or a Chorographicall Description*, trans. Philemon Holland (1637), 491 ('uncivil' was Philemon Holland's translation of Camden's '*incultus*'; in 1695 Edmund Gibson translated it as 'uncivilized'); *The Life of Edward, Earl of Clarendon ... by Himself* (Oxford, 1857), vol. 1, 53; William Dugdale, *The History of Imbanking and Drayning of Divers Fenns and Marshes* (1662), 171; Nathanael Carpenter, *Geographie Delineated Forth in Two Bookes* (2nd edn, Oxford, 1635), 24.
86. *The Somersetshire Quarterly Meeting of the Society of Friends*, ed. Stephen C. Marland (Somerset Rec. Soc., 1978), 4; J. W. Gough, *The Mines of Mendip* (rev. edn, Newton Abbot, 1967), 224.
87. S[tephen] P[rimatt], *The City and Country Purchaser and Builder* (2nd edn by William Leybourne, 1680), 32; Andy Wood, *The Politics of Social Conflict* (Cambridge, 1999), 3.
88. J. V. Beckett, 'Elizabeth Montagu', *Huntington Lib. Qtly* 49 (1986), 157.
89. G. R. Lewis, *The Stannaries* (1908; Truro, 1965), 217.

90. See, e.g., David Levine and Keith Wrightson, *The Making of an Industrial Society* (Oxford, 1991), 296–308, 430–32 (on the miners of Tyneside).

91. David Marcombe, '"A Rude and Heady People"', in *The Last Principality*, ed. Marcombe (Nottingham, 1987), 117, 121; Puttenham, *Arte of English Poesie*, 144.

92. Diarmaid MacCulloch, *Thomas Cranmer* (New Haven, CT, 1996), 178; *Correspondence of Matthew Parker*, ed. John Bruce and Thomas Thomason Perowne (Parker Soc., Cambridge, 1853), 123; Steven G. Ellis, *Tudor Frontiers and Noble Power* (Oxford, 1995), 56–68, 260, and id., 'Civilizing Northumberland', *Journ. of Hist. Sociology* 12 (1999).

93. T. F., *Newes from the North* (1585), sig. Lii^{r-v}.

94. *The Earl of Strafforde's Letters and Despatches*, ed. William Knowler (1739), vol. 1, 51; Plume, in Hacket, *Century of Sermons*, iii.

95. J. M. Fewster, *The Keelmen of Tyneside* (Woodbridge, 2011), 100–101.

96. James Pilkington, A *View of the Present State of Derbyshire* (Derby, 1789), vol. 2, 57–59.

97. Markku Peltonen, *Classical Humanism and Republicanism in English Political Thought* (Cambridge, 1995), 60–64; Jonathan Barry, 'Civility and Civic Culture in Early Modern England', in *Civil Histories*, ed. Burke et al.

98. C. W. Brooks, review of Lawrence Stone and Jeanne Fawtier Stone, *An Open Elite?*, in *EHR* 101 (1986), 179; John Brewer, 'Commercialization and Politics', in Neil McKendrick et al., *The Birth of a Consumer Society* (1982), 214–15; Helen Berry, 'Polite Consumption', *TRHS*, 6th ser., 12 (2002), 387–89.

99. Philip E. Jones, *The Butchers of London* (1976), 118–19.

100. John Saltmarsh, *The Practice of Policie in a Christian Life* (1638), 29; Daniel Defoe, *The Complete English Tradesman* (1745; Oxford, 1841), vol. 1, 62; Scott, *Essay of Drapery*, 86; Joseph Collyer, *The Parent's and Guardian's Directory* (1725–27), 45, 110–11, 158, 159; Lawrence E. Klein, 'Politeness for Plebes', in *The Consumption of Culture 1600–1800*, ed. Ann Bermingham and John Brewer (1975), 372; Joel Mokyr, *The Enlightened Economy* (New Haven, CT, 2009), 370–74.

101. *Reliquiae Baxterianae*, vol. 1, 89; *The Travels through England of Dr Richard Pococke*, ed. James Joel Cartwright (Camden Soc., 1888–89), vol. 1, 8.

102. [Béat Louis de Muralt], *Letters describing the Character and Customs of the English and French Nations* (Eng. trans., 1726), 83.

103. Mandeville, *Fable of the Bees*, vol. 1, 349–52; R. Campbell, *The London Tradesman* (1747; Newton Abbot, 1969), 197.

104. R. S. Fitton and A. P. Wadsworth, *The Strutts and the Arkwrights 1758–1830* (Manchester, 1958), 145.

105. Richard Warner, *A Walk through Wales* (Bath, 1798), 9–10, cit. Paul Langford, 'The Uses of Eighteenth-Century Politeness', *TRHS*, 6th ser., 12 (2002), 320.

106. B[ernard] M[andeville], *Free Thoughts on Religion, the Church and National Happiness* (1720), 273; Hutton, *History of Birmingham*, 398; Paul Langford, *Englishness Identified* (Oxford, 2000), 97.

107. CH. ED. [Christian Erndtel], *The Relation of a Journey into England and Holland, in the years 1706, and 1707* (Eng. trans., 1711), 39.

108. Clark, *British Clubs and Societies*, is the authoritative account.

109. *Ben Jonson*, ed. C. H. Herford and Percy and Evelyn Simpson (Oxford, 1925–1947), vol. 11, 360. On Jacobean clubs, see Michelle O'Callaghan, *The English Wits* (Cambridge, 2007), and the chapters by her and by Stella Achilleos, in *A Pleasing Sinne*, ed. Adam Smyth (Cambridge, 2004) and in *'Lords of Wine and Oile'*, ed. Ruth Connolly and Tom Cain (Oxford, 2011).

110. *Polydore Vergil's English History*, ed. and trans. Sir Henry Ellis (Camden Soc., 1846), vol. 1, 24; Carew, *Survey of Cornwall*, fol. 67^v; Lorna Weatherill, *Consumer Behaviour and Material Culture in Britain 1660–1760* (1988), 151–59; Carole Shammas, *The*

Pre-Industrial Consumer in England and America (Oxford, 1990), chap. 6; Mark Overton et al., *Production and Consumption in English Households, 1600–1750* (2004), 90–98; Robert Applebaum, *Aguecheek's Beef, Belch, Hiccup, and Other Gastronomic Interjections* (Chicago, IL, 2006), 42, 84, 201, 207.

111. Stephen Mennell, *All Manners of Food* (Oxford, 1985), 92; Fynes Moryson, *An Itinerary* (Glasgow, 1907–8), vol. 4, 173; Robert Burton, *The Anatomy of Melancholy*, ed. Thomas C. Faulkner et al. (Oxford, 1989–2000), vol. 2, 26 (2. 2. 1. 2); Felicity Heal, *Hospitality in Early Modern England* (Oxford, 1990), chap. 9.

112. *Coffee Houses Vindicated* (1675), 5, cited by Steve Pincus, '"Coffee Politicians Does Create"', *JMH* 67 (1995); Jennifer Richards, 'Health, Intoxication, and Civil Conversation in Renaissance England', in *Cultures of Intoxication*, ed. Phil Withington and Angela McShane (*P&P*, supp. 9, 2014); Jordan Goodman, 'Excitantia', and Woodruff D. Smith, 'From Coffeehouse to Parlour', in *Consuming Passions*, ed. Jordan Goodman et al. (2nd edn, Abingdon, 2007).

113. Hutchinson, *Life of Colonel Hutchinson*, 70.

114. R[obson], *The Choise of Change*, sig. Giv^v.

115. *Reliquiae Baxterianae*, vol. 1, 89.

116. See, e.g., Henry Fielding, *The Covent Garden Journal*, ed. Bertrand A. Goldgar (Oxford, 1988), xlii– xliii, 94–95, 174–75.

117. Donna T. Andrew, 'The Code of Honour and Its Critics', *SocHist* 5 (1980); Phil Withington, *The Politics of Commonwealth* (Cambridge, 2005), 176; Margaret R. Hunt, *The Middling Sort* (Berkeley, CA, 1996); Hannah Barker, 'Soul, Purse and Family', *SocHist* 33 (2008).

118. William Shakespeare, *Henry IV, Part I* (ca. 1597), act 3, scene 1, lines 246–55.

119. T. L. Kington Oliphant, *The New English* (1886), vol. 2, 232.

120. James Nelson, *An Essay on the Government of Children* (1753), 306; and see Vickery, *Gentleman's Daughter*, chap. 1.

121. Richard Whately, *Elements of Rhetoric* (2nd edn, Oxford, 1828), 179n–180n.

122. A seventeenth-century satirist coarsely remarked that it would take a country wench a year 'before she'll know how to shite upon a house of office'; A. Marsh, *The Confessions of the New Married Couple* (1683), 131. For the facilities at Queenhithe, see Dorian Gerhold, *London Plotted* (London Topographical Soc., 2016), 211–12.

123. David Cressy, 'Saltpetre, State Security and Vexation in Early Modern England', *P&P* 212 (2011), 94; *Commons Debates 1628*, ed. Robert C. Johnson et al. (New Haven, CT, 1977–83), vol. 4, 350.

124. Giacomo Casanova, *History of My Life*, trans. Willard R. Trask (vols. 9 and 10, 1970), 251.

125. Martin Ingram, 'Sexual Manners', and Sara Mendelson, 'The Civility of Women in Seventeenth-Century England', in *Civil Histories*, ed. Burke et al.

126. [Francis Grose], *Lexicon Balatronicum* (1811), sig. M3.

127. Godfrey Goodman, *The Fall of Man* (1616), 5, 51; Archibald Alison, *Essays on the Nature and Principles of Taste* (4th edn, Edinburgh, 1815), vol. 2, 393–94.

128. John Weaver, *An Essay towards an History of Dancing* (1712), 23; J[ohn] B[ulwer], *Chirologia* (1644), vol. 2, 117.

129. W[illiam] K[empe], *The Education of Children in Learning* (1588), sig. E3^v; Margaret Cavendish, Duchess of Newcastle, *The Life of William Cavendish, Duke of Newcastle*, ed. C. H. Firth (n.d.), 157; BL, Addl. MS 28, 531 (James Boevey, 'The Art of Building a Man', fol. 17; Brian W. Hill, *Robert Harley* (New Haven, CT, 1988), 4; Bryson, *Courtesy to Civility*, 133–34.

130. William Darrell, *The Gentleman Instructed* (11th edn, 1738), 16.

131. *The Voyages and Colonising Enterprises of Sir Humphrey Gilbert*, ed. David Beers Quinn (Hakluyt Soc., 1940), vol. 2, 361; Jenny Uglow, *A Gambling Man* (2009), 56; Antonio Gramsci, *Il Risorgimento* (Turin, 1949), 199–200.

132. W. P., *Foure Great Lyers* (1585), sig. E6ᵛ; Gervase Markham, *Cavelarice, or the English Horseman* (1607), bk 5, 18–19.

133. Roderick Floud, Kenneth Wachter and Annabel Gregory, *Height, Health and History* (Cambridge, 1990), 1–3, and chap. 5; other references in Floud, 'The Dimensions of Inequality', *Contemporary British History* 16 (2002), and id. et al., *The Changing Body* (Cambridge, 2011), 34, 135, 229–30; Louis Simond, *Journal of a Tour and Residence in Great Britain during the Years 1810 and 1811* (2nd edn, Edinburgh, 1817), vol. 1, 30–31, 266; Matthew McCormack, 'Tall Histories', *TRHS*, 6th ser., 26 (2016), 87–89.

134. David Hume, *A Treatise of Human Nature*, ed. David Fate Norton and Mary J. Norton (Oxford, 2000), 259 (2. 3. 1).

135. George Owen of Henllys, *The Description of Pembrokeshire* (1603), ed. Dillwyn Miles (Llandysul, 1994), 48.

136. John Locke, *Some Thoughts on the Conduct of the Understanding in the Search of Truth* (Glasgow, 1754), 21.

137. Dennis Smith, *Norbert Elias and Modern Social Theory* (2002), 163.

138. Joseph Bettey, '"Ancient Custom Time Out of Mind"', *Antiquaries Journ.* 89 (2009), 316; Jeremy Boulton, 'Going on the Parish', and Pamela Sharpe, '"The Bowels of Compassion"', in *Chronicling Poverty*, ed. Tim Hitchcock et al. (Basingstoke, 1997), 32–33, 100–103; *Warwick County Records*, ed. S. C. Ratcliff and H. C. Johnson (Warwick, 1936), vol. 2, 85.

139. Steve Hindle, *On the Parish?* (Oxford, 2004), 161, 164; id., 'Civility, Honesty and the Identification of the Deserving Poor', in *Identity and Agency in England, 1500–1800*, ed. Henry French and Jonathan Barry (Basingstoke, 2004); K. D. M. Snell, *Parish and Belonging* (Cambridge, 2006), 297; Jonathan Healey, *The First Century of Welfare* (Woodbridge, 2014), 119–20. On 'honesty' see Alexandra Shepard, *Meanings of Manhood in Early Modern England* (Oxford, 2003), 73–74, 87, 248; and ead., 'Honesty, Wealth and Gender in Early Modern England', in *Identity and Agency*, ed. French and Barry.

140. Alexandra Shepard, *Accounting for Oneself* (Oxford, 2015), esp. 180–90; Mark Hailwood, *Alehouses and Good Fellowship in Early Modern England* (Woodbridge, 2014), 49, 51.

141. Bernard Capp, 'The Double Standard Revisited', *P&P* 162 (1999). On the sixteenth- and seventeenth-century language of insult, see Laura Gowing, *Domestic Dangers* (Oxford, 1996), chaps. 3 and 4; Bernard Capp, *When Gossips Meet* (Oxford, 2003), esp. 189–204, 230–32, 252–63; Shepard, *Meanings of Manhood in Early Modern England*, index, s.v. 'defamation', 'sexual insult' and 'verbal abuse'; Fiona Williamson, *Social Relations and Urban Space* (Woodbridge, 2014), 134–37; Martin Ingram, *Carnal Knowledge* (Cambridge, 2017), 69–75, 184–86, 194.

142. Mendelson, 'Civility of Women'; Laura Gowing, *Common Bodies* (New Haven, CT, 2003), 96, 103, 104; David M. Turner, *Fashioning Adultery* (Cambridge, 2002), 49, 78–92, 195–96; and, especially, Ingram, 'Sexual Manners'.

143. Penelope J. Corfield, 'Walking the Streets', *Journ. of Urban History* 16 (1990); Robert B. Shoemaker, *The London Mob* (2004), 174–75; Tim Reinke-Williams, *Women, Work and Sociability in Early Modern London* (Basingstoke, 2014), 6, 127, 150–56.

144. Ingram, 'Sexual Manners', 99; Laura Gowing, *Domestic Dangers* (Oxford, 1996), 73; Christopher Haigh, *The Plain Man's Pathways to Heaven* (Oxford, 2007), chap. 8.

145. John Rushworth, *Historical Collections* (1721), vol. 2, 88; Ingram, 'Sexual Manners', 100–102; Paul Griffiths, *Lost Londons* (Cambridge, 2008), 43.

146. Capp, *When Gossips Meet*, 88, 190, 219, 220, 230, 257.

147. *Calendar of Wynn (of Gwydir) Papers 1515–1690* (Aberystwyth, 1926), 68.

148. Joseph Moxon, *Mechanick Exercises on the whole Art of Printing (1683–4)*, ed. Herbert Davis and Harry Carter (2nd edn, 1962; New York, 1978), 323–27; Adrian Johns, *The Nature of the Book* (Chicago, IL, 1998), 188, 197; Philip J. Stern, *The Company-State* (Oxford, 2011), 36.

149. Thomas Churchyard, *The Worthines of Wales* (1587; 1776), vi, vii, 3, 4, 89–90; *Records of Early English Drama: Norwich 1540–1642*, ed. David Galloway (Toronto, 1984), 294–95; Thomas Tusser, *Five Hundreth Points of Good Husbandry* (1573), fol. 7.

150. Fynes Moryson, *Shakespeare's Europe*, ed. Charles Hughes (2nd edn, New York, 1967), 474; William Brenchley Rye, *England as Seen by Foreigners in the Days of Elizabeth and James the First* (1865), 7, 186; [Thomas] P[ritchard], *The Schoole of Honest and Vertuous Lyfe* (1579), 40; *Two Italian Accounts of Tudor England*, trans. C. W. Malfatti (Barcelona, 1953), 36.

151. *Stuart Royal Proclamations*, vol. 1, 508–11, 588–90; Mary Carleton, *The Case of Madam Mary Carleton* (1663), 128–29; D. A., *The Whole Art of Converse* (1683), 119–20; *The Writings of John Evelyn*, ed. Guy de la Bedoyère (Woodbridge, 1985), 78; *M. Misson's Memoirs and Observations in his Travels over England*, trans. [John] Ezell (1719), 310.

152. Langford, *Englishness Identified*, 221–25.

153. Henry Fielding, *The Journal of a Voyage to Lisbon*, ed. Martin C. Battestin (Oxford, 2008), 569.

154. Richard Gough, *Antiquities and Memoirs of the Parish of Myddle* (Shrewsbury, 1875), 56, 113, 115, 122, 135, 139, 146, 147, 150.

155. Gainsford, *The Rich Cabinet Furnished*, fol. 29; Ingram, 'Sexual Manners', 102–3; Capp, *When Gossips Meet*, 261; Reinke-Williams, *Women, Work and Sociability*, 113–14, 130–31.

156. Ingram, 'Sexual Manners', 108.

157. Tim Hitchcock and Robert Shoemaker, *London Lives* (Cambridge, 2015), 267.

158. Robert Roberts, *The Classic Slum* (Harmondsworth, 1973), 14–19. See also R. Q. Gray, *The Labour Aristocracy in Victorian Edinburgh* (Oxford, 1976), chap. 7 ('The Meaning of Respectability'); J. M. Golby and A. W. Purdue, *The Civilisation of the Crowd* (1984), 185–87; F. M. L. Thompson, *The Rise of Respectable Society* (1988), 198–204.

159. Ames, *Conscience*, bk 4, 267; M. Dorothy George, *London Life in the XVIIIth Century* (1925), 276–77; Ian McCalman, *Radical Underworld* (Cambridge, 1988), 26–29; Anna Clark, *The Struggle for the Breeches* (1995), 33.

160. Thomas, *Ends of Life*, 164–65; Carolyn Steedman, *An Everyday Life of the English Working Class* (Cambridge, 2013), 111–12 (and see 93–94, 108–9); Clark, *Struggle for the Breeches*, 35–36, 43, 51, 54, 61, 248.

161. David A. Postles, *Social Proprieties* (Washington, DC, 2006), 2.

162. Peter Chamberlen, *The Poore Mans Advocate* (1649), 9; Mandeville, *Fable of the Bees*, vol. 1, 269–70.

163. John St John, *Observations on the Land Revenue of the Crown* (1787), appendix, 4, 12, 14.

164. Andy Wood, *The Memory of the People* (Cambridge, 2013), 343.

165. Jo[hn] Streater, *A Glympse of that Jewel, Judicial, Just, Preserving Libertie* (1653), 15; Samuel Hartlib, *Londons Charitie* (1648), 5; [Daniel Defoe], *Some Considerations on the Reasonableness and Necessity of Encreasing and Encouraging the Seamen* (1728), 44.

166. John Brinsley, *A Consolation for our Grammar Schooles* (1622), sig. *3ᵛ; John Gauden, *Hieraspistes* (1653), 400; Nicholas Carlisle, *A Concise Description of the Endowed Grammar Schools* (1818), vol. 1, 809.

167. Carlisle, *Concise Description*, vol. 1, 420; John Locke, *Some Thoughts concerning Education*, ed. John W. and Jean S. Yolton (Oxford, 1989), 208.

168. Thomas Killigrew, *The Prisoners and Claracilla* (1641), sig. A2ᵛ (and Edmund Spenser, *The Faerie Queene* (1596), bk 6, canto 1, st. 1); John Stow, *A Survey of London*, ed. Charles Lethbridge Kingsford (Oxford, 1908), vol. 2, 211.

169. *Desiderata Curiosa*, vol. 2, 444; D. A., *Whole Art of Converse*, sig. A2ᵛ.

170. R. O. Bucholz, *The Augustan Court* (Stanford, CA, 1993), chap. 7; Joanna Marschner, *Queen Caroline* (New Haven, CT, 2014), 19; Chesterfield, in *The World* 148 (30 Oct. 1755), in *British Essayists*, ed. Lynam, vol. 17, 182; David Scott, *Leviathan* (2013), 272–73.

171. David Starkey, 'The Court', *Journal of the Warburg and Courtauld Institutes* 45 (1982); John Aubrey, *Brief Lives and Other Selected Writings*, ed. Anthony Powell (1949), 9; David Norbrook, '"Words more than civil"', in *Early Modern Civil Discourses*, ed. Jennifer Richards (Basingstoke, 2003), 71; Jonathan Swift, 'Hints on good manners', in *A Proposal for Correcting the English Tongue*, 221.

172. Thomas Milles, *The Catalogue of Honor* (1610), 16 (translating Robert Glover, *Nobilitas Politica vel Civilis* (1608)).

173. [Richard Overton], *The Araignement of Mr Persecution* (1645), 33; Cavendish, *Life of William Cavendish*, 51.

174. *Cyvile and Uncyvile Life*, sig. Hiv^v; Gerard Leigh, *The Accedens of Armory* (3rd edn, 1612), 216; Botero, *Relations of the Most Famous Kingdomes*, 75; Mark Girouard, *Life in the English Country House* (New Haven, CT, 1978), 7–8.

175. S. J. Watts with Susan J. Watts, *From Border to Middle Shire* (Leicester, 1975), 192; *HMC, Cowper*, vol. 2, 51.

176. Boemus, *Manners, Lawes and Customes of All Nations*, 450 (Aston's interpolation).

177. David Coke and Alan Borg, *Vauxhall Gardens* (New Haven, CT, 2011), 41.

178. Norbert Elias, *On the Process of Civilisation*, trans. Edmund Jephcott (*Collected Works of Norbert Elias*, Dublin, 2006–14, vol. 3), 195.

179. Daniel E. Thiery, *Polluting the Sacred* (Leiden, 2009).

180. Watts, *From Border to Middle Shire*, 87.

181. See, e.g., *The Workes of . . . M[aster] W[illiam] Perkins* (Cambridge, 1608–31), vol. 1, 50, 634; vol. 2, 150–52; Shelford, *Lectures or Readings upon Proverbs*, 14–17; Richard Rogers, *Seven Treatises* (1603), 168–69; William Gouge, *Of Domesticall Duties, Eight Treatises* (3rd edn, 1634), 538–39; *A Compleat Collection of the Works of . . . John Kettlewell* (1719), vol. 1, 123, 315; Bejan, *Mere Civility*, 40–41.

182. John Jackson, *The True Evangelical Temper* (1641), 5–6.

183. 'A Briefe Narrative of the Life and Death of Mr Thomas Hall' (Dr Williams' Library, London, MS 61.1), 53; and see Denise Thomas, 'The Pastoral Ministry of Thomas Hall (1610–1665) in the English Revolution', *Midland History* 38 (2013).

184. Bernard Capp, *England's Culture Wars* (Oxford, 2012); and works cited by Martin Ingram, 'Reformation of Manners in Early Modern England', in *The Experience of Authority in Early Modern England*, ed. Paul Griffiths et al. (Basingstoke, 1996), notes 17 and 20.

185. William Prynne, *Canterburies Doome* (1646), 141–42; Carew, *Survey of Cornwall*, fol. 69^{r-v}; Thomas G. Barnes, 'County Politics and a Puritan Cause Célèbre', *TRHS*, 5th ser., 9 (1959); *Epistolary Curiosities*, ed. Rebecca Warner (1818), vol. 1, 186.

186. Thomas Secker, *Fourteen Sermons* (1766), 121; *Spectator* 112 (9 July 1711), ed. Donald F. Bond (Oxford, 1965), vol. 1, 460; Hugh Blair, *The Importance of Religious Knowledge to the Happiness of Mankind* (1750), 23; *Boswell's Life of Johnson*, vol. 3, 437. On vicars' wives as 'a civilizing element', see Mrs Henry Sandford, *Thomas Poole and His Friends* (1888), vol. 1, 56.

187. Thomas Walter Laqueur, *Religion and Respectability* (New Haven, CT, 1976), chap. 7; Pilkington, *View of the Present State of Derbyshire*, vol. 2, 58–59; Anne Stott, *Hannah More* (Oxford, 2003), 167.

188. George Heath, *The New History, Survey and Description of the City and Suburbs of Bristol* (Bristol, 1794), 75. On them, see Robert W. Malcolmson, '"A Set of Ungovernable People"', in *An Ungovernable People*, ed. John Brewer and John Styles (1980).

189. Anthony Armstrong, *The Church of England, the Methodists and Society, 1700–1850* (1973), 92–94; Prys Morgan, 'Wild Wales', in *Civil Histories*, ed. Burke et al., 280.

190. *The Autobiography of Francis Place*, ed. Mary Thale (Cambridge, 1972), 82. See also Carew, *Survey of Cornwall*, fol. 66^{r-v}; John Money, *Experience and Identity* (Manchester, 1977), 90; Langford, *Englishness Identified*, 223–25; Jonathan White, 'The Laboring-Class Domestic Sphere in Eighteenth-Century British Social Thought', in *Gender,*

Taste and Material Culture in Britain and North America 1700–1830, ed. John Styles and Amanda Vickery (New Haven, CT, 2006), 251–52.

191. *William Warner's Syrinx*, ed. Wallace A. Bacon (Evanston, IL, 1950; New York, 1970), 183; Sir Harry Beaumont [Joseph Spence], *Crito: or, a Dialogue on Beauty* (Dublin, 1752), 43. Cf. Pierre Bourdieu, *Distinction*, trans. Richard Nice (Cambridge, MA, 1984), 190–93.

192. Keith Thomas, 'Bodily Control and Social Unease', in *The Extraordinary and the Everyday in Early Modern England*, ed. Angela McShane and Garthine Walker (Basingstoke, 2010), 15; William Bullein, *A Newe Booke Entituled the Gouernement of Healthe* (1558), sig. Fviii (I have taken 'heares' to be 'hairs', not 'ears'); also id., *Bulleins Bulwarke of Defence againste all Sicknes, Sornes, and Woundes* (1579), sig. bbb2ᵛ.

193. [John Norden], *The Fathers Legacie* (1625), sig. A7ʳ⁻ᵛ. For other comments on the smell of the lower orders: Brents Stirling, *The Populace in Shakespeare* (New York, 1947), 65–73; Henry More, *A Modest Enquiry into the Mystery of Iniquity* (1664), sig. A3ᵛ; M. G. Smith, *Pastoral Discipline and the Church Court* (Borthwick Papers, York, 1982), 38; Mark Jenner, 'Civilization and Deodorization', in *Civil Histories*, ed. Burke et al., 139; Paul Griffiths, 'Overlapping Circles', in *Communities in Early Modern England*, ed. Alexandra Shepard and Phil Withington (Manchester, 2000), 119.

194. Elizabeth Mary Wright, *Rustic Speech and Folk-Lore* (1913), 6.

195. John Styles, *The Dress of the People* (New Haven, CT, 2007), esp. chap. 4.

196. Nathaniel Hawes, quoted by Peter Linebaugh, 'The Tyburn Riot against the Surgeons', in Douglas Hay et al., *Albion's Fatal Tree* (1975), 111. Although they convey Hawes's sentiment, the words attributed to him seem to have been composed by a nineteenth-century historian; Arthur Griffiths, *The Chronicles of Newgate* (1884), vol. 1, 253.

197. Capp, *When Gossips Meet*, 189–200, 230, 257; Tim Hitchcock, *Down and Out in Eighteenth-Century London* (2004), 99–101; Peter D. Jones, '"I Cannot Keep My Place without Being Deascent"', *Rural History* 20 (2009). Cf. the comments of the social observer Margaret McMillan on the dirt of London slum dwellers at the beginning of the twentieth century: *Labour and Childhood* (1907), 12–14.

198. Keith Thomas, 'Cleanliness and Godliness in Early Modern England', in *Religion, Culture and Society in Early Modern Britain*, ed. Anthony Fletcher and Peter Roberts (Cambridge, 1994), 77–78.

199. William Vaughan, *Naturall and Artificial Directions for Health* (1602), sig. E1ᵛ; Joseph P. Hart, *The Parish Council of Bletchingley* (n. pl., 1955), 7; William Buchan, *Domestic Medicine* (2nd edn, 1772), 114; Thomas, 'Cleanliness and Godliness', 77–78.

200. David Underdown, *Revel, Riot, and Rebellion* (Oxford, 1985), 64; Thomas Fuller, *The Holy State* ([1648] 1840) 148–49 (echoing [Robert Sanderson], *A Soveraigne Antidote against Sabbatarian Errours* (1636), 24); Christopher Marsh, *Music and Society in Early Modern England* (Cambridge, 2010), 335, 382.

201. James Sharpe and J. R. Dickinson, 'Homicide in Eighteenth-Century Cheshire', *SocHist* 41 (2016).

202. Charles Phythian-Adams, 'Rituals of Personal Confrontation in Late Medieval England', *Bull. John Rylands Lib.* 73 (1991).

203. *The Clarke Papers*, ed. C. H. Firth (Camden Soc., 1890–1901), vol. 4, 300.

204. Shepard, *Meanings of Manhood*, 147–49; *Misson's Memoirs and Observations*, 304–6; Muralt, *Letters*, 42; J. M. Beattie, *Crime and the Courts in England 1660–1800* (Oxford, 1986), 91–94; Shoemaker, *London Mob*, 194–200; Adam Fox, 'Vernacular Culture and Popular Customs in Early Modern England', *CultSocHist* 9 (2012), 334; Sharpe and Dickinson, 'Homicide in Eighteenth-Century Cheshire', 199–200; Langford, *Englishness Identified*, 46, 149–50.

205. Capp, *When Gossips Meet*, 221–22.

206. Ibid., 219–20; Jennine Hurl-Eamon, *Gender and Petty Violence in London, 1680–1720* (Columbus, OH, 2005).

207. Norbert Elias and Eric Dunning, *The Quest for Excitement* (*Collected Works of Norbert Elias*, vol. 7); Shoemaker, *London Mob*, chaps. 3, 6 and 7; Craig Koslofsky, *Evening's Empire* (Cambridge, 2011), chap. 5.

208. Richard Holt, *Sport and the British* (Oxford, 1989), 18–20; Carolyn A. Conley, *The Unwritten Law* (New York, 1991), 49–52; J. Carter Wood, *Violence and Crime in Nineteenth-Century England* (2004), chap. 4; Steedman, *Everyday Life of the English Working Class*, chap. 4 and 109–10.

209. William Blackstone, *Commentaries on the Laws of England*, ed. Wilfrid Prest (Oxford, 2016), vol. 1, 287 (I. xv); Mandeville, *Fable of the Bees*, vol. 2, 306; Elizabeth Foyster, *Marital Violence* (Cambridge, 2005), 79 (for Nicholl) and passim; James Sharpe, *A Fiery & Furious People* (2016), 174–75, 187–89, 414–15.

210. Martin Ingram, *Church Courts, Sex and Marriage in England, 1570–1640* (Cambridge, 1987), 162–63; id., *Carnal Knowledge*, index, s.v. 'antenuptial incontinence'; Keith Thomas, 'The Double Standard', *JHI* 20 (1959), 206; Bridget Hill, 'The Marriage Age of Women and the Demographers', *HWJ* 28 (1989), 143–44; John R. Gillis, *For Better or Worse* (New York, 1985), 110–11, 179–82, 186, 197–209; Levine and Wrightson, *The Making of an Industrial Society*, 299–305; Richard Adair, *Courtship, Illegitimacy and Marriage in Early Modern England* (Manchester, 1996), 81, 109, 142–48; Faramerz Dabhoiwala, *The Origins of Sex* (2012), 11, 19, 41, 204–6.

211. Peter Laslett, *Family Life and Illicit Love in Earlier Generations* (Cambridge, 1977), chap. 3; E. A. Wrigley and R. S. Schofield, *The Population History of England 1541–1871* (1981), 194–95, 304–5, 427, 429–30; E. A. Wrigley, 'Marriage, Fertility and Population Growth in Eighteenth-Century England', in *Marriage and Society*, ed. R. B. Outhwaite (1981), 155–63; Nicholas Rogers, 'Carnal Knowledge', *JSocHist* 23 (1989); Adrian Wilson, 'Illegitimacy and Its Implications in Mid-Eighteenth-Century London', *Continuity and Change* 4 (1989); E. A. Wrigley et al., *English Population History from Family Reconstitution 1580–1837* (Cambridge, 1997), 54, 219, 421–22; Clark, *Struggle for the Breeches*, 42–44, 61.

212. David Levine and Keith Wrightson, 'The Local Context of Illegitimacy in Early Modern England', in *Bastardy and Its Comparative History*, ed. Peter Laslett et al. (1980); Rebecca Probert, *Marriage Law and Practice in the Long Eighteenth Century* (Cambridge, 2009), 100–101, 256.

213. Hunt, *The Middling Sort*, chap. 8; and particularly, Turner, *Fashioning Adultery*, 11–12, 36, 82, 192, 195–96.

214. Margaret Cavendish, Duchess of Newcastle, *CCXI Sociable Letters* (1664), 113–14; *Misson's Memoirs and Observations*, 332.

215. Thomas, *Ends of Life*, 97–98, 304n56; Tim[othy] Nourse, *A Discourse upon the Nature and Faculties of Man* (1686), 320; Bernard Capp, '"Jesus Wept" but Did the Englishman?' *P&P* 224 (2014), 93, 104; S. C., *The Art of Complaisance* (1673), 41–42; Henry Chettle, *Kind-Harts Dream* (1592), ed. Edward F. Rimbault (Percy Soc., 1841), 18.

216. William Harrison, *The Description of England*, ed. Georges Edelen (Ithaca, NY, 1968), 131–32.

217. J[ohn] B[ulwer], *Pathomyotomia* (1649), 130; 'A Divine of the Church of England' (Thomas Bray), *A Course of Lectures upon the Church Catechism* (Oxford, 1696), vol. 1, 200; Obadiah Walker, *Of Education* (1673), 227.

218. Edw[ard] B[ysshe], *The Art of English Poetry* (1702), vol. 2, 1.

219. John Earle, *Micro-Cosmographie* (1628), ed. Edward Arber (Westminster, 1895), 50; *The Works of Symon Patrick*, ed. Alexander Taylor (Oxford, 1858), vol. 9, 238; Henry Peacham, *The Truth of our Times* (1638), 125.

220. D. A., *Whole Art of Converse*, 35–36.

221. Adam Smith, *Lectures on Rhetoric and Belles Lettres*, ed. J. C. Bryce (Oxford, 1983), 198; Thomas Sheridan, *British Education* (1756), 437–38; *Essays of George Eliot*, ed. Thomas Pinney (1963), 217.

222. Mandeville, *Fable of the Bees*, vol. 2, 305; James Beattie, *Essays on Poetry and Music as they affect the Mind* (Edinburgh, 1776), 438–39.
223. B. Lowsley, *A Glossary of Berkshire Words and Phrases* (Eng. Dialect Soc., 1888), 177; Jonathan Swift, *Irish Tracts, 1720–1723 and Sermons*, ed. Louis Landa (Oxford, 1948), 65; Fox, 'Vernacular Culture and Popular Customs', 334.
224. Capp, *When Gossips Meet*, 197–200.
225. Mandeville, *Fable of the Bees*, vol. 2, 295.
226. Bulwer, *Chirologia*, 173–76; Capp, *When Gossips Meet*, 232.
227. Keith Wrightson and David Levine, *Poverty and Piety in an English Village* (1979; Oxford, 1995), 124–25; [William Vaughan], *The Spirit of Detraction Coniured and Convicted in Six Circles* (1611), 103. See, more generally, John Walter, 'Gesturing at Authority', in *The Politics of Gesture*, ed. Michael J. Braddick (*P&P*, supp. 4, Oxford, 2009).
228. *Spectator* 354 (16 Apr. 1712), ed. Bond, vol. 3, 322. On the repertoire of manual gesture ('the dialect of the fingers'), see Bulwer, *Chirologia*, and on farting as a deliberately offensive 'speech act', Thomas, 'Bodily Control and Social Unease'.
229. *Bishop Still's Visitation 1594*, ed. Derek Shorrocks (Somerset Rec. Soc., 1998), 142; Garthine Walker, 'Expanding the Boundaries of Female Honour in Early Modern England', *TRHS*, 6th ser., 6 (1996), 240.
230. Edward Reynell, *The Life and Death of the Lady Lucie Reynell* (1654), cited in Wilford, *Memorials and Characters*, 456.
231. Harrison, *Description of England*, 131; Pilkington, *View of the Present State of Derbyshire*, vol. 2, 54–55; Heal, *Hospitality in Early Modern England*, chap. 9; David Cressy, *Birth, Marriage, and Death* (Oxford, 1997); R. A. Houston, *Bride Ales and Penny Weddings* (Oxford, 2014).
232. John Spicer, *The Sale of Salt* (1611), 258.
233. Adam Petrie, *Rules of Good Deportment* (Edinburgh, 1720), 97; Samuel Cradock, *Knowledge and Practice* (1659), 493; *OED*, s.v. 'shot'. On the importance of alehouse drinking for working men, see Hailwood, *Alehouses and Good Fellowship*, chaps. 3 and 4; Clark, *Struggle for the Breeches*, 81.
234. *Autobiography of Thomas Raymond and Memoirs of the House of Guise*, ed. Godfrey Davies (Camden, 3rd ser., 1917), 115.
235. Thomas, *Ends of Life*, 220; Hans Medick, 'Plebeian Culture in the Transition to Capitalism', in *Culture, Ideology and Politics*, ed. Raphael Samuel and Gareth Stedman Jones (1982), 92. Cf. Pierre Bourdieu on the French working class's 'ethic of convivial indulgence'; Bourdieu, *Distinction*, 179.
236. George, *London Life in the XVIIIth Century*, 273–74; Clark, *Struggle for the Breeches*, 34.
237. Mendelson, 'Civility of Women', 116–17; Angus J. L. Winchester, *The Harvest of the Hills* (Edinburgh, 2000), 39–40, 45–47, and chap. 5; Capp, *When Gossips Meet*, 56–57; and references cited in Thomas, *Ends of Life*, 339n26.
238. William Clagett, *Of the Humanity and Charity of Christians* (1687), 5.
239. *Cyvile and Uncyvile Life*, sig. E1ᵛ; Arnold Hunt, *The Art of Hearing* (Cambridge, 2010), 264.
240. Harrison, *Description of England*, 144. Cf. the eating arrangements of Breton peasants described by Pierre-Jakez Hélias, *Les Autres et les miens* (Paris, 1977), 69–71.
241. Sir Frederic Morton Eden, *The State of the Poor* (1797), vol. 1, 524. Contrast the evidence for chronic hunger in Jane Humphries, *Childhood and Child Labour in the British Industrial Revolution* (Cambridge, 2010), 97–100.
242. Samuel Bamford, *Early Days* (1849), 105; Christopher Dyer, *Standards of Living in the Later Middle Ages* (Cambridge, 1989), 160; id., *An Age of Transition?* (Oxford, 2005), 136–37.
243. Sidney W. Mintz, *Sweetness and Power* (New York, 1985), 114–17; Peter King, 'Pauper Inventories and the Material Lives of the Poor in the Eighteenth and Nineteenth

Centuries', in *Chronicling Poverty*, ed. Hitchcock et al.; Adrian Green, 'Heartless and Unhomely?', in *Accommodating Poverty*, ed. Joanne McEwen and Pamela Sharpe (Basingstoke, 2011).

244. William Godwin, *The Enquirer* ([1797]; New York, 1975), 335.
245. Paul Johnson, 'Conspicuous Consumption and Working-Class Culture in Late Victorian and Edwardian England', *TRHS*, 5th ser., 38 (1988), 36–37.
246. *A Collection of the Several Writings . . . [of] James Parnel* (1675), 96.
247. Edward Phillips, *The Mysteries of Love & Eloquence* (1658), sigs. a3ᵛ–4; Chesterfield, in *The World* 148 (30 Oct. 1755), in *British Essayists*, vol. 17, 182.
248. *Letters of Chesterfield*, vol. 1, 325.
249. Edward Search [Abraham Tucker], *The Light of Nature Pursued*, vol. 3, pt 2 (1777), 376; James Fenimore Cooper, *The American Democrat* (1838), ed. George Dekker and Larry Johnston (Harmondsworth, 1969), 200–201.
250. Hobbes, *Leviathan*, ed. Malcolm, vol. 2, 232 (chap. 15).
251. *Guardian* 162 (16 Sept. 1713).
252. David Fordyce, *The Elements of Moral Philosophy* (1754), ed. Thomas D. Kennedy (Indianapolis, IN, 2003), 94.
253. *Letters of Chesterfield*, vol. 1, 387.
254. 'Plus il y a dans une nation qui ont besoin d'avoir des ménagements entr'eux et de ne pas déplaire, plus il y a de politesse'; 'L'Esprit des Lois', in Montesquieu, *Oeuvres complètes*, ed. Roger Caillois (Paris, 1951), vol. 1, 582. The same belief in human interdependence as the source of the civilized virtues was held by Baron d'Holbach later in the century; Jean Fabien Spitz, 'From Civism to Civility', in *Republicanism*, ed. Martin Van Gelderen and Quentin Skinner (Cambridge, 2002), vol. ii.
255. Elias, *On the Process of Civilisation*, 405–7, 414, 418–20.
256. *The Man of Manners*, title page.
257. *Memoirs of Joseph Priestley to the year 1795, written by himself* (1806), 74–75.
258. See chapter 6.
259. Ingram, 'Sexual Manners', 109; *Tracts on Liberty in the Puritan Revolution 1638–1647*, ed. William Haller (New York, 1934), vol. 3, 242.

3 The Civilized Condition

1. Richard Hakluyt, *Diuers Voyages touching the Discouerie of America* (1582), sigs. H1, J4ᵛ; Sir Thomas Palmer, *An Essay of the Meanes how to Rule our Travailes, into Forraine Countries* (1606), 60. Palmer's book was indebted to a Latin treatise by Theodor Zwinger, *Methodus Apodemica* (Basel, 1577).
2. Roger Williams, *George Fox Digg'd out of his Burrowes* (Boston, MA, 1676), 258.
3. Algernon Sidney, *Discourses concerning Government* (3rd edn, 1751), 281.
4. 'Statutes of Corpus Christi College', 48, in *Statutes of the Colleges of Oxford* (Oxford, 1853); George Buchanan, *Rerum Scoticarum Historia* (Edinburgh, 1682), sig. Aijᵛ.
5. Richard Sherry, *A Treatise of the Figures of Grammer and Rhetorike* (1555), fol. iiii; Quintilian, *Institutio Oratoria*, bk 1, sect. 5, lines 10–16.
6. James Simpson, 'Ageism', *New Medieval Literatures*, vol. 1 (Oxford, 1997), 229–33.
7. *The Dictionary of Syr Thomas Eliot Knyght* (1538), sigs. Biv–v.
8. EEBO's search facility supersedes the dates given in the *OED*.
9. 'A View of the Progress of Society in Europe', in *The Works of the Late William Robertson*, ed. R. Lynam (1826), vol. 3, 114.
10. There is a useful collection of contemporary definitions of the 'barbarous' in *Race in Early Modern England*, ed. Ania Loomba and Jonathan Burton (Basingstoke, 2007), 279–83. See also Charles Estienne, *Dictionarium Historicum, Geographicum, Poeticum*, revised by Nicolas Lloyd (new edn, 1686), vol. 1, sig. M2 (s.v. 'barbari').
11. Roger Williams, *The Bloudy Tenent Yet More Bloody* (1652), 120.

12. *The Complete Works of M. de Montesquieu* (Eng. trans., 1777), vol. 1, 365 ('The Spirit of Laws', bk 18, chap. 11); Adam Ferguson, *An Essay on the History of Civil Society 1767*, ed. Duncan Forbes (Edinburgh, 1966), 82. See François Furet, 'Civilization and Barbarism', in *Edward Gibbon and the Decline and Fall of the Roman Empire*, ed. G. W. Bowersock et al. (Cambridge, MA, 1977), 163–64; J. G. A. Pocock, *Barbarism and Religion* (Cambridge, 1999–2015), vol. 4, 2–5, and chap. 9.

13. For examples, see EEBO.

14. John Gillingham, *The English in the Twelfth Century* (Woodbridge, 2000), 10; id., 'Civilizing the English?', *HistRes* 74 (2001), 20.

15. Denys Hay, *Polydore Vergil* (Oxford, 1952), 78, 183.

16. Denys Hay, *The Idea of Europe* (Edinburgh, 1957), chap. 5.

17. E.g., Robert Pont, 'Of the Union of Britayne', in *The Jacobean Union*, ed. Bruce R. Galloway and Brian P. Levack (Scottish Hist. Soc., 1985), 25. See also Franklin L. Baumer, 'Europe, the Turk, and the Common Corps of Christendom', *AHR* 50 (1944); id., 'The Conception of Christendom in Renaissance England', *JHI* 6 (1945), and Joan-Pau Rubiés, 'Introduction' and 'Christianity and Civilization in Sixteenth-Century Ethnological Discourse', in *Shifting Cultures*, ed. Henriette Bugge and Joan-Pau Rubiés (Münster, 1995).

18. Thomas Fuller, *The Holy State and the Profane State* ([1648]; 1840), 179; R. Junius [Richard Younge], *The Drunkard's Character* (1638), 808 (for 'a civilized pagan'); Wil[liam] Annand, *Fides Catholica* (1661), 326.

19. John Locke, *An Essay Concerning Toleration and Other Writings on Law and Politics 1667–1683*, ed. J. R. Milton and Philip Milton (Oxford, 2006), 327–29; William Penn, *The Great Question to be Considered* (1679); John Coffey, 'Puritanism and Liberty Revisited', *HJ* 41 (1998).

20. Roger Williams, *The Bloudy Tenent, of Persecution, for Cause of Conscience, Discussed* (1644), 103. On Williams, see Teresa Bejan, *Mere Civility* (Cambridge, MA, 2017), chap. 2.

21. George Sandys, *A Relation of a Iourney begun An. Dom. 1610* (1615), 60; Sir Thomas Sherley, 'Discours of the Turkes', ed. E. Denison Ross, in *Camden Miscellany*, vol. 16 (Camden Soc., 1936), 3, 12; Fulgenzio Micanzio, *Lettere a William Cavendish (1615–1628)*, ed. Roberto Ferrini (Rome, 1987), 131; Paul Rycaut, *The Present State of the Ottoman Empire* (1668), 113; Daniel Defoe, *Serious Reflections during the Life and Surprising Adventures of Robinson Crusoe* (1720), 128, 131; Daniel J. Vitkus, 'Early Modern Orientalism', in *Creating East and West*, ed. Nancy Bisaha (Philadelphia, PA, 2004); Norman Housley, *Crusading and the Ottoman Threat, 1453–1505* (Oxford, 2012), 19–20.

22. On the disintegration of the notion of Christendom by 1650, see Mark Greengrass, *Christendom Destroyed* (2014), and on its afterlife, Stephen Conway, *Britain, Ireland, and Continental Europe in the Eighteenth Century* (Oxford, 2011), chap. 6.

23. M. E. Yapp, 'Europe in the Turkish Mirror', *P&P* 137 (1992), esp. 142–45.

24. For this expression, see, e.g., Samuel Purchas, *Hakluytus Posthumus or Purchas his Pilgrimes* ([1625]; Glasgow, 1905–7), vol. 1, 13.

25. Paul MacKendrick, *The Philosophical Books of Cicero* (1989), 19; Thomas N. Mitchell, *Cicero, the Senior Statesman* (New Haven, CT, 1991), 37–38; Quentin Skinner, *Reason and Rhetoric in the Philosophy of Hobbes* (Cambridge, 1996), 77–78.

26. Sir Thomas Elyot, *The Boke Named the Gouernour*, ed. Henry Herbert Stephen Croft (1883), vol. 2, 88–89; and *OED*, s.v. 'humanity, 1'.

27. E.g., Sir Richard Barckley, *The Felicitie of Man* (1631), 29, 335; Joseph Hall, *The Shaking of the Olive-Tree* (1660), 88; Henry Rowlands, *Mona Antiqua Restaurata* (Dublin, 1723), 55. For the translation of *humanissimus* as 'civilized', see, e.g., *The Relation of a Journey into England and Holland* (1711), 16, an English version of CH. ED. [Christian Erndtel], *De Itinere suo Anglicano et Batavo* (Amsterdam, 1711), 46.

28. Thomas Smith, *Remarks upon the Manners, Religion and Government of the Turks* (1678), 1–4.

29. Thomas Starkey, *A Dialogue between Pole and Lupset*, ed. T. F. Mayer (Camden ser., 1989), 7, 2, 8–9, 71; id., *A Preface to the Kynges Highnes* (1536), fol. 40ᵛ.

30. John Watts, '"Common Weal" and "Commonwealth"', in *The Languages of Political Society*, ed. Andrea Gamberini et al. (Rome, 2011), 149; *The Works of . . . Richard Hooker*, ed. John Keble (6th edn, Oxford, 1874), vol. 1, 250 (I. x. 12); Cicero, *De Republica*, bk 1, sect. 49 (*civilis societatis vinculum*); id., *De Oratore*, bk 2, sect. 68. '*Societas civilis*' was Leonardo Bruni's translation (1438) of Aristotle's κοινωνία πολιτική. For early uses of the term, see Sir Thomas Smith, *De Republica Anglorum*, ed. Mary Dewar (Cambridge, 1982), 57, 59, 60 (written 1562–65); John Vowell alias Hooker, *Orders enacted for Orphans and for Their Portions within the Citie of Excester* (1575), sig. Cii; Thomas Cooper, *Thesaurus Linguae Romanae & Britannicae* (1578), s.v. 'Insociabilis'; Richard Mulcaster, *Positions* (1581), ed. Robert Henry Quick (1887), 145; Gervase Babington, *A Very Fruitfull Exposition of the Commaundements* (1583), 206.

31. *Works of Richard Hooker*, vol. 1, 241 (I. x. 3), 250 (I. x. 12).

32. *Cal. SP, Foreign, 1569–71*, 363; *HMC, Salisbury*, vol. 11, 340, and *Cal. SP, Domestic, 1671*, 190.

33. John Barston, *The Safegarde of Societie* (1576), fol. 62; J[ohn] A[p Robert], *The Yonger Brother His Apology* (St Omer, 1618), 44. On the changing meanings of the term, see John Keane, 'Despotism and Democracy', in *Civil Society and the State*, ed. Keane (1988); Norbert Bobbio, *Democracy and Dictatorship*, trans. Peter Kennealy (Cambridge, 1989), xvi–xvii and chap. 2; Fania Oz-Salzberger, introduction to Adam Ferguson, *An Essay on the History of Civil Society*, ed. Oz-Salzberger (Cambridge, 1995); John Ehrenberg, *Civil Society* (New York, 1999); *Civil Society*, ed. Sudipta Kaviraj and Sunil Khilnani (Cambridge, 2001); Jose Harris, 'From Richard Hooker to Harold Laski', in *Civil Society in British History*, ed. Harris (Oxford, 2003); Jürgen Kocka, 'Civil Society from a Historical Perspective', *European Rev.* 12 (2004); James Livesey, *Civil Society and Empire* (New Haven, CT, 2009).

34. George Puttenham, *The Arte of English Poesie*, ed. Gladys D. Willcock and Alice Walker (Cambridge, 1936), 7.

35. G[eorge] S[andys], *Ovids Metamorphosis Englished, Mythologized, and Represented in Figures* (1640), 263; John St John, *Observations on the Land Revenue of the Crown* (1787), appendix, 3–4 ('Norden's Project'); *The Works of George Savile, Marquis of Halifax*, ed. Mark N. Brown (Oxford, 1989), vol. 1, 181.

36. John Locke, *Two Treatises of Government*, ed. Peter Laslett (Cambridge, 1960), 342 (II. para. 87).

37. Bernard Mandeville, *The Fable of the Bees*, ed. F. B. Kaye (Oxford, 1924), vol. 2, 283.

38. Sir William Temple, *Miscellanea: The Second Part* (4th edn, 1696), 275.

39. Williams, *Bloody Tenent yet more Bloody*, 120.

40. Colm Lennon, *Sixteenth-Century Ireland* (Dublin, 1994), 56.

41. 'The History of America', in *Works of William Robertson*, vol. 5, 332–33; James H. Merrell, '"The customes of our countrey"', in *Strangers within the Realm*, ed. Bernard Bailyn and Philip D. Morgan (Chapel Hill, NC, 1991), 143.

42. Purchas, *Hakluytus Posthumus*, vol. 5, 331; Adam Smith, *The Theory of Moral Sentiments*, ed. D. D. Raphael and A. L. Macfie (Oxford, 1976), 86 (II. 2. 3).

43. Anthony Fletcher, *Reform in the Provinces* (New Haven, CT, 1986), 372; C. W. Brooks, *Lawyers, Litigation and English Society since 1450* (1998), 3.

44. Sir Frederick Pollock and Frederic William Maitland, *The History of English Law before the Time of Edward I* (2nd edn, Cambridge, 1911), vol. 2, chap. 8; John Hudson, *The Oxford History of the Laws of England*, vol. 2 (Oxford, 2012), chaps. 7, 16 and 27.

45. Mervyn James, *Society, Family, Lineage, and Civil Society* (Oxford, 1974), 'Conclusion'; id., *Society, Politics and Culture* (Cambridge, 1986), 9–11, 270–78; R. R. Davies, 'The

Survival of the Bloodfeud in Medieval Wales', *History* 54 (1969); Keith M. Brown, *The Bloodfeud in Scotland, 1573–1625* (Edinburgh, 1986); *Cal. Border Papers*, vol. 1, 13, 106–8; vol. 2, 163. At the end of the seventeenth century, however, the inhabitants of Westmorland were still said to be 'much addicted to revenge'; Adam Fox, 'Vernacular Culture and Popular Customs in Early Modern England', *CultSocHist* 9 (2012), 334.

46. Matthew Lockwood, *The Conquest of Death* (New Haven, CT, 2017).

47. C. W. Brooks, *Pettyfoggers and Vipers of the Commonwealth* (Cambridge, 1986), chaps. 4 and 5; id., *Lawyers, Litigation and English Society*, chap. 4; id., *Law, Politics and Society in Early Modern England* (Cambridge, 2008), chap. 9; Steve Hindle, 'The Keeping of the Public Peace', in *The Experience of Authority*, ed. Paul Griffiths et al. (Basingstoke, 1996); Craig Muldrew, 'The Culture of Reconciliation', *HJ* 39 (1996); Derek Roebuck, *Arbitration and Mediation in Seventeenth-Century England* (Oxford, 2017).

48. J. M. Beattie, 'Violence and Society in Early-Modern England', in *Perspectives in Criminal Law*, ed. Anthony M. Doob and Edward L. Greenspan (Aurora, ON, 1984), 41–46.

49. Peter King, *Crime and Law in England, 1750–1840* (Cambridge, 2006), chaps. 7 and 8; Greg Smith, 'Violent Crime and the Public Weal in England, 1700–1900', in *Crime, Law and Popular Culture in Europe, 1500–1900*, ed. Richard McMahon (Cullompton, 2008).

50. See the comments of Andy Wood, 'The Deep Roots of Albion's Fatal Tree', and Brendan Kane, 'Ordinary Violence?', both in *History* 99 (2014).

51. On which see Lawrence Stone, *The Crisis of the Aristocracy* (Oxford, 1965), chap. 5.

52. Adam Smith, *An Inquiry into the Nature and Causes of the Wealth of Nations*, ed. R. H. Campbell and A. S. Skinner (Oxford, 1976), vol. 2, 706 (V. i. a. 40).

53. Adam Smith, *Essays on Philosophical Subjects*, ed. W. P. D. Wightman and J. C. Bryce (Oxford, 1980), 322.

54. *Glossographia Anglicana Nova* (1707), s.v. 'civilize'.

55. *The English Works of Thomas Hobbes*, ed. Sir William Molesworth (1839–45), vol. 1, 6. Cf. Jacqueline de Romilly and Jeanne Ferguson, 'Docility and Civilization in Ancient Greece', *Diogenes* 28 (1980).

56. *The Works of the Learned Benjamin Whichcote* (Aberdeen, 1751), vol. 4, 96; William Hubbard, *The Benefit of a Well-Ordered Conversation* (Boston, MA, 1684), 212–13.

57. Michael Dalton, *The Countrey Justice* (6th edn, 1635), 9, 190–3; Keith Thomas, *Religion and the Decline of Magic* (1971), 528–30; Martin Ingram, '"Scolding Women Cucked or Washed"', in *Order and Disorder in Early Modern England*, ed. Anthony Fletcher and John Stevenson (Cambridge, 1985); Brooks, *Law, Politics and Society*, 259–60; Donald Spaeth, 'Words and Deeds', *HWJ* 78 (2014).

58. [John Cheke], *The Hurt of Sedicion* (1549), sig. F1; John Walter, 'Faces in the Crowd', in *The Family in Early Modern England*, ed. Helen Berry and Elizabeth Foyster (Cambridge, 2007), 119.

59. *The Political Works of James I*, ed. Charles Howard McIlwain (Cambridge, MA, 1918), 25; *Register of the Privy Council of Scotland*, vol. 6, ed. David Masson (Edinburgh, 1884), 594.

60. Markku Peltonen, *The Duel in Early Modern England* (Cambridge, 2003), 138.

61. Nicholas Carlisle, *A Concise Description of the Endowed Grammar Schools* (1818), vol. 1, 660, 680, 730.

62. For the end of town walls, see Oliver Creighton and Robert Higham, *Medieval Town Walls* (Stroud, 2005), 233–40; and for the decline of weapon carrying, James Sharpe, *A Fiery & Furious People* (2016), 126–27.

63. For a summary of previous research on this subject and some valuable new evidence, see J. A. Sharpe and J. R. Dickinson, 'Revisiting the "Violence We Have Lost"', *EHR* 131 (2016), and 'Homicide in Eighteenth-Century Cheshire', *SocHist* 41 (2016). See also Sharpe, *Fiery & Furious People*, 46–47, 125–27.

64. See Drew Gray, *Crime, Policing and Punishment in England, 1660–1914* (2016), 57–63, 73–75.
65. Malcolm M. Feeley and Deborah L. Little, 'The Vanishing Female', *Law and Society Rev.* 25 (1991); Robert B. Shoemaker, *Prosecution and Punishment* (Cambridge, 1991), 213; Martin J. Wiener, 'The Victorian Criminalization of Men', in *Men and Violence*, ed. Pieter Spierenburg ([Columbus], OH, 1998), 199; Garthine Walker, *Crime, Gender and Social Order in Early Modern England* (Cambridge, 2003), 24–25, 75, 135.
66. Sharpe, *Fiery & Furious People*, chap. 6.
67. See Anthony Pagden, *The Fall of Natural Man* (Cambridge, 1982), chap. 2; Denis Crouzet, 'Sur le concept de barbarie au XVIe siècle', in *La Conscience européenne au XVe et au XVIe siècle* (Paris, 1982); James Hankins, 'Renaissance Crusaders', *Dumbarton Oaks Papers* 49 (1995); J. G. A. Pocock, 'Barbarians and the Redefinition of Europe', in *The Anthropology of the Enlightenment*, ed. Larry Wolff and Marco Cipolloni (Stanford, CA, 2007).
68. Sir Clement Edmondes, *Observations upon the First Five Bookes of Caesar's Commentaries* (1604), 4th commentary, chap. 1, and 1st commentary on the Civil Wars, chap. 9; Palmer, *Essay of the Meanes*, 61.
69. John Dalrymple, *An Essay towards a General History of Feudal Society* (2nd edn, 1758), 258.
70. Francesco Patrizi, *A Moral Methode of Civile Policie*, trans. Rycharde Robinson (1576), 3; [William Warburton], *The Alliance between Church and State* (1736), 12.
71. David Hume, *Essays Moral, Political and Literary*, ed. T. H. Green and T. H. Grose (1875), vol. 1, 180 (subsequently cited by William Wilberforce, *A Letter on the Abolition of the Slave Trade* (1807), 73); id., *A Treatise of Human Nature*, ed. David Fate Norton and Mary J. Norton (Oxford, 2007), 259 (2. 3. 1); Duncan Forbes, *Hume's Philosophical Politics* (Cambridge, 1975), 296–97, 322.
72. *Works of William Robertson*, vol. 3, 35; *The Writings and Speeches of Edmund Burke*, ed. Paul Langford et al. (Oxford, 1981–2015), vol. 8, 148.
73. For parallels with China and other Asian countries, see James C. Scott, *The Art of Not Being Governed* (New Haven, CT, 2009), x–xi, 98–126, 337.
74. Samuel, Baron Pufendorf, *Of the Law of Nature and Nations*, trans. Basil Kennet[t] (3rd edn, 1711), 1st pagination, 105n12 (by Jean Barbeyrac).
75. Starkey, *Dialogue*, 68–69; T. F. Mayer, *Thomas Starkey and the Commonweal* (Cambridge, 1989), chap. 5.
76. Giles Fletcher, *Of the Rus Commonwealth*, ed. Albert J. Schmidt (Ithaca, NY, 1966), 155.
77. John Berkenhead, *A Sermon preached before His Majestie at Christ-Church in Oxford* (Oxford, 1644), 21.
78. Locke, *Two Treatises of Government*, 344 (II, para. 90).
79. Hume, *Essays*, vol. 1, 160–61, 186; W. A. Speck, *The Butcher* (Oxford, 1981), 175.
80. [James I], *A Counterblaste to Tobacco* (1604), sig. B1ᵛ; Thomas Coryat, *Coryat's Crudities* ([1611]; Glasgow, 1905), vol. 2, 174–75; Kerry Downes, *Vanbrugh* (1977), 257; Montagu Burrows, *Worthies of All Souls* (1874), 394.
81. *Boswell's Life of Johnson*, ed. George Birkbeck Hill, revised by L. F. Powell (Oxford, 1934–50), vol. 2, 130.
82. Edmondes, *Observations upon Caesar's Commentaries*, 4th commentary, chap. 11.
83. Gillingham, 'Civilizing the English?' 35–36.
84. C. S. L. Davies, 'Slavery and Protector Somerset', *EcHR*, 2nd ser., vol. 19 (1966), 547.
85. [John Streater], *Observations Historical, Political and Philosophical upon Aristotle's First Book of Political Government*, 4 (25 Apr.–2 May 1654), 26–27; Leonard Willan, *The Exact Politician* (1670), 157; John Cramsie, *British Travellers and the Encounter with Britain 1450–1750* (Woodbridge, 2015), 237.
86. Dalrymple, *General History of Feudal Property*, 26–27; William C. Lehmann, *John Millar of Glasgow 1735–1801* (Cambridge, 1960), 299–303; James Ramsay, *An Essay on the Treatment and Conversion of African Slaves in the British Sugar Colonies* (1784), 18–19; William Coxe, *Travels in Poland, Russia, Sweden and Denmark* (5th edn, 1802), vol. 3, 158.

87. Purchas, *Hakluytus Posthumus*, vol. 5, 517.
88. See, e.g., R. Koebner, 'Despot and Despotism', *Journ. of the Warburg and Courtauld Institutes* 14 (1951); Roland Minuti, 'Oriental Despotism', *Europäische Geschichte Online*, http://www.ieg-ego.eu/.
89. Aristotle, *Politics*, 1327b; Josafa Barbaro and Ambrogio Contarini, *Travels to Tana and Persia*, trans. William Thomas and N. A. Roy (Hakluyt Soc., 1863), 2.
90. Guy Miège, *A Relation of the Embassies from His Sacred Majesty Charles II to the Great Duke of Muscovy* (1669), 57. On attitudes to Russian despotism, see Marshall T. Poe, *'A People Born to Slavery'* (Ithaca, NY, 2001).
91. *The Embassy of Sir Thomas Roe to the Court of the Great Mogul, 1615–1619*, ed. William Foster (Hakluyt Soc., 1899), vol. 1, 120; Sidney, *Discourses concerning Government*, 448 (presumably drawing on Robert Knox, *An Historical Relation of the Island of Ceylon* (1681)); Daniel Defoe, *Serious Reflections during the Life and Surprising Adventures of Robinson Crusoe* (1720), 138.
92. Edward, Earl of Clarendon, *A Brief View and Survey of the Dangerous and Pernicious Errors to Church and State in Mr. Hobbes's Book Entitled Leviathan* (2nd imprn., Oxford, 1676), 30.
93. Sir William Temple, *Miscellanea* (2nd edn, 1681), vol. 1, 47.
94. Sidney, *Discourses concerning Government*, 256; Ferguson, *Principles of Moral and Political Science*, vol. 1, 252 (I. iii. ix); Fania Oz-Salzberger, *Translating the Enlightenment* (Oxford, 1995), 148–49.
95. Andrew Boorde, *The Fyrst Boke of the Introduction of Knowledge*, ed. F. J. Furnivall (EETS, 1870), 132; Edmund Spenser, *A View of the Present State of Ireland*, in *Spenser's Prose Works*, ed. Rudolf Gottfried (Baltimore, MD, 1949), 49–52 (this work is in dialogue form, but it is reasonable to assume that Spenser's own views were close to those of the dominant speaker, Irenius).
96. Clarendon, *Brief View and Survey*, 108–9; Rycaut, *Present State of the Ottoman Empire*, sig. A4ᵛ.
97. *The Jesuit's Memorial for the Intended Reformation of England*, ed. Edward Gee (1690), 237.
98. Clarendon, *Brief View and Survey*, 111.
99. Locke, *Two Treatises of Government*, 346 (II. para. 94), 307 (II. para. 30).
100. Henry Home [Lord Kames], *Historical Law-Tracts* (3rd edn, Edinburgh, 1776), 90–91; Adam Smith, *Lectures on Jurisprudence*, ed. R. L. Meek et al. (Oxford, 1978), 64.
101. William Gilpin, *Observations relative chiefly to Picturesque Beauty, . . . particularly in the High-Lands of Scotland* (1789), vol. 1, 210–11; Hume, *Treatise of Human Nature*, 313–14 (3. 2. 2.).
102. Adam Ferguson, *Principles of Moral and Political Science* (Edinburgh, 1792), vol. 1, 252; [T. R.] Malthus, *An Essay on the Principle of Population* (1798), 236–37; Catherine Hall, *Macaulay and Son* (New Haven, CT, 2012), 158–59.
103. Robert Bartlett, *Gerald of Wales 1146–1223* (Oxford, 1982), 165–66; Alberico Gentili, *De Iure Belli Libri Tres* (1612), trans. John C. Rolfe (Oxford, 1933), 238 (II. xvii); Hume, *Essays*, vol. 1, 39.
104. Steve Pincus, *1688* (New Haven, CT, 2009), 375; *Cal. Home Office Papers of the Reign of George III, 1760–1765*, ed. Joseph Redington (1878), 467.
105. Gerrit W. Gong, *The Standard of 'Civilization' in International Society* (Oxford, 1984), 24.
106. *Elizabethan Casuistry*, ed. P. J. Holmes (Catholic Rec. Soc., 1981), 71; Lambeth Palace, MS 565, fol. 22ᵛ ('*incivilitas seu rusticitas*').
107. [S. C.], *A New and True Description of the World* (1673), 20; Olga Dimitrieva, 'The Purge that Failed', in *Frontiers of Faith*, ed. Eszter Andor and István György Tóth (Budapest, 2001); William Sheils, ' "Getting On" and "Getting Along" in Parish and Town', in *Catholic Communities in Protestant States* (Manchester, 2009); Carys Brown,

'Militant Catholicism, Interconfessional Relations, and the Rookwood Family of Stanningsfield, Suffolk, c. 1688–1737', *HJ* 60 (2017).

108. *The Workes of M(aster) W(illiam) Perkins* (Cambridge, 1608–31), vol. 1, 279; Robert Bolton, *Some Generall Directions for a Comfortable Walking with God* (2nd edn, 1626), 73; [John Dod and Robert Cleaver], *A Plaine and Familiar Exposition of the Ten Commandements* (1618), 275; Alexandra Walsham, 'In Sickness and in Health', in *Living with Religious Diversity in Early Modern Europe*, ed. C. Scott Dixon et al. (Farnham, 2009); ead., 'Supping with Satan's Disciples', in *Getting Along*, ed. Nadine Lewycky and Adam Morton (Farnham, 2012).

109. *The Complete Works of Richard Sibbes*, ed. Alexander Balloch Grosart (Edinburgh, 1862–64), vol. 3, 13.

110. [Roger Williams], *Queries of Highest Consideration* (1644), 13; id., *The Examiner Defended, in a Fair and Sober Answer* (1652), 76, 95; and see Bejan, *Mere Civility*, chap. 2.

111. W[illiam] Bedell, *An Examination of Certaine Motives to Recusancie* (Cambridge, 1628), 1–4.

112. *The Works of Robert Sanderson*, ed. William Jacobson (Oxford, 1854), vol. 5, 55–56; Thomas Browne, *Religio Medici* (1643), para. 6; Toby Barnard, *Making the Grand Figure* (New Haven, CT, 2004), 320.

113. Thomas Barlow, *Several Miscellaneous and Weighty Cases of Conscience* (1692), parts 5, 8, and 1, 14.

114. Locke, *Essay Concerning Toleration*, 297; John Marshall, *John Locke: Resistance, Religion and Responsibility* (Cambridge, 1994), 179; id., *John Locke, Toleration and Early Enlightenment Culture* (Cambridge, 2006).

115. John Locke, *Some Thoughts Concerning Education*, ed. John W. and Jean S. Yolton (Oxford, 1989), 122–26 (para. 67), 200 (para. 143); *The Correspondence of John Locke*, ed. E. S. de Beer (Oxford, 1976–), vol. 3, 689 ('*mutuae charitatis vinculum quo omnes in unum corpus colligantur*'). On this, see Bejan, *Mere Civility*, chap. 4.

116. *Spectator* 399 (7 June 1712), ed. Donald F. Bond (Oxford, 1965), vol. 3, 495.

117. Daniel Defoe, *A Tour thro' the Whole Island of Great Britain* ([1724–26]; 1927), vol. 1, 210.

118. Alexandra Walsham, *Charitable Hatred* (Manchester, 2006), 273–77; Benjamin J. Kaplan, *Divided by Faith* (Cambridge, 2007), 334–54; *Living with Religious Diversity in Early Modern Europe*, ed. Dixon et al., 9; Scott Sowerby, *Making Toleration* (Cambridge, MA, 2013), 68.

119. Samuel Sorbière, *A Voyage to England* (Eng. trans., 1709), 36–37.

120. [Thomas Gordon and John Trenchard], *The Independent Whig* (1721), 33; *Some Familiar Letters between Mr Locke and Severall of His Friends* (1708), 'To the Reader'; Steven Shapin, *A Social History of Truth* (Chicago, IL, 1994), 114–25, 308–9; Anne Goldgar, *Impolitic Learning* (New Haven, CT, 1995), 7, 99, 167, 215–18, 227, 236, 239–40; Adrian Johns, *The Nature of the Book* (Chicago, IL, 1998), chap. 7; Marshall, *John Locke, Toleration and Early Enlightenment Culture*, 516–19; Claire Preston, *Thomas Browne and the Writing of Early Modern Science* (Cambridge, 2005), chap. 1.

121. *Complete Prose Works of John Milton*, ed. Don M. Wolfe et al. (New Haven, CT, 1959–83), vol. 4(1), 114–15, 252–54.

122. J. R. Maddicott, *The Origins of the English Parliament, 924–1327* (Oxford, 2010), 38–41. On rules of debate at village leet meetings, see Michael J. Braddick, *State Formation in Early Modern England c. 1500–1700* (Cambridge, 2000), 74. More generally, see Wilbert van Vree, *Meetings, Manners and Civilization*, trans. Kathleen Bell (1999).

123. *Observations, Rules and Orders of the House of Commons*, ed. W. R. McKay (1989), 55–64; Phil Withington, *The Politics of Commonwealth* (Cambridge, 2005), 176–78; Steve Hindle, 'Hierarchy and Community in the Elizabethan Parish', *HJ* 42 (1999), 848–49.

124. Archibald S. Foord, *His Majesty's Opposition 1714–1830* (Oxford, 1964); J. A. W. Gunn, *Factions No More* (1972); Max Skjönsberg, 'Lord Bolingbroke's Theory of Party and Opposition', *HJ* 59 (2016); Ferguson, *Essay on the History of Civil Society*, 188.

125. Edward Daunce, *A Brief Discourse of the Spanish State* (1590), 24; Sir Philip Sidney, *The Countess of Pembroke's Arcadia (The Old Arcadia)*, ed. Katherine Duncan-Jones (Oxford, 1994), 349; Edmondes, *Observations upon Caesar's Commentaries*, 3rd commentary, chap. 4. Cf. Cicero, *De Officiis*, bk 1, chaps. 50–51; bk 3, chap. 69; Richard Tuck, *The Rights of War and Peace* (Oxford, 1999), 36–39.

126. Hugo Grotius, *The Rights of War and Peace* (Eng. trans., 1738), 13–15 (bk 1, chap. 1, sect. 12); John Selden, *The Dominion, or Ownership of the Sea*, trans. Marchmont Nedham (1652), 42, 45. Jean Barbeyrac, 'An Historical and Critical Account of the Science of Morality', in Pufendorf, *Law of Nature and Nations*, 72.

127. In the first category came John Barston, *The Safegarde of Societie* (1576), fol. 7; Gentili, *De Iure Belli*, 9 (I. i); Thomas Hobbes, *Leviathan*, ed. Noel Malcolm (Oxford, 2012), vol. 2, 552 (chap. 30), and Pufendorf, *Law of Nature and Nations*, 1st pagination, 149–52 (II. iii. 23). In the second category were the canon lawyers cited by John Donne, *Biathanatos*, ed. Ernest W. Sullivan II (Cranbury, NJ, 1984), 42 (1. 1. 9), along with Grotius, *Rights of War and Peace*, 15 (I. i. xiv), 568 (III. iv. 16); the Oxford professor and judge Richard Zouche, *Iuris et Iudicii Fecialis* [1650], ed. Thomas Erskine Holland (Washington, DC, 1911), vol. 1, 1; the barrister Robert Ward, *An Enquiry into the Foundations and History of the Law of Nations in Europe* (1795), vi–vii, xiv, xli. For other opinions, see Christopher N. Warren, *Literature and the Law of Nations* (Oxford, 2015).

128. William Fulbecke, *The Pandectes of the Law of Nations* (1602), sig. A2ᵛ, fol. 16ᵛ; *The Whole Works of the Right Rev. Jeremy Taylor*, ed. Reginald Heber, rev. Charles Page Eden (1849–61), vol. 9, 281.

129. Martti Koskenniemi, 'What Should International Legal History Become?', in *System, Order, and International Law*, ed. Stefan Kadelkbach et al. (Oxford, 2017), 392.

130. William Blackstone, *Commentaries on the Laws of England*, ed. Wilfrid Prest et al. (Oxford, 2016), vol. 4, 44 (IV. iv).

131. Rycaut, *Present State of the Ottoman Empire*, 83–88. Alberico Gentili claimed that even barbarians recognized the rights of embassies; *De Legationibus Libri Tres* (1594 edn; New York, 1924), vol. 1, 61 (I. i).

132. John Byrom, *The Necessity of Subjection Asserted* (1681), 1.

133. *Works of Richard Hooker*, vol. 1, 250–52 (I. x. 12–13).

134. Virgil, *Aeneid*, bk 1, 539–43, although in practice it was also to be found among many 'barbarian' peoples.

135. Francis Bacon, *The Essayes or Counsels, Civill and Morall*, ed. Michael Kiernan (*The Oxford Francis Bacon*, Oxford, 1985), 40; Thomas Wright, *The Passions of the Minde in Generall* (1604), 242; *The Correspondence of John Locke*, ed. E. S. de Beer (Oxford, 1976–), vol. 3, 794; also vol. 4, 413–22.

136. Vitoria, *Political Writings*, ed. Anthony Pagden and Jeremy Lawrance (Cambridge, 1991), 278–79; *Works of Richard Hooker*, vol. 1. (I. x. 13); Grotius, *Rights of War and Peace*, 151–56 (II. ii. xii–xvi); and see Georg Cavallar, *The Rights of Strangers* (Farnham, 2002); Naomi Baker, 'Grace and Favour', and Gideon Baker, 'Right of Entry or Right of Refusal?', both in *Hospitality and World Politics*, ed. Baker (Basingstoke, 2013).

137. *William Penn's Journal of His Travels in Holland and Germany in 1677* (4th edn [ed. John Barclay], 1835), 79.

138. E.g., *Cyvile and Uncyvile Life* (1579), sig. Fiv; Richard Carew, *The Survey of Cornwall*, ed. John Chynoweth et al. (Devon and Cornwall Rec. Soc., 2004), fol. 59.

139. Robert P. Adams, *The Better Part of Valor* (Seattle, WA, 1962); *Advice to a Son*, ed. Louis B. Wright (Ithaca, NY, 1962), 11; Edmondes, *Observations upon Caesar's Commentaries*, 6th commentary, chap. 10 (in the expanded 1609 edn); William Ames, *Conscience with*

the Power and Cases thereof (n. pl., 1639), bk 3, 184; [Margaret, Marchioness of Newcastle], *Poems and Fancies* (1653), 91.

140. [John Sheffield, Earl of Mulgrave], *An Essay upon Satyr* (1680), 62; H[umphrey] B[rooke], *The Durable Legacy* (1681), 19.

141. Marquis de Chastellux, *An Essay on Public Happiness* (Eng. trans., 1774), i. xix.

142. Smith, *Wealth of Nations*, vol. 2, 689–96 (v. i. 2–11).

143. Vicesimus Knox, *Essays Moral and Literary* (new edn, 1782), vol. 2, 77.

144. *Works of George Savile, Marquess of Halifax*, vol. 3, 71.

145. Cicero urged that the defeated should be spared, provided they had not behaved with exceptional savagery during the fighting; *De Officiis*, bk 1, chap. 35.

146. Edward Gibbon, *The History of the Decline and Fall of the Roman Empire*, ed. J. B. Bury (5th edn, 1912), vol. 3, chap. 26. On changes in the conduct of war after the Norman Conquest, see Gillingham, *The English in the Twelfth Century*, chaps. 3, 10 and 12; 'Surrender in Medieval Europe – an Indirect Approach', in *How Fighting Ends*, ed. Holger Afflerbach and Hew Strachan (Oxford, 2012); and 'Women, Children and the Profits of War', in *Gender and Historiography*, ed. Janet L. Nelson et al. (2012).

147. On the medieval laws of war, I follow Maurice Keen, *Laws of War in the Late Middle Ages* (1965); Theodore Meron, *Henry's Wars and Shakespeare's Laws* (Oxford, 1993); *The Laws of War*, ed. Michael Howard et al. (New Haven, CT, 1994); Matthew Strickland, *War and Chivalry* (Cambridge, 1996); and Nigel Saul, *For Honour and Fame* (2011), 136–43.

148. Edmondes, *Observations upon Caesar's Commentaries*, 3rd commentary, chap. 4; *Works of Richard Hooker*, vol. 1, 251 (I. x. 13).

149. Neil Murphy, 'Violence, Colonization and Henry VIII's Conquest of France, 1544–1546', *P&P* 233 (2010).

150. See Rémy Ambühl, *Prisoners of War in the Hundred Years War* (Cambridge, 2013).

151. Geoffrey Parker, *Empire, War and Faith in Early Modern Europe* (New Haven, CT, 2002), chap. 6; John Childs, 'The Laws of War in Seventeenth-Century Europe and their Application during the Jacobite War in Ireland, 1688–91', in *Age of Atrocity*, ed. David Edwards et al. (Dublin, 2007), 299; Barbara Donagan, *War in England 1642–1649* (Oxford, 2008), chap. 8; Henry Dunthorne, *Britain and the Dutch Revolt* (Cambridge, 2013), 86, 95; Edmund Spenser, *Selected Letters and Papers*, ed. Christopher Burlinson and Andrew Zurcher (Oxford, 2009), 18–19; and more generally, *Prisoners in War*, ed. Sibylle Scheipers (Oxford, 2010), 3–5, and chaps. 1–3.

152. Matthew Sutcliffe, *The Practice, Proceedings, and Lawes of Armes* (1593), 33; Gentili, *De Iure Belli*, 208–40 (II. xvi–xviii); William Segar, *Honor Military, and Civill* (1602), 401; Fulbecke, *Pandectes of the Law of Nations*, fols. 38, 47–48; Richard Bernard, *The Bible-Battells* (1629), 251.

153. David Hume of Godscroft, *The British Union*, ed. and trans. Paul J. McGinnis and Arthur H. Williamson (Aldershot, 2002), 80–83; id., *The History of the Houses of Douglas and Angus* (Edinburgh, 1644), 102–3.

154. Heinz Duchhardt, 'War and International Law in Europe, Sixteenth to Eighteenth Centuries', in *War and Competition between States*, ed. Philippe Contamine (Oxford, 2000), 295; Pufendorf, *Law of Nature and Nations*, 3rd pagination, 91 (VIII. vi. 7); 1st pagination, 151 (II. iii. 23).

155. Fynes Moryson, *Shakespeare's Europe*, ed. Charles Hughes (2nd edn, New York, 1967), 131; Edmondes, *Observations upon Caesar's Commentaries*, 1st commentary on *The Civil Wars*, chap. 5; John H. L. Keep, *Soldiers of the Tsar* (Oxford, 1985), 217; Sir James Porter, *Observations on the Religion, Law, Government, and Manners of the Turks* (2nd edn, 1771), 171. Ironically, it has been suggested that it was as a result of their contact with Islamic practice that twelfth-century Crusaders relinquished their original habit of taking no prisoners and moved to accepting ransoms from those who could offer them; Yvonne Friedman, *Encounter between Enemies* (Leiden, 2002).

156. *The Voyages and Colonizing Enterprises of Humphrey Gilbert*, ed. David Beers Quinn (Hakluyt Soc., 1940), vol. 2, 450; Perkins, *Workes*, vol. 3, 698; Grotius, *Rights of War and Peace*, 565–67 (III. iv. x–xiii).

157. [Algernon] Sidney, *Court Maxims*, ed. Hans W. Blom et al. (Cambridge, 1996), 199–200; Locke, *Two Treatises of Government*, 302–3 (II. 23–24), 340 (II. 85); Blackstone, *Commentaries*, vol. 1, 427 (I. xiv).

158. *Tudor Royal Proclamations*, ed. Paul L. Hughes and James F. Larkin (New Haven, CT, 1964–69), vol. 1, 116. It is likely that this rule was made not out of humanity but in order to safeguard the possibility of a ransom.

159. *Lawes and Ordinances set down by Robert Earl of Leicester* (1586), 8; R. B. Wernham, *After the Armada* (Oxford, 1984), 109.

160. Robert Ward, *Animadversions of Warre* (1639), vol. 2, 65.

161. *Lawes and Ordinances of Warre, established by His Excellence the Earle of Northumberland for the Better Conduct of the Service in the Northern Parts* (1640), sig. C2. This is recognized as a turning point by Meron, *Henry's Wars and Shakespeare's Laws*, 151–52; he also cites the Scottish Ordinances and Articles of War of 1643, which declared flatly that 'murder is no less unlawful and intolerable in the time of war than in time of peace, and is to be punished with death'. In her authoritative *War in England*, 146–47, Barbara Donagan regards the Earl of Arundel's articles of 1639 as crucially influential, but they appear to be less explicit on this topic.

162. Matthew Carter, *A True Relation of that Honorable, though Unfortunate Expedition of Kent, Essex and Colchester in 1648* (2nd edn, Colchester, 1789), 183; *Complete Prose Works of John Milton*, vol. 7, 327; Joshua Sprigg, *Anglia Rediviva* (1647; Oxford, 1854), 151; J. W. Willis Bund, *The Civil War in Worcestershire* (Birmingham, 1905), 191; [William Waller], *Vindication of the Character and Conduct of Sir William Waller* (1793), 8; Henry Reece, *The Army in Cromwellian England* (Oxford, 2013), 100–101.

163. *A Royalist's Notebook*, ed. Francis Bamford (1936), 119; Sprigg, *Anglia Rediviva*, 326.

164. Edward Symmons, *A Militarie Sermon . . . preached at Shrewsbury* (1644), 26; *The Memoirs of Edmund Ludlow*, ed. C. H. Firth (Oxford, 1894), vol. 1, 82–83.

165. J. D. Davies, *Pepys's Navy* (Barnsley, 2008), 131.

166. For an estimate of the casualties, see Charles Carlton, *Going to the Wars* (1992), 211–14.

167. Ibid., 255–64; Will Coster, 'Massacres and Codes of Conduct in the English Civil War', in *The Massacre in History*, ed. Mark Levene and Penny Roberts (New York, 1999); Ian Gentles, 'The Civil Wars in England', in *The Civil Wars*, ed. John Kenyon and Jane Ohlmeyer (Oxford, 1998), 112–13; Donagan, *War in England*, 135–36, 157–65, 162–63, 341. Frank Tallett, 'Barbarism in War', in *Warrior's Dishonour*, ed. George Kassimeris (Abingdon, 2016).

168. Edward Hyde, Earl of Clarendon, *The History of the Rebellion and Civil Wars in England*, ed. W. Dunn Macray (Oxford, 1888), vol. 3, 115, 369–70, 418, 465, 528, 530; vol. 4, 483, 497; vol. 5, 184.

169. Samuel R. Gardiner, *History of the Great Civil War 1642–1649* (new edn, 1893), vol. 2, 362–65.

170. E.g., Lucy Hutchinson, *Memoirs of the Life of Colonel Hutchinson*, ed. James Sutherland (1973), 261, 275, 277; *A Perfect Relation of the Causes and Manner of the Apprehending by the King's Souldiers . . . with their Inhumane Usage* (1643); [John Gauden], *Cromwell's Bloody Slaughter-House* (1660), 9, 17, 122; Donagan, *War in England*, 162, 163, 203; Nigel Smith, *Andrew Marvell* (New Haven, CT, 2010), 69–70; Fiona McCall, *Baal's Priests* (Farnham, 2013), 157, 194.

171. *A Catalogue of the . . . Gentlemen of Worth and Quality Slain* (1647), single sheet; or 'civil, uncivil wars', as in *Englands Wolfe with Eagles Clawes* (1646), single sheet.

172. C. G. Cruickshank, *Army Royal* (Oxford, 1969), 121; Thomas Churchyard, *A Generall Rehearsall of Warres* (1579), sigs. Qi, Qii–iii^v; Gentili, *De Iure Belli*, 234, 235 (II. xviii),

320 (II. vii); Fulbecke, *Pandectes of the Law of Nations*, fols. 39ᵛ, 46ᵛ, 81ᵛ; Zouche, *Iuris et Iudicii Fecialis*, vol. 2, 37–38 (I. vii. 5).

173. Carlton, *Going to the Wars*, 240–41; Donagan, *War in England*, 376–82.

174. Geoffrey Plank, *Rebellion and Savagery* (Philadelphia, PA, 2006), chaps. 1 and 2.

175. Peter Wilson, *German Armies* (1998), 84–85.

176. Ferguson, *Essay on the History of Civil Society*, 198–201; Hume, *Essays*, vol. 1, 303.

177. Edward Search [Abraham Tucker], *The Light of Nature Pursued* (1777), vol. 3, pt. 2, 387.

178. Gibbon, *Decline and Fall*, vol. 3, 70 (chap. 27); Adam Smith, *Lectures on Jurisprudence*, ed. R. L. Meek et al. (Oxford, 1978), 7, 549–50.

179. *Cal. Home Office Papers, 1760–5*, 469; *Works of William Robertson*, vol. 3, 16.

180. David Parrott, *The Business of War* (Cambridge, 2012), 318–19.

181. Introduction by Albert de Lapradelle to E. de Vattel, *Le Droit des gens ou principes de la loi naturelle* (Washington, DC, 1916), iii, xlviii–li; Geoffrey Best, *Humanity in Warfare* (1980), chap. 1; Armstrong Starkey, *War in the Age of the Enlightenment, 1700—1789* (Westport, CT, 2003), 93–98; David A. Bell, *The First Total War* (2007), 5, 44–47, 71–72; Peter H. Wilson, 'Prisoners in Early Modern Warfare', in *Prisoners in War*, ed. Scheipers, 46.

182. Conway, *Britain, Ireland, and Continental Europe*, 11, 282–83, 287–89.

183. I follow James Q. Whitman, *The Verdict of Battle* (Cambridge, MA, 2012). On the very different warfare of the 1790s, see Bell, *The First Total War*.

184. *John Ledyard's Journey through Russia and Siberia 1787–1788*, ed. Stephen D. Watrous (Madison, WI, 1966), 190; T. R. Malthus, *An Essay on the Principle of Population* (2nd edn, 1803), 35–36 (a vivid account based on travel literature).

185. Carl Becker, *The Declaration of Independence* (New York, 1922), 14; Jack P. Greene, *Evaluating Empire and Confronting Colonialism in Eighteenth-Century Britain* (Cambridge, 2013), 206, 218–19, 227, 231, 242.

186. Helger Hoock, 'Mangled Bodies', *P&P* 230 (2016).

187. Hume of Godscroft, *History of the Houses of Douglas and Angus*, 103; Edith Hall, *Inventing the Barbarian* (Oxford, 1989), 158–59; W. R. Jones, 'The Image of the Barbarian in Medieval Europe', *CSSH* 13 (1971), 378, 391; Bartlett, *Gerald of Wales*, 165–67; Pagden, *Fall of Natural Man*, 18; John Bullokar, *An English Expositor* (1616), s.v. 'barbarisme'; *OED*, s.v. 'barbarity' and 'barbarous'.

188. Thomas Aquinas, *Summa Theologiae*, 2a, 2ae, q. 159.

189. Thomas Scot, *Christs Politician and Salomons Puritan* (1616), part 2, 2.

190. *The Essays of Montaigne*, trans. John Florio, ed. George Saintsbury (1892), vol. 2, 119.

191. Thomas Hobbes, *De Cive, The Latin Version*, ed. Howard Warrender (Oxford, 1983), 113 (iii. xi), 118 (iii. xxvii); *Leviathan*, ed. Malcolm, vol. 2, 232 (chap. 15), and 90–91 (chap. 6), where it is defined as having 'little sense of the calamity of others' (*alienae calamitatis contemptus*).

192. Herodotus, *Histories*, bk 4, chaps. 1–2, 64–66; James William Johnson, 'The Scythian', *JHI* 20 (1959); François Hartog, *The Mirror of Herodotus*, trans. Janet Lloyd (Berkeley, CA, 1988), pt 1.

193. *Polydore Vergil's English History*, ed. Sir Henry Ellis (Camden Soc., 1846), 74; Barnaby Rich, *A New Description of Ireland* (1610), 15 (also Moryson, *Shakespeare's Europe*, 238–39); Hankins, 'Renaissance Crusaders', 136–37, 142–44; Housley, *Crusading and the Ottoman Threat*, 19; Andrea Cambini, *Two Very Notable Commentaries the One of the Originall of the Turcks*, trans. J. Shute (1562), sig. A1; Rycaut, *Present State of the Ottoman Empire*, 3; Joshua Poole, *The English Parnassus* (1677), 213; Nancy Bisaha, '"New Barbarian" or Worthy Adversary?', in *Western Views of Islam in Medieval and Early Modern Europe*, ed. David R. Blanks and Michael Frassetto (Basingstoke, 1999), 193; Joseph de Acosta, *The Naturall and Morall Historie of the East and West Indies*, trans. E[dward] G[rimestone] (1604), 381–90; Fletcher, *Of the Rus Commonwealth*, 155.

194. *Holinshed's Chronicles of England, Scotland and Ireland* (1807–8), vol. 2, 516; vol. 3, 34; Jones, 'Image of the Barbarian', 169–70; Hume, *Essays*, vol. 1, 307; Henry Home, Lord Kames, *Sketches of the History of Man* (Edinburgh, 1774), vol. 1, 242.

195. Cadwallader Colden, *The History of the Five Indian Nations Depending on the Province of New-York* (New York, 1727), 16; *Boswell's Life of Johnson*, vol. 1, 437; *Captain Cook's Voyages of Discovery* (Everyman's Lib., 1906), 348. (This edition is an unacknowledged reprint of *Cook's Voyages of Discovery*, ed. John Barrow (Edinburgh, 1860), a work that sometimes attributes sentiments to Cook which he may have held, but never himself articulated.)

196. [William and Edmund Burke], *An Account of the European Settlements in America* (1757), vol. 1, 188–94; *The Memoirs of Lieut. Henry Timberlake* (1765), 52–53, 57–58; Wayne E. Lee, *Barbarians and Brothers* (Oxford, 2011), 130–67; Armstrong Starkey, *European and Native American Warfare, 1675–1815* (1998), chap. 2; Jill Lepore, *The Name of War* (New York, 1998), 13–14, 180, 257n35; Peter Way, 'The Cutting Edge of Culture', in *Empire and Others*, ed. Martin Daunton and Rick Halpern (1999), 131–34.

197. Smith, *Theory of Moral Sentiments*, 204–11 (V. 2. 8–16).

198. Raymond Firth, *Elements of Social Organisation* (5th edn, 1971), 198, 200; Daniel de Moulin, 'A Historical-Phenomenological Study of Bodily Pain', *Bull. History of Medicine* 48 (1974), 569.

199. James Ross, 'The Battle of Towton (1461)', *Magazine of the Friends of the National Archives* 22 (2011), 13.

200. Arnold Oskar Meyer, *England and the Catholic Church under Queen Elizabeth*, trans. J. R. McKee (1916), 182; Christopher Highley, *Catholics Writing the Nation in Early Modern Britain and Ireland* (Oxford, 2008), 36, 55–57, 69, 72; *The Troubles of Our Catholic Forefathers*, ed. John Morris (1872–77), 3rd ser., 68–70, 74, 87, 96, 98; Richard Challoner, *Memoirs of Missionary Priests* (1741–42), vol. 1, 38, 44, 230; vol. 2, 100.

201. Patrick Gordon of Ruthven, *A Short Abridgement of Britane's Distemper, 1639–49* (Aberdeen, 1844), 160.

202. William Burton, *The Rowsing of the Sluggard* (1595), 152; *Proceedings in the Parliaments of Elizabeth I*, ed. T. E. Hartley (Leicester, 1981–95), vol. 2, 185; *A New Enterlude No Less Wittie than Pleasant, Entituled New Custome* (1573), sig. Ciii^v; Philip Stubbes, *A Motive to Good Workes* (1593), 97–98.

203. Thomas Deloney, *A New Ballet of the Straunge and Most Cruell Whippes which the Spanyards had prepared to Whippe and Torment English Men and Women* (1588).

204. Lancelot Andrewes, *XCVI Sermons* (1629), 893.

205. H. J. Moule, *Descriptive Catalogue of the Charters, Minute Books and Other Documents of the Borough of Weymouth and Melcombe Regis* (Weymouth, 1883), 198.

206. *Works of Whichcote*, vol. 2, 224.

207. Bartholomé de las Casas, *The Spanish Colonie*, trans. M. M. S. (1583); id., *The Tears of the Indians*, trans. J[ohn] P[hillips] (1656). D'Avenant's opera was initially intended to support Cromwell's war with Spain; see Janet Clare, 'The Production and Reception of Davenant's "Cruelty of the Spaniards in Peru"', *Modern Language Rev.* 89 (1994).

208. William Burton, *Davids Evidence, or the Assurance of Gods Love* (1596), 23–24; Sidney, *Discourses concerning Government*, 125. See, more generally, J. H. Elliott, *The Old World and the New* (Cambridge, 1970), 94–96; William S. Maltby, *The Black Legend in England* (Durham, NC, 1971).

209. Daniel Defoe, *Robinson Crusoe* ([1719]; Oxford, 1927), vol. 1, 198–99; id., *Serious Reflections*, 206–7.

210. Margaret Meserve, *Empires of Islam in Renaissance Historical Thought* (Cambridge, MA, 2008), 67, 95.

211. Carla Gardina Pestana, 'Cruelty and Religious Justifications for Conquest in the Mid-Seventeenth-Century English Atlantic', in *Empires of God*, ed. Linda Gregerson and Susan Juster (Philadelphia, PA, 2011), 503.

212. From the translation of the Latin version (possibly by John Milton) issued in 1738, presumably as part of the run-up to war with Spain in 1739. The original English text referred to 'the common brotherhood between all mankind, which in some sort may interest them in the horrid and enormous injuries of each other'; *A Manifesto of the Lord Protector* (2nd edn, Eng. trans., 1738), 6; *Scriptum Dom. Protectoris . . . in quo huius Reipublicae Causa contra Hispanos justa esse demonstratur* (1655), 6. See also *A Declaration of His Highnes, by the Advice of His Council* (1655).

213. Tuck, *Rights of War and Peace*, 34–47; Thomas More, *Utopia*, ed. George M. Logan and Robert P. Adams (Cambridge, 1989), 87; Gentili, *De Jure Belli*, 67–73 (I. xv), 122–23 (I. xxv); *Humanitarian Intervention in History*, ed. Brendan Simms and D. J. B. Trim (Cambridge, 2011), is useful, but makes no mention of Cromwell's West Indian intervention.

214. S. J. Connolly, *Divided Kingdom* (Oxford, 2008), 98; [James Cranford], *The Teares of Ireland* (1642), 3.

215. *Certaine Informations from Severall Parts of the Kingdome*, 56 (2–15 Feb. 1644), 436–37; *The Kings Letters Intercepted Coming from Oxford* (1644), sig. A3ᵛ; Nehemiah Wallington, *Historical Notes of Events Occurring Chiefly in the Reign of Charles I*, [ed. R. Webb] (1869), vol. 1, 290; and see Mark Stoyle, 'The Road to Farndon Field', *EHR* 128 (2008).

216. Brian Magee, 'The Protestant Wind', *Month* 177 (1941); William L. Sachse, 'The Mob and the Revolution of 1688', *JBS* 4 (1964); J. Anthony Williams, 'No-Popery Violence in 1688', in *Studies in Seventeenth-Century English Literature, History and Bibliography*, ed. G. A. M. Janssens and F. G. A. M. Aarts (Amsterdam, 1984), 251; Pincus, *1688*, 247–49.

217. Gilbert Burnet, preface to his translation of L. C. F. Lactantius, *A Relation of the Death of the Primitive Persecutors* (Amsterdam, 1687), 24–25.

218. *The Works of . . . Henry St John, Lord Viscount Bolingbroke* (new edn, 1809), vol. 4, 38; (Pierre) Bayle, *A Philosophical Commentary on Those Words of the Gospel, Luke, XIV. 23* (Eng. trans., 1708), vol. 1, 29.

219. *Considerations upon War, upon Cruelty in General, and Religious Cruelty in Particular* (1758), 220–28.

220. Bulstrode Whitelocke, *Memorials of the English Affairs* (Oxford, 1853), vol. 3, 225.

221. *The Childrens Petition* (1669), 51; Sir Samuel Morland, *The Urim of Conscience* (1695), 120–22; W. A. L. Vincent, *The Grammar Schools* (1969), 61.

222. Bolton, *Some Generall Directions*, 156; *The Actors Remonstrance* (1643), 4; 'A Gentleman at London', *The Tricks of the Town Laid Open* (1746), 55; *The Miscellaneous Works of the Right Honourable Edward, Earl of Clarendon* (2nd edn, 1751), 347; Robert W. Malcolmson, *Popular Recreations in English Society* (Cambridge, 1973), 119, 121, 135–37; Keith Thomas, *Man and the Natural World* (1983), chap. 4; Emma Griffin, *England's Revelry* (British Academy, Oxford, 2005), 127–30.

223. Gibbon, *Decline and Fall*, vol. 3, 72–73 (chap. 26).

224. Samuel Hoard, *Gods Love to Mankind* (1633); Will[iam] Whiston, *The Eternity of Hell Torments Considered* (1740), 18, 137; D. P. Walker, *The Decline of Hell* (1964), esp. 62, 101, 108–9, 112, 201; Ava Chamberlain, 'The Theology of Cruelty', *Harvard Theological Rev.* 85 (1992).

225. Sir John Fortescue, *On the Laws and Governance of England*, ed. Shelley Lockwood (Cambridge, 1997), 31–34; Larissa Tracy, *Torture and Brutality in Medieval Literature* (Cambridge, 2012), 16, 246, 285, 294–95; Smith, *De Republica Anglorum*, 117–18 (I have omitted '[be-]heading', which Smith, surprisingly, regarded as non-English).

226. Described in Moryson, *Shakespeare's Europe*, 67–69, and, with illustrations, in *The Travels of Peter Mundy in Europe and Asia, 1608–1667*, ed. Sir Richard Carnac Temple (Hakluyt Soc., 1907–36), vol. 1, 55–58.

NOTES to pp. 155–158

227. *Russia at the Close of the Sixteenth Century*, ed. Edward A. Bond (Hakluyt Soc., 1856), 172–73.

228. Lisa Silverman, *Tortured Subjects* (Chicago, IL, 2001), 74–75; Robert Muchembled, *A History of Violence*, trans. Jean Birrell (2012), 130–31; Gregory Hanlon, 'The Decline of Violence in the West', *EHR* 128 (2013), 372, 385.

229. John H. Langbein, *Torture and the Law of Proof in Europe and England in the Ancien Régime* (Chicago, IL, 2006), 73–139; Sir John Baker, *The Oxford History of the Laws of England*, vol. 6 (Oxford, 2003), 512; William Cecil, *The Execution of Justice in England*, ed. Robert M. Kingdon (Ithaca, NY, 1965), 47, 50.

230. *The Laws and Liberties of Massachusetts* ([1648]; Cambridge, MA, 1929), 50.

231. *The Diaries and Papers of Sir Edward Dering, Second Baronet, 1644 to 1684*, ed. Maurice F. Bond (1976), 214–15. For torture in Bridewell and Newgate, see Paul Griffiths, *Lost Londons* (Cambridge, 2008), 243, 249, 253–54.

232. *The Diary of William Lawrence*, ed. G. E. Aylmer (Beaminster, 1961), 36–37; *The Diary of Thomas Burton*, ed. John Towill Rutt (1828), vol. 1, 158; *Cal. SP, Domestic, 1661–62*, 285; *The Petty Papers*, ed. Marquess of Lansdowne (1927), vol. 2, 213; Timothy Nourse, *Campania Foelix* (1700), 230–31; J. R., *Hanging, not Punishment Enough, for Murtherers, High-Way Men, and House-Breakers* (1701); J. M. Beattie, *Crime and the Courts in England 1660–1800* (Princeton, NJ, 1986), 78, 525–28; id., *Policing and Punishment in London, 1660–1750* (Oxford, 2001), 311.

233. Fortescue, *Laws and Governance of England*, 111; Estienne Perlin, *Description des Royaulmes d'Angleterre et d'Escosse* (Paris, 1558; London, 1775), 28.

234. Philip Jenkins, 'From Gallows to Prison?' *Criminal Justice History* 7 (1986), 52.

235. Nicholas Geffe, 'A discourse of his own', 13, attached to his translation of Olivier de Serres, *The Perfect Use of Silk-Wormes and Their Benefits* (1607).

236. Cesare Beccaria, *An Essay on Crimes and Punishments* ([1764]; Eng. trans., 14th edn, 1785), translator's preface, viii.

237. Starkey, *Dialogue*, 129; 22 Hen. VIII, c. 9; Baker, *Oxford History of the Laws of England*, vol. 6, 587.

238. *The Lisle Letters*, ed. Muriel St Clare Byrne (Chicago, IL, 1981), vol. 2, 476 (these would have been the executions of three Carthusians and a Bridgettine monk; *Letters and Papers of Henry VIII*, vol. 8, 250–51); *Barrington Family Letters*, ed. Arthur Searle (Camden ser., 1983), 239.

239. Stephen Alford, *The Watchers* (2012), 144.

240. *Proceedings in the Parliaments of Elizabeth I*, ed. T. E. Hartley (Leicester, 1981–95), vol. 2, 84–85; *Cobbett's Complete Collection of State Trials*, ed. T. B. and T. J. Howell (1809–28), vol. 1, cols. 1158, 1160–62.

241. Henry Foley, *Records of the English Province of the Society of Jesus* (1875–83), vol. 1, 375; Richard Challoner, *Memoirs of Missionary Priests*, ed. John Hungerford Pollen (1924), 427.

242. Edward Coke, *The Third Part of the Institutes of the Laws of England* (1644), sig. Kk1.

243. *The Life and Times of Anthony Wood*, ed. Andrew Clark (Oxford Hist. Soc., 1891–1900), vol. 1, 186.

244. *The Diary of John Evelyn*, ed. E. S. de Beer (Oxford, 1955), vol. 3, 28–29.

245. Reginald Scot, *The Discoverie of Witchcraft* (1584), ed. Brinsley Nicholson ([1886]; Wakefield, 1973), 14.

246. Starkey, *Dialogue*, 80; *The Writings of William Paterson*, ed. Saxe Bannister (1859), vol. 1, 86; Donald Veall, *The Popular Movement for Law Reform 1640–1660* (Oxford, 1970), 128–31.

247. Steve Hindle, *The State and Social Change in Early Modern England, c. 1550–1640* (Basingstoke, 2000), 133–34.

248. *Examen Legum Angliae* (1656), 54; Whitelocke Bulstrode, *Essays upon the Following Subjects* (1724), 127; *Acts and Ordinances of the Interregnum*, ed. C. H. Firth and

R. S. Rait (1911), vol. 2, 419, 918; William M. Hamlin, *Montaigne's English Journey* (Oxford, 2013), 138 (cf. *Essays of Montaigne*, vol. 2, 121).

249. *Henry Brinklow's Complaynt of Roderyck Mors*, ed. J. Meadows Cowper (EETS, 1874), 30–32; J. F. Mozley, *John Foxe and His Book* (1940), 86–91; Walsham, *Charitable Hatred*, 58; Ian Atherton and David Como, 'The Burning of Edward Wightman', *EHR* 120 (2005), 1247.

250. [William Eden], *Principles of Penal Law* (1771), 87; Barlow, *Several Miscellaneous and Weighty Cases of Conscience*, vol. 1, 37; Marshall, *John Locke, Toleration and Early Enlightenment Culture*, 619–20; *Acts and Ordinances of the Interregnum*, vol. 1, 1133–36; vol. 2, 412; 29 Car. II, c. 9 (1677).

251. John March, *Amicus Reipublicae* (1651), 144, 147. On it see Andrea McKenzie, 'This death some strong and stouthearted man doth choose', *Law and History Rev.* 23 (2005).

252. 1 William and Mary, sess. 2, c. 2 (1689); *The Entring Book of Roger Morrice 1677–1691*, vol. 3, ed. Tim Harris (Woodbridge, 2007), 5–6; *The Laws and Liberties of Massachusetts*, 46, 50; Anthony F. Granucci, 'Nor Cruel and Unusual Punishments Inflicted', *California Law Rev.* 57 (1969).

253. *M. Misson's Memoirs and Observations in His Travels over England*, trans. [John] Ozell (1719), 325; Eden, *Principles of Penal Law*, 189–90; Blackstone, *Commentaries*, vol. 4, 243 (IV. 29).

254. J. A. Sharpe, *Crime in Early Modern England 1550–1750* (Harlow, 1984), 63–71; id., 'Civility, Civilizing Processes, and the End of Public Punishment in England', in *Civil Histories*, ed. Peter Burke et al. (Oxford, 2000), 218–19; Jenkins, 'From Gallows to Prison?'; Peter King, *Crime, Justice, and Discretion in England 1740–1820* (Oxford, 2000), 277–78.

255. Peter King and Richard Ward, 'Rethinking the Bloody Code in Eighteenth-Century Britain', *P&P* 228 (2015).

256. Cynthia Herrup, 'Punishing Pardon', in *Penal Practice and Culture*, ed. Simon Devereaux and Paul Griffiths (Basingstoke, 2004); Beattie, *Crime and the Courts*, 500–6; id., *Policing and Punishment in London*, 290–96, 301–4, 308–9, 364–68, and chap. 9; A. Roger Ekirch, *Bound for America* (Oxford, 1987).

257. Because of the squeamishness of those who had to administer it; Simon Devereaux, 'The Abolition of the Burning of Women in England Reconsidered', *Crime, histoire et sociétés* 9 (2005).

258. Leon Radzinowicz, *A History of Criminal Law and Its Administration from 1750* (1948–86), vol. 1, 232–38; vol. 2, 1–2; Michael Ignatieff, *A Just Measure of Pain* (1978), vol. 13, 18–19; Beattie, *Crime and the Courts*, chaps 8, 9 and 10; id., *Policing and Punishment*, part 2; Sharpe, 'Civility, Civilizing Processes, and the End of Public Punishment in England'; King, *Crime, Justice and Discretion*, 266–67; Simon Devereaux, 'England's Bloody Code in Crisis and Transition', *Journ. of Canadian Hist. Association* 24 (2013).

259. Richard J. Evans, *Rituals of Retribution* (Oxford, 1996), 228–29, and id., *The Pursuit of Power* (2016), 433.

260. Anthony Ashley Cooper, 3rd Earl of Shaftesbury, *Second Characters or the Language of Forms*, ed. Benjamin Rand (Cambridge, 1914), 170; John Brown, *An Estimate of the Manners and Principles of the Times* (2nd edn, 1757), 21; Smith, *Theory of Moral Sentiments*, 100–101 (II. iii. 2. 4); Blackstone, *Commentaries*, vol. 4, 210–13.

261. Thomas Sheridan, *A Discourse of the Rise and Power of Parliaments* (1677), 48; Randall McGowen, 'The Problem of Punishment in Eighteenth-Century England', in *Penal Practice and Culture, 1500–1800*, ed. Simon Devereaux and Paul Griffiths (Basingstoke, 2004), 215; Anthony Page, *John Jebb and the Enlightenment Origins of British Radicalism* (Westport, CT, 2003), 231.

262. Andrea McKenzie, 'Martyrs in Low Life', *JBS* (2003), 190–91; Ann Thompson, *The Art of Suffering and the Impact of Seventeenth-Century Anti-Providential Thought*

(Aldershot, 2003), vii, 4, 95; Esther Cohen, *The Modulated Scream* (Chicago, IL, 2009), 25–42; Jan Frans Van Dijkhuizen, *Pain and Compassion in Early Modern English Literature and Culture* (Woodbridge, 2012); Hannah Newton, *The Sick Child in Early Modern England, 1580–1720* (Oxford, 2012), 129, 192–93, 201–8; Joanna Bourke, *The Story of Pain* (Oxford, 2014), chap. 4; Alexandra Walsham, 'The Happiness of Suffering', in *Suffering and Happiness in England 1550–1850*, ed. Michael J. Braddick and Joanna Innes (Oxford, 2017).

263. Katherine Royer, *The English Execution Narrative* (2014), 35, 46–48; Henry Home, Lord Kames, *Sketches of the History of Man* (2nd edn, Edinburgh, 1778), vol. 1, 377–78.

264. Baron Lahontan, *New Voyages to North America* (Eng. trans., 2nd edn, 1735), vol. 1, 179; and see Karen Halttunen, 'Humanitarianism and the Pornography of Pain in Anglo-American Culture', *AHR* 100 (1995), esp. 303–7; Greg T. Smith, 'Civilized People Don't Want to See That Sort of Thing', in *Qualities of Mercy*, ed. Carolyn Strange (Vancouver, BC, 1996); Silverman, *Tortured Subjects*, 119, 149–51; Lynn Hunt, *Inventing Human Rights* (New York, 2007), chap. 2.

265. John Stuart Mill, 'Civilisation', in *Essays in Politics and Society*, vol. 1, ed. J. M. Robson (*Collected Works of John Stuart Mill*, vol. 18, Toronto, 1977), 130.

266. Most notably by the French writer Michel Foucault, though even he conceded the 'attenuated severity' of the new system; *Discipline and Punish*, trans. Alan Sheridan (1977), 82.

267. In his powerful work *The Hanging Tree* (Oxford, 1994), V. A. C. Gatrell suggests that popular sympathy for the hanged had little impact on the administration of the law. For some effective criticism of this view, see Randall McGowen, 'Revisiting *The Hanging Tree*', *British Journ. of Criminology* 40 (2000), and Devereaux, 'England's Bloody Code in Crisis and Transition'.

268. A. Ruth Fry, *John Bellers 1654–1725* (1935), 76. Cf. Georg Rusche and Otto Kirchheimer, *Punishment and Social Structure* (New York, 1939), chaps. 3–5.

269. Beccaria, *Essay on Crimes and Punishments*, 178; Kames, *Sketches of the History of Man*, vol. 1, 251; William Smith, *Mild Punishments Sound Policy* (1777), 6.

270. *Gentleman's Magazine* 60 (1790), 1185, cited in Beattie, 'Violence and Society', 55–56; Henry Dagge, *Considerations on Criminal Law* (2nd edn, 1774), vol. 2, 10; Randall McGowen, 'The Body and Punishment in Eighteenth-Century England', *JMH* 59 (1987), 677–78; id., 'Punishing Violence, Sentencing Crime', in *The Violence of Representation*, ed. Nancy Armstrong and Leonard Tennenhouse (1989), 142, 145–46; id., 'Civilizing Punishment', *JBS* 33 (1994); James Gregory, *Victorians against the Gallows* (2012), 8.

271. Tucker, *Light of Nature*, vol. 3, pt 2, 376.

272. *Letters from Mrs Elizabeth Carter, to Mrs Montagu, between the Years 1755 and 1800* (1817), vol. 1, 261.

273. George Hakewill, *An Apologie or Declaration of the Power and Providence of God in the Government of the World* (Oxford, 1630), 327; Edmond Howes, 'An Historicall Preface', in John Stow, *Annales, or, a Generall Chronicle of England*, continued by Howes (1631), sig. C4v; Ferguson, *Essay on the History of Civil Society*, 194–95; Kames, *Sketches*, vol. 1, 248–49.

274. John Favour, *Antiquitie Triumphing over Noveltie* (1619), 410; Gilpin, *Observations, Relative Chiefly to Picturesque Beauty in the Highlands*, vol. 2, 149–50; Kames, *Sketches*, vol. 1, 190–91.

275. Smith, *Theory of Moral Sentiments*, 207–9 (V. 2. 10–13), and 9 (I. 1. 1); Thomas, *Man and the Natural World*, 187–88; W. Hutton, *An History of Birmingham* (3rd edn, 1795), 171.

276. See, for example, Alan Macfarlane's review of Beattie, *Crime and the Courts*, in *London Rev. of Books* 8 (24 July 1986), 8–9.

277. *Spectator* 397 (5 June 1712), ed. Donald F. Bond (Oxford, 1965), vol. 3, 486; Gordon and Trenchard, *Independent Whig*, 312–13; *An Appeal to Humanity, in an Account of the Life and Cruel Actions of Elizabeth Brownrigg* (1767), 1–2; Norman S. Fiering, 'Irresistible Compassion', *JHI* 37 (1986), 204–5; James A. Steintrager, *Cruel Delight* (Bloomington, IN, 2004), xiv; Margaret Abruzzo, *Polemical Pain* (Baltimore, MD, 2011), chap. 2.

278. On this aspect of eighteenth-century joke books, see Simon Dickie, *Cruelty and Laughter* (Chicago, IL, 2011).

279. Palmer, *Essay of the Meanes*, 61.

280. Rowlands, *Mona Antiqua Restaurata*, 257; *The Literary Life of the Late Thomas Pennant, Esq., by himself* (1793), 55.

281. Sir Philip Sidney, *The Defence of Poesie*, ed. Albert Feuillerat (Cambridge, 1923), 42; a criticism reiterated by Sir Balthazar Gerbier, *A Brief Discourse concerning the Three Chief Points of Magnificent Building* (1664), 7.

282. Roger Williams, *A Key into the Language of America* (1643), 184; Spenser, *View*, 99–102, 111; Moryson, *Shakespeare's Europe*, 212–14; Sir William Herbert, *Croftus*, ed. Arthur Keaveney and John A. Madden (Dublin, 1992), 82–84; John Patrick Montaño, *The Roots of English Colonialism in Ireland* (Cambridge, 2011), 378–79.

283. *Spectator* 631 (10 Dec. 1714), ed. Bond, vol. 5, 157; Michael Hunter, 'Pitcairneana', *HJ* 59, no. 2 (2016), 605n35; William Buchan, *Domestic Medicine* (8th edn, 1784), 113–14; T. R. Malthus, *An Essay on the Principle of Population* (3rd edn, 1806), 56–57.

284. Guy Miège, *A Relation of the Three Embassies from His Sacred Majestie Charles II to the Great Duke of Muscovie* (1669), 341; *An Embassy to China*, ed. J. L. Cranmer-Byng (1963), 225.

285. Kames, *Sketches*, vol. 1, 233.

286. J[ean] Gailhard, *The Compleat Gentleman* (1678), vol. 1, 87.

287. Bernard Picart, *The Ceremonies and Religious Customs of the Known Peoples of the World* (abridged Eng. trans., 1741), 294; Pagden, *Fall of Natural Man*, 185.

288. Captain John Smith, *Works*, ed. Edward Arber (Westminster, 1895), vol. 2, 529.

289. Roger Williams, *George Fox Digg'd out of his Burrowes* (Boston, MA, 1676), 308.

290. Thomas Morton, *New English Canaan or New Canaan* (Amsterdam, 1637), 40; Rebecca Earle, *The Body of the Conquistador* (Cambridge, 2012), 119–21.

291. Purchas, *Hakluytus Posthumus*, vol. 7, 303; Graham Kew, *The Irish Sections of Fynes Moryson's Itinerary* (Dublin, 1998), 111; André Thevet, *The New Found Worlde, or Antarcktike* (trans. [Thomas Hacket], 1568), fol. 26ᵛ; [Edward Long], *History of Jamaica* (1774), vol. 2, 382.

292. Robert Boyle, *Occasional Reflections upon Several Subjects* (1665), vol. 2, 19.

293. Richard Hakluyt, *The Principall Navigations . . . of the English Nation* (Glasgow, 1903–5), vol. 7, 224; William Wood, *New Englands Prospect* (1634), 67; *Memoirs of Lieut. Henry Timberlake*, 35.

294. Sherley, 'Discours of the Turks'; Purchas, *Hakluytus Posthumus*, vol. 4, 15; Thomas Herbert, *A Relation of Some Yeares Travaile* (1634), 149; Long, *History of Jamaica*, vol. 2, 383.

295. Miège, *Relation of Three Embassies*, 435; *An Embassy to China*, 225.

296. Alex[ander] Niccholes, *A Discourse of Marriage and Wiving* (1615), 6.

297. Millar, 'Origin of Ranks', in Lehmann, *John Millar of Glasgow*, 183–84; *Voyages of Humphrey Gilbert*, vol. 2, 285.

298. Kames, *Sketches*, vol. 1, 190; Richard Payne Knight, *The Progress of Civil Society* (1796), 53 (bk 3, lines 103–4).

299. Sharpe, *A Fiery & Furious People*, 187–89, 415; W[illiam] H[eale], *An Apologie for Women* (1609), 7 (repeated in *The Great Advocate and Orator for Women* (1682), 1); A Lady [Judith Drake?], *An Essay in Defence of the Female Sex* (3rd edn, 1697), 22.

300. *Spectator* 236 (30 Nov. 1711), ed. Bond, vol. 2, 417–18; Joanne Bailey, *Unquiet Lives* (Cambridge, 2003), 115, 124; Elizabeth Foyster, *Marital Violence* (Cambridge, 2005), 47, 63, 65–66, 169, 195.

301. Henry Cornelius Agrippa, *Female Pre-Eminence*, trans. H[enry] C[are], 'with additional advantages' (1670), 71 (this passage is one of the translator's interpolations).
302. Anna Suranyi, *The Genius of the English Nation* (Newark, DE, 2008), chap. 6; Cramsie, *British Travellers*, 225; William Eton, *A Survey of the Turkish Empire* (1798), 247.
303. Richard Baxter, *A Christian Directory* (1673), 396.
304. Hume, *Essays*, vol. 1, 233–34.
305. Adam Smith, *Lectures on Jurisprudence*, ed. R. L. Meek et al. (Oxford, 1978), 150–59.
306. Kames, *Sketches*, vol. 1, 190–93, 213; *The Letters of Richard Brinsley Sheridan*, ed. Cecil Price (Oxford, 1966), vol. 1, 49.
307. Sir George Staunton, *An Authentic Account of an Embassy from the King of Great Britain to the Emperor of China* (Dublin, 1798), vol. 1, 51–52; vol. 2, 328–29.
308. *Relations of Golconda in the Early Seventeenth Century*, ed. W. H. Moreland (Hakluyt Soc., 1931), 29.
309. Meenakshi Jain, *Sati* (New Delhi, 2016), xiv–xv, 85, 188; Kate Teltscher, *India Inscribed* (New Delhi, 1999), chap. 2; Andrea Major, *Pious Flames* (New Delhi, 2006).
310. Bathsua Makin, *An Essay to Revive the Antient Education of Gentlewomen* (1673), 28; *ODNB*, 'Makin, Bathsua'; Daniel Defoe, *An Essay upon Projects* (1697), ed. Joyce D. Kennedy et al. (New York, 1999), 108.
311. Kames, *Sketches*, vol. 1, sketch 6.
312. Malthus, *Essay on the Principle of Population*, vol. 1, 27; Lehmann, *John Millar of Glasgow*, 192–94; *Memoirs of Lieut. Henry Timberlake*, 76; Hume, *Essays*, vol. 1, 193, 301–2.
313. Dalrymple, *Essay towards a General History of Feudal Property*, 185–86; Kames, *Sketches*, vol. 1, 191. On this theme see Silvia Sebastiani, *The Scottish Enlightenment*, trans. Jeremy Carden (New York, 2013), chap. 5.
314. 'Origin of Ranks', chap. 1, in Lehmann, *John Millar of Glasgow*.
315. *Writings and Speeches of Edmund Burke*, vol. 2, 357 (and vol. 9, 243).
316. Francis Jeffrey, *Contributions to the Edinburgh Review* (2nd edn, 1846), vol. 1, 229–33; Ian Maclean, *Woman Triumphant* (Oxford, 1977), chap. 5; Dena Goodman, *The Republic of Letters* (Ithaca, NY, 1994), chap. 3; Antoine Lilti, *The World of the Salons*, trans. Lydia G. Cochrane (Oxford, 2005), 236, 248n11; Philippe Raynaud, *La Politesse des lumières* (Paris, 2013), 3, 11.
317. Sylvana Tomaselli, 'The Enlightenment Debate on Women', *HWJ* 20 (1985); Rosemarie Zagarri, 'Morals, Manners, and the Republican Mother', *American Quarterly* 44 (1992); *Women, Gender and Enlightenment*, ed. Sarah Knott and Barbara Taylor (Basingstoke, 2005), 70, 695; Harriet Guest, *Empire, Barbarism, and Civilisation* (Cambridge, 2007), 57, 111; Karen O'Brien, *Women and Enlightenment in Eighteenth-Century Britain* (Cambridge, 2009).
318. *The Journals of Captain Cook*, ed. J. C. Beaglehole (Hakluyt Soc., 1955–74), vol. 3 (2), 933, 1366.
319. William Alexander, *The History of Women* (1779), vol. 1, 103.
320. *An Embassy to China*, ed. J. L. Cranmer-Byng (1962), 223.
321. Hobbes, *Leviathan*, ed. Malcolm, vol. 2, 192 (chap. 13).
322. Locke, *Two Treatises of Government*, 311–12 (II. paras. 36–37), 319–20 (II. paras. 49–50); *Locke on Money*, ed. Patrick Hyde Kelly (Oxford, 1991), vol. 2, 410; Mandeville, *Fable of the Bees*, vol. 2, 349; *Complete Works of Montesquieu*, vol. 1, 367 ('The Spirit of Laws', bk 1, chap. 15).
323. 'The Answer of Mr Hobbes', in *Sir William Davenant's Gondibert*, ed. David F. Gladish (Oxford, 1971), 49 (one of Hobbes's three earlier accounts of the distinctive benefits of civil society; the others are in *The Elements of Law* (completed 1640), ed. Ferdinand Tönnies (2nd edn, 1969), 65–66 (I. 13. 3), and *De Cive: the Latin Version* (1642), ed. Howard Warrender (Oxford, 1983), 171 (x. 1)).

324. Margaret T. Hodgen, *Early Anthropology in the Sixteenth and Seventeenth Centuries* (Philadelphia, PA, 1964), 196–201; Michèle Duchet, *Anthropologie et histoire au siècle des Lumières* (Paris, 1971), 11; Ferguson, *Essay on the History of Civil Society*, 75.

325. Thomas Hobbes, *The Questions concerning Liberty, Necessity, and Chance* (1656), 239.

326. Hobbes, *Elements of Law*, 65–66 (I. 13. 3); 'The Answer of Mr Hobbes', 49; id., *Leviathan*, ed. Malcolm, vol. 3, 1054 (chap. 46); *Principes de la Philosophie*, preface, 2, in *Oeuvres de Descartes*, ed. Charles Adam and Paul Tannery (Paris, 1897–1913), ix; Pierre D'Avity, *The Estates, Empires, & Principallities of the World*, trans. Edw[ard] Grimstone (1615), 268.

327. Thevet, *New Found Worlde*, sig. *ii; Francis Bacon, *The Instauratio Magna, Part II: Novum Organum and Associated Texts*, ed. Graham Rees with Maria Wakely (Oxford, 2004), 194–95; Purchas, *Hakluytus Posthumus*, vol. 1, 52 (and 32); Greengrass, *Christendom Destroyed*, 25. On the low state of navigation in late eighteenth-century China, see Staunton, *Authentic Account*, vol. 1, 37–39.

328. Richard Cumberland, *An Essay towards the Recovery of the Jewish Measures and Weights* (1686), 133.

329. Smith, *Wealth of Nations*, vol. 2, 708 (V. i. a. 44); 'Elements of the Philosophy of the Human Mind', in *The Collected Works of Dugald Stewart*, ed. Sir William Hamilton and John Veitch (Edinburgh, 1854–60), vol. 2, 242. Cf. Philip T. Hoffman, 'Prices, the Military Revolution, and Western Europe's Comparative Advantage', *EcHR* 64 (2011).

330. John Locke, *An Essay concerning Human Understanding*, ed. Peter H. Nidditch (Oxford, 1975), 646 (IV. xii. 11); John Ray, *The Wisdom of God Manifested in the Works of Creation* (1691; 12th edn, 1759), 96. The classic statement of the importance of metals was book 1 of Rodulphus Agricola, *De Re Metallica* (Basel, 1556). An English translation was planned by Sir John Pettus in 1636, but never published; see the translation by Herbert Clark Hoover and Lou Henry Hoover (New York, 1950), xviii.

331. *Memoirs and Correspondence of Francis Horner*, ed. Leonard Horner (1843), vol. 1, 113; Paul Mantoux, *The Industrial Revolution in the Eighteenth Century*, trans. Marjorie Vernon (rev. edn, 1928), 397; Jean-Jacques Rousseau, 'Discours sur l'origine et les fondemens de l'inégalité', in *Oeuvres complètes*, ed. Bernard Gagnebin (Paris, 1964), vol. 3, 171; Gibbon, *Decline and Fall*, vol. 1, 220 (chap. 9); *Works of William Robertson*, vol. 6, 140–41.

332. Purchas, *Hakluytus Posthumus*, vol. 1, 486; Matthew Hale, *The Primitive Origination of Mankind* (1677), 150; *Works of William Robertson*, vol. 3, 76–78; Mandeville, *Fable of the Bees*, vol. 2, 269, 283; Gibbon, *Decline and Fall*, vol. 1, 218 (chap. 9).

333. See W. B. Stephens, 'Literacy in England, Scotland, and Wales, 1500–1900', *History of Education Qtly* 30 (1990), and David Cressy, 'Literacy in Context', in *Consumption and the World of Goods*, ed. John Brewer and Roy Porter (1993).

334. *Boswell's Life of Johnson*, vol. 2, 170, vol. 3, 37; Knud Haakonssen, *Natural Law and Moral Philosophy* (Cambridge, 1996), 233, 286.

335. E.g., John Banister, *A Needefull, New, and Necessarie Treatise of Chyrurgerie* (1575), sig. *ij.

336. John Whitgift, *The Defense of the Aunswere to the Admonition* (1574), 450; id., *An Answere to a Certen Libel* (1572), 225; Edward Waterhouse, *An Humble Apologie for Learning and Learned Men* (1653), 111–12.

337. John Gauden, *Hieraspistes* (1653), 400, 403; 'Of Dramatick Poesie', in *The Works of John Dryden* (Berkeley, CA, 1956–2000), vol. 17, 63.

338. Jamie C. Kassler, *The Honourable Roger North (1651–1734)* (Farnham, 2009), 229; F. J. M. Korsten, *Roger North (1651–1734)* (Amsterdam, 1981), 80.

339. Thomas Sprat, *The History of the Royal Society*, ed. Jackson I. Cope and Harold Whitmore Jones (St Louis, WA, 1959), 57, 124; William Marsden, *The History of Sumatra* (1783), 170n; David Hume, *The Natural History of Religion*, ed. Tom L. Beauchamp (Oxford, 2007), 38–39; Guest, *Empire, Barbarism, and Civilisation*, 40–41;

James Ramsay, *An Essay on the Treatment and Conversion of African Slaves* (Dublin, 1784), 191, 224.

340. *Mélanges inédits de Montesquieu*, ed. Baron de Montesquieu (Bordeaux, 1892), 129–31.

341. [John] Logan, *Elements of the Philosophy of History* (Edinburgh, 1781), 7; William Wilkinson, *A Confutation of Certain Articles Delivered unto the Familye of Love* (1579), fol. 35ᵛ; Fletcher, *Of the Rus Commonwealth*, 68, 154; Miège, *Relation of the Three Embassies*, 65–66; Hale, *Primitive Origination of Mankind*, 159.

342. *Works of Benjamin Whichcote*, vol. 2, 223.

343. *The Works of Michael Drayton*, ed. J. William Hebel (Oxford, 1961), vol. 3, 207; Roger Ascham, *English Works*, ed. William Aldis Wright (Cambridge, 1904), 48; *The Works of Francis Bacon*, ed. James Spedding et al. (1857–59), vol. 7, 22; Sherley, 'Discours of the Turkes', 4; Smith, *Manners, Religion and Government of the Turks*, 2–3, 226; P. J. Marshall and Glyndwr Williams, *The Great Map of Mankind* (1982), 142–43; Bisaha, ' "New Barbarian" or Worthy Adversary?', 190–93; Noel Malcolm, 'The Study of Islam in Early Modern Europe', in *Antiquarianism and Intellectual Life in Europe and China, 1500–1800*, ed. Peter N. Miller and François Louis (Ann Arbor, MI, 2012), 276–78.

344. George Sandys, *A Relation of a Journey begun anno Dom. 1610* (1615), 72.

345. Jonathan Richardson, *Two Discourses* (1719), pt 2, 57.

346. The *Letters of David Hume*, ed. J. Y. T. Greig (Oxford, 1932), vol. 2, 111; Hume, *Essays*, vol. 1, 223, 301–3; id., *An Enquiry Concerning the Principles of Morals*, ed. Tom L. Beauchamp (Oxford, 1998), 62–63.

347. Marshall and Williams, *Great Map of Mankind*, 146.

348. Kenneth Pomeranz, *The Great Divergence* (Princeton, NJ, 2000), and id., 'Without Coal?' in *Unmaking the West*, ed. Philip E. Tetlock et al. (Ann Arbor, MI, 2006).

349. Claude Lévi-Strauss, *Race and History* (Paris, 1968), 25. Cf. E. A. Wrigley, *Continuity, Chance and Change* (Cambridge, 1988); Vaclav Smil, *Energy in World History* (Boulder, CO, 1994), chap. 5; Ian Morris, *The Measure of Civilization* (2013), 53, 62–66, 87.

350. [Thomas Bentley], *Letters on the Utility and Policy of Employing Machines to Shorten Labour* (1780), 3.

351. Charles Hall, *The Effects of Civilization on the People in European States* (1805), 131–32.

352. Barbaro and Contarini, *Travels to Tana and Persia*, 1.

353. Malthus, *Essay on the Principle of Population*, vol. 1, chap. 3; Smith, *Wealth of Nations*, vol. 1, 10 (Introduction), 22 (I. i. 10).

354. Michael Adas, *Machines as the Measure of Men* (Ithaca, NY, 1989), esp. chap. 4; John Stuart Mill, 'Guizot's Lectures on European Civilization', in *Essays on French History and Historians*, ed. John M. Robson (*Collected Works of John Stuart Mill*, vol. 20) (Toronto, 1985), 374, and 'Civilization', in *Essays on Politics and Society*, 1.

355. R. G. Collingwood, *The New Leviathan* ([1942]; Oxford, 1947), 291, 299.

356. J. R. Seeley, *The Expansion of England* (1883), 4.

357. 'The Manifesto of the Communist Party', in Karl Marx and Frederick Engels, *Selected Works* (1950).

358. James Dunbar, *Essays on the History of Mankind* (1780), 142, 145.

4 The Progress of Civilization

1. On these authors, see Arthur O. Lovejoy and George Boas, *Primitivism and Related Ideas in Antiquity* (Baltimore, MD, 1935; New York, 1965); Erwin Panofsky, *Studies in Iconology* ([1939]; New York, 1972), chap. 2; Ludwig Edelstein, *The Idea of Progress in Classical Antiquity* (Baltimore, MD, 1967).

2. Thomas Starkey, *A Dialogue between Pole and Lupset*, ed. T. F. Mayer (Camden ser., 1989), 35–36. For similar accounts, see Arthur B. Ferguson, *Clio Unbound* (Durham, NC, 1979), chap 10, and id., *Utter Antiquity* (Durham, NC, 1993), chap. 4, and 152n2; Richard Tuck, *Natural Rights Theories* (Cambridge, 1979), 33–34, 37, 43, 93, 103.

3. Cicero, *De Oratore*, bk 1, sect. 33–34; *Wilson's Arte of Rhetorique 1560*, ed. G. H. Mair (Oxford, 1903), preface, sig. Avii; William Webbe, *A Discourse of English Poetrie* (1586), sigs. Biii^v–iiii; George Puttenham, *The Arte of English Poesie*, ed. Gladys Doidge Willcock and Alice Walker (Cambridge, 1936), 6 (I. iii); *The Poems of George Chapman*, ed. Phyllis Brooks Bartlett (New York, 1941), 362; Joseph Warton, *An Essay on the Writings and Genius of Pope* (1756), 60–61.

4. Sir William Temple, *Miscellanea: The Second Part* (4th edn, 1696), 151.

5. Joannes Boemus, *The Fardle of Facions*, trans. William Watreman (1555), sig. Biiij; *Wilson's Arte of Rhetorique*, sig. Avi^v; Francis Bacon, *New Atlantis* ([1627]; 1906), 273–74; Henry Parker, *Observations upon Some of His Majesties Late Answers and Expresses* (1642), 13; John Woodward, *An Essay toward a Natural History of the Earth* (1695), 56–57, 94–95, 102.

6. George Sandys, *A Relation of a Iourney begun An. Dom. 1610* (1615), 20.

7. Quentin Skinner, *The Foundations of Modern Political Thought* (Cambridge, 1978), vol. 2, 116–18, 340–41.

8. *Bishop Overall's Convocation Book MDCVI* [ed. William Sancroft] (1690), 3–4.

9. John Byrom, *The Necessity of Subjection Asserted* (1681), 2.

10. *The Works of the Most Reverend Father in God John Bramhall* [ed. A. W. H(addan)] (Oxford, 1842–45), vol. 4, 567.

11. E.g., Gabriel Towerson, *An Explication of the Decalogue* (1686), 332 (citing Lactantius, *Divine Institutes*, 6. 10. 13–15).

12. Samuel Parker, *A Discourse of Ecclesiastical Politie* (1670), 118.

13. Adam Smith, *Essays on Philosophical Subjects*, ed. W. P. D. Wightman and J. C. Bryce (Oxford, 1980), 293.

14. William Wood, *New Englands Prospect* (3rd edn, 1764), 94n; *Letters of Roger Williams*, ed. John Russell Bartlett (Pubs. of the Narrangansett Club, Providence, RI, 1866–74, vol. 6), 276; William Walter Hening, *The Statutes at Large; Being a Collection of All the Laws of Virginia* ([1823]; Charlottesville, VA, 1969), vol. 1, 395.

15. [George Abbot], *A Briefe Description of the Whole Worlde* ([1599]; Amsterdam, 1970), sig. B1^v.

16. He had read Cicero's account in *De Oratore* of humanity's early condition, as can be seen from his *Expugnatio Hibernica*, ed. and trans. A. B. Scott and F. X. Martin (Dublin, 1978), 10. For the possible influence on him of a passage in Sallust's *Jugurtha*, see Michael Staunton, *The Historians of Angevin England* (Oxford, 2017), 98.

17. Gerald of Wales, *The History and Topography of Ireland*, trans. J. J. O'Meara (Harmondsworth, 1981), 101–2, and *The Description of Wales*, trans. Lewis Thorpe (Harmondsworth, 1978), 233–35; John Gillingham, 'Civilizing the English?', *HistRes* 74 (2001), 26–27 (who provocatively calls it 'a much more explicitly developmental and progressive view of history than anything written in England in the sixteenth and seventeenth centuries'; he presumably discounts the English translations of Boemus, d'Avity, Le Roy et al.); Edward Gibbon, *The History of the Decline and Fall of the Roman Empire*, ed. J. B. Bury (5th edn, 1912), vol. 3, chap. 26 (quotation at 72). On Gerald's ethnography, see Robert Bartlett, *Gerald of Wales 1146–1223* (Oxford, 1982), chap. 7.

18. *Gesta Stephani*, ed. and trans. K. R. Potter (Oxford, 1976), 14–15, 20–21, 54–55 (paras. 8, 11, 26), though the author does not make the analytic link between pastoralism and warfare that Gillingham, who cites these passages, suggests; 'Civilizing the English?', 27.

19. Edmund Spenser, *A View of the Present State of Ireland*, in *Spenser's Prose Works*, ed. Rudolf Gottfried (Baltimore, MD, 1949), 217–18 (and 98).

20. Samuel Purchas, *Hakluytus Posthumus, or Purchas His Pilgrimes* ([1625]; Glasgow, 1905–7), vol. 7, 303.

21. Fynes Moryson, *Shakespeare's Europe*, ed. Charles Hughes (2nd edn, New York, 1967), 201.

22. Kenneth Nicholls, 'Gaelic Society and Economy', in *A New History of Ireland*, vol. 2, ed. Art Cosgrove (Oxford, 1993), 413–14; R. A. Butlin, 'Land and People, *c.* 1600', in *A New History of Ireland*, vol. 3, ed. T. W. Moody et al. (Oxford, 1978), 152–53; John Patrick Montaño, *The Roots of English Colonialism in Ireland* (Cambridge, 2011), 8–10; Andrew Hadfield, *Edmund Spenser* (Oxford, 2012), 216–18; Fynes Moryson, *An Itinerary* (Glasgow, 1907–8), vol. 2, 330.

23. Nicholas Canny, 'The Ideology of English Colonization', *WMQ*, 3rd ser., vol. 30 (1973), 597.

24. *Forty-Six Lives* (from Boccaccio, *De Claris Mulieribus*), trans. Henry Parker, Lord Morley, ed. Herbert G. Wright (EETS, 1943), 21–23; Barbette Stanley Spaeth, *The Roman Goddess Ceres* (Austin, TX, 1996), 34–41.

25. [Sir Thomas Smith and Thomas Smith], *A Letter sent by I. B. Gentleman unto his very Friend and Master R. C. Esquire* (1572), sigs. Ei, Div; Mary Dewar, *Sir Thomas Smith* (1964), 166; Spenser, *View*, 225; *Cal. SP, Ireland, 1588–1592*, 168; Moryson, *Shakespeare's Europe*, 201. On the centrality of agricultural cultivation to the sixteenth-century 'civilizing' of Ireland, see Montaño, *Roots of English Colonialism*.

26. Andrew Boorde, *The Fyrst Boke of the Introduction of Knowledge*, ed. F. J. Furnivall (EETS, 1870), 126, 132; *The Jacobean Union*, ed. Bruce R. Galloway and Brian P. Levack (Scottish Hist. Soc., 1985), 22; Alison Games, *The Web of Empire* (Oxford, 2008), 119.

27. *The Journal of John Stevens*, ed. Robert H. Murray (Oxford, 1912), 140.

28. [Peter Chamberlen], *The Poore Mans Advocate* (n.d. [1649]), 9; Spenser, *View*, 219.

29. William Wood, *New Englands Prospect* (1634), 78; Letter by John Eliot, in Thomas Shepard, *The Clear Sun-shine of the Gospel Breaking Forth upon the Indians in New-England* (1648), 17.

30. *The Works of Isaac Barrow* (Edinburgh, 1842), vol. 1, 477; *A Letter from a Gentleman in Ireland to his Brother in England* (1677), 12 ('step to civility'). Similarly Jo[hn] Streater, *A Glympse of That Jewel, Judicial, Just, Preserving Libertie* (1653), 15; John Cary, *An Account of the Proceedings of the Corporation of Bristol* (1700), 4.

31. Thomas F. Mayer, *Thomas Starkey and the Commonweal* (Cambridge, 1989), 120.

32. James Buckley, 'A Vice-Regal Progress through the South and West of Ireland in 1567', *Journ. of the Waterford and South-East of Ireland Archaeol. Soc.* 12 (1909), 72–73; *Cal. SP, Foreign, Jan.–June 1583*, 491; Spenser, *View*, 225.

33. *The Voyages and Colonizing Enterprises of Humphrey Gilbert*, ed. David Beers Quinn (Hakluyt Soc., 1940), vol. 1, 181; Edward Waterhouse, *A Declaration of the State of the Colony and Affaires in Virginia* (1622), 24.

34. M. Iuniani Iustinus, *Epitoma Historiarum Philippicarum Pompei Trogi*, ed. Marco Galdi (Turin, 1923), bk 43, para. 4: translated by Arthur Golding as 'a more civil trade of living' (*The Abridgment of the Histories of Trogus Pompeius* (1563), fol. 178), and by Robert Codrington as 'a more refined course of life' (*The Historie of Iustine* (1654), 507).

35. *Registrum Epistolarum Fratris Johannis Peckham*, ed. Charles Trice Martin (Rolls Ser., 1882–85), vol. 3, 776–77; Gillingham, 'Civilizing the English?', 38–40.

36. T[homas] H[eywood], *The Generall History of Women* (1657), 634; Spenser, *View*, 225; *'Reform' Treatises on Tudor Ireland*, ed. David Heffernan (Irish MSS Commission, Dublin, 2016), 21.

37. 'A discourse of the names and first causes of the institution of cities and peopled townes', in John Stow, *A Survey of London*, ed. Charles Lethbridge Kingsford (Oxford, 1908), vol. 2, 196–98. Similarly, John Barston, *The Safegarde of Societie* (1576), fols. 26–27ᵛ.

38. Purchas, *Hakluytus Posthumus*, vol. 5, 359.

39. 'A View of the Progress of Society in Europe', in *The Works of the Late William Robertson*, ed. R. Lynam (1826), vol. 3, 61; Adam Smith, *An Inquiry into the Nature and Causes of the Wealth of Nations*, ed. R. H. Campbell and A. S. Skinner (Oxford, 1976), vol. 1, 412–22 (III. iv. 1–18).

40. Francesco Patrizi, *A Moral Methode of Civile Policie*, trans. Richard Robinson (1576), fol. 5.
41. Steven G. Ellis, 'Civilizing the Natives', in *Frontiers and Identities*, ed. Lud'a Klusáková and Steven G. Ellis (Pisa, 2006), 81.
42. Edmund Hogan, *The Description of Ireland* ([1598]; Dublin, 1878), 65; Debora Shuger, 'Irishmen, Aristocrats, and Other White Barbarians', *Renaissance Qtly* 50 (1997), who rightly recognizes in the Irish tracts 'a rare contemporary analysis of the infrastructural bases of the civilizing process' (521–22).
43. *Cal. SP, Ireland, 1611–14*, 501–2.
44. Thomas Churchyard, *A Prayse, and Reporte of Maister Martyne Forboishers Voyage to Meta Incognita* (1578), sig. Bvii.
45. Samuel Purchas, *Purchas His Pilgrimage* (1626), 230; id., *Hakluytus Posthumus*, vol. 9, 100; Lancelot Addison, *West Barbary* (Oxford, 1671), 138.
46. [Sir Dalby Thomas], *An Historical Account of the Rise and Growth of the West-India Collonies [sic]* (1690), 6; Smith, *Wealth of Nations*, vol. 1, 10 (Introduction), 22 (I. i).
47. See, particularly, J. G. A. Pocock, *The Machiavellian Moment* ([1975]; 2nd edn, Princeton, NJ, 2003), chaps. 13 and 14, and afterword; 'Gibbon and the Shepherds', *History of European Ideas* 2 (1981), 194–96; 'Cambridge Paradigms and Scottish Philosophers', in *Wealth and Virtue*, ed. Istvan Hont and Michael Ignatieff (Cambridge, 1983), 240–45; and *Virtue, Commerce and History* (Cambridge, 1985), 49–50 ('ideological need'), 114–15, 235–38.
48. *The Complete Works of M. de Montesquieu* (1777), vol. 2, 1–3 (xx. 1–2).
49. *The Political and Commercial Works of . . . Charles D'Avenant*, ed. Charles Whitworth (1771), vol. 2, 275; David A. G. Waddell, 'The Career and Writings of Charles Davenant (1656–1714)' (D.Phil. thesis, Univ. of Oxford, 1954).
50. William Fulbecke, *The Pandectes of the Law of Nations* (1602), fol. 65ᵛ.
51. Jacob Viner, *The Role of Providence in the Social Order* (Amer. Philos. Soc., Philadelphia, 1972), chap. 2; David Harris Sacks, 'The True Temper of Empire', *Renaissance Studies*, 26 (2012), 534–40.
52. William Thomas, *The Pilgrim*, ed. J. A. Froude (1861), 4; André Thevet, *The New Found World, or Antarctike*, trans. Thomas Hacket (1568), fol. 74.
53. Purchas, *Hakluytus Posthumus*, vol. 1, 10–11; vol. 19, 223; [Sir Thomas Smith?], *A Discourse of the Commonweal*, ed. Mary Dewar (Charlottesville, VA, 1969), 62; Charles Richardson, *A Sermon against Oppression and Fraudulent Dealing* (1615), 17; Nathanael Carpenter, *Geographie Delineated Forth in Two Bookes* (1625), vol. 2, 274; *The Arrivall and Intertainemens of the Embassador, Alkaid Jauvar Ben Abdella* (1637), 1–3; William Gray, *Chorographia, or a Survey of Newcastle* (1649), 26; 'Preface in Defence of Trade and Commerce', in Edmund Bolton, *The Cities Great Concern* (1674) (not in the original edition of 1629), sigs. A1ᵛ–2; Peter Heylyn, *Cosmography in Four Books* (1674), 4; William Molyneux, *Sciothericum Telescopicum* (Dublin, 1686), 2; [John Streater], *Observations Historical, Political and Philosophical upon Aristotle's First Book of Political Government*, 4 (25 Apr.–2 May 1654), 28.
54. Sir James Perrott, *The Chronicle of Ireland 1584–1608*, ed. Herbert Wood (Dublin, 1933), 16.
55. Stephen Conway, *Britain, Ireland, and Continental Europe in the Eighteenth Century* (Oxford, 2011), 260–65; Thomas Wemyss Fulton, *The Sovereignty of the Sea* (Edinburgh, 1911), 206–8.
56. Joyce Appleby, *Economic Thought and Ideology in Seventeenth-Century England* (Princeton, NJ, 1978), 118–19; Craig Muldrew, *The Economy of Obligation* (Basingstoke, 1998), chap. 5.
57. Games, *Web of Empire*, esp. 24, 51, 78, 79, 113, 115, 320; Roxann Wheeler, *The Complexion of Race* (Philadelphia, PA, 2000), 103; Adam Smith, *Lectures on Jurisprudence*, ed. R. L. Meek et al. (Oxford, 1978), 538.

58. Thomas Sprat, *History of the Royal Society*, ed. Jackson I. Cope and Harold Whitmore Jones (St Louis, MO, 1959), 408; Aylett Sammes, *Britannia Antiqua Illustrata* (1676), 15, 73; John Evelyn, *Navigation and Commerce* (1674), 4, 11; id., *The History of Religion*, ed. R. M. Evanson (1850), vol. 2, 195.

59. *The Diary and Autobiography of Edmund Bohun Esq*, ed. S. Wilton Rix (Beccles, 1853), 134.

60. William Dampier, *A New Voyage around the World* (1697), 115–16.

61. Bernard Mandeville, *The Fable of the Bees*, ed. F. B. Kaye (Oxford, 1924), vol. 2, 349; Malachy Postlethwayt, *The Universal Dictionary of Trade and Commerce* (1751), 3; *Works of William Robertson*, vol. 3, 123.

62. Edward Graves, *A Brief Narration and Deduction* (1679), 6; *John Locke on Money*, ed. Patrick Hyde Kelly (Oxford, 1991), vol. 2, 410; *The Constitution of the Office of Land Credit Declared in a Deed by Hugh Chamberlen* (1696), 2; Matthew Henry, *A Sermon on Acts XXVIII*, 22 (1699), 20. On 'civilizing trade', see Albert O. Hirschman, *The Passions and the Interests* (Princeton, NJ, 1977), 51–52, 58–63, 70–80; id., *Rival Views of Market Society and Other Recent Essays* (New York, 1986), 107–9; Anthony Pagden, *Lords of All the World* (New Haven, CT, 1995), 178–87.

63. William Wood, *New Englands Prospect* (3rd edn, 1764), 94.

64. Smith, *Lectures on Jurisprudence*, 14–16, 459–60; *Turgot on Progress, Sociology and Economics*, trans. and ed. Ronald L. Meek (Cambridge, 1973), 65–69. For discussion, see Ronald L. Meek, *Social Science and the Ignoble Savage* (Cambridge, 1976), esp. chap. 4; Andrew S. Skinner, *A System of Social Science* (Oxford, 1979), 71–90; Peter Stein, *Legal Evolution* (Cambridge, 1980), chap. 2, and 'The Four Stage Theory of the Development of Societies', in his *The Character and Influence of the Civil Law* (1988); Knud Haakonssen, *The Science of a Legislator* (Cambridge, 1981), chap. 7; Christopher J. Berry, *Social Theory of the Scottish Enlightenment* (Edinburgh, 1997), 93–99, and *The Idea of Commercial Society in the Scottish Enlightenment* (Edinburgh, 2013), chap. 2 (a particularly precise analysis); J. G. A. Pocock, *Barbarism and Religion* (Cambridge, 1999–2016), vol. 2, 309–45; vol. 4, 100, 166–71; Frank Palmeri, *Stages of Nature, Stages of Society* (New York, 2016), introduction and chap 1.

65. Christopher J. Berry, 'Rude Religion', in *The Scottish Enlightenment*, ed. Paul Wood (Rochester, NY, 2000).

66. Lovejoy and Boas, *Primitivism and Related Ideas*, esp. chaps. 7, 8, 9, 12; Thomas Cole, *Democritus and the Sources of Greek Anthropology* (Cleveland, OH, 1967), 26, 149, 184.

67. [Johannes Boemus], 'Preface of the Authour', in *The Fardle of Facions*, trans. William Watreman (1555), and in id., *The Manners, Lawes, and Customes of All Nations*, trans. Ed. Aston (1611). On him, see C. Phillip E. Nothaft, 'The Early History of Man and the Uses of Diodorus in Renaissance Scholarship', in *For the Sake of Learning*, ed. Ann Blair and Anja-Silvia Goeing (Leiden, 2016).

68. Louis le Roy, *Of the Interchangeable Course, or Variety of Things in the Whole World*, trans. R[obert] A[shley] (1594), bk 3, esp. fols. 27ᵛ–28ᵛ; Pierre d'Avity, *The Estates, Empires and Principallities of the World*, trans. Edward Grimstone (1615), 266–67 (on degrees of barbarism), 267–68 (on stages of development); Geoffroy Atkinson, *Les Nouveaux Horizons de la Renaissance française* (Paris, 1935), 37–80; Federico Chabod, *Giovanni Botero* (Rome, [1934]), 80; Rosario Romeo, *Le scoperte americane nella coscienza italiana del Cinquecento* (Milan, 1954), 93–106.

69. Istvan Hont, 'The Language of Sociability and Commerce', in his *Jealousy of Trade* (Cambridge, MA, 2005), 160–84, 364–70.

70. Jed Z. Buchwald and Mordechai Feingold, *Newton and the Origin of Civilization* (Princeton, NJ, 2013), 428.

71. *Complete Works of Montesquieu*, vol. 1, 363, 365–69 ('The Spirit of Laws', bk 18, 8, 11–17).

72. Smith, *Lectures on Jurisprudence*, 61, 69–70 (where five times in two successive paragraphs he calls the Scottish system of entails 'absurd'), 70–71, 467–69, 524–25;

id., *Wealth of Nations*, 383–86 (III. ii. 7); Henry Home, Lord Kames, *Historical Law-Tracts* (Edinburgh, 1758), vol. 1, 219. By contrast, another proponent of the four-stage theory, John Dalrymple, showed how the fourth (commercial) stage led to the alienation of landed property, but deplored its consequences; John Dalrymple, *An Essay towards a General History of Feudal Property in Great Britain* (2nd edn, 1758), chaps. 3 and 4; id., *Considerations upon the Policy of Entails in Great Britain* (Edinburgh, 1764).

73. Berry, *Idea of a Commercial Society*, 38.

74. Kames, *Historical Law-Tracts*, vol. 1, 77n–80n, 126–29, 139–40, 146.

75. Adam Ferguson, *An Essay on the History of Civil Society 1767*, ed. Duncan Forbes (Edinburgh, 1966).

76. John Brown, *A Dissertation on the Rise . . . of Poetry and Music* (1763). No attention appears to have been paid in seventeenth-century England to the brilliantly original account of the stages of mankind's intellectual progress offered by the Czech educational and religious reformer Jan Amos Komenský (Comenius) in his *Via Lucis* (Amsterdam, 1668, but written twenty-six years earlier), trans. E. T. Campagnac as *The Way of Light* (Liverpool, 1938), chap. 13.

77. [William and Edmund Burke], *An account of the European Settlements in America* (1757), vol. 1, 167.

78. Donald R. Kelley, *Foundations of Modern Historical Scholarship* (New York, 1970), 64, 83; Robert Burton, *The Anatomy of Melancholy*, ed. Thomas C. Faulkner et al. (Oxford, 1989–2000), vol. 2, 154; Ferguson, *Essay on the History of Civil Society*, 208.

79. Bartlett, *Gerald of Wales*, 190; Spenser, *View*, 96, 113–20; William Camden, *Britain* (1610), 2nd pagination, 148; Richard A. McCabe, *Spenser's Monstrous Regiment* (Oxford, 2002), 140.

80. George Hakewill, *An Apologie or Declaration of the Power and Providence of God* (3rd edn, 1635), vol. 5, 58.

81. Nicholas Tyacke, 'An Oxford Education in the Early Seventeenth Century', *History of Universities*, vol. 27 (2013), 37.

82. Benjamin Farrington, *The Philosophy of Francis Bacon* (Liverpool, 1964), 109; Sprat, *History of the Royal Society*, 22–23, 389; *The Petty Papers*, ed. Marquess of Lansdowne (1927), vol. 2, 24. See Paul Slack, *The Invention of Improvement* ([2014]; Oxford, '2015'), index, s.v. 'progress'.

83. By contrast, the fourteenth-century Arab philosopher Ibn Khaldûn believed that, when development had reached an optimum point, a society would inexorably decline; Muhsin Mahdi, *Ibn Khaldûn's Philosophy of History* (1957), 202.

84. Joseph Hall, *The Discovery of a New World* (1609), sig. A4.

85. William C. Lehmann, *John Millar of Glasgow 1735–1801* (Cambridge, 1960), 176; *Works of William Robertson*, vol. 3, 21; Hugh Blair, *Sermons* (19th edn, 1794), vol. 4, 253; and more generally, David Spadafora, *The Idea of Progress in Eighteenth-Century Britain* (New Haven, CT, 1990).

86. Temple, *Miscellanea: The Second Part*, 173, 196.

87. *An Embassy to China*, ed. J. L. Cranmer-Byng (Hamden, CT, 1963), 226, 222; P. J. Marshall and Glyndwr Williams, *The Great Map of Mankind* (1982), 135, 147, 177; P. J. Marshall, *'A Free though Conquering People'* (Aldershot, 2003), chap. 11, 22–24.

88. Duncan Forbes, *Hume's Philosophical Politics* (Cambridge, 1975), 296–97; Dalrymple, *Essay towards a General History of Feudal Property*, ix–x; Ferguson, *Essay on the History of Civil Society*, 1; Lehmann, *John Millar of Glasgow*, 99–100; *Works of William Robertson*, vol. 1, 21; Thomas Babington Macaulay, *The History of England from the Accession of James II* ([1848–61]; 1905), vol. 1, 378 (chap 3); Spadafora, *Idea of Progress*, chap. 7.

89. Kames, *Historical Law-Tracts*, vol. 1, v.

90. E.g., Sir Richard Blackmore, *Creation* (3rd edn, 1715), 71–74, and Richard Payne Knight, *The Progress of Civility* (1796), both basing their accounts on Lucretius.

91. W. Baring Pemberton, *Lord Palmerston* (1954), 141.

92. John Webb, *An Historical Essay Endeavoring the Probability That the Language of the Empire of China Is the Primitive Language* (1669), 21 (citing Sir Walter Ralegh, *The History of the World* (1617), 115–16).

93. Purchas, *Hakluytus Posthumus*, vol. 1, 81, 252.

94. Sir Clement Edmondes, *Observations upon the First Five Bookes of Caesar's Commentaries* (1604), 5th commentary, chap. 4; Thomas Hobbes, *Decameron Physiologicum* (1678), 5; Sprat, *History of the Royal Society*, 5. On the idea's medieval origins, see Clarence J. Glacken, *Traces on the Rhodian Shore* (Berkeley, CA, 1967), 276–78.

95. Purchas, *Hakluytus Posthumus*, vol. 1, 249–51; *Autobiography of Thomas Raymond and Memoirs of the Family of Guise of Elmore, Gloucestershire*, ed. G. Davies (Camden, 3rd ser., 1917), 101; [Johann Amos Comenius], *A Generall Table of Europe* (1670), 2; Robert Morden, *Geography Rectified* (1688), 10.

96. Larry Wolff, *Inventing Eastern Europe* (Stanford, CA, 1994).

97. M. Balfoure, 'To the Reader', in Sir Andrew Balfour, *Letters write [sic] to a Friend* (1700), 11; David Hume, *Essays Moral, Political, and Literary*, ed. T. H. Green and T. H. Grose (1875), vol. 1, 307.

98. On this huge subject, see Marshall G. S. Hodgson, *Rethinking World History*, ed. Edmund Burke III (Cambridge, 1993), chap. 4; Kenneth Pomeranz, *The Great Divergence* (Princeton, NJ, 2000); C. A. Bayly, *The Birth of the Modern World, 1780–1914* (Oxford, 2004), 60–63; John Darwin, *After Tamerlane* (2007), chap. 3; *Unmasking the West*, ed. Philip E. Tetlock et al. (Ann Arbor, MI, 2009), chaps. 9 (by Kenneth Pomeranz) and 10 (by Joel Mokyr).

99. Michael Wintle, *The Image of Europe* (Cambridge, 2009), 53–67, and index, s.v. 'Eurocentrism.'

100. *The Writings and Speeches of Edmund Burke*, ed. Paul Langford et al. (Oxford, 1981–2015), vol. 9, 248–49; *The Correspondence of Edmund Burke*, ed. Thomas W. Copeland (Cambridge, 1958–78), vol. 7, 387; vol. 9, 306–7; Georges Gusdorf, *Les Principes de la pensée au siècle des Lumières* (Paris, 1971), pt 1, chap. 1; *Penser l'Europe au XVIIIe siècle*, ed. Antoine Lilti and Céline Spector (Oxford, 2014).

101. John Aubrey, *Wiltshire: The Topographical Collections*, ed. John Edward Jackson (Devizes, 1862), 4; John Bridges, *A Sermon, Preached at Paules Crosse* (1571), 17; *Camden's Britannia*, ed. Edmund Gibson (1695; facsimile, 1971), col. 4; Carpenter, *Geographie Delineated*, vol. 2, 281.

102. *The Letters of Sir Thomas Browne*, ed. Geoffrey Keynes (new edn, 1946), 351; Michael Hunter, *John Aubrey and the Realm of Learning* (1975), 175; Thomas Hariot, *A Briefe and True Report of the New Found Land of Virginia* (1590), appendix, sig. E1; Purchas, *Hakluytus Posthumus*, vol. 1, 80, 162.

103. *Writings and Speeches of Edmund Burke*, vol. 1, 348.

104. Thomas Digges, *Foure Paradoxes, or Politique Discourses* (1604), 3rd pagination, 82; William Strachey, *The Historie of Travell into Virginia Britania* (1612), ed. Louis B. Wright and Virginia Freund (Hakluyt Soc., 1953), 24.

105. Inigo Jones, *The Most Notable Antiquity of Great Britain, Vulgarly Called Stone-Heng* (1655), 13 (following Tacitus, *Agricola*, 21).

106. *Complete Prose Works of John Milton*, ed. Don M. Wolfe et al. (New Haven, CT, 1953–82), vol. 5(i), 61 (echoing Camden, *Britain*, 1st pagination, 63); *Diary and Autobiography of Edmund Bohun*, 134–35. There is much on this theme in Richard Hingley, *The Recovery of Roman Britain 1585–1906* (Oxford, 2008), esp. chap. 1.

107. *Complete Prose Works of John Milton*, vol. 5(i), 142; Spenser, *View*, 202–3; David Hume, *The History of England from the Invasion of Julius Caesar to the Revolution in 1688* (new edn, 1773), vol. 1, 229.

108. William of Malmesbury, *Gesta Regum Anglorum*, ed. and trans. R. A. B. Mynors et al. (Oxford, 1998–99), vol. 1, 118–19, 152–53, 190–95, 456–61; id., *The Deeds of the Bishops of England (Gesta Pontificorum Anglorum)*, trans. David Preest (Woodbridge,

2002), 127, 281; John Gillingham, *The English in the Twelfth Century* (Woodbridge, 2000), 5–6, and 'Civilizing the English?', 35–43.

109. *The Miscellaneous Works of the Right Honourable Edward Earl of Clarendon* (2nd edn, 1751), 236; Sir William Temple, *An Introduction to the History of England* (1695), 315. For eighteenth-century views of the Anglo-Saxons, see Rosemary Sweet, *Antiquaries* (2004), chap. 6.

110. *Writings and Speeches of Edmund Burke*, vol. 3, 115.

111. George Hakewill, *An Apologie or Declaration of the Power and Providence of God* (1630), 327–50; Roger North, *Of Building*, ed. Howard Colvin and John Newman (Oxford, 1981), 108; Daniel Defoe, *Serious Reflections during the Life and Surprising Adventures of Robinson Crusoe* (1720), 130, 255.

112. Philip Kinder, *The Surfeit: To A. B. C.* (1656), 27.

113. Joseph Priestley, *Lectures on History and General Policy* (1793), vol. 2, 283; 'An Historical and Moral View of the French Revolution', in *The Works of Mary Wollstonecraft*, ed. Janet Todd and Marilyn Butler (1989), vol. 6, 111n.

114. John Prise, *Historiae Britannicae Defensio* (1573), ed. and trans. Ceri Davies (Toronto, 2015), 36–37, 50–51; Humphrey Llwyd, *The Breviary of Britayne* (1573), fols. 42ᵛ–43.

115. George Saltern, *Of the Antient Lawes of Great Britaine* (1605), sig. F1; *The Works of Michael Drayton*, ed. J. William Hebel (Oxford, 1961), vol. 4, 208 (*Polyolbion*, song 10, 298–99).

116. *Camden's Britannia*, ed. Gibson, cols. 648, 672; Graham Parry, *The Trophies of Time* (Oxford, 1995), 345–55.

117. *ODNB*, s.v. 'Parker, Matthew'; William Camden, *Remains*, ed. R. D. Dunn (Toronto, 1984), 13, 16–17, 24, 27, 29.

118. Puttenham, *Arte of English Poesie*, 59–60 (I. xxxi); Starkey, *Dialogue*, 129; J. Fidoe et al., *The Parliament Justified in Their Late Proceedings against Charls Stuart* (1648 [1649]), 14; Bulstrode Whitelocke, *Memorials of the English Affairs* (Oxford, 1853), vol. 3, 263, 269; Thomas Carte, *A General History of England*, I (1747), 449–51; and more generally, Samuel Kliger, *The Goths in England* (Cambridge, MA, 1952); Christopher Hill, 'The Norman Yoke', in *Puritanism and Revolution* (1958).

119. *The Works of the Late Right Honourable Henry St John, Lord Viscount Bolingbroke* (new edn, 1809), vol. 7, 414–15; *The Complete Writings of William Blake*, ed. Geoffrey Keynes (1957), 577; Sweet, *Antiquaries*, chaps. 4 and 6.

120. Keith Thomas, *The Perception of the Past in Early Modern England* ([1984]), 9–10.

121. Wallace K. Ferguson, *The Renaissance in Historical Thought* (Cambridge, MA, 1948), chaps. 1–3, remains an excellent account. On the supposed aesthetic barbarism of the Middle Ages, see also Keith Thomas, 'English Protestantism and Classical Art', in *Albion's Classicism*, ed. Lucy Gent (New Haven, CT, 1995), 228.

122. James Simpson, 'Ageism', *New Medieval Literatures*, vol. 1 (1997), 230; Spenser, *View*, 54; Francis Bacon, *Early Writings 1584–1596*, ed. Alan Stewart with Harriet Knight (Oxford, 2012), vol. 1, 362; Barston, *Safegarde of Societie*, fols. 22ᵛ–23.

123. Richard Helgerson, *Forms of Nationhood* (Chicago, IL, 1992); Spenser, *View*, 118; Gabriel Harvey, *Pierces Supererogation* (1593), 14; Francis Osborne, *Advice to a Son*, ed. Edward Abbott Parry (1896), 67; Anthony Ashley Cooper, 3rd Earl of Shaftesbury, *Characteristicks of Men, Manners, Opinions, Times*, ed. Philip Ayres (Oxford, 1999), vol. 2, 201; Hume, *Essays*, vol. 1, 346.

124. Thomas, *Perception of the Past*; [Robert Persons], *An Epistle of the Persecution of Catholickes in England* (Douai, 1582), 136–37.

125. Henry Wotton, *The Elements of Architecture* ([1624]; 1903), viii; S[imon] P[atrick], *A Brief Account of the New Sect of Latitude-Men* (1662), 23.

126. Wotton, *Elements of Architecture*, 40–41; Hakewill, *Apologie* (1630 edn), 318–20; Matthew Hale, *The History of the Common Law of England* (3rd edn, 1739), 152; *Works of William Robertson*, vol. 3, 45–51.

127. Christopher Wren, *Parentalia: Or, Memoirs of the Family of the Wrens*, ed. Stephen Wren (1751), 307–8; Terry Friedman, *The Eighteenth-Century Church in Britain* (New Haven, CT, 2011), 186–87, 648n10; Hugh Blair, *Sermons* (1790), vol. 3, 234; Lord Ernle, *English Farming Past and Present* (6th edn, 1961), 199–200.
128. Camõens, *The Lusiads*, trans. William Julius Mickle (Oxford, 1776), introduction, xii–xvi.
129. 'A View of the Progress of Society in Europe', in *Works of William Robertson*, vol. 3, 39; Jonathan Richardson, *Two Discourses* (1719), vol. 2, 221.
130. *A Brief History of Trade in England*, 121–22.
131. *New Letters of David Hume*, ed. Raymond Klibansky and Ernest C. Mossner (Oxford, 1954), 198–99; John Locke, *Two Treatises of Government*, ed. Peter Laslett (Cambridge, 1960), 314–15 (II. 41); Smith, *Lectures on Jurisprudence*, 338–39 (and *Wealth of Nations*, vol. 1, 24 (I. i), where the king is African); Hume, *History of England*, vol. 3, 296.
132. Hume, *History of England*, vol. 5, 459–60; vol. 3, 46.
133. Mandeville, *Fable of the Bees*, vol. 2, 306; William Hutton, *The Beetham Repository*, ed. John Rawlinson Ford (Cumberland and Westmorland Archaeol. and Antiqn Soc., 1906), 125.
134. Woodward, *Essay toward a Natural History*, 95; similarly, Clarendon, *Miscellaneous Works*, 195; Algernon Sidney, *Discourses concerning Government* (3rd edn, 1751), 281.
135. Carpenter, *Geography Delineated*, vol. 2, chaps. 14–15, gives a detailed exposition. On climatic explanations of human differences, see Glacken, *Traces on the Rhodian Shore*; Waldemar Zacharasiewicz, *Die Klimatheorie in der englischen Literatur und Literaturkritik von der Mitte des 16. bis zum frühen 18. Jahrhundert* (Vienna, 1977); Mark Harrison, *Climates and Constitutions* (Oxford, 1999); Mary Floyd-Wilson, *English Ethnicity and Race in Early Modern Drama* (Cambridge, 2003).
136. Sir Thomas Palmer, *An Essay of the Meanes how to Make our Travailes, into Forraine Countries* (1606), 60–62; John Ogilby, *America* (1671), 472.
137. William Vaughan, *The Newlanders Cure* (1630), 3; Sir Matthew Hale, *The Primitive Origination of Mankind* (1677), 154; and more generally, Rebecca Earle, *The Body of the Conquistador* (Cambridge, 2012).
138. Le Roy, *Of the Interchangeable Course, or Variety of Things*, fol. 27ᵛ; Ogilby, *America*, 33; Thomas Hobbes, *De Cive*, ed. Howard Warrender (Oxford, 1983), I. xiii (Latin version, 96; English version, 49).
139. R. R. Davies, *The First English Empire* (Oxford, 2000), chap. 5, for an excellent analysis of the cultural differences between the Welsh and their English neighbours. See also W. R. Jones, 'England against the Celtic Fringe', *Cahiers d'Histoire Mondiale* 12 (1971), and Bartlett, *Gerald of Wales*, 194–200.
140. *Polychronicon Ranulphi Higden Monacho Cestrensis*, ed. Charles Babington (Rolls ser., 1865–86), vol. 1, 410–11. On Edward I's achievement, see J. Goronwy Edwards, *The Principality of Wales* (Caernarvonshire Hist. Soc., n. pl., 1969), 9–16.
141. *Polydore Vergil's English History*, ed. Sir Henry Ellis (Camden Soc., 1846), vol. 1, 13; Boorde, *Fyrst Boke of the Introduction of Knowledge*, 127.
142. Edwards, *Principality of Wales*, 20–26; Peter R. Roberts, 'Wales and England after the Tudors', in *Law and Government under the Tudors*, ed. Claire Cross (Cambridge, 1988); Ciarán Brady, 'Comparable Histories', in *Conquest and Union*, ed. Stephen G. Ellis and Sarah Barber (1995).
143. James Spedding, *The Letters and the Life of Francis Bacon* (1862–74), vol. 3, 384; *Early Chronicles of Shrewsbury, 1372–1603*, ed. W. A. Leighton (n. pl., 1880), 19.
144. Edward Yardley, *Menevia Sacra*, ed. Francis Green (Cambrian Archaeol. Assn, 1927), 388.
145. D. Lleufer Thomas, 'Further Notes on the Court of the Marches', *Y Cymmrodor* 13 (1900), 124, and appendix D; Richard Suggett, 'The Welsh Language and the Court of Great Sessions', in *The Welsh Language before the Industrial Revolution*, ed. Geraint

H. Jenkins (Cardiff, 1997), 153–54; Penry Williams, *The Council in the Marches of Wales under Elizabeth I* (Cardiff, 1958), 61–65, 83–84.

146. Peter Roberts, 'The English Crown, the Principality of Wales and the Council in the Marches, 1534–1641', in *The British Problem, c. 1534–1707*, ed. Brendan Bradshaw and John Morrill (Basingstoke, 1966), 145–46.

147. Humphrey Lluyd, *The Breviary of Britayne*, trans. Thomas Twyne (1573), fol. 60ᵛ (Lluyd died in 1568).

148. *Historical Tracts by Sir John Davies* (1786), 107; Edmondes, *Observations upon Caesar's Commentaries* (2nd pagination), 7th commentary, chap. 2, 49–50; Ed. Aston, in Boemus, *Manners, Lawes, and Customes of All Nations*, 399.

149. W[illiam] R[ichards], *Wallography* (1682); John Cramsie, *British Travellers and the Encounter with Britain, 1450–1700* (Woodbridge, 2015), 315, 390.

150. Bodl., MS Don. d.187, fol. 73 (James Dallaway, 1756); *An American Quaker in the British Isles*, ed. Kenneth Morgan (British Academy, Oxford, 1992), 227; *The Torrington Diaries*, ed. C. Bruyn Andrews (1934–36; 1970), vol. 1, 291, 302; vol. 3, 277, 301, 311. See, more generally, Prys Morgan, 'Wild Wales', in *Civil Histories*, ed. Peter Burke et al. (Oxford, 2000).

151. *Camden's Britannia*, ed. Gibson, col. 885; G. W. S. Barrow, *The Kingdom of the Scots* (2nd edn, Edinburgh, 1973), 336. On the origins of the Highland/Lowland distinction, see *John of Fordun's Chronicle of the Scottish Nation*, trans. Felix J. H. Skene, ed. W. F. Skene (Edinburgh, 1872), 37–38; Alexander Grant, 'Aspects of National Consciousness in Medieval Scotland', in *Nations, Nationalism and Patriotism in the European Past*, ed. Claus Bjørn et al. (Copenhagen, 1994); Charles Withers, 'The Historical Creation of the Scottish Highlands', in *The Manufacture of Scottish History*, ed. Ian Donnachie and Christopher Whatley (Edinburgh, 1991); Arthur H. Williamson, 'Scots, Indians and Empire', *P&P* 150 (1996), 59–66, and, especially, Jane Dawson, 'The Gaidhealtacd and the Emergence of the Scottish Highlands', in *British Consciousness and Identity*, ed. Brendan Bradshaw and Peter Roberts (Cambridge, 1998).

152. *The Political Works of James I*, ed. Charles Howard McIlwain (Cambridge, MA, 1918), 22.

153. Williamson, 'Scots, Indians and Empire', 64–66; David Armitage, 'Making the Empire British', *P&P* 155 (1997), 42–45; Anna Groundwater, 'The Chasm between James VI and I's Vision of the Orderly "Middle Shires" and the "Wickit" Borderers, 1587 to 1625', *Renaissance and Reformation* 30 (2006–7); Jane H. Ohlmeyer, '"Civilizinge of Those Rude Parts"', in *The Origins of Empire*, ed. Nicholas Canny (*Oxford History of the British Empire*, vol. 1, Oxford, 1998).

154. Allan I. Macinnes, 'Crown, Clans and *Fine*', *Northern Scotland* 13 (1993); Julian Goodare, 'The Statutes of Iona in Context', *Scottish Hist. Rev.* 77 (1998), 46; Colin Kidd, *British Identities before Nationalism* (Cambridge, 1999), 126–27; Ohlmeyer, 'Civilizinge of Those Rude Parts', 134.

155. Sherrilyn Theiss, 'The Western Highlands and Central Government, 1616–1645', and Danielle McCormack, 'Highland Lawlessness and the Cromwellian Regime', in *Scotland in the Age of Two Revolutions*, ed. Sharon Adams and Julian Goodare (Woodbridge, 2014); and see the entries for 'feuds' in the superb indexes to the *Registers of the Privy Council of Scotland*.

156. *M. Misson's Memoirs and Observations in his Travels over England*, trans. (John) Ozell (1719), 286; P. Hume Brown, *Early Travellers in Scotland* (Edinburgh, 1891), 203, 205, 241; Cramsie, *British Travellers*, 400–401, 404–6, 417.

157. Henry Fielding, *The True Patriot and Related Writings*, ed. W. B. Coley (Oxford, 1987), 113.

158. 19 George II, chap. 39 (1746); 20 George II, chap. 20, 50–51 (1747).

159. Samuel Johnson, *A Journey to the Western Islands of Scotland*, ed. J. D. Fleeman (Oxford, 1985), 51. Similarly, William Gilpin, *Observations, relative chiefly to Picturesque Beauty,*

made in the Year 1776, on Several Parts of Great-Britain; particularly the High-Lands of Scotland (1789), vol. 1, 209–10.

160. *Letters and Papers Illustrating the Relations between Charles the Second and Scotland in 1650*, ed. Samuel Rawson Gardiner (Scottish Hist. Soc., 1894), 136–37; An English Gentleman [Thomas Kirke], *A Modern Account of Scotland* (1679), 6; Hume Brown, *Early Travellers in Scotland*, 97, 102–3, 142–43, 231; Alan Bell, *Sydney Smith* (Oxford, 1982), 15; *Letters and the Second Diary of Samuel Pepys*, ed. R. G. Howarth (1933), 139.

161. Joseph Taylor, *A Journey to Edenborough in Scotland*, ed. William Cowan (Edinburgh, 1903), 134. On the efforts of the Edinburgh Council to keep the streets clean, see Leona J. Skelton, *Sanitation in Urban Britain 1560–1700* (2016), 111, 121–28, 172.

162. Horace Bleackley, *Life of John Wilkes* (1917), 323.

163. *The Economic Writings of Sir William Petty*, ed. Charles Henry Hull (Cambridge, 1899), vol. 1, 154–55.

164. Gerald of Wales, *History and Topography of Ireland*, 92–125; W. R. Jones, 'Giraldus Redivivus', *Eire-Ireland* 9 (1974), 101–3; Michael Richter, 'Giraldiana', *Irish Historical Studies* 22 (1979); John Gillingham, 'Images of Ireland, 1170–1600', *History Today* 37 (1987); id., *The English in the Twelfth Century*, chap. 9; Andrew Hadfield, *Edmund Spenser's Irish Experience* (Oxford, 1997), 25–29, 53, 92–94; Hiram Morgan, 'Giraldus Cambrensis and the Tudor Conquest of Ireland', in *Political Ideology in Ireland, 1541–1641*, ed. Morgan (Dublin, 1999).

165. Stanford E. Lehmberg, *The Later Parliaments of Henry VIII 1536–1547* (Cambridge, 1977), 142; Walter Bourchier Devereux, *Lives and Letters of the Devereux, Earls of Essex* (1853), vol. 1, 74.

166. Sir Thomas Elyot, *The Boke Named the Gouernour*, ed. Henry Herbert Stephen Croft (1883), 87–89 (i. xi); Spenser, *View*, 90 and index, s.v. 'Scythians'; Andrew Hadfield, 'Briton and Scythian', *Irish Historical Studies* 28 (1993).

167. Francis Bacon, *Early Writings, 1584–1596*, ed. Alan Stewart with Harriet Knight (Oxford, 2012), 82; *The Clarke Papers*, ed. C. H. Firth (Camden Soc., 1891–1901), vol. 2, 205. See, more generally, Nicholas P. Canny, *The Elizabethan Conquest of Ireland* (Hassocks, 1976), chap.6; Joep Leerssen, *Mere Irish and Fior Ghael* (Cork, 1996), 33–84; Eamon Darcy, *The Irish Rebellion of 1641 and the Wars of the Three Kingdoms* (Woodbridge, 2013), chap. 1; Ian Campbell, *Renaissance Humanism and Ethnicity before Race* (Manchester, 2013), chap. 2.

168. Nicholas Canny, 'Revising the Revisionists', *Irish Hist. Studies* 30 (1996), 250; Darcy, *Irish Rebellion of 1641*, 46.

169. David Beers Quinn, *The Elizabethans and the Irish* (Ithaca, NY, 1966), 29, 31–33, 58–59.

170. *Economic Writings of Sir William Petty*, vol. 1, 204; Jones, 'Giraldus Redivivus', 13–20; Brendan Bradshaw, 'Geoffrey Keating', in *Representing Ireland*, ed. Bradshaw et al. (Cambridge, 1993); [John Lynch], *Cambrensis Eversus*, ed. and trans. Matthew Kelly (Celtic Soc., Dublin, 1848–51), esp. vol. 2, 198–222; Leerssen, *Mere Irish and Fíor-Ghael*, 291–434; Campbell, *Renaissance Humanism and Ethnicity*, chap. 3.

171. Kidd, *British Identities, 157–62, 200*; Clare O'Halloran, *Golden Ages and Barbarous Nations* (Cork, 2004).

172. Quinn, *Elizabethans and the Irish*, 64–71; Fynes Moryson, *An Itinerary* (Glasgow, 1907–8), vol. 4, 198–203, 236–38; id., *Shakespeare's Europe*, 485; *Trevelyan Papers*, vol. 3, ed. Walter Calverley Trevelyan and Sir Charles Edward Trevelyan (Camden Soc., 1872), 103; BL, Cotton MS, Faustinus 109 ('A Discourse upon the Reformation of Ireland'), fol. 40ᵛ; John Derricke, *The Image of Irelande*, ed. John Small (Edinburgh, 1883); Graham Kew, *The Irish Sections of Fynes Moryson's Unpublished Itinerary* (Dublin, 1998), 40, 102–3, 105, 106; Barnabe Rich, *A New Description of Ireland* (1610), 16, 24–27, 40.

173. Barnabe Rich, *A Short Survey of Ireland* (1609), 2; Kew, *Irish Sections of Moryson's Itinerary*, 111; Gerard Boate, *Irelands Naturall History*, published by Samuel Hartlib (1657), 7.

5 Exporting Civility

1. Francisco de Vitoria, *Political Writings*, ed. Anthony Pagden and Jeremy Lawrance (Cambridge, 1991), 278–84; Jose de Acosta, *De Procuranda Indorum Salute*, trans. and ed. G. Stewart McIntosh (Tayport, 1995–96), 86–87 (II. xiv), 111–12 (III. vi).
2. *The Voyages and Colonizing Enterprises of Sir Humphrey Gilbert*, ed. David Beers Quinn (Hakluyt Soc., 1940), vol. 2, 453.
3. Alberico Gentili, *De Iure Belli Libri Tres* (1612), trans. John C. Rolfe (Oxford, 1933), 86–87, 89–90 (I. xix) (though with qualifications); Richard Zouche, *Iuris et Iudicii Fecialis*, ed. Thomas Erskine Holland, trans. J. L. Brierly ([1650]; Washington, DC, 1911), vol. 2, 27 (I. v. 1); *The Original Writings and Correspondence of the Two Richard Hakluyts*, ed. E. G. R. Taylor (Hakluyt Soc., 1935), vol. 2, 342; William Strachey, *The Historie of Travell into Virginia Britania (1612)*, ed. Louis B. Wright and Virginia Freund (Hakluyt Soc., 1953), 22–23; Samuel Purchas, *Hakluytus Posthumus, or Purchas his Pilgrimes* (1625; Glasgow, 1905–7), vol. 19, 223–24; Joseph Hall, *Resolutions and Decisions of Divers Practicall Cases of Conscience* (3rd edn, 1654), 243–44; Thomas Hobbes, *The Elements of Law*, ed. Ferdinand Tönnies (1889), 87 (16.12); Andrew Fitzmaurice, *Sovereignty, Property and Empire, 1500–1800* (Cambridge, 2014), 70–73.
4. Annabel Brett, *Changes of State* (Princeton, NJ, 2001), 14; Hedley Bull, 'The Emergence of a Universal International Society', in *The Expansion of International Society*, ed. Bull and Adam Watson (Oxford, 1984), 120; Purchas, *Hakluytus Posthumus*, vol. 19, 224.
5. Daniel Defoe, *A General History of Discoveries* (n.d.), 97, 133–52; id., *A Plan of the English Commerce* ([1728]; Oxford, 1928), pt 3, chap. 2.
6. *Cal. SP, Foreign, Jan.–June 1583 and Addenda*, 478.
7. For valuable treatments of this much discussed subject, see Anthony Pagden, 'The Struggle for Legitimacy and the Image of Empire in the Atlantic to *c.* 1700', in *The Origins of Empire*, ed. Nicholas Canny (*Oxford History of the British Empire*, vol. 1; Oxford, 1998); Richard Tuck, *The Rights of War and Peace* (Oxford, 1999), 47–50, 105–6, 123–26, 175–76, 182–83; Christopher Tomlins, *Freedom Bound* (Cambridge, 2010), chaps. 3 and 4; Fitzmaurice, *Sovereignty, Property and Empire*, 51–58.
8. Thomas More, *Utopia*, ed. George M. Logan and Robert M. Adams (Cambridge, 1989), 56.
9. *Winthrop Papers*, vol. 2, 1623–1630 (Massachusetts Hist. Soc., 1931), 113, 120, 140–41; John Cotton, 'A reply to Mr Williams', appended to his *The Bloody Tenent, Washed and Made White in the Bloude of the Lambe* (1647), 27–28.
10. John Rolfe, *A True Relation of the State of Virginia Lefte by Sir Thomas Dale* (New Haven, CT, 1951), 41, 36; Jeremiah Dummer, *A Defence of the New-England Charters* (1721), 13–14, 19–21; Francis Jennings, *The Invasion of America* (Chapel Hill, NC, 1975), chap. 8; Andrew Fitzmaurice, *Humanism and America* (Cambridge, 2003), 165–66, 184–86; Stuart Banner, *How the Indians Lost Their Land* (Cambridge, MA, 2005), esp. 21–29.
11. Gentili, *De Iure Belli*, 80–81 (I. xvii); Purchas, *Hakluytus Posthumus*, vol. 1, 82; vol. 19, 222–32; *The Sermons of John Donne*, ed. George R. Potter and Evelyn M. Simpson (Berkeley, CA, 1953–62), vol. 4, 274.
12. Thomas Hobbes, *Leviathan*, ed. Noel Malcolm (Oxford, 2012), vol. 2, 540 (chap. 30); Francis Bacon, *The Essayes or Counsels, Civill and Morall*, ed. Michael Kiernan (Oxford, 1985), 106.
13. Peter Sarris, *Empires of Faith* (Oxford, 2011), 31–32.
14. *Register of the Privy Council of Scotland*, vol. 6, 825; vol. 7, 524–25.
15. Emmer de Vattel, *The Law of Nations*, ed. Béla Kapossy and Richard Whatmore (Indianapolis, IN, 2008), 306 (II. vi. 85), 310–11 (II. vii. 97), 129 (I. vii. 81).

16. *Cal. SP, Colonial, America and West Indies, 1681–1685*, 100–101, 179–81, 197; Hilary Beckles, 'The Genocidal Policy in English-Karifuna Relations in the Seventeenth Century', in *Empire and Others*, ed. Martin Daunton and Rick Halpern (Philadelphia, PA, 1999).

17. Elizabeth Fenn, *Pox Americana* (New York, 2001), 88–89, 155–57.

18. C. A. Bayly, *The Birth of the Modern World* (Oxford, 2004), chap. 13. Tom Lawson, *The Last Man* (2014), is a passionate and highly contentious, but archivally based account of genocide in Tasmania.

19. Hobbes, *Leviathan*, ed. Malcolm, vol. 2, 194 (chap. 13); John Locke, *Two Treatises of Government*, ed. Peter Laslett (Cambridge, 1960), 353 (II. para. 102), 357–58 (II. para. 108); 'Advertisement Touching on Holy Warre', in *The Works of Francis Bacon*, ed. James Spedding et al. (new edn, 1879), vol. 7(i), 29–31 (the speaker is a Roman Catholic 'zelant').

20. Christopher Levett, *A Voyage into New England* (1624), 20; and similarly, Robert Gray, *A Good Speed to Virginia* (1609), sigs. C2ᵛ–4; Robert Johnson, *Nova Britannia* (1609), sig. B4.

21. *Newfoundland Discovered*, ed. Gillian T. Cell (Hakluyt Soc., 1982), 258–69; Tomlins, *Freedom Bound*, 176–77.

22. For differing views, see James Tully, *An Approach to Political Philosophy* (Cambridge, 1993), chap. 5; Noel Malcolm, *Aspects of Hobbes* (Oxford, 2002), 75; Srinivas Aravamurdan, 'Hobbes and America', in *The Postcolonial Enlightenment*, ed. Daniel Carey and Lynn Festa (Oxford, 2009); Pat Moloney, 'Hobbes, Savagery, and International Anarchy', *Amer. Political Science Rev.* 195 (2011); Fitzmaurice, *Sovereignty, Property and Empire*, 61, 73, 77–78, 178–79.

23. Examples are cited by Grotius, *Rights of War and Peace*, 438 (II. xx. 40. 4).

24. Gentili, *De Iure Belli*, 122–25 (I. xxv); *The Works of Sir Walter Ralegh* (Oxford, 1829), vol. 8, 69 (not by Ralegh); *Works of Francis Bacon*, ed. Spedding, vol. 7(i), 28–36; Purchas, *Hakluytus Posthumus*, vol. 19, 224; Hugo Grotius, *The Rights of War and Peace* (Eng. trans., 1738), 436–37 (II. xx. 40–49), 440 (II. xx. 43. 3); Zouche, *Iuris et Iudicii Fecialis*, vol. 2, 115–16 (II. vii. 1–2); James Muldoon, *Popes, Lawyers, and Infidels* (Liverpool, 1979), chap. 2; Tully, *Approach to Political Philosophy*, 142–43; Tuck, *Rights of War and Peace*, 34–35, 39–41, 102–3.

25. Aristotle, *Politics*, 1252b; John Case, *Sphaera Civitatis* (Oxford, 1588), 63–64 (I. v); Greg Woolf, *Becoming Roman* (Cambridge, 1998), esp. chap. 3; Wilfried Nippel, 'The Construction of the "Other"', in *Greeks and Barbarians*, ed. Thomas Harrison (Edinburgh, 2002), 196; Alberico Gentili, *The Wars of the Romans*, trans. David Lupher, ed. Benedict Kingsbury and Benjamin Straumann (New York, 2011), xiv, xvi, 129–31, 337, 349–51; Sir Matthew Hale, *The Primitive Origination of Mankind* (1677), 159.

26. Gillingham, 'Civilizing the English', *HistRes* 74 (2001), 41.

27. Sir William Temple, *Miscellanea: The Second Part* (4th edn, 1696), 172.

28. Joseph Addison, *Cato* (1713), act 1, scene 4.

29. Rolfe, *True Relation of the State of Virginia*, 40.

30. Spedding, *Letters and Life of Francis Bacon*, vol. 2, 131–32.

31. Haly Heron, *The Kayes of Counsaile* (1579), ed. Virgil B. Heltzel (Liverpool, 1954), 78; Gray, *Good Speed to Virginia*, sig. C4ʳ⁻ᵛ.

32. Edmund Bolton, *Nero Caesar, or Monarchie Depraved* (1624), 77; *Historical Tracts by Sir John Davies* (1786), 4; BL, Add. MS 37, 345 (Whitelocke's *Annals*, vol. 5), fol. 244ᵛ.

33. Geoffrey Gates, *The Defence of Militarie Profession* (1579), 13, 15; D. B. Quinn, 'Renaissance Influences in English Colonization', *TRHS*, 5th ser., 26 (1976); David Armitage, *The Ideological Origins of the British Empire* (Cambridge, 2000), 47–52; Nicholas Canny, *Making Ireland British 1580–1650* (Oxford, 2001), 121–23, 197–98, 214; David Harris Sacks, 'The Prudence of Thrasymachus', in *Historians and Ideologues*, ed. Anthony Grafton and J. H. M. Salmon (Rochester, NY, 2001), 102.

34. 'Basilikon Doron', in *The Political Works of James I*, ed. Charles Howard McIlwain (Cambridge, MA, 1918), 22.
35. Christopher Maginn, ' "Surrender and Regrant" in the Historiography of Sixteenth-Century Ireland', *Sixteenth-Century Journ.* 38 (2007).
36. For authoritative accounts of the shifting policies, see Canny, *Making Ireland British*, and S. J. Connolly, *Contested Ireland* (Oxford, 2007).
37. *'Reform' Treatises on Tudor Ireland*, ed. David Heffernan (Irish MSS Commission, Dublin, 2016), 304, 315.
38. *Cal. SP, Ireland, Tudor Period, 1571–1575* (rev. edn, Dublin, 2000), 233 (Smith); Nicholas P. Canny, *The Elizabethan Conquest of Ireland* (Hassocks, 1976), 160; Michael J. Braddick, *State Formation in Early Modern England, c. 1550–1700* (Cambridge, 2000), 341–43, 379–89; S. G. Ellis, 'Promoting "English Civility" in Tudor Times', in *Tolerance and Intolerance in Historical Perspective*, ed. Csaba Lévai and Vasile Vese (Pisa, 2003); S. G. Ellis, 'Civilizing the Natives', in *Frontiers and Identities*, ed. Lud'a Klusáková and Steven G. Ellis (Pisa, 2006); Jane Ohlmeyer, 'A Laboratory for Empire?', in *Ireland and the British Empire*, ed. Kevin Kenny (Oxford, 2005), and 'Conquest, Civilization, Colonization: Ireland, 1540–1660', in *The Princeton History of Modern Ireland*, ed. Richard Bourke and Ian McBride (Princeton, NJ, 2016).
39. *Henry VI, Part II*, act 1, scene 1, lines 11, 191–92.
40. *Cal. SP, Ireland, 1509–1573*, 158; Walter Bourchier Devereux, *Lives and Letters of the Devereux, Earls of Essex* (1853), vol. 1, 74.
41. *Holinshed's Chronicles of England, Scotland, and Ireland* (1807–8), vol. 6, 5, 69.
42. Christopher Maginn, *William Cecil, Ireland, and the Tudor State* (Oxford, 2012), 39; Canny, *Making Ireland British*, 81; *Political Works of James I*, 319–20.
43. *Cal. SP, Ireland, 1509–1573*, 158; similarly, ibid., *1566–1567*, 37; ibid., *1586–1588*, 501–2; ibid., *1603–1606*, 317–23; ibid., *1608–1610*, 266; *Letters and Papers of Henry VIII*, vol. 8, 225; *Cal. SP, Foreign, Jan.–June 1583 and Addenda*, 475. On the enduring concern to inculcate 'civility', see Canny, *Making Ireland British*, esp. 51, 76, 121–23, 129–33, 240–41, 249–50, 279, 281.
44. Dummer, *Defence of the New-England Charters*, 20–21; *Voyages of Sir Humphrey Gilbert*, vol. 2, 451, 468.
45. *Cal. SP, Colonial, 1670–6 and Additional, 1574–5*, 32.
46. Purchas, *Hakluytus Posthumus*, vol. 19, 238; Thomas Hariot, *A Briefe and True Report of the New Found Land of Virginia* (1588), sig. E2ᵛ.
47. Gabriel Glickman, 'Protestantism, Colonization, and the New England Company in Restoration Politics', *HJ* 59 (2016), 375.
48. *Voyages of Sir Humphrey Gilbert*, vol. 1, 161, 357–58; vol. 2, 357, 461; *Original Writings of the Two Hakluyts*, vol. 2, 232.
49. Defoe, *Plan of the English Commerce*, 254–56; *The Life of Olaudah Equiano*, ed. Paul Edwards (1988), 168–69; Jack P. Greene, *Evaluating Empire and Confronting Colonialism in Eighteenth-Century Britain* (Cambridge, 2013), 35–36, 159–60.
50. Daniel Defoe, *Serious Reflections during the Life and Surprising Adventures of Robinson Crusoe* (1720), 250–54, 264–67.
51. John Case, *Sphaera Civitatis* (Frankfurt, 1616), 28–30 (I. iii), 50–51 (I. v).
52. Peter Martyr, *The Decades of the New Worlde*, trans. Richard Eden (1555), sig. aiiᵛ; *ODNB*, s.v. 'Eden, Richard'. Cf. Canny, *Making Ireland British*, 3.
53. Edmund Spenser, *View of the Present State of Ireland*, in *Spenser's Prose Works*, ed. Rudolf Gottfried (Baltimore, MD, 1949), 102, 156–58, 177–80, 219–20, 235–45; Canny, *Making Ireland British*, 62–64; Andrew Hadfield, *Edmund Spenser* (Oxford, 2012), 335–40.
54. *Historical Tracts of Sir John Davies*, 134–40; Hans S. Pawlisch, *Sir John Davies and the Conquest of Ireland* (Cambridge, 1985), chap. 4.
55. James Ware, *The Historie of Ireland, Collected by Three Learned Authors* (Dublin, 1633), sig. ¶3ᵛ; Edward, Earl of Clarendon, *The History of the Rebellion and Civil Wars in*

England, ed. W. Dunn Macray (Oxford, 1888), vol. 1, 94; Padraig Lenihan, *Consolidating Conquest* (Harlow, 2008), 58–59.

56. Edward Waterhouse, *A Declaration of the State of the Colony and Affairs in Virginia* (1622), 24; Purchas, *Hakluytus Posthumus*, vol. 19, 246; *The Records of the Virginia Company of London*, ed. Susan Myra Kingsbury (Washington, DC, 1906–35), vol. 3, 683.

57. BL, Thomason Tract, E.1190(1) (untitled pamphlet, 1644), 9.

58. Malcolm Gaskill, *Between Two Worlds* (Oxford, 2014), 277–78, 284; Dummer, *Defence of the New-England Charters*, 23.

59. On the reasons for this difference, see Sir John Elliott, *Britain and Spain in America* (Reading, 1994), and *Empires of the Atlantic World* (New Haven, CT, 2006), chap. 3. For a belated plea to remedy matters, see John David Hammerer, *Account of a Plan for Civilizing the North-American Indians* (1765).

60. Luís de Camões, *The Lusiad*, trans. William Julius Mickle (Oxford, 1776), introduction, vii–viii.

61. *Gweithiau Morgan Llwyd o Wynedd*, ed. Thomas E. Ellis (Bangor, 1899), 28; *The Complete Prose Works of John Milton*, ed. Don. M. Wolfe et al. (New Haven, CT, 1953–82), vol. 3, 304 (also vol. 5, 40); T. C. Barnard, *Cromwellian Ireland* (Oxford, 1975).

62. Charles Carlton, *Going to the Wars* (1992), 213–14.

63. Sir William Petty, *The Political Anatomy of Ireland* (1691), 102; *M. Misson's Memoirs and Observations in His Travels over England*, trans. (John) Ozell (1719), 149–50; *The Correspondence of Jonathan Swift*, ed. Herbert Williams (Oxford, 1963–65), vol. 5, 58; vol. 2, 433; vol. 4, 33–34.

64. W[illiam] Crashaw, *A Sermon preached in London* (1610), sig. D4; John Brinsley, *A Consolation for our Grammar Schooles* (1622), 3; William Wotton, *Reflections upon Ancient and Modern Learning* (1694), 17.

65. Mark Goldie, 'The Civil Religion of James Harrington', in *The Languages of Political Theory in Early-Modern Britain*, ed. Anthony Pagden (Cambridge, 1987).

66. *The Writings and Speeches of Edmund Burke*, ed. Paul Langford et al. (Oxford, 1981–2015), vol. 8, 141; vol. 1, 349.

67. Thomas Thorowgood, *Jewes in America* (1650), 53.

68. Jo[hn] Jackson, *The True Evangelical Temper* (1641), 102.

69. John Gauden, *Hieraspistes* (1653), 399; Pierre d'Avity, *The Estates, Empires & Principallities of the World*, trans. Edward Grimestone (1615), 268; Purchas, *Hakluytus Posthumus*, vol. 18, 498n.

70. *The Life of the Reverend Humphrey Prideaux* (1748), 152–53.

71. Travis Glasson, *Mastering Christianity* (New York, 2012), 67–72; William Warburton, *The Divine Legation of Moses Demonstrated* (3rd edn, 1742), vol. 1, 318.

72. For a lucid account of the opinions of medieval canonists on this topic, see Muldoon, *Popes, Lawyers, and Infidels*.

73. *Voyages of Sir Humphrey Gilbert*, vol. 1, 188; vol. 2, 261; Richard Hakluyt, *The Principall Navigations Voyages Traffiques and Discoveries of the English Nation* (Glasgow, 1903–5), vol. 8, 289–96; *Cal. SP, Colonial Series, America and West Indies, 1675–1676, also Addenda, 1574–1674*, 25, 32, 37, 70, 72, 73; Francis Newton Thorpe, *The Federal and State Constitutions . . . of . . . the United States* (Washington, DC, 1909), vol. 3, 1169, 1667–68; Ken MacMillan, *Sovereignty and Possession in the English New World* (Cambridge, 2006), 84, 107–8.

74. *Tudor Royal Proclamations*, ed. Paul L. Hughes and James F. Larkin (New Haven, CT, 1964–9), vol. 3, 221–22; *The Reports of Sr. Creswell Levinz*, trans. (William) Salkeld et al. (2nd edn, 1722), vol. 1 (pt 2), 201; Robert, Lord Raymond, *Reports of Cases Argued and Adjudged in the Courts of King's Bench and Common Pleas* (2nd edn), ed. George Wilson (1765), vol. 1, 147.

75. Gentili, *De Iure Belli*, 56–57 (I. xii), 124–25 (I. xxv).

76. Vitoria, *Political Writings*, 284–86; Richard Baxter, *A Holy Commonwealth*, ed. William Lamont (Cambridge, 1994), 103–4; Noel Malcolm, 'Alberico Gentili and the Ottomans',

in *The Roman Foundations of the Law of Nations*, ed. Benedict Kingsbury and Benjamin Straumann (Oxford, 2010), 135; *The Sermons of John Donne*, ed. George Reuben Potter and Evelyn M. Simpson (Berkeley, CA, 1953–62), vii, 372–73; Muldoon, *Popes, Lawyers, and Infidels*, chap. 2.

77. Andrew Porter, *Religion versus Empire?* (Manchester, 2004), chap. 7.

78. Francis Bacon, *The Instauratio Magna, Part II: Novum Organum and Associated Texts*, ed. Graham Rees with Maria Wakely (Oxford, 2004), 194–95; Fynes Moryson, *An Itinerary* (Glasgow, 1907–8), vol. 3, 426–44 (esp. 432).

79. Peter Paxton, *Civil Polity* (1703), sigs. a2–4^v; similarly, the Scottish physician Archibald Pitcairne (1652–1713): Michael Hunter, 'Pitcairneana', *HJ* 59 (2016), 620–21.

80. Bernard Mandeville, *The Fable of the Bees*, ed. F. B. Kaye (Oxford, 1924), vol. 2, 318; James Adair, *The History of the American Indians* (1775), 419, 427.

81. David Hume, *Essays Moral, Political, and Literary*, ed. T. H. Green and T. H. Grose (1875), vol. 1, 249; Edward Gibbon, *The Decline and Fall of the Roman Empire*, ed. J. B. Bury (5th edn, 1912), vol. 3, 71 (chap. 26).

82. Richard Tuck, *The Rights of War and Peace* (Oxford, 1999), 41–42, 47; Gentili, *De Iure Belli*, 53–54 (I. xii). But for some who held it, see Case, *Sphaera Civitatis*, 37–39 (I. iv); John Smyth of Nibley, *A Description of the Hundred of Berkeley*, ed. Sir John Maclean (*The Berkeley Manuscripts*, vol. 3 (Gloucester, 1885)), 43; *Works of Francis Bacon*, ed. Spedding, vol. 7, 29; John Hall of Richmond, *Of Government and Obedience* (1654), 34; Gabriel Towerson, *An Explication of the Decalogue* (1676), 311–12; *Memoirs of the Life of Mr Ambrose Barnes*, ed. W. H. D. Longstaffe (Surtees Soc., 1867), 213; [Algernon] Sidney, *Court Maxims*, ed. Hans W. Blom et al. (Cambridge, 1996), 199–200, and *Discourses concerning Government* (3rd edn, 1751), 64, 90; *Athenian Mercury*, 3 Nov. 1694, cited in Catherine Molineux, *Faces of Perfect Ebony* (Cambridge, MA, 2012), 119.

83. John Milton, 'Samson Agonistes', lines 268–71, and *Complete Prose Works*, vol. 3, 581; vol. 7, 428, on which see Quentin Skinner, *Visions of Politics* (Cambridge, 2002), vol. 2, chap. 11.

84. Sir Thomas Palmer, *An Essay of the Meanes how to Make our Travailes, into Forraigne Countries* (1606), 60–61.

85. Gray, *A Good Speed to Virginia*, sig. C2; Nathanael Carpenter, *Geographie Delineated Forth in Two Bookes* (1635), vol. 2, 281; Canny, *Elizabethan Conquest of Ireland*, 25–26.

86. Morgan Godwyn, *The Negro's and Indians Advocate* (1680), 10; John Locke, *An Essay Concerning Human Understanding*, ed. Peter H. Nidditch (Oxford, 1975), 92 (I. iv. 12); Mandeville, *Fable of the Bees*, vol. 2, 214.

87. Roger Williams, *A Key into the Language of America* (1643), 53; Colin Kidd, *The Forging of Races* (Cambridge, 2006), chap. 3.

88. George Best, *A True Discourse of the Late Voyages of Discoverie* (1578), 29–32; Winthrop D. Jordan, *White over Black* (Chapel Hill, NC, 1968), esp. 4–9, 248–49, 252–53; Alden T. Vaughan, *Roots of American Racism* (New York, 1995), 15–16, 306–7; Ania Loomba, *Shakespeare, Race and Colonialism* (Oxford, 2002), chaps. 1 and 2; *Black Africans in Renaissance England*, ed. T. F. Earle and K. J. P. Lowe (Cambridge, 2005); *Race in Early Modern England*, ed. Ania Loomba and Jonathan Burton (Basingstoke, 2007), 13–15; Francisco Bethencourt, *Racisms* (Princeton, NJ, 2013), 45, 245–46, 368.

89. Purchas, *Hakluytus Posthumus*, vol. 5, 359. This was from John Pory's translation of 1600, which puts into the present a description of African backwardness that its author had placed in the past; Natalie Zemon Davis, *Trickster Travels* (2008), 145.

90. *Japanese Travellers in Sixteenth-Century Europe*, trans. J. F. Moran, ed. Derek Massarella (Hakluyt Soc., 2012), 87, 89, 446–48.

91. Robert Bartlett, *The Making of Europe* (1993), 236–42; id., 'Medieval and Modern Concepts of Race and Ethnicity', *Journ. of Medieval and Early Modern Studies* 31 (2001); Ian Campbell, *Renaissance Humanism and Ethnicity before Race* (Manchester, 2013), 189–90, and chaps. 4 and 5.

92. *Thomas Browne*, ed. Kevin Killeen (Oxford, 2014), 356.

93. Peter Biller, 'Proto-Racial Thought in Medieval Science', in *The Origins of Racism in the West*, ed. Miriam Eliav-Feldon et al. (Cambridge, 2009), 25, chap. 7; Andrea Ruddick, *English Identity and Political Culture in the Fourteenth Century* (Cambridge, 2013), 140–45, 155, 180–81.

94. 'The Memoirs of Father Robert Persons', ed. J. H. Pollen, in *Miscellanea II* (Catholic Rec. Soc., 1906), 91 ('inter Wallos hos verosque Anglos tamquam diversorum populorum soboles').

95. Graham Kew, *The Irish Sections of Fynes Moryson's Unpublished Itinerary* (Dublin, 1998), 49; Sir John Temple, *The Irish Rebellion* (1646), 9–10; Nicholas Canny, 'Rowland White's "Discors touching Ireland", ca. 1569', *Irish Hist. Studies* 20 (1977), 444; Norah Carlin, 'Extreme or Mainstream?' in *Representing Ireland*, ed. Brendan Bradshaw et al. (Cambridge, 1993). Jane H. Ohlmeyer detects English 'convictions of racial superiority', leading to the perception of the Irish as 'a lower form of humanity'; ' "Civilizinge of those rude parts" ', in *Origins of Empire*, ed. Canny, 131.

96. Christopher Brooke, 'A Poem on the Late Massacre in Virginia', introduction by Robert C. Johnson, *Virginia Magazine of History and Biography* 72 (1964), 262.

97. Philippe Rosenberg, 'Thomas Tryon and the Seventeenth-Century Dimensions of Slavery', *WMQ* 61 (2004), 621–22, 626n39; Tomlins, *Freedom Bound*, 409, 413n50, 464–68, 472–75.

98. Rhodri Lewis, *William Petty on the Order of Nature* (Tempe, AZ, 2012), 54–71, 122–25; Campbell, *Renaissance Humanism and Ethnicity*, 182–84.

99. Kate Loveman, 'Samuel Pepys and "Discourses Touching Religion" under James II', *EHR* 127 (2012), 65–67; Temple, *Miscellanea: Second Part*, 166–67; Francis Lodwick, *On Language, Theology and Utopia*, ed. Felicity Henderson and William Poole (Oxford, 2011), 200–201; Siep Stuurman, 'François Bernier and the Invention of Racial Classification', *HWJ* 50 (2000).

100. Margaret T. Hodgen, *Early Anthropology in the Sixteenth and Seventeenth Centuries* (Philadelphia, PA, 1964), 213–14, 424–26; Bethencourt, *Racisms*, chap. 15; Silvia Sebastiani, *The Scottish Enlightenment*, trans. Jeremy Carden (New York, 2013).

101. Hume, *Essays*, vol. 1, 252 (a footnote added to the 1753 edition of an essay first published in 1748); John Immerwahr, 'Hume's Revised Racism', *JHI* 53 (1992), and Aaron Garrett, 'Hume's Revised Racism Revisited', *Hume Studies* 26 (2000).

102. *John Ledyard's Journey through Russia and Siberia 1787–1788*, ed. Stephen D. Watrous (Madison, WI, 1966), 178.

103. Nicholas Hudson, 'From "Nation" to Race', *Eighteenth Century Studies* 29 (1996); Kidd, *Forging of Races*, chap. 4. On the emerging belief that the 'Hottentots' (Khoikhoi) were incapable of being civilized, see Linda E. Merians, *Envisioning the Worst* (Newark, DE, 2001).

104. Edward Long, *The History of Jamaica* (1773), vol. 2, 356, 364; Henry Home, Lord Kames, *Sketches of the History of Man* (Edinburgh, 1774), vol. 1, bk 1, sketch 1 (quotation at 32–33); K. N. Chaudhuri, 'From the Barbarian and the Civilised to the Dialectics of Colour', in *Society and Ideology*, ed. Peter Robb (Delhi, 1993), 32–33; Nicholas Hudson, 'From "Nation" to "Race" ', *Eighteenth-Century Studies* 29 (1996).

105. Eliga H. Gould, 'Zones of Law, Zones of Violence', *WMQ* 60 (2003).

106. Maurice Keen, *Laws of War in the Late Middle Ages* (1965), 58; Gentili, *De Iure Belli*, 293 (III. ii); Frédéric Mégret, 'A Cautionary Tale from the Crusades', in *Prisoners in War*, ed. Sibylle Scheipers (Oxford, 2010), 3; David Hume, *An Enquiry Concerning the Principles of Morals*, ed. Tom L. Beauchamp (Oxford, 1998), 16.

107. Wilbur Cortez Abbott, *The Writings and Speeches of Oliver Cromwell* (Cambridge, MA, 1939–47), vol. 2, 205.

108. Dan Edelstein, *The Terror of Natural Right* (Chicago, IL, 2007), prologue; Walter Rech, *Enemies of Mankind* (Leiden, 2013). On the different standards observed in

so-called 'transcultural wars', see *Transcultural Wars from the Middle Ages to the 21st Century*, ed. Hans-Henning Kortüm (Berlin, 2006).

109. Robert Bartlett, *Gerald of Wales 1146–1223* (Oxford, 1982), 166–67, 197; Matthew Strickland, *War and Chivalry* (Cambridge, 1994), chap. 11; John Gillingham, *The English in the Twelfth Century* (Woodbridge, 2000), 54–55, 58; Frederick Suppe, 'The Cultural Significance of Decapitation in High Medieval Wales and the Marches', *Bulletin of the Board of Celtic Studies* 36 (1989).

110. Bernard W. Sheehan, *Savagism and Civility* (Cambridge, 1980), 174; Bernard Bailyn, *Atlantic History* (Cambridge, MA, 2005), 64–70; Tomlins, *Freedom Bound*, 176–77; Wayne E. Lee, *Barbarians and Brothers* (Oxford, 2011).

111. Rech, *Enemies of Mankind*, 11–13.

112. Andy Wood, 'The Deep Roots of Albion's Fatal Tree', *History* 99 (2014), 417; Smuts, 'Organized Violence in the Elizabethan Monarchical Republic', *History* 99 (2014), 434.

113. Canny, *Elizabethan Conquest of Ireland*, 118.

114. Joseph de Acosta, *The Naturall and Morall Historie of the East and West Indies*, trans. E[dward] G[rimestone] (1604), sig. a4ᵛ, 362–63; A Plain Man, 'The True State of the Question (1792)', in *The Slave Trade Debate*, ed. John Pinfold (Oxford, 2007), 304–5; Thomas Clarkson, *The History of the Rise, Progress, and Accomplishment of the Abolition of the African Slave Trade* (1808), vol. 1, 480; Thomas Churchyard, *A Generall Rehearsall of Warres* (1579), sig. Qiiiᵛ. On atrocities in the Anglo-Irish wars, see *Age of Atrocity*, ed. David Edwards et al. (Dublin, 2007); Mícheál Ó Siochrú, *God's Executioner* (2008); Rory Rapple, *Martial Power and Elizabethan Political Culture* (Cambridge, 2009), chap. 6; Brendan Kane, 'Ordinary Violence?' *History* 99 (2014).

115. *Acts and Ordinances of the Interregnum*, ed. C. H. Firth and R. S. Rait (1911), vol. 1, 554–55; Roger B. Manning, *An Apprenticeship in Arms* (Oxford, 2006), 222; Barbara Donagan, *War in England, 1642–1649* (Oxford, 2006), 205–9; Elaine Murphy, 'Atrocities at Sea and the Treatment of Prisoners of War by the Parliamentary Navy in Ireland, 1641–1649', *HJ* 53 (2010).

116. Ó Siochrú, *God's Executioner*, 43, 49.

117. Clarendon, *History of the Rebellion*, vol. 3, 530.

118. See Mark Stoyle, *Soldiers and Strangers* (New Haven, CT, 2005), 29–30, 48, 51–52, 149–50.

119. Alberico Gentili, *De Legationibus Libri Tres* ([1595]; New York, 1924–26), vol. 1, 85–88 (II. viii).

120. Thomas Waring, *A Brief Narration of the Plotting, Beginning and Carrying of That Execrable Rebellion and Butcherie in Ireland* (1650), 42, 64; and see Carlin, 'Extreme or Mainstream?'

121. Geoffrey Plank, *Rebellion and Savagery* (Philadelphia, 2006), 22, 52.

122. 'A Few Thoughts on Intervention', in *The Collected Works of John Stuart Mill*, ed. John M. Robson et al. (Toronto, 1963–91), vol. 21 (*Essays on Equality, Law and Education*), 118–20; J. F. C. Fuller, *The Reformation of War* (1923), 191; Brett Bowden, *The Empire of Civilization* (Chicago, IL, 2009), 179–82; Alex J. Bellamy, *Massacres and Morality* (Oxford, 2012), 42, 81–86, 95–97.

123. For figures, see *The Eighteenth Century*, ed. P. J. Marshall (*Oxford History of the British Empire*, vol. 2, Oxford, 1998), 2, 15, and chap. 20; Susan Dwyer Amussen, *Caribbean Exchanges* (Chapel Hill, NC, 2007), 41; Herbert S. Klein, *The Atlantic Slave Trade* (2nd edn, Cambridge, 2010), 214–16. On the brutal and/or negligent treatment of slaves and indentured labourers, see, e.g., Richard Pares, *Merchants and Planters* (*EcHR*, supp. 4, 1960), 39–40; Philip D. Morgan, 'British Encounters with Africans and African-Americans, circa 1600–1780', in *Strangers within the Realm*, ed. Bernard Bailyn and Philip D. Morgan (Williamsburg, VA, 1991); Larry Gragg, *Englishmen Transplanted* (Oxford, 2003), 129–30; Trevor Burnard, *Mastery, Tyranny,*

and Desire (Chapel Hill, NC, 2004); Stephanie Smallwood, *Saltwater Slavery* (Cambridge, MA, 2007).

124. John Rushworth, *Historical Collections* (1721), vol. 2, 468.

125. William Salkeld, *Reports of Cases Adjudged in the Court of King's Bench* (3rd edn, 1731), vol. 2, 666; John Dalrymple, *An Essay towards a General History of Feudal Property in Great Britain* (2nd edn, 1758), 27; David Hume, *The History of England from the Invasion of Julius Caesar to the Revolution in 1688* (new edn, 1773), vol. 3, 304.

126. Granville Sharp, *A Representation of the Injustice and Dangerous Tendency of Tolerating Slavery* (1769), 112, 125–26.

127. *Tudor Royal Proclamations*, ed. Paul L. Hughes and James F. Larkin (New Haven, CT, 1964–69), vol. 1, 352, 455–56; C. S. L. Davies, 'Slavery and Protector Somerset', *EcHR*, 2nd ser., vol. 19 (1966).

128. *Acts of the Privy Council, 1592–3*, 486–87; *1601–1604*, 489; *Letters of Philip Gawdy*, ed. Isaac Herbert Jeayes (Roxburghe Club, 1906), 123–24.

129. *Commons Debates 1621*, ed. Wallace Notestein et al. (New Haven, CT, 1935), vol. 7, 54–55; BL, Lansdowne MS 22, fol. 64 (statement of 1576); Bodl., Rawlinson MS A 185 (Pepys papers), fol. 311; Michael J. Rozbicki, 'To Save Them from Themselves', *Slavery and Abolition* 22 (2001); Michael Guasco, *Slaves and Englishmen* (Philadelphia, PA, 2014), 33–38.

130. John Donoghue, '"Out of the Land of Bondage"', *AHR* 115 (2010); Tomlins, *Freedom Bound*, 8, 30, 35, 593–97; Malcolm Gaskill, *Between Two Worlds* (Oxford, 2014), 342; *Building the Atlantic Empires*, ed. John Donoghue and Evelyn P. Jennings (Leiden, 2016), chap. 5. On the harsh treatment of poor white servants, see Richard Ligon, *A True and Exact History of the Island of Barbados* (1657), 43–46.

131. Richard Jobson, *The Golden Trade* (1623), 88–89; *The Works of Robert Sanderson*, ed. William Jacobson (Oxford, 1854), vol. 1, 177.

132. Amussen, *Caribbean Exchanges*, 129–35; Tomlins, *Freedom Bound*, 452–75.

133. G. E. Aylmer, 'Slavery under Charles II', *EHR* 114 (1999).

134. Locke, *Two Treatises of Government*, 302n–303n (II. 23–24).

135. Abigail L. Swingen, *Competing Visions of Empire* (New Haven, CT, 2015), 197–98.

136. Peter Heylyn, *Cosmography in Four Books*, ed. Edmund Bohun (1703), 941–42.

137. *Boswell's Life of Johnson*, ed. George Birkbeck Hill, rev. L. F. Powell (Oxford, 1934–50), vol. 3, 201.

138. Perry Gauci, *William Beckford* (New Haven, CT, 2013), 81, 203; David Brion Davis, *The Problem of Slavery in Western Culture* (Ithaca, NY, 1966), 108–9; John Darwin, 'Civility and Empire', in *Civil Histories*, ed. Burke et al., 325–26.

139. Adam Smith, *Lectures on Jurisprudence*, ed. R. L. Meek et al. (Oxford, 1978). 452–53.

140. Tomlins, *Freedom Bound*, 464–67, 473; Molineux, *Faces of Perfect Ebony*, 113.

141. Christopher Leslie Brown, *Moral Capital* (Chapel Hill, NC, 2006), 52.

142. Aristotle, *Politics*, 1252b; Euripides, *Iphigenia at Aulis*, lines 1400–1; John E. Coleman, 'Ancient Greek Ethnocentrism', in *Greeks and Barbarians*, ed. Coleman and Clark A. Walz (Bethesda, MD, 1997), 201–2.

143. Amussen, *Caribbean Exchanges*, 139 (and 133).

144. Mandeville, *Fable of the Bees*, vol. 2, 199.

145. Carpenter, *Geographie Delineated*, vol. 2, 222; [Richard Nisbet], *Slavery Not Forbidden by Scripture* (Philadelphia, PA, 1773), 21–25, 307; Long, *History of Jamaica*, vol. 2, 377–78; Anthony J. Barker, *The African Link* (1978), 77, 141, 191–97; P. J. Marshall and Glyndwr Williams, *The Great Map of Mankind* (1982), 231, 239, 252; Loomba, *Shakespeare, Race and Colonialism*, 127, 155; Srividya Swaminathan, *Debating the Slave Trade* (Farnham, 2009), 165–66; Swingen, *Competing Visions of Empire*, 180–81.

146. *The Miscellaneous Writings of Sir Thomas Browne*, ed. Geoffrey Keynes (new edn, 1946), 126–27; James Ramsay, 'An Inquiry into the Effects of Putting a Stop to the African Slave Trade (1784)', in *The Slave Trade Debate*, 52.

147. *Boswell's Life of Johnson*, vol. 3, 204; Davis, *Problem of Slavery*, 186, 202; 'A Plain Man', 'The True State of the Question', in *The Slave Trade Debate*, 301–3; Clarkson, *History of the Abolition of the African Slave-Trade*, vol. 1, 481; [Captain Macart], *An Appeal to the Candour and Justice of the People of England in Behalf of the West India Merchants and Planters* (1792), 21.

148. Barker, *The African Link*, 160, 166; Marshall and Williams, *Great Map of Mankind*, 233; John Taylor, *Newes and Strange Newes from St Christophers* (1638), 2.

149. Morgan Godwyn, *The Negro's and Indians Advocate* (1680), sig. A4ᵛ; Richard S. Dunn, *Sugar and Slaves* (1973), 249–50; *Boswell's Life of Johnson*, vol. 2, 476; William C. Lehmann, *John Millar of Glasgow, 1735–1801* (Cambridge, 1960), 303; Bernard Bailyn, *The Ideological Origins of the American Revolution* (Cambridge, MA, 1967), 237, 242; Philip Gould, *Barbaric Traffic* (Cambridge, MA, 2003).

150. See, e.g., *Enduring Western Civilization*, ed. Silvia Federici (Westport, CT, 1995), xii–xiii.

151. Karl Marx, *Grundrisse*, trans. Martin Nicolaus (Harmondsworth, 1973), 409; Karl Marx and Frederick Engels, *Selected Works* (1950), vol. 1, 36–37.

152. [Sir Thomas Smith and Thomas Smith], *A Letter sent by I. B. Gentleman unto his very Friend and Master R. C. Esquire* (1572), sig. Ciiiᵛ.

153. Armitage, *Ideological Origins of the British Empire*, 51–52; Sir Thomas More, *Utopia*, ed. J. H. Lupton (Oxford, 1895), 118; id., *Utopia*, trans. Gilbert Burnet (1684), 66; Spenser, *View*, 149.

154. *Original Writings of the Two Hakluyts*, vol. 2, 368; *The Complete Works of Captain John Smith (1580–1631)*, ed. Philip L. Barbour (Williamsburg, VA, 1968), vol. 2, 437, and vol. 3, 277.

155. Chris Durston, 'Let Ireland Be Quiet', *HWJ* 21 (1986), 111; *The Political Works of James Harrington*, ed. J. G. A. Pocock (Cambridge, 1977), 328.

156. Warburton, *Divine Legation of Moses*, vol. 1, 319; Robert Henry, *Revelation the Most Effective Way of Civilizing and Reforming Mankind* (Edinburgh, 1773), 4–5.

157. William Wilberforce, *A Letter on the Abolition of the Slave Trade* (1807), 73–74.

6 Civilization Reconsidered

1. For an extreme statement, see Wendy Brown, *Regulating Aversion* (Princeton, NJ, 2006).

2. Edward Keene, *Beyond the Anarchical Society* (Cambridge, 2002), 159.

3. See the trenchant remarks of Claude Lévi-Strauss, *Race and History* (Paris, 1968), 31–38.

4. This aspect of Herder's thought was much emphasized, and indeed exaggerated, by Isaiah Berlin, who saw in Herder's work an anticipation of his own belief in the incommensurability of values. See his crisp summary in 'The Counter-Enlightenment', in *Dictionary of the History of Ideas*, ed. Philip P. Wiener (New York, 1968–74), 105–6, and his more extensive treatment in 'Vico and Herder', in *Three Critics of the Enlightenment* (2nd edn, 2013); 'Alleged Relativism in Eighteenth-Century European Thought', in *The Crooked Timber of Humanity*, ed. Henry Hardy (2nd edn, 2013); and *The Roots of Romanticism*, ed. Henry Hardy (1999), 58–67. Contrast Kevin Hilliard, '"Populism, Expressionism, Pluralism" – and God?', in *Isaiah Berlin and the Enlightenment*, ed. Laurence Brockliss and Ritchie Robertson (Oxford, 2016), chap. 12.

5. In 'Vico and Herder', 289–93, 297, Berlin concedes that Herder holds these values, but dismisses them as a relatively subordinate element in his thought.

6. See, e.g., Herder, *Outlines of a Philosophy of the History of Man* [*Ideen zur Philosophie der Geschichte der Menschheit*], trans. T. Churchill (1800), 136–45 145, 213, 253, 255, 264 (on civilization), 289, 292, 293 (on bodily appearance), 255, 289, 295, 300, 303 (on the civilized and the barbarous), 213, 309 (on *Sati*). Herder's translator usually renders his '*Cultur*' and '*Bildung*' as 'civilization', and his '*gesittet*' and '*gebildet*' as 'civilized.'

7. *J. G. Herder on Social and Political Culture*, trans. and ed. F. M. Barnard (Cambridge, 1969), 23–24, 27, 35–37, 181–223; Herder, *Philosophical Writings*, trans. and ed. Michael N. Forster (Cambridge, 2002), xvii, xxv–xxx, 324–31, 342, 380–82, 385–86, 394–95, 398–99. For perceptive, though differing, assessments of this most contradictory of thinkers, see F. M. Barnard, *Herder's Social and Political Thought* (Oxford, 1965); Anthony Pagden, *European Encounters with the New World* (New Haven, CT, 1993), 172–78; Robert J. C. Young, *Colonial Desire* (1995), 36–43; Sankar Muthu, *Enlightenment against Empire* (Princeton, NJ, 2003), chap. 6; Sonia Sikka, *Herder on Humanity and Cultural Difference* (Cambridge, 2011); Michael N. Forster, *After Herder* (Oxford, 2010); T. J. Reed, *Light in Germany* (Chicago, IL, 2015), 58–61.

8. Herodotus, *The Histories*, bk 38; *The Cynic Epistles*, ed. Abraham J. Malherbe (Missoula, MT, 1977), 37; Ovid, *Tristia*, bk 5, chap. 10, lines 37–38; 1 Corinthians 14:11. For other examples, see Lynette Mitchell, *Panhellenism and the Barbarian in Ancient and Classical Greece* (Swansea, 2007), 28–29.

9. Joachim du Bellay, *Defence and Illustration of the French Language*, trans. Gladys M. Turquet (1939), 23; Bartolomé de Las Casas, *Apologètica Historia Sumaria*, ed. Edmundo O'Gorman (Mexico, D. F., 1967), vol. 2, 639, 654.

10. *Sextus Empiricus*, trans. R. G. Bury (1955), vol. 1, 84–93 (I. xiv. 145–93), 455–511 (III. xxiv–xxxi); C. B. Schmitt, 'The Rediscovery of Ancient Skepticism', in *The Skeptical Tradition*, ed. Myles Burnyeat (Berkeley, CA, 1983), esp. 237–38; Quentin Skinner, *Visions of Politics* (Cambridge, 2002), iii, chap 4.

11. J. H. Elliott, *The Old World and the New* (Cambridge, 1970), 29, 46; Anthony Pagden, *The Fall of Natural Man* (Cambridge, 1982), 125.

12. *The Essays of Montaigne*, trans. John Florio, ed. George Saintsbury (1892–93), vol. 1, 221 (I. xxx), vol. 3, 236 (III. ix); Peter Burke, *Montaigne* (Oxford, 1981), esp. chap. 7. In his 'Lessons of the New World', *Yale French Studies* 64 (1983), Edwin M. Duval argues that Montaigne regarded the faculties of reason and judgement as themselves relative.

13. Pierre Charron, *Of Wisdome*, trans. Samson Lennard ([1608?]), 308–9.

14. *Essays of Montaigne*, vol. 1, 226 (I. xxx); Charron, *Of Wisdome*, 278–79. On Montaigne as 'an unwitting universalist' rather than a relativist, see Tzvetan Todorov, *On Human Diversity* (1993), 39–43.

15. Robert Wedderburn, *The Complaynt of Scotland*, ed. A. M. Stewart (Scottish Text Soc., 1979), 83–84.

16. George Puttenham, *The Arte of English Poesie*, ed. Gladys Doidge Willcock and Alice Walker (Cambridge, 1936), 250 (III. xxii). This did not inhibit Puttenham from characterizing other peoples as 'rude', 'savage' or 'barbarous' (at 11 (I. vi), and 47 (I. xxiv)); see the comments of Carlo Ginzburg, *No Island Is an Island* (New York, 2000), 34–38.

17. Samuel Daniel, *Poems and A Defence of Ryme*, ed. Arthur Colby Sprague (1950), 139–40, 142–43.

18. Gerard de Malynes, *A Treatise of the Canker of Englands Common Wealth* (1601), 66–67, and id., *Consuetudo, vel Lex Mercatoria* (1636), 62; Sir Thomas Palmer, *An Essay of the Meanes how to make our Travailes, into Forraigne Countries, the more Profitable and Honourable* (1606), 67; *Locke: Political Essays*, ed. Mark Goldie (Cambridge, 1997), 29.

19. *The Traveiler of Ierome Turler* (Eng. trans., [1575]), 39–40; E[d]. A[ston], 'To the friendly reader', in Ioannes Boemus, *The Manners, Lawes, and Customes of all Nations*, trans. Aston (1611); Antoine de Courtin, *The Rules of Civility*, Eng. trans. (1671), 7; Hannah Woolley, *The Gentlewomans Companion* (1675), 46.

20. Adam Smith, *The Theory of Moral Sentiments*, ed. D. D. Raphael and A. L. Macfie (Oxford, 1976), 204 (V. 2. 7).
21. R[obert] B[oyle], *Occasional Reflections upon Several Subjects* (1665), vol. 2, 6, 19.
22. Paul Rycaut, *The Present State of the Ottoman Empire* (1668), sigs. A2ᵛ–A3; John Oldmixon, *The British Empire in America* (1708), vol. 1, 161; Simon Ockley, *The History of the Saracens* (2nd edn, 1718), vol. 2, xi.
23. *The Works of John Dryden*, ed. H. T. Swedenborg et al. (Berkeley, CA, 1956–89), vol. 9, 30.
24. L. P. [possibly John Toland], *Two Essays sent in a Letter from Oxford, to a Nobleman in London* (1695), iii.
25. F. J. M. Korsten, *Roger North (1651–1734)* (Amsterdam, 1981), 9–20; Henry Rowlands, *Mona Antiqua Restaurata* (Dublin, 1723), 256; Benjamin Martin, *Lingua Britannica Reformata* (1749), 111.
26. H[enry] B[lount], *A Voyage into the Levant* (2nd edn, 1636), 2, 17, 75, 108.
27. J[ohn] B[ulwer], *Chirologia* (1644), 145.
28. Lancelot Addison, *West Barbary* (Oxford, 1671), sigs. A2ᵛ–3, 111, 201. On him, see William J. Bulman, *Anglican Enlightenment* (Cambridge, 2015), 106–14, and on his assessment of the Jews, Elliott Horowitz, '"A Different Mode of Civility"', in *Christianity and Judaism*, ed. Diana Wood (*Studies in Church History* 29, Oxford, 1992).
29. John Bulwer, *Anthropometamorphosis* (1653), 184; Samuel Purchas, *Hakluytus Posthumus or Purchas his Pilgrimes* ([1625]; Glasgow, 1905–7), vol. 9, 532–33.
30. Apparently echoing José de Acosta, *The Naturall and Morall Historie of the East and West Indies*, trans. E[dward] G[rimstone] (1604), 495.
31. Palmer, *Essay of the Meanes how to make our Travailes*, 62–64.
32. [A. Roberts], *The Adventures of (Mr. T. S.) an English Merchant taken Prisoner by the Turks of ARGIERS* (1690), 161–62 (on its authorship, see Gerald M. MacLean, *The Rise of Oriental Travel* (Basingstoke, 2004), chap. 15); William Smith, *A New Voyage to Guinea* (1744), 100–101, 123, 135, 195; Philip D. Morgan, 'British Encounters with Africans and African-Americans, circa 1600–1780', in *Strangers in the Realm*, ed. Bernard Bailyn and Philip D. Morgan (Chapel Hill, NC, 1991), 214.
33. Smith, *New Voyage to Guinea*, 244–45; similarly, Ockley, Preface to *Sentences of Ali, Son of Mahomet*, in *History of the Saracens*, vol. 2, fol. 6ʳ⁻ᵛ.
34. M. E. Yapp, 'Europe in the Turkish Mirror', *P&P* 137 (1992); MacLean, *Rise of Oriental Travel*; Joan-Pau Rubiés, *Travellers and Cosmographers* (Aldershot, 2007), chap. 4; James Mather, *Pashas* (New Haven, CT, 2009), esp. 92–95, 99–102, 179–88; John-Paul Ghobrial, *The Whispers of Cities* (Oxford, 2013), chap. 3; Noel Malcolm, 'Positive Views of Islam and of Ottoman Rule in the Sixteenth Century', in *The Renaissance and the Ottoman World*, ed. Anna Contadini and Claire Norton (Farnham, 2013), 198–200; Jerry Brotton, *This Orient Isle* (2016).
35. Rycaut, *Present State of the Ottoman Empire*, sig. A3; Fynes Moryson, *An Itinerary* (Glasgow, 1907–8), vol. 2, 94, 100; vol. 3, 41–42; vol. 4, 125; Thomas Smith, *Remarks upon the Manners, Religion and Government of the Turks* (1678), 1–2, 36–38, 46–49, 209; Anna Suranyi, *The Genius of the English Nation* (Newark, DE, 2008), 55–59, 110–16, 166–67.
36. Scott Sowerby, *Making Toleration* (Cambridge, 2013), 72, 74.
37. Gerald MacLean and Nabil Matar, *Britain and the Islamic World, 1558–1713* (Oxford, 2011), 6; Alexander Bevilacqua and Helen Pfeifer, 'Turquerie', *P&P* 221 (2013).
38. Ockley, Preface to *Sentences of Ali, Son of Mahomet*, sigs. Cc5ᵛ–6.
39. *The Complete Letters of Lady Mary Wortley Montagu*, ed. Robert Halsband (Oxford, 1965), vol. 1, 313, 327; [Sir James Porter], *Observations on the Religion, Law, Government, and Manners of the Turks* (2nd edn, 1771), xiv (but for a strongly contrary view, see W. Eton, *A Survey of the British Empire* (1798)).
40. Karen Ordahl Kupperman, *Settling with the Indians* (1980), 39, 112, 144, 146; Richard Hakluyt, *The Principall Navigations Voyages Traffiques and Discoveries of the English*

Nation (Glasgow, 1903–5), vol. 8, 300; Roger Williams, *A Key into the Language of America* (1643), 1, 7, 9–10, 16.

41. Frederick B. Tolles, 'Non-Violent Contact', *Procs. of the Amer. Philosophical Soc.* 107 (1963).

42. Kupperman, *Settling with the Indians*, 50–51, 120–21, and *Indians and English* (Ithaca, NY, 2000), esp. chaps. 3 and 5; [Andrew White], *A Relation of the Successful Beginnings of the Lord Baltemore's Plantation in Mary-land* (1634), 7; *Johnson's Wonder-Working Providence 1628–1651*, ed. J. Franklin Jameson (New York, 1910), 162; Thomas Morton, *New English Canaan or New Canaan* (Amsterdam, 1637), 26 (where 'nations' has been misprinted as 'natives').

43. William Penn, *The Peace of Europe* (Everyman's Lib., n.d.), 288.

44. A. L. Rowse, *The Elizabethans and America* (1959), 96; John Josselyn, *An Account of Two Voyages to New-England* (1674), 124–25; [Robert Molesworth], *An Account of Denmark, as it was in the year 1692* (1694), sigs. a5ᵛ–6; Morton, *New English Canaan*, 33–34; *The Mirror* 18 (27 Mar. 1779; by Lord Abercromby), in *The British Essayists*, ed. Robert Lynam (1827), vol. 24, 69.

45. William Strachey, *The History of Travell into Virginia Britannia* (1612), ed. Louis B. Wright and Virginia Freund (Hakluyt Soc., 1953), 84; William Wood, *New England's Prospect*, ed. Alden T. Vaughan (Amherst, MA, 1977), 92.

46. Loren E. Pennington, 'The Amerindian in English Promotional Literature 1575–1625', in *The Westward Enterprise*, ed. K. R. Andrews et al. (Liverpool, 1978).

47. *ODNB*, s.v. 'Morton, Thomas (1580x95–1646/7)'; Williams, *Key into the Language of America*, 9–10, 29, 76, 135.

48. John Forster, *Englands Happiness Increased* (1664), 18; *The Miscellaneous Writings of Sir Thomas Browne*, ed. Geoffrey Keynes (1946), 395. Jared Diamond, *The World until Yesterday* (2012), is a modern work in this tradition.

49. James Tyrrell, *Patriarcha non Monarcha* (1681), 110; H[umphrey] B[rooke], *The Durable Legacy* (1681), 19.

50. John Locke, *Some Thoughts concerning Education*, ed. John W. and Jean S. Yolton (Oxford, 1989), 206 (para. 145). See also his *Two Treatises of Government*, ed. Peter Laslett (Cambridge, 1960), 201 (I, para. 58).

51. [Joseph-François] Lafitau, *Moeurs des sauvages Amériquaines* (Paris, 1724), vol. 1, 97.

52. William Smellie, *The Philosophy of Natural History* (1790), 199; *Captain Cook's Voyages of Discovery* (Everyman's Library, 1906), 68; also 21, 32, 34, 38, 147; *The Journals of Captain Cook on His Voyages of Discovery*, ed. J. C. Beaglehole (Hakluyt Soc., 1955–67), vol. 2, 271; vol. 3, pt 1, 307, 312, 459; vol. 3, pt 2, 954.

53. Adam Smith, *Lectures on Jurisprudence*, ed. R. L. Meek et al. (Oxford, 1978), 439; id., *Theory of Moral Sentiments*, 204–8 (V. ii. 7–10).

54. 'Ductor Dubitantium', in *The Whole Works of the Right Rev. Jeremy Taylor*, ed. Reginald Heber, rev. Charles Page Eden (1849–61), vol. 9, ed. Alexander Taylor, 287.

55. Sir Tho[mas] Pope Blount, *Essays on Several Subjects* (1692), 73–74; *Spectator* 50 (27 Apr. 1711), ed. Donald F. Bond (Oxford, 1965), vol. 1, 215.

56. Muthu, *Enlightenment against Empire*; Larry Wolff, 'Introduction', in *The Anthropology of the Enlightenment*, ed. Wolff and Marco Cipolloni (Stanford, CA, 2012).

57. David Hartley, *Observations on Man* (1749), vol. 1, 485; Adam Ferguson, *Essay on the History of Civil Society*, ed. Duncan Forbes (Edinburgh, 1966), 205; 'Remarks concerning the Savages of North America', in *The Writings of Benjamin Franklin*, ed. Albert Henry Smyth (New York, 1907), vol. 10, 97; *An Embassy to China*, ed. J. L. Cranmer-Byng (1962), 230.

58. On the limits to Franklin's sympathy with the Native American way of life, see Élise Marienstras, 'Sauvagerie et civilisation chez Benjamin Franklin', in *Barbares et sauvages*, ed. Jean-Louis Chevalier et al. (Caen, 1994), 155–58.

59. Sir Humphrey Gilbert, *A Discourse of a Discoverie for a New Passage to Cataia* (1576), sig. 102.

60. See also P. J. Marshall and Glyndwr Williams, *The Great Map of Mankind* (1982), chap. 5 and 169–81; Peter Burke, 'A Civil Tongue', in *Civil Histories*, ed. Burke et al. (Oxford, 2000), 34. For an unusually negative assessment, see William Julius Mickle's translation of Camöens, *The Lusiad* (1776), 468n–472n.

61. *Sir John Chardin's Travels in Persia*, trans. Edmund Lloyd (1720), vol. 2, 130; *Sir Anthony Sherley his Relation of his Travels into Persia* (1613), 29.

62. *The Works of Sir William Jones* (1807), vol. 3, 50.

63. *The Letters of Sir William Jones*, ed. Garland Cannon (Oxford, 1970), vol. 2, 766; *Works of Sir William Jones*, vol. 3, 17, 34; Garland Cannon, *The Life and Mind of Oriental Jones* (Cambridge, 1990); Richard Fynes, 'Sir William Jones and the Classical Tradition', in *Sir William Jones 1746–1794*, ed. Alexander Murray (Oxford, 1998); *The Writings and Speeches of Edmund Burke*, ed. Paul Langford et al. (Oxford, 1981–2015), vol. 5, 389–90; and see Geoffrey Carnall, 'Robertson and Contemporary Images of India', in *William Robertson and the Expansion of Empire*, ed. Stewart J. Brown (Cambridge, 1997).

64. P. J. Marshall, *Problems of Empire* (1968), 60–61, 69–73, 191; Philip J. Stern, *The Company-State* (New York, 2011), 110–17; Meenakshi Jain, *Sati* (New Delhi, 2016), 444–56; Sir Penderel Moon, *The British Conquest and Dominion of India* (1989), 225.

65. Georgius Trapezuntius [George of Trebizond], *Comparatio Platonis et Aristotelis* (Venice, 1523; written 1457–58), sig. R3.

66. Aziz Al-Azmeh, 'Barbarians in Arab Eyes', *P&P* 134 (1992); Moryson, *Itinerary*, vol. 3, 414; Addison, *West Barbary*, 150; Natalie Zemon Davis, *Trickster Travels* (2007), 148–49.

67. David Hume, *Essays Moral, Political, and Literary*, ed. T. H. Green and T. H. Grose (1898), vol. 1, 266.

68. K. N. Chaudhuri, 'From the Barbarian and the Civilised to the Dialectics of Colour', in *Society and Ideology*, ed. Peter Robb et al. (Delhi, 1993), 37–38.

69. *Japanese Travellers in Sixteenth-Century Europe*, trans. J. F. Moran, ed. Derek Massarella (Hakluyt Soc., 2012), 137.

70. Sir George Staunton, *An Authentic Account of an Embassy from the King of Great Britain to the Emperor of China* (Dublin, 1798), vol. 1, 329.

71. Sir William Temple, *Miscellanea, The Second Part* (4th edn, 1696), 170; Frank Dikötter, *The Discourse of Race in Modern China* (1992), chap. 1; Harry G. Gelber, *The Dragon and the Foreign Devils* (2007), 33–35; Joseph Hall, *The Discovery of a New World* (1609), sig. A4.

72. Ferguson, *Essay on the History of Civil Society*, 75, 95.

73. Peter de La Primaudaye, *The French Academie*, trans. T. B. (1586), 576.

74. John Smith, *A Map of Virginia* (Oxford, 1612), in *Works 1608–1631*, ed. Edward Arber (Birmingham, 1884), 79 (echoed by Alexander Whitaker, *Good Newes from Virginia* (1613), 26); Williams, *Key into the Language of America*, 47; Kupperman, *Settling with the Indians*, 47, 49–50; Peter King, '"A King in Every Countrey"', *Journ. of Canadian Hist. Assocn* 14 (2013). Contrast Thomas Hobbes, *Leviathan*, ed. Noel Malcolm (Oxford, 2013), vol. 2, 194 (chap. 13), and other commentators cited in vol. 2, 195, note g.

75. John Ogilby, *Atlas* (1670), sig. c5ᵛ, and 8–9; Richard Boothby, *A Breife Discovery or Description of the Most Famous Island of Madagascar* (1646), 17.

76. Peter Paxton, *Civil Polity* (1703), 3.

77. David Hume, *A Treatise of Human Nature*, ed. David Fate Norton and Mary J. Norton (Oxford, 2000), 346 (3. 2. 8); similarly, John Locke, *Two Treatises of Government*, ed. Peter Laslett (Cambridge, 1960), 357–58 (II. para.108).

78. James Dunbar, *Essays on the History of Mankind in Rude and Cultivated Ages* (1780), 147–48. Cf. Lévi-Strauss, *Race and History*, 31–38.

79. Philippe Bénéton, *Histoire de mots* (Paris, 1975), 40–42. An isolated French instance from 1767 is cited in Joachim Moras, *Ursprung und Entwicklung des Begriffs der Zivilisation in Frankreich, 1756–1830* (Hamburg, 1930), 41. The first plural citation in the *OED* is for 1857: 'civilization', 3c.

80. J. P. Arnason, 'Civilizational Analysis, History of', in *International Encyclopedia of the Social and Behavioral Sciences*, ed. Neil J. Smelser et al. (Amsterdam, 2001), 1910.

81. 'Coleridge', in *Collected Works of John Stuart Mill*, ed. John M. Robson et al. (Toronto, 1963–91), vol. 10, 139–40.

82. Daniel A. Segal, '"Western Civ" and the Staging of History', *AHR* 105 (2000), 799–800; David Hollinger, 'Cultural Relativism', in *The Cambridge History of Science*, vol. 7, ed. Theodore M. Porter and Dorothy Ross (Cambridge, 2003), 712; *OED*, s.v. 'culture'; Émile Durkheim and Marcel Mauss, 'Note on the Concept of Civilisation', and Mauss, 'Civilisations, Their Elements and Forms', in Marcel Mauss, *Techniques, Technology, and Civilisation*, ed. Nathan Schlanger (New York, 2006).

83. R. H. Tawney, preface to Raymond Firth, *Primitive Economics of the New Zealand Maori* (1929), xiii.

84. 'Le barbare, c'est d'abord l'homme qui croit à la barbarie'; Claude Lévi-Strauss, *Race et histoire* (Paris, 1961), 22. See the comments of Raymond Aron, 'Le Paradoxe du même et de l'autre', in *Echanges et Communications*, ed. Jean Pouillon and Pierre Maranda (The Hague, 1970), and Charles Taylor, 'Comparison, History, Truth', in *Myth and Philosophy*, ed. Frank Reynolds and Derek Tracy (Albany, NY, 1990), 47.

85. Francisco de Vitoria, *Political Writings*, ed. Anthony Pagden and Jeremy Lawrance (Cambridge, 1991), 278–84; Alberico Gentili, *De Iure Belli Libri Tres*, trans. J. C. Rolfe (Oxford, 1933), 86–87, 88–90 (I. xix). Luis de Molina, *De Iustitia Tomus Primus, Complectens Tractatum Primum, et ex Secundo Disputationes* (Cuenca, 1593), cols. 566–67 (*Disputatio*, 105).

86. John Selden, *Of the Dominion, or, Ownership of the Sea*, trans. Marchamont Nedham (1652), 123–26; id., *Opera Omnia*, ed. David Wilkins (1726), vol. 2, pt 2, cols. 1250–52; Toomer, *Selden*, vol. 1, 407; and see Richard Tuck, *The Rights of War and Peace* (Oxford, 1999), 51–52, 68–70, 119–20.

87. Richard Zouche, *Iuris et Iudicii Fecialis* [1650], ed. Thomas Erskine Holland (Washington, DC, 1911), vol. 2, trans. J. L. Brierly, 109–10 (II. v. 9); Robert Skinner, *Reports of Cases adjudged in the Court of King's Bench* (1728), 91–93, 168.

88. Thomas Hobbes, *The Elements of Law*, ed. Ferdinand Tönnies (2nd edn, 1969), 87 (I. 16. 12); *Leviathan*, ed. Malcolm, vol. 2, 392 (chap. 24); Pat Moloney, 'Hobbes, Savagery, and International Anarchy', *Amer. Political Science Rev.* 105 (2011), 197–98.

89. [Samuel], Baron Pufendorf, *The Laws of Nature and Nations*, trans. Basil Kennet[t] (3rd edn, 1717), 2nd pagination, 32–36 (III. iii. 9–12), 168 (IV. v. 10); Gideon Baker, 'Right of Entry or Right of Refusal?' *Rev. of International Studs.* 37 (2012), 50–54.

90. Muthu, *Enlightenment against Empire*, 75, 85, 103–4, 192–97; *Journals of Captain Cook*, ed. Beaglehole, vol. 2, 493 and 493n; Dan O'Sullivan, *In Search of Captain Cook* (2008), 139–42.

91. *The Correspondence of Roger Williams*, ed. Glenn W. Lafantasie (Hanover, NH, 1988), vol. 1, 19; John Cotton, 'A Reply to Mr. Williams his Examination', in *The Bloudy Tenent Washed, and Made White in the Bloud of the Lambe* (1647), 2nd pagination, 27–28. Anthony Pagden points out that Williams's concern to establish the natives' property in their land may have been motivated by his desire to establish the right (disputed by the Crown) of the Salem colonists to buy it; 'The Struggle for Legitimacy and the Image of Empire in the Atlantic to c. 1700', in *The Origins of Empire*, ed. Nicholas Canny (*Oxford History of the British Empire*, vol. 1, Oxford, 1998), 47.

92. Tuck, *Rights of War and Peace*, 157–58, 172–73, 181, 183–84, 190–91.

93. Robin F. A. Fabel, *Colonial Challenges* (Gainesville, FL, 2000), chaps. 8–11; Jack P. Greene, *Evaluating Empire and Confronting Colonialism in Eighteenth-Century Britain* (Cambridge, 2013), 1–19.

94. *The Reports of Sir Edward Coke*, ed. George Wilson (1777), vol. 4, pt 7, fol. 17^{r-v} (Calvin's Case); Richard Brownlow and John Goldesborough, *Reports of Divers Choice Cases in Law* (1651), 2nd pagination, 296–97; Sir Edward Coke, *The Second Part of the Institutes of the Laws of England* (1817), 154–55.

95. *Cobbett's Complete Collection of State Trials*, ed. T. B. Howell et al. (1809–28), vol. 10, cols. 372–554; lucidly discussed by Richard Tuck, 'Alliances with Infidels in the European Imperial Expansion', in *Empire and Modern Political Thought*, ed. Sankar Muthu (Cambridge, 2012), though Tuck does not note that, in his judgment, Jeffreys observed (col. 545) that, though irrelevant to the case under consideration, Coke's opinion was in itself good law.

96. Michael Dalton, *The Countrey Justice* (6th edn, 1635), 165; William Salkeld, *Reports of Cases adjudged in the Court of King's Bench* (4th edn, 1742–43), vol. 1, 46; Henry Cowper, *Reports of Cases adjudged in the Court of King's Bench from Hilary Term . . . 1774 to Trinity Term . . . 1778* (1783), 209.

97. Edward Coke, *The First Part of the Institutes of the Laws of England*, 15th edn, ed. Francis Hargrave and Charles Butler (1794), 6b; *Reports of Adjudged Cases in the Court of Common Pleas during the time Lord Chief Justice Willes Presided*, ed. Charles Durnford (Dublin, 1800), 542–43.

98. Muldoon, *Popes, Lawyers, and Infidels*, chap. 2; Purchas, *Hakluytus Posthumus*, vol. 1, 38–45; vol. 19, 220.

99. *The Voyages and Colonizing Enterprises of Sir Humphrey Gilbert*, ed. David Beers Quinn (Hakluyt Soc., 1940), vol. 2, 450–58.

100. Bartolomé de Las Casas, *In Defense of the Indians*, trans. and ed. Stafford Poole (DeKalb, IL, 1974), 47–48.

101. *Selections from Three Works of Francisco Suárez, S. J.*, ed. James Brown Scott (Oxford, 1944), vol. 2, trans. Gwladys L. Williams et al., 825–26.

102. Roger Williams, *The Bloody Tenent Yet More Bloody* (1652), 276.

103. Jos[eph] Hall, *Resolutions and Decisions of Divers Practicall Cases of Conscience* (3rd edn, 1654), 236. Though noting that 'the learned professors of Complutum [Alcalá] and Salamanca' had exposed the Spaniards' unjust usurpation (234, 239–42), Hall followed them in maintaining that Europeans were entitled to travel where they pleased and to use force if that was the only way of securing the right to trade with the natives.

104. 'Ductor Dubitantium', in *Whole Works of Jeremy Taylor*, vol. 9, 281–82.

105. Sir Thomas More, *Utopia*, ed. George M. Logan and Robert M. Adams (Cambridge, 1989), 56; 'Of Coaches', in *Essays of Montaigne*, vol. 3, 142–51. Armitage, 'Literature and Empire', in *Origins of Empire*, ed. Canny, 106–12, is an excellent discussion of the conflicting ingredients of the classical legacy.

106. *Tyrannipocrit, Discovered with his Wiles* (1649), in *British Pamphleteers*, ed. George Orwell and Reginald Reynolds, vol. 1 (1948), 90–91, 105; *Leveller Manifestoes of the Puritan Revolution*, ed. Don M. Wolfe ([1944]; New York, 1967), 318; *ODNB*, s.v. 'Marten, Henry'; *A New Engagement* (1648); *The English Souldiers Standard to Repaire to* (1649), 9–10; *The Souldiers Demand* (Bristol, 1649), 12–13; *Walwins Wiles* (1649), in *The Leveller Tracts 1647–1653*, ed. William Haller and Godfrey Davies (New York, 1944), 288, 310. See Chris Durston, 'Let Ireland Be Quiet', *HWJ* 21 (1986); Norah Carlin, 'The Levellers and the Conquest of Ireland in 1649', *HJ* 30 (1987); Christopher Hill, 'Seventeenth-Century English Radicals and Ireland', in *A Nation of Change and Novelty* (1990). Although the Leveller leaders were reluctant to take a public stand on Ireland, it is too much to say, as does Mícheál Ó Siochrú in *God's Executioner* (2008), 64–65, that these objections were invented by the government's supporters and attributed to the Levellers in order to discredit them.

107. Algernon Sidney, *Discourses concerning Government* (3rd edn, 1753), 40; Locke, *Two Treatises of Government*, 296–300, 406 (ii. 16–20, 180).

108. Edward Stillingfleet, *A Sermon Preached on the Fast-Day, November 13, 1678* (1678), 31; *Barlow's Journal*, ed. Basil Lubbock (1934), vol. 2, 401.

109. See, in general, Muthu, *Enlightenment against Empire*. For the British dimension, see the excellent account in Greene, *Evaluating Empire and Confronting Colonialism*. For

Diderot and Raynal, see *Raynal's 'Histoire des Deux Indes': Colonialism, Networks and Global Exchange*, ed. Cecil Courtney and Jenny Mander (Oxford, 2015).

110. Denis Diderot, *Political Writings*, trans. and ed. John Hope Mason and Robert Wokler (Cambridge, 1992), 177.
111. John Lawson, *A New Voyage to Carolina* (1709), 236; Samuel Johnson, *The Lives of the Most Eminent English Poets*, ed. Roger Lonsdale (Oxford, 2006), vol. 3, 163; *Idler* 81 (3 Nov. 1759); *Gentleman's Magazine* 8 (June 1738); and see Clement Hawes, *The British Eighteenth Century and Global Critique* (New York, 2005), 179–83.
112. David Hume, *An Enquiry concerning the Principles of Morals*, ed. Tom L. Beauchamp (Oxford, 2014), 18.
113. *Journals of Captain Cook*, ed. Beaglehole, vol. 1, 514.
114. Thomas Parker, *Evidence of our Transactions in the East Indies* (1782), iii.
115. William MacIntosh, *Travels in England, Asia, and Africa* (1782), vol. 2, 73; Parker, *Evidence of our Transactions*, v; P. J. Marshall, *'A Free though Conquering People'* (Aldershot, 2003), vol. 1, 8–9; Greene, *Evaluating Empire*, chap. 4.
116. *Writings and Speeches of Edmund Burke*, vols. 5, 6 and 7; Jennifer Pitts, *A Turn to Empire* (Princeton, NJ, 2005), chap. 3.
117. *An Historical Disquisition concerning the Knowledge the Ancients Had of India*, in *The Works of the Late William Robertson* (1826), vol. 2, 483–84.
118. Malachy Postlethwayt, *The Universal Dictionary of Trade and Commerce* (3rd edn, 1766), vol. 1, vii; Granville Sharp, *A Representation of the Injustice and Dangerous Tendency of Tolerating Slavery* (1769), 112–26, 104–5.
119. *The Diary of Thomas Burton*, ed. John Towill Rutt (1828), vol. 4, 255–73, 301–8.
120. John Donoghue, *Fire under the Ashes* (Chicago, IL, 2013), 265–67, 270–74, 276, 277–78.
121. Richard Baxter, *A Christian Directory* (1673), 538–39.
122. Philippe Rosenberg, 'Thomas Tryon and the Seventeenth-Century Dimensions of Antislavery', *WMQ*, 3rd ser., 61 (2004); Christopher Leslie Brown, *Moral Capital* (Chapel Hill, NC, 2006), chap. 1; Greene, *Evaluating Empire*, 54–60.
123. See, e.g., Peter Gay, *The Enlightenment* (1970), vol. 2, 412–19; Greene, *Evaluating Empire*, 164.
124. Granville Sharp, *The Law of Liberty, or, Royal Law* (1776), 33; and for an early statement, George Keith, *An Exhortation & Caution to Friends Concerning Buying or Keeping of Negroes* (New York, 1693).
125. Anthony Page, *John Jebb and the Enlightenment Origins of British Radicalism* (Westport, CT, 2003), 226.
126. David Brion Davis, *The Problem of Slavery in the Age of Revolution 1770–1823* (Ithaca, NY, 1975), 258.
127. *The Complete Antislavery Writings of Anthony Benezet 1754–1783*, ed. David L. Crosby (Baton Rouge, LA, 2013), 71; John Wesley, *Thoughts Upon Slavery* (1774), 9–17; John Ady, *The Case of our Fellow-Creatures the Oppressed Africans* (1784), 7; 'Papers relative to our treatment of the people of Africa', 40–42, 46–47, appended to Parker, *Evidence of our Transactions*; 'Charity', in *The Poems of William Cowper*, ed. John D. Baird and Charles Ryskamp (Oxford, 1980–95), vol. 1, 341.
128. 'A Serious Thought (1775)', in *The Complete Writings of Thomas Paine*, ed. Philip S. Foner (New York, 1945), vol. 2, 19–20.
129. For the abolitionists' case, see Wylie Sypher, *Guinea's Captive Kings* (Chapel Hill, NC, 1942), chap. 2; David Brion Davis, *The Problem of Slavery in Western Culture* (Ithaca, NY, 1966); Roger Anstey, *The Atlantic Slave Trade and British Abolition, 1760–1810* (1975); Brown, *Moral Capital*, chaps. 6 and 7; and Greene, *Evaluating Empire*, chap. 5.
130. See the University College London, 'Legacies of British Slave-Ownership' project; www.ucl.ac.uk/lbs.
131. Postlethwayt, *Universal Dictionary*, vol. 1, sig. G1.

132. Anstey, *Atlantic Slave Trade*, chaps. 8 and 9; Brown, *Moral Capital*, chaps. 6 and 7.
133. Bartolomé de Las Casas, *In Defense of the Indians*, trans. and ed. Stafford Poole (DeKalb, IL, 1974), 47–48; José de Acosta, *De Procuranda Indorum Salute*, trans. and ed. G. Stewart McIntosh (Tayport, 1995–96), vol. 1, 113 (III. vii); D. A. Brading, *The First Americans* (Cambridge, 1991), chaps. 3 and 4; Tuck, *Rights of War and Peace*, 69–72.
134. John Donne, *Biathanatos*, ed. Ernest W. Sullivan II (Newark, DE, 1984), 40.
135. Alberico Gentili, *De Iure Belli Libri Tres*, trans. John C. Rolfe (Oxford, 1936), 53–55 (I. xii); Hugo Grotius, *The Free Sea*, trans. Richard Hakluyt, ed. David Armitage (Indianapolis, IN, 2004), 15 (chap. 2); id., *De Iure Praedae Commentarius*, vol. 1, trans. Gwladys L. Williams and Walter H. Zeydel (Oxford, 1950), 222 (chap. 12); id., *Rights of War and Peace*, 436–40 (II. xx. 40–43), 478–79 (II. xxii. 10 and 12).
136. G. W. Leibniz, *New Essays on Human Understanding*, trans. Peter Remnant and Jonathan Bennett (Cambridge, 1996), 87–88, 93; Muthu, *Enlightenment against Empire*; Jonathan Israel, *Enlightenment Contested* (Oxford, 2006), 590–603 (but mentioning no British author); id., *Democratic Enlightenment* (Oxford, 2011), pt 3; Melvin Richter, 'The Comparative Study of Regimes and Societies', in *The Cambridge History of Eighteenth-Century Political Thought*, ed. Mark Goldie and Robert Wokler (Cambridge, 2006), chap. 5.
137. Pufendorf, *Law of Nature and Nations*, 1st pagination, 126–28 (II. iii. 7–9); 2nd pagination, 18–20 (III. ii. 8); 3rd pagination, 90–91 (VIII. vi. 5); see also Tuck, *Rights of War and Peace*, 158–62. Pufendorf's earlier reflections on the impossibility of agreement on which peoples were barbarous and which were civilized ('*moratiores*') occur in a letter of 1663; Fiammetta Palladini, 'Le due lettere di Pufendorf al Barone di Boineburg', *Nouvelles de la République des Lettres*, vol. 1 (1984), 135–36.
138. Christian Thomasius, *Foundations of the Law of Nature and Nations* (1705), ed. and trans. Thomas Ahnert (Indianapolis, IN, 2011), 619.
139. Emmer de Vattel, *The Law of Nations*, ed. Béla Kapossy and Richard Whatmore (Indianapolis, IN, 2008), 265 (II. 1. 7); Daniel Gordon, 'Uncivilised Civilisation', in *Raynal's 'Histoire des Deux Indes'*, ed. Courtney and Mander.
140. Robert Ward, *An Enquiry into the Foundation and History of the Law of Nations in Europe* (1795), vol. 1, xiv, 135–39, 163–65.
141. Temple, *Miscellanea, Second Part*, 47, 163.
142. Thomas Burnet, *The Sacred Theory of the Earth* (7th edn, 1759), vol. 2, 21.
143. Paxton, *Civil Polity*, sig. a4.
144. *The Briton* (1722), 36 (act 3, scene 8).
145. Jonathan Swift, *Gulliver's Travels* ([1726]; 1919), 292–93 (bk 4, chap. 5).
146. *The Poetical Works of Richard Savage*, ed. Clarence Tracy (Cambridge, 1962), 253.
147. Bulwer, *Anthropometamorphosis*, 155; Smith, *Theory of Moral Sentiments*, 199 (v. i. 9).
148. Richard McCabe, *Spenser's Monstrous Regiment* (Oxford, 2002), 123; George Bishop, *New-England Judged* (1661; repr. 1703), 29, 123.
149. John Underhill, *Newes from America* (1638), 42–43.
150. Elliott, *Old World and the New*, 26.
151. Thomas Fuller, *The Holy State and the Profane State* (1840), 156.
152. Bernard Mandeville, *The Fable of the Bees*, ed. F. B. Kaye (Oxford, 1924), vol. 2, 215; 'Fragments, or Minutes of Essays', in *The Works of the Right Honourable Henry St John, Viscount Bolingbroke* (new edn, 1809), vol. 7, 467.
153. Williams, *Key into the Language of America*, 180; Ira D. Gruber, 'Atlantic Warfare, 1440–1763', in *The Oxford Handbook of the Atlantic World*, ed. Nicholas Canny and Philip Morgan (Oxford, 2011), 420–21.
154. John Hippisley, *Essays* (1764), 13.
155. The classic account of their horrors is Albert Sorel, *Europe and the French Revolution* [1885], trans. and ed. Alfred Cobban and J. W. Hunt (1969), 108–15.

156. Daniel Defoe, *Serious Reflections during the Life and Surprising Adventures of Robinson Crusoe* (1720), 124–25.

157. Joseph Fawcett, *Poems* (1798), 187–242; Henry Roscoe, *The Life of William Roscoe* (1833), vol. 1, 296.

158. *The Complete Works of Gerrard Winstanley*, ed. Thomas N. Corns et al. (Oxford, 2009), vol. 2, 80.

159. John Brown, *An Estimate of the Manners and Principles of the Times* (1760), 93. On this much-discussed subject, see John Sekora, *Luxury* (Baltimore, MD, 1977); David Spadafora, *The Idea of Progress in Eighteenth-Century Britain* (New Haven, CT, 1990), 15–16, 35–36, 215–17, 317–18; James Raven, *Judging New Wealth* (Oxford, 1992), chap. 8; Christopher J. Berry, *The Idea of Luxury* (Cambridge, 1994), chaps. 5 and 6; *Luxury in the Eighteenth Century*, ed. Maxine Berg and Elizabeth Eger (Basingstoke, 2003), chap. 1; E. J. Clery, *The Feminization Debate in Eighteenth-Century England* (Basingstoke, 2004); Keith Thomas, *The Ends of Life* (Oxford, 2009), 132–37.

160. Smith, *Lectures on Jurisprudence*, 540–41.

161. *The Complete Works of M. de Montesquieu* (Eng. trans., 1777), vol. 2, 1–3 ('The Spirit of Laws', bk 20, chaps. 1–2).

162. William Letwin, *The Origins of Scientific Economics* (1963), 43–44; Alexander Hamilton et al., *The Federalist*, ed. Max Beloff (Oxford, 1948), 20–25; Muthu, *Enlightenment against Empire*, 97–99; and see Paul Slack, *The Invention of Improvement* (Oxford, 2014 [2015]), 190.

163. *Writings and Speeches of Edmund Burke*, vol. 8, 130–31.

164. Roscoe, *Life of William Roscoe*, vol. 1, 269–70; *Journals of Captain Cook*, ed. Beaglehole, vol. 2, 174–75 (and similar sentiments in George Forster, *A Voyage Round the World* (1777), vol. 1, 303).

165. See Mark Harrison, *Contagion* (2012), 276.

166. Ferguson, *Essay on Civil Society*, 183.

167. W. R. Scott, *Adam Smith as Student and Professor* (Glasgow, 1937), 326; Adam Smith, *An Inquiry into the Nature and Causes of the Wealth of Nations*, ed. R. H. Campbell and A. S. Skinner (Oxford, 1976), vol. 2, 781–88 (v. i. f.); *Lectures on Jurisprudence*, 539–40.

168. 'Lectures on Political Economy, I', in *The Collected Works of Dugald Stewart*, ed. Sir William Hamilton (1854–60), vol. 8, 317.

169. Dunbar, *Essays on the History of Mankind*, 146–47, 165, 424.

170. Denis Diderot, *Political Writings*, trans. and ed. John Hope Mason and Robert Wokler (Cambridge, 1992), 72, 173, 185–88, 193–97, 199, 212–14; Jean-Jacques Rousseau, *Oeuvres complètes*, ed. Bernard Gagnebin and Marcel Raymond, vol. 3 (Paris, 1964), at, e.g., 164–80, 258.

171. *Mirror* 18 (27 Mar. 1779; by Lord Abercromby), in *British Essayists*, vol. 24, 70.

172. Forster, *Voyage Round the World*, vol. 1, 365–67; vol. 2, 31–35.

173. *The Works of Mary Wollstonecraft*, ed. Janet Todd and Marilyn Butler (1989), vol. 6, 220; vol. 5, 215; *The Life and Major Writings of Thomas Paine*, ed. Philip S. Foner (Secaucus, NJ, 1974), 398, 610.

174. T. R. Malthus, *Essay on the Principle of Population* (1798), 344; Charles Hall, *The Effects of Civilization on People in European States* (1805), 131–32.

175. Alexis de Tocqueville, *Journeys to England and Ireland*, trans. George Lawrence and K. P. Mayer, ed. J. P. Mayer (New York, 1968), 96.

176. Thomas Churchyard, *A Prayse, and Reporte of Maister Martyne Forboishers Voyage to Meta Incognita* (1578), sig. Bii.

177. *A View of the Present State of Ireland*, in *Spenser's Prose Works*, ed. Rudolf Gottfried (Baltimore, MD, 1949), 55, and *A Brief Note of Ireland*, in *Spenser's Prose Works*, 239–40; Samuel Daniel, *The Queenes Arcadia* (1606), sig. K2.

178. Colin Lennon, 'Political Thought of Irish Counter-Reformation Churchmen', in *Political Ideology in Ireland, 1541–1641*, ed. Hiram Morgan (Dublin, 1999), 189, 202;

Patricia Palmer, *Language and Conquest in Early Modern Ireland* (Cambridge, 2001), 212; Ian Campbell, *Renaissance Humanism and Ethnicity before Race* (Manchester, 2013), chap. 3.

179. Gerard Boate, *Irelands Naturall History*, published by Samuel Hartlib (1652), 89, 130 (drawing on information from Irish Protestant refugees and from Sir John Temple, *The Irish Rebellion* (1646), vol. 1, sig. b1, 83; vol. 2, 41).

180. *The Works of George Savile, Marquis of Halifax*, ed. Mark N. Brown (Oxford, 1989), vol. 3, 171; Alfred Owen Aldridge, 'Franklin's Letter on Indians and Germans', *Amer. Philos. Soc. Procs.* 14 (1950), 392–93.

181. Colin G. Calloway, *New Worlds for All* (2nd edn, Baltimore, MD, 2013), 192–96; Baron Lahontan, *New Voyages to North-America* (Eng. trans., 1703; 2nd edn, 1705), vol. 2, 21–31, 38–39.

182. Ottobah Cugoano, *Thoughts and Sentiments on the Evil and Wicked Practice of the Slavery and Commerce of the Human Species* (1787), 138–39.

183. John Streater, *Observations Historical, Political, and Philosophical upon Aristotles First Book of Political Government*, no. 4 (25 Apr.–2 May 1654), 28.

184. Ian K. Steele, *Warpaths* (New York, 1994), 39–40; Ester Boserup, *The Conditions of Agricultural Growth* (1965), 24–25; Jill Lepore, *The Name of War* (New York, 1998), 95–96.

185. *The History of America* (1777), in *Works of William Robertson*, vol. 5, 395–97; *The Memoirs of Lieut. Henry Timberlake* (1765), 51.

186. John Demos, *The Unredeemed Captive* (New York, 1994); Calloway, *New Worlds for All*, 160–63; Juliana Barr, 'Captivity, Native American', in *The Princeton Companion to Atlantic History*, ed. Joseph C. Miller (Princeton, NJ, 2015).

187. Edward D. Neill, *Virginia Vetusta* (Albany, NY, 1885), viii; Malcolm Gaskill, *Between Two Worlds* (Oxford, 2014), 285; Nicholas Canny, 'The Permissive Frontier', in *The Westward Enterprise*, ed. Andrews, 30–35 (quotation at 34).

188. James Axtell, *The European and the Indian* (New York, 1981), 156; Peter Way, 'The Cutting Edge of Culture', in *Empire and Others*, ed. Martin Daunton and Rick Halpern (Philadelphia, PA, 1999), 141–43; J. Hector St John de Crèvecoeur, *Letters from an American Farmer* (Dublin, 1782), 237–38. In 'Crossing the Cultural Divide', *Procs. Amer. Antiquarian Soc.* 90 (1980), Alden T. Vaughan and Daniel K. Richter arrive at a much lower figure; see also Alden T. Vaughan and Edward W. Clark, *Puritans among the Indians* (Cambridge, MA, 1981), 15.

189. Aldridge, 'Franklin's Letter on Indians and Germans', 392. On this subject, see Axtell, *The European and the Indian*, 156, 161, 279–84, and 'The White Indians of Colonial America', in *American Encounters*, ed. Peter C. Mancall and James H. Merrell (2nd edn, New York, 2007); Richard VanDerBeets, *The Indian Captivity Narrative* (Lanham, MD, 1984), 47; Linda Colley, *Captives* (2002), 195–98; Evan Haefeli and Kevin Sweeney, *Captors and Captives* (Amherst, MA, 2003), 151–52; Alison Games, *The Web of Empire* (Oxford, 2008), 130–31.

190. *ODNB*, s.v. 'Verney, Sir Francis'; Simon Ockley, *An Account of South-West Barbary* (1713), 125; Kenneth Parker, 'Reading "Barbary" in Early Modern England', *Seventeenth Century* 19 (2004), 80, 91–93.

191. Smith, *Remarks upon the Turks*, 144–45; Joseph Pitts, *A True and Faithful Account of the Religion and Manners of the Mahometans* (Exeter, 1717), chap. 9; Rycaut, *Present State of the Ottoman Empire*, 79–80.

192. Sir Thomas Sherley, 'Discours of the Turkes', ed. E. Denison Ross, 4, in *Camden Miscellany*, vol. 16 (Camden, 3rd ser., 52 (1936)).

193. Smith, *Remarks upon the Turks*, 41–43; Addison, *West Barbary*, 197.

194. Henry Byam, *A Return from Argier* (1628), 74. See, in general, Nabil Matar, *Turks, Moors, and Englishmen in the Age of Discovery* (New York, 1999); *Three Turkish Plays from Early Modern England*, ed. Daniel J. Vitkus (New York, 2000), introduction;

Robert C. Davis, *Christian Slaves, Muslim Masters* (Basingstoke, 2003); Tobias P. Graf, *The Sultan's Renegades* (Oxford, 2017).

195. David Allan, 'Manners and Mustard', *CSSH* 37 (1995).

196. [Marc Lescarbot], *Nova Francia*, trans. P. E[rondelle] (1609), esp. 95, 97, 203, 227–28, 247, 283.

197. Moryson, *Itinerary*, vol. 3, 369–70.

198. Morton, *New Englands Caanan*, 56–58; *The Writings of William Walwyn*, ed. Jack R. McMichael and Barbara Taft (Athens, GA, 1989), 82–83; Derek Hirst, 'A Happier Man', *Seventeenth Century* 27 (2012), 59–60, 68.

199. John Lynch, *Cambrensis Eversus* (1662), trans. Matthew Kelly (Dublin, 1848–54), vol. 2, 222–23, 284–85; Thomas Traherne, *Poems, Centuries and Three Thanksgivings*, ed. Anne Ridler (1966), 269–70; John Aubrey, *Monumenta Britannica, Parts 1 and 2*, ed. John Fowles (Sherborne, 1980–82), 194.

200. James Thomson, *The Seasons*, ed. James Sambrook (Oxford, 1981), 242 ('Winter', lines 843–45, 847–48, 851–53); John Scheffer, *The History of Lapland* (Eng. trans., 1704), 35–36, 169.

201. *Journals of Captain Cook*, ed. Beaglehole, vol. 1, 399, 508–9; vol. 2, 271.

202. *John Ledyard's Journal through Russia and Siberia, 1787–8*, ed. Stephen D. Watrous (Madison, WI, 1966), 169.

203. On this tradition, see Arthur O. Lovejoy and George Boas, *Primitivism and Related Ideas in Antiquity* (Baltimore, MD, 1935); Alan Dugald McKillop, *The Background of Thomson's Seasons* (Minneapolis, MN, 1942), chap. 3; Ludwig Edelstein, *The Idea of Progress in Classical Antiquity* (Baltimore, MD, 1967), 43–51, 58–62, 93–95; George Boas, *Essays on Primitivism and Related Ideas in the Middle Ages* (Baltimore, MD, 1948); Elizabeth Armstrong, *Ronsard and the Age of Gold* (Cambridge, 1968), chap. 2; Robert Bartlett, *Gerald of Wales 1146–1223* (Oxford, 1982), 172–73, 186, 198–99; Andrew Fitzmaurice, *Humanism and America* (Cambridge, 2003), 157–63; Gordon Lindsay Campbell, *Lucretius on Creation and Evolution* (Oxford, 2003), 12–15, 336–53.

204. W[illiam] Watreman, preface to Joannes Boemus, *The Fardle of Facions*, trans. Watreman (1555), sigs. Ai–ii^v; 'The Shepheards Garland, 8th Eclog', in *The Works of Michael Drayton*, ed. J. William Hebel (Oxford, 1961), vol. 1, 86–87; *The Works of the Learned Benjamin Whichcote* (Aberdeen, 1751), vol. 2, 223; Locke, *Two Treatises of Government*, 360 (II. 110).

205. Edward Gibbon, *The Decline and Fall of the Roman Empire*, ed. J. B. Bury (6th edn, 1912), vol. 1, 227; *Works of William Robertson*, vol. 5, 281; *Works of Mary Wollstonecraft*, vol. 6, 235.

206. Campbell, *Lucretius on Creation and Evolution*, 14; Catherine Wilson, 'Political Philosophy in a Lucretian Mode', in *Lucretius and the Early Modern*, ed. David Norbrook et al. (Oxford, 2015); Lovejoy and Boas, *Primitivism and Related Ideas*, 47–48, 93–95, 117–52, 239–42.

207. On conflicting opinions within the early and medieval Church, see Peter Garnsey, *Thinking about Property* (Cambridge, 2007), chaps. 3–5, and for the Franciscan view, see William of Ockham, *A Letter to the Friars Minor and Other Writings*, ed. Arthur Stephen McGrade and John Kilcullen (Cambridge, 2007), 37, 88–89, 264, 286–87.

208. Henry Parker, Lord Morley, *Forty-Six Lives Translated from Boccaccio's De Claris Mulieribus*, ed. Herbert G. Wright (EETS, 1943), 22–24. Perhaps significantly, a mid-fifteenth-century verse translation of this work omits the section in which Boccaccio describes the unfortunate consequences of Ceres's invention; *On Famous Women: The Middle English Translation of Boccaccio's De Mulieribus Claris*, ed. Janet Cowen (Heidelberg, 2015), 69.

209. 'Discours contre fortune', in *Oeuvres complètes de Ronsard*, ed. Hugues Vaganay (Paris, 1923), vol. 4, 53–54; Lescarbot, *Nova Francia*, 285 (also 280).

210. Morris Palmer Tilley, *A Dictionary of the Proverbs in England* (Ann Arbor, MI, 1950), 459; Pufendorf, *Law of Nature and Nations*, 2nd pagination, 151–52 (IV. iv. 7), 216 (IV. xii. 5).

211. Lahontan, *New Voyages to North-America*, vol. 1, sig. A4ᵛ.
212. Mandeville, *Fable of the Bees*, vol. 2, 309; Henry Home, Lord Kames, *Sketches of the History of Man* (Edinburgh, 1774), vol. 1, 242; Gilbert Stuart, *A View of Society in Europe* (Edinburgh, 1778), 2, 75–76; 'The Task' (v. 11. 220–29), in *The Poems of William Cowper*, ed. John D. Baird and Charles Ryskamp (Oxford, 1980–95), vol. 2, 216; Rousseau, *Oeuvres*, vol. 3, 164–76.
213. 'A Short Discourse on the preceeding Comedy', in *The World's Idol: Plutus*, trans. H. H. B. (1659), 33–46. The BL catalogue attributes this work to the Irish (Old English Catholic) playwright Henry Burnell, but the attribution is implausible and, as the entry for Burnell in the *ODNB* remarks, there is no evidence for it. It is unclear whether the author's initials were H. H. B. or just H. H., as 'H. H.' is italicized, whereas 'B.' is not and may therefore be some other kind of descriptor.
214. For a modern discussion, see Rosie Wyles, 'Publication as Intervention', in *Aristophanes in Performance 421 BC–AD 2007*, ed. Edith Hall and Amanda Wrigley (Leeds, 2007).
215. Greg Woolf, *Becoming Roman* (Cambridge, 1998), 60. For the rhetorical skill of arguing *in utramque partem*, on the assumption that there are always two sides to every question, see Quintilian, *Institutio Oratoria*, xii. i. 35, and Quentin Skinner, *Reason and Rhetoric in the Philosophy of Hobbes* (Cambridge, 1996), 9–10, 27–30, 97–99, 172–73.
216. J. G. A. Pocock, *Barbarism and Religion* (Cambridge, 1999–2015), vol. 4, 238.
217. François Guizot, *The History of Civilization*, trans. William Hazlitt, ed. Larry Siedentop (1997), xviii–xix.
218. On the change, see Pitts, *A Turn to Empire*.
219. Kathleen Wilson, *The Island Race* (2003), 82.
220. 'On Liberty' (1859), in *Collected Works of John Stuart Mill*, vol. 18, 224. In the same work, however, Mill declared, 'I am not aware that any community has the right to force another to be civilized' (291).

7 Changing Modes of Civility

1. John Crowther, 'Musae Faciles or an Easy Ascent to Parnassus', ed. Nicholas Tyacke, in *History of Universities* 27 (2013), 12.
2. Lucy Hutchinson, *Memoirs of the Life of Colonel Hutchinson*, ed. James Sutherland (1973), 11.
3. Keith Thomas, *The Ends of Life* (Oxford, 2009), chap. 2.
4. George Buchanan, *The History of Scotland* (Eng. trans., 1690), 23–24.
5. Sir Clement Edmondes, *Observations upon Caesar's Commentaries* (1604), vol. 2, 31 (bk 6, chap. 9).
6. *The Negotiations of Sir Thomas Roe, in his Embassy to the Ottoman Porte from the year 1621 to 1628* (1740), 16.
7. Nathanael Carpenter, *Geographie Delineated* (1635), vol. 2, 283.
8. [Richard Allestree], *The Ladies Calling* ([1673]; 1720), 13; Jean Gailhard, *The Compleat Gentleman* (1678), vol. 2, 49; S. C., *The Art of Complaisance* (1673), 121; *HMC, Salisbury*, vol. 20, vii; Anna Bryson, *From Courtesy to Civility* (Oxford, 1998), 229–30; Michèle Cohen, *Fashioning Masculinity* (1996), 9, 42–43, 61–62; Philip Carter, *Men and the Emergence of Polite Society, Britain 1660–1800* (Harlow, 2001), esp. chap. 4; Emma Major, *Madam Britannia* (Oxford, 2012), 197–98.
9. [Thomas Gainsford], *The Rich Cabinet* (1646), fol. 38ᵛ; Adam Smith, *The Theory of Moral Sentiments*, ed. D. D. Raphael and A. L. Macfie (Oxford, 1976), 209 (V. 2. 13).
10. *The Political Works of James I*, ed. Charles Howard McIlwain (Cambridge, MA, 1918), 44; Bryson, *Courtesy to Civility*, 229.
11. *Tatler* 244 (31 Oct. 1710), ed. Donald F. Bond (Oxford, 1987), vol. 3, 251.
12. *Negotiations of Sir Thomas Roe*, 16; *Spectator* 236 (30 Nov. 1711), ed. Donald F. Bond (Oxford, 1965), vol. 2, 418.

13. David Hume, *Essays Moral, Political, and Literary*, ed. T. H. Green and T. H. Grose (1875), vol. 1, 304–5.
14. Jennifer Richards, ' "A Wanton Trade of Living" ', *Criticism* 42 (2000); Michèle Cohen, ' "Manners" Make the Man', *JBS* 44 (2005); Sheldon Rothblatt, review of Martha Vicinus, *A Widening Sphere*, in *Journ. of Interdisciplinary History* 10 (1979), 175.
15. *Diary of John Manningham*, ed. John Bruce (Camden Soc., 1868), 110.
16. *The Works of . . . William Laud*, ed. William Scott and James Bliss (Oxford, 1847–60), vi (ii), 377.
17. *The Works of Thomas Nashe*, ed. Ronald B. McKerrow (Oxford, 1966), vol. 1, 361; T[homas] J[ones], *Of the Heart and Its Right Soveraign* (1678), 11.
18. John Earle, *Micro-cosmographie* (1628), sig. G5; [John Leslie], *A Treatise of Treasons against Q. Elizabeth* ([Louvain], 1572), 144; Anthony Stafford, *Meditations, and Resolutions, Moral, Divine, Politicall* (1612), 60; John Smyth, *The Lives of the Berkeleys*, in *The Berkeley Manuscripts*, ed. Sir John Maclean (Gloucester, 1883–85), vol. 2, 386; William Cole, *A Journal of My Journey to Paris in the Year 1765*, ed. Francis Griffin Stokes (1931), 300.
19. [Barnabe Rich], *A Souldiers Wishe to Britons Welfare* (1604), 56.
20. Sir Thomas Palmer, *An Essay of the Meanes how to Make our Travailes* (1606), 42.
21. *Parochial Collections . . . by Anthony à Wood and Richard Rawlinson*, ed. F. N. Davis (Oxon. Rec. Soc., 1920–29), 226, and *The Poems of Edmund Waller*, ed. G. Thorn Drury (1893), vol. 2, 109.
22. Peter Chamberlen, *The Poore Mans Advocate* (1649), 7; Susan Whyman, *Sociability and Power in Late-Stuart England* (Oxford, 1999), 106–7; 'A lover of his country' [William Sprigge], *A Modest Plea for an Equal Common-wealth* (1659), 68–69.
23. Fynes Moryson, *An Itinerary* (Glasgow, 1907–8), vol. 3, 396–97, 421–22.
24. *Letters of John Holles 1587–1637*, ed. P. R. Seddon (Thoroton Soc., 1975–86), vol. 1, 52.
25. William Harrison, *The Description of England*, ed. Georges Edelen (Ithaca, NY, 1968), 131; William Shakespeare, *King Henry V* (1600), act 5, scene 2; *Parochial Collections by Wood and Rawlinson*, vol. 1, 81; Timothy Nourse, *Campania Foelix* (1700), 15; Sir Thomas Pope Blount, *Essays on Several Subjects* (3rd edn, 1697), 78.
26. *Gentleman's Magazine* 1 (1731), 384. A Jacobite, he presumably had in mind the Germans who came over with the Hanoverian monarchs.
27. [Béat Louis de Muralt], *Letters describing the Character and Customs of the English and French Nations* (1726), 6; David H. Solkin, *Painting for Money* (New Haven, CT, 1993), 99–102; Herbert M. Atherton, *Political Prints in the Age of Hogarth* (Oxford, 1974), 267–70; Vic Gatrell, *City of Laughter* (2006), esp. 110–29.
28. *Gentleman's Journal* (Apr. 1692), 18, cited in Lawrence E. Klein, 'The Figure of France', *Yale French Studies* 92 (1997), 43.
29. Philomusus [John Gough?], *The Academy of Complements* (4th edn, 1641), sigs. A8ᵛ–9; Whyman, *Sociability and Power*, 106; Nicholas Breton, *The Court and Country* (1618), sig. B1.
30. *The Plays and Poems of Robert Greene*, ed. J. Churton Collins (Oxford, 1905), vol. 2, 214. For a fine account of this enduring Yorkshire tradition of 'sour rudeness', see Elizabeth C. Gaskell, *The Life of Charlotte Bronte* (1857; World's Classics, 1919), 9–13. See also John Crawshey, *The Country Mans Instructor* (1636), sig. A3; Joseph Hunter, *The Rise of the Old Dissent, Exemplified in the Life of Oliver Heywood* (1842), 75; *OED*, s.v. 'Yorkshire, 2'.
31. See, e.g., J[ohn] Ray, *A Collection of English Proverbs* (2nd edn, 1678), 68–69; *The English Dialect Dictionary*, ed. Joseph Wright (Oxford, 1870), s.v. 'fine', 'Marry! Come up', 'knack', 'skyome'; Samuel Bamford, *Dialect of South Lancashire* (Manchester, 1850), 196–97; B. Lowsley, *A Glossary of Berkshire Words and Phrases* (Eng. Dialect Soc., 1888), 177.

32. *The Correspondence of John Locke*, ed. E. S. de Beer (Oxford, 1976–), vol. 1, 119.

33. Robert B. Shoemaker, *The London Mob* (2004), 294–95; John Tosh, 'Gentlemanly Politeness and Manly Simplicity in Victorian England', *TRHS*, 6th ser., 12 (2002), 468; John Styles, *The Dress of the People* (New Haven, CT, 2007), chap. 12.

34. Smyth, 'The Lives of the Berkeleys', in *The Berkeley Manuscripts*, vol. 2, 386; Ulpian Fulwell, *The First Parte of the Eyghth Liberal Science: Entituled Ars Adulandi* (1579); *Cyuile and Uncyuile Life* (1579), sig. Miv^v.

35. R. H. Sweet, 'Topographies of Politeness', *TRHS*, 6th ser., 12 (2012), 371.

36. Paul Langford, *Englishness Identified* (Oxford, 2000), 17; Philomusus [John Gough?], 'To the Reader', *Academy of Complements* (1640), sigs. A8^v–9; Joseph Hall, *The Great Impostor* (1623), 34–35; Hume, *Essays*, vol. 1, 191.

37. J[ohn] Saltmarsh, *The Practice of Policie in a Christian Life* (1639), 29–30.

38. *Spectator* 557 (21 June 1714), ed. Donald F. Bond (Oxford, 1965), vol. 4, 504.

39. Daniel Javitch, *Poetry and Courtliness in Renaissance England* (Princeton, NJ, 1978), chap. 4; Sydney Anglo, *The Courtier's Art* (Swansea, 1983); Bryson, *Courtesy to Civility*, 203–5; Susan Brigden, *Thomas Wyatt* (2012), 200, 260–61; Andrew Hadfield, *Lying in Early Modern English Culture* (Oxford, 2017), chap. 5.

40. *The Works of Sir Walter Ralegh* (Oxford, 1829), vol. 6, 459; Sir Henry Wotton, *A Philosophical Survey of Education* (1938), 27; [William Cavendish?], *A Discourse against Flatterie* (1611), 4.

41. A. D. B. [Ambrosius de Bruyn], *The Court of the Most Illustrious and Most Magnificent James, the First* (1619), 163.

42. Edward Waterhous[e], *The Gentlemans Monitor* (1665), 241; *Works of George Savile, Marquis of Halifax*, ed. Mark N. Brown (Oxford, 1989), vol. 3, 328; Bernard Mandeville, *The Fable of the Bees*, ed. F. B. Kaye (Oxford, 1924), vol. 1, 77, 79; and see Markku Peltonen, *The Duel in Early Modern England* (Cambridge, 2003), 30–31, 279–85.

43. A Gentleman, *The Baboon A-la-Mode* (1704), 11.

44. *The Workes of M(aster) W(illiam) Perkins* (Cambridge, 1608–31), vol. 2, 339; Daniel Defoe, *The Complete English Tradesman* (2nd edn, 1727), vol. 1, 235; *New Letters of David Hume*, ed. Raymond Klibansky and Ernest C. Mossner (Oxford, 1954), 83.

45. Henry Stubbe, *A Light Shining out of Darkness* (rev. edn, 1659), 163–65; [Meric Casaubon], *A Treatise of Use and Custom* (1638), 160. On the shift to less deferential endings to letters, see Keith Thomas, 'Yours', in *The State of the Language*, ed. Christopher Ricks and Leonard Michaels (Berkeley, CA, 1990).

46. Hannah More, *Thoughts on the Manners of the Great* (1798), in *The Works of Hannah More* (Philadelphia, PA, 1853), vol. 2, 255–56.

47. Bryson, *Courtesy to Civility*, 197–99, 220, 225, 229–30.

48. [John Wilford], *Memorials and Characters* (1741), 9.

49. *Works of William Laud*, vol. 4, 247; J. C. Davis, 'Against Formality', *TRHS*, 6th ser., 3 (1993); Bryson, *Courtesy to Civility*, 209–10.

50. [John Taylor], *Religions Enemies* (1641), 6.

51. *Workes of Perkins*, vol. 2, 339.

52. Jer[emiah] Dyke, *Good Conscience* (1624), 102–3.

53. *The Complete English Works of Thomas Brooks*, ed. Alexander Balloch Grosart (Edinburgh, 1866–67), vol. 4, 88; *Christ A Compleat Saviour*, ed. W. R. Owens, in *The Miscellaneous Works of John Bunyan* (Oxford, 1976–94), vol. 13, 278; John Bunyan, *The Pilgrim's Progress*, ed. W. R. Owens (Oxford, 2003), 24.

54. 'The Plain-Dealer' (published 1677), in *The Plays of William Wycherley*, ed. Arthur Friedman (Oxford, 1979), 378–79 (I. i).

55. William Gouge, *Of Domesticall Duties* (3rd edn, 1634), 539; Mandeville, *Fable of the Bees*, vol. 2, 281.

56. Gouge, *Domesticall Duties*, 539.

57. *Workes of Perkins*, vol. 1, 277 ('275'); Thomas Manton, *A Practical Commentary . . . on the Epistle of Jude* (1657), 40–42; George Downame, *The Christians Freedome* (1635), 119; James Janeway, *Invisibles, Realities* (1674), 53–54.

58. John White, *Two Sermons* (1615), 81; James Hart, Κλινική, *the Diet of the Diseased* (1633), 220; Richard Rogers, *Seven Treatises* (1603), 63.

59. *Oliver Heywood's Life of John Angier of Denton*, ed. Ernest Axon (Chetham Soc., 1937), 149–50; Hutchinson, *Memoirs of Colonel Hutchinson*, 28; *Works of George Savile*, vol. 3, 181.

60. Samuel Clarke, *The Lives of Sundry Eminent Persons in this Later Age (1683)*, vol. 1, 165; Nehemiah Rogers, *Christian Curtesie* (1621), 32.

61. Richard Baxter, 'To the Reader', in *Mr Thomas Wadsworth's Last Warning to Sinners* (1677), sig. C4.

62. Richard Younge, *The Drunkard's Character* (1638), 744; Samuel Torshell, *The Hypocrite Discovered and Cured* (1644), 13.

63. G. H. Turnbull, *Hartlib, Drury and Comenius* (Farnborough, 1968), 120; R[obert] B[oyle], *Occasional Reflections upon Several Subjects* (1665), 2nd pagination, 130–31.

64. Ephraim Pagitt, *Heresiography* (1662), 194; *The Lives of Dr Edward Pocock* [et al.], ed. A[lexander] C[halmers] (1816), vol. 1, 93; Caroline Francis Richardson, *English Preachers and Preaching 1640–1670* (1928), 58–65; Arnold Hunt, *The Art of Hearing* (Cambridge, 2010), 86–88; Michael J. Braddick, 'Introduction', in *The Politics of Gesture*, ed. Braddick (*P&P*, supp., 2009), 22–23.

65. *Heywood's Life of John Angier*, 50.

66. Thomas Wilson, *Davids Zeal for Zion* (1641), 17.

67. Samuel Parker, *A Discourse of Ecclesiastical Politie* (1670), viii, xiii; [John Gill], *An Essay on the Original of Funeral Sermons* (1729), 24, 37.

68. Geraint H. Jenkins, *The Foundations of Modern Wales* (Oxford, 1987), 383.

69. [Strickland Gough], *An Enquiry into the Causes of the Decay of the Dissenting Interest* (1730), 43.

70. Thomas, *Ends of Life*, 135, 221–22.

71. *The Works of George Herbert*, ed. F. E. Hutchinson (Oxford, 1941), 277; [Edward Reynolds], *Imitation and Caution for Christian Woman* (1659), 6.

72. Richard Strange, *The Life and Gests of S. Thomas Cantilupe* (1674), 185.

73. *The Practical Works of the Late Reverend and Pious Mr Richard Baxter* (1707), vol. 1, 294, 308; George Gascoigne, 'A Delicate Diet for Daintiemouthed Droonkards' (1571), in *The Glasse of Government*, ed. John W. Cunliffe (Cambridge, 1910), 467.

74. Nath[aniel] Parkhurst, *The Faithful and Diligent Christian* (1684), 155–56.

75. *Workes of Perkins*, vol. 2, 113; vol. 1, 446; Thomas, *Ends of Life*, 221–22.

76. See, e.g., *Workes of Perkins*, vol. 1, 456, 479, 636.

77. Ibid., 634.

78. [Theodosia Alleine], *The Life and Death of Mr Joseph Alleine* (1672), 35; Clarke, *Lives of Sundry Eminent Persons*, vol. 1, 96, 119, 144; vol. 2, 148, 172, 193, 198, 211; Anthony Walker, *The Holy Life of Elizabeth Walker* (1690), 68.

79. For an excellent account of early Quaker speech, manners and bodily comportment, see Adrian Davies, *The Quakers in English Society, 1655–1725* (Oxford, 2000), chap. 3. The authoritative statement of Quaker principles was Robert Barclay, *An Apology for the Christian Divinity* (Latin edn, 1676; 5th English edn, 1703), esp. 512–71.

80. W[illiam] C[ovell], *Polimanteia* (1595), sig. Bb3; Nathaniel Homes, *Daemonologie, and Theologie* (1650), 196; [Bruno Ryves], *Mercurius Rusticus* (1685), 31; John Strype, *Collections of the Life and Acts of . . . John Aylmer* (1821), 176; William C. Braithwaite, *The Beginnings of Quakerism* (1912), 23; Claus-Peter Clasen, *Anabaptism* (Ithaca, NY, 1972), 146; Christopher Hill, *The World Turned Upside Down* (1972), 198; *The Collected Essays of Christopher Hill* (Brighton, 1986), vol. 2, 99; Penelope Corfield, 'Dress for Deference and Dissent', *Costume* 23 (1989).

81. Arthur O. Lovejoy and George Boas, *Primitivism and Related Ideas in Antiquity* ([1935]; New York, 1965), chap. 4; *The Cynics*, ed. R. Bracht Branham and Marie-Odile Goulet-Cazé (Berkeley, CA, 1996).

82. George Fox et al., *A Battle-Door for Teachers & Professors to Learn Singular and Plural* (1660); *The Journal of George Fox*, ed. Norman Penney (Cambridge, 1914), vol. 2, 7.

83. Samuel Fisher, *Rusticus ad Academicos* (1660), vol. 1, 43–46; B[enjamin] F[urly], *The Worlds Honour Detected* (1663), 7; John Whitehead, *A Manifestation of Truth* (1662), 13–16.

84. Francis Higginson, *A Brief Relation of the Irreligion of the Northern Quakers* (1653), 29.

85. Barclay, *Apology for the Christian Divinity*, 515, 519, 524, 367, 369, 372, 376; Whitehead, *Manifestation of Truth*, 13–16; Furly, *Worlds Honour Detected*, 7; Richard Bauman, *Let Your Words Be Few* (Cambridge, 1983), chap. 4.

86. *A Shield of the Truth* (1655), in *A Collection of the Several Writings [of] James Parnel* (1675), 91; Oz Almog, *The Sabra*, trans. Haim Watzmann (Berkeley, CA, 2000), xv (and 145–46, 245–46); Tamar Katriel, *Talking Straight* (Cambridge, 1986).

87. Furly, *Worlds Honour Detected*, 8; Thomas Clarkson, *A Portraiture of Quakerism* (3rd edn, 1807), vol. 1, 361.

88. Clarkson, *Portraiture of Quakerism*, vol. 1, 359; Bunyan, *Christ a Compleat Saviour*, 278.

89. John Gauden, *The Case of Ministers Maintenance by Tithes* (1653), 3.

90. Whitehead, *Manifestation of Truth*, 14; *The Life, Diary, and Correspondence of Sir William Dugdale*, ed. William Hamper (1827), 85n.

91. R. H., *The Character of a Quaker* (1671), 2.

92. [John Parry], *A Resolution of a Seasonable Case of Conscience* (Oxford, 1660), 2; R[oger] W[illiams], *George Fox Digg'd out of his Burrowes* (Boston, MA, 1676), 5.

93. Jonathan Clapham, *A Full Discovery and Confutation of the Wicked and Damnable Doctrines of the Quakers* (1656), 66–71.

94. Thomas Fuller, *The Church History of Britain* (new edn, 1837), vol. 2, 364.

95. *A Shield of the Truth* (1655), 27, in *A Collection of the Writings of James Parnel*.

96. Furly, *Worlds Honour Detected*, 12–13.

97. George Keith, *The Magick of Quakerism* (1707), 11.

98. Stubbe, *Light Shining out of Darkness*, 89.

99. *The Written Gospel-Labours of . . . John Whitehead* (1709), 144–45.

100. Parnel, *Shield of the Truth*, 91.

101. *The Theological Works of the Most Reverend John Sharp* (Oxford, 1829), vol. 3, 310; vol. 4, 207–12.

102. Edward Fowler, *The Design of Christianity* (1671), 39; Lawrence E. Klein, *Shaftesbury and the Culture of Politeness* (Cambridge, 1994), 158–60, 163–65.

103. [Thomas Gordon], *The Independent Whig* (1721), 116.

104. Clarkson, *Portraiture of Quakerism*, vol. 1, 356; vol. 3, 225–27; Keith Thomas, 'Cleanliness and Godliness in Early Modern England', in *Religion, Culture and Society in Early Modern England*, ed. Anthony Fletcher and Peter Roberts (Cambridge, 1994), 64; Leslie Hannah, 'The Moral Economy of Business', in *Civil Histories*, ed. Peter Burke et al. (Oxford, 2000), 292.

105. Thomas Hobbes, *Leviathan* (1651), ed. Noel Malcolm (Oxford, 2012), vol. 2, 232 (chap. 15).

106. Richard Rogers, *A Commentary upon the Whole Booke of Judges* (1615), 628.

107. 'Of sincerity towards God and Man' (1694), in *The Works of . . . Dr John Tillotson*, ed. Ralph Barker (4th edn, 1728), vol. 2, 6–8.

108. Gerald Newman, *The Rise of English Nationalism* (Basingstoke, 1997), chap. 6; Langford, *Englishness Identified*, 87–88.

109. Fenela Childs, 'Prescriptions for Manners in English Courtesy Literature, 1690–1760, and their Social Implications' (Oxford University, DPhil thesis, 1984), 123–30.

110. Messieurs du Port Royal, *Moral Essays*, trans. A Person of Quality (2nd edn, 1696), vol. 2, 149; Jean Pungier, *La Civilité de Jean-Baptiste de La Salle* (Rome, 1996–2000).

111. Mandeville, *Fable of the Bees*, vol. 1, 349.

112. *Misery's Virtues Whetstone: Reliquiae Gethinianae* (1699), 52; *New Letters of David Hume*, vol. 2, 83. Similarly, William Paley, *Principles of Moral and Political Philosophy* ([1785]; 13th edn, 1801), vol. 1, 185–86; Bryson, *Courtesy to Civility*, 221–22. On this theme see Jenny Davidson, *Hypocrisy and the Politics of Politeness* (Cambridge, 2004).

113. Immanuel Kant, *The Metaphysics of Morals*, trans. Mary Gregor (Cambridge, 1991), 227, and *Anthropology from a Pragmatic Point of View*, in id., *Anthropology, History, and Education*, ed. Günter Zöller and Robert B. Louden (Cambridge, 2007), 263–64; Émile Durkheim, *Cours de philosophie fait au Lycée de Sens (1883–4)*, sections C, D, and E, 149 (available in 'Les Classiques des sciences sociales', on the website of the University of Quebec); 'Good Manners and Hypocrisy', in Bertrand Russell, *Mortals and Others*, ed. Harry Ruja (1975–98), ii.

114. N[athaniel] Waker, *The Refin'd Courtier* (1663), 65; Davidson, *Hypocrisy and the Politics of Politeness*, 13. For some interesting reflections on this subject by the Victorian scholar James Spedding, see his *The Letters and the Life of Francis Bacon* (1861–74), vol. 4, 31–32.

115. Jean Baptiste Poquelin de Molière, *The Misanthrope*, trans. Richard Wilbur (1958), 9.

116. William Godwin, *The Enquirer* ([1797]; New York, 1965), pt 2, essay 10; *Analytical Rev.* 27 (Jan.–June 1798), 489.

117. Jean-Jacques Rousseau, 'Julie, ou la nouvelle Héloïse', pt 2, ltr. 14, and *Émile*, bk 4, in *Oeuvres complètes*, ed. Bernard Gagnebin and Marcel Raymond (Paris, 1964–69), vol. 2, 231–35; vol. 4, 665–69. See also Marshall Berman, *The Politics of Authenticity* (1971). Montesquieu attacked 'false politeness' (*une politesse fausse*) in his unpublished 'Éloge de la sincérité', *Mélanges inédits de Montesquieu*, ed. Baron de Montesquieu (Bordeaux, 1892), 18.

118. *The Journals of Captain James Cook on His Voyages of Discovery*, ed. J. C. Beaglehole (Hakluyt Soc., 1955–74), iii (2). 1406; Mary Wollstonecraft, *Letters Written during a Short Residence in Sweden, Norway and Denmark* ([1796]; Fontwell, 1970), 40.

119. Tacitus, *Agricola*, para. 21.

120. *Complete Prose Works of John Milton*, ed. Don M. Wolfe et al. (New Haven, CT, 1953–82), vol. 5, pt 1, line 85.

121. *Reliquiae Wottonianae* (2nd edn, 1654), 150.

122. Paul Langford, 'Manners and the Eighteenth-Century State', in *Rethinking Leviathan*, ed. John Brewer and Eckhart Hellmuth (Oxford, 1999), 297.

123. Blount, *Essays on Several Subjects*, 78; Joseph Marshall, *Travels ... in the years 1768, 1769, and 1770* (1772), vol. 2, 297.

124. Roger Crab, *The English Hermite* (1655), 7; Robert Coster, *A Mite Cast into the Common Treasury* (1649), 3–4. See also K. D. M. Snell, 'Deferential Bitterness', in *Social Orders and Social Classes in Europe since 1500*, ed. M. L. Bush (Harlow, 1992).

125. *Records of Early English Drama, Norwich, 1540–1642*, ed. David Galloway (Toronto, 1984), 294.

126. Phil Withington, *The Politics of Commonwealth* (Cambridge, 2005), 148; Sir Henry Spelman, *The History and Fate of Sacrilege*, 4th edn by C. F. S. Warren (1895), 126; and more generally, Lawrence Stone, *The Crisis of the Aristocracy 1558–1641* (Oxford, 1979), 747–50.

127. Andy Wood, '"Poore men woll speke one daye"', in *The Politics of the Excluded, c. 1500–1850*, ed. Tim Harris (Basingstoke, 2001), chap. 3; Paul Griffiths, *Lost Londons* (Cambridge, 2008), 42–47; Mark Hailwood, *Alehouses and Good Fellowship in Early Modern England* (Woodbridge, 2014), 64–73; David Cressy, *Charles I and the People of England* (Oxford, 2015), 42–45, 119–22, 240–42, 283–85, 290–91, 300–1.

128. For discussion of recent work on this subject, see Andy Wood, *Riot, Rebellion and Popular Politics in Early Modern England* (Basingstoke, 2002); Adrian Randall, *Riotous Assemblies* (Oxford, 2010); Keith Thomas, 'John Walter and the Social History of Early Modern England', in *Popular Culture and Political Agency in Early Modern England and Ireland*, ed. Michael J. Braddick and Phil Withington (Woodbridge, 2017).

129. John Walter, 'Gesturing at Authority', in *Politics of Gesture*, ed. Braddick, 114–16.

130. J. S. Morrill, *The Revolt of the Provinces* (1976), 36; John Walter, *Understanding Popular Violence in the English Revolution* (Cambridge, 1999); id., *Covenanting Citizens* (Oxford, 2017), 70; David Cressy, *England on Edge* (Oxford, 2006), esp. chap. 16; Braddick, 'Introduction', *Politics of Gesture*, ed. Braddick, 21–26.

131. Edward, Earl of Clarendon, *The History of the Rebellion and Civil Wars in England*, ed. W. Dunn Macray (Oxford, 1888), vol. 2, 318.

132. 'The Shepheards Oracles' (1646), in *The Complete Works in Prose and Verse of Francis Quarles*, ed. Alexander B. Grosart (1880–81), vol. 3, 236.

133. Frank Grace, '"Schismaticall and Factious Humours"', in *Religious Dissent in East Anglia*, ed. David Chadd (Norwich, 1996), 99; *HMC*, vol. 5, 163.

134. Hutchinson, *Memoirs of Colonel Hutchinson*, 89–90, on which see David Norbrook, '"Words more than civil"', in *Early Modern Civil Discourses*, ed. Jennifer Richards (Basingstoke, 2003).

135. Thomas Edwards, *Gangraena* (1646), pt 2, 154.

136. Frances Parthenope Verney, *Memoirs of the Verney Family during the Civil War* ([1892]; 1971), vol. 2, 312.

137. *Complete Prose Works of Milton*, vol. 7 (rev. edn), 426, 428.

138. *Original Letters and Papers of State Addressed to Oliver Cromwell*, ed. John Nickolls (1743), 102; *Middlesex County Records*, ed. John Cordy Jeaffreson (Mddx County Records Soc., 1886–92), vol. 3, 231.

139. *The Life and Times of Anthony Wood*, ed. Andrew Clark (Oxford Hist. Soc., 1891–1900), vol. 1, 299; John Evelyn, *A Character of England* (1659), in *The Writings of John Evelyn*, ed. Guy de la Bédoyère (Woodbridge, 1995), 73.

140. Parry, *Resolution of a Seasonable Case of Conscience*, 2–3.

141. *The Life of Edward Earl of Clarendon by Himself* (Oxford, 1857), vol. 1, 305.

142. TNA, *SP* 29/69/21 (3 Mar. 1662–63).

143. Paul Griffiths, *Youth and Authority* (Oxford, 1996), 26–27.

144. (William Aglionby), *Painting Illustrated in Three Diallogues* (1686), sig. b3; Klein, *Shaftesbury and the Culture of Politeness*, 164–65; Samuel Parker, *A Demonstration of the Divine Authority of the Law of Nature and of the Christian Religion* (1681), iii–iv.

145. Brian Weiser, *Charles II and the Politics of Access* (Woodbridge, 2003), 36–37, 55.

146. Nicholas Breton, *The Court and the Country* (1618), sig. B1ᵛ; Richard Braithwaite, *The English Gentleman* (1630), epistle dedicatory; Thomas Heywood, *Machiavels Ghost* (1641), sig. B3ᵛ; Daniel Price, *Lamentations for the Death of the Late Illustrious Prince Henry* (1613), 18.

147. Logan Pearsall Smith, *The Life and Letters of Sir Henry Wotton* (Oxford, 1907), vol. 2, 335; *The Works of Isaac Barrow* (Edinburgh, 1842), vol. 1, 491; Bryson, *Courtesy to Civility*, 208–12; Peltonen, *Duel in England*, 227–31.

148. Hutchinson, *Memoirs of Colonel Hutchinson*, 4; Jonathan Swift, *A Proposal for Correcting the English Tongue*, ed. Herbert Davis and Louis Landa (Oxford, 1957), 213, 215–16, 221; *The Letters of the Earl of Chesterfield to His Son*, ed. Charles Strachey (1901), vol. 2, 165.

149. Anthony Ashley Cooper, 3rd Earl of Shaftesbury, *Second Characters or the Language of Forms*, ed. Benjamin Rand (Cambridge, 1914), 128–29; William Enfield, *The Speaker* (1774), xxix; Childs, 'Prescriptions for Manners', 175–76; *Galateo of Manners* (Eng. trans., 1703), sig. a2ᵛ.

150. Sir Thomas Browne, *Religio Medici and Other Works*, ed. L. C. Martin (Oxford, 1964), 85; *Correspondence of John Locke*, vol. 8, 7, 177–78; *John Locke: Selected Correspondence*, ed. Mark Goldie (Oxford, 2002), xxii.

151. Thomas Sprat, *History of the Royal Society*, ed. Jackson I. Cope and Harold Whitmore Jones (St Louis, MO, 1959), 406–7. Cf. Harrison, *Description of England*, 132.

152. F. J. M. Korsten, *Roger North (1651–1734)* (Amsterdam, 1981), 119 (date unknown).

153. *Life of Edward Earl of Clarendon*, vol. 1, 305.

154. Seneca, *De Beneficiis*, bk 1, chap. 10, sect. 1; *Works of Sir Walter Ralegh*, vol. 2, 349. For later instances, see Elizabeth More, 'Some Remarks on the Change of Manners in My Own Time', in *Selections from Family Papers Preserved at Caldwell*, pt 1 (New [Maitland] Club ser., Paisley, 1883); Algernon West, 'Some Changes in Social Life during the Queen's Reign', *Nineteenth Century* 242 (April 1897), 649.

155. [John Dod and Robert Cleaver], *A Plaine and Familiar Exposition of the Ten Commandements* (1618), 249.

156. *The Works of Robert Sanderson*, ed. William Jacobson (Oxford, 1854), vol. 2, xxxv; Giles Firmin, *The Real Character* (1670), 268; Gabriel Towerson, *An Explication of the Decalogue* (1676), 239–40; John Shower, *Family Religion* (1694), 105.

157. George Estie, *A Most Sweete and Comfortable Exposition, upon the Tenne Commaund-ments* (1602), sig. P5; Gouge, *Domesticall Duties*, 443–45; Edward Elton, *Gods Holy Minde touching Matters Morall* (1648), 130; Thomas Fuller, *A Comment on the Eleven First Verses of the Fourth Chapter of S. Matthew's Gospel concerning Christ's Temptations* (1652), 158; Laur[ence] Claxton [Clarkson], *The Lost Sheep Found* (1660), 5; Moryson, *Itinerary*, vol. 3, 352.

158. *Winthrop's Journal*, ed. James Kendall Hosmer (New York, 1908), vol. 2, 324; Deodat Lawson, *The Duty and Property of a Religious Housholder* (Boston, MA, 1693), 51; *The Correspondence of John Cotton*, ed. Sargent Bush (Chapel Hill, NC, 2001), 343–44.

159. Roger North, *Notes of Me*, ed. Peter Millard (Toronto, 2000), 84; César de Saussure, *A Foreign View of England in the Reigns of George I and George II*, trans. and ed. Mme Van Muyden (1902), 296.

160. [John Garretson], *The School of Manners* (4th edn, 1706; repr. 1983), 29. Similar advice was offered in [Eleazer Moody], *The School of Good Manners* (5th edn, Boston, MA, 1769), 9.

161. Gilly Lehmann, 'Représentations du comportement à table dans les manuels de civilité anglais de 1660 à 1880', in *Convivialité et politesse*, [ed. Alain Montandon] (Clermont-Ferrand, 1993); Korsten, *Roger North*, 120.

162. Hesther Lynch Piozzi, *Anecdotes of Samuel Johnson*, ed. S. C. Roberts (Cambridge, 1932), 72.

163. *Spectator* 119 (17 July 1711), ed. Bond, vol. 1, 486–87.

164. *Collectanea*, 2nd ser., ed. Montagu Burrows (Oxford Hist. Soc., 1890), 391 (following John Locke, *Some Thoughts concerning Education*, ed. John W. and Jean S. Yolton (Oxford, 1989), 203 (para. 144)). On George I's preference for simplicity, see John M. Beattie, *The English Court in the Reign of George I* (Cambridge, 1967), 257–58.

165. *M. Misson's Memoirs and Observations in his Travels over England*, trans. [John] Ozell (1719), 7; Penelope Corfield, 'Dress for Deference and Dissent', *Costume* 23 (1989); Langford, *Englishness Identified*, 275–79; Louis Simond, *Journal of a Tour and Residence in Great Britain during the Years 1810 and 1811* (Edinburgh, 1817), vol. 1, 26.

166. Anne Buck, *Dress in Eighteenth-Century England* (1979), 55–59, 138, 204; Paul Langford, 'Politics and Manners from Sir Robert Walpole to Sir Robert Peel', *Procs. Brit. Acad.*, 94 (1997), 109–10; id., 'The Uses of Eighteenth-Century Politeness', *TRHS*, 6th ser., 12 (2002), 329–30; Styles, *Dress of the People*, 189–93.

167. *Rambler* 200 (15 Feb. 1752), in *The British Essayists*, ed. Robert Lynam (1827), vol. 12, 406; also *Rambler* 172 (9 Nov. 1751), in *The British Essayists*, ed. Lynam, vol. 13, 301.

168. *The New Bath Directory, for the year, 1792* (Bath, 1792), 5.

169. Alexis de Tocqueville, *Democracy in America*, trans. Henry Reeve and Francis Bowen, ed. Phillips Bradley (New York, 1954), vol. 2, 179 (II. 3. 2); Paul Langford, 'British Politeness and the Progress of Western Manners', *TRHS*, 6th ser., 7 (1997). Significantly, nearly all the evidence for English reserve adduced in this excellent article relates to the late eighteenth and early nineteenth centuries.

170. Jane Austen, *Pride and Prejudice* (1813), 190–93 (chap. 4, last para.).

171. Francis Hawkins, *Youths Behaviour, or Decency in Conversation amongst Men* (4th edn, 1646), 19; Charles Barber, *Early Modern English* (1976), 208–13.

172. Barber, *Early Modern English*, 150–52; *OED*, s.v. 'Mr, 1a'; Paul Langford, *A Polite and Commercial People* (Oxford, 1989), 66; David A. Postles, *Social Proprieties* (Washington, DC, 2006), 133; Amy Louise Erickson, 'Mistresses and Marriage', *HWJ* 78 (2014). Della Casa had recommended that strangers should be given the benefit of the doubt; *Galateo of Maister John Della Casa*, trans. Robert Peterson (1576), 43.

173. Edward Chamberlayne, *Angliae Notitia* (3rd edn, 1669), 60–61; Muralt, *Letters Describing the English and French Nations* (1726), 2–3.

174. R. T. [Sir Peter Pett], *A Discourse concerning Liberty of Conscience* (1661), 33; Sprat, *History of the Royal Society*, 407.

175. Thorstein Veblen, *The Theory of the Leisure Class* ([1899]; New York, 1912), 46.

176. Henry Fielding, *The Covent-Garden Journal*, ed. Bertrand A. Goldgar (Oxford, 1988), 270; Penelope Corfield, 'Walking the City Streets', *Journ. of Urban History* 16 (1990), 156, and 'Dress for Deference and Dissent', 72–74.

177. *Elizabeth Ham by Herself 1783–1820*, ed. Eric Gillett (1945), 27; *The Torrington Diaries*, ed. C. Bruyn Andrews ([1935]; 1970), vol. 2, 149.

178. Richard Price, *Political Writings*, ed. D. O. Thomas (Cambridge, 1991), 164.

179. Hume, *Essays*, vol. 1, 187–88.

180. 'Spirit of the Laws', in *The Complete Works of Montesquieu* (1777), vol. 1, 37–39 (bk 4, chap. 2), 417–18 (bk 19, chap. 17); Godwin, *Enquirer*, 335–36.

181. Henry Home, Lord Kames, *Sketches of the History of Man* (2nd edn, Edinburgh, 1778), vol. 1, 332–33.

182. Joseph Priestley, *Lectures on History, and General Policy* (1793), vol. 2, 281–82.

183. *Boswell on the Grand Tour: Germany and Switzerland 1764*, ed. Frederick A. Pottle (1953), 271, 298.

184. *Reflections on the Revolution in France*, in *The Writings and Speeches of Edmund Burke*, ed. Paul Langford et al. (Oxford, 1981–2015), vol. 8, 120–21; Alfred Soboul, *Les Sans-culottes parisiens en l'an II* (Paris, 1958), 655–57. For attempts by some supporters of the Revolution to develop a theory of 'republican civility' based on equality and respect for others, see Roger Chartier, *Lectures et lecteurs dans la France d'Ancien Régime* (Paris, 1987), 75–79.

185. Thomas Paine, *The Rights of Man*, in *The Life and Major Writings of Thomas Paine*, ed. Philip S. Foner (Secausus, NJ, 1974), 267.

186. Godwin, *Enquirer*, 326; *The Works of Mary Wollstonecraft*, ed. Janet Todd and Marilyn Butler (1989), vol. 5, 237.

187. Stephen Conway, *Britain, Ireland and Continental Europe in the Eighteenth Century* (Oxford, 2011), 131–32; Mrs Henry Sandford, *Thomas Poole and His Friends* (1888), vol. 2, 312.

188. Herbert Spencer, *An Autobiography* (1904), vol. 1, 47.

189. Thomas Hobbes, *Behemoth or the Long Parliament*, ed. Paul Seaward (Oxford, 2010), 274.

190. See, e.g., Iris Marion Young, *Justice and the Politics of Difference* (Princeton, NJ, 1990), 136–38; Randall Kennedy, 'The Case against "Civility"', *American Prospect* 41 (Nov.–Dec. 1998); James Schmidt, 'Is Civility a Virtue?' in *Civility*, ed. Leroy S. Rouner (Notre Dame, IN, 2000), 36–37; Linda M. G. Zerilli, 'Against Civility', in *Civility, Legality and Justice in America*, ed. Austin Sarat (Cambridge, 2014).

191. P. F. Clarke, *Liberals and Democrats* (Cambridge, 1978), 34.
192. John Osborne, 'They Call It Cricket', in Lindsay Anderson et al., *Declaration*, ed. Tom Maschler (1957), 83.
193. On the assumption that the primary purpose of 'a society of formal manners' was to create and sustain class distinctions, the distinguished Israeli philosopher Avishai Margalit maintains that it is no longer necessary; *The Decent Society*, trans. Naomi Goldblum (Cambridge, MA, 1996), 192–94.
194. Nicola Lacey, *A Life of H. L. A. Hart* (Oxford, 2004), 266. On Israeli manners as reflecting a belief in the importance of sincerity and truthfulness, see Shoshana Blum-Kulka, 'The Metapragmatics of Politeness in Israeli Society', in *Politeness in Language*, ed. Richard J. Watts et al. (Berlin, 1992).
195. *Correspondence of the Family of Hatton*, ed. Edward Maunde Thompson (Camden Soc., 1878), vol. 1, 47.
196. Archibald Alison, *Essays on the Nature and Principles of Taste* (4th edn, Edinburgh, 1815), vol. 2, 292.
197. Clarkson, *Portraiture of Quakerism*, vol. 1, 398–400; Dan Cruickshank and Neil Burton, *Life in the Georgian City* (1990), 40–43; William Stafford, 'The Gender of the Place', *TRHS*, 6th ser., 13 (2003), 309; Mme [Germaine] de Staël, *Corinne, or Italy*, trans. and ed. Sylvia Raphael (Oxford, 1998), 244.
198. *Works of Mary Wollstonecraft*, ed. Todd and Butler, vol. 5, 114, 129–30.
199. Arthur M. Schlesinger, *Learning How to Behave* ([1946]; New York, 1968), vii–viii; Michael Zuckerman, 'Tocqueville, Turner, and Turds', *Journ. of Amer. History* 85 (1998); C. Dallett Hemphill, *Bowing to Necessities* (New York, 1999), 136, 212.
200. James Fenimore Cooper, *The American Democrat* (1838), ed. George Dekker and Larry Johnston (Harmondsworth, 1969), 202–5; Jack Larkin, *The Reshaping of Everyday Life 1790–1840* (New York, 1988), 155–57; Kenneth Cmiel, *Democratic Eloquence* (New York, 1990), 67–70, 127–28; Matthew McCormack, *The Independent Man* (Manchester, 2005), 109; Dallett Hemphill, 'Manners and Class in the Revolutionary Era', *WMQ*, 3rd ser., 63 (2006).
201. *A Journal by Thos. Hughes*, with an introduction by E. A. Benians (Cambridge, 1947), 25; Frances Trollope, *Domestic Manners of the Americans* (5th edn, 1839), ed. Richard Mullen (Oxford, 1984), 15, 37–40, 190, 197; Charles Dickens, *American Notes and Pictures from Italy* (Everyman's Lib., 1907), 111–12, 121, 147 (though cf. 23–24); John F. Kasson, *Rudeness and Civility* (New York, 1990), 58–59, 186–87; Cooper, *American Democrat*, 205.
202. Tocqueville, *Democracy in America*, vol. 2, 179–80 (II. 3. 2), 228–31 (II. 3. 14); Cooper, *American Democrat*, 201–2; Hemphill, *Bowing to Necessities*. For a balanced assessment, see Stephen Mennell, *The American Civilizing Process* (Cambridge, 2007).
203. Margaret Cavendish, Marchioness of Newcastle, *CCXVI Sociable Letters* (1664), 137; Michael Farrelly and Elena Seoane, 'Democratization', in *The Oxford Handbook of the History of English*, ed. Terttu Nevalainen and Elizabeth Closs Traugott (Oxford, 2012).
204. 'Dipsychus', scene 3, in *The Poems of Arthur H. Clough*, ed. H. F. Lowry et al. (Oxford, 1951), 237.
205. Jose Harris, 'Tradition and Transformation', in *The British Isles since 1945*, ed. Kathleen Burk (Oxford, 2003), 123.
206. Norbert Elias, *On the Process of Civilization*, trans. Edmund Jephcott, ed. Stephen Mennell, in *Collected Works of Norbert Elias* (Dublin, 2006–14), vol. 13, 139; id., *Studies on the Germans*, trans. Eric Dunning and Stephen Mennell, in *Collected Works*, vol. 9, 33–35, 41–43, 84–85; Cas Wouters, *Informalization* (2007), 141; Stephen Mennell, *Norbert Elias* (1989), 241–46 (explaining Elias's argument that, in a world of informality, even more self-control is required).
207. For the much higher homicide rate in the Middle Ages, see James Sharpe, *A Fiery & Furious People* (2016), chap. 1 and p. 622.

208. 'The Spirit of Laws', xix, 6, 14, 16, in *Complete Works of Montesquieu*, vol. 1, 390–91, 396, 398.
209. John C. Lassiter, 'Defamation of Peers', *Amer. Journ. of Legal History* 22 (1978).
210. Teresa M. Bejan, *Mere Civility* (Cambridge, MA, 2017), 43–47; Hobbes, *Leviathan*, vol. 2, 276 (chap. 18).
211. John Locke, 'First Tract of Government' (1660), in *Locke: Political Essays*, ed. Mark Goldie (Cambridge, 1990), 22–24; id., *A Letter concerning Toleration and Other Writings*, ed. Mark Goldie (Indianapolis, IN, 2010), 182; Bejan, *Mere Civility*, 46, 125–26, 170–71.
212. Martin Ingram, 'Ridings, Rough Music, and the "Reform of Popular Culture" in Early Modern England', *P&P* 105 (1984); id., 'Ridings, Rough Music and Mocking Rhymes in Early Modern England', in *Popular Culture in Seventeenth-Century England*, ed. Barry Reay (1985); E. P. Thompson, 'Rough Music', in *Customs in Common* (1991), chap. 8; Bernard Capp, *When Gossips Meet* (Oxford, 2003), 268–81.
213. Peter King, *Crime and Law in England, 1750–1840* (Cambridge, 2006), 17.
214. William Blackstone, *Commentaries on the Laws of England*, ed. Wilfrid Prest et al. (Oxford, 2016), vol. 4, 106–15.
215. Robert B. Shoemaker, 'The Decline of Public Insult in London, 1600–1800', *P&P* 169 (2000).
216. Hume, *Essays*, vol. 1, 192–93; 'First Letter on a Regicide Peace' (1796), in *Writings and Speeches of Burke*, vol. 9, 242. Also 'Reflections on the Revolution in France', in vol. 8, 129–31, and Montesquieu, *Complete Works*, vol. 1, 406–8 ('The Spirit of Laws', bk 19, chaps. 23–26), and vol. 3, 57–58 ('Considerations of the Causes of the Grandeur and Decline of the Roman Empire', chap. 8).
217. *William Lambarde and Local Government*, ed. Conyers Read (Ithaca, NY, 1962), 68–69 (echoing Horace, *Odes*, bk 3, no. 24, lines 35–36).
218. [Henry Home, Lord Kames], *Elements of Criticism* (Edinburgh, 1762), vi; Adam Ferguson, *An Essay on the History of Civil Society*, ed. Duncan Forbes (Edinburgh, 1966), 237; Smith, *Theory of Moral Sentiments*, 163 (III. 5. 2–3), 85–86 (II. 3. 2–4); id., *An Inquiry into the Nature and Causes of the Wealth of Nations*, ed. R. H. Campbell and A.S. Skinner (Oxford, 1976), vol.1, 26–27 (I. 11. 12).
219. See, in particular, the German law of insult, as described by James Q. Whitman, 'Enforcing Civility and Respect', *Yale Law Journ.*, 109 (2000).
220. See the observations of Michael Power, *The Audit Society* (Oxford, 1991); Onora O'Neill, *A Question of Trust* (Cambridge, 2002); and Lord [Jonathan] Sumption, 'The Limits of Law', *27th Sultan Azlan Shah Lecture, Kuala Lumpur*, 3, https://www.supremecourt.uk/docs/speech–131120.pdf.
221. See W. Michael Reisman, *Law in Brief Encounters* (New Haven, CT, 1999).
222. Chartier, *Lectures*, 73; Cooper, *American Democrat*, 200–201.
223. R. G. Collingwood, *The New Leviathan* (Oxford, 1947), 291 (para. 35, 4), on which see Peter Johnson, 'R. G. Collingwood on Civility and Economic Licentiousness', *International Journ. of Social Economics*, 37 (2010). For other reflections on the moral and political importance of manners, see the contributions by Edward Shils, Charles R. Kessler and Clifford Orwin to *Civility and Citizenship in Liberal Democratic Societies*, ed. Edward C. Banfield (New York, 1992); and Sarah Buss, 'Appearing Respectful', *Ethics*, 109 (1999).
224. As is powerfully argued by Camille Pernot, *La Politesse et sa philosophie* (Paris, 1996).
225. John Darwin, 'Civility and Empire', in *Civil Histories*, ed. Burke et al., 323.
226. John Rawls, *A Theory of Justice* (Cambridge, 1971), 355.
227. In 'Civility and Civic Virtue in Contemporary America', *Social Research* 41 (1974), 598, Michael Walzer rightly hails the reliance of the United States income tax system upon individual citizens conscientiously calculating and paying what they owe as 'a triumph of civilization'.

228. Joan Scott, letter in *New York Rev. of Books* (11 Feb. 2016), 45–46. There is an excellent discussion of these issues, in both their seventeenth- and twenty-first-century contexts, in Bejan, *Mere Civility*. See also *Extreme Speech and Democracy*, ed. Ivan Hare and James Weinstein (Oxford, 2009).
229. Mark Kingswell, *A Civil Tongue* (University Park, PA, 1995), 26; Bejan, *Mere Civility*, 1–4, 209n. See also Kenneth Cmiel, 'The Politics of Civility', in *The Sixties*, ed. David Farber (Chapel Hill, NC, 1994), and *Civility, Legality, and Justice in America*, ed. Sarat.
230. E.g., Jeremy Waldron, *The Harm in Hate Speech* (Cambridge, MA, 2012).
231. E.g., Ronald Dworkin, 'Foreword', *Extreme Speech and Democracy*; Timothy Garton Ash, *Free Speech* (2016), esp. 211–12; John A. Hall, *The Importance of Being Civil* (Princeton, NJ, 2013), 32.
232. For representative discussion of these issues, see John Rawls, *Political Liberalism* (New York, 1996), 217, 219–20, 226, 236, 242; id., *The Law of Peoples* (Cambridge, MA, 1999), 55–56, 59, 62, 67, 135–36; id., *Justice as Fairness*, ed. Erin Kelly (Cambridge, MA, 2001), 90, 92, 117; Janet Holmes, *Women, Men and Politeness* (1995), 4–5; Richard Boyd, *Uncivil Society* (Lanham, MD, 2004), 26–28, 38–39, 248–49; Jacob T. Ley, 'Multicultural Manners', in *The Plural States of Recognition*, ed. Michel Seymour (Basingstoke, 2010); Dieter Rucht, 'Civil Society and Civility in Twentieth-Century Theorizing', *European Rev. of History* 18 (2011).
233. As is pointed out by Keith J. Bybee, *How Civility Works* (Stanford, CA, 2016), 68–69.
234. *The Early Essays and Ethics of Robert Boyle*, ed. John T. Harwood (Carbondale, IL, 1991), 240; Williams, *George Fox Digg'd out of his Burrowes*, 308.
235. Godwin, *Enquirer*, 336.
236. Chesterfield, in *The World*, 148 (30 Oct. 1755), in *British Essayists*, ed. Lynam, vol. 17, 182.
237. B. H. Liddell Hart, *The Revolution in Warfare* (1946), 93; F[rancis] R[eginald] Scott (1899–1985), 'Degeneration', in *Selected Poems* (1966), 98.
238. See the reflections of Norbert Elias, *Studies on the Germans*, trans. Eric Dunning and Stephen Mennell, in *Collected Works of Norbert Elias*, vol. 11, 190, 206, 213, and chap. 5; Georg Schwarzenberger, 'The Standard of Civilisation in International Law', *Current Legal Problems* 8 (1955), 229–30; and Eric Hobsbawm, 'Barbarism: A User's Guide', in *On History* (1997).
239. On the GDR's belief that etiquette and good manners, founded on equality and mutual respect rather than social hierarchy, were indispensable ingredients of socialist civilization, see Paul Betts, *Within Walls* (Oxford, 2010), 136–41, 168.

INDEX

Civil Wars, English *see* wars, English Civil
civility (as manners), xiii, 7, 15, 16–17, 20,
29, 111: of the aristocracy, 31, 62, 64,
77–8, 113; of the common people, 90–3,
108, 110, 113–14; a conservative force,
75–6, 322–4, 342; and duelling, 33–5;
English distinctiveness, 44, 197, 202,
255, 301; guides to, 17–18, 23;
international 137–40; late arrival in
England, 17, 45, 203–5; medieval
antecedents, 21–3; of the middling
classes, 83–7, 110, 112, 113; in modern
Britain, 337; and morality, 24–6; other
peoples' notions of, 113–14, 254–61;
pressures to adopt, 112–13; prudential
value, 70–3; and religion, 135–6, 307–10,
314–16, *see also* Quakers; resistance to,
296–302, 321–3; respects social
differences, 65–70, 74; of servants, 40;
social effects, 36–7, 67–76, 111; of towns,
23, 78, 80–1, 85–6, 186–7; in war, 144–5;
of women, 47–8; *see also* 'civility',
meanings of the term; politeness
'civility', meanings of the term: civil order
and government, 6, 16, 120, 121; the
civilized condition, xv, 6, 15, 115–16,
183, 185–8, 208, 222, 225, 284–8, 346,
see also civil society; conversational
decorum, 342–3; good citizenship, 6, 16,
342; good manners, xiii, 7, 15, 16–17, 20,
24, 27, 29, 111, 113–14; law-abidingness,
16, 94, 115–16, 186, 208, 222, 223–4,
226; *see also* affability; benevolence;
cleanliness; compassion; 'compleasance';
condescension; connoisseurship;
conversation; conviviality; courtesy;
decency; decorum; good breeding;
honesty; humanity; manners; meekness;
mildness; modesty; neighbourliness;
politeness; respect; self-control; sincerity;
sociability; urbanity
civilization: British, 196; Christian, 118; a
contentious term, 248; European, 171,
197; defects of, 282–4; ingredients of, 8,
121–3, 125–6, 127–8, 130–40, 163,
166–79, 245, 247–8, 266, 295; origins of
the term, xv, 6–7, 351n18; plurality of,
266; a relative term, 9; standard of, 7–8;
Western, 245, 247–8, 266, 295; *see also*
cultures
'civilized world, the', 116, 119, 175, 215
civilizing mission, 8: in England, 93–9;
involving force, 219–22, 225–6; in

Ireland, 221–4, 228; a moral obligation,
245–6; in North America, 224–5, 227;
opposition to, 270–4, 276–9, 294
civilizing process *see* Elias, Norbert
Clarendon, Edward Hyde, 1st Earl, 37,
131–2, 145, 199, 227, 239, 320–2, 325
Clarke, Samuel, 310
cleanliness, bodily, 52–3, 86–7, 100–1,
164–5, 315, 317
clergy, as civilizers, 97–9
climate, influence of, 131, 206, 231, 232,
236, 254; denied, 231–2
Clive, Robert, Baron, 271
clothes *see* dress
Clough, Arthur Hugh, 335
clubs, 58, 81, 85, 176, 301
coachmen, 102
Cobden, Richard, 166n
coffeehouses, 58, 81, 86
Coke, Sir Edward, 44, 157, 269–70
Colden, Cadwallader, 149
Cole, William, 51
Colet, John, 140
Collingwood, R. G., 8, 34, 341
Collins, Samuel, 27
colonization by force: criticized, 269,
270–2; justified, 216–22
commerce: Age of, 192; civilizing
influence, 84–5, 99, 188–92, 215; ill
effects, 189, 281–2; right to conduct,
214, 267–8
common people: authentic, 106, 318;
civility and manners, 88–93, 100–1,
105–6; civilizing of, 93–9; conviviality,
107–8; deference, 90, 319–23, 329;
language, 106; sociability, 104; violence,
101–3
communications, impact of, 80, 99;
see also roads
compassion, 60, 163
'compleasance', 111–12
compliments, 30, 59, 110, 316–17; disliked,
299–300, 301, 302, 306–7, 311, 315, 323,
332
condescension, 66, 73, 327
'conjectural history', 183, 192; *see also*
stadial theory
Connecticut, 287
connoisseurship, 228–9
conversation, 58–61, 77, 343: civil, 17, 141;
godly, 310
conviviality, 85, 108; *see also* clubs;
sociability